The World and Its People

THE UNITED STATES AND ITS NEIGHBORS

Annotated Teacher's Edition

SILVER BURDETT COMPANY

MORRISTOWN, NEW JERSEY

Glenview, Ill. · San Carlos, Calif. · Dallas · Atlanta

The World and Its People

THE UNITED STATES

SERIES AUTHORS

Val E. Arnsdorf, Professor,
College of Education, University of Delaware, Newark, Delaware

Carolyn S. Brown, Principal,
Robertson Academy School, Nashville, Tennessee

Kenneth S. Cooper, Professor of History, Emeritus,
George Peabody College for Teachers, Vanderbilt University, Nashville, Tennessee

Alvis T. Harthern, Professor of Education,
University of Montevallo, Montevallo, Alabama

Timothy M. Helmus, Middle School Teacher,
Harrison Park Middle School, Grand Rapids, Michigan

Bobbie P. Hyder, Elementary Education Coordinator,
Madison County School System, Huntsville, Alabama

Theodore Kaltsounis, Professor and Chairman of Curriculum and Instruction,
College of Education, University of Washington, Seattle, Washington

Richard H. Loftin, Director of Curriculum and Staff Development,
Aldine Independent School District, Houston, Texas

Norman J.G. Pounds, Former University Professor of Geography,
Indiana University, Bloomington, Indiana

Edgar A. Toppin, Professor of History and Dean of the Graduate School,
Virginia State University, Petersburg, Virginia

PROGRAM CONTRIBUTORS

Paula Allaert, Third Grade Teacher,
St. Therese School, Portland, Oregon
Carol Armour, Third Grade Teacher,
Marie V. Duffy Elementary School, Wharton, New Jersey
Sandra Breman, Fifth Grade Teacher,
Whitney Young Magnet School, Fort Wayne, Indiana
Vivian Brown, Fifth Grade Teacher,
Silver Spur Elementary School, Rancho Palos Verdes, California
Kim Eyler, Former Elementary School Teacher,
Wyckoff, New Jersey
Sharon Gaydon, Sixth Grade Teacher,
Thompson Middle School, Alabaster, Alabama
Janet Glenn, Second Grade Teacher,
Greene School, Greensboro, North Carolina
Viola Gonzalez, Fifth – Sixth Grade Teacher,
Ryan Elementary School, Laredo, Texas
Ellen Gremillion, Third Grade Teacher,
Parkview Elementary School, Baton Rouge, Louisiana
Lucy Hatch, Fifth – Sixth Grade Teacher,
Taylor Elementary School, Abilene, Texas
Judy Hobson, Fourth Grade Teacher,
Elmdale Elementary School, Springdale, Arkansas
Peggy Hogg, Fourth Grade Teacher,
Dartmouth Elementary School, Richardson, Texas
Geoffrey Kashdan, Special Education Teacher,
Hanover Avenue School, Morris Plains, New Jersey
Gloria Lemos, First Grade Teacher,
Emerson Elementary School, Pasco, Washington
William Lentino, Fifth Grade Teacher,
Lloyd Harbor Elementary School, Huntington, New York
Carolyn Lombardo, Third Grade Teacher,
Ferrara Elementary School, East Haven, Connecticut
Mary Lou Martin, Social Studies Resource Teacher, K – 6,
San Diego Unified School District, San Diego, California
Patricia McWey, Second Grade Teacher,
Martin Luther King School, Providence, Rhode Island
Sandra Murphy Mead, Second Grade Teacher,
L.W. West School, Endicott, New York
Ray Ringley, Fifth Grade Teacher,
Powell Valley Primary School, Big Stone Gap, Virginia
Elaine Sisselman, Fourth Grade Teacher,
Biscayne Gardens Elementary School, Miami, Florida
Katharyn Smith, First Grade Teacher,
The Meadows School, College Park, Georgia
Jan Talbot, Sixth Grade Teacher,
Pope Avenue Elementary School, Sacto, California
Patricia Terai, First Grade Teacher,
Woodin Elementary School, Bothell, Washington
William Tucker, Sixth Grade Teacher,
Alanton Elementary School, Virginia Beach, Virginia
Sister Catherine Zajac, S.S.J., Fourth – Sixth Grade Teacher,
St. Agnes School, Dalton, Massachusetts

ISBN 0-382-02727-2

AND ITS NEIGHBORS

AUTHORS

VAL E. ARNSDORF

Professor
College of Education
University of Delaware
Newark, Delaware

TIMOTHY M. HELMUS

Middle School Teacher
Harrison Park Middle School
Grand Rapids, Michigan

NORMAN J.G. POUNDS

Former University Professor of Geography
Indiana University
Bloomington, Indiana

EDGAR A. TOPPIN

Professor of History and Dean of the Graduate School
Virginia State University
Petersburg, Virginia

Annotated Teacher's Edition

CONTENTS

PROGRAM RATIONALE

The Silver Burdett social studies program THE WORLD AND ITS PEOPLE was developed to help students understand the world around them and to instill in them the knowledge and skills necessary for responsible citizenship. Built on a solid factual foundation, the program examines the students' world in an ever-widening circle. THE WORLD AND ITS PEOPLE begins with a study of self and family in Grade 1 and expands in Grades 2 through 6 to a study of neighborhood, community, state, region, nation, and world.

Each book in the series reflects the following belief: *Students need to know, to appreciate, and to do.* A grasp of basic facts is essential in gaining an understanding of social studies. To that end, a wealth of materials is provided. Lesson checkups, chapter and unit reviews, and chapter tests ensure the students' understanding of the text material. Opportunities for development of language, reading, and social studies skills are provided throughout the series through vocabulary study, skills development exercises, and other skills-related activities. Parental involvement is encouraged through the use of a letter to parents provided periodically in the Teacher's Editions.

THE WORLD AND ITS PEOPLE involves much more than a passive acceptance of facts. The program involves *doing.* Students work with maps, charts, graphs, tables, and time lines as a vital part of the learning process. Students build models, conduct interviews, hold debates, and take part in a variety of other activities. In short, students are *active participants.*

While facts are emphasized, it is recognized that those facts, to be meaningful, must be utilized. The function of factual knowledge in THE WORLD AND ITS PEOPLE is to enable students to appreciate themselves, the world around them, and their role as citizens of the United States. Students are led to understand some of the important links between them and their families, community, state, region, nation, and world. In doing so, they develop an appreciation of historic and geographic factors and economic and political relationships that have shaped their world. Moreover, students are given specific suggestions for assuming a responsible role—in a capacity commensurate with age and ability—in their community, state, region, nation, and world. THE WORLD AND ITS PEOPLE not only prepares students for the future but also helps them function meaningfully and effectively in the present.

FEATURES OF THE PUPIL'S EDITION

Feature	Description
A Letter to You from the Author	Preceding the first unit is a letter of introduction from the author(s) to the pupils. The purpose of the letter is to tell the pupils about the book.
Vocabulary	A vocabulary list precedes each lesson. This list consists of the key social studies vocabulary for the lesson. These vocabulary words are in boldface type in the text. All words in boldface are defined in the Glossary. These words may be used to introduce the lesson.
Pronunciations	Words that pupils may find difficult to pronounce are followed by pronunciations in parentheses when the words first appear. A Key to Pronunciation Symbols appears on the first page of the index. In recent years, Pinyin, a new system of spelling Chinese names, has been coming into general use. This system is now used by state departments and communications media. In this series, the traditional Wade-Giles spellings are followed by the Pinyin spellings in parentheses.
Checkup	At the end of each lesson are questions labeled Checkup. These questions, covering the main points of the lesson, may be used in a variety of ways. The pupils may use them to check their grasp of the material. The teacher may wish to use these questions for class discussion or written homework.
Chapter Review	At the end of every chapter is a Chapter Review. The Chapter Review has four categories: Key Facts, Vocabulary Quiz, Review Questions, and Activities.
Key Facts	Key Facts or main ideas from the chapter are listed, providing a valuable tool for reviewing the content of the chapter.
Vocabulary Quiz	Items such as true/false, matching, completion sentences, and multiple choice are used to review or to test vocabulary.
Review Questions	Review Questions cover all lessons in the chapter. The majority of the questions are recall. Some are thinking questions that involve comparing and contrasting, interpreting, applying, generalizing, and synthesizing.
Activities	Activities that require little or no teacher direction are given.
Skills Development	A Skills Development page follows the Chapter Review in each book. This page consists of questions and/or activities that develop reading, language arts, and social studies skills. Some reading skills included are identifying topic sentence and main idea, summarizing, understanding and defining words, following directions, understanding sequence, and recalling information. Language arts skills such as letter writing, outlining, book reports, and oral reports are included. Social studies skills included are reading of maps, time lines, tables, graphs, photographs, drawings, and source materials. Scope and sequence charts for map and globe, reading, and language arts skills, as well as scope and sequence charts for reasoning and societal skills begin on page T14.

FEATURES OF THE PUPIL'S EDITION

Feature	Description
Unit Review	A Unit Review is found at the end of each unit. The Unit Review includes a list of the main ideas of the unit. These ideas may come from individual chapters, or they may synthesize information from a combination of chapters. Each idea is followed by a question and/or activity dealing with recall, opinion, interpretation, or application. At least one activity in each Unit Review is appropriate for extra credit and is so indicated.
Map Skills	Each book devotes an entire chapter to map skills. The chapter develops the essential map-reading skills in a logical and systematic way. Starting with the most basic skills and simplest maps in Grade 1, the series develops those skills and builds on them at each grade level. In addition, the many maps included in the other chapters of each book provide the means for reinforcing the skills presented in the map chapter. There are 260 maps located throughout the texts of Grades 1 through 6 in THE WORLD AND ITS PEOPLE series.
Atlas	An Atlas, located in the back of each book, beginning at Grade 3, includes a variety of political and/or physical maps.
Gazetteer	The Gazetteer, which appears in Grades 3 – 6, lists most of the places discussed in the text. For each entry the Gazetteer provides the following information: 1. latitude and longitude (when appropriate), rounded off to the nearest full degree 2. a statement or two about the place 3. a reference to a map, included in the text, where the place can be located
Glossary	All social studies vocabulary words that are listed prior to each lesson appear in the Glossary.
Tables/Graphs	Some of the many tables and graphs provided throughout the text are the following: 　In Grade 3, a Graph Appendix is located in the back of the book. The Appendix includes pie graphs, bar graphs, and line graphs, and reinforces graph skills introduced in Chapter 1. This special graph section presents information about population, land division, average monthly rainfall, average monthly temperature, and production of certain natural resources for the United States and other countries. 　In Grade 4, "Facts About" boxes provide information about a state or a country. These are located throughout the text. Data provided include population, area, official language, capital, chief cities, and percentage of rural and urban area. 　In Grade 5, at the end of each chapter dealing with the geography of a United States region is a table giving important facts about each state in the region. In addition to such data as population, capital city, and chief products, the tables show in graphic form the outline of each state and the state bird, flower, tree, and flag. Similar tables are found at the end of the chapters on Canada and Latin America. 　In Grade 6, the Appendix contains tables giving important facts about the countries of the Eastern Hemisphere. The categories include data on land area, population, population density, the capital city and its population, languages, and so on.

FEATURES OF THE TEACHER'S EDITION

Feature	Description
Program Content Outline	A listing of the program content for THE WORLD AND ITS PEOPLE is located on pages T10–T13.
Program Skills Scope and Sequence	Various skills that are introduced and/or developed throughout the program are listed in scope and sequence charts. The categories of skills include the following: Map and Globe Skills, Reading Skills in social studies, Language Arts Skills in social studies, Reasoning Skills, and Societal Skills.
Letter to Parents	For each unit, a letter to parents is provided in the teacher's lesson plans. The purpose of this letter is to inform parents of what pupils will be learning about in the unit.
Bulletin-Board Display(s)	Ideas and directions for one or more bulletin-board displays, appropriate for the unit of study, are provided.
Getting Started	Introductory activities or projects relating to the unit are suggested under the heading Getting Started.
Chapter Theme	The theme of each chapter is stated as a guide for the teacher in the teacher's lesson plans.
Chapter Projects	Projects relating to the chapter content are suggested. These projects usually require more time than a single class session to prepare and complete.
Lesson Goals	The lesson goals are guides of what the pupil can be expected to have learned on completion of the lesson content. A lesson is a plan for developing a block of material in the Pupil's Edition; it does not necessarily refer to one class session. The teacher's lesson plans provide Pupil's Edition page references for each lesson.

FEATURES OF THE TEACHER'S EDITION

Feature	Description
Teaching Suggestions	Suggestions and activities for each lesson are given in the teacher's lesson plans. Descriptive headings provide a guide for the teacher in selecting desired suggestions and activities. Some examples of these descriptive headings are Map Reading, Reading Recall, Discussion, Making a Chart, Community Resources, Creative Writing, and Research Reports. Vocabulary reinforcement is emphasized in many of the activities. A variety of activities are suggested, but it is not expected that every activity be used. Suggested questions and direct discourse for teachers to quote are provided.
	This symbol ● designates expanded activities that contain suggestions for use with pupils who have difficulty grasping the concepts and/or pupils who need a challenge.
Supplementary Information	Supplementary Information is provided when needed. It may give some historical background, focus on human interest material, provide information on unit opening art, or give fun-to-know kinds of information.
Annotations	Questions and information are surprinted on the pupil's page of the Teacher's Edition. Often answers to such questions will be given in parentheses. Annotations include interesting facts, unusual information, photo comparisons, supplementary information, and photo-reading questions.
	The pupil's page of the Teacher's Edition will contain underscoring of some of the key definitions and some of the important ideas.
	Photographs that can be identified by latitude and longitude will carry an annotation indicating the latitude and longitude in degrees and minutes.
Books and Other Media	This section includes materials of general interest to teachers and pupils. Among these materials are books, films, filmstrips, and records. They are listed by unit with chapter references after the entry when appropriate.

PROGRAM CONTENT OUTLINE

PROGRAM CONTENT OUTLINE

PROGRAM CONTENT OUTLINE

EUROPE, AFRICA, ASIA, AND AUSTRALIA

PROGRAM CONTENT OUTLINE

MAP AND GLOBE SKILLS

SKILLS	GRADES	1	2	3	4	5	6
Globe		■	■	■	■	■	■
Continents and Oceans		■	■	■	■	■	■
Landform Identification			■	■	■	■	■
Shape Identification		■	■	■	■	■	■
Cardinal Directions		■	■	■	■	■	■
Legend (Key)		■	■	■	■	■	■
Symbols		■	■	■	■	■	■
Color		■	■	■	■	■	■
Political Boundaries		■	■	■	■	■	■
Pictorial		■	■	■	■	■	■
Abstract		■	■	■	■	■	■
Transition from Photo to Map		■	■	■	■	■	■
Comparative Size		■	■	■	■	■	■
Labels		■	■	■	■	■	■
Location		■	■	■	■	■	■
Inset Maps		■	■	■	■	■	■
Picture Maps		■	■	■			
Directional Arrows		■	■	■			
North Pole			■	■	■	■	■
South Pole			■	■	■	■	■
Floor Plan			■	■		■	■
Thematic Maps				■	■	■	■
Atlas				■	■	■	■
Intermediate Directions				■	■	■	■
Compass Rose				■	■	■	■
Latitude				■	■	■	■
Equator				■	■	■	■
Arctic Circle				■	■	■	■
Antarctic Circle				■	■	■	■

MAP AND GLOBE SKILLS

SKILLS	GRADES	1	2	3	4	5	6
Latitude (continued)							
Tropic of Cancer				■	■	■	■
Tropic of Capricorn				■	■	■	■
Longitude				■	■	■	■
Prime Meridian				■	■	■	■
Using a Coordinate System				■	■	■	■
Hemispheres				■	■	■	■
Shaded Relief				■	■	■	■
Scale				■	■	■	■
Elevation Tints					■	■	■
Mileage Chart				■		■	
Subway Map				■			
Railroad Map						■	
Physical-Political Map					■	■	■
Road Map					■	■	
Isolines (e.g., contour lines)					■	■	
Profile Maps					■	■	■
Travel Routes						■	■
Historical Maps						■	■
Weather Map							■
Time Zones							■
Projections							■
Diagrams				■	■	■	■
Graphs							
Pictograph		■		■	■		■
Pie Graph			■	■	■		■
Bar Graph			■	■	■	■	■
Line Graph				■	■	■	■
Climograph						■	■

READING SKILLS

SKILLS	GRADES	1	2	3	4	5	6
VOCABULARY BUILDING							
Understanding and defining words by:							
Using objects		■	■	■	■	■	■
Using illustrations		■	■	■	■	■	■
Using a glossary		■	■	■	■	■	■
Using a dictionary				■	■	■	■
Using context clues				■	■	■	■
Alphabetical Order		■	■	■	■	■	■
Synonyms/Antonyms		■	■	■	■	■	■
Prefix/Suffix				■	■	■	■
Acronyms/Abbreviations				■	■	■	■
Word Origins				■	■	■	■
DEVELOPING READING COMPREHENSION							
Understanding and identifying the main idea		■	■	■	■	■	■
Following directions		■	■	■	■	■	■
Understanding relationships		■	■	■	■	■	■
Understanding sequence		■	■	■	■	■	■
Understanding cause and effect		■	■	■	■	■	■
Recalling information		■	■	■	■	■	■
Recognizing attitudes and emotions		■	■	■	■	■	■
Understanding different literary forms		■	■	■	■	■	■
Understanding that facts support main idea			■	■	■	■	■

READING SKILLS

SKILLS	GRADES	1	2	3	4	5	6
DEVELOPING READING COMPREHENSION (continued)							
Identifying purpose for reading			■	■	■	■	■
Reading schedules and calendars			■	■	■	■	■
Identifying topic sentence				■	■	■	■
Distinguishing between the main idea and details				■	■	■	■
Skimming				■	■	■	■
Distinguishing between fact and opinion				■	■	■	■
Summarizing				■	■	■	■
Reading mileage charts				■	■	■	■
Reading and interpreting facts from tables				■	■	■	■
Using details to support main idea					■	■	■
Distinguishing between relevant and irrelevant data						■	■
Paraphrasing						■	■
Recognizing and identifying author's or speaker's purpose						■	■
Understanding primary and secondary sources						■	■
Recognizing propaganda						■	■

LANGUAGE ARTS SKILLS

SKILLS GRADES	1	2	3	4	5	6
Writing Skills						
Letter Writing (personal)	■	■	■	■	■	■
Descriptive Writing		■	■	■	■	■
Narrative Writing		■	■	■	■	■
Report Writing		■	■	■	■	■
Letter Writing (business)		■	■	■	■	■
Book Reports			■	■	■	■
Writing a Diary			■	■	■	■
Outlining			■	■	■	■
Persuasive Writing				■	■	■
SPEAKING SKILLS						
Expressing a Point of View	■	■	■	■	■	■
Oral Reports		■	■	■	■	■
Debate					■	■
LIBRARY SKILLS						
Choosing References			■	■	■	■
Card Catalog			■	■	■	■
Encyclopedia			■	■	■	■
Newspapers and Magazines			■	■	■	■
Vertical File				■	■	■
Readers' Guide to Periodical Literature					■	■
Almanac					■	■

REASONING SKILLS

SKILLS	GRADES	1	2	3	4	5	6
Identifying and expressing preferences and opinions		■	■	■	■	■	■
Generalizing		■	■	■	■	■	■
Making inferences		■	■	■	■	■	■
Drawing conclusions		■	■	■	■	■	■
Comparing and contrasting		■	■	■	■	■	■
Classifying		■	■	■	■	■	■
Interpreting cause and effect			■	■	■	■	■
Gathering information							
Observing		■	■	■	■	■	■
Interviewing			■	■	■	■	■
Using primary sources				■	■	■	■
Using secondary sources				■	■	■	■
Polling						■	■
Identifying a problem				■	■	■	■
Identifying alternatives				■	■	■	■
Recognizing and identifying points of view					■	■	■
Defending a point of view				■	■	■	■
Predicting					■	■	■
Developing objectivity					■	■	■
Making or withholding judgment					■	■	■
Evaluating relevance of information						■	■

SOCIETAL SKILLS

SKILLS	GRADES	1	2	3	4	5	6
LIFE SKILLS							
Telling time		■	■				
Reading a calendar		■	■				
Practicing pedestrian and bicycle safety		■	■				
Reading traffic signs		■	■	■			
Recognizing warning signs and symbols		■	■	■			
Knowing full name and address		■	■	■			
Understanding the importance of good nutrition		■	■	■			
Knowing fire drill procedure		■	■	■			
Knowing when and how to call fire or police help		■	■	■			
Practicing basic safety techniques in home and school		■	■	■			
Knowing emergency telephone numbers		■	■	■			
Using a telephone		■	■	■	■	■	■
Becoming aware of job opportunities		■	■	■	■	■	■
Budgeting and banking		■	■	■	■	■	■
Addressing an envelope			■	■	■	■	■
Using a telephone directory				■	■	■	■
Reading a schedule				■	■	■	■
Filling out forms and applications				■	■	■	■
Reading newspaper ads						■	■
HUMAN RELATIONS							
Developing personal friendships		■	■				
Developing respect for self		■	■	■	■	■	■
Developing respect for others		■	■	■	■	■	■
Working in groups		■	■	■	■	■	■
Recognizing interdependence among people		■	■	■	■	■	■

SOCIETAL SKILLS

SKILLS	GRADES	1	2	3	4	5	6
HUMAN RELATIONS (continued)							
Understanding the importance of courtesy		■	■	■	■	■	
Recognizing other points of view				■	■	■	■
CITIZENSHIP AND VALUES							
Respecting our American heritage and beliefs		■	■	■	■	■	■
Understanding the democratic process		■	■	■	■	■	■
Understanding the role of the citizen in a democracy		■	■	■	■	■	■
Understanding and accepting the need for laws		■	■	■	■	■	■
Developing a respect for rules and laws		■	■	■	■	■	■
Appreciating ethnic heritage		■	■	■	■	■	■
Appreciating such basic values as honesty, equality, loyalty, dependability, cooperation, fair play, and human dignity		■	■	■	■	■	■
Appreciating the dignity in all occupations		■	■	■	■	■	■
Developing pride in one's own work		■	■	■	■	■	■
Developing good work and job habits, e.g., punctuality, neatness, dependability		■	■	■	■	■	■
Understanding the importance of responsibility		■	■	■	■	■	■
Participating in decision making		■	■	■	■	■	■
Understanding the importance of leisure time					■	■	
Respecting the rights of others while exercising one's own						■	■
Recognizing that responsibility and freedom are closely related						■	■
Recognizing and avoiding negative stereotypes						■	■

UNIT ONE
BOOKS FOR PUPILS

Early Man. F. Clark Howell. Time-Life Books Inc.† (2)*

First Books of Maps and Globes. Sam Epstein and Beryl Epstein. New York: Franklin Watts, Inc. (1)

The Metric System. Joan E. Rahn. New York: Atheneum Pubs. (Distributed by Book Warehouse, Inc., Paterson, N.J.) (1)

Life History of the United States, 12 vols. Time-Life Books Inc.† (2)

The Mississippi. Susan Darell-Brown. Wayland Pubs., Ltd.† (2)

Search for the Past: An Introduction to Archaeology. Michael Avi-Yonah. Minneapolis, Minn.: Lerner Pubs. Co. (2)

The World of Maps and Mapping: A Creative Learning Aid. Norman Thrower. New York: McGraw-Hill, Inc. (1)

BOOKS FOR TEACHERS

Be Expert with Map and Compass: The Orienting Handbook, rev. ed. Bjorn Kjellstrom. New York: Charles Scribner's Sons. (1)

Building a Map Skills Program. Beth Arnold. Palo Alto, Calif.: Education Today Co., Inc. (1)

From Freedom to Slavery: A History of Negro Americans. John Hope Franklin. New York: Alfred A. Knopf, Inc. (2)

A History of Women in America. Carol Hymowitz and Michaele Weissman. New York: Bantam Books, Inc. (2)

The Oxford History of the American People, vols. 1–3. New York: New American Library, Inc. (2)

Maps and Their Makers: An Introduction to the History of Cartography. A.R. Crone. Hamden, Conn.: Shoe String Press, Inc. (1)

OTHER MEDIA
Filmstrips

Building Maps and Globe Skills. Chicago: Encyclopaedia Britannica Educational Corp. Set of 5, 64 frames, cassettes, teacher's guide. (1)

Exploring Maps: Skills for Today. Columbus, Ohio: Xerox Educational Pubs. Set of 6, cassettes, teacher's guide, color. (1)

Finding Our Way with Maps and Globes. Burbank, Calif.: Walt Disney Educational Media Co. Set of 7, records or cassettes, teacher's guide, color. (1)

Learning to Use Maps. Chicago: Encyclopaedia Britannica Educational Corp. Set of 6, 47 frames, captions. (1)

Map Competency. Chicago: Coronet Instructional Films. Set of 6, cassettes, teacher's guide. (1)

Videocassette (¾ inch)

Other People's Garbage. Washington, D.C.: Public Broadcasting Service. 60 min, videocassette, color. (2)

Multimedia Kits

Where and Why. Chicago: A.J. Nystrom & Co. 1 diagnostic test, 23 cassettes, 3 teacher's guides, 23 copymaster tests, 21 symbols chart, reductions, storage/display box. (1)

Records

"The Hammer Song." *Silver Burdett Music 5*, Record 4. (2)

"It's a Small World." *Silver Burdett Music 5*, Record 2. (1)

UNIT TWO
BOOKS FOR PUPILS

America's Paul Revere. Esther Forbes. Houghton Mifflin Co. (5)

Amos Fortune, Free Man. Elizabeth Yates. New York: E.P. Dutton Pub. Co., Inc. (5)

Ancient Skyscrapers. Sherry Paul. Contemporary Perspectives, Inc.† (5)

The Aztecs. Judith Crosher. Macdonald Educational Ltd.† (3)

Discoveries of the New World. Joseph Berger and Lawrence Wroth. New York: American Heritage Pub. Co., Inc. (4)

The Explorers. Richard Humble. Time-Life Books Inc.† (4)

Indian Tribes of America. Marion E. Aridley. Chicago: Rand McNally & Co.

BOOKS FOR TEACHERS

The European Discovery of America: The Northern Voyages. New York: Oxford University Press, Inc. (4)

The Formative Years, 1607–1763. Clarence L. Ver Steeg. New York: Hill & Wang, Inc. (5)

We Talk, You Listen: New Tribes, New Turf. Vine Deloria, Jr. New York: Dell Pub. Co., Inc. (3)

The World of the American Indian. Washington, D.C.: National Geographic Society. (3)

OTHER MEDIA
Filmstrips

Exploring and Colonizing America—Who Won the Great Race. Baldwin, N.Y.: Bear Film's Inc. and Audiovisual Associates. Script, 42 frames, color. (4)

Life in Early America. Chicago: Encyclopaedia Britannica Educational Corp. Set of 6, 52 frames, color. (5)

Video Cassettes (¾ inch)

The Chaco Legacy (Odyssey Series). Washington, D.C.: PBS Video (Public Broadcasting Service). Color. (3)

Cree Hunters of the Mistassini (Odyssey Series). Washington, D.C.: PBS Video (Public Broadcasting Service). Color. (3)

The Incas (Odyssey Series). Washington, D.C.: PBS Video (Public Broadcasting Service). Color. (3)

Seeking the First Americans (Odyssey Series). Washington, D.C.: PBS Video (Public Broadcasting Service). Color. (3)

Records

"Rock-a-My Soul." *Silver Burdett Music 5*, Record 8. (5)

"Thanksgiving Chorale." *Silver Burdett Music 5*, Record 4. (3)

"Winds of Morning." *Silver Burdett Music 5*, Record 4. (4)

UNIT THREE
BOOKS FOR PUPILS

Black Heroes of the American Revolution. Burke Davis. New York: Harcourt Brace Jovanovich, Inc. (6)

The California Gold Rush. Mary McNeer. New York: Random House, Inc. (8)

The First Blue Jeans. Ricki Dru. Contemporary Perspectives, Inc.† (8)

The First Book of the Founding of the Republic. Richard B. Morris. New York: Franklin Watts, Inc. (6)

Louisiana Purchase. Robert Tallant. New York: Random House, Inc. (7)

Mexicans in America. Jane Pinchot. Minneapolis, Minn.: Lerner Pubs. Co. (8)

On to Oregon. Honore Morrow. New York: William Morrow & Co., Inc. (8)

Susan B. Anthony. Iris Noble. New York: Julian Messner. (7)

Zenas and the Shaving Mill. F.N. Monjo. New York: Coward, McCann & Geoghegan, Inc. (6)

BOOKS FOR TEACHERS

The Black West: A Documentary and Pictorial History. William Loren Katz. New York: Doubleday & Co., Inc. (3)

Eyewitness to Wagon Trains West. James Hewitt. New York: Charles Scribner's Sons. (8)

A History of the Mexican American People. Julian Samora and Patricia Vandel Simon. South Bend, Ind.: University of Notre Dame Press. (8)

The Nation Takes Shape: Seventeen Eighty Nine to Eighteen Thirty Seven. Chicago: University of Chicago Press. (7)

The Reinterpretation of the American Revolution, 1763–1789. Jack P. Green, ed. New York: Harper & Row, Pubs., Inc. (6)

OTHER MEDIA
Filmstrips

The American Woman: A Social Chronicle. Mt. Kisco, N.Y.: Teaching Resources Films. Set of 6, color. (7)

*Refers to the chapter to which this material is particularly appropriate.
†Distributed by Silver Burdett Company, Morristown, N.J.

BOOKS AND OTHER MEDIA

Eighteen Twelve—Mr. Madison's War. Stamford, Conn.: Multi Media Productions. 79 frames, cassette or script, color. (7)

Famous Patriots of the American Revolution. Chicago: Coronet Instructional Films. Set of 6, color. (6)

Films (16 mm)

Pioneer Home. Chicago: Coronet Instructional Films. 10 min, color. (8)

The Spanish in the Southwest. Santa Monica, Calif.: BFA Educational Media. 13 min, color. (8)

The Westward Movement. West Hollywood, Calif.: Handel Film Corp. 15 min, color. (8)

Records

"America." *Silver Burdett Music 4,* Record 8. (6)

"Clementine." *Silver Burdett Music 5,* Record 9. (8)

"The Star-Spangled Banner." *Silver Burdett Music 5,* Record 9. (7)

UNIT FOUR
BOOKS FOR PUPILS

All This Wild Land. Ann Nolan Clark. New York: The Viking Press. (11)

Appomatox: Closing Struggle of the Civil War. Burke Davis. New York: Harper & Row, Pubs., Inc. (9)

The First Book of the Civil War. Dorothy Levenson. New York: Franklin Watts, Inc. (9)

Frederick Douglas: Slave—Fighter—Freeman. Arna Bontemps. New York: Alfred A. Knopf, Inc. (9)

Gettysburg. MacKinlay Kantor. New York: Random House, Inc. (9)

Indian Paintbrush. Edna Walker Chandler. Chicago: Albert Whitman & Co. (10)

Inventions That Made History. David C. Cooke. New York: G.P. Putnam's Sons. (11)

The Pioneers. Huston Horn. Time-Life Books Inc.† (10)

The Railway. L.W. Cowie. Macdonald Educational Ltd.† (10)

Reconstruction: The Great Experiment. Allen W. Trelease. New York: Harper & Row, Pubs., Inc. (9)

When the Rattlesnake Sounds: A Play About Harriet Tubman. Alice Childress. New York: Coward, McCann & Geoghegan, Inc. (9)

Wingman. Manus Pinkwater. New York: Dell Pub. Co., Inc. (11)

BOOKS FOR TEACHERS

Abraham Lincoln: From His Own Work and Contemporary Accounts. Roy E. Appleman, ed. Washington, D.C.: U.S. Government Printing Office. (9)

Bury My Heart at Wounded Knee: An Indian History of the American West. Dee Brown. New York: Holt, Rinehart & Winston, Inc. (10)

A Diary from Dixie. Mary Boykin Chestnut.

Ben Ames Williams, ed. Boston: Houghton Mifflin Co. (9)

Ebony Pictorial History of Black Americans, Vol. 1. *Ebony,* eds. Boulder, Colo.: Johnson Pub. Co., Inc. (9)

Immigrants in American Life: Selected Readings. Arthur Mann. Boston: Houghton Mifflin Co. (11)

OTHER MEDIA
Filmstrips

Civil War and Reconstruction. Chicago: Encyclopaedia Britannica Educational Corp. Set of 6, 89 frames, cassette, color. (9)

Growth of Towns and Cities. Chicago: Coronet Instructional Films. 51 frames, record or cassette, color. (11)

Films (16 mm)

Abraham Lincoln: The War Years. Capistrano Beach, Calif.: Linc Films. 16 min, color. (9)

Cities and History: Changing the City. New York: McGraw-Hill, Inc. (11)

The Frontier Experience. New York: Learning Corp. of America. 25 min, color. (10)

Immigration. New York: McGraw-Hill, Inc. Optical Sound, color. (11)

Records

"Buffalo Gals." *Silver Burdett Music 5,* Record 9. (10)

"Lazybones." *Silver Burdett Music 5,* Record 2. (11)

"Pay Me My Money Down." *Silver Burdett Music 5,* Record 3. (9)

UNIT FIVE
BOOKS FOR PUPILS

The American Heritage Picture History of World War Two. Cyrus L. Sulzberger. New York: Simon & Schuster, Inc. (12)

The Fighting Redtails: Americas First Black Airmen. Warren Halliburton. Contemporary Perspectives, Inc.† (12)

The First Woman in Congress: Jeanette Rankin. Judy Rachel Black. Contemporary Perspectives, Inc.† (13)

The Home Front: U.S.A. Ronald Bailey. Time-Life Books Inc.† (12)

Ludell. Brenda Wilkinson. New York: Harper & Row, Pubs., Inc. (13)

Protectors of the Wilderness: The First Forest Rangers. Teri Crawford. Contemporary Perspectives, Inc.† (13)

Teddy Roosevelt and the Roughriders. Henry Castor. New York: Random House, Inc. (12)

Women of Courage. Dorothy Nathan. New York: Random House, Inc. (13)

World War One. Robert Hoare. Macdonald Educational Ltd.† (12)

World War Two. Robert Hoare. Macdonald Educational Ltd.† (12)

BOOKS FOR TEACHERS

Affluence and Anxiety: America Since Nine-

teen Forty Five. Carl N. Segler. Glenview, Ill.: Scott, Foresman & Co. (13)

American Diplomacy: 1900 – 1950. George F. Kennan. Chicago: University of Chicago Press. (12)

The Influence of Seapower Upon History. Alfred T. Mahan. Boston: Little, Brown & Co. (12)

OTHER MEDIA
Filmstrips

America Becomes a Great Power. New York: Pathescope Educational Films, Inc. 61 frames, sound or audiotape, color. (13)

World War II. New York: McGraw-Hill, Inc. Set of 5, color. (13)

Films (16 mm)

Eye to Eye (Brown vs. Blue—Lesson on Discrimination). Syracuse, N.Y.: Syracuse University Film Library. Optical Sound, 20 min, color. (13)

Sufferin' Until Sufferage. Middletown, Conn.: Xerox Films. 3 min, color. (13)

Records

"Big Rock Candy Mountain." *Silver Burdett Music 5,* Record 1. (13)

"Simple Gifts." *Silver Burdett Music 5,* Record 9. (12)

UNIT SIX
BOOKS FOR PUPILS

Automobile Factory. Melvin Berger. New York: Franklin Watts, Inc. (19)

First Book of Coal. Betsy H. Craft. New York: Franklin Watts, Inc. (16, 17)

First Book of Graphs, rev. ed. Dino Lowenstein. New York: Franklin Watts, Inc. (14)

First Book of Nuclear Energy. Dan Halacy. New York: Franklin Watts, Inc. (16)

First Book of Oil and Natural Gas. Betsy H. Craft. New York: Franklin Watts, Inc. (18, 21)

First Book of Textiles. Roz Abisch and Boche Kaplan. New York: Franklin Watts, Inc. (15, 17)

Food Processing Plant. Melvin Berger. New York: Franklin Watts, Inc. (15 – 21)

Hurricanes: Monster Storms from the Sea. Ruth Brindze. New York: Atheneum Pubs. (Distributed by Book Warehouse, Inc., Paterson, N.J.) (17)

Indian Paintbrush. Edna Walker Chandler. Chicago: Albert Whitman & Co. (20)

Mañana Is Now. Alberta Eisman, New York: Atheneum Pubs. (Distributed by Book Warehouse, Inc., Paterson, N.J.) (21)

The Mexican American. Gilbert T. Martinez and Jane Edwards. Boston: Houghton Mifflin Co. (21)

New Enchantment of America State Books, rev. ed. (Series: 1 book for each state). Allen Carpenter. Chicago: Childrens Press. (15 – 21)

Printing Plant. Melvin Berger. New York: Franklin Watts, Inc. (16)

Scenic Wonders of America. Readers' Digest, ed. New York: W.W. Norton & Co., Inc. (14 – 21)

T23

Simple Gifts: The Story of the Shakers. Jane Yolen. New York: The Viking Press. (15)

Steel Mill. Melvin Berger. New York: Franklin Watts, Inc. (16)

BOOKS FOR TEACHERS

The American Wilderness (series). Time-Life Books Inc.† (15−21)

America's Inland Waterways. Allen C. Fisher, Jr. Washington, D.C.: National Geographic Society. (14)

New York. Anthony Burgess. Time-Life Books Inc.† (16)

OTHER MEDIA
Filmstrips

A Geography of the United States and Its People. Chicago: Encyclopaedia Britannica Educational Corp. 5 series (set of 4−5 each), 65−75 frames, cassettes, teacher's guide. (14−21)

Geology Series. Santa Monica, Calif.: BFA Educational Media. Set of 4, cassettes or records, study guide. (14, 19, 21)

Industry and Technology. Burbank, Calif.: Walt Disney Educational Media Co. Set of 4, records or cassettes, teacher's guide, color. (14−21)

The Jelly Bean Company: A Career Activity Program. Santa Monica, Calif.: BFA Educational Media. 2 series (set of 6 each), cassettes or records, study guide, color. (17)

The Many Americans, Parts 1 and 2. New York: Learning Corp. of America. Set of 8, cassettes, study guides, color. (14−21)

Regions of the United States. Mahwah, N.J.: Troll Associates. Set of 8, 66 frames, cassettes, color. (15−21)

The Story of Salt. Santa Monica, Calif.: BFA Educational Media. Set of 4, cassettes or records, study guides, color. (18)

Records

"Fisherman's Song." *Silver Burdett Music 4,* Record 2. (15)

"Mountain Sound." *Silver Burdett Music 5,* Record 2. (20)

"Nani Wale Na Hala." *Silver Burdett Music 5,* Record 5. (21)

"Old Texas." *Silver Burdett Music 5,* Record 8. (18)

"On Top of Old Smokey." *Silver Burdett Music 5,* Record 3. (17)

"Shrimp Boats." *Silver Burdett Music 5,* Record 1. (16)

"Thank God I'm a Country Boy." *Silver Burdett Music 5,* Record 3. (19)

"This Land Is Your Land." *Silver Burdett Music 4,* Record 10. (14)

UNIT SEVEN
BOOKS FOR PUPILS

Canada. Linda W. Ferguson. New York: Charles Scribner's Sons. (22)

Canada. Theo L. Hills and Jane Hills. Grand Rapids, Mich.: The Fideler Co. (22)

Enchantment of South America (A series: books on individual countries). Allen Carpenter. Chicago: Childrens Press. (23)

Fifteen Famous Latin Americans. Helen Bailey and Maria Grijalva. Englewood Cliffs, N.J.: Prentice-Hall, Inc. (23)

The First Book of Puerto Rico, rev. ed. Antonio Colorado. New York: Franklin Watts, Inc. (23)

The First Book of South America, rev. ed. William Carter. New York: Franklin Watts, Inc. (23)

Llamas of South America. Gladys Conklin. New York: Holiday House, Inc. (23)

Looking at Canada. Josephine Earn. Philadelphia: J.B. Lippincott Co. (23)

Mexico. Robert Marett. New York: Walker & Co. (23)

Mexico. Patricia F. Ross. Grand Rapids, Mich.: The Fideler Co. (23)

Portraits of Nations, (Land and People series). Philadelphia: J.B. Lippincott Co. (23)

BOOKS FOR TEACHERS

Beauty of Canada. Lorne Greene. New York: Mayflower Books, Inc. (22)

Canada. Edmund Nagele. New York: Mayflower Books, Inc. (22)

Canada: A Guide to the Peaceable Kingdom. William Kilbourn. New York: St. Martin's Press, Inc. (22)

Canada A to Z, rev. ed. Robert S. Kane. Garden City, N.Y.: Doubleday & Co., Inc. (22)

Colour of Canada, 3rd ed. Hugh Maclennan. Boston: Little, Brown & Co. (22)

Maya Land in Color. Walter R. Aguiar. New York: Hastings House, Pubs., Inc. (23)

OTHER MEDIA
Filmstrips

Canada: Challenge of Change. Chicago: Society for Visual Education, Inc. Set of 4, 72 frames, cassettes, teacher's guide, color. (22)

The Canadians. Chicago: Encyclopaedia Britannica Educational Corp. Set of 5, 77 frames, record or cassette, teacher's guide, color. (22)

Central America: A Regional Study. New York: Eye Gate Media, Inc. Set of 4, cassette, color. (23)

Central America and the Caribbean. Chicago: Encyclopaedia Britannica Educational Corp. Set of 6, 80 frames, record or cassette, teacher's guide, color. (23)

Lifeways of the People: South America. New York: Eye Gate Media, Inc. Set of 6, cassette or record, color. (23)

Mexico: A Regional Study. New York: Eye Gate Media, Inc. Set of 4, cassette, color. (23)

People and Geography of South America. New York: Eye Gate Media, Inc. Set of 6, cassette or record, color. (23)

South America: Land of Many Faces. Chicago: Society for Visual Education. Set of 5, 63 frames, cassette, teacher's guide, color. (23)

Records

"Banana Boat Loaders." *Silver Burdett Music 5,* Record 3. (23)

"Vive La Canadienne!" *Silver Burdett Music 5,* Record 1. (22)

PROFESSIONAL BOOKS
FOR TEACHERS

The Blue Book of Occupational Education. Max M. Russell, ed. New York: CCM Information Corporation.

Crucial Issues in the Teaching of Social Studies: A Book of Readings. Byron G. Massialas and Andreas M. Kazamais, eds. Englewood Cliffs, N.J.: Prentice-Hall, Inc.

Discovering the Structure of Social Studies. James G. Womack. Encino, Calif.: Bruce & Glencoe, Inc.

Economics and Its Significance. Richard S. Martin and Reuben G. Miller. Columbus, Ohio: Charles E. Merrill Pub. Co.

The Geography of Population: A Teacher's Guide. Paul Griffin, ed. The 1970 Yearbook of The National Council for Geographic Education. Belmont, Calif.: Fearon Pubs., Inc.

Handicapped People in Society: Ideas and Activities for Teachers. Ruth-Ellen K. Ross, and others. Morristown, N.J.: Silver Burdett Company.

Skill Development in Social Studies. (Thirty-third Yearbook of the National Council for the Social Studies). Helen McCracken Carpenter, ed. Washington, D.C.: National Council for the Social Studies.

The Slow Learner in the Classroom. Newell C. Kephart. Columbus, Ohio: Charles E. Merrill Pub. Co.

The Social Studies and the Social Sciences. Gordon B. Turner, et al. New York: Harcourt Brace Jovanovich, Inc.

The Social Studies: Eightieth Yearbook of the National Society for the Study of Education, Part II. Howard D. Mehlinger and O. L. Davis, Jr., eds. Chicago: University of Chicago Press.

Social Studies Through Problem Solving. Maxine Dunfee and Helen Sagl. New York: Holt, Rinehart & Winston, Inc.

Sociology: The Study of Man in Society. Caroline B. Rose. Columbus, Ohio: Charles E. Merrill Pub. Co.

The Study and Teaching of Social Science Series. Raymond H. Muessig, ed. New York: Charles E. Merrill Pub. Co.

Teaching Ethnic Studies. James A. Banks, ed. Belmont, Calif.: Fearon Pubs., Inc.

Teaching Social Studies in the Elementary School. Theodore Kaltsounis. New York: Prentice-Hall, Inc.

THE UNITED STATES AND ITS NEIGHBORS

THE UNITED

AUTHORS

Val E. Arnsdorf, Professor,
College of Education, University of Delaware,
Newark, Delaware

Carolyn S. Brown, Principal,
Robertson Academy School, Nashville, Tennessee

Kenneth S. Cooper, Professor of History, Emeritus,
George Peabody College for Teachers, Vanderbilt
University, Nashville, Tennessee

Alvis T. Harthern, Professor of Education,
University of Montevallo, Montevallo, Alabama

Timothy M. Helmus, Middle School Teacher,
Harrison Park Middle School, Grand Rapids,
Michigan

Bobbie P. Hyder, Elementary Education Coordinator,
Madison County School System, Huntsville, Alabama

Theodore Kaltsounis, Professor and Chairman of
Curriculum and Instruction,
College of Education, University of Washington,
Seattle, Washington

Richard H. Loftin, Director of Curriculum and Staff
Development,
Aldine Independent School District, Houston, Texas

Norman J. G. Pounds, Former University Professor
of Geography,
Indiana University, Bloomington, Indiana

Edgar A. Toppin, Professor of History and Dean of
the Graduate School,
Virginia State University, Petersburg, Virginia

PROGRAM CONTRIBUTORS

Paula Allaert, Third Grade Teacher,
St. Therese School, Portland, Oregon

Carol Armour, Third Grade Teacher,
Marie V. Duffy Elementary School, Wharton, New Jersey

Sandra Breman, Fifth Grade Teacher,
Whitney Young Magnet School, Fort Wayne, Indiana

Vivian Brown, Fifth Grade Teacher,
Silver Spur Elementary School, Rancho Palos Verdes,
California

Kim Eyler, Former Elementary School Teacher,
Wyckoff, New Jersey

Sharon Gaydon, Sixth Grade Teacher,
Thompson Middle School, Alabaster, Alabama

Janet Glenn, Second Grade Teacher,
Greene School, Greensboro, North Carolina

Viola Gonzalez, Fifth-Sixth Grade Teacher,
Ryan Elementary School, Laredo, Texas

Ellen Gremillion, Third Grade Teacher,
Parkview Elementary School, Baton Rouge, Louisiana

Lucy Hatch, Fifth-Sixth Grade Teacher,
Taylor Elementary School, Abilene, Texas

Judy Hobson, Fourth Grade Teacher,
Elmdale Elementary School, Springdale, Arkansas

Peggy Hogg, Fourth Grade Teacher,
Dartmouth Elementary School, Richardson, Texas

Geoffrey Kashdan, Special Education Teacher,
Hanover Avenue School, Morris Plains, New Jersey

Gloria Lemos, First Grade Teacher,
Emerson Elementary School, Pasco, Washington

William Lentino, Fifth Grade Teacher,
Lloyd Harbor Elementary School, Huntington, New York

Carolyn Lombardo, Third Grade Teacher,
Ferrara Elementary School, East Haven, Connecticut

Mary Lou Martin, Social Studies Resource Teacher, K–6,
San Diego Unified School District, San Diego, California

Patricia McWey, Second Grade Teacher,
Martin Luther King School, Providence, Rhode Island

Sandra Murphy Mead, Second Grade Teacher,
L. W. West School, Endicott, New York

Ray Ringley, Fifth Grade Teacher,
Powell Valley Primary School, Big Stone Gap, Virginia

Elaine Sisselman, Fourth Grade Teacher,
Biscayne Gardens Elementary School, Miami, Florida

Katharyn Smith, First Grade Teacher,
The Meadows School, College Park, Georgia

Jan Talbot, Sixth Grade Teacher,
Pope Avenue Elementary School, Sacto, California

Patricia Terai, First Grade Teacher,
Woodin Elementary School, Bothell, Washington

William Tucker, Sixth Grade Teacher,
Alanton Elementary School, Virginia Beach, Virginia

Sister Catherine Zajac, S.S.J., Fourth-Sixth Grade Teacher,
St. Agnes School, Dalton, Massachusetts

STATES AND ITS NEIGHBORS

TIMOTHY M. HELMUS
Middle School Teacher, Harrison Park Middle School, Grand Rapids, Michigan

VAL E. ARNSDORF   Professor, College of Education,
University of Delaware, Newark, Delaware

EDGAR A. TOPPIN   Professor of History and Dean of the Graduate School,
Virginia State University, Petersburg, Virginia

NORMAN J. G. POUNDS   Former University Professor, Geography,
Indiana University, Bloomington, Indiana

SILVER BURDETT COMPANY   **Morristown, N.J.**
Glenview, Ill. • San Carlos, Calif. • Dallas • Atlanta

CONTENTS

ACKNOWLEDGMENT

Page 125: From THE WINTER AT VALLEY FORGE, by F. Van
Wyck Mason. Copyright 1953 by F. Van Wyck Mason.
Reprinted by permission of Random House, Inc., and
Harold Matson Company, Inc.

MAPS

A LETTER TO YOU FROM THE AUTHORS

Dear Student:

We hope you will enjoy using this book that we have written for you. It is all about the countries of North and South America, especially your country, the United States.

You will learn about the first Americans who lived here, the explorers who came here, and the people from other lands who settled here. You will also learn the wonderful story of the birth and growth of a new nation—the United States of America. And you will see how the United States became a world leader.

In this book we have divided the United States into seven geographic regions. You will learn many interesting facts about these different parts of the country. In addition to the written material in The United States and Its Neighbors, there are maps, charts, tables, and many pictures to help you.

We hope you will come to appreciate the beauty and variety of the land and the people in your country and in the rest of the Western Hemisphere. We hope you will also learn that what people have done in the past affects us today, and that what we do today will affect the future.

Most of all, we hope that this will be an exciting year for you.

Sincerely,

Timothy M. Helmus

Dal Amsdorf

Edgar Allan Toppin

Norman J. G. Pounds

Tools for Learning About Your Country

These figures represent the uses and functions of geography and history. The boy holds a globe, a proportional representation of the earth's surface. The woman is reading a road map. The man and girl are taking part in a historical process by studying a family album together.

Where Is It?

Have pupils make a rebus for the lyrics to "America the Beautiful."

┌─VOCABULARY──────────────────┐

hemisphere	longitude
North Pole	Arctic Circle
equator	Antarctic Circle
South Pole	Tropic of Cancer
continent	Tropic of Capricorn
compass rose	meridian
latitude	prime meridian

└──────────────────────────────┘

Our nation: a big, beautiful land   We live in one of the biggest countries in the world, the United States of America. We live in one of the most beautiful countries on earth, also. Few other nations have as many different and interesting kinds of people and places as ours. Poets and songwriters have written about the great size and beauty and the rich history of our land. You have probably sung this song many times.

> O beautiful for spacious skies,
> For amber waves of grain,
> For purple mountain majesties
> Above the fruited plain!
> America! America! God shed His grace on
>   thee
> And crown thy good with brotherhood
> From sea to shining sea!

Ask pupils to define *patriot* and name famous American patriots they know. Relate to Grade 5 content.

> O beautiful for patriot dream
> That sees beyond the years
> Thine alabaster cities gleam,
> Undimmed by human tears!
> America! America! God shed His grace on
>   thee

> And crown thy good with brotherhood
> From sea to shining sea!

Do you remember this song? Do you know what its words mean? The song is "America, the Beautiful." Its words were written in 1893 by an American teacher who was also a fine poet. Her name was Katharine Lee Bates. As you read this book, you will learn a great deal about what the poet meant when she wrote the words. You will learn about our people, our land, and our history.

Hemispheres   Let's begin our study of the United States by imagining that you and your family are planning a trip. You are going to a place that is far from home. What do you need to know in order to make your plans?

First, you will want to know just where you're going. Suppose your mother and father have said that you will be going to Yellowstone National Park. Unless you have been there before, or have learned about national parks in school, you probably do not know where Yellowstone is. How might your parents go about telling you where it is?

They might begin by telling you that it is in the Northern Hemisphere (hem' ə sfir). A **hemisphere** is one half of the earth's surface. (Words in heavy type are in the Glossary at the end of the book.) The Northern Hemisphere includes all of the

Have pupils write a poem or short essay on "What America Means to Me" or "America the Beautiful."
This photograph shows the rugged beauty of Yellowstone National Park.

Yellowstone (45°58′N/110°42′W) is the oldest national park in the United States. The Yellowstone River plunges down the canyon walls creating the Lower Falls (308 ft, 94 m) and the Upper Falls (109 ft, 33m).

earth's surface between the **North Pole** and the **equator.**

The North Pole is the most northern place in the world. North is the direction toward the North Pole. The North Pole is at the opposite end of the earth from the **South Pole.** The South Pole is the most southern place in the world. South is the direction toward the South Pole.

Halfway between the North Pole and the South Pole is the line called the equator. The equator circles the whole earth. Mapmakers use this line to divide the earth into the Northern Hemisphere and the Southern Hemisphere. You will learn more about the equator a little later. Look at the maps at the top of page 5. These maps show the Northern Hemisphere and the Southern Hemisphere. Find Yellowstone National Park in the Northern Hemisphere.

There is another way to divide the earth into halves. It can be divided into a Western Hemisphere and an Eastern Hemisphere. Look at the maps at the bottom of page 5. In which of these two hemispheres do you find Yellowstone National Park?

When you face north, east is the direction to your right. West is to your left. East and west are opposite each other just as north and south are opposite each other.

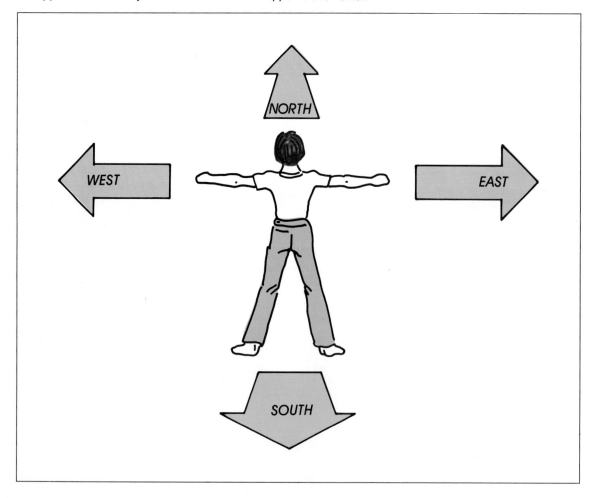

Where appropriate in the teacher's edition, we have provided the locations of places in degrees and minutes.

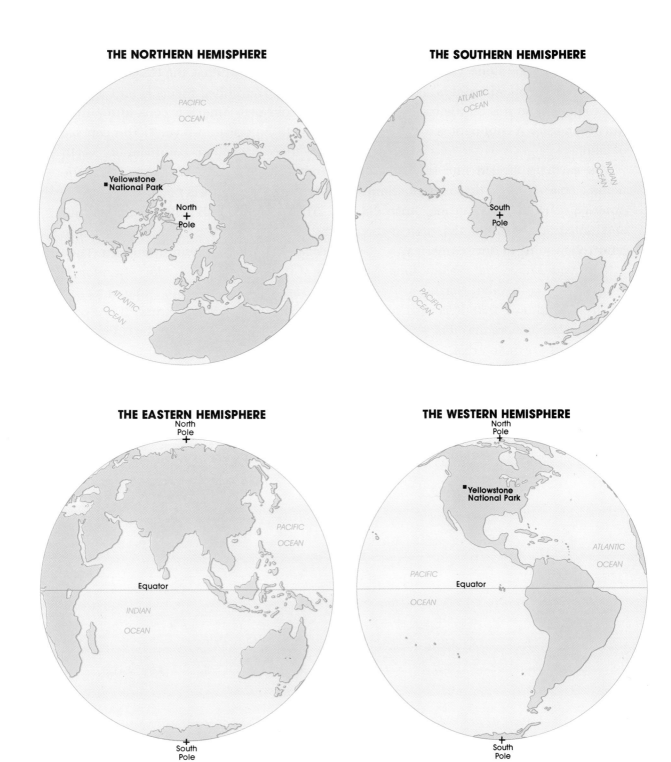

THE NORTHERN HEMISPHERE

PACIFIC
OCEAN

Yellowstone
National Park

North
+
Pole

ATLANTIC
OCEAN

THE SOUTHERN HEMISPHERE

ATLANTIC
OCEAN

INDIAN
OCEAN

South
+
Pole

PACIFIC
OCEAN

THE EASTERN HEMISPHERE

North
Pole
+

PACIFIC
OCEAN

Equator

INDIAN

OCEAN

South
+
Pole

THE WESTERN HEMISPHERE

North
Pole
+

Yellowstone
National Park

ATLANTIC
OCEAN

PACIFIC

OCEAN

Equator

South
+
Pole

Dividing the earth at the equator gives you the Northern Hemisphere and the Southern Hemisphere. Dividing the earth in half along a line passing through the North and South Poles results in the Eastern Hemisphere and the Western Hemisphere.

After pupils have read about the continents on p. 6, ask them to identify the continents shown in each hemisphere above.

Continents   Of course, if you are traveling to Yellowstone you will have to know more about where it is. It will help you to know that it is on the **continent** of North America. A continent is a huge area of land.

The earth is divided into seven continents. They are North America, South America, Africa, Asia, Europe, Australia, and Antarctica. Look at the map below. Find Yellowstone in North America.

Now you know that Yellowstone National Park is in the Northern Hemisphere. You know that it is also in the Western Hemisphere and that it is on the continent of North America.

Countries   Yellowstone National Park is also in our country, the United States of America. The United States is on the continent of North America. Look at the map of North America on page 7. You can see that there are other countries in North America. Mexico is our neighbor to the south. What country is north of us?

The map of North America also shows the countries of Central America. There are six countries in Central America. They are Guatemala, El Salvador, Honduras, Nicaragua, Costa Rica, and Panama. Belize is not an independent country. It is a part of the United Kingdom. The map also shows the Caribbean Islands.

Find the four major oceans of the world on this map. What are their names? Sometimes people think of Europe and Asia as one continent. They call it Eurasia.

THE EARTH'S CONTINENTS

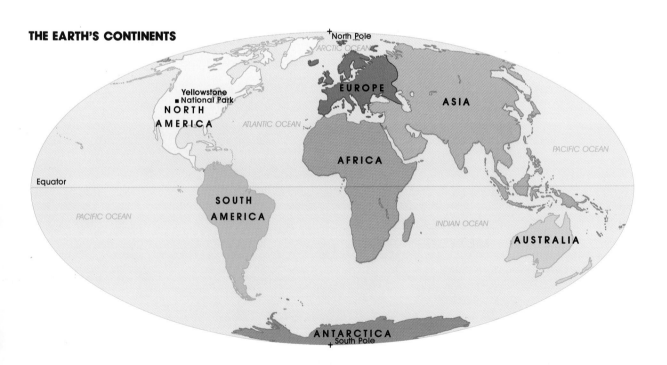

The map on page 7 shows the capital cities of North America, as well as all the countries. What is the capital of Mexico?

Some scientists think that the continents were connected as one large landmass 200 million years ago. Observe the shapes of the continents and discuss how they might have been connected. Ask: Which continent is the largest? (Asia)

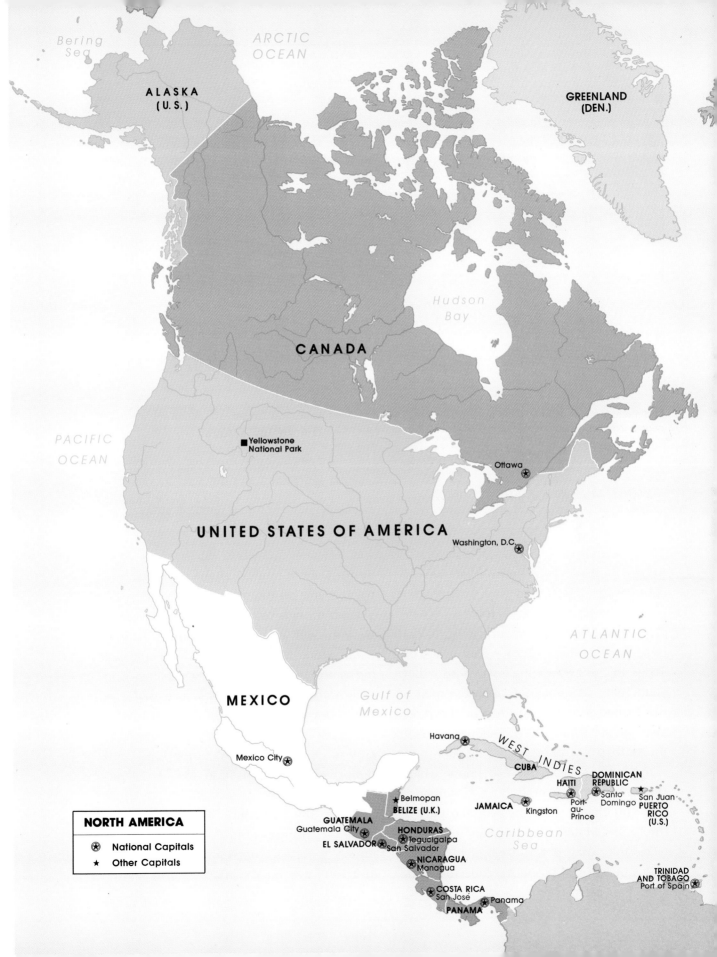

Bering Sea

ARCTIC OCEAN

ALASKA (U.S.)

GREENLAND (DEN.)

CANADA

Hudson Bay

PACIFIC OCEAN

■Yellowstone National Park

Ottawa ⊛

UNITED STATES OF AMERICA

Washington, D.C. ⊛

ATLANTIC OCEAN

MEXICO

Gulf of Mexico

Mexico City ⊛

Havana ⊛

WEST INDIES

CUBA

DOMINICAN REPUBLIC

HAITI

Port-au-Prince ⊛

⊛ Santo Domingo

San Juan ★

PUERTO RICO (U.S.)

JAMAICA

Kingston ⊛

★ Belmopan

BELIZE (U.K.)

GUATEMALA

Guatemala City ⊛

HONDURAS

⊛ Tegucigalpa

EL SALVADOR ⊛

San Salvador

NICARAGUA

Managua ⊛

Caribbean Sea

TRINIDAD AND TOBAGO

Port of Spain ⊛

COSTA RICA

San José ⊛

Panama ⊛

PANAMA

NORTH AMERICA

⊛ National Capitals

★ Other Capitals

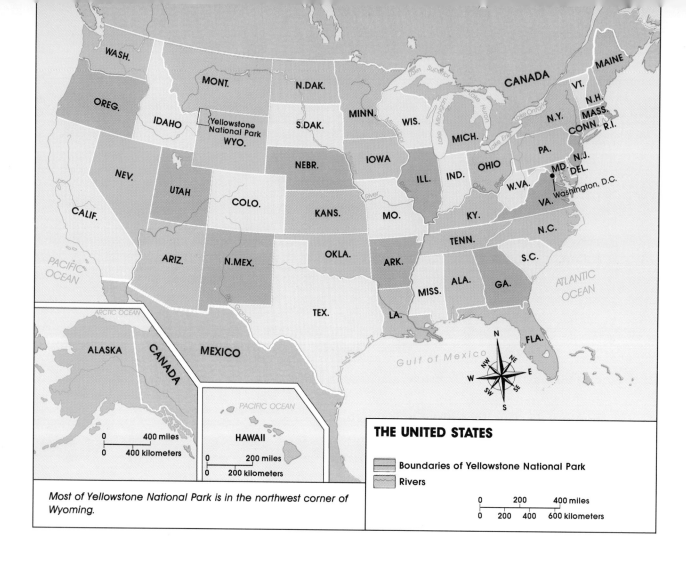

Most of Yellowstone National Park is in the northwest corner of Wyoming.

THE UNITED STATES

Boundaries of Yellowstone National Park
Rivers

States   Now you know that Yellowstone is in the United States. But what part of the United States is it in?

As you know, our country is divided into parts called states. There are 50 states in the United States. To find which state Yellowstone is in, look at the map of the United States at the top of the page. You will see that most of Yellowstone is in the state of Wyoming.

But what if you did not know where Wyoming is? It would help if someone told you that it is in the western part of the United States. It would also help if you were told that it is surrounded by the states of Idaho, Utah, Colorado, Nebraska,

South Dakota, and Montana. Find each of these states on the map above.

Even though you know where Wyoming is, you still might not be able to find Yellowstone National Park. Wyoming is a big state. But you could probably find Yellowstone if someone told you that it is in the northwest corner of the state.

Compass rose   Directions help you find places on maps and globes. Sometimes directions are shown by a small drawing on the map. This drawing is called a **compass rose**, or a direction finder. It shows where north, south, east, and west are on the map. It also shows where the in-between directions are. It shows you how to find northwest (NW), northeast (NE), southwest (SW), and southeast (SE). On the map on page 8 find Yellowstone National Park in the northwest corner of Wyoming.

Latitude   A more exact way to tell you where to find a place is to give you its **latitude** and **longitude.** Look at the map on this page. The lines drawn on this map are called lines of latitude. You can see that these lines stretch east and west.

You have already learned the name of a very important line of latitude. It is the equator. You know that the equator is halfway between the North Pole and the South Pole. The lines of latitude north of the equator are called lines of north latitude. The lines south of the equator are called lines of south latitude.

The equator itself is numbered 0. All other lines of latitude measure distances north or south of the equator. These distances are measured in degrees. The sign for degrees is (°). So the equator is always marked 0° and is read "zero degrees." Find the equator on the map on this page. Now find the line marked 15°N. This is read "15 degrees north." How do you read 15°S? 30°N? 30°S?

There are other lines of latitude that have names. Two of them are the **Arctic Circle** and the **Antarctic Circle.** The Arctic Circle is at 66½° north. The Antarctic circle is at 66½° south. The other two named lines are the **Tropic of Cancer** and the **Tropic of Capricorn.** The Tropic of Cancer is at 23½° north. The Tropic of Capricorn is at 23½° south. Find these four lines on the map.

THE IN-BETWEEN DIRECTIONS

The letters NW stand for northwest. What does NE stand for? SE? SW? What are the 5 named lines of latitude on the map below?

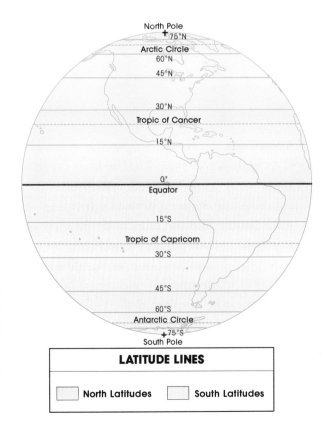

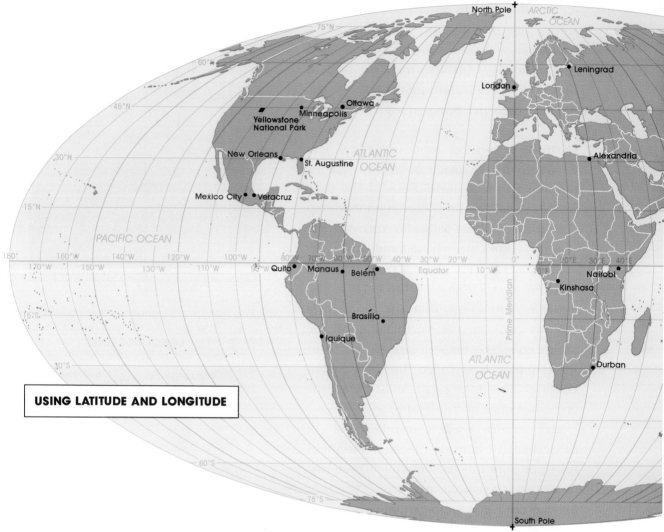

Longitude   Now look at the map on the right side of page 11. The lines on this map are lines of longitude. Another name for these lines is **meridians** (mə rid′ ē ənz). Notice that the lines of longitude run north and south from Pole to Pole.

A very important line of longitude is called the **prime meridian.** Like the equator, it is numbered 0°. However, the equator is 0° latitude. The prime meridian is 0° longitude. All the other <u>lines of lon-</u> <u>gitude measure distances in degrees east</u> <u>or west of the prime meridian.</u> This line passes through Greenwich (gren′ ich), a

part of London, England. Half of all lines of longitude are west of Greenwich. The others are east of Greenwich.

Using latitude and longitude   Now you know something about lines, of latitude and longitude. Let us see how they can help you locate Yellowstone.

A good way to tell you how to find Yellowstone is to say that it is at 45° north latitude and 110° west longitude. Look at the map above. This map of the world shows both lines of longitude and lines of latitude. Put one finger on the line

Ask pupils to name the cities located at the following coordinates: 2°S/48°W (Belem); 52°N/0° (London); 2°S/36°E (Nairobi); 15°N/122°E (Manila); 30°N/82°W (St. Augustine); 41°S/175°E (Wellington).

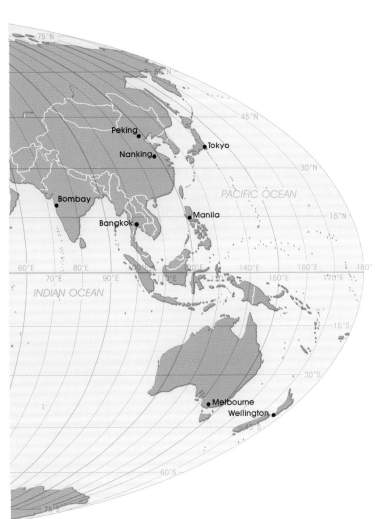

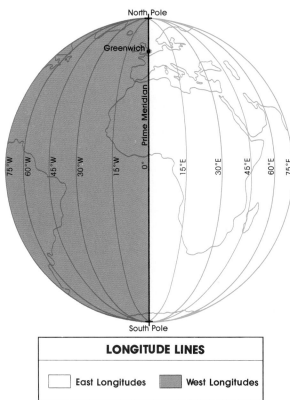

The prime meridian divides the world into east longitudes and west longitudes. Find the latitude and longitude of the cities shown on the world map.

LONGITUDE LINES

☐ East Longitudes   ■ West Longitudes

marked 45° north latitude. Put a finger of your other hand on the line marked 110° west longitude. Now move your fingers toward each other on these lines. The place where these two lines meet is Yellowstone National Park.

In telling someone where Yellowstone National Park is, you could say, "It is in the northwest corner of the state of Wyoming. Wyoming is in the United States. The United States is on the continent of North America. North America is in the Western Hemisphere." But you can see how much more exact it is to say that

Yellowstone National Park can be found at 45° north latitude and 110° west longitude.

You can find any place in the world on a map if you know its latitude and longitude. Almost all globes and maps have these lines marked to help you locate places quickly and easily.

CHECKUP

1. In which hemisphere is Yellowstone found?
2. On which continent is the United States found?
3. In which state is Yellowstone found?
4. Which lines measure distances north and south of the equator?
5. Which lines measure distances east and west of the prime meridian?

You may wish to point out to your more advanced pupils that by using minutes and seconds as well as degrees, latitude and longitude can be used to pinpoint locations. Point out that each degree (°) is divided into 60 minutes (′) and that each minute can be further divided into 60 seconds (″).

11

How Far Is It?

Scale   Now you know where Yellowstone National Park is. But if you are going there on your trip you will also want to know how far it is from your home. To find out, you can use a map **scale.** Let's see how such a scale works. Of course, distances on maps must be smaller than the real distances on the earth. So a certain number of inches on a map stand for a certain number of miles on the earth. On a map of a very small area, 1 inch can stand for a certain number of feet. The numbered line that gives you this information is called the scale. The map scale tells you the relationship between the real distance on the earth and the distance shown on the map.

Look at the drawing of a Little League baseball field below. This drawing is a kind of map. On this map, 1 inch stands for 50 feet. The scale at the bottom of the

Ask: How far is home plate from the pitcher's rubber? (46 ft; 14 m) How far is home plate from second base? (84 ft 10 in.; 26.9 m) How far is second base from third base? (60 ft; 18 m)

The scale tells you the relationship between the real distance on the earth and the distance shown on the map.

Have pupils use graph paper to draw their school or classroom to scale.

LITTLE LEAGUE FIELD

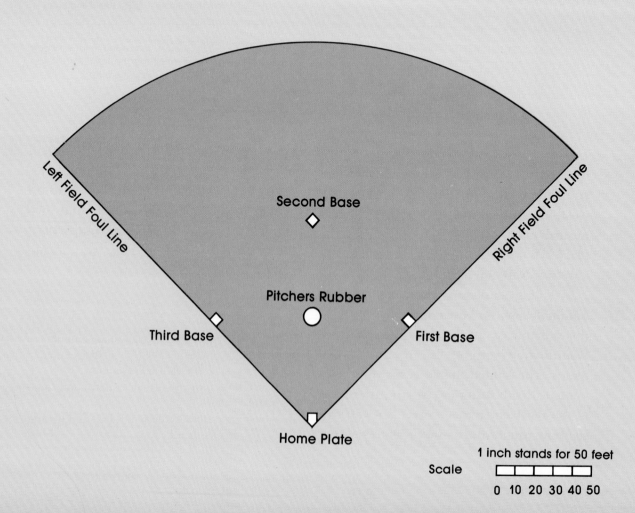

1 inch stands for 50 feet

Scale

0 10 20 30 40 50

THE METRIC SYSTEM OF MEASUREMENT

In the section below, you will read that one kilometer (km) and a little more than half a mile are about the same distance. A kilometer is a unit of measure in the metric system.

This system is used for measuring distance. It is also used for measuring such things as weight, capacity, and heat. The metric system is in use or being introduced in all the major countries of the world except the United States. However, plans are being made to "go metric" here also.

To prepare you for this change, we have used both U.S. and metric measurements in this book. When a U.S. measurement appears in this book, it is followed in parentheses ( ) by the metric measurement that is about equal to it. Inches are changed to centimeters (cm), feet and yards to meters (m), miles to kilometers (km), and acres to hectares (ha). Pounds are changed to kilograms (kg), and quarts to liters (L). Degrees Fahrenheit (°F) are changed to degrees Celsius (°C).

map tells you that. Place a ruler along the right-field foul line. You will see that it is 4 inches from home plate to the end of the right-field foul line.

Remember, each inch on the map stands for 50 feet on a real baseball field. To find out how far it is from home plate to the end of the right-field foul line, you multiply 4 by 50. By doing this you will see that on a real Little League baseball field, home plate is 200 feet from the end of the right-field foul line.

Miles and kilometers On pages 14 – 15 is a map of the United States. Look at the map scale. Notice that this map scale gives distances in **kilometers** (kil' ə mē terz) as well as in miles. Kilometers are a measure of distance in the *metric system*. A kilometer (km) is a little more than half a mile. You can find out more about the metric system above.

On this map 1 inch stands for 200 miles. The map scale also tells you that 2 **centimeters** (cm) stand for 250 kilometers. Find Yellowstone on the map. Now

find Washington, D.C., our nation's capital. Lay a ruler between Washington, D.C., and Yellowstone National Park. You will see that the distance on the map is about 8½ inches. You know that the scale on this map is 200 miles to an inch. So by multiplying 8½ by 200, you find that it is 1,700 miles from Washington, D.C., to Yellowstone National Park.

Find your state on the map on pages 14 – 15. Then find your community. No map can show every city and town in the United States. Don't be surprised if yours is not on the map. Just find on the map the city you think is nearest where you live. Using what you know about scale, find out how many miles it is to Yellowstone. How many kilometers is it?

CHECKUP

1. What part of a map helps you find out how far one place is from another?
2. How long is a kilometer?
3. Kilometers and centimeters are units of measure in what system?

Seattle
Olympia ⊛ WASHINGTON
Spokane

Portland
⊛ Salem OREGON
Eugene

Great Falls Missouri River
Helena ⊛ MONTANA
Billings

NORTH DAKOTA
Bismarck ⊛
Grand Forks
Fargo

Boise IDAHO
Idaho Falls
Pocatello

WYOMING
Casper

SOUTH DAKOTA
⊛ Pierre
Rapid City
Sioux Falls
Missouri River

Sacramento ⊛
Reno NEVADA
Carson City ⊛

Oakland
San Francisco
San Jose CALIFORNIA
Fresno

Great Salt Lake
Ogden
⊛ Salt Lake City
Provo
UTAH

Laramie
Cheyenne ⊛

NEBRASKA
Grand Island
Omaha
Lincoln ⊛

Las Vegas
Colorado River

Denver ⊛
Aurora
COLORADO
Colorado Springs

KANSAS
Topeka ⊛
Wichita
Arkansas River

Los Angeles Anaheim
Long Beach Santa Ana
San Diego

ARIZONA
Phoenix ⊛
Mesa
Tucson

Albuquerque
⊛ Santa Fe
NEW MEXICO

OKLAHOMA
Oklahoma City ⊛
Tulsa
Lawton
Red River

PACIFIC OCEAN

Las Cruces
El Paso

MEXICO

Fort Worth Dallas
TEXAS
Brazos River

Austin ⊛
San Antonio
Corpus Christi

HAWAII
Honolulu ⊛ Kailua
PACIFIC OCEAN
Hilo

0   100 miles
0   150 kilometers

ARCTIC OCEAN
U.S.S.R.

Arctic Circle

ALASKA
Fairbanks

CANADA

Anchorage

Juneau ⊛

PACIFIC OCEAN

0   200 miles
0   200 kilometers

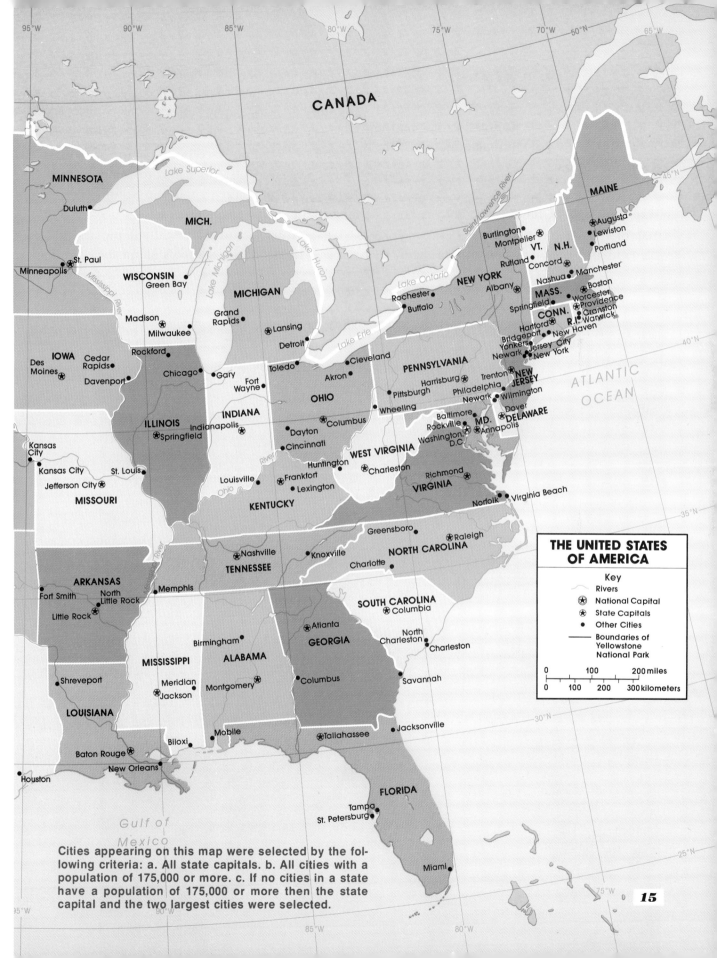

THE UNITED STATES OF AMERICA

Key
- ～～ Rivers
- ✪ National Capital
- ✵ State Capitals
- • Other Cities
- —— Boundaries of Yellowstone National Park

0		100		200 miles
0	100	200	300 kilometers	

15

Cities appearing on this map were selected by the following criteria: a. All state capitals. b. All cities with a population of 175,000 or more. c. If no cities in a state have a population of 175,000 or more then the state capital and the two largest cities were selected.

Volcanic molten rock, or magma, beneath the surface of the parklands heats more than 200 active geysers and thousands of hot springs found in Yellowstone National Park.

The Language of Maps

Map key and symbols   Look at the map of Yellowstone National Park on page 17. Find the map **key.** As you probably know, the map key is one of the most important parts of any map. This part of a map is called the key because it unlocks the map's secrets for you. It also tells you about all the **symbols** used on the map.

Maps use symbols, or signs, to show where places are and to tell you something about them. Sometimes letters are used as symbols. Sometimes small pictures are used. All the symbols stand for

Old Faithful is a geyser. It shoots steamy water into the air once every hour.

For over 80 years Old Faithful has erupted for an average of 4 minutes of every hour. The water shoots between 120 and 150 ft (37–46 m) high.

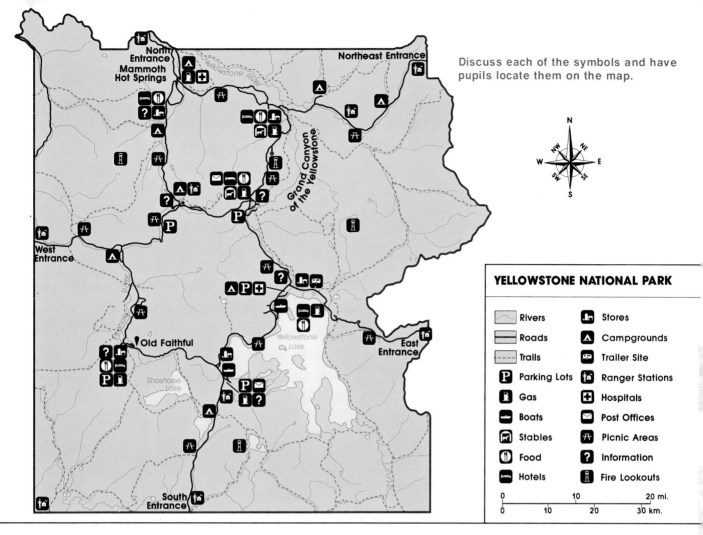

Discuss each of the symbols and have pupils locate them on the map.

YELLOWSTONE NATIONAL PARK

Rivers		Stores
Roads		Campgrounds
Trails		Trailer Site
Parking Lots		Ranger Stations
Gas		Hospitals
Boats		Post Offices
Stables		Picnic Areas
Food		Information
Hotels		Fire Lookouts

0   10   20 mi.
0   10   20   30 km.

Yellowstone National Park was the first national park in our nation. It was made a national park in 1872.

real things and places. The map key tells you just what real things and places the symbols stand for. For example, a cross is one symbol in the key on the map of Yellowstone National Park above. If you were to go to each place marked on the map with a cross, you would find a real hospital. What symbol would you look for if you wanted to find a picnic area? What symbol would you look for if you wanted to find a parking lot? A ranger station?

Labels   Quite often map symbols do not tell you everything you might want to know. If you want to find Yellowstone Lake on the map above, the key will not help you. There is no symbol for lake in the key. You will have to look at the lakes on the map and find the one labeled "Yellowstone Lake." On page 16 is a picture of Old Faithful. Look on the map above to find the label that shows where Old Faithful is.

The map key shows you the symbol for rivers. But the key does not tell you the names of the rivers in Yellowstone National Park. To find a certain river you have to look for its label on the map. Find the Firehole River on the map.

Drawing a map   In this chapter, you have seen many maps. As you know, a map is a special kind of drawing of the earth's surface. It shows what the earth, or part of the earth, looks like from straight overhead. If you were far enough out in space, you could see about one half of the earth's surface. But what would the earth look like if you were only a couple thousand feet (600 m) above it?

The photograph on page 19 was taken from about 1,500 feet (460 m) above the earth's surface. The map on page 19 shows you what a **cartographer** (kär tog′ rə fər), or mapmaker, can do with such a photograph. The photograph and the map show the same area. But the map shows it in a very special way. The cartographer has picked out the most important features of the photograph and used symbols to show them. Find a parking lot in the photograph. Look in the key to find the symbol used on the map to stand for the parking lot. Then find the parking lot on the map. Find the football field and the water tank in the same way.

This is one of the cartographers who made the maps in this book. He is working on the map shown on page 19.

Ask pupils to make a map from one of the photographs on p. 264. Remind them to make a map key for their map.

FROM PHOTOGRAPH TO MAP

| 0 | 100 | 200 Feet |
| 0 | 50 Meters | |

Houses	Running Track	Baseball Diamonds
Roads	Tennis Courts	School Buildings
Woods	Football Field	School Grounds
Water Tank	Soccer Field	Other Land
Parking Lots	Basketball Court	

Grand Teton National Park is 6 miles (10 km) south of Yellowstone. Have pupils locate the park on the map, p. 21. The Tetons rise 7,000 ft (2,100 m) to the highest peak, Grand Teton, which is 13,770 ft (4,197 m). The park also has glacial lakes and is a wildlife preserve for elk, deer, moose, mink, marten, and beaver.

Road map symbols   Many people in the United States travel by car. In 1976 there were more than 110 million cars in this country. If you go to Yellowstone National Park, there is a good chance that you will go by car. Suppose someone handed you a road map and said, "What roads will you take?" Could you read the map? If not, you should learn, because road maps can help you in many ways.

If you go to Yellowstone you may want to take the widest road you can find. Wide highways have many lanes for cars to travel on. Highways with many lanes are sometimes called *expressways*. Cars can move along on them without having to stop for traffic lights. *Interstate highways* are expressways. Interstate highways are roads that connect two or more states. Some of these big highways run through many states.

Look at the map key on page 21. Then on the map find Routes 16, 34, 80, and 85. Which is wider, Route 16 or Route 85? Route 80 or Route 34? What symbols in the map key and on the map helped you answer? You can see how important it is to understand the symbols on a road map.

This map also uses symbols to show the size of cities. Find Casper on the map. It is on Route 220. Notice that the symbol used to show Casper is a large yellow dot. By looking at the key you will see that this means that Casper has a **population** of between 25,000 and 60,000. In other words, between 25,000 and 60,000 people live in the city of Casper.

Remember, symbols stand for real things and places. What other information can the symbols on this map give you?

This camper is traveling on a road in Grand Teton National Park in Wyoming. Find this park on the map on page 21. Which road might the camper be using?

Ask pupils to bring in road maps of areas in which they have traveled. Have each pupil trace his or her route with a felt tip pen.

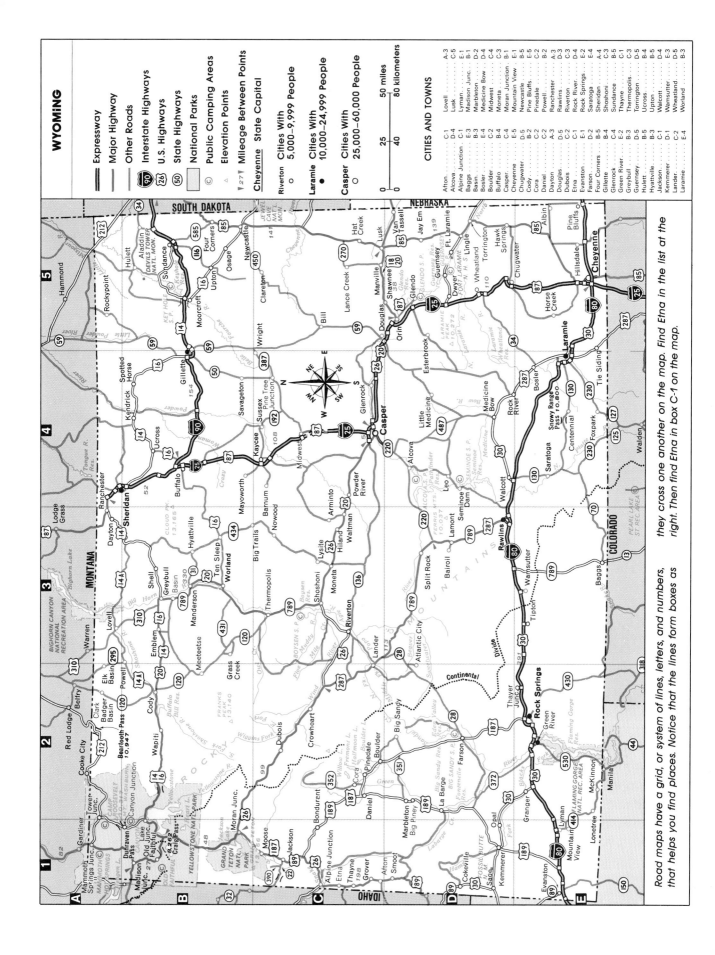

WYOMING

Legend

- Expressway
- Major Highway
- Other Roads
- **90** Interstate Highways
- **26** U.S. Highways
- **50** State Highways
- National Parks
- © Public Camping Areas
- △ Elevation Points
- ▼27▼ Mileage Between Points
- **Cheyenne** State Capital

Riverton o Cities With 5,000–9,999 People

Laramie • Cities With 10,000–24,999 People

Casper ⊙ Cities With 25,000–60,000 People

| 0 | 25 | 50 miles |
| 0 | 40 | 80 kilometers |

CITIES AND TOWNS

Afton	C-1	Lovell	A-3
Alcova	D-4	Lusk	C-5
Alpine Junction	C-1	Lyman	E-1
Baggs	E-3	Madison Junc.	B-1
Basin	B-3	Marbleton	D-2
Bosler	E-4	Medicine Bow	D-4
Boulder	C-2	Midwest	C-4
Buffalo	B-4	Moneta	C-3
Casper	C-4	Moran Junction	B-1
Cheyenne	E-5	Mountain View	E-1
Chugwater	D-5	Newcastle	B-5
Cody	B-2	Pine Bluffs	E-5
Cora	C-2	Pinedale	C-2
Daniel	C-2	Powell	B-2
Dayton	A-3	Ranchester	A-3
Douglas	D-3	Rawlins	D-3
Dubois	C-1	Riverton	C-3
Etna	C-1	Rock River	D-4
Evanston	E-1	Rock Springs	E-2
Farson	D-2	Saratoga	E-4
Four Corners	A-4	Sheridan	A-4
Gillette	B-4	Shoshoni	C-3
Glenrock	C-4	Sundance	B-5
Green River	E-2	Thayne	C-1
Greybull	B-3	Thermopolis	C-3
Guernsey	D-5	Torrington	D-5
Hulett	B-5	Upton	B-5
Hyattville	B-3	Walcott	D-4
Jackson	C-1	Wamsutter	E-3
Kemmerer	D-1	Wheatland	D-5
Lander	C-2	Worland	B-3
Laramie	E-4		

Road maps have a grid, or system of lines, letters, and numbers, that helps you find places. Notice that the lines form boxes as they cross one another on the map. Find Etna in the list at the right. Then find Etna in box C-1 on the map.

Mileage Chart

	Boston	Chicago	Dallas	Denver	Kansas City	Los Angeles	Miami	Montreal	New Orleans	New York	St. Louis	San Francisco	Seattle	Washington, D.C.
Chicago	990		960	995	510	2120	1370	850	945	790	285	2195	2020	705
Dallas	1805	960		780	495	1425	1370	1780	505	1565	650	1785	2165	1375
Denver	1990	995	780		600	1170	2135	1900	1295	1760	875	1270	1385	1645
Kansas City	1420	510	495	600		1610	1530	1320	830	1185	255	1890	1925	1050
Los Angeles	3085	2120	1425	1170	1610		2820	2985	1920	2765	1820	390	1180	2725
Miami	1565	1370	1370	2135	1530	2820		1680	870	1300	1265	3160	3425	1115
Montreal	310	850	1780	1900	1320	2985	1680		1665	370	1100	3060	2800	585
New Orleans	1550	945	505	1295	830	1920	870	1665		1320	710	2295	2695	1115
New York	215	790	1565	1760	1185	2765	1300	370	1320		950	2930	2825	220
St. Louis	1160	285	650	875	255	1820	1265	1100	710	950		2140	2175	805
San Francisco	3190	2195	1785	1270	1890	390	3160	3060	2295	2930	2140		825	2875
Seattle	2950	2020	2165	1385	1925	1180	3425	2800	2695	2825	2175	825		2845
Washington, D.C.	445	705	1375	1645	1050	2725	1115	585	1115	220	805	2875	2845	
Yellowstone N.P.	2410	1385	1310	575	1135	1105	2560	2125	1860	2135	1380	985	785	2065

How far is it from Miami to New York? 1,300 miles

Ask pupils to tell the distances between a variety of cities shown on this chart.

Road distances Earlier you learned how to use a map scale to find out how far one point is from another. However, when you are going by car, just measuring the distance on a map may not work. The roads you take might not go in a straight line. You need another way to tell how far you have to drive.

Often road maps have **mileage charts** like the one above. This chart tells the number of *road miles* between one place and another.

Suppose you want to find the distance between Los Angeles, California, and Yellowstone. Find *Yellowstone* on the left side of the chart. Put a finger on *Yellowstone*. Now find *Los Angeles* at the top of the chart. Put a finger of your other hand on *Los Angeles*. Move both fingers, one across and one down, until they meet. They should meet at **1,105**. That is the number of road miles between Los Angeles and Yellowstone. How far would you have to drive from Dallas, Texas, to Yellowstone? 1,310 miles

CHECKUP

1. What do map symbols tell you?
2. What does *population* mean?
3. When you read a road map, why might you need a mileage chart in addition to a map scale?

Mass Transit

---VOCABULARY---
mass transit	schedule
subway	express

Other ways to go   So far you have been learning about traveling by automobile. And many people do drive around our country. But there are other ways to visit the different parts of the United States. People can go by train, bus, or plane. The name for all these ways of travel is **mass transit**. *Mass* means "a great amount." *Transit* means "the moving of people or things from one place to another." Mass transit is a way of moving a great many people at the same time. You might use mass transit to go to and from school. Perhaps your parents use it to get to and from work. Mass transit gives people a way of going places without having to use an automobile.

Trains   There are about 335,000 miles (540,000 km) of railroad track in the United States. Our country is tied together by railroad lines that reach from the Pacific Ocean to the Atlantic Ocean and from Mexico to Canada. You can travel thousands of miles across the country by train.

Of course, many trains go only short distances. Some of these trains connect large cities like San Francisco, California, or New York City with smaller communities nearby.

Subways   Trains are also helpful for getting around in some of our country's large cities. Often these trains run under the ground. Then they are called **subways.** New York City; San Francisco; Chicago, Illinois; Philadelphia, Pennsylvania; Boston, Massachusetts; and Washington, D.C., all have subways.

This is part of the Metro system in Washington, D.C. Metro trains run above ground and underground.
(38°54′N/77°1′W)

Because the trains are so quiet, the station lights are flashed to warn waiting passengers of their approach.

There are more than 50 glaciers in Glacier National Park. The largest glacier, Blackfoot Glacier, is about 3 sq mi (8 sq km). Iceberg Lake, elevation 6,000 ft (1,800 m), has icebergs even on warm summer days.

People can take a bus and see their country. This bus is in Glacier National Park in Montana.

Have pupils write creative stories that describe how people might travel in the future.

Buses   Buses, like trains, connect all parts of our country. People can visit almost every part of the United States by bus. As in a train, they can sit back in comfortable seats. They can watch our country's beautiful scenery pass by their windows.

Like trains, buses are helpful when traveling within a city. Most big cities have bus systems that take people from one part of their city to another.

Planes   People who want to get somewhere very quickly often fly. All of our big cities and many smaller cities and towns have airports.

Many airplanes that fly from city to city in the United States are huge. They carry about 375 people. They fly about 560 miles (900 km) an hour. Most planes fly so high that they are above the clouds. All you can see from the windows are white clouds below and blue sky above.

Schedules   When you want to take a train, bus, or plane, it is helpful to read a **schedule.** These schedules tell you when a train, bus, or plane leaves one place and arrives at another. Why is it important to know these facts?

The schedule shown on page 25 tells you about buses that go into and out of New York City. You will see that the numbers in red are for the **express** service. Express buses are those that make the fewest stops to pick people up or let them off. They take less time to get from one place to another than other buses.

If you left Hackettstown at 6:30 on an express bus, you would be in New York City by 8:00. The ride would take an hour and a half. However, if you left Hackettstown at 7:25 on a nonexpress bus, you would get into New York City at 9:20. That ride would take 1 hour and 55 minutes. It would take 25 minutes longer than the ride on the express bus.

Look at the schedule again. If you left Netcong at 2:10, what time would you be in New York City? Would you have been riding on an express or a nonexpress bus?

3:40 pm; express

CHECKUP

1. Name three kinds of mass transit.
2. What is a subway?
3. What do schedules tell you?

Suggested research projects for extra credit: 1. The Historical Development of Trains, Automobiles, or Airplanes 2. The Development of Transportation in Our Community 3. Subway Systems Around the World 4. All About Hydrofoils

SCHEDULES SHOWN IN RED INDICATE EXPRESS HIGHWAY SERVICE

LEAVE — MON. through FRI. — *Eastbound to N.Y.C.* — ARRIVE

HACKETTSTOWN	MT. OLIVE BUDD LAKE	NETCONG	LAKE HOPATCONG	SPARTA	MINE HILL KENVIL	DOVER	ROCKAWAY	DENVILLE	MT. LAKES RT. 46 & BLVD.	BOONTON	LINCOLN PARK	PINE BROOK	MT. VIEW CIRCLE	NEW YORK
–	–	–	–	–	–	5:30	5:40	5:45	5:48	–	–	6:00	6:10	6:40
–	–	–	–	–	–	5:45	5:55	6:00	–	6:10	–	6:25	6:35	7:05
–	–	–	–	–	–	6:00	6:10	6:15	–	6:25	6:40	–	6:50	7:20
–	–	–	–	–	–	6:15	6:25	6:30	6:33	–	–	6:45	6:55	7:25
–	–	–	–	6:25	–	–	–	–	6:58	–	–	–	–	7:45
–	–	–	–	–	–	–	–	–	–	6:35	–	7:00	7:10	7:45
–	–	–	–	–	–	6:30	6:40	6:45	–	6:55	–	–	–	7:45
–	–	–	–	–	–	–	–	–	–	–	–	7:25	7:35	8:05
–	–	–	–	–	–	6:45	6:55	7:00	–	–	–	7:25	7:35	8:05
–	–	–	–	–	–	–	–	–	–	7:15	7:30	–	7:40	8:10
–	–	–	–	–	–	7:00	7:10	7:15	7:18	–	–	7:30	7:40	8:10
6:30	6:45	6:50	6:55	–	–	–	–	EXPRESS		–	–	–	–	8:00
–	–	–	–	6:55	–	–	–	–	–	–	–	7:40	7:50	8:10
–	–	–	–	–	–	–	–	–	–	7:25	–	–	–	8:25
–	–	–	–	–	–	7:15	7:25	7:30	7:33	–	–	7:45	7:55	8:25
–	–	–	–	–	–	7:30	7:40	7:45	–	7:55	–	8:10	8:20	8:50
–	–	–	–	–	–	8:00	8:10	8:15	–	8:25	–	8:40	8:50	9:20
–	–	–	–	–	–	8:30	8:40	8:45	8:48	–	–	9:00	9:10	9:40
–	–	–	–	–	–	9:00	9:10	9:15	–	9:25	–	9:40	9:50	10:20
–	–	–	–	–	–	9:30	9:40	9:45	9:48	–	–	10:00	10:10	10:40
–	9:35	9:40	9:45	–	9:55	10:00	10:10	10:15	–	10:25	10:40	–	10:50	11:20
–	–	–	–	10:00	–	10:30	10:40	10:45	10:48	–	–	11:00	11:10	11:40
–	–	–	–	–	–	11:00	11:10	11:15	–	11:25	–	11:40	11:50	12:20
–	–	–	–	–	–	11:30	11:40	11:45	11:48	–	–	12:00	12:10	12:40
–	–	–	–	–	–	12:00	12:10	12:15	–	12:25	–	12:40	12:50	1:20
–	–	–	–	–	–	12:30	12:40	12:45	12:48	–	–	1:00	1:10	1:40
–	–	–	–	–	–	1:00	1:10	1:15	–	1:25	1:40	–	1:50	2:20
–	–	–	–	–	–	1:30	1:40	1:45	1:48	–	–	2:00	2:10	2:40
–	–	–	–	–	–	2:00	2:10	2:15	–	2:25	–	2:40	2:50	3:20
–	2:05	2:10	2:15	–	2:25	2:30	2:40	2:45	2:48	–	–	3:00	3:10	3:40
–	–	–	–	–	–	3:00	3:10	3:15	–	3:25	–	3:40	3:50	4:20
–	–	–	–	–	–	3:30	3:40	3:45	–	3:55	4:10	–	4:20	4:50
–	–	–	–	–	–	4:00	4:10	4:15	–	4:25	–	4:40	4:50	5:20
–	–	–	–	–	–	4:30	4:40	4:45	4:48	–	–	5:00	5:10	5:40
–	–	–	–	–	–	5:00	5:10	5:15	–	5:25	–	5:40	5:50	6:20
–	–	–	–	–	–	6:00	6:10	6:15	–	6:25	–	6:40	6:50	7:20
–	–	–	–	–	–	7:00	7:10	7:15	–	7:25	–	7:40	7:50	8:20
–	–	–	–	7:30	–	–	–	7:50	7:53	–	–	8:05	8:15	8:45
7:25	7:35	7:40	7:45	–	7:55	8:00	8:10	8:15	–	8:25	–	8:40	8:50	9:20
–	–	–	–	–	–	9:00	9:10	9:15	–	9:25	–	9:40	9:50	10:20
–	9:35	9:40	9:45	–	9:55	10:00	10:10	10:15	–	10:25	–	10:40	10:50	11:20
–	–	–	–	–	–	11:30	11:40	11:45	–	11:55	–	12:10	12:20	12:50

SCHEDULES SHOWN IN RED INDICATE EXPRESS HIGHWAY SERVICE

LEAVE — MON. through FRI. — *Westbound from N.Y.C.* — ARRIVE

RUSH HOUR – NUMBERED CODE	NEW YORK	MT. VIEW CIRCLE	PINE BROOK	LINCOLN PARK	BOONTON	MT. LAKES RT. 46 & BLVD.	DENVILLE	ROCKAWAY	DOVER	MINE HILL KENVIL	SPARTA	LAKE HOPATCONG	NETCONG	BUDD LAKE MT. OLIVE	HACKETTSTOWN
	7:00	7:25	7:35	–	–	7:45	7:50	7:55	8:00	–	–	–	–	–	–
	7:30	7:55	–	8:05	8:20	–	8:30	8:35	8:40	–	–	–	–	–	–
	7:45	8:10	8:20	–	–	8:30	8:35	–	–	–	–	8:45	8:50	9:00	–
	8:00	8:25	8:35	–	–	8:45	8:50	8:55	9:00	–	–	–	–	–	–
	8:30	8:55	9:05	–	9:20	–	9:30	VIA RT. 80		–	10:00	–	–	–	–
	9:00	9:25	9:35	–	–	9:45	9:50	9:55	10:00	–	–	–	–	–	–
	9:30	9:55	10:05	–	10:20	–	10:30	10:35	10:40	–	–	–	–	–	–
	10:00	10:25	10:35	–	–	10:45	10:50	10:55	11:00	–	–	–	–	–	–
	10:30	10:55	11:05	–	11:20	–	11:30	11:35	11:40	–	–	–	–	–	–
	11:00	11:25	11:35	–	–	11:45	11:50	11:55	12:00	–	–	–	–	–	–
	11:30	11:55	–	12:05	12:20	–	12:30	12:35	12:40	–	–	–	–	–	–
	12:00	12:25	12:35	–	–	12:45	12:50	12:55	1:00	1:05	–	1:15	1:20	1:30	–
	12:30	12:55	1:05	–	1:20	–	1:30	1:35	1:40	–	–	–	–	–	–
	1:00	1:25	1:35	–	–	1:45	1:50	1:55	2:00	–	–	–	–	–	–
	1:30	1:55	2:05	–	2:20	–	2:30	2:35	2:40	–	–	–	–	–	–
	2:00	2:25	2:35	–	–	2:45	2:50	2:55	3:00	–	–	–	–	–	–
	2:30	2:55	–	3:05	3:20	–	3:30	3:35	3:40	–	–	–	–	–	–
	3:00	3:25	3:35	–	–	3:45	3:50	3:55	4:00	–	–	–	–	–	–
	3:30	3:55	4:05	–	4:20	–	4:30	4:35	4:40	–	–	–	–	–	–
	4:00	4:25	4:35	–	–	4:45	4:50	4:55	5:00	–	–	–	–	–	–
	4:20	4:45	4:55	–	–	5:05	5:10	5:15	5:20	–	–	–	–	–	–
	4:30	4:55	–	5:05	5:20	–	5:30	5:35	5:40	–	–	–	–	–	–
46	4:50	5:15	5:25	–	–	5:35	5:40	5:45	5:50	–	–	–	–	–	–
1	5:00	5:25	5:35	–	5:50	–	6:00	6:05	6:10	–	–	–	–	–	–
80	5:15	–	–	–	–	–	–	–	VIA RT. 80		–	6:20	6:30	6:40	6:50
99	5:20	–	–	–	EXPRESS		–	–	–	–	6:35	–	–	–	–
22	5:30	6:00	–	6:10	6:25	–	6:35	6:40	6:45	–	–	–	–	–	–
46	5:30	5:55	6:05	–	–	6:15	6:20	6:25	6:30	–	–	–	–	–	–
32	5:30	–	6:00	–	–	–	–	–	–	–	–	–	–	–	–
10	5:40	–	–	–	–	–	–	–	–	–	–	6:50	6:55	–	–
1-B	5:40	6:10	6:20	–	–	–	6:45	6:50	6:55	–	–	–	–	–	–
1	5:50	6:20	6:30	–	6:45	–	6:55	7:00	7:05	–	–	–	–	–	–
46	6:00	6:25	6:35	–	–	6:45	6:50	6:55	7:00	–	7:25	–	–	–	–
	6:10	6:40	6:50	–	7:05	–	7:15	7:20	7:25	–	–	–	–	–	–
	6:20	6:50	7:00	–	–	7:10	7:15	7:20	7:25	–	–	–	–	–	–
	6:30	6:55	–	7:05	7:20	–	7:30	7:35	7:40	–	–	–	–	–	–
	6:45	7:10	7:20	–	–	7:30	7:35	7:40	7:45	–	–	–	–	–	–
	7:00	7:25	7:35	–	–	7:45	7:50	7:55	8:00	8:05	–	8:15	8:20	8:25	–
	7:30	7:55	8:05	–	8:20	–	8:30	8:35	8:40	–	–	–	–	–	–
	8:00	8:25	8:35	–	–	8:45	8:50	8:55	9:00	–	–	–	–	–	–
	8:30	8:55	9:05	–	9:20	–	9:30	9:35	9:40	–	–	–	–	–	–
	9:00	9:25	9:35	–	–	9:45	9:50	9:55	10:00	10:05	–	10:15	10:20	10:25	–
	9:30	9:55	10:05	–	10:20	–	10:30	10:35	10:40	–	–	–	–	–	–
	10:30	10:55	11:05	–	11:20	–	11:30	11:35	11:40	–	–	–	–	–	–
	11:30	11:55	12:05	–	12:20	–	12:30	12:35	12:40	–	–	–	–	–	–
	1:00	1:25	1:35	–	1:50	–	2:00	2:05	2:10	–	–	–	–	–	–

When would you be in New York City if you left Denville at 6:45 in the morning? 7:45 am

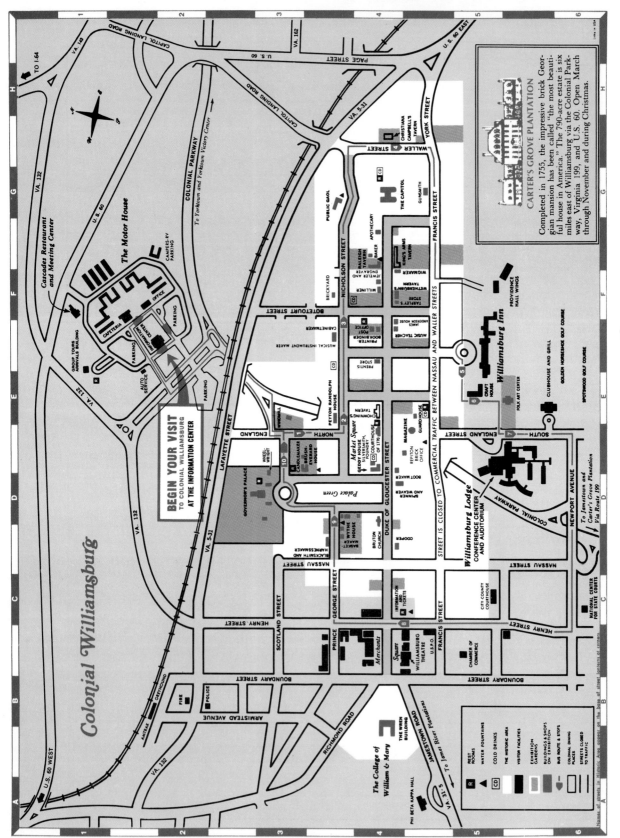

What to See in Colonial Williamsburg

Colonial Williamsburg

BEGIN YOUR VISIT TO COLONIAL WILLIAMSBURG AT THE INFORMATION CENTER

CARTER'S GROVE PLANTATION

Completed in 1755, the impressive brick Georgian mansion has been called "the most beautiful house in America." The 790-acre estate is six miles east of Williamsburg via the Colonial Parkway, Virginia 199, and U.S. 60. Open March through November and during Christmas.

Could you find your way from the Governor's Palace to the Capitol?   (37°16′N/76°43′W)

26

Have pupils plan a day at Colonial Williamsburg. Have them describe in writing the route they would use to enter the parking lot, and the route they would follow in visiting the various attractions.

Maps Are Important

┌─VOCABULARY─────────────────┐
resort   event
└────────────────────────────┘

Living with maps By this time, you should have a good idea about how important maps are for planning a trip. Yellowstone National Park is just one of the thousands of places in our country you might visit. And of course there are places in other countries that you might visit one day. If you can read a map, chances are you will not get lost. You might even find some other interesting places to visit that you didn't know about before.

There are many other times when you will find it helpful to read maps. It is not possible to show you all the maps that you might use in your life. It would take more pages than there are in this book to do that. However, there will be many times when a map will be useful. Here are some of them.

1. To find your way on the subway in New York City, Washington, D.C., or San Francisco
2. To find your seat at a football game at the Houston Astrodome in Houston, Texas, or at Three Rivers Stadium in Pittsburgh, Pennsylvania
3. To find your seat at a basketball game at the Spectrum in Philadelphia or at the Boston Garden in Boston
4. To find the animals that you are most interested in at the zoo in St. Louis, Missouri, or in San Diego, California
5. To find the ride you want to go on at Disney World, in Orlando, Florida, or at Great Adventure, in Jackson, New Jersey

6. To pick the ski trail you want to try at a ski **resort** in Aspen, Colorado; Stowe, Vermont; or Lake Placid, New York
7. To find the theater you are looking for at the Lincoln Center for the Performing Arts in New York City
8. To plan a tour of Colonial Williamsburg in Virginia

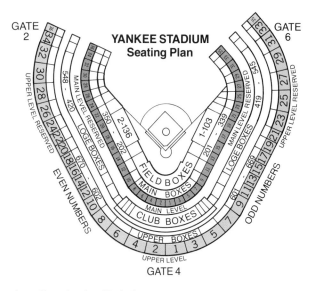

A seating plan is a kind of map.

Textbook maps Maps are important to the study of our country. Many of the facts about our country's history and geography will be shown on the maps in this book. The **events** and places you will be reading about will become more interesting and will mean more to you when you look carefully at the maps in this book.

CHECKUP

1. Give three examples of when you might use a map.
2. Why are maps important to the study of our country's history?

1/CHAPTER REVIEW

KEY FACTS

1. A hemisphere is half the earth.
2. The seven continents of the earth are North America, South America, Asia, Europe, Africa, Australia, and Antarctica.
3. The most exact way of locating places on the earth is to use latitude and longitude.
4. A map scale gives the relationship between distance on the map and distance on the earth.
5. Maps use symbols, labels, and colors.
6. There are many kinds of mass transit in the United States.

VOCABULARY QUIZ

Write the letter of the term next to the number of its description. Write on a sheet of paper.

a. equator   **f.** kilometer
b. hemisphere   **g.** schedule
c. prime meridian   **h.** longitude
d. latitude   **i.** compass rose
e. mileage chart   **j.** subway

c **1.** This line of longitude is labeled 0° and goes through Greenwich, England.
g **2.** This chart tells you when a bus (or any other kind of mass transit) leaves and arrives.
h **3.** These lines go from the North Pole to the South Pole.
i **4.** This drawing tells you the directions on a map.
a **5.** This line of latitude is halfway between the North Pole and the South Pole.
e **6.** This chart tells you the distance between cities.
d **7.** These lines measure distances north and south of the equator.
j **8.** This kind of mass transit travels underground.
b **9.** This word means "half the earth."
f **10.** This is the name given to a unit of measure in the metric system.

REVIEW QUESTIONS

1. What are the four hemispheres?
2. In which two hemispheres is the United States found?
3. How would you describe the North Pole and the South Pole?
4. What is a continent?
5. On which continent is the United States found?
6. What does a map scale tell you?
7. What does a map key tell you?
8. What is mass transit?
9. Name three kinds of mass transit.
10. Give two examples of times when you might want to use a map.

ACTIVITIES

1. Get a road map of your state. Plan a trip from your home to a place you would like to visit. On paper, list the routes you would take and any places you would like to visit along the way. How far would you have to travel? What would you take with you on the trip?
2. Trace a map of the United States. Label each state. Use several different colors for the different states.
3. Find a map of your state in an atlas. What is the latitude and longitude of your community?
4. Trace a map of the world. Label the continents and the oceans. Use a different color for each continent.

OUTLINING

One way of reviewing, summarizing, or organizing what you have learned is to make an outline. An outline shows the important ideas in an orderly way. Below is the beginning of an outline of Unit 1. Look at it to see how an outline works.

I. Reading Maps
  A. Where Is It?
    1. Our nation: a big, beautiful land
      a. "America, the Beautiful"
      b. Katharine Lee Bates
    2. Hemispheres
      a. Hemisphere: half the earth
      b. North Pole: most northern place

In the above outline, the title of Chapter 1 is Roman numeral I. Notice that Chapter 1 is divided into five main sections, the first of which is *Where Is It?* This heading becomes capital letter A in the outline. The headings of the other four sections would be letters B, C, D, and E.

Each main section is in turn divided into smaller parts. There are nine such parts in the first main section of Chapter 1. We have shown only the first two of those headings: *Our nation: a big, beautiful land* and *Hemispheres*. They appear in the outline beside the Arabic numerals 1 and 2. Lowercase letters are used to show some of the information found under those headings.

Look through Unit 1 of your text to answer these questions about the outline.

1. What information should be listed as lowercase letter c under *Hemispheres?*
2. What should appear as Arabic numeral 3?
3. What should appear as capital letter B?
4. What should appear as Roman numeral II?

Outlines are also used to organize ideas for reports. Suppose you want to report on your state's geography. The first question to ask is, What broad topics do I want to cover? You might choose *Land, Climate, People, Agriculture, Industry,* and *Cities. Land* would be Roman numeral I; *Climate,* II; *People,* III; and so forth.

Each of those broad topics can be divided into smaller topics. For example, under *Land,* you could write about *Lakes, Mountains,* and *Plains.* Each of these would be shown as a capital letter in your outline.

Next you would break each smaller topic into even smaller parts. Under *Lakes,* you might discuss *Uses of Lakes, Names of Lakes,* and *Locations of Lakes.* You would give each of those topics an Arabic numeral.

You could divide the topic *Uses of Lakes* into still smaller topics. These topics would be shown by lowercase letters. Then the beginning of your outline would look like the partial outline shown below.

I. Land
  A. Lakes
    1. Uses of Lakes
      a. Fishing
      b. Swimming
      c. Boating
      d. Drinking water

To get some practice in outlining, either complete this outline using some of the headings suggested above, or make an outline for a report of your own.

2 Our History

What Is History?

> **VOCABULARY**
>
> chronological   factories
> order   swamp
> transportation

The story of a family Suppose your teacher gives you the task of writing about your family. You are to find out about your family as far back as you can. What would you write? Where would you begin? Would you write everything there is to say about your family? Would you tell about the bad things as well as the good? How would you decide what to write?

You might begin by writing about some important things that happened in your family even before you were born. These events may have been passed down to you in stories told by your parents or grandparents.

You could tell about important people in your family. You might tell about your great-great-great-grandmother Annie, who once held Abraham Lincoln's horse. Perhaps you could tell what your great-grandfather Carlos, who was the first member of your family to live in the United States. Maybe you could tell about your great-great-uncle Tony, who had the first car in town.

You could tell about important events, like the time your parents were teenagers and went to hear President John F. Kennedy make a speech. Or maybe you could write about the fireworks your older brother or sister saw when this country celebrated its two hundredth birthday.

You could write about yourself, of course. You could give the date of your birth. You could share other important points in your life. You might tell about the prize you once won for swimming. You might write about the time you had to stay in the hospital with a broken leg. Maybe you could tell about the summer you drove to Yellowstone National Park.

You might end your story by telling what you are doing right now. This would bring your family's story up to the present day.

The story you write about your family would be your family's *history.* Families have a history. So do countries. The history of a country tells the story of how the country was born and how it grew. It tells about people and events that were important in the life of the country.

History is a telling of what happened in the past. History is often told in **chronological** (kron ə loj´ ə kəl) **order.** That means events are told in the order in which they happened. You would be likely to write in chronological order when writing your family's history. The history of countries is also written in chronological order.

Draw pupils' attention to the photograph on p. 31. Ask: Do you recognize the statue shown here? Why would the Statue of Liberty be included in our Bicentennial celebration? (40°43′N/74°1′W)

A special Fourth of July celebration takes place in New York Harbor in 1976.

Discuss the meaning of *bicentennial* with pupils. Explain to them that we celebrated our Bicentennial here in the United States on July 4, 1976.

People affect history People make history happen. History is the story of great people. History is the story of great leaders, such as George Washington. It is the story of inventors, such as Thomas Edison. It is the story of freedom workers, such as Martin Luther King, Jr. It is the story of brave people, such as Amelia Earhart.

But history is not only about well-known people. When people vote, they are making history. Their votes decide who will lead the country. When large numbers of people move from one place to another, they make history. This happened about a hundred years ago in the United States when people moved west.

People cause events to happen. You cannot tell a family's history without telling about the people in the family. And you cannot tell a country's history without telling about its people.

The sculptured heads are about 60 ft (18 m) high. They were designed by Gutzon Borglum. Construction began on the project and was continued by Borglum's son after his father's death in 1941.

Mt. Rushmore honors four Presidents. Can you tell who they are? Both monuments are at approximately 44°N/103°W.

The sculptor of the Chief Crazy Horse statue is Korczak Ziolkowski, seen in this picture with his wife. He has been carving the mountain for over 30 years, using his own funds and private donations.

Someday this mountain will look like the statue of Chief Crazy Horse.

When completed the monument will be 641 ft (195.4 m) long by 563 ft (171.6) high.

Events affect history People make events happen. If your team wins a game, that is an event. But who made the event happen? People, of course. Sometimes people make events happen that cause other people to make other events happen. So you might say that events themselves make history happen. Suppose you wanted to watch a favorite television show last night. But your parents said that before you could watch the show you had to do your homework. Your parents made something happen. They made sure you would do your homework. Doing your homework was an event. That event made it possible for something else to happen. It made it possible for you to watch television. That was another event.

One event leads to another. Events are connected to each other. Events cause other events to happen. Can you think of an event in your life that caused something else to happen? Of course, it still takes people to make things happen.

Geography affects history The third thing that affects history is geography. Geography is a study of the earth. When you study geography you learn about the different forms that the earth's surface takes. You study the different kinds of weather all over the world. You learn about the waters of the earth. You study plants and animals. And you study where people live on the earth and what they do. What might all this have to do with things that happened in the past? What does it have to do with history?

Imagine that it is almost 150 years ago. It is 1840. You are a farmer looking for a good place to farm. What kind of place would you want to live in? You would try to choose a place with a lot of flat land, good soil, and the right amount of rain. You would want a place where it is warm long enough for you to raise good crops.

You would also try very hard to find a place near a river. A river would give you good **transportation.** Transportation means moving people and things from one place to another. A riverboat would be a good way to get farm products to market.

Suppose you wish to work in a city. You would find that most early cities and towns are near a river. The river makes it easier to get things and people to and from the city. The river makes a good place to build **factories.** A factory is a building where goods are made by machines. The moving water in the river could be used to run the machines in the factories. The first factories in the United States were built next to rivers.

The rushing water supplied power for this mill.

The photograph shows the restoration of one of Samuel Slater's mills. It is located in Pawtucket, RI at the Slater Mill Historical Site. The mill was first built in 1793 and enlarged throughout the 19th and into the 20th centuries.

How did Francis Marion use his knowledge of geography against the British?

The flat land, good soil, rainfall, and warm weather the farmer would have looked for are all part of geography. So are the rivers that were so important to both the farmer and city worker of 1840. You can see that geography had a lot to do with what people did and where they lived.

The history of our country is full of examples that show how geography affected what happened in the past. Geography helped the Americans during the Revolutionary War. One famous leader of that time was Francis Marion. He was called the "Swamp Fox." This was because he knew the wet, muddy **swamp** lands of what is now the state of South Carolina.

Marion made daring raids on the British soldiers. He would hide among the thick trees and bushes of the swamps. The British could not follow him without getting lost. He was able to escape capture because he knew geography. Marion and many others used geography to affect American history.

Geography is just as important right now. Later in this book you will learn more about geography and how it affects the people of this country.

CHECKUP

1. What is history?
2. In what order is history generally told?
3. What three things affect history?

How Do We Learn About the Past?

VOCABULARY

oral history	artifact
archaeologist	historian

Oral history   You might wonder how it is possible to find out so much about the past. Think again about trying to write your family history. Where might you get information about your family? One of the best ways might be to ask older family members. They can tell you stories from long before you were born. They can tell you about life when they were young.

This is called **oral history**, or spoken history. People who take part in an event can tell about it. Or it can be passed down through your family from parent to child. In some places in the world, this is the only kind of history people have.

Written records   But there are events that happened so long ago that no one who was there is still living. Suppose nothing was passed down orally. How would you find out about these events? You would have to find written records. Letters, family Bibles, newspapers of the time, diaries, and business records are examples of written records.

One way to learn about history is to ask older people what they remember.

Pictures. Pictures or paintings can also tell you much about the past. They can show what life was like in earlier times. The picture on this page shows you what life was like in an American city more than a hundred years before you were born. The picture was made by an artist in 1830. What do you see in this picture that is different from what you might see in an American city today?

Archaeologists Often we want to find out about things that happened before written records were kept. Or we might wish to find out about things for which the records have been lost or destroyed. What do we do then?

This is when **archaeologists** (är kē ol′ ə jists) can help. Archaeologists are people who study plant and animal remains, ruins of buildings, and other **artifacts**, or objects. These things left by people who lived long ago may be found buried in the ground. Archaeologists dig in places where they think people once lived. They must be very careful so that no clues are lost. Each thing is important. Each bone, pot, or tool helps to tell a story about people from the past.

Finding out about the past in this way is like trying to solve a giant jigsaw puzzle with only a few of the pieces. However, trained archaeologists can tell us a great deal from a few objects. Whole groups have had their story told in this way.

Suppose archaeologists found some stone arrowheads when they were digging where people lived hundreds of years ago. Would that tell you something about how these people got their food?

Many times findings of archaeologists are used together with written records and oral history. This gives us a more complete history.

The building at the left of center is P.T. Barnum's Museum. Across Broadway from the museum is Matthew Brady's photography studio. The building with the columns near Brady's studio is St. Paul's Chapel.

This is Broadway in New York City. Do you think you would have enjoyed a visit to the building to the left of center in the picture? In the distance is the steeple of Trinity Church. St. Paul's Chapel and Trinity Church can still be seen today.

Be sure pupils observe details such as the crosswalk made of wood, the unpaved roads, and the omnibuses, as well as the private carriages.

Plastic sheets and old tires protect an archaeological dig from the weather.
Ask pupils to describe what they think the people in the archaeological expedition are doing.

Historians   If you wrote your family history, you would be doing the job of a **historian**. Historians are people who work at understanding and writing about the past. Doing this kind of work is like being a detective. Historians have to go back and find clues. They must try to put the clues together in a way that makes sense. They use oral history. They use the things that archaeologists have discovered. They also use written records and pictures. In our country historians have many written records. This makes it possible for us to know a great deal about the past of the United States.

It would be hard for you to write about everything that ever happened in your family history. It would also be hard to write a history about everything that happened in the United States. The job of the historian is to choose only those happenings that are very important. The authors of this book have done that. They will tell you what our country was like years ago.

CHECKUP

1. What is the difference between oral history and written records?
2. How do pictures help us learn about the past?
3. What does an archaeologist do?
4. How do artifacts help us learn about the past?

37

Why Study United States History?

Understanding the present There are many reasons why people should study the history of their country. Think back to your family history. Your family history is about *you*. When you learn about the past of your family, you understand more about yourself.

United States history is about you, too. It is a big part of your own story. To understand the past of your country helps you to understand more about how you live today. It helps you see why you do the things you do.

You are in this school now because long ago Americans decided that all young people had the right to learn. You and your family are free to belong to any religious group you want. This is because long before you or your parents were born, great Americans fought for your right to this freedom.

You have many such freedoms. You live in a free country. Why is that? It is because Americans who have lived before you have been willing to work for and defend that freedom.

Do you like to go to the movies? Do you enjoy talking to a friend on the telephone? Do you think it's fun to fly in a plane? You can enjoy all these things and many more because of Americans who lived before you. They worked hard on inventions that

This Marine Corps War Memorial in Arlington, Va. honors all marines who have died in action since 1775, when the corps was established. The battle of Iwo Jima was the largest marine battle in history, it was also one of the bloodiest battles of World War II.

Marines are raising the American flag after the battle of Iwo Jima in 1945.

You may want to share and discuss the lyrics of the *Marine's Hymn* with the class:
From the Halls of Montezuma
To the shores of Tripoli,
We fight our country's battles
In the air, on land, and sea,
First to fight for right and freedom,
And to keep our honor clean,
We are proud to claim the title of
United States Marine.

Not all Americans subscribe to the melting pot theory. Some Americans feel that they should not forget their heritage from another part of the world but instead should combine the old culture with the new.

The United States has been called a melting pot of people because Americans have come from all parts of the world.

Ask: How do the children shown in the picture represent the idea of America being a melting pot?

changed the world. Imagine what your life would be like without these things. The past makes it possible for you to live the way you do. Studying history helps you to understand life today.

You are part of United States history right now. People in years to come may look back at your life today to understand how people lived. You may even be written about in future history books. You are like a bridge between the past and the future. Things that have happened in the past have important meaning for your life today. Things that happen now may be important for the future.

Learning from the past Studying United States history is important because it really is a family history. You could think of the United States as one enormous family. In this family are men and women and children of all ages, religions, skin colors, and languages. Everybody in this "family" came from other lands. Some, like the **Native Americans**, who are also called American Indians, came long before anyone else. Other members of the family have come to the United States much more recently.

We are proud of the good things the people of our American family have done.

Note the balloon in the upper lefthand corner. Balloons were used by the Union Army to observe artillery placements and cavalry movements.

Americans from Northern states fought Americans from Southern states in the Civil War.
This picture is a Currier and Ives print of the battle of Fair Oaks. It was drawn many years after the battle took place.

We want to learn about these people and what they did. We want to try to be like the many fine Americans who lived before us.

Sometimes, as you know, families are not happy. They go through bad times. Brothers and sisters fight. They are cruel to each other. When these things happen families try to learn from their mistakes. They try not to repeat them.

This is part of United States history, also. Once we had slavery in this country. Some members of the American family treated other Americans cruelly. We had a war in which one part of the great American family fought against another part.

All families and countries have these sad times. But the United States has always had people who wanted to learn from the past. They wanted to make life better. And United States history shows that things are getting better. We still have problems. We are not perfect. But we are trying. We want to learn from our mistakes and avoid them in the future. We study history to do just that.

Good citizenship There is another very good reason for studying United States history. You live in this country. You are a **citizen** of the United States. That means you are a member of this nation. It is necessary for you to be a good citizen.

Suppose you tried to put together a model airplane without reading the instructions first. What might happen? The airplane probably would not fly very well. It might not fly at all. It might even fall apart very quickly.

Some day you are going to have to help run the affairs of the United States. It will be up to you to see that things stick together and run smoothly. To do this well you must understand how this country was put together in the first place. History tells you that. An understanding of history helps you play your part as a citizen of the United States.

CHECKUP

1. What does history have to do with your being in school today?
2. How can learning about mistakes made in the past help us in the future?
3. Why is it important to learn how this country was put together?

Taking part in school government helps train you to be a good citizen.

You may want to set up a democratic form of government in your classroom so that pupils may actually experience the governmental process.

KEY FACTS

1. History tells of what happened in the past.

2. People, events and geography all affect history.

3. We learn about the past through oral history, written records, pictures, and artifacts.

4. We must study United States history in order to understand the present, to learn from the past, and to be good citizens.

VOCABULARY QUIZ

Use the vocabulary listed here to fill in the correct words in this story. Write your answers on a separate sheet of paper.

oral history

artifacts

Native Americans

historian

citizen

history

chronological order

geography

archaeologist

transportation

"Hello! I am a person who works hard at understanding and writing about the past. I am a (1) ___historian___ . What happened in the past is called (2) ___history___ . When I write about the past, I write about events in the order in which they happened. This is called (3) chronological order .

"Sometimes when I write about the past, I have to study old objects, called (4) ___artifacts___ . These objects are found by an (5) archaeologist , a person who studies remains and ruins from people of long ago. Some of these people, the (6) Native Americans were the first to come to America.

"The study of the past is important for any member of this country who wants to be a good (7) ___citizen___ . Study of the past includes many things. It involves a study of the earth, called (8) ___geography___ . It involves understanding (9) transportation , or the different ways of moving people and goods from place to place. Sometimes you even get to hear about the past from people who lived it. This is one form of (10) ___oral history___ . Studying the past is very interesting."

REVIEW QUESTIONS

1. Describe one thing you might do during a day at work if you were a historian; a geographer; an archaeologist.

2. In what four ways do historians learn about the past?

3. Why is it important for you to study United States history?

ACTIVITIES

1. Become a historian and write your family's history. In telling your story, make use of as many of the following tools as possible: oral history from older family members, pictures, written records, and objects.

2. What kind of artifacts would be most helpful to future archaeologists who wanted to study about life today? Draw pictures of ten of these artifacts. You could use pictures cut from magazines instead of drawing if you like. Or you could make a list of these artifacts. Be ready to explain why you chose as you did.

3. Many inventions from the past help you in your life today. Design or build an invention which would be helpful for people in the future. Be prepared to tell how it would work and what problem it would solve.

USING TIMELINES

A timeline is one way to organize information in history. It helps you put things in the order in which they happened. Events which happened longest ago are farthest left on this timeline. Events which happened closer to the present are farther right.

Look carefully at the timeline on this page. It is divided into two parts, B.C. and A.D. The letters B.C. mean "before Christ." The year 10,000 B.C. would be 10,000 years *before* the birth of Jesus. What would 20,000 B.C. mean? 30,000 B.C.? Which came first in history— 20,000 B.C. or 30,000 B.C.?

The letters A.D. refer to the Latin words *anno Domini.* That means "in the year of our Lord." A.D. 1000 means 1,000 years *after* the birth of Jesus. What would A.D. 2000 mean? You can see that there is much less time in A.D. than B.C. Most of American history has happened since A.D. 1492. What happened in A.D. 1492?

Two rules apply when finding the number of years between events.

1. To find the number of years between two B.C. events or two A.D. events, *subtract.*
Examples: The amount of time between 30,000 B.C. and 20,000 B.C. is 10,000 years. The amount of time between A.D. 1000 and A.D. 1492 is 492 years.

2. To find the number of years between a B.C. event and an A.D. event, *add.*
Example: The amount of time between 10,000 B.C. and A.D. 1000 is 11,000 years.

Use the timeline on this page to answer the following questions.

1. What came first, A.D. or B.C.?

2. Which covers more time, A.D. or B.C.?

3. Except for Native American history, does American history take place in B.C. or A.D.?

4. The events which happened longest ago are on the ___left___ side of the timeline.

5. The events which happened nearest the present are on the ___right___ side of the timeline.

6. Which came first, 40,000 B.C. or 10,000 B.C.?

7. Which came nearest the present, 10,000 B.C. or A.D. 1000?

8. How many years between 40,000 B.C. and 20,000 B.C.? 20,000

9. How many years between A.D. 1492 and the present? at least 490

10. How many years between 40,000 B.C. and A.D. 1492? 41, 492

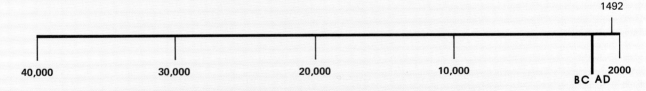

43

I/UNIT REVIEW

1. A hemisphere is half the earth. — *Name the four hemispheres. Be ready to locate them on a globe.*

2. The earth has seven continents. — *Name them. Be ready to label all seven on an outline map of the world.*

3. There are five named lines of latitude: the Arctic Circle, the Antarctic Circle, the Tropic of Cancer, the Tropic of Capricorn, and the equator. — *Be ready to label these five lines, as well as the North Pole and the South Pole, on an outline map of the world.*

4. All lines of longitude are measured east and west of longitude 0°, which goes through Greenwich, England. — *What is the name given to 0° longitude?*

5. Latitude and longitude help us locate places on the earth. — *Explain how you can find the city of San Diego, California, using latitude and longitude. What is San Diego's latitude and longitude?*

6. The four cardinal directions are north, south, east, and west. — *What are the four in-between directions?*

7. Maps use scale, colors and other symbols, and labels. — *Make a map of your classroom. Include a scale, and use labels and colors and other symbols. Make a key to explain the colors and other symbols.*

8. There are many kinds of mass transit in the United States. — *Name at least three kinds.*

9. People, events, and geography affect history. — *Give an example of how a person, an event, and geography have affected history.*

10. We learn about the past through oral history, written records, and artifacts. — *From which of these sources, do you think, have we learned most of the history of the United States?*

11. We must study United States history to understand the present, to learn from the past, and to be good citizens. — *What kinds of things do good citizens do? Make a montage, picture, or cartoon showing people being good citizens.*

For extra credit

An Age of Adventure

Native American

Christopher Columbus

Conquistador

Pilgrim

3 The First Americans

An excellent learning tool would be to have pupils maintain a personal glossary of the vocabulary words plus any other words in the text that are unfamiliar to them.

Native Americans

> **VOCABULARY**
>
> | strait | mound |
> |--------|-------|
> | tribe | culture |
> | descendant | custom |

How did they get here? Native Americans were the very first Americans. They were here long before any other people. Where did they come from? How did they get here? How did they spread out through all of North and South America?

Look at the map on page 48. Find a place where only a narrow stretch of water separates the continent of Asia from North America. This small body of water is called the Bering (bir′ ing) Strait. A **strait** is a narrow waterway that connects two large bodies of water.

Once, thousands and thousands of years ago, the Bering Strait was dry land. The first Americans probably crossed over from Asia to America on this narrow strip of land. These people from Asia were hunters. They needed animals for their food. They needed animal skins for their clothes. They needed the bones of animals to make their spears. These Asian hunters depended on animals in order to live. Most likely they followed herds of animals from Asia across the narrow land bridge that is now the Bering Strait. They discovered America by walking to it!

No one is really sure how long ago this happened. There is proof that human beings lived in North America over 12,000 years ago. Other people say the first Americans arrived as long ago as 70,000 years. And, of course, these early people did not all arrive at the same time. Small groups of Asian hunters came to America over a period of many hundreds of years.

Spreading out These earliest Americans did not just stay in one place. For a time they would live where hunting was good. If the animals moved on, the hunters would follow them. If the animals became scarce, the hunters moved on, looking for new supplies.

Sometimes, after many years, a group might get too large. It was hard to find food for everyone. So a part of that group would move to another place. Sometimes a group, or **tribe**, would move to avoid war with another group.

This kind of moving from place to place went on for many years. At last almost all parts of North and South America were settled by these earliest Americans and their **descendants**. There were hundreds of tribes in the Americas by 1492. That was the year Christopher Columbus arrived in America from Europe and called the people he found here Indians.

Perhaps the people who became the first Americans looked like this.

This 40 ft (12.2 m) high mural can be seen in the George C. Page Museum in Los Angeles, CA.

The first Americans relied on their spears for hunting food and for protection.

Notice that the first Americans transported their belongings on their backs or by dragging them on sled-like frames.

Notice the clothing. Ask: Of what material do you think their clothing was made?

Now would be a good time for pupils to visit a local museum that has artifacts, either with the class or with their families. You may want to invite an archaeologist from a local college to talk to the class.

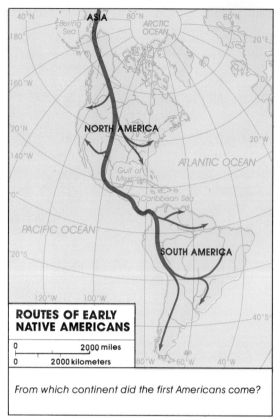

ROUTES OF EARLY NATIVE AMERICANS

0   2000 miles
0   2000 kilometers

From which continent did the first Americans come?

Digging for history   By digging where they believed that people once lived, archaeologists have discovered a number of things about early people in America.

They found spear points near the bones of animals. From these finds they could tell that the first Americans hunted big animals. From the bones they knew that some of these animals looked like giant buffalo, some were very large elephant-like beasts, and some were huge cats like tigers. All these animals died out long ago.

Besides the spear points, archaeologists found sharp arrowheads made of stone. They found well-made tools of bone as well as stone. They discovered that the first Americans used fire to cook their meat. They found out that these early

48

hunters even kept tame dogs. Archaeologists think these dogs might have been used to carry loads or to help in the hunt.

Mound Builders   Beginning about 3,000 years ago, some Native Americans built huge piles of earth called **mounds**. Many different groups of Mound Builders built these piles all through the middle and eastern parts of what is now the United States.

The mounds were different shapes. Some were round. Some were square. Some had wide bases and smaller, flat tops. Some were made in the shape of animals like turtles or snakes. Many of these piles of earth were used as burial places for great leaders.

Archaeologists have learned a great deal by digging in these mounds. Sharp stone axes found inside the mounds told that these Native Americans could cut down

Animals such as this mammoth were hunted by the Native Americans.

14 ft
(4.3m)

The tusks could grow as long as 13 ft (4 m).

Some mammoth bodies were found perfectly preserved in ice. Ask: What present-day animal looks similar to the mammoth?

Size: 1,330 ft (405 m) long; 15 to 20 ft (4 to 6 m) wide; 3 to 5 ft (1 to 2 m) high. Age: 2,000 years

This mound is in Ohio. What animal does it represent?

near Cincinnati, OH

Note that Mound Builders lived in plains areas. Because there was not an abundant supply of wood, sod became an important building material. Pupils may want to make miniature mounds from sod.

trees and make things from wood. Stone arrowheads and knives proved that they killed animals for food. Stone scraping tools and bone needles showed that they knew how to clean animal skins and sew them into clothing. Farm tools such as hoes showed that they knew how to grow food.

Also in the mounds were found fine pieces of artwork, like small stone figures, beautiful pots, and masks made of wood and shell. These things meant that the Mound Builders were very skilled craftworkers. Archaeologists found things in the mounds that came from far away. This meant that the builders were travelers and traders.

Our debt to the first Americans
Americans today owe a great deal to the first Americans. Over half of our states and many of our cities, rivers, and streets still have Native American names. Words such as *skunk, canoe, chipmunk, moccasin,* and *succotash* all come from American Indian languages. In fact, nearly 500 Indian words are part of everyday English.

Many foods, such as potatoes, corn, peanuts, turkey, tomatoes, cocoa, beans, and squash were borrowed by later settlers from the Native Americans. It was from the Indians that other Americans learned how to use rubber. Indians taught them how to travel over snowy land on snowshoes and on the water in canoes.

You may at some time have slept in a hammock. You may have raced down a snowy hill on a toboggan. It was the Native Americans who first taught other people to use these things.

The mounds were used as storehouses, platforms for the homes of important citizens, burial grounds, and for religious ceremonies.

Several healing medicines used for fevers and other sickness were also borrowed from the Native Americans. In fact, without the help of the Native Americans many other early settlers might never have survived.

Many cultures   What was life like for these Native Americans who lived here when the first European settlers began to arrive? What did they eat? What did they wear? What was their daily life like?

These questions are not easy to answer. They are hard because there were so many Native American tribes and **cultures**. The culture of a people means their way of life. Native Americans did not all live in the same way. They had different **customs**, or special ways of doing things. They wore different kinds of clothes. They spoke different languages. What was true for one group might not have been true for another.

We must look at more than one group and more than one way of life in order to get some idea of what Native Americans were like long ago. We will start by looking at some Native American groups who lived in what was to become the United States. These groups were here when the first settlers began to arrive from Europe and Africa.

If there is cultural diversity within the community, encourage pupils to discuss and compare the special traditions they have observed in each culture.

CHECKUP

1. How did the first Americans get to America?
2. Why did they spread out throughout the Americas?
3. How do we know that the earliest Americans were hunters?
4. List five things that have been borrowed from the Native Americans.

Iroquois, Sioux, and Pueblo

┌─VOCABULARY─────────────────┐
longhouse   tepee
league   desert
└────────────────────────────┘

The Iroquois: people of the Eastern Woodlands   The picture on this page shows you what much of the eastern part of America looked like when the Eastern Woodland peoples lived there. It was a land of trees and lakes and rivers. It was a good land for hunting and fishing. The summers were warm enough and there was enough rain for people to grow some of their food.

In this rich land lived many Indian groups. One of the largest and most important were the Iroquois (ir′ ə kwoi). The Iroquois lived in the northeastern part of the Eastern Woodlands area.

Let us now find out a little about what life was like for an Iroquois boy long long ago.

The Eastern Woodland peoples lived in an area that looked much like this.

There are 10 players to a team. The name comes from the French *la crosse* meaning "the stick."

Ask: Why are the players wearing gloves and helmets?

Lacrosse, a Native American game, is a popular sport in many schools today.

An Iroquois boy   Two Rivers was excited. But he did not want anyone to know. An Iroquois warrior should never show his feelings. That would be a sign of weakness.

For all of his 12 years Two Rivers had prepared to be a warrior. He practiced long-distance running on the trails around his home. Some of his older friends were great runners. They could cover a hundred miles in a day! Two Rivers had also taken part in the game of lacrosse. In this tough game teams had to try to get a ball into a goal using webbed sticks. Many players got hurt. The game was not for the weak or cowardly.

Two Rivers had practiced using weapons, also. He was quite good with a tomahawk and bow and arrows. He had learned to move quietly through the woods in his soft deerskin moccasins.

Running the gauntlet   Why was Two Rivers excited? Iroquois warriors had just come back from battle. They had brought back many captives. Two Rivers was sad that some brave Iroquois had been killed. But heroes of battle would receive great honors both in this life and the next, he believed.

Now the captives were being put to a test. This was the Iroquois way of replacing their dead warriors. The Iroquois wanted only the best of the captives. To prove he was worth keeping alive, the captive had to run the gauntlet. This meant running and dodging between two rows of women and children holding sticks, whips, or clubs. They tried to hit the captive. If he ran through bravely and without getting badly hurt, he was made a member of the tribe. If he did not run the gauntlet well, he was killed.

The longhouse   Later in the day Two Rivers returned with his family to the **longhouse**. The longhouse was his home. There were over 100 such houses in Two Rivers's village. The longhouse was about 80 feet (24 m) long and 18 feet (5.4 m) wide. It was made of poles covered with the bark of trees. There were four fires on the floor down the middle of the house. One family lived in a small section on each side of the fire. Each family had a raised sleeping platform. A family also had a shelf for its belongings. At one end of the longhouse was a large meeting room.

Food   When Two Rivers and his family got home it was time for the evening meal. Two Rivers always ate well. The men fished and hunted in the rich streams and forests. They also cleared the land for farming. But it was the job of the women to plant the "Three Sisters"— corn, beans, and squash. Each family had its own field. The village also had fields on which to raise food for festivals and for visitors.

Iroquois government   After eating, Two Rivers's grandfather told a story. It was Two Rivers's favorite story. He always listened to it carefully. One day he could tell his own children. It was the story of the great leader, Hiawatha.

The Iroquois nation was really five different tribes. These tribes often fought each other until the time of Hiawatha. Hiawatha believed in peace. He went to all five tribes. He convinced them to live in

What material was used to build a longhouse?

In the late 1800's almost the entire bison population was killed. Today they are protected and the herds are growing.

The animal we call the buffalo is actually the American bison, not a buffalo at all. Notice the lighter color of the calves and the short grass on which bison graze.

peace. These five tribes would be called the League of Iroquois. A **league** is a group of people joined together for a common purpose.

There were 50 sachems (sā′ chəmz), or leaders, in the league. Each year they held a peace council.

"What a great honor it is to be a sachem!" thought Two Rivers. Such a leader has to understand his people very well. He has to be honest and work hard. If he does not do a good job, the women of the tribe will replace him.

Women could not be sachems. But the women chose these leaders. The women were the real rulers of the tribe. Besides choosing the government leaders, the women also chose the religious leaders. They chose the Pine Trees, too. These were a group of warriors who decided when the League of Iroquois would fight. Two Rivers could not know that many years later a great American leader, Benjamin Franklin, would point to the Iroquois League as a way for the 13 colonies to follow in joining together. Before he fell asleep, Two Rivers's head was full of the things he had seen and thought about this day. He hoped that when he grew up he would be a Pine Tree or a sachem. He wanted to bring honor to his family.

The Sioux: people of the Plains   A young person who belonged to one of the Sioux (sü) tribes lived a very different kind of life from Two Rivers. The Sioux were Plains Indians.

This land was not the rich, forested country of the Eastern Woodlands. The Sioux and many other tribes lived on wide, open land, covered with short, tough grass. It was not easy land to farm. The ground was hard, and often dry. There were few trees to give the Sioux wood and bark for building. But these Native Americans had something very important. They had the buffalo.

Buffalo   Great herds of buffalo roamed the grasslands where the Sioux lived. These animals gave the people almost everything they needed in order to live.

The Sioux ate fresh buffalo meat. What could not be eaten right away was dried in the sun and saved to eat later. The thick hairy hides of the buffalo were used for warm robes and blankets. The skins without the hair were used to make shoes, shirts, leggings, and dresses. The women sewed several hides together to make coverings for their homes. Not a single part of the buffalo was wasted. Even the hooves and stomach were used. Hooves were boiled and made into glue. Stomachs were used for cooking pots.

True buffalo have 13 ribs; these bison have 14 ribs.
Weight: Bull 1,600–2,000 lbs (726–910 kg); Cow 900 lbs (410 kg).   **53**

The hunt   Life for the Sioux, as well as for other Plains tribes, depended on the buffalo. So hunting was the most important job in their lives.

It was a dangerous job to hunt buffalo on foot with bow and arrows. Sometimes the hunters tried to kill the animals by driving them over cliffs. In the winter the hunters tried to drive them into deep snow or onto icy lakes where the animals found it hard to move. But this was a risky way to get food. And it didn't always work.

Horses   Later on, people from Europe came to these grassy lands. And with them came the horse. The horse made a great difference in the life of the Native Americans.

With a horse a hunter could move faster than an angry buffalo. He could shoot it with his bow and arrows more easily. It became much easier and less dangerous for the Sioux hunters to bring down these great beasts on which their people depended.

Tepees   When scouts signaled that buffalo were nearby, the men quickly dashed off. The women had to pick up camp, homes and all, and follow.

Each Sioux family lived in a buffalo-skin tent. These tents were called **tepees**. These tent homes weighed very little. They could easily be taken apart, carried to a new camp, and quickly set up again.

The tepees were good homes. They were waterproof and they kept out the wind. Fires burning inside kept them warm. The smoke was let out by little flaps in the buffalo-skin covering. These

Ask: Why was the village shown below set up near water? Notice the number of poles needed to support the tent.

Notice the canoe.

A teepee is made of skins and poles. How is it different from the longhouse?

homes were very different from Two Rivers's longhouse. But they fit the life of the Sioux very well indeed.

War   Sioux men, like the Iroquois, were expected to be good warriors. As boys, they too had to be good runners. They had to wrestle. They were taught to swim in the ice-cold water. They had to learn to do without food for a long time. They had to learn to take a great deal of pain without complaining.

All this training was to make them good fighters. War was just as important to the Sioux as hunting. The great heroes of the Sioux were the bravest warriors.

The Pueblo: people of the Southwest   The Native Americans we call the Pueblo (pweb' lō) lived in still different ways from those of the Eastern Woodland and Plains tribes. *Pueblo* is the Spanish word for "village." The same

54

word is used to describe the people and the towns and buildings in which they lived.

The land of the Pueblo is very dry. It is so dry that some of it might be called **desert** land. There are few trees and it is often very hot. The picture on this page shows you what much of the Pueblos' land looks like.

Now let us look at one exciting event in the life of a Pueblo girl.

The fields were on the plateau 100 ft (30.5m) above the pueblos. The farmers reached the fields by ladder.

Pueblos were often built into the sides of cliffs as protection from enemies and the weather.

Sandstone cliff

Called Cliff Palace, these pueblos can be seen today in Mesa Verde, Colo. What modern-day buildings do the pueblos resemble?

A Pueblo girl   "Run! Run! The Navajo are coming!" Tuma was washing her hair in a little stream. But she ran home as quickly as she could. The Navajo were another tribe who lived nearby. They tried to raid Pueblo villages in search of food and other supplies. The peace-loving Pueblo people did not like to fight. But they could not allow their food to be stolen. They would fight for their food.

"Hurry, Tuma," cried Yonga, her older brother. Tuma scrambled up the ladder. Yonga pulled it up after them.

Tuma's building was like an apartment house. One room was stacked on top of another. More than 300 families lived in this tall pueblo made of stone and clay. The only way to get from one floor to another was by ladder. Under attack, all the ladders were pulled up. It became very hard for an enemy to reach the people inside.

Tuma climbed down through the roof and through the homes of many families. At last she reached the room she shared with her family. Meanwhile the men of the village hurried to the roof to defend their home.

There are 200 rooms for approximately 400 people.

Farming   Tuma thought back to all the work the men had done to grow the corn that the Navajo wanted so badly. They built fences so the soil would not blow away. They dug ditches to bring water to the fields from a nearby stream. They were careful not to plant the seed too early in the growing season. They offered many prayers for a good crop.

The women and girls did not help plant the corn. But they spent hours grinding it into cornmeal. They made many different

Show a sample of corn meal to the class. You may want to
have the class participate in preparing and tasting an
American Indian recipe using corn meal.

foods from the corn. Much of their time
was also spent making clay pots for the
corn. Plain pots were used for cooking
the corn. Beautifully painted pots were
used for storing the corn.

Everyone in a Pueblo village depended
on this important food. They all worked
and prayed for it. They would not let the
Navajo take it away from them.

Pueblo religion   Tuma hugged her
kachina (kä chē′ nə) doll as she listened
to sounds of fighting from the roof. The
Pueblo people believed that kachinas were
good spirits who protected them and
their crops. Boys and girls alike had dolls
made to look like the different kachina
spirits. That way children could learn to
know the different kachina masks worn
by dancers at religious festivals.

The Pueblo held many religious ceremonies each year. There was much sing-

ing and dancing at these ceremonies.
Each song and dance was a prayer to
bring rain and to make the corn grow tall.

Homes   Tuma looked around her
home. It was a good home. Thick walls
kept it cool in the hottest summer. A
cooking fire burned brightly in the firepit.
When she grew up she would receive this
home from her mother's family. When
she married, her husband would come to
her home to live.

"The women have their homes; the men
have their kivas (kē′ vəz)," she thought.
Kivas were underground rooms. The Pueblo men used them for religious ceremonies. But in the winter, the men gathered
in kivas to tell stories, weave blankets,
and teach the younger boys.

A sharp bang frightened Tuma! It was
Yonga. He had dropped his club in returning from the roof. He was out of breath
but happy.

"The Navajo have gone away," he said.
"They used tree trunks to climb our pueblo. But we drove them away . . . this
time."

Tuma gave her kachina doll a hug. She
was happy too. She knew why the Navajo
had been driven away. She must remember to thank the good spirit who
protected her people.

CHECKUP

1. What were the homes of the Iroquois, Sioux, and
   Pueblo peoples called? What were they like?
   How did the area in which each group lived
   influence the kind of housing in which they
   lived?
2. Which people got their food by hunting, fishing,
   and farming? Which got their food mostly by
   hunting? By farming?

Dolls helped children recognize the Kachina spirits.

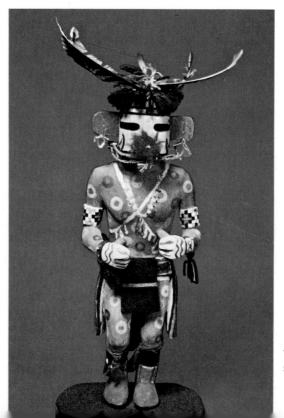

This is the spotted corn kachina or Qá-ö. Notice the breech clout,
sash and moccasins—typical dress of the Southwest Indians.

Have pupils draw Mayan, Aztec, and Inca designs for the bulletin board after showing them some examples. You may want to work with the art teacher on this activity.

Mayas, Aztecs, and Incas

VOCABULARY

civilization	causeway
human sacrifice	canal
empire	terrace

Great civilizations   About 8,000 years ago somewhere in Middle America, a great discovery was made. People learned how to plant and grow corn.

Before this discovery people had to hunt animals or gather wild plants for their food. Everybody had to help in the search for food. They had very little time for anything else. But when people learned to grow their own food, many ways of life began to change. People had time to do other things. Cities, trade, government, writing, art, and science developed. These can all be called marks of a **civilization**.

Civilizations grew up in Middle and South America. Most early Native Americans lived in these places. You are going to learn about two early Middle American cultures and one early South American culture.

Mayan farming   The Mayas (mä′ yəz) were one group of Native Americans whose ways of life were changed by the new way of getting food. The Mayas lived in Central America and in the southern parts of what is now Mexico. On the map on page 58 find the lands of the Mayas.

The Mayas had good soil for growing crops. They raised squash, beans, sweet potatoes, and chili peppers as well as corn.

After a while Maya farmers became able to raise more food than they needed for themselves. This meant that while most Mayas continued to farm, not everyone had to be a farmer. Some people could do other kinds of work.

Mayan cities   The Mayas became very good at many new jobs. Some learned to weave beautiful cloth. Others became fine builders. Some learned to be artists. Some became traders.

Because of all these new skills and many others, it became possible to build cities. There were Mayan cities more than 1,600 years ago. They were beautiful cities. They had huge pyramids made of earth and stone, with fine temples at the top. There were wide courtyards and palaces with many rooms.

Religious festivals were held in the cities. So were market days when all kinds of goods were for sale. Traders traveled to faraway places to bring back goods for the city markets.

The priests climbed the four steep stairways to the temple.

The temples built on top of the pyramids were the scenes of important Mayan religious ceremonies.

The main temple

The stones of the pyramids, although different sizes and shapes, fit together precisely. The pyramids have survived many earthquakes.

Of all Native Americans, the Mayans developed the most advanced system of writing. Their symbols stood partly for ideas and partly for sounds.

Maya priests   While each city had one main ruler, the priests were also very important in the life of the Mayas. They did much more than lead the people in worship. They helped govern the cities. Many of the things that people did were directed by the priests. The builders and craftworkers were under the priests' orders. Roads and many important buildings were built under their orders.

The priests were also scientists. They studied the stars. They learned to tell by the stars when the rainy seasons would come. How did this help the farmers?

The priests invented a system of arithmetic and a calendar. They also worked out a way to write their language. This made it possible for them to keep records of Mayan history.

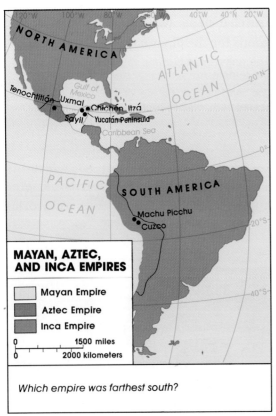

MAYAN, AZTEC, AND INCA EMPIRES

☐ Mayan Empire
■ Aztec Empire
■ Inca Empire

0   1500 miles
0   2000 kilometers

Which empire was farthest south?

Aztecs: a warlike people   The Aztecs (az' teks) and Mayas were alike in many ways. The Aztecs lived in what is now Mexico. Their homes, clothes, arts, science, farming, foods, and writing were almost the same as the Mayas'.

The religion of each group called for **human sacrifice**. Both groups killed people as offerings to their gods. But the Aztecs made many more such sacrifices to their gods than the Mayas did. Unlike the Mayas, the Aztecs went to war often to get enough prisoners to sacrifice.

Every Aztec boy was trained for war. The Aztec warriors defeated many other groups of Native Americans. The Aztecs built a huge **empire** by taking the lands of the people they defeated in battle. Find the Aztec empire on the map. This great country was very carefully governed and it lasted for at least 300 years.

The Aztecs had no alphabet; they used picture symbols.

Tenochtitlán   The great Aztec city of Tenochtitlán (tā näch tē tlän') was one of the largest cities in the world only 400 years ago. Up to 300,000 people may have lived there at one time. Tenochtitlán was the center of Aztec government and trade.

Tenochtitlán was built on an island in the middle of a lake. **Causeways**, or land bridges, were made by building earth up above the water in narrow strips. Goods and people could move along these land bridges to get from the city to the mainland. Wooden bridges were added to the land bridges. These could be moved away, leaving empty spaces in the land bridges. This made it hard for enemies to enter the city.

Tenochtitlán was always busy. It was always full of people. All roads led to the

Ask: What are the latitude and longitude coordinates for: Tenochtitlán? (19° N, 99° W), Sayil? (19° N, 90° W), Cuzco? (17° S, 71° W)

causeways

removeable bridges

(19° 24′ N/99° 1′ W)

A modern Mexican artist, using old maps and drawings as sources, painted this mural of Tenochtitlan.

Notice the woman carrying the basket on her head.

Stones were brought from these mountains to build the Pyramid in the center of the city.

center of the city. There were also **canals,** or waterways dug out for boats. These also led to the center of the city. In the city center, on top of large pyramids, were temples for each of the Aztec gods.

The Inca empire   Over 500 years ago the empire of the Incas stretched along the western mountains of South America. This huge land took in all of what is now the country of Peru and parts of present-day Chile, Ecuador, and Bolivia. On the map on page 58, find the land of the Incas.

In 1450 this empire, 3,000 miles (4,800 km) long, held over 4 million people. The tribes conquered by the great Inca armies were treated well. Some tribes even asked to be made part of the Inca empire. The Incas protected them. In return, they allowed the Incas to rule them.

The Incas were great builders. They were able to build fine roads over the steep mountains. They could build bridges across the deep valleys. These roads helped the Inca government keep in touch with everything that was going on.

The rulers and rich people among the Incas lived in great stone palaces. They ate from gold plates. They wore beautiful jewelry made by Inca artists. A great many people waited on them and worked for them.

But most Incas were not rich. They lived in small mud, stone, or reed houses. Their main food was potatoes. They also ate corn, beans, squash, and tomatoes. They raised guinea (gin′ ē) pigs for meat. The llama was very important to the Incas. They used its wool to make clothes. They used it to carry loads. They even ate llama meat.

The name Tenochtitlán means "near the cactus." According to an Aztec tale, the War God told the Aztecs to build their great city where they saw an eagle perched on a cactus holding a snake in its beak. That vision is the present-day symbol used on Mexico's coat-of-arms.

Getting it Straight: the Americas

The terms North America, South America, Central America, Middle America, and Latin American can be confusing. The Western Hemisphere, our half of the globe, really has only two continents, or large masses of land. These are North and South America.

North America means everything north of South America (see map 1). This includes Panama and the small countries northwest of Panama, the islands in the Caribbean Sea, Mexico, the United States, and Canada. South American means only the large continent south of the entire area of North America (see map 2).

Sometimes it is helpful to refer to certain regions in this area. Central America (see map 3) really means only the narrow part of North America connecting the larger part of North America with South America. It includes Guatemala, Belize, El Salvador, Honduras, Nicaragua, Costa Rica, and Panama. Middle America (see map 4) is the whole area south of the United States and north of South America. It also includes the islands in the Caribbean Sea.

Latin America is a helpful term we use to identify part of the Americas by language. Latin America means all the countries south of the United States. Many of the people in these countries speak a language based on the old Latin language. Often this language is Spanish.

1.

2.

3.

4.

The silver llama was found on the Island of the Sun at Lake Titicaca in the late 1800's. These figures were sometimes used as ceremonial offerings. Notice the fine detail on the blanket.

This llama made of silver shows the skill of the Inca artists.
The silver was covered with minerals to add color.

Inca farming Most Incas were farmers. They learned to grow crops on the steep sides of the mountains as well as in the valleys. They cut **terraces**, or rows of steps, into the mountainsides to plant their crops. Stone walls kept the soil from washing away during heavy rains.

The government owned all the land. The people were allowed to farm it. But in return they had to give part of their crop to the government. The government stored some of this food in special buildings. Then when times were hard and crops were poor, the people had food to eat.

Ask: Why was the llama so important to the Incas?

Inca religion The Incas had many gods. One of the most important was the sun god. The Incas even called their land the Kingdom of the Sun.

The Incas, like the Mayas and the Aztecs, believed their gods wanted sacrifices. But the Incas generally sacrificed animals instead of people.

The priests had an important place in the lives of the Incas. These religious leaders were also the doctors. They took care of the people who became sick. Some of them became so skilled that they were even able to operate on people's heads!

Inca education Most Inca children did not go to school. They learned by working with their parents every day. But some of the children of rich people did go to school. The boys were sent to the capital city of Cuzco to learn to become government workers. They studied history, war, religion, and language.

They did not learn to write. The Incas did not have writing. But they did have a way of remembering things and of counting by using knotted strings of different lengths and colors.

Some 10-year-old girls were also picked to go to a special school. Here they learned how to work in the emperor's palace. They learned how to be the wives of rich and important men.

Inca arts and crafts The Incas were fine artists and craftworkers. They made beautiful pottery. They made jewelry, tools, and many other things out of different metals. They wove fine cloth from wool and cotton.

The Incas were famous for their stonework. They could build stone walls that fit tightly together without cement. Some of these walls have stood for hundreds of years.

CHECKUP

1. What are the marks of a civilization? Which of them were found among the Mayas? Aztecs? Incas?
2. Why was it possible for Mayas to develop skills other than farming?

61

KEY FACTS

1. Native Americans came to America long before any other groups.

2. Americans today have learned a great deal from Native Americans.

3. To understand what early Native Americans were like you must study many different tribes, because each tribe is different.

4. A civilization is marked by cities, farming, trade, government, writing, art, and science.

5. Many Native American groups had very advanced civilizations.

VOCABULARY QUIZ

Write **T** if the statement is true and **F** if it is false. If the statement is false, change the underlined word to make the statement true.

1. The first Americans came to America by crossing a <u>causeway</u>. F strait

2. A <u>civilization</u> is marked by government, science, and art. T

3. Another name for a group of Native Americans is a <u>crowd</u>. F tribe

4. Huge piles of earth in which archaeologists have found clues about how some Native Americans lived are called <u>terraces</u>. F mounds

5. <u>Human sacrifice</u> is the practice of killing people and offering them to the gods. T

6. A large land area ruled by one leader or group is called a <u>longhouse</u>. F empire

7. A <u>desert</u> is a dry, often hot, land with few trees. T

8. Native Americans had many <u>cultures</u>, or ways of life. T

9. Waterways dug out for boats are called <u>canals</u>. T

10. A group of people joined together for a common purpose is a <u>sachem</u>. F league

REVIEW QUESTIONS

1. What is the importance of a "land bridge" in the coming of the first people to the Americas?

2. What do you think was the greatest accomplishment of the Iroquois? The Sioux? The Pueblo?

3. Prove that the Mayas, Aztecs, and Incas were great civilizations by naming at least three of the marks of civilization for each.

ACTIVITIES

1. Native Americans had to develop a written language. They did this by making pictures or symbols for their words. Some of these written languages still have not been entirely solved.

Make your own secret code by giving each letter in the alphabet a symbol. For example: "A" could be #. Write a note and share it with a friend or the whole class. See if they can solve the code or if they need help from you.

2. Draw a scene from the chapter that you found interesting. Some suggestions could be, "Running the gauntlet," "A game of lacrosse," "Buffalo hunting," "A religious ceremony,"or "Human sacrifice."

3. You learned in this chapter that there are over 500 Native American words in the English language. Make a list of words you know or think are of Native American origin. Look in a dictionary to check those words of which you are not sure. Also check your spelling.

Now make a picture dictionary. First put the words in alphabetical order. Illustrate each word with a picture you have drawn or cut from an old magazine. Write a definition for each word and its picture. Make your work as neat and attractive as possible.

READING FOR CONCLUSIONS

All religions tell the story of creation. Native Americans have many songs and stories that tell about how the world began.

The Chippewa (chip′ ə wä) are a tribe of Native Americans. Once they lived in the forests around what is now called Lake Superior. There are many stories in the Chippewa religion that tell of the beginnings of the people. The story that follows tells how man and woman came to be.

The Great Manitou was a ruling spirit. Long, long ago he took the form of a giant bird. This giant bird had an egg in its nest. The Great Snake found the nest. The egg looked good to eat. As the Snake came near, the egg moved. The Manitou heard the egg move. He took a big rock in his claws and killed the Great Snake. But he also broke open the egg.

A man came out of the broken egg. The man could not move far. He had a large rock on his feet. The Manitou wanted to teach the man many things. Soon the man learned how to make tools and to hunt. He learned how to make clothing and grow food. At last he learned enough. One day he awoke to find a woman beside him.

The Manitou removed the rock from his feet. The two people ran away. These people were Native Americans. They were the first people to live on earth.

To "draw conclusions" means to take information and use it in a new way. A story does not have to say something clearly. Because of the way the story is written, however, you can draw conclusions that certain things are true.

Some of the following statements are correct conclusions from the story. Some are not. Write **T** if the statement is true and **F** if it is false.

1. The Great Manitou and the Great Snake were enemies. T

2. The Chippewa believe that all birds are gods. F

3. The Great Manitou built a nest of straw. F

4. The man could not move because his feet were pinned by a rock. T

5. The Chippewa believe humans came from godlike animals. T

6. The Great Manitou would not let the man go free until he had learned to take care of himself. T

7. The Chippewa are the descendents of the two people who ran away. T

8. The skills of hunting and farming came to the Chippewa from the Great Manitou. T

Early Explorers

VOCABULARY

explore

What is an explorer?   Have you ever gone exploring? Perhaps you have hiked deep into a wood, deeper than you had ever been before. You might have discovered trees or flowers or insects there that were new to you. Maybe you found a stream you didn't know about. You probably brought back a leaf or a plant to show your parents or friends. Or perhaps you moved to another home and went for a walk around your new neighborhood. You might have found streets and buildings you had never seen before and people you had never met. You probably told your family what you had seen.

If you have ever done anything like these things, you were exploring. To **explore** means to search for new things or places. It means making discoveries.

A great age   There was a time in the history of Europe when there were many great explorers. They were daring people who voyaged to unknown lands. They made wonderful discoveries. They brought back plants and treasures and even people that no one at home had ever seen before. They brought back information that people at home had never heard

about before. Some of these daring adventurers found their way to America. We often call the time of the great explorers the "Age of Exploration."

Who was first?   We know that people came to America from Asia many thousands of years ago. These were the Native Americans. But who were the first people to come to America *after* the Native Americans? Who were the first explorers to discover America?

Many claims have been made that different groups from Africa, Asia, or Europe were the first to arrive in America. But no real proof has been found for any of these claims except one.

The Vikings   The Vikings (vī′ kingz) were a bold and brave sailing people. They came from the countries we now call Norway, Denmark, and Sweden. Find these northern European countries on the map on page 474 in the Atlas. Some of these daring people had left their home country and settled on the small northern island of Iceland. Others had gone still farther west. They had made settlements on the large island of Greenland. Find Iceland and Greenland on the map on pages 466–467. Stories about these settlements made many hundreds of years ago became part of Viking oral history.

This painting is from the collection at the Naval Academy in Annapolis, Md.

Point out to pupils that there were no engines, only sails, by which to make the journey across the oceans. Ask: Would you like to sail the ocean in one of these ships?

This is what the Santa Maria, *Christopher Columbus's flagship, might have looked like on the evening of October 11, 1492.*

Historians estimate that the Santa Maria was from 75 to 90 ft (23 to 27 m) long. The Niña and Pinta, smaller ships, were about 70 to 75 ft (21 to 23 m) long. These vessels were made of wood. Cooking was done in a firebox on deck and only the highest ranking officers had bunks.

The Viking trading ships called knorrs were about 50 ft (15 m) long. The warships, called long ships, were 65 to 95 ft (20 to 29 m) long and 17 ft (5 m) wide.

Leif Ericson The Vikings also passed down stories about a great explorer named Leif (lāv) Ericson. The stories told that in the year 1000 Leif Ericson had sailed west across the north Atlantic from a Viking settlement in Greenland to a new and unknown land. He named the new land Vinland. The stories also said that after Leif's discovery, other groups of Vikings settled in this new land. They built stone houses. They planted crops and raised cattle.

But old stories alone are not proof that something really happened. If there had been settlements, they had disappeared. Certainly no other European settlers had followed the Vikings to the new land. However, about 20 years ago, archaeologists discovered the remains of some old stone buildings in Newfoundland. Look at the map on page 470. Find Newfoundland on the eastern coast of Canada. You can see that it is not very far from Greenland.

The archaeologists could prove that the oldest stone buildings they found had

Danish sea scouts built this replica of a Viking ship. Imagine crossing an ocean in such a ship!

During which years did most of the exploration of North America take place?

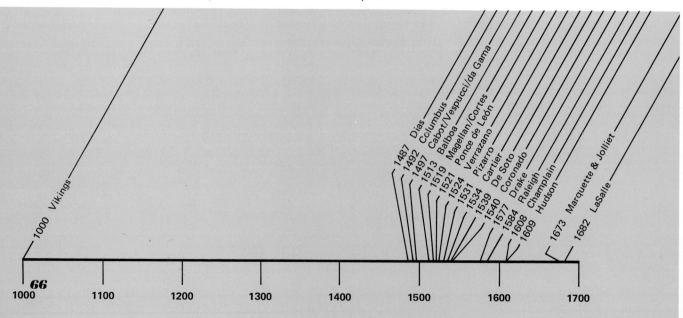

Historians have learned about Scandinavian kings, wars, and customs from stories or sagas written in Iceland between the 1100s and the 1300s. Also, Icelandic poems, or eddas, revealed legends about Scandinavian kings as well as their mythology.

been built by the Vikings. They were able to tell that these buildings had been built about A.D. 1000. Many Viking artifacts were also discovered nearby. Now there was real proof that the Vikings had come to North America as early as the year 1000.

A forgotten discovery The Vikings were probably the first Europeans in America. But they had no idea that Vinland was part of a whole new world. And they found nothing valuable to take back home with them. After a very few years their settlements died out. As far as the rest of Europe was concerned, the Vikings' great discovery went almost unnoticed. Only in the old Viking tales was Leif Ericson's adventure remembered. Nearly 500 years later another discovery would cause much more excitement.

CHECKUP

1. What does an explorer do?
2. What proof has been found that the Vikings came to America about 1,000 years ago?

Christopher Columbus

┌─VOCABULARY─
 colony

Land ho! "¡Tierra! ¡Tierra!" The cry of the watchman drove the sleep from the eyes of the sailors. A cheer went up. It was early morning, October 12, 1492. The land sighted was a small island southeast of what is now the state of Florida. The cheering sailors were part of the crew of the Spanish sailing ship the *Santa Maria*. Perhaps no one on board the *Santa Maria* was happier than the captain, Christopher Columbus.

A boy who wanted to be a sailor Columbus had been born in 1451, the son of a wool weaver in the busy Italian seaport of Genoa on the Mediterranean Sea. Genoa was one of the busiest trading ports in Europe. Christopher loved the sea. As a boy he had spent many happy hours watching the tall sailing ships come and go in Genoa's harbor.

In the 1200s and 1300s Genoa and Venice vied for control of trade in the eastern Mediterranean Sea. Genoa has been an important port city throughout history. Notice the style of dress and hair of Columbus's youth.

The harbor of Genoa looked like this when Christopher Columbus was a boy.

44°25′N/8°57′E

More than anything else young Christopher wanted to go to sea. And while he was still a teenager, Christopher Columbus became a sailor. He spent many years sailing to foreign lands. He was a brave sailor and a good one. He learned much about the seas and about the ships that sailed on them. And after a while Christopher Columbus became a captain.

Trade routes   At that time every important country in Europe wanted to find an all-water route to India, the Spice Islands, and China—all the lands that people then called the Indies. From these far-off places came jewels, ivory, and silks. The spices, such as nutmeg and cinnamon, cloves and pepper, were almost as valuable as jewels. They were used to keep food from spoiling.

The young Columbus had watched these precious goods being taken off the ships in Genoa's harbor. But they had not made their whole journey by ship. A large part of their trip had been overland on the backs of camels or other pack animals. The trade routes across deserts, over mountains, and through valleys were long and hard. They were also very dangerous. Robbers lay in wait for the richly laden animal trains. Even the parts of the journeys made by ship were risky. Pirates often attacked these treasure ships, robbing, burning, and killing.

Most people talked about the possibility of sailing around the southern tip of Africa and then northward across the Indian Ocean to India. From there ships could sail to the Spice Islands. They might even sail on to China. Find this route on the map on page 466 in the Atlas.

A different idea   Captain Christopher Columbus was as much interested as anyone else in finding a new route to the Indies. He knew if he could find such a route he would become rich and famous. Besides, it would be such a great adventure! And Columbus had a new idea. He believed, as did many people of the time, that the world was round. "If that is true," thought Columbus, "why not sail west to get to the East?"

Portugal   It is one thing to have a good idea. It is another and sometimes harder thing to make that idea work. Voyages cost a great deal of money. Where would Columbus get enough money to try out his idea?

He decided to go to the king of Portugal for help. He asked the king for three ships. And he asked for the title of admiral. He wanted to keep some of the gold and other riches he believed he would find for himself. And he wanted to rule any new lands he might discover. The king of Portugal refused to agree to Columbus's demands. He felt that Columbus was asking too much.

There was another reason that the king refused Columbus. Columbus had said that Asia was only 2,400 miles (3,860 km) west of Europe. The king's geographers believed that this distance was not correct. It was too short. They believed that it was really about four times as far to Asia. It just was not possible, they felt, to make such a long voyage.

The king's geographers were much more nearly correct than Columbus about the distance between Europe and Asia. Of course neither they nor Columbus knew that the huge continents of the Americas lay between Europe and Asia.

Columbus was not the kind of person who gives up easily. This was part of what made him a great man. He wanted riches for himself and his family. He was also sure that God wanted him to make this voyage. If Portugal would not help him, he would try Spain!

Ferdinand and Isabella   King Ferdinand and Queen Isabella of Spain were very interested in Columbus's idea. But Spain was at war. Wars are very expensive. Spain had no money to pay for such a costly voyage. Columbus would have to wait.

While he was waiting, Portuguese explorers were sailing farther and farther down the coast of Africa. Finally, in 1488, Bartholomeu Dias, a Portuguese sea captain, rounded the southern tip of Africa. While he did not sail on to India, a new trade route to the Indies was ready to open. And Columbus still had not been able to test his idea. At last he decided to leave Spain early in 1492.

While on the road home, Columbus was stopped by a messenger from the palace. King Ferdinand and Queen Isabella had finally decided to help him. Spain still had very little money to spare, but Columbus must sail!

A dream comes true   Columbus's dream was going to come true. He went about the work of getting ships and crews together. In August of 1492, Columbus set sail. He had 90 sailors in three ships, the *Niña*, the *Pinta*, and the *Santa Maria*. The ships stopped at the Canary Islands for supplies. Find the Canary Islands on the map on page 71. Then in September Columbus and his sailors set out into the vast Atlantic Ocean.

After they had been out of sight of land for a month, the sailors began to get frightened. No one had ventured out this far upon the "Sea of Darkness" before. They were afraid that if they went any farther, they would never be able to return home safely. The sailors talked of taking over the ships and turning back to Spain. Columbus reminded them of the gold they would surely get if they completed the voyage. But still the sailors threatened to take over and turn the ships back.

Just as it seemed they would go no farther, they saw branches and leaves in the water. This was a sure sign that land was near. Then on October 12, 1492, the welcome call was heard that land had been sighted.

Columbus, about to set sail on his first voyage, says good-bye to Ferdinand and Isabella.

Notice the style of clothing on the people and the rigging on the ships. Ask: What do you think the priest is doing? Why do you think Columbus is bowing to Queen Isabella?

Ask: If you had been a sailor on the Niña, Pinta, or Santa Maria would you have been afraid? Why or why not?

69

Later that morning Columbus went on shore and claimed the land he had found for King Ferdinand and Queen Isabella of Spain. He named the small island San Salvador. *San Salvador* means "Holy Savior" in Spanish.

Columbus's mistake   San Salvador is one of a group of islands we call the Bahamas. Look at the map on page 71. Find these islands off the southern tip of Florida. Columbus made a mistake. He was sure that he had reached the East Indies, islands very close to Asia. He even called the friendly people he found on the island "Indians" after the term "Indies." The islands became known as the West Indies. Columbus never knew that he had discovered a whole New World.

With the help of the Native Americans, Columbus explored some of the other islands. He sailed along the coast of a larger island we call Cuba. And as he sailed farther east he found still another island. He named this smaller island Hispaniola. You can find these islands on the map on page 71. Columbus found white beaches, beautiful forests, and colorful birds and flowers. He saw people smoking tobacco, something no European had ever seen. He saw corn growing in the fields. Nowhere in Europe did people grow corn. But he found very little gold and no silks or spices. Still Columbus believed that he had reached the outposts of Asia and that all the riches of the Indies were almost within his grasp.

After a long, stormy journey, Columbus arrived back in Spain in March 1493. He was received as a great hero by King Ferdinand and Queen Isabella. He had not brought home much gold. But he had proved that brave sailors could cross the huge unknown sea and return home safely. And he had claimed new lands for Spain. Besides, everyone was sure that on future voyages to the new lands Columbus would find all the riches of the East to bring back to Spain.

Other voyages   Columbus made three other voyages to what we now know was a new world to Europeans. You can follow each voyage on the map on page 71. On his second trip he started the **colony** of Isabela. A colony is land that is settled far from the country that governs it. It was on the third trip that he first set foot on the American mainland in what is now Venezuela. Columbus's forth voyage was started in 1502. He wanted to find a water passage through these unknown lands. But he could not find a passage that was not there.

San Salvador is called Watlings Island today. Columbus reported that the native inhabitants called the island Guanahani. 24°N/74°30′W

Columbus thought he was landing on an island off the coast of Asia.

Ask: How did American astronauts leave evidence that they had landed on the moon? Relate the fact that the American flag was planted on the surface of the moon to the fact that explorers usually planted the flag of their homeland on newly discovered land.

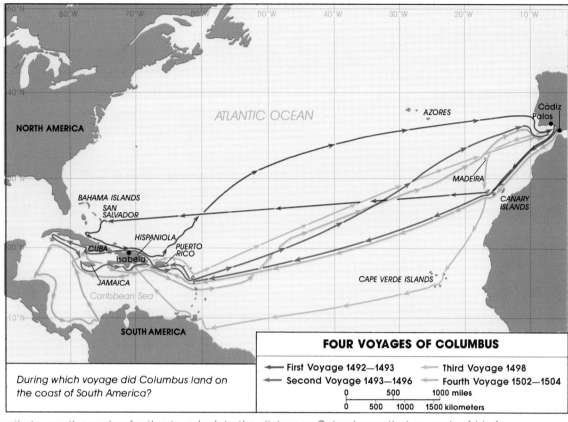

During which voyage did Columbus land on the coast of South America?

FOUR VOYAGES OF COLUMBUS

← First Voyage 1492—1493   ← Third Voyage 1498
← Second Voyage 1493—1496   ← Fourth Voyage 1502—1504

Ask pupils to use the scale of miles to calculate the distances Columbus sailed on each of his four voyages.

On this last voyage Columbus stayed on the island we now call Jamaica for a whole year. In order to get food, Columbus played a trick on the people who lived on the island. He told them to bring him food or his God would take away the light in the night sky. They did not believe him. But before long it became very dark and the moon was gone from the sky. Soon people with food were coming from all over. They begged Columbus to put back the light. What do you think happened? Have you ever seen an eclipse of the moon?

It may help pupils to refer to a diagram of the eclipse of the moon, probably found in their science text.

The contributions of Columbus   In 1506, two years after he returned from his last voyage, Columbus died. He was poor and disgraced. He had never found the

Ask: Do you think Columbus should have felt disgraced after his last voyage? Why or why not?

gold he expected. He had not found a new route to Asia.

It is true that Columbus made mistakes. But he was a man of great courage and skill. And he made one of the greatest discoveries in history. He is the explorer who opened a whole New World to Europe. And his discovery was not forgotten, like that of the Vikings. More and more people learned of Columbus's great discovery. It was not very long before hundreds and then thousands of people followed where he had led.

CHECKUP

1. What was Columbus's new idea?
2. What was the date of Columbus's discovery of America?
3. Why was Columbus's discovery more important than that of the Vikings?

71

Explorers for Spain and Portugal

"First come, first served"   Columbus had been the first to reach the New World. He claimed the land he found for King Ferdinand and Queen Isabella of Spain. Only 4 years later Spain built its first lasting settlement on Hispaniola.

The news of Columbus's discovery spread throughout Europe. Other countries became interested in the new lands beyond the Atlantic. Many explorers and settlers came after Columbus. Each group claimed land for the country that sent them. Generally the first country to have explorers and settlers in an area would be able to control it and profit from it. The rule for claiming New World lands seems to have been "First come, first served."

A claim for Portugal   In 1500 a Portuguese sailor, Pedro Cabral (kä bräl'), was trying to sail around Africa to Asia. He somehow got off course and landed on the coast of what we now call Brazil in South America. Cabral claimed this land for Portugal. Find the area he claimed for Portugal on the map on page 74. Another explorer sailing for Portugal also landed on that coast. Find the area claimed by Amerigo Vespucci (ve spü' chē).

Portugal was not as interested in the New World at that time as were other European countries. Three years earlier another Portuguese sailor, Vasco da Gama, had become the first to sail around Africa and on to India. The trade route from Lisbon in Portugal around the southern tip of Africa and across the Indian Ocean had become a reality. Portuguese trading ships had been sailing up and down the coast of Africa for some years. Traders and sailors knew the area pretty well. So da Gama's route seemed to them the easiest way to get to the Indies. Trace this route on the map on page 466 in the Atlas.

Brazil was to remain Portugal's only claim to the New World. Spain explored and claimed almost everything else in the southern part of the Americas.

Ponce de León   One of the first Spanish explorers was Juan Ponce de León (pons də' lē' ən). He had sailed with Columbus on his second voyage. Ponce de León lived in the West Indies for many years. He went on several **expeditions** in search of gold. An expedition is a journey for a certain purpose. Ponce de León's purpose was to look for gold. In 1508 he did find some gold on the island we now know as Puerto Rico. And he claimed that land for Spain.

Ponce de León had heard stories about a wonderful fountain whose waters could make people young again. In 1513 he sailed off to find this Fountain of Youth. Of course Ponce de León never found this magic fountain. But he did find a beautiful warm land filled with flowers. He named this land Florida and claimed it for Spain. It was here that the first Spanish settlement in North America, St. Augustine, was started. Find St. Augustine on the map on page 74.

ler, who was making a new map of the world including the newly discovered lands, suggested after reading Vespucci's letters that the new land be named "America" in honor of Vespucci. Modern historians question the validity of Vespucci's letters.

Balboa   Also in 1513 another Spaniard, Vasco Núñez de Balboa (vas′ kō nü(n)əs′ də bal bō′ ə), was leading an expedition in the New World. He, too, was looking for gold. But he was also looking for a water passage through the land. Such a passage, many Europeans felt, would allow ships to continue sailing westward to Asia. Balboa was leading his group through the Isthmus of Panama. An **isthmus** (is′ məs) is a narrow strip of land connecting two larger pieces of land. It has water on both sides. Find the Isthmus of Panama on the map on page 74.

Climbing a high mountain after a hard journey through thick wet forests, Balboa saw a huge body of water before him. He called this body of water the "South Sea" and claimed for Spain all the land which its waters touched. Balboa had discovered the Pacific Ocean.

Magellan   Ferdinand Magellan (mə jel′ an) is thought by many people to be the greatest sailor in the history of the world. In 1519 Magellan sailed southwest from Spain. He, like so many others, was looking for a new water route to the Indies.

When he reached the New World, he sailed south along the coast of South America. Trace his route on the map on page 466 in the Atlas. At the tip of South America he discovered the water passage that led through the land to the west. Today we call this passage the Strait of Magellan.

It took Magellan a long time to sail through this narrow, rough waterway. But when he did, he became the first European to sail on the great ocean that Balboa had named the South Sea. Magellan found this ocean so calm that he called it Pacific, meaning "peaceful."

The Strait of Magellan is known for its high winds, heavy rains, and rough seas throughout the year.

Magellan had great difficulty getting his ships through the strait at the tip of South America.

Magellan's five ships were the Santiago, the San Antonio, the Concepción, the Trinidad, and the Victoria. The Santiago was destroyed by a winter storm. The crew of the San Antonio refused to go through the Strait of Magellan and decided to return to Spain. The Concepción was abandoned because there were

South America was the last land Magellan and his crew would see for 14 weeks. They ran out of food and water as they sailed across this vast, calm ocean. They became so hungry they were eating shoe leather, rats, and sawdust. Many of them were dying.

At last they reached the island of Guam. Here they were able to rest and get fresh water and food. Magellan and his crew then sailed for the Philippine Islands. Here Magellan was killed in a battle between two groups of islanders. But his men continued the journey westward

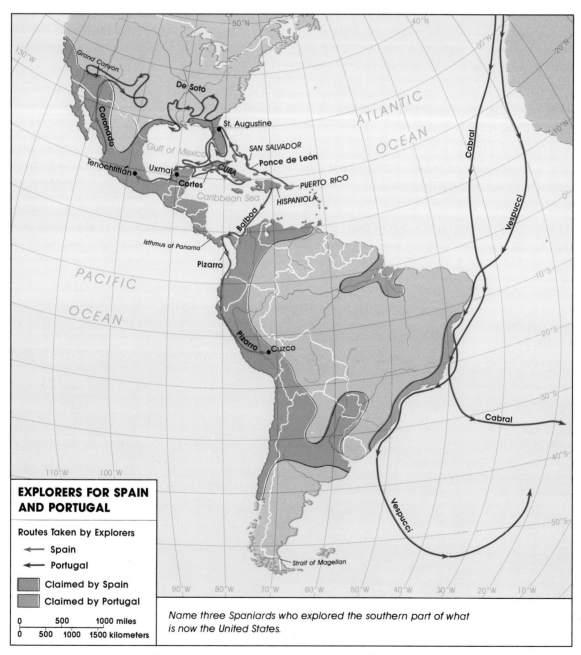

EXPLORERS FOR SPAIN AND PORTUGAL

Routes Taken by Explorers

← Spain

← Portugal

Claimed by Spain

Claimed by Portugal

| 0 | 500 | 1000 miles |
| 0 | 500 1000 | 1500 kilometers |

Name three Spaniards who explored the southern part of what is now the United States.

too few men left to sail it by the time they were ready to leave the Philippines. The Trinidad was forced to return to the Spice Islands as a result of bad weather and disease. Only the Victoria succeeded in making the full trip back to Spain.

until they reached the Spice Islands. They bought some precious spices and rested again. Then they set sail for Africa. They sailed west around the tip of Africa and up the coast. They finally limped into their home port in Spain in 1522, exhausted and ill. Trace the voyage from the Strait of Magellan back to Spain on the Atlas map on page 466.

Five ships and 240 men had left Spain in 1519. One ship and 17 men returned in 1522. The price had been great. But human beings had sailed all the way around the world for the first time! <u>The huge size of the world was understood for the first time. For the first time and for all time it had been proven that the East could be reached by sailing west.</u>

Cortes   Hernando Cortes (kôr′ tiz) had been in the New World since he was 19. He had helped conquer Cuba for Spain and had become very rich. But he wanted still more! Reports of the great riches of the Aztec empire in the land we call Mexico had reached Cuba. In 1519 Cortes left Cuba and set out for Mexico. With him he brought a small army of well-armed Spanish soldiers.

Cortes found that the Aztecs possessed gold and silver even beyond his dreams. And these Native Americans, although very brave, were no match for the Spanish soldiers with their horses, guns, and swords. By 1521 the Spaniards had conquered the Aztecs. They tore down the beautiful Aztec capital city of Tenochtitlán and made the proud Aztecs slaves. Turn back to page 59 to see what Tenochtitlán looked like. The great Aztec empire now belonged to Spain.

Pizarro   Ten years later the bold Spanish explorer Francisco Pizarro (pə zar′ rō) sailed from Central America to the rich empire of the Incas on the west coast of South America.

In order to gain control of this empire, Pizarro and his soldiers killed thousands of unarmed Incas. He took the Inca ruler captive. And after taking all his gold, Pizarro had him put to death. Pizarro soon won the whole huge Inca empire for Spain.

De Soto   Spain had almost complete control of Latin America by 1540. But Spanish explorers also made claims in the southern part of what is now the United States.

Hernando de Soto was one of these explorers. In 1539 he began a search for gold that took him from Florida and across the Southeast. He never did find gold. But he did discover what the American Indians called the Mississippi, the "Father of Waters." Why, do you think, was it given this name?

Coronado   Francisco Coronado was another Spanish explorer. In 1540 he left Mexico and went searching for the "Seven Cities of Gold" in the southwestern part of what is now the United States. He had heard about these cities from a black explorer named Estevánico (es tə va nē′ kō).

For about two years, Coronado and Estevánico, along with many Spanish soldiers, searched in vain for these cities of gold, which did not really exist. However, some of Coronado's men were the first Europeans to see the Grand Canyon in what is now the state of Arizona. And

De Soto died of fever near the Mississippi River. His men weighted his body and buried him in the river. In his earlier years of exploration, de Soto was one of the leaders, along with Pizarro, who conquered the Incan empire.

75

This artist's portrayal of the Coronado expedition shows the various elements that were common to most Spanish exploration ventures: soldiers, priests, Native American guides, horses, mules, and weapons. The guides were not always willing to join the expeditions as depicted here.

In his search for gold, Coronado traveled as far north as what is now Kansas.

Coronado was able to claim the wide lands of the American Southwest for Spain.

Spanish leadership ends   Spain had taken the lead in exploring, conquering, and settling the New World. By 1580 thousands of Spanish people were living in the New World. Gold and silver from the Americas were pouring into the Spanish treasury. Spain led the world in wealth and power.

However, in 1588 the Spanish sent an **armada** (är mä′ də), or group of armed ships, to raid England. The English were able to crush this Spanish fleet. With this defeat, Spain began to decline as a world power. Spanish growth in America slowed. The French, Dutch, and English would soon be starting permanent settlements in America.

CHECKUP

1. How was Portugal able to claim Brazil? Why did Portugal claim only Brazil?
2. What was the major accomplishment of each of the following Spanish explorers: Ponce de León, Balboa, Magellan, Cortes, Pizarro, De Soto, and Coronado?
3. At what point did Spanish growth in America decline?

French, Dutch, and English in America

VOCABULARY
Northwest
  Passage
missionary

Northwest Passage   France, England, and the Netherlands, or Holland, which was the country of the Dutch people, had long been looking for a way to get around or through North America by water. They still wanted a short route to Asia and the Indies. Many brave explorers tried and failed to find such a **Northwest Passage.** But because of their journeys they were able to give their home countries much valuable information about the New World. And as a result of their searches they were able to claim new lands for their countries.

Verrazano   French beginnings in the New World were small and slow. French fishing boats had been working off the coast of Canada since 1504. But no explorers came from France until Giovanni Verrazano (vär rə zä′ nō) sailed for the New World in 1524.

Verrazano had been hired by French merchants to find a Northwest Passage. He did not succeed in this. But he did explore the northeast coast of what is now the United States. Trace Verrazano's route on the map on page 78. He discovered New York Bay and entered the mouth of the Hudson River. He sailed up the coast as far as what is now Newfoundland in Canada before he returned to France.

One of the first maps of the North American coast was made from the rough drawings Verrazano had done during this voyage.

Cartier   In 1534 a fine French sailor named Jacques Cartier (kär tēā′) made the first of several voyages to the New World. He too was looking for a Northwest Passage. He was not able to find this water route through the continent. But he discovered the Gulf of St. Lawrence and the great St. Lawrence River in Canada. He sailed westward up this mighty river and claimed it for France. The land that is now called Canada became known as New France.

You can follow Cartier's route on the map on page 78.

Champlain   French fur companies began sending explorers and traders to Canada. The Native Americans were happy to trade furs for metal tools. The French got along well with the Indians. They did not try to conquer them as the Spanish had done in Mexico and Peru.

In 1603 one of the French fur companies sent Samuel de Champlain (sham plān′) to New France. For over 30 years Champlain explored the New World, trading for furs and searching for a Northwest Passage.

He explored the coast of what is now New England. He also explored northeastern Canada all the way to the Great Lakes area. Everywhere he went he drew maps and made pictures of the places he saw and the people he met. He also wrote long reports about them and sent much information back to France.

Cartier named the river for Saint Lawrence because he found it on the saint's feast day. He also named a mountain Mont Real. That mountain is the present day site of the city of Montreal. Cartier established excellent relations with the Iroquois Indians.

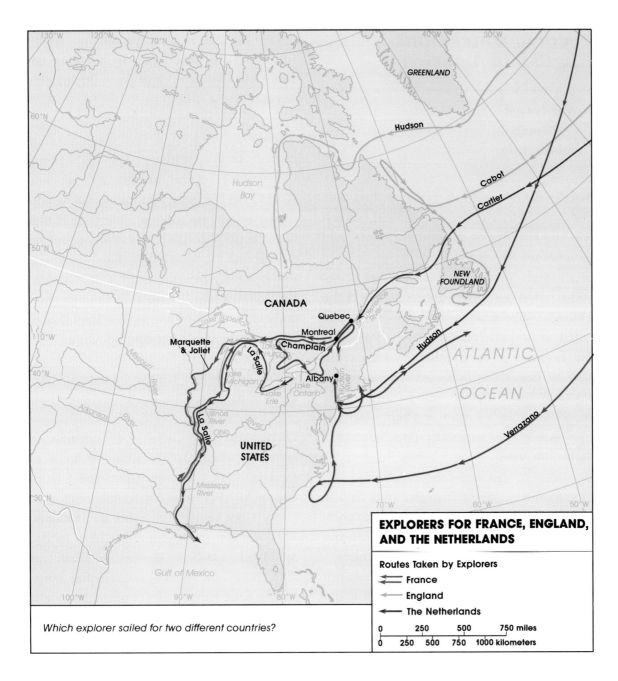

CANADA
Quebec
Montreal
Champlain
Marquette
& Joliet
Albany
La Salle
La Salle
UNITED
STATES
GREENLAND
Hudson
Cabot
Cartier
NEW
FOUNDLAND
Hudson
ATLANTIC
OCEAN
Verrazano

Hudson
Bay

Lake Superior
Lake Michigan
Lake Huron
Lake Erie
Lake Ontario
Missouri River
Arkansas River
Illinois River
Ohio River
Mississippi River
Gulf of Mexico
St. Lawrence River
Hudson River

Which explorer sailed for two different countries?

EXPLORERS FOR FRANCE, ENGLAND, AND THE NETHERLANDS

Routes Taken by Explorers
France
England
The Netherlands

0   250   500   750 miles
0   250   500   750   1000 kilometers

In 1608 Champlain founded the city of Quebec. Find Quebec on the map on this page. Quebec was the first lasting settlement in New France. It started as a small trading post on the St. Lawrence River. Now it is one of the leading cities in Canada. French is still spoken by the people who live in this lovely old city.

Marquette and Jolliet Many **missionaries** also came to the New World from France. A missionary is a person sent to teach religion and provide help for people who need it. One of the French missionaries was Father Jacques Marquette (mär ket'). He wanted to teach Christianity to the American Indians.

The Hudson River has played an important part in United States history and has become one of the most important United States trade waterways. The rivers' mouth flows into the ocean at New York City. The river is 306 miles (492 km) long.

Champlain discovered this lake, which was later named after him.
Lake Champlain is part of the border between Vermont and New York state.

It was from these Native Americans that Father Marquette first heard stories of a "great water" which led to an even greater water. Father Marquette thought that these waters must certainly be part of the Northwest Passage. And in 1673 he set off to find the passage. With him was a French fur trader named Louis Jolliet (zhō lēā′) and several others.

They paddled south along the shores of Lake Michigan and eventually found the broad Mississippi River. They saw that the river flowed north and south, not east and west. It could not be the Northwest Passage after all. However, Marquette and Jolliet followed the Mississippi River as far as the mouth of the Arkansas River before turning back.

You can follow the route of Marquette and Jolliet on the map on page 78.

La Salle In 1682 another Frenchman, Robert de La Salle, became the first European to travel the whole length of the Mississippi River to the Gulf of Mexico. He added greatly to French lands in the New World by claiming all the land along the river for France. La Salle named the whole Mississippi Valley "Louisiana" for King Louis XIV of France.

Henry Hudson Henry Hudson, an Englishman, made four trips to America looking for the Northwest Passage. He explored much of the eastern coast of North America while sailing for the Dutch in 1609. In his small ship, the *Half Moon,* Hudson was the first European to sail up the Hudson River. Find the Hudson River on the map on page 78. Follow the river northward to where the city of Albany now stands. This is the point Hudson reached before turning back.

Of course the Hudson River was not the great Northwest Passage. But Hudson was able to claim much of the beautiful land along the Hudson for the Dutch. It was good land with rich soil and many fur-bearing animals. The land that Henry Hudson claimed for the Dutch came to be known as New Netherland when a settlement was started there.

In 1611, Hudson, his son, and seven loyal sailors were set adrift in a small boat in James Bay by the rest of the crew who were anxious to return to England.

One of the first Dutch settlements in the New World was built on an island at the mouth of the Hudson River. The Dutch named this settlement New Amsterdam for a city in Holland. This small Dutch fur-trading settlement would eventually become New York City.

In 1610 Henry Hudson was hired by England to look for the Northwest Passage. This time he sailed farther north then he had done before. He discovered the huge Hudson Bay in Canada. Hudson and his crew spent the long, cold winter there. This bay is so large that it is little wonder Hudson thought it might be the Pacific Ocean. Hudson Bay did not, of course, prove to be part of the Northwest Passage to the East. But England was able to claim a large part of Canada because of Henry Hudson's voyage.

Cabot   Henry Hudson was not the first explorer to be sent to the New World by England. An Italian called John Cabot believed, as Columbus did, that he could reach the Indies and all the wealth of the East by sailing westward. In the spring of 1497 Cabot was sent by England to test this idea.

Cabot's voyage across the cold and stormy North Atlantic was a rough one in his small ship. But on June 24 he became the first known European to set foot on North America since Leif Ericson. The land he discovered was an island off the eastern coast of Canada.

He found no spices or jewels or gold. He had not reached the Indies any more than Columbus had. But his voyage gave England its first claim to much of North America.

While exploring for the Dutch in his ship, the Half Moon, *Henry Hudson sailed up the river later named for him.*
The Half Moon was about 75 ft (23 m) long. Hudson had a crew of only about 20 men including his son, John.

Drake   From the time of Cabot to the time of Sir Francis Drake, England did very little exploring in the New World. Drake was an explorer, a sea captain, and a great adventurer. His looting of Spanish treasure ships as they returned from America brought great wealth to England.

In December of 1577 England sent Drake on a voyage of exploration to the New World. On December 12 he left Plymouth, England, on a journey that was to take him around the world.

One of the things Drake wanted to do was to find the western outlet of the Northwest Passage into the Pacific Ocean. He sailed through the Strait of Magellan and up the Pacific coasts of both South America and North America. He claimed land along the northern coast of what is now California for England. Some histo-

Cabot grew up in Venice, Italy, and became a trader and mapmaker. After hearing about Columbus's voyage in 1492, he decided that he could find a shorter route to Asia by sailing farther north. Although he found no spices, jewels, or gold, he found the rich fishing area called the Grand Banks today.

rians believe that he claimed land for England as far north as the southern coast of Oregon.

Drake sailed back to England by traveling westward across the Pacific and Indian oceans, around the southern tip of Africa, and northward up the coast of Africa. He reached his home port of Plymouth in September of 1580. He was the first person from England to sail around the world. Turn to the map on pages 466–467 in the Atlas and trace Drake's route around the world.

Raleigh and Roanoke Just a few years after Drake's famous voyage, another Englishman, Sir Walter Raleigh, started a colony in the New World. Raleigh called the new land "Virginia." For many years this name was used to describe a huge piece of land. It stretched from our present-day state of Pennsylvania to what we now call North Carolina.

Raleigh's group settled on Roanoke Island off the coast of North Carolina in 1585. But the colony was a failure. The people found life too hard. Many of them became sick. The settlers returned to England within a year.

However, Raleigh decided to try again in 1587. This time his ships carried 117 men, women, and children. This new group also settled on Roanoke Island. Soon after they arrived a baby was born. She was named Virginia Dare. Virginia Dare was the first English baby born in the New World.

Because England was at war with Spain, Raleigh was not able to get supplies to Roanoke for 3 years. When the supply ships finally arrived, the colony had disappeared. The sailors found empty buildings, but not a single person remained. The sailors also found the word "Croatoan" carved into a tree. This was the name of a friendly group of American Indians who lived on an island about 100 miles (160 km) from Roanoke.

No one ever found out what happened to the English people of Roanoke. To this day that early settlement is known as the "Lost Colony of Roanoke."

The name of an Indian tribe carved on a tree was all that remained of the colony on Roanoke Island.

CHECKUP

1. What were most of the explorers from France, Holland, and England looking for in the New World?
2. Why was Canada once known as New France?
3. On what basis could the Dutch claim the area around what is now New York City?
4. Who was the first English person to sail around the world?

4/CHAPTER REVIEW

KEY FACTS

1. The Vikings were probably the first Europeans to discover America.

2. Christopher Columbus's discoveries made the rest of Europe aware of the new world.

3. Explorers from Spain, Portugal, France, England, and the Netherlands made claims for their countries in the New World. Usually claims were made on the basis of which country got explorers and settlers to an area first.

4. The Spanish had a huge empire in the southern part of the New World long before lasting French and English colonies were begun to the north.

VOCABULARY QUIZ

Match these terms with the definitions. Use a separate sheet of paper.

a. explore
b. Vikings
c. colony
d. isthmus
e. strait
f. Northwest Passage
g. Quebec
h. St. Augustine
i. armada
j. expedition

b **1.** First Europeans to reach America
h **2.** First Spanish settlement in North America
j **3.** A journey for a certain purpose
f **4.** Many explorers looked for this
a **5.** To search for new things or places
d **6.** Narrow strip of land connecting two larger pieces of land
g **7.** First French settlement in North America
e **8.** Narrow water passage connecting large bodies of water

9. Place far from the country that rules it. c

10. A group of armed ships i

REVIEW QUESTIONS

1. Why was Columbus's discovery of America so important?

2. Why did the Spanish have the greatest and earliest claims to the New World?

3. What are the differences between Spanish and French treatment of Native Americans?

4. What seem to be some of the difficulties in starting a settlement or a colony?

ACTIVITIES

1. Use an encyclopedia or some other library book to answer these questions.
(a) What did Ponce de León do in the New World besides discovering Florida?
(b) Why was Balboa in the New World?
(c) How did Estevanico get to the New World?
(d) Where is Father Marquette buried?
(e) Why was Sir Francis Drake in the area of the Roanoke colony in 1586?

2. Find out as much as you can about one of the early explorers or settlers mentioned in this chapter. Read a book or look him or her up in the encyclopedia. Present the person you studied to the class by pretending you are that person. Tell about your life. Answer questions about your life as though you are that person.

3. Make a chart of famous explorers. Tell what country each explored for and the areas he explored. Include the following explorers: Leif Ericson, Christopher Columbus, John Cabot, Hernando de Soto, Juan Ponce de León, Jacques Cartier, Robert de La Salle, and Francis Drake.

4/SKILLS DEVELOPMENT

USING THE LIBRARY

In reading this chapter you have learned about the people who explored North and South America. Perhaps you would like to know more about them. Or maybe you would like to know more about the kinds of ships on which they sailed. Do you know what instruments they used to sail such great distances on unknown seas? Do you know about other, more modern explorers? Who discovered the North Pole? The South Pole? Are people still exploring today?

The answers to these questions can be found in books on the shelves of your school or public library. There is a great deal of material available in the library. It is divided into several sections.

First there is the reference section. Here you will find encyclopedias, almanacs, atlases, dictionaries, and other books of general information. An encyclopedia is a good place to start if you do not know very much about a topic. It is a good place to go for background information.

You will also find the *Reader's Guide to Periodical Literature* in the reference section of most libraries. This guide tells you if any magazine articles have been written about the topic in which you are interested. Many libraries have magazines of general interest. For a report on exploration or exploring, magazines such as *National Geographic, Smithsonian,* and *Natural History* may help.

Admiral of the Ocean is a book about Chris-Christopher Columbus written by Samuel Eliot Morison. You can find out if your library has this book by looking in the card catalog. You could look under the author—Morison,

Samuel Eliot. Or you could look for the title—*Admiral of the Ocean Seas.* You can also look under the name of the subject—Columbus. Looking at a subject name is a good way to see how many books the library has on that topic. You should be able to find one of interest to you.

Many libraries also have collections of pictures, illustrations, and maps. These are kept in the vertical file. They are usually stored alphabetically by subject. The library may also have files of pamphlets and articles cut from newspapers. These, too, are usually arranged by subject.

Let's see how good you are at using the library. Pick one of the topics listed below. You may, if you wish, choose an explorer or a topic dealing with exploration that is not on the list. Go to the library. Using the books and articles you find there, do enough research to write a short essay on the topic of your choice. Be sure to list, at the end of your essay, the library resources you used.

Roald Amundsen
Robert E. Peary/Matthew A. Hensen
Richard E. Byrd
Henry Morton Stanley
Roy Chapman Andrews
John W. Powell
Robert Gray
Robert F. Scott
Edwin E. Aldrin
James Cook
Explorers' Club
Navigation Instruments
Ships
Northwest Passage

The First Colonies

VOCABULARY

London Company	burgess
journal	House of Burgesses
peninsula	pilgrim
indentured servant	Separatist
representative	Mayflower Compact

The London Company Other people shared Sir Walter Raleigh's dream of an English colony in Virginia. But they had learned from Raleigh's experience that starting a colony was too costly for one person. So a number of these people got together and formed the **London Company.** That way they could share the costs. Of course they also had to share any earnings. In 1607 Jamestown, Virginia, the first lasting English settlement in America, was founded by the London Company.

A settler's journal What was it like to be part of this new adventure? Suppose one of the first settlers had kept a **journal.** Parts of it might look like this:

20 December 1606 Great Excitement! Today 120 men sail from London in three ships, *Susan Constant, Godspeed,* and *Discovery.* We are to find gold and farm the land of Virginia.

Ask: How many months were the first settlers at sea? (Approximately 4½)

26 April 1607 After 18 weeks at sea, land at last! It will feel so good to step on firm ground again! Sixteen of our number died on the long voyage. . . .

14 May 1607 Today our leaders, Captain Christopher Newport and Captain John Smith, chose a small **peninsula** for the settlement. We named it Jamestown in honor of the king. With water on three sides, Jamestown will be easy to defend against enemies. But I worry that it is too low and swampy. There is no freshwater spring. It may not be healthful to live here.

Ask: Do you think this settler was right in being concerned about settling in a low and swampy area?

26 May 1607 Problems already! The "gentlemen" among us refuse to help with the work. They want only to search for gold. It's lucky everyone does not feel that way. We had just finished building our shelters when we were raided by Indians. I do not care to think what might have happened to us without the shelters.

Already we are running out of food and supplies. Captain Newport will sail to England soon to get more.

25 December 1607 I cannot remember a more unhappy Christmas! Only 53 of us are still alive. Disease and hunger are our worst enemies. If Captain Smith had not obtained food from Chief Powhatan, we might all be dead.

Ask: How many men had died from December 1606 to December 1607? (67)

A struggle to survive You can see from the journal that life at Jamestown was not easy. However, the colony struggled on. Shortly after New Year's Day in 1608, Captain Newport returned with supplies and more settlers, two of whom

The worker on top of the log was known as the sawyer; the one below him, the pitman. Here the logs are placed on a sawhorse. More often a saw pit was dug.

Logs were laid across the sawhorses and sawed into usable lengths. Skilled workers became important members of the Jamestown settlement. 37°12'N/76°46'W

Have pupils observe how the sawed lumber was used in building the frame for the second house from the left. The wall space between the timbers was filled with wattle and daub: a simple weave of saplings or reeds daubed with mud, or clay. Bundles of reeds and grasses were used to thatch the roof.

This full-scale reconstruction of the first Jamestown settlement is part of the Jamestown Festival Park in Virginia. Have pupils note the style of clothing.

were women. Captain Smith made a strict new rule: "No work, no food." Everyone had to work in the fields. For a while it seemed as though things were going well. But then Captain Smith was hurt and had to return home. Without his leadership, the settlers went back to their old ways.

By the fall of 1609, almost 500 people had come to Jamestown. But by June of 1610, the old enemies—sickness and hunger—had taken all but 60 of the settlers. These few survivors decided to leave Jamestown. Just as they set sail, they met a ship carrying supplies and 300 new settlers. The Jamestown group decided to join the new settlers.

Indentured servants   Many people wanted to come to the colony but they were too poor to pay the fare on the ship. So they came as **indentured servants.** Someone in the colony would agree to pay the fare of the poor person who in turn would agree to work without pay for a certain length of time—sometimes as long as 7 years. The master would have to give the servant food, clothing, and a place to live. When the time of service was up, the person was free. Both men and women came to the New World as indentured servants. This way of getting enough people to settle and work in the new land was used throughout the English colonies.

Tobacco   After several more years of hard work, the Jamestown settlement began to hold its own. In 1611 each settler was given land. In return a part of the crops was given to the London Company. Soon the colonists began growing tobacco, which proved to be very well suited to the area. In no time, ships loaded with tobacco to sell to England were sailing from Jamestown. Tobacco was used for money. It was even planted in the streets of the town. Some settlers became very wealthy, even though King James I at first tried to stop the tobacco trade. He said smoking was "hateful to the nose, harmful to the brain, dangerous to the lungs. . . ."

Ask: Is tobacco still an important crop in the United States today? Do you agree or disagree with King James I's opinion of tobacco? Why?

How many years were there between the settlement of the first English colony and the last?

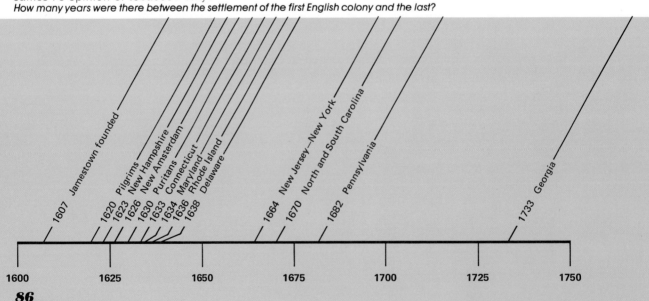

86

By 1700 there were about 60,000 inhabitants of the Virginia colony. Jamestown declined as a settlement because of the marshy lands. Williamsburg became the capital of the Virginia colony in 1699.

POPULATION OF JAMESTOWN, 1619–1624

Year	Number of people arriving	Total population
1619	—	1,000
1620	100 (est.)	866
1621	1,051	843
1624	4,000	1,277

Success at last   In 1619 the colonists were given the right to make their own laws. They voted for **representatives** called **burgesses.** They met as the **House of Burgesses.** Also in that year the first Africans were brought to Jamestown. They were put to work on the farms as indentured servants to pay their fare from Africa.

Let's look once more at the journal before we leave Jamestown:

> **25 December 1619** This is my thirteenth Christmas in Jamestown. When I think back over the years, I am sad. So many people have lost their lives here. We still have lots of sickness, and the natives are a constant threat.

Yet this has been my best year ever! My tobacco crop was excellent. I own my own farm and am thought to be quite rich. [Each settler was given 100 acres in 1616. All the crops grown on that land belonged to the settler.] And I got married! A shipload of women was brought to Jamestown by the London Company. They could choose a husband from the 1,000 men here. Each husband had to pay for his wife's passage. It is good to have a home at last!

As you can see from the journal, Jamestown was going well. Many good things had happened. The people had land and family life. They were free to choose their own representatives for their own government. The English had one successful colony in America. Another would soon be started.

Pupils living in the Virginia area may want to visit Williamsburg and Jamestown.

The Pilgrims   In 1620 another group of people came to America. These were the Pilgrims. A **pilgrim** is a person who travels for religious reasons. The story of the Pilgrims begins in England. There they were called **Separatists** because they

Patrick Henry delivered a speech against the Stamp Act in this building.

The House of Burgesses met here in the Capitol Building at Williamsburg.

had broken away from the English church. Because of this some of them were put in prison or watched closely. Others lost their jobs or had to leave their homes. Things got so bad in England that the Separatists decided to move to the Netherlands. Here, they heard, they could worship as they pleased.

The Separatists found religious freedom in the Netherlands. But they did not feel at home. They were country people in the city, strangers in a strange land. They did not like having their children grow up learning a different language and way of life. Many decided to move again, this time to Virginia.

The *Mayflower* In September 1620, about 100 people set sail for Virginia on a small ship called the *Mayflower*. Most of

the travelers were Separatists. Others came for different reasons. None of the Pilgrims knew what they would find when they got to this new land.

After about 2 months the Pilgrims finally saw land. They were off the coast of what is now Massachusetts, far to the north of Virginia. They fell to their knees and thanked God for their safe arrival. Only one person had died in crossing.

Since they were so far from Virginia, the Pilgrims realized that they would need to make their own laws. So before they left the *Mayflower,* they made a compact, or agreement, with each other. They agreed to make laws as needed for the colony's good. They agreed to obey these laws. The paper, signed by the men of the new colony, was called the **Mayflower Compact.**

Remind pupils that in addition to the passengers and crew the *Mayflower* carried tools, provisions for the voyage, and provisions including livestock for the settlement.

The Mayflower *was only 90 feet (27 m) long—there was very little room for passengers and crew.*

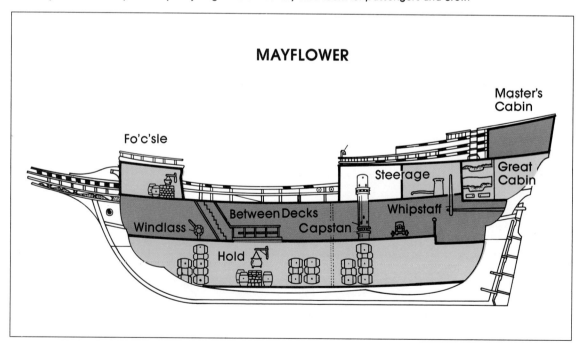

MAYFLOWER

The Pilgrim leaders lived in the great cabin. The ship's officers berthed in the steerage area. The crew was berthed in the fo'c'sle. The main group of Pilgrims lived, ate, and slept in the area between decks.

88

The first year   After a few weeks of exploring, the little group finally chose an area to make their home. Here were a good harbor, fresh water, and a cleared field. They first went ashore on December 16, 1620. They called the area where they settled Plimoth Plantation.

Soon they were building houses and settling in. It was winter, and their clothing was not warm enough. They were alone, and they feared wild animals and what they called "wild men." Yet they trusted God for their help. By the end of 2 or 3 months half of the group had died. Disease and the cold were too much for them. At times there were only six or seven people well enough to care for the rest.

Some pupils may enjoy reading a biography of Squanto.

Squanto   In the spring of 1621, a Native American named Samoset came to visit the Pilgrims. He made it possible for them to meet Squanto, who spoke English well. Squanto had been taken to England some years before. When he returned, he found his entire tribe was dead from disease. Samoset also brought together the Pilgrims and Massasoit (mas ə soit'), the chief of the Wampanoags (wom' pä nōgz). The Native Americans and the Pilgrims agreed not to hurt one another or steal from one another. They would live together in peace. They would help each other in case of attack.

Squanto stayed on with the Pilgrims. They felt he was a special help sent from God. He showed them where to fish. He taught them how to plant corn. Fish heads and tails were put in the ground with the corn seed. This helped the corn grow. He also acted as a guide.

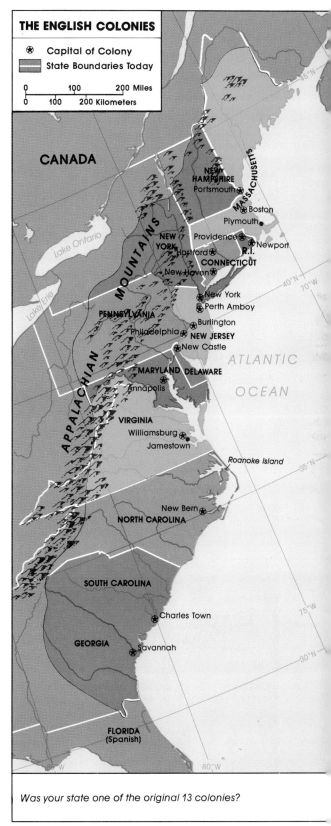

THE ENGLISH COLONIES

⊛ Capital of Colony

State Boundaries Today

Was your state one of the original 13 colonies?

The first Thanksgiving The crops were good that first year. The Pilgrims decided to give thanks to God. They asked their new friends, the Wampanoags, to come to a feast. The Indians brought turkey and deer meat. They celebrated together for three days in the fall of 1621.

After 1621 The Plymouth Colony lasted because the Pilgrims were willing to put up with hardships. No one returned to England after that first terrible year. They stayed and worked together. They farmed and traded. They had a new life. And they were free.

CHECKUP

1. What were the first two lasting English settlements in North America? When was each begun? Where was each located?
2. Who were each of the following people: Captain John Smith, the Pilgrims, and Squanto?
3. Why were the Mayflower Compact and the House of Burgesses important?

New England Colonies

Massachusetts Bay Colony Ten years after the Pilgrims started the Plymouth Colony, English **Puritans** started coming to America. Like the Pilgrims, the Puritans wanted to worship in their own way. But they didn't want to leave the Church of England. Instead they wanted to "purify" it, or change it. The Puritans in England were treated just as badly as the Pilgrims. That was one reason they left England for America. They also came because they felt they could make a better living for themselves in America. The colony the Puritans started was the Massachusetts Bay Colony. Its chief city was Boston. Massachusetts Bay became the

The first group of Puritans settled in Salem, Mass. Boston was established in 1630.
John Winthrop led a group of Puritan settlers ashore to start a new colony.

most powerful New England colony. The Plymouth Colony founded by the Pilgrims became part of Massachusetts Bay Colony in 1691. Maine was a part of Massachusetts until 1820 when it became a state.

New Hampshire and Connecticut People moved from the Massachusetts Bay Colony into New Hampshire and Connecticut. New Hampshire remained a part of Massachusetts until 1679. The broad river valleys of Connecticut with their rich soil were good for farming. There were fine harbors on the coast. Fishing and shipping soon became important ways to make a living.

Rhode Island The Puritans of Massachusetts Bay Colony felt that everyone had to believe as they did. People who held other beliefs were punished.

This puzzled and angered Roger Williams. Williams was a minister in the Massachusetts Bay Colony. He taught that all people had the right to their own religious beliefs. He wondered how a colony such as Massachusetts Bay could punish people for holding different beliefs. Had it not been founded by people seeking religious freedom?

The Puritans felt Roger Williams had to be punished for his new ideas. He would be sent back to England. But Williams did not want this. He escaped with several followers and lived with Native Americans for a time. In 1636 Williams started a town that would later become the capital of Rhode Island. He named the town Providence, because he believed that God had "provided" the place.

Anne Hutchinson defied the church leaders of the Massachusetts Bay Colony and was banished. Some pupils may enjoy reading a biography of Anne Hutchinson and sharing information about her life with the class.

Another of the first settlers of Rhode Island was Anne Hutchinson. She was sent out of the Massachusetts Bay Colony for her religious beliefs. Because of people like Anne Hutchinson and Roger Williams, Rhode Island became known as a place in which people could believe as they pleased without fear of punishment. Their ideas about freedom of religion are still basic in the United States.

New England towns The early colonists found that the rocky soil and hilly land of New England were not good for large farms. But most families could grow enough food for themselves and their animals. The settlers also found rapidly moving rivers and a coastline with many harbors. Fishing, shipping, and trading soon became more important ways to make a living than farming.

Ask: Can people in the United States today practice their religious beliefs without fear of punishment? Is that true of all countries in the world?

91

Towns quickly sprang up along the rivers and on the coast of New England. The largest of these was Boston, on Massachusetts Bay.

At the center of most New England towns was the green, or **common.** The common land was owned by all the people in the town. Here they could put their animals to graze. At the edge of the common stood the most important building in the town—the meeting house and the church.

The meeting house was used for the **town meeting.** Not everyone who lived in the town could take part in the town meeting. Only those men who owned property could discuss and vote on town business. Women and people who did not own land did not have a voice in running the town. The town meeting is, nevertheless, one of the earliest forms of **democracy** in America. Democracy means rule, or government, by the people.

Ask: How do your parents express their views in your town or city government?

Church was very important to the people of New England. No work could be done on Sunday. Worship services often lasted 3 hours or more. There were morning and evening services. The minister of the church was one of the most important people in the town.

Schooling and apprenticeship By law, every Puritan town of a certain size had to have a school. Let us follow a young boy of Boston and see what his education was like. This boy's name is Paul. His first school was a dame school, which met in the house of a townswoman. There were both boys and girls in the dame school. Here Paul was taught to read and write, to do a little arithmetic, and to mind his manners. If he did well, he was sometimes given a little cake. Children who did poorly had to wear the duncecap. Those who misbehaved were beaten.

Ask: What would the early settlers of Cohasset have called the open land in front of this meeting house? (The common)

This meeting house in Cohasset, Massachusetts, has been in use for over 200 years.

Often the same building was used for the church and the meeting house.

In 1647 the Massachusetts Bay Colony passed the first law in all the colonies that required public schools to educate children at the elementary level. In 1636 the first university of higher learning in all the colonies was founded in Massachusetts Bay Colony. It is a well-known college in the United States today.

Ask: Do you know what college it is? (Harvard)

When he was 8, Paul went to another school. Here he improved his reading and writing. He went on with his arithmetic. This school was usually for boys only. Girls, it was thought, did not need a good education.

At age 13 Paul became an **apprentice.** This means he became the pupil of a master craftworker in order to learn a trade. Many boys had to leave home to become apprentices. But Paul was lucky. He would learn how to be a silversmith from his own father. By the time he was 18 he was as good as his father.

As a teenager, Paul learned to ring the church bells. This way he could earn extra money. From high in the church tower Paul could look over Boston. He could see what a busy, crowded town it was. He could look over the harbor and see how important ships were to this port city. Almost everyone who lived in Boston was connected with shipping or fishing in some way.

Paul would have a great deal more to do in this city of Boston when he grew up. It would be helpful for him to know the city well. For Paul, the silverworker from old Boston, was also Paul Revere, patriot. He would play a big part in the colonies' struggle for independence. You will learn about this in the next chapter.

This is a famous portrait by Copley of Paul Revere, the silversmith.

CHECKUP

1. What was the difference between the Pilgrims and the Puritans? What colony did each group start?
2. Why was New England not really good for farming, but good for fishing, shipping, and trading?
3. How was the town meeting a form of democracy? In what way was it not democratic?
4. What did a child learn in a dame school?

The Southern Colonies

```
─VOCABULARY────────────────────────
naval stores        indigo
debt                Middle Passage
plantation          spiritual
```

Virginia   You have learned that the first of the 13 colonies to be settled was Virginia. It always had more people than any other southern colony. By 1760 it was the largest colony in America.

The other four southern colonies were Maryland, North and South Carolina, and Georgia. Can you find all five southern colonies on the map on page 89?

Proprietors of the southern colonies found that the best way to attract settlers was to offer free land often amounting to 100 acres (40 ha).

The Carolinas King Charles II gave eight of his friends land in North America. They called the colony Carolina in honor of the king. (Charles is Carol in Latin.) The northern part of the colony was settled by people moving south from Virginia. They lived on small farms and grew enough food to feed their families. There were forests of pine trees. Ship masts, pitch, tar, and turpentine can be made from pine trees. These goods, called **naval stores** because they were used by the navy, were sent to England. The climate in the southern part of the colony was better for growing crops such as rice and **indigo**, a plant from which a blue dye is made. There were many good harbors in this part of the colony. Charleston, founded in 1670, was the major port from which these crops were shipped. In 1729 the king bought the colony back from his friends and divided it into two colonies—North and South Carolina.

Georgia The last of the original 13 colonies was begun by James Oglethorpe. He felt sorry for English people who owed money and had been put in jail until they could pay their **debts.** As long as they were in jail, how could they earn money to pay the debts?

Oglethorpe went to King George II and asked to start a colony. Some of its settlers would be people from debtors' prisons. King George II feared that the Spanish in Florida would try to take over his North American colonies. He wanted a colony between South Carolina and Florida for protection. He allowed Oglethorpe to settle this region. It was named Georgia in the king's honor.

Lord Baltimore and his grandson are shown here with a map of the Maryland colony.

Ask: Why was the Chesapeake Bay important to the growth and prosperity of Maryland?

Maryland Cecilius Calvert, Lord Baltimore, was a friend of King Charles I. Calvert was a Catholic. It was hard for Catholics to practice their religion in England at that time. King Charles listened to his friend's plea for a colony in America. It was to be a haven for Catholics.

Many Catholics settled in Maryland. In a short time people other than Catholics also came to Maryland. A law had been passed that allowed freedom of religion to any Christian. Maryland soon became a prosperous colony. The settlers grew many crops. The most important was tobacco. Many of these crops were sent back to England to be sold.

In 1632 Lord Baltimore received a charter for 10 to 12 million acres (4 to 4.9 million ha) in the upper Chesapeake Bay area. He became ruler of the colony. His son Charles became governor of Maryland in 1660. Maryland was named in honor of King Charles I's queen.

Many southern plantations are historically preserved and can be visited by tourists. Some southern plantations are still working farms with paid workers.

Oglethorpe and 114 settlers started their colony at Savannah in 1733. Not too many debtors ever came. But those who did could thank James Oglethorpe for a fresh start.

Pupils may want to make a bulletin-board display or model of a southern plantation.

Life on a southern plantation The South was very different from New England. There were not as many large towns. There was a great deal of flat land with rich soil. Many people in the South became farmers.

Many of the southern farms were called **plantations.** These were large farms where often only one main crop was grown. The main crops at this time were tobacco, rice, and indigo. Most plantations were built along the banks of rivers. This made it easier to load the crops on the ships that would take them to England to be sold.

The center of the plantation was the big house set in the middle of green grass, flower beds, and vegetable gardens. There would be several smaller buildings around the big house. There was usually a kitchen building, for it was too hot to cook inside the main house. There were barns for the horses. There might also be a separate school building. The sons and daughters of plantation owners were educated at home. There was often a tutor for the boys. Girls were usually taught to read and write by their mother. Some girls, however, received just as good an education as the boys.

Set off at a distance from the big house were the slave quarters. These were small houses. They had dirt floors and few windows. There was very little furniture. Sometimes the houses had small vegetable gardens.

Even though the large plantations could be nearly self-supporting, plantation owners were often in debt to English merchants for items such as furniture and clothing for the family.

Nearly everything the people on a large plantation needed could be grown or made there.

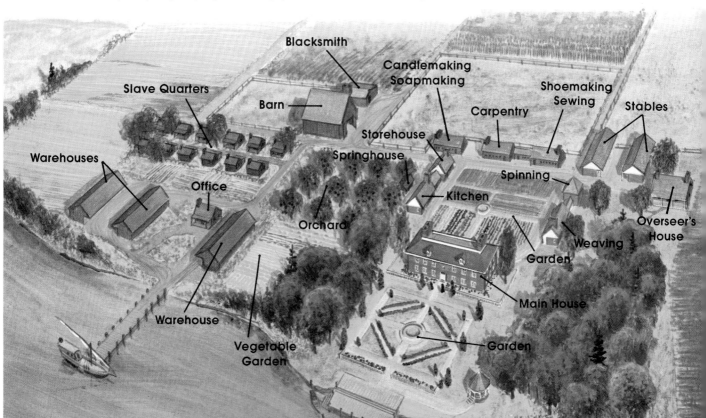

The "Middle Passage" was the second lap of the "triangular trade." Goods from England were traded in Africa for slaves. The slaves were traded in the West Indies and American colonies for agricultural products such as sugar, rice, and tobacco which were taken back to England.

Only the very wealthy lived on plantations. Most people in Virginia were small farmers. They had few slaves, if any. They raised most of their own food and traded very little.

Many other people lived in small towns or villages. Williamsburg was the capital of Virginia. This is where the House of Burgesses met.

Slavery in the colonies   By 1760 the English were the largest group of people to settle in the American colonies. The second largest group were Africans. The English came freely. After 1650 nearly all the Africans came as slaves.

Perhaps the cruelest part of the slave trade was the **Middle Passage.** This was what the trip from Africa to America on the slave ship was called. Slave ships were very overcrowded. Traders felt they could make more money by filling the ships. Slaves were squeezed in and chained together. Some were laid on rough boards. There was not room for exercise. The smell was terrible. The people were covered with filth.

Living like this caused much illness and death. Many slaves wished they could die. Often they tried to jump overboard. If caught they would be savagely whipped.

Most of these slaves were separated from their families. The ship and the way of life were new to them. There was a fear

COLONIAL POPULATION BY RACE
(selected colonies and years)

Colony	Black	White	Total
Virginia (1756)	120,156	173,316	293,472
North Carolina (1756)	19,000	60,000	79,000
South Carolina (1765)	90,000	40,000	130,000
Georgia (1766)	8,000	10,000	18,000
Maryland (1750)	40,000	100,000	140,000
New York (1771)	19,883	148,124	168,007
New Jersey (1745)	4,606	56,797	61,403
Massachusetts (1764)	5,235	218,950	224,185
Rhode Island (1749)	3,079	28,439	31,518
Connecticut (1756)	3,587	128,212	131,799

The mortality rate on a voyage could be as high as 20 percent. It is estimated that in the 1700s over 6 million Africans were shipped to North or South America.

The Middle Passage was a terrible experience for people to go through.

Slaves worked long, hard hours, especially those who worked in the fields.

in not knowing where they were being taken. The Middle Passage showed how cruel humans could be to each other. It was a taste of the life in slavery that was to come.

There were slaves in every one of the 13 colonies by 1760. Because plantations were so large and needed so many workers, there were far more slaves in the southern colonies than in the middle colonies or New England. Yet only one out of four southerners owned slaves.

Life as a slave The worst thing about slavery was the lack of freedom. Food, clothing, and shelter all came from the master. Slaves had no legal rights. They could not be taught to read and write in most colonies. They could not own property. They could not even marry legally.

Slavery was for the most part constant hard work. Most slaves worked in the fields. Slaves said they worked from "can-see" (dawn) until "can't-see" (dusk). After field work there were other chores, such as mending roads and fences. It was usually late in the day before they could eat their first hot meal of the day. This kind of hard work went on 6 days a week, every week of the year.

Other slaves worked as servants in the big house. They often had easier lives than the field slaves. But they, too, worked all day, 6 days a week. House servants

You may want to read to the class excerpts about slave life from *Roots* by Alex Haley.

97

had to cook, clean, weave, sew, mend, and nurse. Slaves were also skilled crafts-workers, such as carpenters, masons, blacksmiths, potters, and silversmiths.

Slaves usually ate the same plain food day after day. Pork and cornmeal were most common. Clothes were old and patched. Shoes were provided only in winter. You have already read a description of the slave quarters on a plantation. Sometimes these quarters were little more than shacks that did not keep out the rain and cold.

Some owners treated their slaves well. Kindness worked the best in keeping the loyalty of slaves. Unfortunately many owners used force and punishment. Beatings, whippings, torture, less food, and threats of being sold away from family members were all used to make slaves obey. Because there were so many slaves in the South, owners feared the slaves would harm them. Many slaves tried to run away. Some tried to fight back.

Most slaves were very religious. Their belief in a better life after death helped many live with hope. Their **spirituals**, or religious songs, are often sung today.

These slaves helped get the United States started. They helped build the country with their labor. But as we shall see, the treatment of blacks as slaves led to many problems.

CHECKUP

1. Name the five southern colonies. Which was the first to be settled? The last?
2. Which was the largest group of people to come to the colonies? Second largest?
3. Why did the South have so many more slaves than other parts of the country?

The Middle Colonies

VOCABULARY
Quaker

Why "middle" colonies?   Turn to the map on page 89. Find the colonies of New York, Pennsylvania, New Jersey, and Delaware. These are called the "middle colonies." Notice they are between the New England and southern colonies. Does this give you a clue as to how the middle colonies got their name?

The middle colonies were a mixture of New England and southern colonies. They were like New England in that people worked in shipping, lumbering, and fishing. They were like the southern colonies because there were also large farms.

Pennsylvania   William Penn received land in America as payment for a debt owed by the king to Penn's father. He called the new land *Pennsylvania,* which means "Penn's woods." He wanted to start a colony on this land where people of any religion would be free to worship as they pleased.

William Penn belonged to a religious group called **Quakers**. Because of their love for all people, Quakers called themselves simply "Friends." Quakers believed God had made all men and women equal. They refused to take part in war. During the 1600's they were being jailed and even killed in England. This was because their beliefs were different from those of the Church of England.

Beginning in 1682, Quakers and others quickly settled Penn's colony. In 2 years

39°57'N/75°7'W

Philadelphia has been a busy port since the eighteenth century.
Buildings labeled 1, 4, 5, and 7 are churches. Building 2 is the State House, building 6 is the Court House, and the windmill, labeled 14, is where the corn was milled. This view of Philadelphia is taken from the Jersey shore.

there were 8,000 colonists in Pennsylvania. The Native Americans and Penn made a treaty of friendship very quickly. He paid them for their land. Because of this, the two groups got along well.

Philadelphia, the largest city in Pennsylvania, was on its way to becoming the leading city in the colonies. It was already very busy. It was the chief port for newcomers to America. It was a center of trade for the many small farms that dotted the countryside of the middle colonies. Many groups of people with different jobs and different religions lived together peacefully here. Philadelphia had public libraries, a fire department, and the first hospital in America. The city had some well-lighted, paved streets, and police protection. There were three newspapers, a college, and discussion groups to talk about problems. Philadelphia became the most advanced city in America.

New York Henry Hudson claimed much of the New World for the Dutch in 1609. The area he claimed was named New Netherland. Early Dutch settlers traded furs with the Native Americans.

In 1625 the Dutch began settling New York City, which they called New Amsterdam. Peter Minuit, their leader, bought Manhattan Island, part of New York City, from the Native Americans for goods worth $24.00.

In 1664 the Netherlands and England were at war. The king of England decided to take over New Netherland. He gave his brother, the Duke of York, four warships to capture it.

The leader of New Netherland was Peter Stuyvesant. He was not well-liked by the Dutch settlers. When the English came with their warships, the Dutch would not fight under Stuyvesant. New Netherland was taken by the English without a shot being fired! It was renamed New York.

The Dutch had a lasting influence on New York. Brooklyn and Yonkers are Dutch names. Three presidents of the United States, Martin Van Buren and Theodore and Franklin Roosevelt, had Dutch ancestors in New York.

New Jersey   The Duke of York gave a large part of his huge colony to two friends, George Carteret and John Berkeley. Carteret had defended the island of Jersey in the English Channel during a war. So the area was called New Jersey. There were already some Dutch settlers here near the Hudson River. There were also some Swedish settlers near the mouth of the Delaware River. Find these rivers on the map on page 89.

Land in New Jersey was sold for low prices so that people would come there to live. There was also religious freedom. By 1702 there were so many new settlers in New Jersey that it was decided to separate it from New York. It became a colony with its own government.

Delaware   The first European settlement in Delaware was made by Swedes. They called the colony New Sweden. These early settlers made a very important contribution to life in the colonies. In Sweden, where they came from, people lived in houses made of logs rather than planks or boards. They built the same

Notice the fort, the windmill, and the gallows—all part of the colony of New Amsterdam. Why, do you think, was each important to the colony?   40°43′N/74°1′W

kinds of houses in New Sweden. Other settlers liked these easy-to-build houses and copied them.

In time New Sweden became part of the New Netherlands colony and then part of New York. The Pennsylvania colony wanted a way to reach the Atlantic Ocean. William Penn bought Delaware from the Duke of York. In 1704 it finally became a separate colony.

CHECKUP

1. What colonies were known as the middle colonies? Why?
2. Who started Pennsylvania? Why was there total religious freedom there?
3. Why was Philadelphia a leading city of the time?
4. What colonies started out as New Netherland and New Sweden?
5. With what colony are Carteret and Berkeley connected?

Use this table as a basis for a review of the information from Chapter 5. Pupils may want to ask each other questions based on the information given here.

THE ENGLISH COLONIES

Colony	Place and date of first settlement	Founders	Facts
Virginia	Jamestown, 1607	English	Founded to make profit for company and to improve settlers' fortunes.
Massachusetts	Plymouth, 1620	English	Established so that settlers could live according to their religious beliefs
New Hampshire	Dover, 1623	People from Massachu-setts	Settlers sought greater opportunity.
New York	Fort Orange (Albany), 1624	Dutch	Dutch set up trading posts. English seized colony, 1664.
Connecticut	Windsor, 1633	People from Massachu-setts	Settlers sought land and religious freedom.
Maryland	St. Mary's City, 1634	English	Founded by Cecilius Calvert, Lord Baltimore, as a refuge for Catholics.
Rhode Island	Providence, 1636	People from Massachu-setts	Founder Roger Williams sought religious freedom.
Delaware	Fort Christina (Wilmington), 1638	Swedes	Small Swedish towns, taken over by Pennsylvania after 1681.
New Jersey	Pavonia (Jersey City), about 1640	Dutch	Early Dutch settlements. Land granted to Englishmen John Berkeley and George Carteret, 1664.
Pennsylvania	Tinicum Island, 1643	Swedes, English	Early small Swedish colony. William Penn founded English colony as refuge for Quakers and others.
North Carolina	Albemarle County, about 1653	People from Virginia	Eight men given area later divided into North and South Carolina.
South Carolina	Charlestown, 1670	English	(See above.)
Georgia	Savannah, 1733	English	Founded by James Oglethorpe as refuge for debtors and others.

5/CHAPTER REVIEW

KEY FACTS

1. The first English colonies were started at Jamestown, Virginia, in 1607, and Plymouth, Massachusetts, in 1620.

2. Thirteen colonies in three areas, New England, the middle colonies, and the southern colonies, had been started by 1760. Each area had its own characteristics and way of life.

3. Geography played an important part in where the first settlements were located and in the types of jobs colonists in different parts of America would have.

4. Black Americans were forced to come to America as slaves almost from the beginning. A large part of the southern way of life depended on their labor.

VOCABULARY QUIZ

Match these terms with the definitions. Write your answers on a separate paper.

a. peninsula	**f.** democracy
b. burgesses	**g.** town meeting
c. pilgrim	**h.** apprentice
d. Mayflower Compact	**i.** plantation
e. Puritans	**j.** slavery

b **1.** Representatives who made laws in Virginia

f **2.** Rule by the people

e **3.** Settled Massachusetts Bay Colony

i **4.** Large farm

h **5.** Person learning a trade from a master craftworker

j **6.** Being treated as less than human

a **7.** Land with water on three sides

d **8.** Agreement made by Plymouth settlers to govern themselves

g **9.** Gathering to vote on matters of concern to all

c **10.** Person who travels for religious reasons

REVIEW QUESTIONS

1. In what ways were the people of Jamestown and the Pilgrims helped by the Native Americans?

2. Why is the Mayflower Compact important to United States history?

3. In what way did geography help New Englanders decide what jobs to do?

4. Why were the middle colonies called by that name?

5. Explain the statement, "The South was built on the backs of blacks."

ACTIVITIES

1. Make your own map and map key of the original 13 colonies. The map should give the name and location of each of the colonies. Identify the colonies by group—New England, Middle, Southern—in the key. Use the map on page 89 as a guide, but think of your own key.

2. Benjamin Franklin, who lived in Philadelphia, was one of the first of many people to work with electricity. It has become very important to all of us. Make a poster or scrapbook on one of the following themes: "Uses of Electricity," "Life Without Electricity," or "How I Can Save Electricity."

3. Write and act out a two-person play on one of the following ideas or one of your own.

(a) Captain John Smith explaining why the "No work, no food" rule was important

(b) Penn making a treaty with the Native Americans

(c) An apprentice looking for a master craftworker to learn from

(d) Slaves talking about their life on a southern plantation

INTERPRETING PROVERBS

Benjamin Franklin earned lasting fame as the publisher of *Poor Richard's Almanac*. This small book with a paper cover was put out yearly from 1733 to 1758. People in all the colonies read it. The almanac had information about holidays, weather, tides, quarters of the moon, jokes, and much more.

Perhaps *Poor Richard's Almanac* is best remembered for the many wise sayings or proverbs Franklin put in it. Some sayings were about good manners. Others were about the value of hard work or saving money. Most of the important parts of daily living were the subjects of these proverbs. Franklin's ideas were stated clearly and often in a funny way. They were easy to remember. People were always repeating them to each other. Here are some of these sayings.

Fish and visitors smell in three days.

God helps those that help themselves.

A small leak will sink a great ship.

A word to the wise is enough.

Early to bed and early to rise makes a man healthy, wealthy, and wise.

A penny saved is a penny earned.

When the well is dry, you know the worth of water.

He that goes a borrowing goes a sorrowing.

To be sure that you understand what Benjamin Franklin meant by each of these sayings, rewrite them in your own words. Now choose one of these wise sayings and write a story from your own life that helps to show that the saying is true.

What do the proverbs around the border of the painting mean?

2/UNIT REVIEW

1. Native Americans arrived in the Americas long before any other settlers. — *What is one theory about the way they came?*

2. There were many different Native American cultures throughout North and South America. — *Can you name a Native American group that used to live or still lives in your area?*

3. Native Americans made many contributions to the way of life in the United States. — *What foods have you eaten recently that were developed by Native Americans? What Native American words have become part of the English language?*

4. Explorers had to be very brave. — *Compare an early explorer such as Columbus with modern explorers such as the astronauts.*

5. Many European countries sent explorers to the New World. — *On an outline map of North and South America, show the claims made by various explorers.*

6. Each group of settlers that came here helped the country to grow and develop the way it is today. — *Cut out pictures of many different Americans. Use old newspapers and magazines. Paste your pictures on a large piece of cardboard or around an empty cereal box. Cover the whole surface. Title your montage "Americans All."* **For extra credit**

7. Early settlers came for many different reasons: desire for riches, religious freedom, a chance to make a new life, or because they were forced to. — *Name at least one group of settlers that fits each reason.*

8. Thirteen English colonies were located along the Atlantic coast. They have been divided into New England, Southern, and Middle colonies. — *Name which colonies were New England colonies, Southern colonies, and Middle colonies. Tell who settled each colony.*

A New and Growing Nation

Revolutionary War soldier

George Washington

Davy Crockett

Pioneer

CHAPTER

6 Birth of a Nation

Bad Feelings Grow Between Britain and the Colonies

┌─VOCABULARY─────────────────┐
│ independence   Boston Tea   │
│ revolution   Party   │
│ Parliament   Continental   │
│ massacre   Congress   │
│ Committees of   │
│   Correspondence   │
└──────────────────────────────┘

The French and Indian War   In 1763 Britain and the colonies ended a 7-year war with the French and Indians. As a result of this war France was driven out of North America. Britain would now rule Canada and other lands that had belonged to France. This brought peace to the American colonies. The colonists no longer had to fear attacks from Canada. The Americans were happy to be a part of Britain in 1763. Yet a dozen years later, these same people would be fighting the British for **independence**, or freedom from Great Britain's rule. This war was called the War for Independence, or the American **Revolution.** A revolution changes one type of government or way of thinking and replaces it with another. In this chapter, you will learn about the American Revolution and the changes it brought about.

"No taxation without representation!" The British lawmaking body was and still is called **Parliament**. The colonists were not members. The British Parliament started passing laws to tax the colonies. Britain thought the colonists should pay their share of the cost of the French and Indian War. The taxes would also help pay for keeping British soldiers in America. The soldiers would serve along the borders of the colonies to protect the settlers from Indian attacks. It seemed fair to the British that the colonists share these costs too. They put taxes on legal papers and everyday items such as glass, paint, and tea.

The colonists got very upset about these taxes. Their own colonial assemblies had not voted for them. They did not welcome Parliament's tax laws. Their motto became, "No taxation without representation." People would not buy anything British. Colonial assemblies would not collect the taxes. Perhaps the most excitement was caused by groups called the Sons of Liberty. They destroyed tax collectors' homes and drove some tax people out of town.

Trouble in Boston   British soldiers in America became special targets of the colonists' anger. They were constant reminders of British control.

Drummers and fifers had an important role on the battlefield. They gave signals for troop movements.

This famous painting is called "The Spirit of '76." Can you tell why?
Archibald M. Willard completed this painting for the Centennial Exposition of 1876. The three persons in the painting bear likenesses to people Willard knew.

106

In March 1770, a crowd gathered near some British soldiers in Boston. The crowd waved sticks, threw snowballs and stones, and yelled at them.

After some time the soldiers feared for their safety and fired into the crowd. Five people died. Among them was Crispus Attucks, a freedom-loving runaway slave. Colonial leaders called this sad event a **massacre.** A massacre is a killing of many people who cannot defend themselves very well.

Committees of Correspondence Things quieted down for a few years. In 1770 most of the hated taxes were ended. Parliament and the king felt that collecting the taxes was too much trouble. But what had happened in Boston was only a sample of what was to come.

In order to keep contact between colonies, leaders started groups called **Committees of Correspondence.** They kept in touch by writing letters. In these days before telephone, radio, and television, this was the best way to get news from one colony to another. Many leaders, such as Samuel Adams, Thomas Jefferson, and Patrick Henry, were members of these committees.

Boston Tea Party George III, the king of England, said that there had to be a tax on something to prove that the British had the right to tax. So there was still a small tax on tea. The colonists remained firm. They would not pay any tax passed by Parliament. Colonial women refused to buy or serve tea.

British merchants were not selling much tea. So Parliament passed a law that greatly lowered its price. Boat loads of tea were sent to America. Since it was cheaper than ever, the British thought that surely the colonists would buy tea now!

They were wrong. Tea was burned. Tea was left to rot. Ships loaded with it were not allowed in ports. In Boston the Sons of Liberty dressed up as Indians. Late at

In what year did the Constitution become the law of the land?

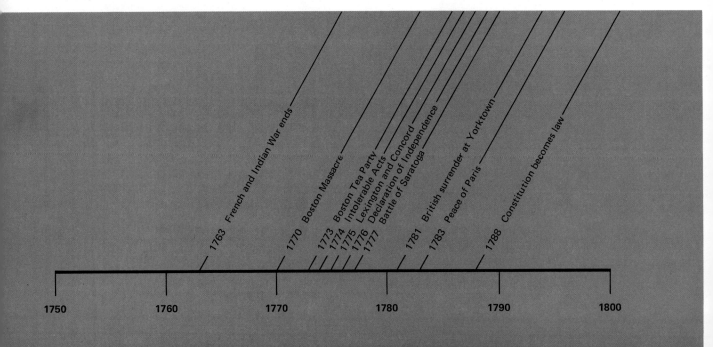

The Boston Tea Party took place the night of December 16, 1773.   42°20'N/71°05'W
Paul Revere was one of
the Sons of Liberty.

night they went to Boston Harbor and threw over 300 chests of tea into the water. This action was called the **Boston Tea Party.**

The Intolerable Acts

The British were very angry! Within a few months, they passed what the colonists called the Intolerable Acts. Intolerable means unbearable. These acts were meant to punish the people of Boston. The port of Boston was closed. No self-government was allowed in Massachusetts. British troops had to be housed and fed by the Massachusetts colonists.

The Committees of Correspondence acted quickly—letters were sent telling what was happening in Boston. Other colonies sent help and supplies. People wondered if their colony would be the next to feel the anger of Great Britain. The colonies agreed to meet together in late summer of 1774.

First Continental Congress

The first meeting of the group of representatives from the colonies was called the **Continental Congress.** It was held in Philadelphia on September 5, 1774. Efforts were made to keep peace with Great Britain. Parliament was asked to agree that the colonists had the same rights as citizens who lived in England. The colonists decided to meet again the next spring.

But events were almost out of control already. King George III was too stubborn to give in. He said that the king and Parliament would rule the colonies! Before the Congress met again, the first shots of the American Revolution had been fired.

CHECKUP

1. What were the results of the French and Indian War?
2. How did Britain try to get the colonies to pay for keeping soldiers in America?
3. What did the colonists mean by the slogan "No taxation without representation"?

The Move To Independence

┌─ VOCABULARY ──────────────────┐

Minuteman **Declaration of**
preamble **Independence**

└───────────────────────────────┘

"The British are coming!" It was early morning, April 19, 1775. Captain John Parker was getting tired. He was waiting with a group of **Minutemen.** These were farmers and other citizens who were ready to fight "with a minute's warning." They had been up since midnight.

Paul Revere had galloped through Lexington warning everyone that the British soldiers were on their way from Boston. The British wanted to capture colonial leaders John Hancock and Samuel Adams, who were in Lexington. They also wanted to get the military supplies that were stored in Concord.

Now it was nearly dawn. Parker paced the floor of the tavern in which he was waiting. Many men had gone home. Would the British come? What would he do if they did come?

Suddenly a rider broke the morning silence. "The British are coming! They are nearly here!" The men sprang to action. There was shouting and beating of drums. About 70 citizens of Lexington followed Captain Parker to the grassy area in the center of town called the green. The British marched up. They found themselves facing a group of proud colonists who refused to go home when told to do so.

Parker said, "Don't fire unless fired upon, but if they mean to have a war, let it begin here." A shot was fired, but whether by a British soldier or a Minuteman, no one knows. Other shots fol-

Ask: How can you tell from the painting that Paul Revere alerted people to the coming of the British?

The midnight ride of Paul Revere is a popular story in American history.
Grant Wood painted "Midnight Ride of Paul Revere" in 1931.

lowed. Eight colonists were killed and ten wounded. Only one British soldier was wounded. The war for independence had begun.

". . . the shot heard round the world"   The British went on to Concord. They destroyed military supplies and fought with another group of minutemen at Concord Bridge. Adams and Hancock were not captured. The British then started back to Boston. It seemed that Minutemen were behind every tree and rock on the way. The Minutemen fired at the British as they marched past. Almost one third of the British soldiers were killed or wounded on the return trip to Boston. Find Lexington and Concord on the map on page 115.

Second Continental Congress   The representatives from the colonies met again on May 10, 1775. Perhaps at no time in our history has a finer group ever met together. Samuel Adams, John Adams, John Hancock, John Jay, Patrick Henry, Thomas Jefferson, George Washington, and Benjamin Franklin were only a few of the outstanding people who gathered in Philadelphia. They would lead the country through the war.

The Continental Congress soon got news of armed fights. Ethan Allen and the Green Mountain Boys captured Fort Ticonderoga in New York (see map on page 115). In June of 1775 the Battle of Bunker Hill was fought in Boston (see map on page 115). The British won the hill, but lost over a thousand men. Peter Salem, a freed slave, was given credit for killing the British leader. The Americans

New Yorkers pull down the statue of George III on the Bowling Green after they get the news of the signing of Declaration of Independence. There is a park there today.

learned that they could fight the British successfully. But the colonies were still not ready to declare independence.

George Washington   The Second Continental Congress picked Washington as commander in chief of the Continental Army. George Washington was a tall, quiet man. He was well known for being wise and kind. Washington was raised on a large Virginia plantation. As a 16-year-old boy he explored lands in western Virginia. Later he gained experience as a soldier and became well-known in the French and Indian War.

After that war Washington married and settled down to a life as a farmer and land owner. He became one of the richest men in the colonies. He was a member of the Virginia House of Burgesses for 15 years. He was elected to both the First and Second Continental Congresses. Washington did not want war. But he saw no other way. He would prove to be an outstanding leader.

John Adams (left), Thomas Jefferson (center), Benjamin Franklin (right), Roger Sherman (left rear), and Robert Livingston (right rear) present the Declaration to the Congress.

Independence comes at last   Loyalty to England and the king was still very strong in the colonies as late as 1775. Many people still thought of themselves as subjects of the king. War was a very serious matter. But the Continental Army had been formed and battles were being fought. England was doing nothing to try to keep the peace. A booklet called *Common Sense* was getting more people to favor independence. The author was Thomas Paine, an Englishman who came to live in Philadelphia in 1774. In *Common Sense* Paine gave good reasons why the colonists should be free from "the royal brute of England."

Finally, in June of 1776, a committee was chosen to write a declaration of independence. Thomas Jefferson wrote the draft of the declaration based on the committee's suggestions. On July 4, 1776, after two days of discussion, Congress passed the **Declaration of Independence**. Church bells rang all over Philadelphia to make independence known.

John Hancock, the president of the Continental Congress, was the first to sign. According to legend he wrote his name in large letters, "so the king of England could read it without his glasses." When Hancock mentioned the need for complete agreement on the

112

Declaration, Ben Franklin commented, "We must all hang together or we shall all hang separately." This remark showed the great risk each of the signers was taking.

The Declaration of Independence gave reasons for fighting the American Revolution. It has served as a guide to freedom-loving people throughout the world.

The Declaration of Independence

There are four parts to the Declaration of Independence. They are the **Preamble**, or introduction; a Statement of Rights, telling what rights all people should have; a list of wrongs done by King George III, and, finally, a Statement of Independence. The following summary gives some of the ideas that Thomas Jefferson put into the Declaration.

IN CONGRESS, JULY 4, 1776 All 13 of the United States of America agree on this Declaration—

The Preamble   Sometimes in history people have to free themselves from control by other people. They have to make their place with the nations of the world, in keeping with the laws of nature and the laws of God. When people do this, it is only right that they give their reasons.

A Statement of Rights   Jefferson said we believe these truths: People are created equal. God gives people certain rights that cannot be taken away. Among these are the right to life, the right to liberty, and the right to try to be happy.

Government should help people keep these rights. Governments get their power from the people they govern.

When government does not protect people's rights, the people must change the government or get rid of it. They then must start a new government based on these rights. It is only wise that a change in government not be made lightly. It is such a serious matter that most people throughout history would rather suffer than change governments. However, when people's rights are taken away over and over again, it is their right and duty to get rid of the old government and start a new one.

List of George III's Wrongs   Jefferson believed that this is what happened in the colonies. Therefore the people have to start a new government. The king of Great Britain has a history of trying to take away freedoms. These facts are presented to the world.

A Statement of Independence   In spite of all these things, we have tried to get along. We have not been helped. George III has proved he cannot rule a free people. The British people have been no better. We have warned them, reminded them, and asked them to consider our freedom. They have turned a deaf ear to us.

Therefore, we in Congress, representatives of the good people of these colonies, with God as our Judge, declare the following:

That these colonies are now free states and they have the right to be free states.

That these states have no connection at all with Great Britain.

That because they are free states, they have the right to make war and peace, make friends, trade, and do everything free states can do.

In support of this Declaration, with God's protection, we pledge to each other our lives, our wealth, and our honor.

CHECKUP

1. Why are the events at Lexington and Concord important?
2. Who took a midnight ride? Captured Fort Ticonderoga? Was made commander in chief of the Continental Army? Was a hero at Bunker Hill? Wrote *Common Sense?* Wrote the Declaration of Independence?
3. On what date was the Declaration of Independence passed by the Continental Congress?
4. What are the four major parts of the Declaration of Independence? What is each section about?

The original Declaration of Independence is displayed along with the Constitution in the National Archives Building in Washington, D.C. See picture on page 123.

WAR!

Outlook bad   Most of Washington's army thought they could go home after independence was declared. John Adams knew better. He said, "We shall have a long and bloody war to go through." The war would go on for 5 hard years. The peace treaty was not signed for another 2 years.

The new United States of America faced a tough challenge in 1776. Britain had the best navy in the world. The United States had no navy. Britain had a well-trained army and also hired soldiers from other countries. In the beginning most of the United States army was made up of state **militia**, such as the Minutemen of Massachusetts. These men agreed to serve in the army for a period of time. When that time was up, they went home. As the war went on, a small, full-time regular army was built up. British soldiers were well supplied. George Washington had to beg Congress for proper food, clothing, and weapons for his troops.

The United States had a population of less than 3 million people. Of that number perhaps 500,000 were **Loyalists**, who still supported England and George III. Many fought in the king's army. Also,

The winter at Valley Forge is often called the "Winter of Despair." See material on p. 125.

The winter of 1777–1778 spent at Valley Forge was one of the most difficult of the war.   40°06′N/75°27′W

"Washington Reviewing His Troops" (1883), a painting by William Trego, hangs in the museum of the Valley Forge Historical Society, Valley Forge, Pa.

The Valley Forge National Historical Park preserves the historical landmarks and monuments associated with Washington's winter at Valley Forge.

114

about one third of the Americans took no side. They really did not care who won. The remaining **Patriots**, however, gave their best for the cause of liberty.

War in the Northeast In late 1776 General George Washington had to take a chance. His army was in poor shape. Many soldiers had been killed, captured, or had simply left for home. British soldiers had taken New York City. If British General Howe had pushed a bit harder in New York, Washington could have lost his entire army.

On Christmas night, 1776, Washington sent soldiers across the ice-blocked Delaware River. They were to attack the **Hessians** who were celebrating Christmas in Trenton, New Jersey. Hessians were German soldiers hired to fight for the British. The plan worked! The Hessians were totally surprised. Almost 1,000 prisoners were taken.

In 1777 much fighting took place in Pennsylvania. When the British captured Philadelphia, the Continental Congress had to leave the city. But the turning point of the war was the battle of Saratoga in New York. The British under General "Gentleman Johnny" Burgoyne were badly defeated. About 5,000 British soldiers surrendered. One of the American heroes was General Benedict Arnold.

This great American victory brought France into the war. The French had not forgotten the loss of the North American colonies to the British in 1763. But France wanted some sign that the colonists could win against the British. The battle of Saratoga showed the French that the colonists had a good chance of winning their

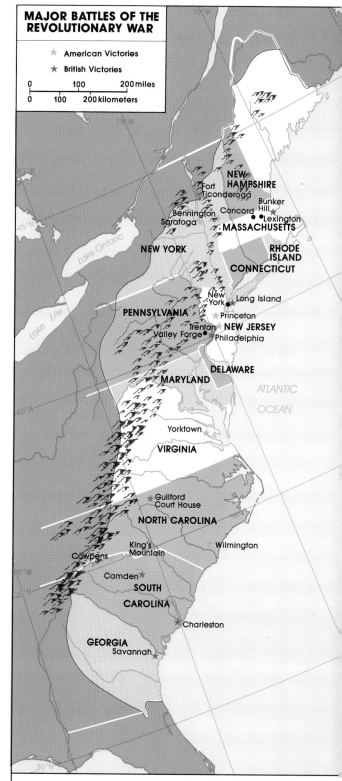

MAJOR BATTLES OF THE REVOLUTIONARY WAR

☆ American Victories
★ British Victories

Were most of the American victories shown on this map in the north or in the south?

independence. This was especially true if the Patriots could get help from European powers. Later Spain and Holland also joined the Patriots against the British. Find the sites of these battles on the map on page 115.

War at sea   The United States did very well at sea fighting the world's most powerful navy. One reason was because of the **privateers.** These were small privately owned ships. They were armed with cannons. The owners were given permission by Congress to attack the British in the name of the United States government. By the end of the war the 2,000 privateers had sunk or captured 600 enemy ships. The Continental Congress also started a national navy. It, together with the navies of 11 states, numbered no more than 100 ships. Yet they managed to destroy or capture twice that many British ships.

37°14′N/76°32′W

This Currier and Ives print honors the British surrender at Yorktown. It was made many years after the event.

The greatest American naval officer was John Paul Jones. He was daring. He attacked ships off the British coast. In a famous battle, Jones's ship, the *Bonhomme Richard* fought the British ship *Serapis*. At one point in the battle Jones's ship was sinking. When asked to give up, Jones answered, "I have not yet begun to fight!" He went on to win.

John Paul Jones can be considered the founder of the American Navy.

Battles in the South   After the battle of Saratoga, the major land battles were fought in the South. For a time the British were very successful. They controlled most of Georgia. Americans suffered their greatest defeat of the war at Charleston, South Carolina.

But Americans would not give up. People like Francis Marion, "the Swamp Fox," made constant daring raids on the British. Washington put General Nathanael Greene in charge of the army in the South. The Americans began to win some battles.

The British general, Lord Cornwallis, tried hard to capture Greene's army. He was unable to do so and marched his army north to Yorktown, Virginia. See the map on page 115. Notice that Yorktown is on a peninsula. Can you see how Cornwallis and his army could be trapped there?

Washington raced his army south from New York. He used the French army and navy to complete the trap of the British. The British could not win against such a combination of fighting forces. There was nowhere they could retreat to. Cornwallis had to surrender at Yorktown on October 19, 1781. This was the last big battle of the war. With Cornwallis's surrender, the British were ready to make peace.

Why the Americans won   The Americans won the war in spite of great odds against them. But some things favored the Patriots. They were fighting for their homes and families. They knew the land they were fighting for. Their sources of supplies and new soldiers were nearby.

Perhaps the greatest strength of the United States was its people. While not everyone was for the war, those who favored it were willing to die for what they believed. The people's courage and belief in freedom started our country.

The leadership of the United States was outstanding. George Washington was a wise and respected general. His skill held things together when all seemed lost. And he was helped by a number of other able leaders—Samuel Adams, John Adams, Benjamin Franklin, Robert Morris, John Hancock. The list of names could be a long one.

Many great leaders came from foreign countries. They believed in the ideas for which the Americans were fighting. Marquis de Lafayette came from France. He became one of Washington's most trusted aides. Thaddeus Kosciusko from Poland helped build important defenses such as the fort at West Point. Another Pole, Casimir Pulaski, bravely fought in the South. He was killed leading the charge at Savannah, Georgia. Baron de Kalb, a German, served well and died of wounds he got in battle. In the hard winter at Valley Forge, Baron von Steuben of Prussia taught the soldiers how to drill. These soldiers proved to be the equal of the British.

Toward the end of the war a young British officer wrote that even if all the American men were defeated, the British would still have to beat the women. His remark was correct. Women played an important part in the American victory. Some women ran farms and businesses while the men in their families went off to fight in the war. Others marched with their husbands. They worked in army camps. They served as nurses. They made clothing and gunpowder.

Some women fought. Molly McCauley of New Jersey was one. She carried pitchers of water to her husband and others during a battle on a very hot day. Because of this soldiers called her Molly Pitcher. When her husband was wounded, she took his place and helped fire his cannon.

Deborah Sampson Gannett took a male name and joined the army. She fought for 18 months and was wounded. After the war Paul Revere helped her receive money for her service to the country.

Molly Pitcher earned her reputation as a hero of the Revolution at the Battle of Monmouth. This battle took place in June 1778.   40°22′N/74°33′W

Women served as spies. Deborah Champion carried important information to George Washington. She rode for two days on horseback. General Howe chose Lydia Darragh's Philadelphia home for a headquarters. She secretly listened to his staff meetings. She then sent her son to Washington's camp with important news about the British plans. This information once saved the American army from a surprise attack.

Signing a treaty   Americans played many different roles in the struggle for freedom. Benjamin Franklin spent the war in France. His efforts gained vital French help. He was in Paris to sign the peace treaty in 1783. Joining Franklin were John Adams, John Jay, and Henry Laurens.

The treaty said three things:

The United States was an independent nation bounded by the Mississippi River, the Great Lakes and Canada, and Florida.

The United States would have fishing rights off Canada's coast.

All war debts had to be paid by both sides.

The new states had met their goal. They were free and independent. But they were not yet united.

CHECKUP

1. Name at least three things that were against the Americans at the beginning of the Revolutionary War.
2. Why was the battle of Saratoga so important?
3. When, where, and how did the Revolutionary War end?
4. Give at least three reasons why Americans were able to win the war.

118

The Constitution of the United States

┌─ VOCABULARY ─────────────────┐

Articles of Confederation	legislative branch
Constitution	executive branch
republic	judicial branch
federal	amendment
separation of powers	Bill of Rights
	census
	ratify

└──────────────────────────────┘

Articles of Confederation   With independence came many problems. The United States were joined together under one government by the **Articles of Confederation.** The articles listed the powers of the central government and the powers of the states. There was a national Congress made up of representatives from each state. But Congress had almost no power at all. The 13 states acted like 13 separate little nations. There were many times when states would not cooperate with the central government. They were too busy quarreling with each other. The United States was in danger of failing.

A Constitutional Convention   In May 1787, a meeting began in Philadelphia to change the Articles of Confederation. Representatives from all the states except Rhode Island were present. It was soon decided that a whole new **constitution** had to be written. A constitution is a set of laws by which a country is governed.

This meeting became known as the Constitutional Convention. George Washington was chosen president of the convention. Adding his wisdom was 81-year-old Benjamin Franklin. A new group of first-rate leaders were at this meeting. Among these leaders were James Madison and Gouverneur Morris. Madison made a careful written record of the meetings. Morris headed a committee that drew up the Constitution. He put the final touches on it. The people who attended the convention did their job very well. The Constitution has lasted to the present.

A new plan of government   What kind of government would be best for the United States? The delegates all agreed that the new government should continue to be a **republic.** This means that the people would elect representatives to manage their country.

Other things were not so easy to decide. The delegates knew they wanted a **federal** government. In such a government the power is divided between the national and the state governments. But how much power should go to the states? And how much to the national government?

They solved this problem by writing just which powers the national government would have. It would collect taxes and borrow money. It would control trade with foreign countries and between states. The national government would print or coin money. It alone could declare war. All other powers were left to the states. Matters within a state would be settled by that state.

Separation of powers   The Constitutional Convention wanted a government that would protect the people's rights, not take them away. So they divided the government's power into three parts or branches. This is called **separation of powers**.

The **legislative branch** was the Congress. Its major job was to make laws. The **executive branch** was the president and his helpers. It was their job to carry out the laws the Congress passed. The **judicial branch** was the courts. They had to decide the meaning of laws.

This is a model for a part of a frieze at the State Capitol of Nebraska entitled "Drafting the Constitution." Seated left to right are Benjamin Franklin, George Washington, and Alexander Hamilton.

The people who came together at the Constitutional Convention knew they had an important job to do. Can you find Benjamin Franklin in this picture?

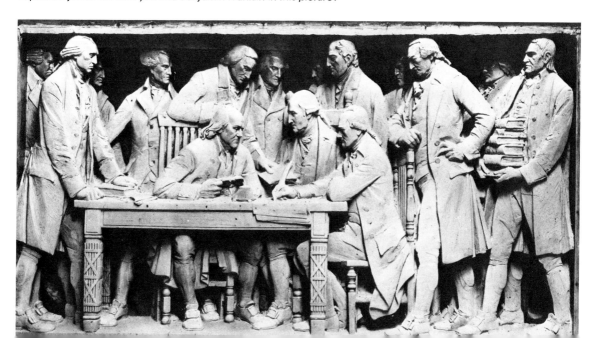

The four freedoms are freedom of speech, freedom of worship, freedom from want, and freedom from fear.

Each branch had some power over the other two. No one branch would be allowed more power than the others.

Congress A big debate at the convention was over the matter of who would control Congress. Large states wanted representatives to Congress based on the number of people in the state. Small states wanted an equal vote with the larger states. This problem was solved by giving Congress two parts. Regardless of size each state would send two representatives to the Senate, one part of Congress. States with more people would send more delegates to the House of Representatives, the other part of Congress. In order for a law to be passed, it had to go through both parts of Congress.

Changing the Constitution The new Constitution included a way to make changes, called **amendments.** If things did not work out, or if the United States grew or changed, the Constitution could be amended without being entirely changed. This was to prove helpful very soon.

Bill of Rights Nine state governments had to approve the Constitution before it could become the law of the land. Many states refused to do so unless the Constitution listed people's rights as well as the rights of the government. They argued that important freedoms must be written down. Once the states were promised that this would happen, the Constitution would become law.

James Madison saw to it that these freedoms were written down. Madison

This man is using his right to speak freely.

Printed by permission of the Estate of Norman Rockwell and its agent, Raines & Raines, New York.
Reprinted from *The Saturday Evening Post.*
© 1943 The Curtis Publishing Company.

had been very active at the Constitutional Convention. After the convention he worked hard to explain the Constitution to the people. Once the new government was started, Madison wrote many amendments that would make rights like freedom of the press, speech, and worship part of the Constitution. Ten of these amendments were passed by the states. These first ten amendments to the Constitution are known as the **Bill of Rights.**

CHECKUP

1. Why was the United States government in danger of failing when the Articles of Confederation were the law of the land?
2. What were the roles of George Washington, James Madison, and Gouverneur Morris at the Constitutional Convention?
3. What powers did the new Constitution give to the national government? To the states?
4. Why were powers divided among three branches of government?
5. Why was Congress divided into two parts?
6. Why was it necessary to add a Bill of Rights to the Constitution?

"Freedom of Speech," one in Norman Rockwell's series *Four Freedoms,* was published in 1943 as a *Saturday Evening Post* cover. It was reproduced as a poster during World War II.

A SUMMARY OF THE CONSTITUTION OF THE UNITED STATES

PREAMBLE

Reasons for Constitution   The people of the United States made this Constitution and put it into practice for the following reasons: (1) to have a better government than under the Articles of Confederation, (2) to give everyone fair treatment, (3) to keep peace within the country, (4) to defend the country from enemies, (5) to live comfortably and well, and (6) to keep people free both now and in the future.

ARTICLE I—LEGISLATIVE BRANCH

Description (Section 1)   The legislative branch of government, or Congress, makes all the laws. It has two parts, or houses, the Senate and the House of Representatives.

House of Representatives (Section 2)   Members of the House of Representatives serve a 2-year term. They are elected by the people. Representatives must be at least 25 years old, citizens of the United States for at least 7 years, and citizens of the state they represent.

The number of representatives from each state depends on that state's population. In order to decide on the number of representatives from each state, the government must count the people every 10 years. This is called a **census.**

The Senate (Section 3)   The Senate is made up of two senators from each state. Senators have a 6-year term. Senators must be at least 30 years old, citizens of the United States for at least 9 years, and citizens of the state they represent.

The Vice President of the United States is in charge of the Senate, but may only vote in case of a tie.

Rules (Sections 4–7)   Instructions on how to operate both the House and the Senate are covered. Behavior of members, record keeping, pay, and how a bill becomes a law are covered.

Duties (Section 8–10)   The exact jobs of Congress are listed. Congress makes all money and trade laws. Congress decides how people can become citizens of the United States and can declare war if necessary. Powers Congress and the states do *not* have are also listed.

ARTICLE II—EXECUTIVE BRANCH

Description (Section 1)   The executive branch is made up of the President of the United States and those who help carry out laws passed by Congress. The President manages the government. A President and Vice President are elected to a 4-year term.

A President must have been born in the United States, must be at least 35 years old, and must have lived in the United States for at least 14 years.

Duties (Sections 2–4)   Some of the President's jobs include carrying out the laws made by Congress, responsibility for all the armed forces, pardoning crimes, and reporting to Congress at least once a year on what the nation is doing. The President makes treaties and appoints government leaders; the Senate must give its approval.

If the President does wrong, he may be removed from office.

ARTICLE III—JUDICIAL BRANCH
Description (Section 1)   The judicial branch of government is the federal court system. The Supreme Court is the nation's highest court. It has the final say in all matters of law. Judges are appointed, not elected to office.

Duties (Section 2)   The federal courts have a say in all cases that are not entirely within a state.

Treason (Section 3)   The crime of treason, trying to overthrow the government, is explained.

ARTICLE IV—THE STATES
Rules about the states (Sections 1–4)   All states must accept acts, records, and laws of other states. A citizen of one state must be given the same rights as the citizens of another state he or she may be in. The governor of one state may send an accused criminal from another state back to that state for trial.

New states may be added to the United States. The United States government will protect all states from enemies.

ARTICLE V—AMENDMENTS
Making changes   The Constitution may be amended, or changed.

ARTICLE VI—HIGHEST LAW
Above all others   The Constitution of the United States is the highest law in the land. State laws must be under this law. All national and state lawmakers and offices must support the Constitution.

ARTICLE VII—PASSING THE CONSTITUTION
Ratification   This Constitution becomes law when 9 of the 13 states **ratify** it, or approve it.

AMENDMENTS
Amendment I   Congress may not make rules to change freedom of religion, freedom of speech, freedom of the press, or the right of people to come together in a peaceful way or to send petitions to their government.

Amendment II   The people have the right to keep and bear arms.

Amendment III   During peacetime, the government cannot make citizens put up soldiers in their homes.

Amendment IV   People or their homes may not be searched unreasonably.

Amendment V   Persons accused of serious crimes have the right to a jury trial. They may not be forced to give evidence against themselves. Their lives, freedom, and property may not be taken from them unfairly. If the government takes a person's property for public use, it must pay the owner for it.

Amendment VI   Persons accused of serious crimes have the right to a speedy and public trial. They must be told what they are accused of. They have the right to have a lawyer. They have the right to see and question those who accuse them.

Amendment VII   In most cases, there must be a right to a jury trial.

Amendment VIII   Punishment may not be cruel and unusual.

Amendments IX and X   If the Constitution does not give a certain right to the United States government, and also does not forbid a state government to have that right, then the states and the people have it.

Amendment XI   The power of the judicial branch is limited to certain kinds of cases.

Amendment XII   Electors vote for President and Vice President separately.

Amendment XIII   Slavery may not exist in the United States.

Amendment XIV   People born in the United States or naturalized here are United States citizens. They are also citizens of the states they live in.

States may not make laws that limit the rights of citizens of the United States. They may not take away a person's life or freedom or property unfairly. They must treat all people equally under the law.

Amendment XV   No citizen may be denied the right to vote because of race.

Amendment XVI   Congress is allowed to pass an income tax law.

Amendment XVII   United States senators are elected by the people.

Amendment XVIII   Liquor may no longer be manufactured or sold in the United States.

Amendment XIX   No citizen may be denied the right to vote because of sex.

Amendment XX   Presidents start their new terms on January 20; Congress starts its new term on January 3.

The Constitution is on display at the National Archives Building in Washington, D.C.

Amendment XXI   The eighteenth amendment to this Constitution is repealed, or taken back.

Amendment XXII   Presidents are limited to two terms in office.

Amendment XXIII   Residents of Washington, D.C., have the right to vote for President.

Amendment XXIV   Citizens need not pay a tax in order to vote for President, senators, or members of Congress.

Amendment XXV   In case the President becomes too ill to carry on the job, the Vice President will take over as Acting President until the President is better.

Amendment XXVI   No citizen who is 18 years of age or older may be denied the right to vote because of age.

6/ CHAPTER REVIEW

KEY FACTS

1. The Revolutionary War was fought because the colonists felt Great Britain was taking away their freedoms.

2. The war started in Lexington, Massachusetts, in 1775 and came to a virtual end at Yorktown, Virginia, in 1781.

3. The Declaration of Independence, signed on July 4, 1776, gave the reasons why the colonists thought they had the right to set up a new government.

4. The United States won the Revolution because of devoted people who fought hard for an idea, because of brilliant leadership, and because the Americans were fighting at home.

5. The type of government created by the Constitution of the United States has lasted to the present without major changes.

VOCABULARY QUIZ

If a statement is true, write **T**. If it is false, write **F** and write the word or words that could replace the underlined word to make it true.

F **1.** The <u>Boston Massacre</u> was a protest against tax on tea. **Tea Party**

F **2.** The <u>Continental Congress</u> made laws for the British. **Parliament**

T **3.** A <u>revolution</u> replaces one type of government or way of thinking with another.

T **4.** <u>Minutemen</u> were colonists who were ready to fight the British on a minute's notice.

F **5.** A <u>Loyalist</u> was a foreign soldier hired by the British. **Hessian**

F **6.** The United States was first governed by the <u>Constitution</u>. **Articles of Confederation**

F **7.** A <u>republic</u> has power divided between the state and national governments. **federal govt.**

T **8.** The <u>legislative</u> branch of government makes the laws.

F **9.** The <u>executive</u> branch of government decides the meaning of laws. **judicial**

F **10.** Changes in the Constitution are called <u>separation of powers</u>. **amendments**

REVIEW QUESTIONS

1. How did a strong desire for freedom lead the colonists to fight the Revolutionary War?

2. Why is the Declaration of Independence such an important writing?

3. What do you think was the most important battle of the Revolutionary War? Explain.

4. Why is the war discussed in this chapter called both the Revolutionary War and the War for Independence?

5. What were the results of the Revolutionary War?

6. Which amendment ended slavery? Guaranteed freedom of speech and press? Allowed both men and women to vote? Repealed another amendment?

ACTIVITIES

1. You can research and recreate one of the battles of the American Revolution. You can make a three-dimensional board and use toy soldiers, do a storyboard, make a drawing, or even act out a famous battle scene. Lexington, Concord, Bunker Hill, Trenton, or the surrender at Yorktown are very exciting possibilities.

2. Write a constitution for your class. Give reasons for writing it and spell out all the rules necessary for your class to get along well together.

3. Find or draw pictures that show life without one of the rights listed in the Bill of Rights. For example, what would life be like without freedom of religion?

BUILDING VOCABULARY

Read the story on this page to find the words that are listed here.

ragtag and bobtail	coarse
realized	rude
despised	Rebels
rabble	brigand
powder	starvation
muskets	pestilence
stout	priceless

On a separate sheet of paper, after you have finished reading, write each word and a short definition. You may be able to define some of the words using context clues found in the reading. You may also use a dictionary if you need it.

The Winter at Valley Forge
F. Van Wyck Mason

Valley Forge—our nation has no prouder chapter . . . than the one written during the winter of 1777 and 1778. That was when George Washington led about ten thousand troops into winter quarters at that place on the Schuylkill River, in Pennsylvania, about twenty miles northwest of Philadelphia.

It was a ragtag and bobtail army that went into Valley Forge. It had suffered many defeats and realized few victories. It was despised by the British who called it "a rabble in arms." It was an army that fought among itself and was led by generals who were jealous of each other.

Some of these men even plotted against George Washington himself. The army had few weapons, not enough powder, almost no discipline. There was a serious lack of meat and flour, shoes and blankets, medicine and muskets.

In Philadelphia, the captured capital of our newborn nation, the British General, Sir William Howe, had everything Washington did not have. He had a well-trained, well-equipped, well-supplied army of Redcoats that had beaten the Americans nearly every time the two forces had met.

Howe spent that bitter winter of 1777 and 1778 in comfort. His "Lobsterbacks" and Hessians left no bloody tracks in that winter's snow. Their feet were protected by stout boots. Howe's men did not eat "firecakes" of coarse flour and water nor did they shiver in rude huts with dirt floors. They ate red beef and juicy pork, and their winter quarters were warm.

"Let the Rebels starve and freeze this winter," said "Dandy Sir Billy" Howe, as he was called. "In the spring we'll waste no time taking care of the ones who are left—if that brigand, Washington, has any men left at all."

But in the spring of '78, out of Valley Forge marched a new army. It was an army that had come through one of the cruelest winters in our country's history. More than that, it was an army that had found itself. During the dark days of snow and cold, starvation and pestilence, the Americans had learned many a priceless lesson.

125

Mount Vernon is on the Potomac River, about 15 mi (24 km) south of Washington, D.C.

Our First President

VOCABULARY

inauguration	term
oath	District of
secretary	Columbia
Cabinet	White House
Chief Justice	
Union	

Everyone's choice   Thomas Jefferson said, "He was, indeed, in every sense of the words a wise, a good, and a great man." Abigail Adams felt ". . . no other man could rule over this great people and unite them into one mighty empire." One of his officers ("Light-Horse" Harry Lee) said he was "First in war, first in peace, and first in the hearts of his countrymen." And Phillis Wheatley, the poet, wrote "Fam'd for thy valour, for thy virtues more,/Hear every tongue thy guardian aid implore!"

All of these statements were made about George Washington. You can see how well loved and respected he was. Washington was trusted and admired. He was the only choice for the honor of being the first President of the United States.

Washington did not want to be President. He wanted to live at his beautiful home, Mount Vernon. But he put his love for his country ahead of his own wishes.

Inauguration day   April 30, 1789, was inauguration day for the young nation's first President. An **inauguration** is the ceremony that puts someone in office. Washington traveled from Mount Vernon to New York City by coach and on horseback. New York City was the nation's first capital. In every city and town along the way people came out to cheer him and wish him well. There were parades, fireworks, dinners, and balls.

A huge crowd came to the inauguration. They watched Washington place his left hand on an open Bible, raise his right hand, and take the **oath** of office. An oath is a promise. The oath the President takes is written in the Constitution. Washington promised to do his best to keep, protect, and defend the Constitution. He ended the oath with the words, "So help me God." Most Presidents since then have added these words.

The Constitution listed the powers and duties of the President. Washington knew what he had to do. But the Constitution did not tell him *how* to carry out his duties. This Washington had to decide. He was a wise and thoughtful man. Many of Washington's acts as President have served as examples to the Presidents that have followed him. See how many you find as you read about President Washington in this chapter.

40°15′N/74°43′W

Washington passed through Trenton, New Jersey on the way to his inauguration in New York City.

At the bridge over the Assunpink Creek, just before Trenton, New Jersey, a group of women and girls gathered to honor Washington. Washington's passing through Trenton was especially significant to people who remembered his victory over the Hessian mercenaries encamped at Trenton twelve years before.

Starting a government The new government was started with a Constitution, a Congress, a President, and little else. The states had been used to going their own way under the Articles of Confederation. Both Washington and the Congress knew that the new government would have to show its strength quickly. With Washington's leadership the new government went to work.

The job of President was too big for one person alone. Congress formed three departments to help Washington. These departments went to work on three of the biggest problems facing the new nation.

The State Department would work on relations with other nations. The War Department would build a national navy and army. The War Department is now called the Department of Defense. The Treasury Department would handle the nation's money problems.

Washington chose able leaders for each of these departments. Each leader would be called a **secretary**. Thomas Jefferson became Secretary of State; Henry Knox, Secretary of War; and Alexander Hamilton, Secretary of the Treasury.

Each of these men advised the President. Final decisions were made by the President, however. This group of advisors became known as the **Cabinet**. Future Presidents would all have a Cabinet.

The Constitution called for a third branch of government—a Supreme Court. All questions about the Constitution and federal law would be settled by this court. Washington appointed John Jay as head of the Supreme Court. He was called the **Chief Justice.**

The government grew stronger In 1791 Congress passed a tax law in order to raise money for the new government. Some people thought they would rather fight than pay these taxes. Washington formed an army to stop them. The new government could not have its laws disobeyed. Washington showed future Presidents how to be a strong leader.

In what year did George Washington begin to serve as President of the United States?

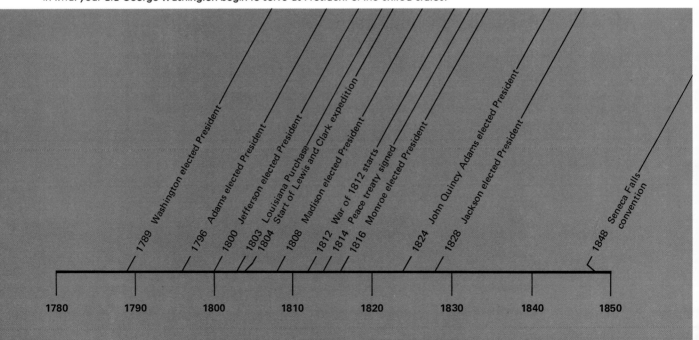

1789 Washington elected President
1796 Adams elected President
1800 Jefferson elected President
1803 Louisiana Purchase
1804 Start of Lewis and Clark expedition
1808 Madison elected President
1812 War of 1812 starts
1814 Peace treaty signed
1816 Monroe elected President
1824 John Quincy Adams elected President
1828 Jackson elected President
1848 Seneca Falls convention

1780 1790 1800 1810 1820 1830 1840 1850

Interesting Notes About the Presidents

Three Presidents held national public office after their terms were over: John Quincy Adams served in the House of Representatives for 17 years; Andrew Johnson represented Tennessee in the Senate; and William Howard Taft was Chief Justice of the Supreme Court from 1921 to 1930.

Woodrow Wilson was the first President to hold regular press conferences and the first President to speak over the radio.

Franklin Delano Roosevelt was the first President to appear on television.

The first President to travel to a foreign country was Theodore Roosevelt.

Eight Presidents died in office: William Henry Harrison, Zachary Taylor, Abraham Lincoln, James Garfield, William McKinley, Warren Harding, Franklin Roosevelt, and John Kennedy.

Three Presidents died on the Fourth of July: John Adams and Thomas Jefferson in 1826; James Monroe in 1831.

Ulysses Grant, Dwight Eisenhower and Jimmy Carter were graduates of United States military service academies; Grant and Eisenhower from West Point and Carter from Annapolis.

The first President to be inaugurated in Washington, D.C., was Thomas Jefferson.

Only one child of a President was born in the White House. That was Esther Cleveland, the daughter of Grover Cleveland, in 1893.

William Henry Harrison made the longest inaugural speech, and caught cold and died one month later. As a result John Tyler became the first President to take office on the death of the previous President.

There have been three sets of presidential relatives: John Adams and John Quincy Adams (father and son); William Henry Harrison and Benjamin Harrison (grandfather and grandson); Theodore Roosevelt and Franklin Delano Roosevelt (cousins).

Van Buren— 1st President to be born a U.S. citizen

Buchanan— only bachelor President

Hoover— 1st President born west of the Mississippi (Iowa)

Eisenhower— 1st President to have a pilot's license

Panama, 1906

The nation also grew and expanded while Washington was President. Three new states—Vermont, Kentucky, and Tennessee—entered the **Union**. When people or groups such as states join together, they form a union. The United States is a union of 50 states.

Washington steps down   Washington could have been President for life. But he did not feel this was right. He had devoted most of his life to helping his country. Now, however, he was 65 years old and had served two **terms**, or 4-year periods, as President. With the exception of Franklin Roosevelt, every President has followed Washington's two-term tradition. In 1951, a constitutional amendment limited all future Presidents to two terms.

"'Tis well."   Washington spent his last years managing his large farm at Mount Vernon. But he remained active for his country. The nation's new capital was being built near his home. The capital was going to be the **District of Columbia**. The district was not part of any state. In time the city would be named in Washington's honor. Washington, D.C., was a planned city. The chief designer was

Pierre L' Enfant (pē′ är län′ fänt), from France. Benjamin Banneker was appointed by President Washington to make a survey of the land. Banneker was the first black person to get a presidential appointment to work for the government.

Then on a wet, snowy day in December of 1799, Washington caught a cold while riding around Mount Vernon. He became seriously ill and died two days later.

Washington's last words, " 'Tis well," are good words by which to remember him. He had been commander in chief during the Revolution, President of the Constitutional Convention, and first President of the United States. He had done well.

Some rooms on the main floor of the White House are open to the public at stated hours.

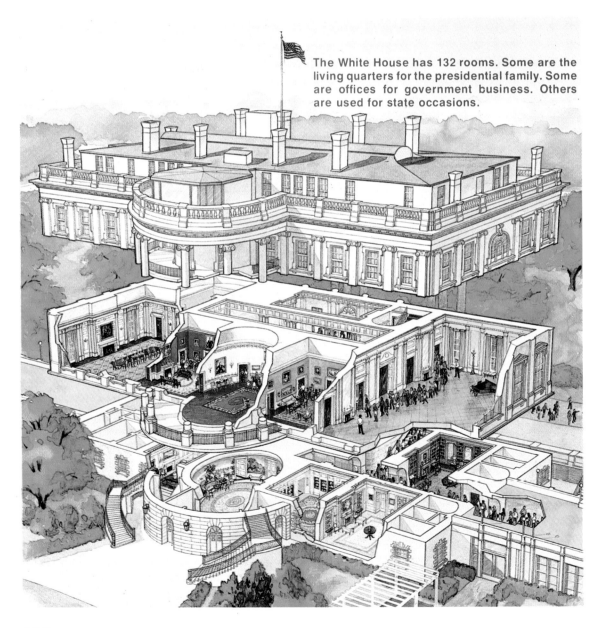

The White House has 132 rooms. Some are the living quarters for the presidential family. Some are offices for government business. Others are used for state occasions.

The President Travels

Once during his time in office, George Washington decided to tour the South. Men to handle the horses and a personal servant went with him on this 3-month tour. The President slept in inns along the way. The innkeepers had no idea he was coming. For almost 2 months his government could not keep track of where he was.

In the summer of 1979 President Carter took a 37-minute train ride from Washington, D.C., to Baltimore, Maryland. Mrs. Carter was with him. There were many guards. Communications experts were along to keep Carter in touch with his government. A train filled with Secret Service people went ahead of the President's train to check the tracks. Three helicopters watched the progress from above. Reporters also came along.

Can you imagine the President today being away from Washington for 3 months? Think about the many changes that have taken place since President Washington took his trip. There were no reporters with Washington. There was no radio or television to let all the people in the country know what the President was doing that day. There were no telephones and telegraphs. And there were no trains, planes, or helicopters.

These two trips show how the Presidency has grown in size and importance since Washington's time.

A growing presidency Washington had two people on his personal staff. When they went on vacation, Washington wrote his own letters. Today the President has over 500 people working just for him.

Washington had three Cabinet advisors. Today there are 13. Under Washington, all three branches of the federal government employed only 350 people. Today almost 3 million people work for just the Executive Branch of the government.

Washington was paid $25,000 a year. He had to pay all his expenses from that. Today the President receives $200,000 per year. He also receives money to pay for transportation, staff, and entertainment. This totals in the millions of dollars.

Washington lived in a small house in Philadelphia, which was the nation's capital from 1790 to 1800. He had to buy furniture with his own money. Today the President lives in the **White House**, a 132-room mansion. It is beautifully furnished at govenmental expense.

Why, do you think, have these great changes been made? The presidency has grown with the United States. There are many more people today than in 1790. They demand many more services. Our government must be able to meet the changing needs of the American people.

CHECKUP

1. Why was Washington "the only choice" for President in 1789?
2. Name at least three things that Washington did that set an example for future Presidents.
3. What three departments made up Washington's Cabinet? Who was the first secretary of each?
4. Name three differences between Washington's presidency and the modern presidency.

Thomas Jefferson, A Remarkable Man

Jefferson modeled the Rotunda of the University of Virginia at Charlottesville after the Pantheon, an ancient temple in Rome. A statue of Jefferson is in front of the Rotunda.

Jefferson designed the building shown here.

---VOCABULARY---
diplomat
architect

A man of many talents He was a lawyer. He wrote the Declaration of Independence. He was the representative of the United States at the court of the king of France. A person who does this kind of work is called a **diplomat**. He was the first Secretary of State, second Vice President, and third President of the United States. While he was President, the size of the country doubled.

He came from Virginia. He served that state as governor and congressman. As an **architect** he drew the plans for many buildings in Virginia. Some of these buildings are the state capitol, buildings at the University of Virginia, and his beautiful home, Monticello.

At the same time, he was also a fine violinist and composer. He studied Native American languages. He knew Greek, Latin, and Hebrew. He could speak French and Italian.

His work as scientist and inventor should not be forgotten. He did practical things such as improving farming methods by inventing a new type of plow. He experimented with different seeds. He developed the swivel chair and the "dumbwaiter," a gadget that brought food from one floor to another. His home is filled with inventions like this.

In his later life he was very proud of his work in education. He started the University of Virginia.

HERE WAS BURIED THOMAS JEFFERSON AUTHOR OF THE DECLARATION OF AMERICAN INDEPENDENCE OF THE STATUTE OF VIRGINIA FOR RELIGIOUS FREEDOM AND FATHER OF THE UNIVERSITY OF VIRGINIA

Jefferson died July 4, 1826 and was buried at Monticello.

The picture on this page shows his tombstone. He chose the words that are on it. They are a list of those acts in his life of which he was most proud. Thomas Jefferson is truly one of the most talented Americans who ever lived.

132

The Louisiana Purchase Jefferson's greatest accomplishment as President was the Louisiana Purchase. At this time, Louisiana included just about all the land from the Mississippi River to the Rocky Mountains. (See the map on page 135.)

The Mississippi River was a highway for those Americans who lived west of the Appalachian Mountains. They took their goods downriver to the port of New Orleans near the mouth of the Mississippi. Find these places on the map. New Orleans was not part of the United States. It belonged to France, which had received the city and the rest of what we call the Louisiana Territory from Spain in 1800.

Americans living in the west were afraid that France would not allow them to use the port of New Orleans for trade. This was because Napoleon, the ruler of France, wanted to start another French empire in America. Jefferson sent James Monroe to join Robert Livingston in France. They were to try to buy New Orleans from the French for $10 million.

A revolution in Haiti helps the United States Haiti was a French colony in the Caribbean Sea. Find Haiti on the map on page 470 in the Atlas. Napoleon needed a strong naval base in Haiti if he wanted a French empire in America. But a former slave, Toussaint L' Ouverture, led the people of Haiti in a successful fight for freedom at this time. Without Haiti, Louisiana lost some of its appeal for Napoleon. It also looked as though France would be fighting Great Britain very soon. If that happened, France would be unable to defend Louisiana. The soldiers would be needed in Europe. "So why not sell the entire Louisiana Territory to the United States?" thought Napoleon.

Livingston had been dealing with the French for some time. He was surprised when he was asked, "What will you give for the whole of Louisiana?" The entire Louisiana Territory was bought for $15 million, or about 3 cents per acre (1 cent per hectare). By this act the United States doubled in size. There would be room to grow and expand.

Lewis and Clark President Jefferson wanted to know more about the Louisiana Territory. He wished to find out about the Native Americans, the animals, the minerals, the climate, and the type of land. To make such an exploration, Jefferson chose Meriwether Lewis, his personal secretary, and William Clark, Lewis's

New Orleans is still one of the busiest seaports in the United States.

Mississippi River

close friend. They were to try to find a route all the way to the Pacific Ocean.

Lewis and Clark kept day-by-day records of their journey, or expedition. The following is based on their records. It will give an idea of what they saw and did.

May 14, 1804 We are now ready to begin our journey. We will leave from St. Louis and follow the Missouri River (see map). We have gathered about 45 men together. Most are regular army soldiers, but there are a few others. York, Clark's black servant, is along. We are also taking supplies and many small gifts to trade with Indians.

June 16 Hunting is excellent. We got two deer and two bear today. But the mosquitoes and other bugs are a real bother.

July 4 We celebrated Independence Day by firing guns. We named Fourth of July Creek and Independence Creek in honor of the day. One of our number was bitten by a rattlesnake.

August 23 We can tell we are getting farther west—we killed our first buffalo today. The Indians are all very friendly so far.

April 7, 1805 We have spent the winter among the Mandan Indians. We have had a good time sharing with them and learning from each other.

We have had the good fortune of taking on a new guide. He is a French Canadian named Toussaint Charbonneau (tü′ sän shər bō′ nō). He brings his wife, Sacagawea (sak ə chə wē′ ə), with him. She is a young woman of the Shoshoni tribe. She was raised in the western lands. She will guide us in the Rocky Mountains.

July 22 We have been traveling over 2 months. Sacagawea recognizes the area we are now in. She was captured from here as a little girl. We have been in sight of the Rocky Mountains for weeks. We believe that no white people have ever been here before.

August 17 When we met the Shoshoni people, Sacagawea recognized some friends. Imagine everyone's surprise when we found that the chief was her long-lost brother!

October 16 Today we had our first bites of tasty salmon from the Columbia River. We will follow this river to the Pacific.

Sacagawea guided Lewis and Clark through the Pacific Northwest. She is pictured here with the two explorers at Three Forks, Montana. 45°54′N/111°32′W

York   Clark   Lewis   Sacagawea

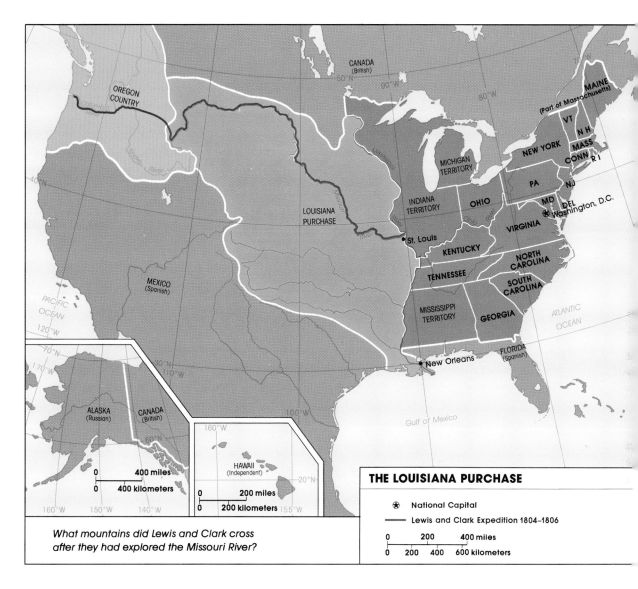

THE LOUISIANA PURCHASE

⊛ National Capital

— Lewis and Clark Expedition 1804–1806

| 0 | 200 | 400 miles |
| 0 | 200 | 400 | 600 kilometers |

What mountains did Lewis and Clark cross after they had explored the Missouri River?

November 7 We are so excited! We can hear the roar of waves crashing on shore. We have finally reached the great Pacific Ocean!

Results   Lewis and Clark built a fort and spent the winter on the shores of the Pacific. In the spring they started the trip home, finally reaching St. Louis in September, 1806.

President Jefferson received an excellent report of their journey. He learned a great deal about the geography of the new territory. He learned about the animals, trees, and plants there. The work of Lewis and Clark gave the United States a claim to the Oregon country. In 1846 this area became part of the United States.

CHECKUP

1. List at least five of Thomas Jefferson's talents or accomplishments.
2. What was the importance of the Louisiana Purchase?
3. What are the two results of the Lewis and Clark journey?

The tune for "The Star-Spangled Banner" was borrowed from a popular English drinking song "To Anacreon in Heaven." John Stafford Smith composed the music in 1777.

Our National Anthem

VOCABULARY

anthem	"Old Ironsides"
War Hawks	Era of Good Feelings

"Oh, say! can you see, by the dawn's
early light,
What so proudly we hailed at the
twilight's last gleaming,
Whose broad stripes and bright stars,
through the perilous fight,
O'er the ramparts we watched were
so gallantly streaming?
And the rockets' red glare, the
bombs bursting in air,
Gave proof through the night that
our flag was still there.
Oh, say, does that star-spangled
banner yet wave
O'er the land of the free and the
home of the brave?

The "star-spangled banner" now is in the Smithsonian.
The flag is 50 ft (15 m) long.

The Spar-Spangled Banner These words were written in 1814 by an American named Francis Scott Key. He was a prisoner on a British warship. This ship was bombing Fort McHenry in Baltimore.

During the bombing Key walked back and forth on the ship's deck. Throughout the night the flag of the United States could be seen as it was lit up by the rockets and bombs. But the smoke and fog got so thick that Key could no longer see. He must have wondered, "Has the fort held out? Is the flag still flying?"

Then, "by the dawn's early light," Key saw the torn and tattered flag. It was still there! Wishing to record his feelings, Key wrote a poem on the back of a letter he was carrying.

When Key was freed the next day, the poem was printed and passed around Baltimore. It was soon set to music. The song spread rapidly, but did not become our country's national **anthem** until 1931.

Why another war with Britain? Americans and British had already been at war for 2 years when the firing on Fort McHenry took place. What were the causes of this War of 1812?

Americans were angry about British conduct on the sea. Britain, always in need of sailors, was stopping American ships and taking sailors. The British said they were taking only runaway British sailors. But many American citizens were also taken. People felt this had to be ended. Britain had also passed laws that interfered with American trade. Many Americans felt that Britain should be shown once and for all that our country was free from British control.

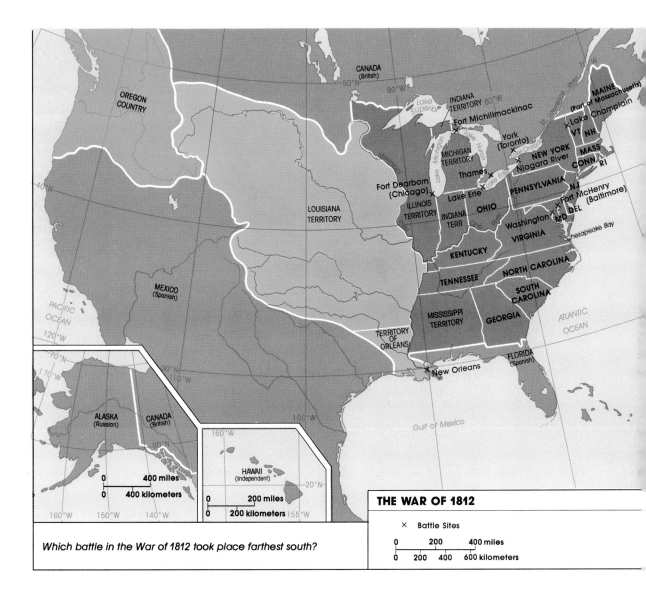

THE WAR OF 1812

× Battle Sites

| 0 | 200 | 400 miles |
| 0 | 200 | 400 | 600 kilometers |

Which battle in the War of 1812 took place farthest south?

Relations between the United States and Great Britain had not been good since the Revolution. Also the British and Canadians were urging Indians to fight settlers. Many Indian groups were already angry with the settlers for taking their land and breaking promises. Americans were angry with the British for causing more trouble. Tecumseh, a great Indian leader, united the tribes to fight the settlers. He later joined the British and was killed in the War of 1812.

Rising feelings of national pride in the United States were another reason for the war. Some Americans felt that Canada rightfully belonged to the United States. Henry Clay and many other leaders in Congress favored fighting Britain. These new leaders were known as the **War Hawks**. There were some Americans, however, especially those from New England and the Middle Atlantic states who were against the war. Strong feelings nearly split the country.

137

The sides of the *Constitution* were made of stout oak.

The Constitution *is the oldest American warship afloat today. It can be seen in Boston harbor.*

Constitution   Guerrière

The War of 1812   There were many Americans who wanted war with Great Britain, but the United States was not ready to fight one. The American navy was small. The British had the largest navy in the world. There was only a small American army. West Point had just begun to train officers. The British, even though they were also fighting a war in Europe, were able to send well-trained troops to fight in America.

The navy provided the high points of the war for the Americans. The wooden warship *Constitution* gained lasting fame by defeating a British ship. It was said that British cannon shots bounced right off the sides of the *Constitution*. Because of this, the ship was given the nickname, **"Old Ironsides."**

The war on the ocean usually did not go well for the Americans. They had better luck on the inland lakes. Oliver Hazard Perry defeated the British on Lake Erie. His report of victory, "We have met the enemy and they are ours," is still a proud part of American naval history. The Americans stopped a British raiding party coming from Canada at the battle of Lake Champlain.

Burning of Washington   In 1814 the British marched into Washington, D.C. The President, James Madison, was with the troops who were trying to defend the city. His wife, Dolley, was left to manage the White House. She stayed in Washington until the last possible minute. She gathered important papers and a few

138 The *Constitution* was to be scrapped in 1830 but Oliver Wendell Holmes' poem "Old Ironsides" aroused such public feeling that it was restored to service in 1833. Drydocked in 1897, it was again commissioned into active service in 1931 after American children helped to raise money to recondition it.

White House treasures for safekeeping. She refused to leave until a famous portrait of George Washington was in safe hands. Dolley Madison finally fled only 2 hours before the British arrived. At the White House the British soldiers ate a hot meal that had been prepared for the President and his Cabinet!

The British burned just about every public building in Washington. They then went on to Baltimore. There British warships in the harbor unsuccessfully bombarded Fort McHenry.

A peace treaty is signed   There were many Americans who had opposed the War of 1812 from the start. As time wore on both sides grew eager for it to end. Finally, in December 1814, a peace treaty was signed. None of the problems that were reasons for the war were settled by the treaty. However, it was agreed as part of the treaty to work out future problems peaceably. Gilbert Stuart made many copies of his original portrait of Washington.

This is the portrait saved by Dolley Madison.

The peace treaty had been signed in Europe. It took many weeks for the news to get back to the United States. So the biggest battle of the war was fought 2 weeks after the peace treaty was signed. Two thousand British were killed or wounded at the battle of New Orleans. The Americans lost 13 men and 58 were wounded. The victory gave the Americans great confidence, but lives were lost in a needless battle.

Second war for independence   The peace treaty itself changed very little. However, there were positive results from the war. Two military leaders in this war were later to become Presidents. Andrew Jackson, "the hero of New Orleans," was elected in 1828. And William Henry Harrison was elected in 1840 because of the battles he fought on the frontier.

In addition to new leaders, the war gave the people of the United States a new way to look at themselves. They were proud of their country. They were proud of their ability to fight a great power. Europe now respected the United States more. Our country was free to go its own way. The War of 1812 is often called "The Second War for American Independence." After the War of 1812 Americans were much more united. New states were added. The young nation was sure of itself.

In 1816 James Monroe was elected President. Things went so smoothly that this time is called the **Era of Good Feelings**.

CHECKUP
1. What caused the War of 1812?
2. Tell one fact about Old Ironsides, Oliver Perry, the battle of New Orleans.

139

Jacksonian Democracy

"Victory for the common man"   Glass and china were smashed. Noses were bloodied. People fainted.

A riot? No. Another British raid on Washington? No. About 4 months earlier Andrew Jackson had been elected President. For weeks thousands of people had fun coming to Washington, D.C., to see his inauguration. Jackson was their hero. His victory was seen as a "victory for the common man."

After Jackson was sworn into office, the crowd followed him to the White House. They jammed themselves in to get food and drink. Most of all they wanted to get closer to their hero. Muddy boots ruined expensive carpets and chairs as people pushed and shoved to see Andrew Jackson.

People cheered Jackson on the way to his inauguration.

Jackson welcomed them at first. But the crushing force of the crowd soon caused him to leave by the back door. He spent his first night as President in a hotel. But he would truly be a President "of the people."

"Old Hickory"   To understand this deep love for Andrew Jackson, you have to understand who Jackson was and where he came from. Andrew Jackson was a fighter. At age 13 he was already fighting the Revolutionary War in the Carolinas. He and his brother were captured by the British and taken to a prison camp. When ordered to clean a British officer's boots, Andy refused. The angry officer slashed Andy with a sword. Andy's brother was also badly cut.

The boys' wounds went untreated. Both caught smallpox. Andy's brother died. Andy was sick for months and carried scars for life. Perhaps Jackson lived because of his fierce temper and stubborn nature.

Jackson had moved to Tennessee as a young man. He was just the kind of man the people of Tennessee liked. Westerners had to be tough, and Jackson was tough. His soldiers later called him "Old Hickory," because hickory wood was the toughest thing they knew.

A man of the people   Jackson served the people of Tennessee as a lawyer, judge, Congressman, and senator. But he won his greatest fame as a soldier. Both before and after the War of 1812 Jackson fought in the wars against the Creeks of Alabama and Georgia and the Seminoles in Florida. Because of his activity in

The painting "Trail of Tears" (1942) by Robert Lindneux depicts a part of the Cherokee removal from their home- land to Indian Territory. The Cherokees set out on their "trail of tears" in the spring of 1838.

Florida the United States was able to take control of that area from Spain.

The people loved this bold, take-charge, fiery fighter. Jackson believed in people. He felt that common people could run the government. This idea has come to be called **Jacksonian democracy**. These people elected Andrew Jackson President in 1828. He gave them their first chance to really have a part in government.

Not everyone benefited while Andrew Jackson was President. Women, blacks, and Native Americans were not able to take part in government. In fact, in some cases, the government worked against them.

Trail of Tears   The Cherokee nation serves as an example of what happened to many Native American tribes and people in Jackson's time. The Cherokees had a great deal of land in Georgia and Alabama. The Cherokees were farmers. They had roads and lived in houses. They had a written language and a weekly newspaper. Their government was democratic. But many whites felt that the Cherokees were in the way. White settlers wanted their land.

The land was promised to the Cherokee nation by treaty. Missionaries, Congressman Henry Clay, and the Supreme Court all said that the Cherokees had

The Trail of Tears led Cherokees west after they had been forced from their homes. How do you think they felt as they traveled to reservations across the Mississippi?

rights to their claims. Even so, the Cherokees were thrown off their land. They were told to go to Oklahoma. With soldiers watching them, they had little choice but to obey.

This journey lasted several months. Disease, hunger, and cold brought death to many. Over 4,000 Cherokees were buried along the **Trail of Tears** that stretched from Georgia to Oklahoma.

Andrew Jackson said that this removal was necessary. Without it, he said, the Cherokees all would have been killed by white settlers looking for more land.

The rise of women   Jackson did a great deal to make people feel a part of government. But as we have just seen, Jackson was not ready to give equality to

Native Americans. A slaveholder all his life, Jackson did not believe in equality for blacks either.

Yet in Jackson's time, some people were starting to oppose slavery. These people were called **abolitionists**. Among the abolitionists were the Grimké sisters. They had been brought up on a southern plantation, but they were against slavery. They wanted equal rights for all humans. In 1838, Angelina Grimké became the first woman ever to speak to a lawmaking group. She spoke to the Massachusetts legislature about equal rights for women and blacks. She tied the two issues together quite easily. She felt that freedom was being denied to large groups of Americans. She thought lawmakers and all people should worry about this.

This stamp and this coin were issued by the United States government to honor the women's rights movement.

Carrie Chapman Catt was very interested in women's rights. She came later in the movement than Stanton and Mott. She was president of the National American Women's Suffrage Association when the Nineteenth Amendment was ratified. Later she founded the League of Women Voters.

Seneca Falls   Another link between the two issues occurred when women were not allowed to speak at the World Anti-Slavery Conference in London in 1840. At that point, two abolitionists, Lucretia Mott and Elizabeth Cady Stanton, decided to start a women's rights group.

Eight years later, in Seneca Falls, New York, Mott and Stanton called a meeting on women's rights. At the **Seneca Falls convention**, a set of goals was agreed upon. Women should have the same rights as men. Women should have free speech. Women should have the chance for equal education. Women should have the right to vote.

Women went to work quickly to meet these goals. But it was a hard job. One early speaker, Lucy Stone, was treated rudely and had things thrown at her. Once in the winter she was sprayed with icy water. She simply pulled her shawl tighter and went on talking. Stone became the "star" speaker of the movement at this time and won many followers.

A team of fighters for women's rights soon developed. In 1851 Elizabeth Cady Stanton met Susan B. Anthony. The two liked each other at once. Stanton was the thinker and the writer. Anthony was the organizer and the person of action. By 1860 they had won some basic rights for women in the state of New York. Other and larger gains would follow in the 50 years they would work together.

Another early worker for human rights was a former slave, Sojourner Truth. In 1851 she made a stirring speech to the women's rights convention in Akron, Ohio. As men tried to shout her down, she went to the platform and said,

Sojourner Truth worked for human rights for all people.

Sojourner Truth is a subject for a biographical report.

"That man over there says that women need to be helped into carriages and lifted over ditches, and to have the best place wherever. Nobody ever helps me into carriages or over mud puddles, or gives me any best place. And ain't I woman? Look at me! I have ploughed and planted and gathered into barns and no man could head [do better than] me. And ain't I a woman? I could work as much and eat as much as a man—when I could get it—and bear the lash [whip] as well.

And ain't I a woman? I have borne thirteen children and seen most all sold off to slavery, and when I cried out with my mother's grief, none but Jesus heard me. And ain't I a woman? . . ."

CHECKUP

1. Why was Andrew Jackson's election called a victory for the common man?
2. What three groups were left out of this victory?
3. Why were the Cherokees removed from their lands in the early 1800s?
4. What roles did Elizabeth Cady Stanton and Susan B. Anthony play in the early women's rights movement?

KEY FACTS

1. The first President of the United States, George Washington, helped to define the powers and duties of the President.

2. The Louisiana Purchase doubled the size of the United States.

3. The war between the United States and Great Britain in 1812 ended without a clear victory for either side. But it did finally establish the independence of the United States.

3. With the election of Andrew Jackson as President in 1828, more and more people took part in government. Yet women, blacks, and Native Americans were not included in this participation.

VOCABULARY QUIZ

Fill in the blanks with the correct word or words. All the words are in this chapter.

1. The capital of the United States is _Washington, D.C._ .

2. The leader of the Supreme Court is the _Chief Justice_ .

3. The President's advisors make up the _Cabinet_ .

4. A formal ceremony to put someone in office is called an _inauguration_ .

5. With the _Louisiana Purchase_ the United States doubled in size.

6. People in Congress who favored the War of 1812 were called _War Hawks_ .

7. "The Star-Spangled Banner" was written during the British bombing of _Fort McHenry_ .

8. The path taken by many Cherokees to Oklahoma was called the _Trail of Tears_ .

9. A person who wanted to end slavery was called an _abolitionist_ .

10. The first convention of the women's rights movement was at _Seneca Falls, N.Y._ .

REVIEW QUESTIONS

1. What was one great accomplishment of President Washington? President Jefferson? President Jackson?

2. Name at least two results of the War of 1812.

3. Give evidence from the time of Andrew Jackson that not all Americans were enjoying equality.

ACTIVITIES

1. You may wish to find out more about Washington, D.C. Use an encyclopedia to learn more about some of the following:

a. Why was this place chosen for the capital of the United States?

b. What was life like there in 1800?

c. How were streets named?

d. Read about some famous government buildings, like the Capitol, White House, Library of Congress, or Supreme Court Building.

e. Find out about some tourist attractions, like the Washington Monument, Jefferson Memorial, Lincoln Memorial, Ford's Theater, or the Bureau of Engraving and Printing.

f. Read about some of its famous museums, like the Smithsonian Institution, the National Gallery of Art, or the Museum of African Art.

g. Learn about some famous nearby attractions like Arlington National Cemetery, Mount Vernon, or the Marine Corps War Memorial.

h. What type of government does Washington, D.C., have?

2. Johnny Appleseed, Daniel Boone, Davy Crockett, Mike Fink, and Jean Laffite were real people. Try to find out at least one true story and at least one tall tale from the life of one of these people. Tell or act out your stories to the class.

STATING A POINT OF VIEW

In this chapter you read parts of the journals kept by Lewis and Clark as they explored the Louisiana Purchase territory. One person who was very important to them on this journey was a Native American woman named Sacagawea. Turn to page 134 and reread what Lewis and Clark wrote about her. Now read the short biography below.

No one knows exactly when or where Sacagawea was born. It is thought that she was born around 1787 in either western Montana or eastern Idaho. She was a Shoshoni and was captured by a slave-hunting party of Indians from the area around North Dakota. She was a young teenager at this time. She was sold to a French Canadian trapper who married her when she was about 18 years old. They joined the Lewis and Clark expedition shortly thereafter. Sacagawea gave birth to a son in February 1805, during the time the expedition wintered with the Mandan Indians. The baby was named Jean Baptiste. In April Lewis and Clark and all the members of the group started out again. Sacagawea and the baby went, too. In May a river that feeds into the Platte was explored and named the Sacagawea River. In June Sacagawea became sick with a bad fever and stomach pains. At the same time the baby was having trouble with his teeth. Captain Lewis gave them both medicine. In August the expedition made its first contact with Sacagawea's people. They were given horses by Sacagawea's brother and they eventually continued their journey. Sacagawea and her husband and baby went on with Lewis and Clark to the coast, wintered on the shores of the Pacific, and began the return journey. When Lewis and Clark went on to Washington, D.C., Sacagawea and her family stayed in the North Dakota area. They never saw Meriwether Lewis again. It is thought, however, that in 1809 they met William Clark in St. Louis and turned Jean Baptiste over to him to be educated. There is a mystery connected to the death of Sacagawea. Some sources say she died at Fort Lisa near present-day Omaha, Nebraska, on December 20, 1812. However, in 1875 an old woman living among the Wind River Shoshoni in Wyoming claimed she was Sacagawea. This woman died in 1884. If she was Sacagawea, then she was nearly 100 years old.

The journals kept by Lewis and Clark told about the expedition from their points of view. What do you think Sacagawea would have written if she had kept a journal? What would have been her feelings about joining the expedition, about returning to her homeland, about seeing her brother again? Use the information in this book as source material and write a journal of the Lewis and Clark expedition from the point of view of Sacagawea.

A Changing Way of Life

┌─ VOCABULARY ─────────────────────┐

turnpike	interchangeable
canal	parts
textile	mass
Industrial	production
Revolution	telegraph
cotton gin	immigrant

└──────────────────────────────────┘

Heading west   Americans had been heading west even before the War for Independence. One of the first great western adventurers was Daniel Boone. He led a group of people to Kentucky. They used a trail that had been used for many years by Native Americans. This trail became the famous Wilderness Road. Find this road on the map on page 148.

Boone made his trips west on foot. But transportation would soon be much improved. Many roads, canals, steamboats, and railroads were built in the early 1800s. And better transportation changed the United States.

Roads   Most roads were built by private companies that charged money for use of the roads. They came to be known as **turnpikes.** This was because a pole, or pike, was set across the road. After people paid their money, the pike was turned so people could pass.

The early roads were nothing like the modern, hard-surfaced roads you know today. Early roads were covered with stone and gravel. In spring they turned to mud. Often traffic was held up by sheep or cattle going to market. But the roads were like today's roads in one way. They cost a lot to build and use.

Canals   While roads were a great help, people soon demanded cheaper forms of transportation to the West. A great time of **canal** building began in 1825. A canal is a waterway dug across land. Rivers and lakes had always been used for transportation in the United States. Canals were dug to join major rivers and lakes. They made transportation of people and goods easier and cheaper.

Perhaps the greatest of the early canals was the Erie Canal. It was begun at the urging of Governor DeWitt Clinton of New York. The Erie Canal connected Buffalo and Lake Erie with Albany on the Hudson River. Goods were then shipped downriver to New York City. Cities grew up around the canal. But most important, the cost of shipping fell. What had once cost $100 a ton to ship overland now cost $10 a ton by canal. Trade between East and West prospered. And more people headed west.

Have pupils note the construction of the wagons—canvas cover, wooden body, and thick wood-rimmed wheels. Such wagons carried the family, supplies for the trip, and household goods and farm tools needed for the new life that would begin when they reached their destination. Ask: What would you take along if you were one of the people in the top picture? *Pioneers moved West in wagon trains. Other methods of transportation, such as canals, opened the settled areas to industry and commerce.*

After pupils have read the pages for this lesson, have them write sentences using the vocabulary words listed below to be sure that they can define the words.

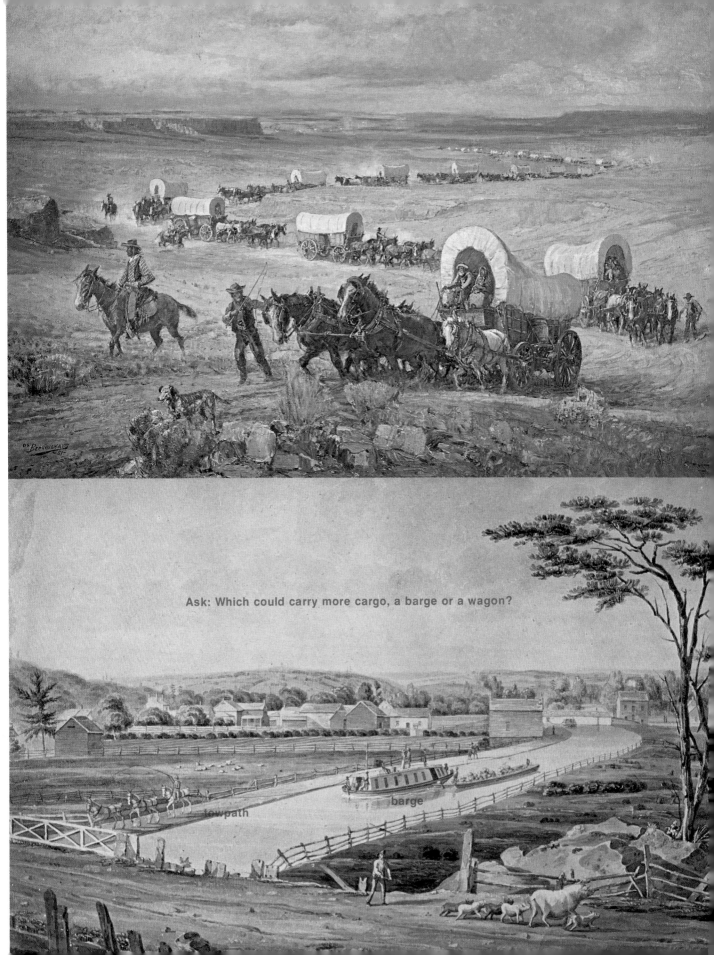

Ask: Which could carry more cargo, a barge or a wagon?

towpath

barge

Have pupils hypothesize why there were more canals and railroads built in the northern part of the country than in the southern part.

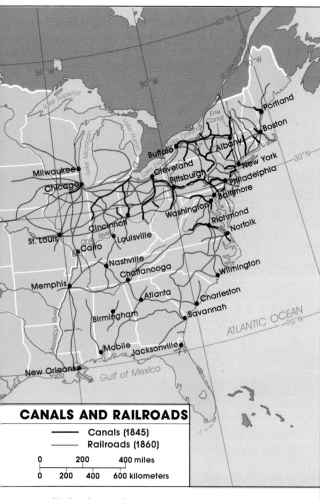

CANALS AND RAILROADS

— Canals (1845)
— Railroads (1860)

0   200   400 miles
0   200   400   600 kilometers

Notice how quickly railroads developed between 1830, when the Tom Thumb race took place, and 1860.

Steamboats   An English invention, the steam engine, helped improve American transportation in the United States. In 1787 John Fitch demonstrated the first steam-powered boat in America. In 1807 Robert Fulton's ship the *Clermont* became the first steamboat to provide regular service.

Steamboats were seen on the Mississippi River by 1820. Twenty years later most of the goods being shipped on that river were sent by steamboat.

Railroads   In 1804 an Englishman put a steam engine on a locomotive. The locomotive pulled a train along a track. This seemed like a good idea to some people in the United States.

In 1830 Peter Cooper's early locomotive, the *Tom Thumb*, ran a famous race with a horse. Cooper had been challenged by a stagecoach owner to see which of the two was faster. The *Tom Thumb* would have won, but it had an engine problem. One of the first locomotives in the United States had been beaten by a horse!

In what year was the first telegraph message sent? Who was President at that time?

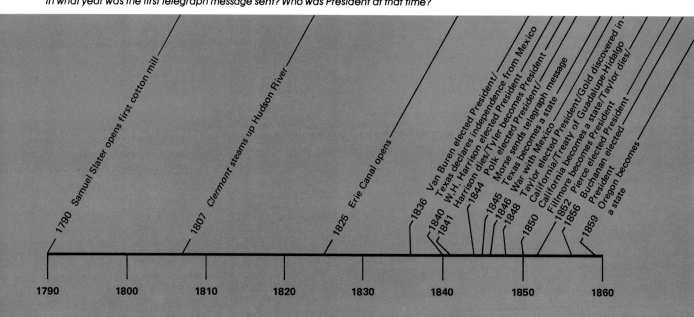

1790 Samuel Slater opens first cotton mill

1807 *Clermont* steams up Hudson River

1825 Erie Canal opens

1836 Van Buren elected President/
1840 Texas declares independence from Mexico
1841 W.H. Harrison elected President/
Harrison dies/Tyler becomes President/
1844 Polk elected President/
Morse sends telegraph message
1845 Texas becomes a state
1846 War with Mexico
1848 Taylor elected President/Gold discovered in California/Treaty of Guadalupe-Hidalgo
1850 California becomes a state/Taylor dies/
Fillmore becomes President
1852 Pierce elected President
1856 Buchanan elected President
1859 Oregon becomes a state

1790   1800   1810   1820   1830   1840   1850   1860

Have pupils observe the dress on the woman worker. Ask: Do you think accidents could happen under the conditions shown here?

Most people were impressed by the railroad. It grew rapidly. By 1860, about 30,000 miles (32,000 km) of railroad tracks linked many parts of the East with the Mississippi River.

Results of improved transportation The effects of these improvements in transportation were amazing. A trip from New York to Chicago took 6 weeks in 1800. The same trip in 1860 took less than 2 days. New areas of the West were opened up because travel to these areas was made much easier. Trade flowed more quickly and cheaply between the factories of the East and the farms of the West. Many towns were started along the trading routes to the Midwest. Improved transportation helped the nation to grow and prosper.

A photo of one of Slater's mills is on p. 33.

The rise of industry The United States was changing in the early 1800s. In 1800 there were 15 farmers to every city dweller. By 1850 there were only five farmers to every nonfarmer. More and more people were working in factories.

This change started in 1789 when young Samuel Slater arrived from England. Slater came with secret knowledge about England's cloth-making, or **textile**, industry. Information about the machines used to make cloth was not supposed to leave England. England wanted to keep the textile business for itself. Nevertheless, Slater built machines and set up the first American textile factory in Rhode Island. He did this all from memorized plans. Soon other factories were built. The rapid building of many factories became known as the **Industrial Revolution.**

Have pupils analyze the term *Industrial Revolution*. Ask: Why is it called a revolution? What great changes were made in the way people lived?

Working long hours among machines could be dangerous, especially for young children.

The life of a Lowell girl would make a very interesting oral report.

One interesting feature of the Industrial Revolution was the beginning of several towns like Lowell, Massachusetts. The factories of Lowell attracted many young women. They were given room, food, and about $2 per week for working 12 to 13 hour days, 6 days per week. Girls as young as 10 years worked these hours. People in the early 1800s were used to working long hours on the farms. They did not think it strange to work long hours in factories, too.

The Lowell girls lived by strict rules. They were required to go to church. They had to remain clean and honest. They could not stay out past 10 o'clock at night. In spite of the long days, the girls still found time to study and attend lectures.

This Industrial Revolution and changes in transportation aided each other. The better transportation became, the more goods were shipped. The easier and cheaper it was to buy these goods, the more people wanted factory products. So many factories were built to make what people wanted. And the greater the number of factories, the more goods there were to ship.

149

Important contributions to industry
Two very important contributions to the growth of industry in the United States were made by Eli Whitney. One was an invention; the other was an idea.

The invention was the **cotton gin.** This machine allowed a worker to pick the seeds out of a ball of cotton quickly and easily. When this was done by hand, a very good worker could clean only a few pounds of cotton a day. Fifty pounds of cotton a day was possible if the cotton gin was used. Now textile factories in the North could count on a steady supply of cotton from the South. The cotton gin was a very important invention.

But even more important was Whitney's idea about **interchangeable parts.** Eli Whitney owned a factory that made guns. Guns were once made by craftworkers called gunsmiths. The gunsmith would make the whole gun—all the parts—and put it together. This would take time and no two guns from the same

The reaper made great changes in the lives of farmers.

worker would be the same. And if part of the gun broke a new part would have to be made for it. Whitney knew that guns could not be made like this in a factory. It was too slow and would cost too much money. Factories had to be used for **mass production**—making large numbers of the same product. If all the parts in one gun were just like all the parts in another gun of the same type then even an unskilled worker, someone who wasn't a gunsmith, could put together a weapon quickly. This was the idea of interchangeable parts. This became basic for most manufacturing industries. Today automobiles, radios, refrigerators, and many other products are all built on this idea.

More invention New inventions brought great changes. Two inventions in the 1830s especially helped farmers. These were the reaper, invented by Cyrus McCormick, and the steel plow, invented by John Deere. These inventions came just at the time the West was being opened up for farming. They saved hours of work in preparing the fields and in harvesting, or reaping, the crops.

A third invention greatly changed communication. In 1844 Samuel Morse sent the first **telegraph** message from Baltimore, Maryland, to Washington, D.C. He used a code to send his message by wire. This code is now called the Morse code. As the crowd watched, Morse tapped out the message, "What hath God wrought?" The age of instant communication had begun. Now Americans would be drawn closer together not only by better transportation, but also by rapid communication.

Ask: What is meant by "instant communication"? What does the last sentence on p. 150 mean? Give examples.

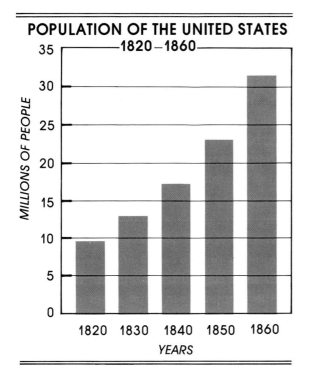

POPULATION OF THE UNITED STATES
1820–1860

MILLIONS OF PEOPLE

35
30
25
20
15
10
5
0

1820 1830 1840 1850 1860

YEARS

Study these graphs carefully. What connection can you see between the increase in the number of immigrants and the increase in population? What effect do you think this had on the expansion of the United States?

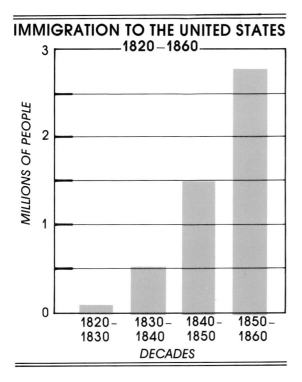

IMMIGRATION TO THE UNITED STATES
1820–1860

MILLIONS OF PEOPLE

3

2

1

0

1820– 1830– 1840– 1850–
1830 1840 1850 1860

DECADES

Immigration   The United States was an exciting place to be. There were new jobs, new land, and new opportunities here because of the Industrial Revolution and changes in transportation. Many people in other parts of the world wanted a new chance in life. Beginning in the 1830s, **immigrants** came to the United States by the thousands. Immigrants are people who leave one country to settle in another.

Almost all of these immigrants came from northern Europe, mostly from England, Scotland, Ireland, and Germany. People had many different reasons for coming to the United States. Hardships in Europe, chances for work on farms and in factories in this country, and a desire for greater freedom were their chief reasons for leaving their old homes and traveling so far.

Unfortunately, there were so many immigrants coming so rapidly that many Americans did not welcome them. They were seen as outsiders who did things differently. There was ill-feeling between immigrants and lifelong Americans. Still the immigrants came. Their hard work and belief in democracy helped shape the United States.

CHECKUP

1. Name four improvements in transportation in the early 1800s.
2. List at least three results of improved transportation.
3. How did the Industrial Revolution begin in the United States?
4. What three inventions helped the United States grow in the 1800s?
5. Why did so many immigrants come to the United States in the early 1800s?

The Lone Star Republic

Americans in the Southwest   In 1820 the vast southwestern part of what is now the United States belonged to Mexico. By 1860 the entire Southwest was controlled by the United States. How did this come about?

Both Presidents Adams and Jackson had tried to buy Texas from Mexico. They were refused. But Mexico did invite people from the United States to settle in Texas. In 1823 Stephen Austin was allowed to bring 300 families to Texas. They were given a large amount of land. By 1830 the number of United States citizens in Texas numbered over 20,000. There were four Americans from the United States for every Mexican there.

Desire for independence   The Mexicans were losing power in Texas. The Mexican government did not like what was happening there. In 1830 no more immigration to Texas from the United States was allowed. But this law was disobeyed by people hungry for land. They came to Texas as fast as ever!

Mexico got a new president, General Antonio Lopez de Santa Anna, (san' tə an' ə) in 1834. He wanted the power in Mexico to be centered in the government in Mexico City. He took away much of the self-government that the people in Texas had enjoyed until that time. The Americans and some Mexicans in Texas reacted quickly. They set up a government and formed an army. The army captured the town of San Antonio.

The Alamo was actually a group of buildings—a church, a monastary, and several outbuildings—surrounded by a high wall. The scene shown in this painting took place the morning of March 6, 1836. The Texans were running low

The battle for the Alamo is an important part of the history of Texas.

of ammunition, so Santa Anna decided to attack in strength. The Mexican troops were able to scale the walls and a great deal of ferocious hand-to-hand fighting took place.

Sam Houston was a fascinating person. He was President of a country—the Republic of Texas; governor of two states—Tennessee and Texas; and a seantor—from Texas.

Alamo is a Spanish word for cottonwood. These trees surrounded the mission.

"Remember the Alamo!" Of course Mexico did not want to lose Texas. General Santa Anna and an army of 4,000 soldiers moved to crush the revolt. A battle took place at an old Spanish mission in San Antonio. The mission was called the **Alamo.** Davy Crockett, the frontier hero, and Jim Bowie, inventor of the Bowie knife, were among the 187 defenders of the Alamo. Santa Anna began the attack on February 23, 1836. It was March 6 before the Alamo fell to the Mexicans. None of the defenders were still alive.

A few weeks later a battle was fought at San Jacinto. With the shout "Remember the Alamo!" to spur them on, the Texans under Sam Houston defeated the Mexican army. Santa Anna was taken captive.

After Texas became a state, Sam Houston served as a United States senator and later as governor of the state.

The independence that the Texans had declared had become a fact. Texas was a free nation. It remained independent of both Mexico and the United States for 10 years. It was called the **Lone Star Republic**, because its flag had only one star. Samuel Houston became its president.

Texas becomes a state Many Americans badly wanted the United States to control all the territory from the Atlantic Ocean to the Pacific Ocean. They wanted the southern border to extend at least to the Rio Grande (see map, page 157). This area included Texas. Most of the Americans living in Texas wanted to become part of the United States. Finally, in 1845, Texas became our twenty-eighth state.

War with Mexico Making Texas a state and the desire of the United States to spread from the Atlantic to the Pacific Ocean did not help relations between this country and Mexico. The two countries could not agree on the southern boundary of Texas. The United States wanted to buy the land between Texas and the Pacific Ocean from Mexico. The President of the United States at the time, James K. Polk, sent troops to the Mexican border. The Mexicans were angry at this show of force. They sent troops north. Trouble was certain to start between the two angry armies. A small American force was attacked and all the soldiers were either killed, wounded, or taken prisoner. President Polk asked Congress to declare war on Mexico, which it did in May 1846.

Treaty of Guadalupe Hidalgo The war with Mexico went well for the United

This type of architecture was well-suited to the climate. Deep arcades provided shade over windows

35°41′N/105°57′W

This was the Palace of the Governor when Santa Fe was part of Mexico. It is the oldest public building still standing in North America.

and doors. Thick adobe walls also helped to keep the rooms cool.

States. It lasted less than 2 years and during this time the United States did not lose a major battle. The American heroes of this war were General Zachary Taylor and General Winfield Scott. Other army officers, such as Robert E. Lee and Ulysses S. Grant, gained military experience that they would use not too many years later in the Civil War.

The Treaty of Guadalupe Hidalgo (gwäd′ əl üp hi dal′ gō) ended the war. Mexico recognized the Rio Grande as the <u>southern boundary of Texas</u>. Mexico also **ceded**, or gave, to the United States the land labeled "Mexican Cession" on the map on page 157. Compare this map with the map of the United States in the Atlas on page 468. Which states were part of the Mexican Cession? In 1853, the United States paid Mexico ten million dollars for the piece of land labeled "Gadsden Purchase" on the map on page 157. This land is now the southern parts of New Mexico and Arizona.

A Mexican heritage   In Chapter 3 you read about the Spanish explorers of the southwestern part of what was to become the United States. The first permanent Spanish-Mexican settlement north of the Rio Grande was made in 1598. The colony was started by Don Juan de Oñate. (ō nya′tä). He was born in Mexico of a Spanish family. His wife was a granddaughter of Cortes and a great-granddaughter of Montezuma, the last Aztec emperor. Oñate was the first colonizer. By 1630 there were 25 settlements and missions scattered throughout what the Spanish were calling New Mexico. Santa Fe, the most important settlement,

was started in 1609. This was only 2 years after the British started their first colony in Virginia.

The Spanish-Mexican settlers brought many changes into New Mexico. Missionaries converted many Native Americans to Christianity. New ways of farming were introduced. Great cattle ranches were started. The cowboy, or *vaquero* (vä kär′ ō), became a common sight. And so too did the Indian on horseback. Two very important parts of the legend of the American West—the cowboy and the Indian—were given their start when the first settlers brought horses into the American Southwest. Spanish **architecture**, or style of building, can still be seen in the area.

Our country still has a large Mexican-American population. A number of Mexican Americans, past and present, have influenced the history of the United States. Father Eusebio Kino was known as the Padre on Horseback. He started a

154

group of missions in what is now southern Arizona and spent 25 years exploring the southwestern part of the country. He was also a mapmaker and was the first white man to prove that California was not an island. José Navarro fought for Texan independence, first from Spain and then from Mexico. He helped write the constitution of the state of Texas. The signature of Romana Banuelos (bän wā′ lōs) appeared on all the paper money printed in this country between 1971 and 1974. She was the treasurer of the United States during this time. Cesar Chavez started the United Farm Workers of America to help farm workers get better wages.

CHECKUP

1. How did defeat at the Alamo help Texans win their war with Mexico?
2. Why did the United States go to war with Mexico?
3. What land did the United States gain by the Treaty of Guadalupe Hidalgo?
4. What was the Gadsden Purchase?

California

┌─ VOCABULARY ──────────────────────┐
presidio
inflation
└───────────────────────────────────┘

Early settlement   California was settled by the sword and the cross. In 1769, Gaspar de Portolá (pôr tō lä′) led a military force north from Baja (lower) California near present-day San Diego and built a **presidio**, or military fort, there. In 1770 he built another presidio at Monterey. Six years later settlers and soldiers established another presidio near what is now known as San Francisco. In time five of these forts were built. The presidios protected the settlers. They also served to hold this part of the Spanish empire from the English. The English claimed land on the west coast of North America because of the voyages of Sir Francis Drake (see Chapter 4).

Five missionaries went with Portolá on his military expedition. They were led by

The missionaries brought a new religion and a different way of life to the Native Americans of California and the Southwest. Nomadic tribes were turned to farming and herding. This did not always go smoothly; there were a
The missions were an important part of life in Spanish California.
number of serious uprisings in which missions were decimated.

Have pupils observe the presence of both soldiers and priests. Missions were often presidios and vice versa.

The culture that developed in this part of the Spanish empire was a combination of Spanish and Indian. Have pupils look for examples in this painting.

Father Junípero Serra (ser′ rä). Father Serra spent the next 15 years building missions up and down the coast. The first was at San Diego. Eventually there were 21 missions between San Diego and San Francisco. The missions were about 30 miles (50 km)—a single day's march—apart. The missions were run by priests who trained local Indians to do the farming and building. The land was fertile and the climate temperate. The missions did well. By the early 1800s the missions had over 30,000 head of livestock and were harvesting more than 30,000 bushels (1,000,000 L) of grain and vegetables each year. Mission workshops made pots, dishes, furniture, and cloth. The California missions, presidios, and pueblos (small villages) were far away from the government in Mexico and even farther away from the king in Spain. The population stayed small and self-supporting. The culture was part Spanish and part Indian.

The Bear Flag Republic   In 1846 most of the population of California was either Native American, Mexican, or Spanish. There were fewer than 1,000 United States citizens living there.

Yet these few people wanted California to be part of the United States. They joined a revolt against the Mexican government and helped form the Republic of California. It was also called the Bear Flag Republic, because the flag showed a bear. Mexico was too busy fighting the United States to do anything about the revolt. United States troops were in California when the war ended. The republic became a United States territory as part of the Treaty of Guadalupe Hidalgo.

California gold fever   In 1849 San Francisco grew from a small, sleepy village to a busy town of 25,000. The population of California went from 15,000 to over 100,000.

People came to California any way they could. They took boats around the tip of

Life in the mining camps was not easy for the men and women who came to California to find fortunes. People who provided services, such as cooking, often became richer than those who looked for gold.

from the stream bed; the water and finer sand grains are drained or washed out, and the residue is carefully searched for gold nuggets.

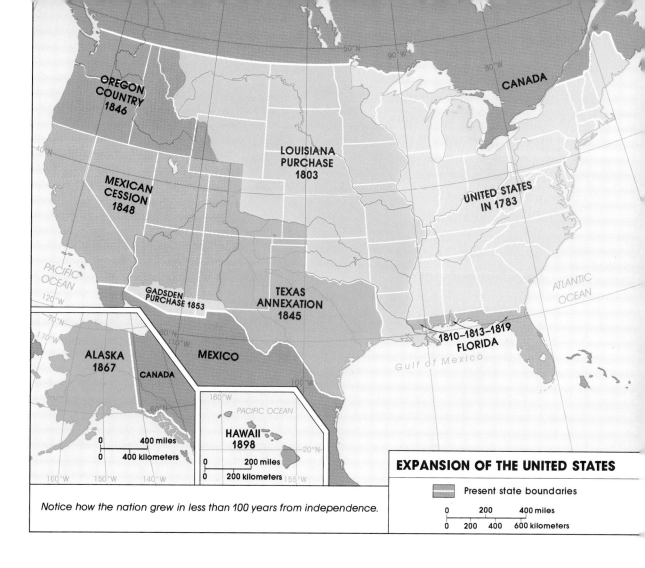

OREGON COUNTRY 1846

LOUISIANA PURCHASE 1803

CANADA

MEXICAN CESSION 1848

UNITED STATES IN 1783

PACIFIC OCEAN

GADSDEN PURCHASE 1853

TEXAS ANNEXATION 1845

ATLANTIC OCEAN

ALASKA 1867

MEXICO

CANADA

1810–1813–1819 FLORIDA

Gulf of Mexico

0   400 miles
0   400 kilometers

PACIFIC OCEAN

HAWAII 1898

0   200 miles
0   200 kilometers

EXPANSION OF THE UNITED STATES

Present state boundaries

0   200   400 miles
0   200   400   600 kilometers

Notice how the nation grew in less than 100 years from independence.

South America. They took covered wagons across dangerous trails. The most important thing in life was getting to California. Why do you think so many people wanted to come to California?

That question can be answered in one word: "Gold!" In January 1848, James Marshall was working at a sawmill near Sacramento for his boss, John Sutter. Suddenly something caught his eye. It had glittered in the small stream beneath his feet. He picked up the small lump. It felt heavy. Could it be gold?

It was gold! Marshall told John Sutter and the two agreed it should be kept secret. But the word got out and spread

rapidly. "Gold! Gold at Sutter's Mill!" The words were whispered and repeated over and over. Soon there was a report in the newspaper.

People caught gold fever. It seemed as though the entire world wanted to come to California and "get rich quick." People on their way to Oregon turned to California instead. People traveled overland by wagon train. Some made long ocean voyages around South America or cut through the jungles of Panama. States back East lost hundreds of citizens to the gold rush. Word spread throughout the world. South Americans, Australians, Chinese, and Europeans all hurried to California.

"Clementine" (*Silver Burdett Music 5*, p. 185; Record 9)   **157**

Gold by the wheelbarrowful in California! You could kick it around! Instant wealth just by bending over and picking it up! This was not true, but the thought of gold made people willing to believe anything. Thousands of miners followed a tale of a lake that had a gold bottom. The slightest rumor of a new discovery caused people to move. And enough people were getting rich to keep the dreams alive.

Perhaps the surest way to get rich was to sell supplies to the miners. Hundreds became wealthy by charging high prices for their goods. Flour was $40.00 a barrel. Picks and shovels were $10.00 each. Tin pans for gold washing were $30.00. So were butcher knives. Eggs were $10.00 a dozen. This **inflation**, or rise in prices, was caused by the large amounts of money and small amounts of goods available on which to spend it.

California becomes a state   California was a rough place to be during the early years of the gold rush. There was little law and order. There was an urgent need for government. In 1850 Californians elected a governor. They chose a legislature to make laws. Later in 1850, California became the thirty-first state.

The excitement over gold died down in a few years. But California has not stopped growing. Today more people live in California than in any other state.

CHECKUP

1. How did Portolá, Serra, and Marshall each contribute to the development of California?
2. What was the Bear Flag Republic?
3. What is inflation?
4. When did California become a state?

158

The Oregon Trail

> VOCABULARY
> **Oregon Trail**
> **mountain men**
> **pioneer**

Oregon fever   The Southwest was not the only place of growth and activity in the 1840s. People from all over the East caught "Oregon fever." They had heard reports of the beautiful land and plentiful game found in the Oregon Country. The **Oregon Trail** was made up of hopes and dreams of men and women who wanted to start new lives in Oregon. With everything they owned in covered wagons, people took on the challenges and dangers of the rugged 2,000-mile (3,200 km) journey west. "Oregon or bust" was the slogan of the day. Thousands came to Oregon. Many died trying.

What are the clothes made of? Why did mountain men wear clothing made of animal skins?
Jim Beckwourth spent his later years running a ranch and trading post near the mountain pass he discovered.

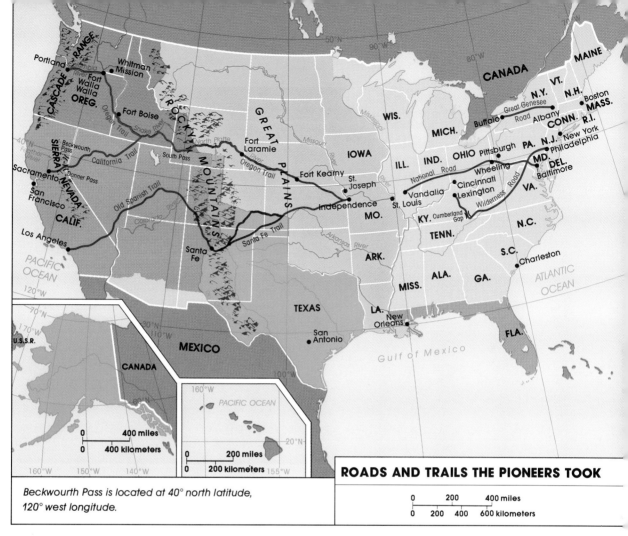

Beckwourth Pass is located at 40° north latitude, 120° west longitude.

	200	400 miles
0	200 400	600 kilometers

Mountain men What kind of people went to Oregon? First there were the **mountain men.** These men went west to get beaver fur. In the nineteenth century, men's hats were made of beaver fur and so there was much demand for it. Mountain men had to be rough and tough in order to survive. They had to go deep into the mountains to trap the animals. Most mountain men got along well with the Native Americans. Kit Carson spent part of his life as a mountain man. Another famous mountain man was Jim Beckwourth. Beckwourth found and explored the pass through the Sierra Nevadas. Find this pass on the map on this page. Because they came to know the land so well, the mountain men served as guides for the pioneers headed to Oregon.

Pioneers Several trading posts were started. Mountain men used them to get supplies. Indians traded furs for manufactured goods such as blankets and iron pots. American churches soon sent missionaries to the area. One such missionary, Narcissa Whitman, was the first white woman from the East to settle west of the Rockies. She came as a young bride in 1836 along with her husband, Dr. Marcus Whitman.

The courage of the **pioneers** who followed the mountain men and the missionaries to Oregon is remarkable. Dis-

Rules of the Road

Why do Americans drive on the right side of the road? The reason is the Conestoga wagon.

These wagons were used to carry goods on the early roads. They were sturdy. Teams of four to six oxen or horses pulled them. The people who drove the wagons rode what was called the left wheelhorse. This was the animal closest to the wagon on the left side. In order to have a clear view of what was ahead, the driver would keep the animals and wagon to the right side of the road or the trail.

The Conestoga wagons were used to carry people and their household goods to the West. Driving on the right side of the road became a habit. Eventually it became the law throughout the United States.

Conestoga wagons were first manufactured in Conestoga, Pennsylvania. They were higher in the front and back so that goods would not roll out when traveling up or down hill. Heavier wagons built to haul freight were often called prairie schooners.

ease, starvation, flooding streams, or deserts with no water were some of the problems they faced. Not wishing to see their land taken, Native Americans constantly threatened attack. Still, between 1841 and 1845 about 5,000 people made the trip to the Oregon Country.

John Sager The story of John Sager shows the courage and determination of the people who went to Oregon. Thirteen-year-old John joined a wagon train to Oregon in the summer of 1844 with his parents, younger brother, and five younger sisters. Sager's father had the dream of helping settle the Oregon Country for the United States. Sadly, both parents died when they were about 500 miles (800 km) from where they wanted to settle. Kit Carson helped the children for a time before he went back east to lead another wagon train. When other members of young Sager's wagon train decided to go to California rather than to Oregon, John decided to take the family to Oregon. He wanted to fulfill his father's dream.

Of course, the adults would not have let him take small children and a baby through dangerous territory. So he left a note saying he had gone back east with Kit Carson. Then he set out for Oregon.

Travel was difficult. The rugged country was very hot during the day and cold at night. After traveling 300 miles (480 km) in several weeks, the Sagers straggled into Fort Boise in Idaho. Their clothes were ragged. They were dirty and hungry and the baby was very sick. Yet when John found that he could get no help for the

Possible topics for extra-credit reports: John Jacob Astor, Hudson Bay Company, Jedediah Smith, Kit Carson; Jim Beckwourth, the Whitmans.

The beauty and richness of the land drew the pioneers to Oregon.

baby here, he decided they would leave again the next day. He was told there would be help at the Whitman mission, 200 miles (320 km) away. Fresh horses and Native American guides were sent along to help them.

Within a few days the guides left with the horses, leaving John and the children alone. The strain on John was terrible. The children often said they would go no farther. John yelled at them and did everything he could to keep them moving toward the Oregon dream.

Getting through the mountains was hard. The oldest sister had broken her leg. This made travel slower. They kept on. Oregon! The oxen were starving and had to be left behind. They kept on. Ore-gon! Feet were nearly frozen, sores went unhealed, hunger was constant. They kept on. Oregon!

Then, finally, after weeks of struggle, a beautiful sight—Oregon! The Whitman mission! Narcissa Whitman took the baby and began caring for her. Dr. Whitman helped the other children. They were invited to stay. Their father's dream came true. They were in Oregon together!

CHECKUP

1. What is meant by the phrases "Oregon fever" and "Oregon or bust"?
2. What three groups of people went to Oregon?
3. Choose three words that describe John Sager. Explain why you chose those words.

161

8/CHAPTER REVIEW

KEY FACTS

1. Due to the development of roads, canals, steamboats, and railroads, transportation became faster and cheaper in the early 1800s.

2. America was changing in the early 1800s due to the rise of industry, new inventions, and immigration to this country.

3. Between 1845 and 1853 America gained a great deal of land in the Southwest from Mexico.

4. Mexican Americans have made and are making great contributions to the United States.

5. Hoping for a better life, pioneers flocked to Oregon in the 1840s.

6. The discovery of gold in California in 1848 caused thousands of people from all over the world to rush to that area in hopes of getting rich quick.

VOCABULARY

On a separate sheet of paper write **T** if the statement is true and **F** if it is false.

T **1.** Many of our clothes are made of textiles.

T **2.** The Lone Star Republic is the first name given to Texas.

F **3.** The Industrial Revolution is a name for a time when a lot of factory workers fought each other.

F **4.** Inflation occurs when prices go down.

T **5.** Many people followed the Oregon Trail west to California and Oregon.

T **6.** A type of road you have to pay money to use is called a turnpike.

T **7.** Someone who comes from one country to live in another country is an immigrant.

F **8.** On the telegraph you can talk to another person.

T **9.** Architecture is the style of a building.

F **10.** Jim Beckwourth and Kit Carson were pioneers in the Oregon Country.

REVIEW QUESTIONS

1. Of all the changes and improvements in transportation in the early 1800s, which do you think was the most important? Explain.

2. How did the Industrial Revolution and changes in transportation help each other?

3. Name at least three events that led up to Texas becoming independent in 1836.

4. What territory did the United States gain as a result of the 1848 war with Mexico?

ACTIVITIES

1. The following headlines could have been found in newspapers of the 1800s. Arrange them in the order in which they happened. Write a brief news story about each one.

PIONEERS CATCH "OREGON FEVER"

HORSE FASTER THAN LOCOMOTIVE!

TEXANS WIN AT SAN JACINTO: "REMEMBER THE ALAMO!" THEY CRY

ERIE CANAL OPENED

GOLD IN CALIFORNIA: GET RICH QUICK

2. Debate with another pupil on one of the following topics or one of your own:

a. Railroads were more important than canals to the growth of our country.

b. The United States got land from Mexico in a proper way.

c. The steel plow was a more helpful invention than the telegraph.

d. Immigrants to the United States have helped the country grow.

8/SKILLS DEVELOPMENT

READING FOR SEQUENCE

Read the following story carefully. Notice especially in what order (sequence) events happened.

Gold!

The discovery of gold in California started the most famous gold rush in American history. So many people came for gold that California became a state within a year. But the California gold rush was not the first in America. About 20 years earlier Georgia had the first gold rush in the history of our country. Even before that, the Spanish had searched hungrily for gold in areas that were to become the United States.

Nor was California the last gold rush. Ten years later thousands of people flocked to Colorado to "get rich quick." Just before the close of the nineteenth century, Alaska had a large gold rush. Still today, whenever the price of gold rises, many people can be found panning for gold in the streams of many of these western areas. They even find tiny amounts once in a while. The dream of sudden wealth has not died.

Place the following statements in the order in which they happened. Write on a separate sheet of paper.

1. California becomes a state.
2. There is a gold rush in Georgia.
3. The Spanish searched for gold.
4. Gold is discovered in Alaska.
5. There is a gold rush in California.
6. People look for gold in Colorado.

Copy the time line on this page. There are six markers on the time line. The first has been filled out for you. Put the items from your list on the time line in the correct order. You may, if you wish, use a history book and an encyclopedia to find dates for these events and add them in the proper places on the time line.

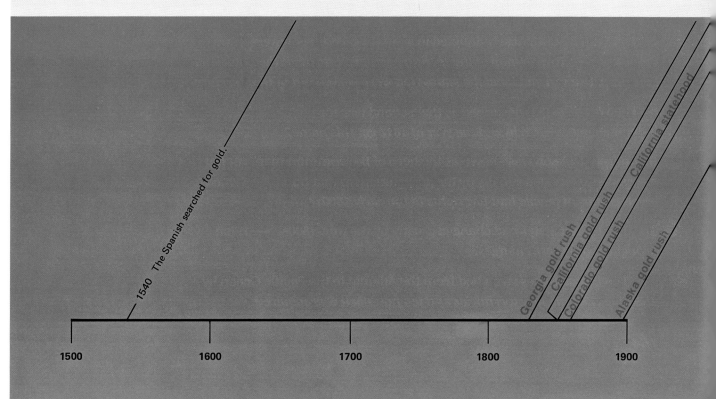

3/UNIT REVIEW

1. The American Revolution was fought because the colonists felt they had lost their rights as British subjects. — *What does the phrase "No taxation without representation" mean?*

2. The Declaration of Independence states ideas of freedom and equality and provides reasons for fighting the Revolution. — *Name the four major parts of the Declaration of Independence.*

3. Americans won the Revolutionary War because of outstanding leadership, help from people in foreign countries, and the strength of the American people. — *Make a chart labeled "Heroes of the American Revolution." Include leaders, foreign helpers, and the ordinary men and women who became heroes.*

4. The Constitution of the United States makes our government a republic divided into three branches on the federal level. — *Make a chart showing the three branches and how each is a separate part of the power of the government.*

5. The Bill of Rights protects our basic freedoms as Americans. — *Which one of these first ten amendments to the Constitution would you least like to give up or do without. Explain your answer.*

6. The presidency has grown enormously since George Washington became our first President. — *Make a scrapbook of newspaper and magazine articles that tell about the work done by the President and staff during a week.* For extra credit

7. The United States nearly doubled in size while Thomas Jefferson was President. — *Draw a map of the territory acquired through the Louisiana Purchase. Draw in and label the states that were carved out of that territory.*

8. The War of 1812 is described as the "second war for independence." — *Why did the War of 1812 get this name?*

9. Andrew Jackson was known as the hero of the common man, yet not everyone was treated equally by the government at that time. — *Which three groups of people had few rights in the early 1800s?*

10. The United States had changed greatly by the mid-1800s. — *What brought about these changes?*

11. The United States stretched from the Atlantic to the Pacific Ocean by 1850. — *List the new territories and tell how each was acquired.*

The United States Comes of Age

Jefferson Davis

Abraham Lincoln

Chief Joseph

Immigrant

9 A Nation Divides and Reunites

Slavery

VOCABULARY

free state   sectionalism

Underground secede
 Railroad

Differences In the early 1800s differences arose among three sections of the United States: the Northeast, Southeast, and West. These three sections had developed in different ways. In all three, farming was the chief means of making a living. But in the Northeast, farms were smaller, factories and trade were important, and those in business were the leading citizens. In the Southeast, farms were larger. Cotton, tobacco, and sugar were the main crops. The leading citizens were the great planters who owned 100 or more slaves. The West had large farms that grew corn and wheat, but milling, meat-packing, and other industries were growing more important.

The sections disagreed on what was best for the country, but for a long time, found ways to settle their arguments. No one section could control Congress. Until the 1840s, West and Southeast generally worked together as people in the West shipped their goods to market down the Mississippi River. From the 1840s onward, West and Northeast tended to unite as canals and railroads linked them in trade and travel. (See map on page 148.)

Slavery The most troublesome issue among the sections was slavery. Originally all 13 American colonies had slavery. After the War for Independence, slavery slowly came to an end in the Northern states where slave labor, as part of the work force, was not important. These became known as **free states.** Slavery was needed in the South, where slaves were a main part of the work force. They were one third of the population. Slaves were owned for life by their masters. They were forced to work without pay, receiving only food, clothing, and housing.

You read in Chapter 5 about the hardships of slaves. Poor food, poor housing, very hard work, and often cruelty were all part of a slave's life. Slaves were able to bear these hardships because of the strong support they gave each other. Many slaveowners tried to break up slave families to make it easier to control slaves. But the strong family ties blacks had when they were free in Africa carried over in the United States. The love and care that slave parents, children, brothers, sisters, and other relatives showed toward each other helped them pull through a rough time.

There were approximately 6 million Southern whites in 1850. Fewer than 350,000 were slave owners. The census that year showed 37,662 white Southerners who owned 20 or more slaves.

One of the most important battles of the Civil War was the one fought at Gettysburg. The battle lasted 3 days. This painting shows a moment during the third day.

166 By 1860 the population of the Western region of the country—states such as Iowa, Michigan, Minnesota, Ohio, Indiana, and Illinois—was over 8 million. This nearly equaled the population of each of the other sections. The alignment of the Northern and Western sections was not seen as a good sign by the South.

Resistance grows   Many slaves fought against slavery. Some fought openly, even though that meant almost certain death. This was the punishment set by law for any slave who raised a hand against a master.

Others fought back in milder but safer ways. They broke their tools on purpose but said it was an accident. Slaves pretended not to know the difference and cut down crops and left weeds standing. They dropped sand or stones into machinery to break it. They set fire to haystacks, barns, and crops in the fields. Some slaves did as little work as possible, slowing down whenever the master or his helpers turned their backs.

Slaves also ran away. Some hid nearby while fellow slaves sneaked food to them. After some weeks, such runaways often were caught or gave up. Their punish-

ment was a severe whipping. Some runaways tried to escape to freedom in the North. They would travel along side roads by night and hide during the day from slave patrols and slave catchers.

There were also revolts in which people were killed. Probably the best known of these was the revolt led by Nat Turner in 1831. He was a slave in Virginia. Before the revolt was finished, over 160 people, white and black, had died. Turner himself was captured, tried, and hanged.

The abolitionists   In 1831, William Lloyd Garrison, editor of a new Boston newspaper, *The Liberator,* called for ending, or abolishing, slavery at once. People who supported this idea called themselves abolitionists. Abolitionists held large meetings to win support for their cause. They sent papers to the South say-

Garrison ceased publication of *The Liberator* in 1865 convinced that with emancipation and the restoration of the Union, black people needed no more help.

In what year did the Civil War begin? In what year did it end?

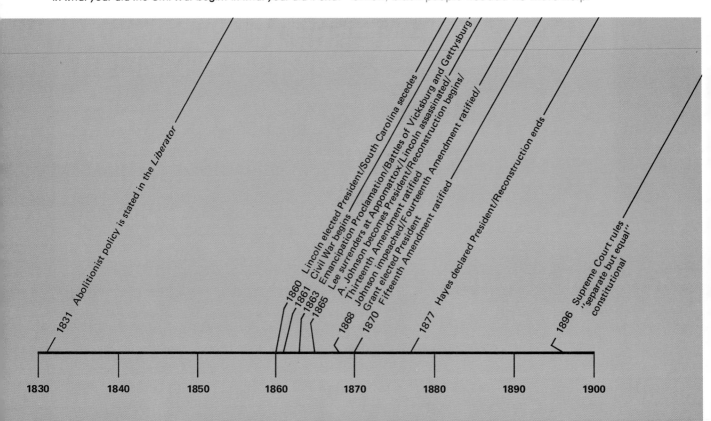

1831 Abolitionist policy is stated in the *Liberator*

1860 Lincoln elected President/South Carolina secedes
1861 Civil War begins
1863 Emancipation Proclamation/Battles of Vicksburg and Gettysburg
1865 Lee surrenders at Appomattox/Lincoln assassinated/A. Johnson becomes President/Reconstruction begins/Thirteenth Amendment ratified
1868 Johnson impeached/Fourteenth Amendment ratified
1870 Grant elected President
Fifteenth Amendment ratified
1877 Hayes declared President/Reconstruction ends
1896 Supreme Court rules "separate but equal" constitutional

1830   1840   1850   1860   1870   1880   1890   1900

ing that slavery was evil. They asked Congress to do away with slavery, without payment to owners.

Many of the leading abolitionists were whites, like Garrison or the Grimke sisters, about whom you read in Chapter 7. Free blacks and runaway slaves also joined the movement. They were active as officers, speakers, and givers of money. Blacks were free if their parents were free, or if their masters set them free. Sometimes relatives and friends bought their freedom. In 1860 about 8 to 10 percent of blacks living in the United States were free. There were more free blacks living in the South than in the North.

Frederick Douglass was the most famous black abolitionist. He was born a slave on a large plantation in Maryland. He was taught to read and write by the wife of his owner. He said that the slave who frees his or her mind by learning to read and to think as a free person is no longer a slave even though still in chains. Douglass escaped to the North. He was skilled in shipbuilding but had a hard time finding a job. He started to speak before small groups about his life as a slave. In time he became an outstanding speaker at large abolitionist meetings. Douglass was a major leader of blacks in the United States from the late 1840s to his death in 1895.

Liberia   Not everyone who wanted to see an end to slavery thought that was something that should happen all at once. Some groups, such as the Quakers, put forth other plans. Some of these plans called for ending slavery slowly and paying the owners for the freed slaves. The freed blacks would then be sent back to Africa to live in colonies of their own.

The American Colonization Society was started in 1822. Over 12,000 blacks were returned to Africa by this group. The colony was called Liberia (for liberty) and the capital, Monrovia, was named in honor of President James Monroe. Liberia became an independent country in 1847. Find Liberia on the map of Africa on page 475.

Underground Railroad   Many slaves escaped on the **Underground Railroad.** On this railroad, a "conductor" was a person guiding slaves, called "passengers," who were escaping from the South to the North. This "train" traveled only at night. The slaves hid in "stations," which were homes and barns, during the day. The "tracks" were the routes followed to the North. The "terminals" were Northern cities, such as Cincinnati or Philadelphia. Here abolitionists helped slave passengers get jobs and start living as free people. Some slaves went even farther north. They left the United States to settle in Canada. Some of them returned after the start of the Civil War. The Underground Railroad was most active in the years between 1830 and 1860. There are no records of how many slaves were helped to escape to freedom during this time.

Harriet Tubman, a conductor on the railroad, was one of the bravest women in American history. She was an escaped slave who returned to the South 19 times to lead 300 slaves to freedom. Rewards of more than $40,000 were posted for her capture, dead or alive. She boasted that she never lost a passenger and that her

After the passage of the Fugitive Slave Law, which was part of the Compromise of 1850, many slaves chose to escape to Canada. They could no longer be assured of remaining free even in the non-slave states. **169**

These slaves have come closer to freedom as they reach an Indiana station on the Underground Railroad.

Ask: Can you imagine what this slave family is feeling? What would it be like to be a conductor? To run a station?

train never jumped the tracks. She never let a slave who got tired on the long and dangerous journey turn back.

Abraham Lincoln   Slavery was ended by a man who did not like slavery but who opposed the abolitionists, Abraham Lincoln. He was born in the slave state of Kentucky. His family was poor. They did not have either the money or the wish to buy a slave. When he was 8, the family moved across the Ohio River to the state of Indiana, later settling in Illinois. Neither of these was a slave state. Lincoln had less than a year of formal schooling. He read every book he could borrow. He read and reread the family Bible. On trips carrying goods down the Mississippi River to New

Orleans, he saw slavery. He did not like what he saw. He said slavery was a "monstrous injustice."

Lincoln became known for his honesty and wit. He was a good speaker. He served four terms in the Illinois state legislature. Meanwhile, he studied law books and became a lawyer in the state capital, Springfield. He later served one term in the United States House of Representatives. Lincoln felt that while slavery was wrong, the government did not have the right to stop slavery where it already existed. What the government could do, and should do, according to Lincoln, was to stop slavery in the territories. When these areas became states, they would be free states. There would be no slavery.

170

Abraham Lincoln became President of a divided nation.

Election of 1860 At the start of this chapter you read about **sectionalism**, how the country was divided into three main areas. The election of 1860 shows that by that time there were really only two sections. They were the North and the South—those states that were against slavery and those that were for it. The question of slavery was tied to another question as well. Did the government in Washington, D.C., have the right to tell the states what they could or could not do?

In the election of 1860 Lincoln did not win in a single slave state. The candidate who was in favor of slavery throughout the United States did not win in a single free state. This showed how clearly the country was divided.

The states in the deep South would not accept Lincoln as President. His victory was looked upon as an insult and a danger. Before the election, Southerners had said that if Lincoln won they would leave the Union. They would **secede.** Now that Lincoln was elected, they would act on that threat.

CHECKUP

1. How was farming different in the sections of the United States in the early 1800s?
2. In what part of the country did most slaves live?
3. What was the Underground Railroad?
4. What did Lincoln feel should happen to slavery in the territories?

A Civil War

VOCABULARY

blockade	emancipate
proclamation	

Secession South Carolina left the Union the month after Lincoln's election. By February 1861, six more states had seceded. At a meeting in Montgomery, Alabama, they formed the Confederate States of America (C.S.A.) and chose Jefferson Davis of Mississippi as their President. Like Lincoln, Davis had been born in Kentucky, but Davis's family moved to Mississippi, a slave state. He graduated from West Point and later became a wealthy cotton planter. He was also a congressman, secretary of war, and United States senator. He left the Senate when Mississippi seceded.

War began on April 12, 1861. The Confederates attacked Fort Sumter at Charleston, South Carolina. Northerners rushed to fight for the Union. Southerners were

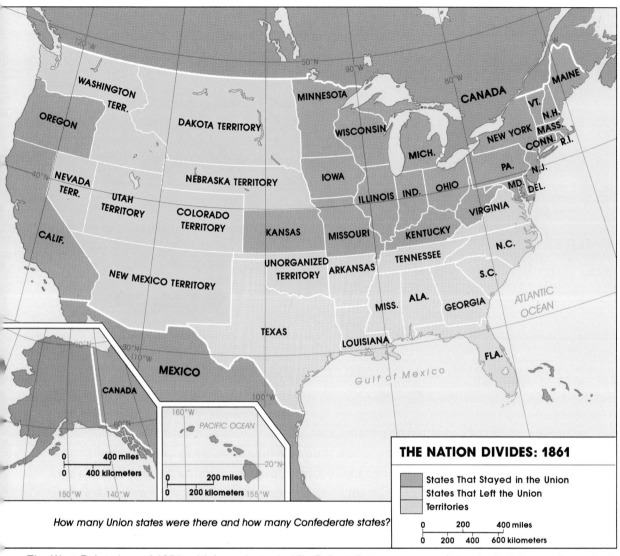

THE NATION DIVIDES: 1861

States That Stayed in the Union
States That Left the Union
Territories

0   200   400 miles
0 200 400 600 kilometers

How many Union states were there and how many Confederate states?

The West Point class of 1854, which graduated while Robert E. Lee was superintendent of the academy, had as its motto "When Our Country Calls." Of these men 23 served as officers in the Union army; 14 with the Confederate.

surprised that Northerners cared enough about keeping the nation together to fight to do so. After Sumter, four more slave states joined the Confederacy, while the other four stayed in the Union. See the map on this page.

Unequal fight? The Union had far more states, people, money, factories, resources, railroads, and ships. The Confederacy did at the start have better generals and more men used to outdoor life.

Southerners graduating from West Point stayed in the army because fewer jobs could be found in the South. When the war began, Southern generals were in charge of five of the nation's six military districts. Also, the Confederacy's 3,500,000 slaves did so much of the work that more of the 5,500,000 whites could fight. The Union had to beat Confederate armies and take over the Confederate states to force them back into the United States. Confederates wanted only to depart from the

Union in peace. They had only to keep the war going until the Union side grew tired of it and stopped fighting, leaving them and their slaves alone. Also, Confederates had an easier time because they were fighting on their own familiar land, while Union troops had to fight on Southern soil.

When the war began, President Lincoln ordered the Union navy to **blockade** or stop shipping from Confederate ports. At first he did not have enough ships. More ships were built and the blockade became more nearly complete. Confederates found it harder and harder to ship their cotton and other goods for sale overseas or to bring in needed supplies.

Two great generals   Robert E. Lee ranked with Lincoln as one of the greatest men of his day. Lee was born into one of America's most famous families. His Father, "Light-Horse Harry" Lee, served with General George Washington. Harry Lee later became governor of Virginia. Other relatives were congressmen, governors, and signers of the Declaration of Independence. Robert E. Lee graduated from West Point and married Martha Washington's granddaughter. He served in the Mexican War, and was a top Union officer when the war began. Lee disliked slavery. He had freed the few slaves he inherited. Lincoln asked him to be field commander of all the Union armies, but he said he could not. Lee went with his state when Virginia seceded. He held minor commands and served as an aide to President Jefferson Davis until June 1, 1862, when he took over one of the Confederate armies. Lee became general-in-

Clara Barton earned the title "Angel of the Battlefield." She went on to become the founder of the American Red Cross.

chief of all the Confederate armies 2 months before the war ended.

The general who led the Union forces to victory was Ulysses S. Grant. He grew up on a farm in Ohio and also graduated from West Point. He became lonely while serving on army posts in the West away from his wife and children. He left the army. When the Civil War began, the Union needed men with West Point training. Grant went back into the army. He soon became one of the best generals in the West.   Ask: What things did Grant and Lee have in common? How were they different?

Early battles   The Confederates won the first big battle of the war. This was at Bull Run in Northern Virginia in July 1861. The Union's army of the Potomac rushed to do battle before the 3-month volunteers who signed up after Sumter returned home. A large crowd came out from Washington to watch. Their picnic mood turned to fear when the Union army, after fighting hard all day, suddenly began to lose. The soldiers ran the 25 miles (40 km) back to Washington, dropping their guns and packs on the way.

Clara Barton fought infection and disease to save the lives of many wounded soldiers.

The battle of Petersburg was actually a siege of the city that lasted for 10 months in 1864–1865. It finally ended in a very costly Union victory.

Have pupils study the picture. They should note the flags of the opposing sides, the men on horseback, the colors of the uniforms, the equipment, etc. You may wish to discuss the feelings aroused by the picture.

They trampled over the people who had come out to see them.

After Bull Run, George B. McClellan became commander of the army of the Potomac. McClellan organized, equipped, and trained his soldiers brilliantly. His men drilled and paraded perfectly, but McClellan was slow to fight. President Lincoln said McClellan had the "slows." He did everything except the most important thing, attack.

McClellan did not obey Lincoln's demands for action for months. President Lincoln was going to replace him when finally he began to move his army south. He planned to capture Richmond, Virginia, the Confederate capital. Find Richmond on the map on page 175. See how close it is to Washington, D.C. For 4 months McClellan moved his army around this part of Virginia, barely avoiding total defeat. He was finally forced to retreat to Washington by General Lee.

Lee's greatest victory against the Union forces came in May 1863, at Chancellorsville, Virginia. The Union general had 130,000 men to Lee's 60,000. Lee's victory was amazing. It gave the Southern troops and their leaders new confidence.

Emancipation Proclamation Blacks tried to join the Union army. They were told "keep out of this, this is a white man's war." President Lincoln said that the war was to "save the union," not to end slavery. After a year he changed his mind: "Things had gone on from bad to worse, until I felt that we must change our tactics, or lose the game. I now determined [decided] upon the adoption of the Emancipation Policy."

The President secretly wrote a **proclamation**, an order, that would **emancipate**, set free, the slaves and let them join the Union army. He believed that black soldiers would help win the war: "Keep

It took three amendments to the Constitution to back up the Emancipation Proclamation. Pupils will learn about them in the following lesson.

[them] and you can save the Union. Throw [them] away and the Union goes also." His Cabinet asked him to wait for a victory before announcing this new policy so that it would not look as if the government needed blacks to save the Union.

Lincoln waited 3 months until a Union army won an important victory. This was the battle of Antietam in September 1862. Lincoln's Emancipation Proclamation of January 1, 1863, declared the slaves in all areas under Confederate control to be "then, thenceforward, and forever free."

Black soldiers   About 180,000 blacks joined the Union army. Forty thousand were free blacks from the North. The rest were Southern blacks, mostly slaves who ran away from their owners. Until mid-1864, blacks were paid less than white Union soldiers. One black regiment took no pay until all were paid equally. One sergeant was tried and shot after he and his men laid down their guns because of unequal pay.

Twenty-one black soldiers and sailors were among the many who won the

THE CIVIL WAR: Some Major Battles

× Battle Sites

0   100   200 miles

0   100   200   300 kilometers

Many of the battles of the Civil War were fought in Virginia.

Medal of Honor for bravery. The first black man to win the medal was Sergeant William Carney of Massachusetts. He was hit by many bullets in the attack on Fort Wagner, Charleston, South Carolina, but kept the flag flying. Blacks made a difference in the last 2 years of the war.

These men are part of a guard detail of a black regiment stationed near Washington, D.C. The regiment fought in the Carolinas later in the war.

The Monitor *and the* Merrimac

In March 1862, the Confederates tried to break the blockade. Sailors on Union ships blocking Virginia's Hampton Roads ports saw a strange looking vessel move boldly toward them. Union guns fired at it but the shells simply bounced off. It was the Confederate ironclad warship, the *Virginia,* better known by its old name, the *Merrimac.* The Confederates had taken the *Merrimac,* an old Union ship, and turned it into an ironclad vessel by putting iron all along its sides. On the front they put extra slabs of metal to make a battering ram. They renamed the ship the C.S.S. *Virginia.*

The *Virginia* steamed to the attack against the wooden ships of the Union navy. Two were destroyed. It seemed that a way had been found to break the blockade.

These hopes were dashed the next day when the *Virginia* returned to the attack. This time the Confederate sailors were surprised to see a strange object in the water. It was a comical sight. It did not look like any ship ever seen. It looked like a box sitting on a raft. It lay flat in the water with guns poking out from a circular turret rising from its center. It was the U.S.S. *Monitor.* The newly built *Monitor* was on

its trial run from the shipyard at New York. It arrived off the Virginia coast just in time to defend the blockade fleet.

The famous duel between the *Monitor* and the *Merrimac* (*Virginia*)—the first in the world between ironclads—lasted all day on March 9, 1862. Neither ship could harm the other, but the *Monitor* stopped the *Virginia* from sinking any more Union ships.

In May, the Confederates sank the *Virginia* to keep the ship from the invading Union army. Later that year, the *Monitor* went down in a storm off Cape Hatteras, North Carolina.

Two important battles The two most important battles of the Civil War were Vicksburg in the West and Gettysburg in the East. They can be called turning points. Victory began to follow the Union armies.

Vicksburg was a Confederate stronghold on the Mississippi River. Find it on the map on page 175. This battle was General Grant's greatest success. His plan was simple. His army would cut off all supplies from Vicksburg. It took 6 weeks before the people in the city and the army gave up. During this time people were so hungry they ate anything, even shoe

leather. Vicksburg surrendered on July 4, 1863.

At nearly the same time—July 1 to 3—but hundreds of miles away, the battle of Gettysburg was taking place. General Lee decided to try again to invade the North, but he failed. Both sides lost many men. Lee returned to Virginia with what was left of his army. He would not try again to invade the North.

The war ends Grant and Lee never fought each other until the last year of the war. Lee was in the East and Grant was in the West. In 1864, however, Grant was put

The battle of Gettysburg is known to many because of the speech President Lincoln gave at the dedication of the cemetery after the battle. You may wish to have your pupils memorize the short, beautifully written, and very eloquent address. See p. 185.

The man who owned the house in which the surrender took place had lived near Manassas. After the second battle of Bull Run, in which his farm was overrun, he moved his family to Appomattox Court House so that the war would not touch them in "this quiet little village."

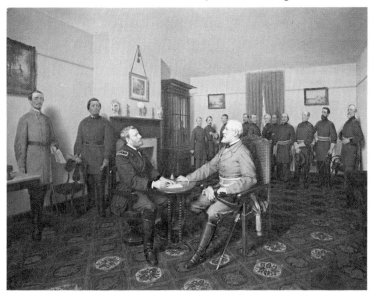

General Grant (left) and General Lee (right) discuss the terms of surrender as they sit in the parlor of a house in the village of Appomattox Court House.

in charge of all the Union armies. Grant's plan to win the war was to attack Lee daily. He would pin him down while other Union forces closed in on Lee from other directions. Many of Grant's men were killed or wounded. In the end, however, Lee was forced to retreat. Lee moved westward. Grant followed, finally catching up with him at Appomattox, Virginia. Lee surrendered on April 9, 1865.

The Civil War ended 4 years after it began. The United States was one nation again. Slavery was about to be ended throughout the land.

CHECKUP

1. How many states were there in the Confederate States of America?
2. Which slave states did not join the Confederacy?
3. At the time of the Civil War, who was President of the United States? Of the Confederate States?
4. Who was the most outstanding Confederate general? Union general?

When Northern troops fired salutes to celebrate the final victory, Grant stopped them because, as he wrote later, "We did not want to exult in their downfall."

Reconstruction

VOCABULARY

Reconstruction	impeachment
Freedmen's Bureau	carpetbagger
	scalawag
refugee	poll tax
sharecropping	grandfather
crop lien	clause

Lincoln dies   Less than a week after the war ended, Abraham Lincoln was dead. He was shot by John Wilkes Booth, an actor. Booth was angry over the South's defeat. When Lincoln died Vice-President Andrew Johnson became President. He was a Democrat, a Southerner, and a former slave-owner. He had been nominated in 1864 to bring wider support for Lincoln and the Republicans in that election.

President Lincoln's leadership was greatly needed during **Reconstruction.** This is the name given to the dozen years after the Civil War, 1865 to 1877. It was during this time that two big questions would have to be answered. Under what conditions would the former Confederate states be given back all their rights and powers? How would real freedom be given to the millions of freed slaves?

After the war   Four years of fighting had left much of the South's railroads, factories, and bridges torn up. Several cities, such as Atlanta, Georgia, and Columbia, South Carolina, had been burned. Many people had been driven from their homes. Some areas had very little food. Others with more than enough had no way to ship food to places in need.

Abraham Lincoln toured Richmond the day after Union troops had the city under control. He sat briefly at Jefferson Davis's desk in the Confederate White House. If you share this anecdote with your pupils, you may wish to ask them what Lincoln could have been thinking about at that moment.

By the end of the war, fire and artillery shells had destroyed most of the city of Richmond, Virginia, which had been the Confederate capital.   37°34'N/77°27'W

Blacks were so eager for education that sometimes whole families would attend the Freedmen's Bureau's schools. There was one school that had four generations of the same family in attendance.

Near the end of the war Congress set up the **Freedmen's Bureau.** It helped the poor and the homeless. It gave food, blankets, and housing to freedmen, persons just set free from slavery, and to **refugees,** whites and blacks who fled from their homes because of the fighting. It also set up schools for black children.

Since the South was mainly a farming region and the soil was not hurt by war, rebuilding would not be hard. All that was needed were seeds, tools, and workers. However, it took money to buy seeds and tools and to pay workers. Confederate money printed during the war was worthless. Freeing the slaves left landowners, especially planters, without their workers. Freed workers, unlike slaves, had to be paid. But landowners had no money to hire anyone. Planters and other large landowners could sell or rent land to the newly freed blacks and to landless whites. These blacks and whites, however, had no money to buy or rent land. After pupils have read "After the war" and "Sharecropping," ask: How would you have solved the problem of getting farming started again?

Sharecropping New ways—**sharecropping** and **crop lien**—were found to solve these problems. In sharecropping, farmers, black and white, paid for the use of the land by giving the owner of the land a part of the crop. It was usually a fourth to a half. Storekeepers sold seeds, tools, supplies, and other needs to landowners and sharecroppers on credit. In return they got a lien, or first claim, on the crop. The storekeepers sold the crops and took what was owed them. Any money left was shared by the landowners and farmers. The Freedmen's Bureau protected blacks who could not

178

read or write from unfair sharecropping and lien agreements.

Some freed blacks tested freedom by wandering and not working. In slavery they had been forced to work all day and could not move about. Most wandering was to find relatives, separated when slaves were sold, or to get back to homeplaces from which they and their masters had fled when battles were fought nearby. Most soon settled down and were ready to work. Many whites, used to free labor from slaves, were not willing, even when they had the money, to pay freed blacks a fair wage. Blacks were unwilling to work for sums so small they could not feed themselves and their families.

Ask: How did these amendments make the Emancipation Proclamation a reality?

Constitutional amendments From 1865 to 1870, three constitutional amendments changed life for blacks. The Thirteenth Amendment, ratified late in 1865, ended all slavery everywhere in the United States. The Fourteenth Amendment made blacks citizens of the United States, equal in rights and status to any other citizen. The Fifteenth Amendment gave blacks everywhere in the United States the right to vote.

Black Codes The South had lost the war, but many Southerners thought that the wishes of the winners, the North, did not matter. The states returning to the Union elected former Confederate generals, congressmen, and cabinet members, as well as the vice-president of the Confederacy, to represent them in the United States Congress. Southern states passed Black Codes. These codes gave freed blacks rights to sue, marry, speak in court, and own property. Other parts of the codes seemed like a return to slavery.

Black youngsters without parents were put under guardians, often their former masters. They would teach the children a trade but also would have full control over them. Black men without jobs were arrested, fined, and jailed. They would have to work a year without wages to repay any employer who paid the fine. When that year ended, the sheriff could start all over again by arresting the man for being without a job.

Johnson and the Radical Republicans The President and Congress could not agree on how to treat the former Confederate states. The leader of the Radical Republicans was Thaddeus Stevens. He was a congressman from Pennsylvania. The Radicals wanted to punish the South. President Johnson wanted to follow Lincoln's plan to let the southern states return "with malice toward none." Ask: What does "with malice toward none" mean?

Congress would not allow the former Confederate leaders to take their seats in the House of Representatives and the Senate. Congress passed laws to protect the rights of blacks and to continue the Freedmen's Bureau. Congress also passed laws that put all the former Confederate states except Tennessee under military rule. To be allowed back into the Union the states had to ratify the Fourteenth Amendment. This was the amendment that made blacks citizens. Tennessee had already ratified this amendment.

When President Johnson tried to block Congress's program, the House of Representatives impeached him. **Impeachment** is saying that an officeholder has done something very wrong. The impeachment charges against the President were not fair. They did show, however, how strong the feelings were against him.

Impeachment   Under the Constitution, the House of Representatives impeaches, but the Senate holds the trial to see if the officeholder is guilty and should be removed from office. There were 54 Senators then. A vote of 36 to 18 was needed to find the President guilty. Thirty-five Senators voted guilty. The other 19 Senators voted not guilty. By the narrow margin of one vote, Johnson stayed in office. He is the only President ever impeached.

Andrew Johnson accepts the notice that the House of Representatives has voted to impeach him and that the Senate will be sitting in judgement of him.

Carpetbaggers and scalawags   **Carpetbaggers** were Northern whites who moved to the South after the war. Most of them were soldiers and officers who had learned during the war that the South had good soil and a pleasant climate. Some were business people who wanted to invest in rebuilding the South. These soldiers, officers, and business people made the South their home. There were other people seeking to make money from the South's troubles. The name *carpetbagger*—given to all Northerners coming South after the Civil War—arose because this last group supposedly entered the South with all their belongings in a carpetbag suitcase.

Scalawags were Southern whites who joined the new state governments that had been set up during Reconstruction. Many Southerners believed that these governments had been forced upon them. The people called scalawags believed that the South would be better off by helping than by fighting these governments. Many scalawags had been respected before, but many lost friends and standing by aiding these governments.

Blacks in office   Most black voters in the South could not read or write. However, most of the blacks they elected to office, especially higher posts, were educated. The two black men elected to the United States Senate, Hiram Revels and Blanche K. Bruce, were born in the South but went to Knox and Oberlin colleges in the North. South Carolina State Supreme Court Justice Jonathan J. Wright was a free black who had graduated from the University of Pennsylvania. Jonathan

Robert Small was a slave who worked as a sailor and pilot on a small Confederate naval vessel called the *Planter*. One night he managed to get his family and the families of other slave crew members on board. He then sailed the ship out of Charleston harbor and surrendered to a Union warship blockading the harbor. Thus the *Planter*

The central figures in this picture are (left to right) Blanche Bruce, Frederick Douglass, and Hiram Revels. Can you tell what part of black history each corner scene shows?

became the first Confederate ship captured during the war. Small joined the Union navy, serving with distinction throughout the war.

Gibbs, who became Florida's state superintendent of education, was a graduate of Dartmouth College. Francis Cardozo, state treasurer and state secretary in his home state of South Carolina, had graduated from the University of Glasgow in Scotland.

There were black lieutenant governors in Louisiana, Mississippi, and South Carolina. P.B.S. Pinchback served 43 days as acting governor of Louisiana when the governor left office a month and half before his term was over.

Twenty blacks served in the United States House of Representatives from 1870 to 1901. One of them, Robert Small of South Carolina, was elected to five terms in Congress. He had been a war hero.

Waste and debt   While Reconstruction governments controlled the South, some state funds were wasted or stolen. Partly as a result of this, the amount of money owed by these states went up greatly. The states were left with debts that took years to pay off.

All the blame for misuse of state funds should not be placed on Reconstruction governments. There was waste and stealing nationwide on all levels of government.

Benefits Some good did result from Reconstruction governments. They began the public school systems in their states. Among these states, only North Carolina already had a sound system of public schools in operation before Reconstruction. Also, these governments had roads, canals, and railroads built. They sold bonds for such projects and for helping businesses, especially from the North, to set up in the South. Bringing in industry improved the South's way of life. It gave farm laborers a chance to work in better-paying factory jobs. In addition, the South became more democratic during the Reconstruction period. More people took part in government than ever before. Up to then, the South had been run by the planters and other people who were rich or successful. The poorer classes, white and black, generally had been left out and had little to say. Under Reconstruction rule, they too had a voice in public affairs.

Building and running school systems also added to the cost of government and state debt. Building more roads, hospitals, state colleges, and mental institutions than ever before to serve the people also added to the cost. Thus much of the rise in state spending and rise in debt was a result of the Reconstruction governments doing more for the people. They did far more than was done before the war, when little attention was paid to the needs of poor people.

Southern reaction Many Southerners could not see any good in the actions of these Reconstruction state governments. They felt that they had not chosen these governments. The federal government in Washington was forcing Reconstruction on them. These Southerners became more and more angry. Sometimes this anger turned to violence.

Secret societies such as the Ku Klux Klan were formed. The Klan started in Tennessee in 1866. Members wore hoods. The Klan was against everyone and everything connected with Reconstruction. They beat and killed blacks. They burned schools and churches. They attacked people who had come to run the Freedmen's Bureaus and to teach in schools. They frightened people to try to keep them from voting or holding office. The Klan grew more violent as the Reconstruction governments grew stronger.

The Klan officially broke up in 1871. Its actions drew so much attention that federal laws were passed. Federal officers began taking steps against it.

The hoods hid the faces of the Klan members so that they could not be identified by their victims. The rest of the costume was supposed to further frighten people.

You may wish to make your pupils aware of the fact that the Klan never disappeared entirely and indeed still exists today in many parts of the country.

1876 election   The 1876 presidential election ended without a clear winner. The Democrat, Governor Samuel Tilden of New York, had 184 of the 185 electoral votes needed to win. The Republican, Governor Rutherford Hayes of Ohio, had only 165 votes. There were 20 other votes that both sides claimed. Of these 20, 19 came from the last three states still under Reconstruction governments, Florida, Louisiana, and South Carolina. A commission set up to settle the argument gave all 20 votes to Hayes. He won 185 to 184. Democrats and Southerners agreed to accept this decision on three conditions: (1) that Hayes put a Southerner in his Cabinet; (2) that federal troops be removed from the South; (3) that Congress give help for building a transcontinental railroad by the southern route (New Orleans to Los Angeles). This agreement is the Compromise of 1877. After Hayes became President in March 1877, he took the federal soldiers out of the South and the last Reconstruction governments fell.

The poll tax, grandfather clause, and similar restrictions have been declared unconstitutional.

Losing what has been won   From 1890 to 1901 Southern states took steps to stop most blacks from voting. All voters had to pay a **poll tax.** Many blacks were too poor. All voters had to take a test to show they could read and understand the state constitution. Often, well-educated blacks were told they had failed while whites with little education were told they passed. The **grandfather clause** let a white who failed the literacy test vote as long as he, his father, or his grandfather had voted before January 1, 1867. Most blacks had not been able to vote before March 1867.

Two black leaders with different points of view on how blacks were to achieve civil rights became prominent at this time. One was Booker T. Washington; the

Blacks also lost the right to use public places, such as trains, streetcars, hotels, theaters, and restaurants, freely. Southern states passed many laws to separate the races in such places. The United States Supreme Court ruled in 1896 that laws ordering "separate but equal" treatment did not take away civil rights given to blacks in the Fourteenth Amendment. However, the separate places were almost never equal. Not until the civil rights movement of the 1950s and 1960s did blacks get back the rights lost between 1890 and 1910.

other was W.E.B. DuBois. Both are excellent subjects for extra-credit reports.

Reconstruction ends   The nation was reunited. The North and South stopped arguing in the 1890s over rights for blacks. The Republicans no longer needed the votes of black Republicans in the South because new western states backed the Republican party. Republicans no longer feared a Democratic party takeover because Southern Democrats supported business interests. The Republicans therefore allowed Southern Democrats to do as they wished in dealing with blacks. A civil war, 1861 – 1865, had made clear that one portion of a country could not pull out and form another country. The 1890s saw an end to much of the bitterness left by that war. The United States of America was firmly one nation indivisible.

CHECKUP

1. What did the Thirteenth Amendment do? The Fourteenth? The Fifteenth?
2. Who was the only President ever impeached?
3. Who were carpetbaggers? Who were scalawags?
4. Name one good thing Reconstruction governments did.

KEY FACTS

1. Slavery was one of the main differences between the South and the rest of the nation.

2. With the election of Abraham Lincoln as President, the Southern states left the Union and formed a new nation.

3. In the Civil War, the Union side was more powerful but the Confederacy started, with better generals, was fighting on its own ground, and merely had to hold on till the North grew tired of the war.

4. The Emancipation Proclamation freed slaves in Confederate areas. After the war the Thirteenth Amendment ended slavery everywhere in the United States.

5. The Fourteenth and Fifteenth Amendments made blacks citizens and gave black men the right to vote.

6. Reconstruction governments wasted some money but also began the public school systems in almost all southern states.

7. Blacks lost many of their rights between 1890 and 1910.

VOCABULARY QUIZ

Choose the word or words from the list that best completes each of the sentences below. Write your answers on a separate sheet of paper.

sharecropping	blockade
Underground Railroad	poll tax
impeachment	scalawags
Reconstruction	carpetbaggers
Freedmen's Bureau	free states
emancipate	crop lien
secede	

1. To free slaves is to __emancipate__ them.

2. Before the 1860s the United States had slave states and __free states__.

3. Eleven southern states decided to __secede__ after the election of 1860.

4. A __blockade__ keeps ships from entering or leaving a port.

5. Many slaves escaped on the __Underground Railroad__.

6. The __Freedmen's Bureau__ was started to help the former slaves.

7. Paying for use of the land by giving the owner of the land part of the crop was known as __sharecropping__.

8. The __poll tax__ and the grandfather clause were used to keep blacks from voting.

9. Northerners who came to the South after the war were called __carpetbaggers__.

10. __Impeachment__ is accusing an officeholder of misconduct and bringing him or her to trial.

REVIEW QUESTIONS

1. What were the main differences between the different parts of the country in the 1830s and 1840s?

2. Compare the Union and Confederate states. What did each have to do to win?

3. How did the Thirteenth, Fourteenth, and Fifteenth Amendments help the freed slaves?

4. Choose three positive acts by Reconstruction governments. Explain your choices.

ACTIVITIES

1. There were many exciting battles during the Civil War. Choose one and write a report describing the battle. You may find it helpful to use maps to show troop movements.

2. Take the role of one of the following: an abolitionist, a southern farmer without slaves, a slaveowner, a free black living in the North, a plantation slave. Pretend it is early 1860 before the election. Write a letter, or a newspaper article, or a speech telling what you feel is going to happen or what should happen.

READING FOR MEANING

People still call President Lincoln's Gettysburg Address one of the best speeches ever given. It was short and simple. People could understand it. Read the speech and find the words listed here. Try to define the words as they seem to be used. Write your answers on a separate sheet of paper. Check your definitions in a dictionary. How close were you to getting the meaning of these words?

score	consecrate
continent	hallow
conceived	advanced
dedicated	devotion
proposition	vain
created	perish
fitting and proper	earth
engaged	

Four score and seven years ago our fathers brought forth, upon this continent, a new nation, conceived in Liberty, and dedicated to the proposition that all men are created equal.

Now we are engaged in a great civil war, testing whether that nation, or any nation, so conceived, and so dedicated, can long endure. We are met here on a great battle-field of that war. We have come to dedicate a portion of it as a final resting place for those who here gave their lives that that nation might live. It is altogether fitting and proper that we should do this.

But in a larger sense we can not dedicate—we can not consecrate—we can not hallow this ground. The brave men, living and dead, who struggled here, have consecrated it far above our poor power to add or detract. The world will little note, nor long remember, what we say here, but can never forget what they did here. It is for us, the living, rather to be dedicated here to the unfinished work which they have, thus far, so nobly carried on. It is rather for us to be here dedicated to the great task remaining before us—that from these honored dead we take increased devotion to that cause for which they here gave the last full measure of devotion—that we here highly resolve that these dead shall not have died in vain; that this nation shall have a new birth of freedom; and that this government of the people, by the people, for the people, shall not perish from the earth.

You may wish to discuss this definition of democracy with your pupils. Ask: Why are these words a good definition of democracy?

10 The Nation Expands

Ask: What does the title tell you about this chapter? In what direction did the nation grow?

Westward Movement

VOCABULARY

survey	land grant
dry farming	homestead
bonanza	recall
open-range	initiative
grazing	referendum

Westward to the mountains　You read in Chapter 8 how brave pioneers have moved westward from the earliest times in our country's history. Daniel Boone, Kit Carson, and Jim Beckwourth led settlers into new areas. The Civil War slowed this movement for a while. But the end of the war saw more and more people, many of them displaced Southerners, moving west. The West was seen as a place where a person could make a new life. The country of the Native Americans and the mountain men was being settled by miners, ranchers, and farmers.

The Great American Desert　Trees were important to the pioneers. Before planting crops, they had forests to cut down. This was hard work. The trees made logs, lumber, and firewood. Trees were used to build forts, houses, and fences. Wood was used to cook meals; and to heat homes. Farmers could easily turn the soft, rich earth because tree roots had kept the soil loose and moist. Tree branches had shaded the soil from the baking sun.

But as pioneers went farther west, especially beyond the Mississippi River, there were fewer trees. Since they did not know how to live without trees, pioneers at first passed by the grassy, treeless prairie and plains. Prairies had grass about 4 to 10 inches high, but the grass on the Great Plains was not so high. The sun-baked soil had a hard crust that a wooden plow could not break through. In 1806, Captain Zebulon Pike explored the plains. He called the region the "Great American Desert." In the 1820s, Major Stephen Long was sent to **survey**, or measure, this area. He said it was "almost wholly unfit for farming." But today this "desert" that stretches from western Iowa to the Rocky Mountains (see map, page 191) is a rich farm region. You will read more about it in Chapter 19.

Learning to live on the Great Plains　The pioneers learned to cope with the prairie and plains. Instead of wooden plows, they used iron plows that could break through the foot or two of grass roots and dried earth to the rich soil beneath. They used substitutes for wood. Wire fences were used in place of wooden fences. Corncobs and grass stalks were used for firewood. Pioneers lived in dugouts, which were cut into the ground or

This Currier & Ives print presents an idealized scene. Have pupils observe the train. The device on the front of the engine is sometimes called a cowcatcher. The baggage car is directly behind

The expansion of the railroads made it easier for people and goods to move West.

the coal car. There are three passenger cars. Ask: What would it have been like to travel on this train?

Even though their sod house was warm in winter and cool in summer, this pioneer family was probably eager to give it up for something more permanent.

then used to build homes. Thick grass was used for the roof.

A hard life Can you imagine how hard it was to live in dugouts and sod houses? When it rained, mud oozed from the walls and dripped from the roof, and the floor became a puddle. Dust was everywhere in dry times. Dirt fell from the roof and walls onto the beds, chairs, tables, dishes, and food. Gophers, snakes, and other creatures burrowed through the walls into the rooms. No wonder some families could not take it and moved back East.

into the sides of small hills. Sod was also used to build houses. Sod is the hard top layer of soil of the prairie and plains. This soil is held together by grass roots and other vegetation. Sod was plowed up in long strips and then sliced into bricks about one foot square. The bricks were set out in the sun to dry and harden and

Dry farming Those who stayed were rewarded when great crops of wheat and corn finally came in. Settlers had to use **dry farming** on the plains because little rain fell. In dry farming, land is plowed in curves rather than straight lines. This holds rainfall until it can soak into the

In what year did the railroads meet at Promontory Point?

1824 Bureau of Indian Affairs established

1859 Gold discovered in Colorado
1862 Homestead Act passed
1867 First big cattle drive from Texas
1869 Women gain voting rights in Wyoming
Territory/Transcontinental railroads join at Promontory Point
1873 Barbed wire invented
1876 Battle of Little Big Horn
1880 Garfield elected President
1881 Arthur becomes President on death of Garfield
1884 Cleveland elected President
1888 Benjamin Harrison elected President
1898 South Dakota allows initiative and referendum

1820   1830   1840   1850   1860   1870   1880   1890   1900

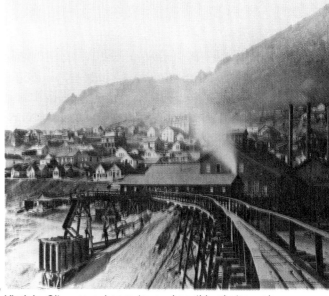

Virginia City is located at 30°19′N/119°39′W, 6,500 ft. (1980 m) in the Sierra Nevadas. It is near Mt. Davidson, the site of the Comstock Lode.

Virginia City was a boom town when this photograph was taken. Today it is a quiet village.

ground. Also, the settlers allowed the land to lie idle every other year to build up moisture. Grain from Europe's steppes, which resembled the Great Plains, replaced the kinds of grain the settlers brought with them from the East, where rainfall was heavier.

The fifty-niners   Many other pioneers pushed onward while farmers were learning to live on the prairie and plains. Leading the way westward were mountain men who trapped fur-bearing animals and traded with Indians for furs. Next to come were miners prospecting for gold. The gold rush of 1849 filled California with people long before the rest of the Far West was settled.

Gold was discovered in Colorado in 1858. The gold rush the next year sent "Fifty-niners" from the East pouring into Colorado, saying "Pikes Peak or Bust." Many went bust.

Bonanzas and boom towns   The biggest mining discovery of all was the Comstock Lode in Nevada. At first prospectors thought it was a gold mine but soon learned it had far more silver. Twelve different **bonanzas**, rich veins of silver ore, were found between 1859 and 1873. The largest vein was the Comstock Lode, the big bonanza of 1873. Virginia City, Nevada, boomed. By 1876 it had 23,000 people, fine homes, an opera house, and theaters. A young reporter who used the name Mark Twain worked for the city's newspaper in the early 1860s.

Good times did not last for the boom towns. When the mines gave out, the towns ran down. This happened to Dead-

wood in South Dakota. The boom town grew with the discovery of gold in the Black Hills in 1874. Among Deadwood's colorful citizens were Calamity Jane and Wild Bill Hickok. They were famous on the frontier. Hickok was killed in a Deadwood saloon. You can visit a cemetery in Deadwood and see his grave. Martha (Calamity) Jane Canary was a native of Missouri who grew up in mining camps and boom towns. She became an expert with a pistol and an excellent horsewoman. She wore men's clothing at a time when women just didn't do that. She settled in Deadwood during the gold rush. A few years later she nursed victims of a smallpox outbreak. Calamity Jane married and moved away but much later returned to Deadwood. She died there in 1903 and is buried near Hickok.

The long drive   The third group that moved west, after the mountain men and miners, were cattle ranchers. To ship their cattle to markets, the ranchers had to get them to a railroad. The nearest rail depot for the ranchers of western Texas was Abilene, Kansas. It was a thousand miles away. Cattle ranchers began walking their herds to Kansas. The first major drive was in 1867. During the next 20 years, some 6,000,000 cattle reached market by the long drive along such trails as the Chisholm Trail to Abilene. Other trails went to Dodge City, Kansas, and St. Louis, Missouri.

The longhorn cattle roamed freely in **open-range grazing**. Each animal was marked by the brand of its owner. In twice-a-year roundups the cattle were driven into corrals. They were separated according to the brands stamped on them. Young calves were given the same brands as their mothers. A calf separated from its mother or whose mother had died was called a stray or maverick. The mavericks were divided up according to how many cattle a rancher had in the roundup. If a rancher owned 15 percent of the cattle, he got 15 percent of the mavericks.

Cowboys   At roundup and long drive times, cowboys lived in the open for days on end. They were far from the ranch bunkhouse. They were fed from the chuck wagon. The wrangler handled their horses. They were led by a tophand, the ranch foreman. The high time of the cowboy was from the 1860s to the 1880s. There were some 40,000 working cowboys at this time; 5,000 of them were black. American cowboys learned a lot from Mexican vaqueros, who were among the world's most skilled cowboys.

The open range ends   When sheep ranchers came west, cattle ranchers fought them. Sheep cropped closely, leaving little grass for cattle. The groups joined to fight off homesteaders, or farmers. The barbed wire fences of the farmers cut up the open range. Also, rapid spread of animal diseases made it necessary to keep herds apart. Many cattle died in the harsh winters from 1885 to 1887. Fewer cowboys were needed.

You may have some pupils who would be able to identify various parts of a cowboy's equipment.

Horse and rider had to be highly skilled to handle the nearly wild cattle during the roundups.

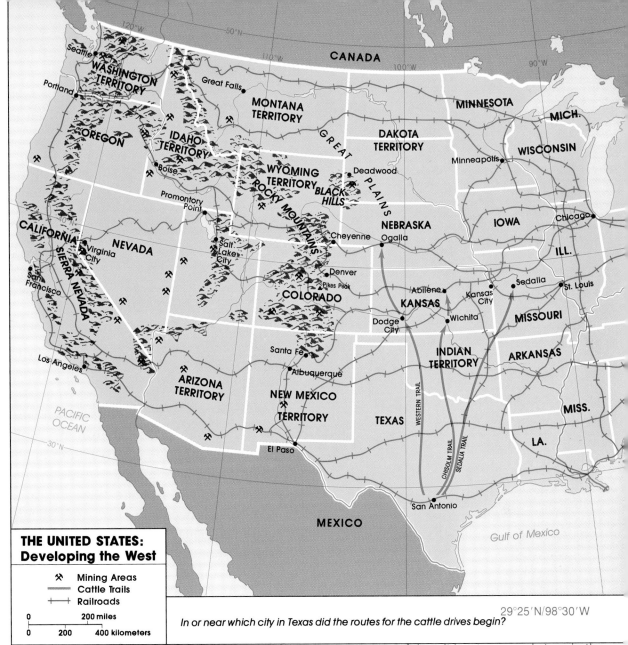

THE UNITED STATES: Developing the West

⚒ Mining Areas
── Cattle Trails
┼──┼ Railroads

0	200 miles
0	200	400 kilometers

29°25′N/98°30′W

In or near which city in Texas did the routes for the cattle drives begin?

Be sure pupils understand that the information on this map covers a span of time. It locates several steps in the development of the West.

Homesteaders The Homestead Act of 1862 helped bring farmers westward. This law gave 160 acres (65 ha) of land free to anyone who settled on the land for 5 years and improved it by planting crops and building a house. The hardships of prairie and plains kept many people from taking full advantage of the plan. Also, the best land was given to railroads and to **land grant** colleges. These were colleges set up in the territories to teach farming.

Moreover, 160 acres (65 ha) was too small an area on which to profitably use the new expensive farm machinery.

Some homesteaders gave up and sold their **homesteads** to land companies. These companies held the land until more people moved to the area. Prices rose enough to make a big profit in selling the land. Some land companies also got homesteads by cheating. A person filing a claim would have to swear that the land

191

WHEN THEY BECAME STATES

State	Year	Order of admission*
Alabama	1819	22
Alaska	1959	49
Arizona	1912	48
Arkansas	1836	25
California	1850	31
Colorado	1876	38
Connecticut	1788	5
Delaware	1787	1
Florida	1845	27
Georgia	1788	4
Hawaii	1959	50
Idaho	1890	43
Illinois	1818	21
Indiana	1816	19
Iowa	1846	29
Kansas	1861	34
Kentucky	1792	15
Louisiana	1812	18
Maine	1820	23
Maryland	1788	7
Massachusetts	1788	6
Michigan	1837	26
Minnesota	1858	32
Mississippi	1817	20
Missouri	1821	24
Montana	1889	41
Nebraska	1867	37
Nevada	1864	36
New Hampshire	1788	9
New Jersey	1787	3
New Mexico	1912	47
New York	1788	11
North Carolina	1789	12
North Dakota	1889	39
Ohio	1803	17
Oklahoma	1907	46
Oregon	1859	33
Pennsylvania	1787	2
Rhode Island	1790	13
South Carolina	1788	8
South Dakota	1889	40
Tennessee	1796	16
Texas	1845	28
Utah	1896	45
Vermont	1791	14
Virginia	1788	10
Washington	1889	42
West Virginia	1863	35
Wisconsin	1848	30
Wyoming	1890	44

*For first 13, year of ratification of the Constitution.

had been improved by putting a house on it. Land companies hired people who took a tiny house on wheels from one plot to another. Each person would lay claim to a number of sites, using a different name each time. The settler could claim that a house had been put on a site and had been slept in. The settler would merely spend one night sleeping in the open with a foot inside the tiny house. Then the claim would be sold to the land company. In the end, only about 14 percent of the land given away free was settled by homesteaders. When homesteaders did settle down and farm, they built fences to protect their crops from the freely roaming cattle and sheep. Cattle trampled down plain wire fences. But barbed wire was invented in 1873. It stopped the cattle from coming through. The end of open-range grazing was in sight.

Homesteading farmers filled the West with enough people to form states. Before 1821, Louisiana was the only state with land west of the Mississippi River to come into the Union. The chart on this page shows the order in which the states entered the Union. How many states were there in 1865? Which state entered the Union 100 years after the signing of the Declaration of Independence? By what year were there 48 states? In what year did the United States reach its present number of states?

Western reforms Westerners often seemed more willing than Easterners to try new ways. Women first gained full voting rights in Wyoming Territory in 1869 and the first three states to let women vote freely were Wyoming in 1890,

In 1790 women in New Jersey could vote. This right was taken away in 1807 when the state revised its voting laws.

This picture, which appeared in a magazine in 1870, showed women in Wyoming voting for the first time.

Colorado in 1893, and Idaho in 1896. The first states with the **recall** were western states. Recall lets voters remove a person from office before that person's term is over. When about 25 percent of the voters sign petitions asking that a person be removed, the office is said to be vacant. A special election is held. South Dakota in 1898 and Oregon in 1902 were the first states with the **initiative** and **referendum.** Initiative allows voters to introduce a bill they would like to see become a law. Referendum allows people to vote on a law instead of leaving it solely to elected representatives.

CHECKUP

1. How were the prairie and the Great Plains different from areas back East? How did metal plows, wire, dugouts, sod houses, and dry farming help settlers in treeless areas?
2. What group of settlers did the Comstock Lode bring to the West?
3. Why did open-range grazing end?
4. Explain recall, initiative, referendum.

The Transcontinental Railroads and the Indian Wars

VOCABULARY

transcontinental	Bureau of
reservation	Indian Affairs

Iron horse The coming of the "Iron Horse"—the name Native Americans gave to railroads—helped destroy the way of life of the Plains Indians. The railroads made it possible for millions of people to move to and fill up the West.

Railroads began operating in the East in the 1830s. They crossed the Appalachian Mountains in the early 1850s, and reached Chicago before 1860. Rail lines from Chicago reached the Mississippi in 1854. The river was bridged 2 years later. Earlier, in 1852, a short rail line began operating on the west side of the river, near St. Louis.

The gold rush filled up California, making it the thirty-first state in 1850. But more than a thousand miles of unsettled country separated California from the nearest states: Texas, Arkansas, Missouri, and Iowa. A rail link was needed to tie California to the rest of the nation.

Federal aid Most eastern railroads were built without federal aid. But the distance to California was so great that business could not build such a railroad unaided. Federal land grants had been given in 1851 to help build an eastern railroad, the Illinois Central, running from Chicago toward the Gulf of Mexico. In 1862, during the Civil War, Congress chartered the first **transcontinental** rail-

193

roads, the Union Pacific. A transcontinental railroad would connect the two sides of the continent—the east or Atlantic coast to the west or Pacific coast. The Union Pacific was to build westward from Omaha, Nebraska, toward Utah to meet the Central Pacific Railroad building eastward from Sacramento, California.

The federal government gave the railroad 1-mile-long (1.6 km) sections of land on alternating sides of the railroad track, running as far back as 10 miles (16 km). Also the government gave the railroad $16,000 for each mile built on level land, $32,000 for each hilly mile, and $48,000 for each mile over mountainous areas.

The golden spike Thousands of Chinese workers built the Central Pacific. Thousands of Irish and blacks worked on the Union Pacific. Many died in the effort. The two roads met at Promontory Point, near Ogden, Utah, on May 10, 1869. Find Promontory Point on the map on page 191. A golden spike was driven into the last rail to signal completion of the first transcontinental railroad. A person could now travel from California to New York on the railroad.

Soon other transcontinental railroads were built. The Atchison, Topeka, & Santa Fe connected Kansas City to Los Angeles in 1881. The Southern Pacific combined

What, do you think, were the feelings of the people who took part in or watched the ceremony when the golden spike was driven to join the two sets of tracks? Promontory Point is at 41° north latitude and 112° west longitude.

41°37'N/112°35'W

Have pupils observe similarities between the parts of the engines in this photo and the one in the picture on p. 187.

with the Texas Pacific in 1882 to provide a line from New Orleans to Los Angeles. The Northern Pacific, completed in 1883, connected Duluth, Minnesota, with Portland, Oregon. The Great Northern ran from Minneapolis – St. Paul, Minnesota, to Seattle, Washington, when it was completed in 1893.

Taming the West The transcontinental railroads finished the conquest of the West. Both coasts, Atlantic and Pacific, were tied firmly together. Railroads brought more settlers to the West. Pioneers had learned new ways to cope with prairie and plains. They were turning what some thought to be a desert into rich farming and grazing country. Unfortunately, the rights of Native Americans to the land were trampled on. Backed by the armed might and power of the United States, settlers ignored the claims of the Native Americans as first occupants of the land.

Two views of the land The settlers moving westward suffered many hardships. They were willing to leave behind the life they knew because there was hope of beginning a better life in the West. That better life included owning land. Each family looked forward to having its own place to settle after the long trip west.

Native Americans looked at the land and all of nature as gifts to be shared. The land was to be cared for and treated with respect. Land belonged to the whole tribe. Crops were used for the good of all. Land was not divided up into farms and ranches for the sole ownership and use of

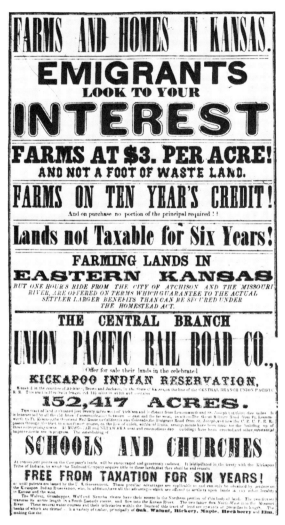

Immigrants, city people, and farmers were all drawn to the West by promises such as those on this poster.

the family that claimed or bought it. Animals were hunted for food and skins, not just for sport.

These two views about the land led to trouble between the settlers moving westward and the Native Americans already living in the West. Each group believed its view of the land was right. Each group expected the government to protect its rights to the land. There were many attempts to settle the differences between the settlers and Native Americans peacefully. Many of these attempts failed.

The land is taken   A famous writer, Helen Hunt Jackson, wrote a book in 1887 about relations with the Indians and titled it *A Century of Dishonor.*

Before the Civil War, most of the tribes living east of the Mississippi River had been driven off their land. They had been sent to live on territory set aside for them in the West. This new land was to be theirs, "as long as the rivers shall run and the grass shall grow." That promise was not kept. Instead, as waves of settlers pushed westward in search of furs, gold, grazing ground, and farms, this new land was also taken from them.

Broken promises   In many treaties the Native Americans were promised supplies and other help for giving up their land. Very little was ever delivered. In many treaties they were promised protection on the lands left to them. Yet settlers kept moving into the new tribal lands set aside for Native Americans.

Some tribes were simply cheated out of their land. Sometimes they were not told what the treaty they signed really said. Sometimes the terms and boundaries were changed after the treaty was agreed to and signed. In other cases, when the real chiefs refused to sell tribal lands, minor chiefs with no power to bargain for the whole tribe would be forced or bribed to sell the land.

Warfare   Some tribes of Native Americans were gentle people who greeted the settlers warmly and tried hard to stay friendly and peaceful. Other tribes had many fierce warriors eager and ready to fight for the land they claimed as their own. The warfare between the settlers and the Native Americans became bitter and brutal. Both settlers and Native Americans suffered.

In 1870 a peaceful village of Piegan Blackfeet was attacked without warning. Only one United States soldier died, but 174 Piegan were killed, including about 90 women and 50 children. Chief Black Kettle, who escaped an earlier attack, was killed in 1868 in still another massacre, this one led by George A. Custer in Indian Territory (now Oklahoma).

Custer's last stand   Custer was a West Point graduate from Ohio who became the Union Army's youngest general, at the age of 23. After the Civil War, he returned to his permanent rank of captain and later advanced to lieutenant-colonel, commanding the Seventh Cavalry Regiment. Custer had a low opinion of the Native American, describing him as "a savage in every sense of the word; not worse, perhaps, than his white brother would be [if he were] similarly born and bred, but one whose cruel and ferocious nature far exceeds that of any wild beast of the desert." At the battle of Little Bighorn on June 25, 1876, Custer and about 250 of his soldiers were killed by Sioux warriors. They were led by Crazy Horse and Sitting Bull.

A losing cause   Despite some victories such as Little Bighorn, Native Americans were doomed to defeat. The odds against them were too heavy. More and more settlers pushed westward. The pressure for land was too great. As Sitting Bull, the great Sioux chief, said in 1889, "They want

196

Sitting Bull (left) and Chief Joseph (right) were two great leaders of their people. Each fought for freedom, but both died on Indian reservations.

The retreat of Chief Joseph and his people is still taught at West Point as an example of a classic retreat maneuver.

us to give up more of our tribal land. This is not the first time or the last time. They will try to gain possession of the last piece of ground we possess."

"Fight no more forever" Chief Joseph and the Nez Percé learned how without hope they were. A few unimportant chiefs signed a treaty with the United States government in 1863 giving up Nez Percé lands in the Wallowa Valley of Oregon. None of those who signed were among the Nez Percé living in that valley. The major tribal chiefs protested. A government commission agreed that the treaty was false and that the Nez Percé could stay on the land. More settlers crowded westward, looking eagerly at Nez Percé holdings. The decision was turned around. In 1877 the Nez

Percé were ordered to pack up and move to other, poorer lands.

Chief Joseph refused at first, but was put in prison until he gave in. As Nez Percé were preparing to leave, some young braves stole away. They killed four white men in revenge for the murder of some braves. Fearing punishment, the tribe fled. They traveled over 1,200 miles (1930 km) in winter weather in an effort to shake off the pursuing troops led by General Oliver Howard and Colonel Nelson Miles. When they were caught and had to surrender, Chief Joseph said:

I am tired of fighting. Our chiefs are dead . . . . It is cold and we have no blankets. The little children are freezing to death. . . . Hear me, my chiefs. I am tired; my heart is sick and sad. From where the sun now stands, I will fight no more forever.

There were a number of Indian uprisings in the 1880s. The government was afraid that Sitting Bull was going to lead one. Troops were sent to arrest him. He and his son resisted and were shot and killed.

Ely Parker appears in the painting of the surrender at Appomattox on p. 177. He is the Union officer standing next to the fireplace.

The buffalo herds   The tribes living on the Great Plains—such as the Arapaho, Blackfeet, Cheyenne, Comanche, and Sioux—needed the buffalo herds for food, fuel, and skins. But in the course of the building of transcontinental railroads, these bison were destroyed by hunters paid to kill off the great herds of some 13,000,000 bison. Without the buffalo, many tribes became very poor. By 1900 the Native American population had dropped to only a quarter of a million.

The Indian Bureau   Many whites felt that Native Americans were standing in the way of settlers trying to conquer the American wilderness. There were some whites, however, who treated them fairly, honestly, and kindly. One such person was Major Edward Wynkoop. He was a friend of Black Kettle and his band of peaceful Cheyenne.

Wynkoop treated Native Americans decently when he was an army officer. He continued to do so when he became an Indian agent. As an agent he worked for the **Bureau of Indian Affairs**. This was the federal agency given the duties of controlling Native Americans and looking out for their interests. Some agents, like Wynkoop, helped the Native Americans. But many agents cheated them of their supplies and lands. The federal government would pay for blankets, meat, grain, ammunition, and other supplies. The dishonest agents stole most of the best goods, leaving the Indians only a small portion of what they needed.

In 1869 President Ulysses Grant appointed a Native American, Ely Parker, to head the Bureau. Parker was an Iroquois and a civil engineer educated at Rensselaer Polytechnic Institute in New York. He served under General Grant in the war, becoming his military secretary. Parker tried to reform the Indian Bureau and get rid of dishonest agents. He was not successful. He resigned in 1871.

The Dawes Act   Until 1887, the United States dealt with Native Americans as tribes, buying their lands and resettling them on land reserved (set aside) for them. On the **reservation** as off, decisions were made by the elders and chiefs for the whole tribe. Some reformers wanted to change this. They wanted individual Native Americans to own land, make decisions for themselves, and more easily fit into the white American way of doing things. The Dawes Act, passed in 1887, did that. It divided tribal land among the members. They were to become farmers. They would be educated to live like other Americans. After 25 years, United States citizenship was to be granted to Native Americans.

The reformers meant well but the act was more harmful than helpful. Few members of the tribes wanted to farm. Many sold their lands. They lived on the money until it ran out, and then had to depend on federal aid. Because of this, an act postponing citizenship for Native Americans was passed in 1906. It was not until 1924 that Indians were made citizens of the United States. In 1934 the Wheeler-Howard Act returned land ownership to the tribes as a whole. They have done better under this arrangement. The Native American population is building toward a million again.

This is the Pine Ridge (S.D.) Indian Reservation around 1884. Many Sioux were still living in their traditional shelters. However, according to the Indian agent's report in 1880, the building of log houses with dirt roofs and floors was going on. Between 300 and 400 had been built that year. This was seen as a great step forward.

43°02′N/102°33′W

Native Americans on the reservations — being almost completely dependent on the government for food, clothing, and shelter, forced to give up old customs and traditions, not having the freedom to hunt and roam — found life very difficult.

The West changes   The untamed wilderness loved and respected by the Native Americans was taken from them to build western ranches, farms, factories, railroads, dams, and cities. The Native Americans fought for the land. They lost and were forced to live on reservations. New states were formed and added to the Union, completing the 48 mainland states.

To the settlers and the nation this was progress. But Native Americans might wonder about that.

CHECKUP

1. What is a transcontinental railroad? Why was it needed?
2. How and why did the federal government aid in the building of the transcontinental railroads?
3. How did the railroad affect the Native American?

Pine Ridge is near Wounded Knee, S.D. Three hundred Native American men, women, and children were killed here by soldiers in 1890. The story of what led to the events at Wounded Knee is good material for an extra-credit report.

10/CHAPTER REVIEW

KEY FACTS

1. Miners, ranchers, and farmers followed the mountain men to settle the West.

2. Settling the Great Plains was a challenge to the pioneers.

3. The coming of the homesteader and the railroad meant an end to open-range grazing and the long drive.

4. The Native Americans could not stop the westward movement of the settlers.

VOCABULARY QUIZ

On a separate sheet of paper mark each of the following statements **T** if it is true or **F** if it is false. If the statement is false, rewrite it so that the statement is the correct definition for the underlined word.

T **1.** A sod house is built largely of soil cut into bricks.

T **2.** Fifty-niners went West to Colorado looking for bonanzas.

T **3.** Ranchers sent their cattle to market on the long drive.

T **4.** Open-range grazing meant that cattle roamed freely.

F **5.** Homesteader is another name for rancher. *farmer*

F **6.** Recall allows voters to introduce a bill they would like to see become a law. *to remove an official from office before his or her term is over*

T **7.** The transcontinental railroad connected the east and west coasts of the United States.

F **8.** Native Americans believed strongly that land belonged to the person who had paid or fought for it. *to the whole tribe*

T **9.** The Bureau of Indian Affairs was formed to take care of and protect the interests of the Native Americans.

T **10.** A reservation was land set aside for the resettlement of Native Americans.

REVIEW QUESTIONS

1. What changes in the way they lived did the pioneers who settled on the Great Plains have to make?

2. What turned Virginia City, Nevada, into a boom town?

3. What was the high time of the cowboy? About how many working cowboys were there at that time?

4. What did the Homestead Act do?

5. How did a homesteader file a claim?

6. How did federal government help build the transcontinental railroads?

7. How did the Native American and the settler differ in their views on land?

8. What did the federal government do to and for Native Americans?

ACTIVITIES

1. Put yourself in the place of a young person moving West with his or her family around 1870. Keep a diary. Describe what you see and what your life is like as you and your family settle on the Great Plains.

2. Draw a diagram on poster board of how a sod house is constructed. You may have to use an encyclopedia to get more information on the subject.

3. You learned in this chapter how the American cowboy was greatly influenced by the Mexican vaquero. A great many Spanish words were taken over by the cowboys. The word *ranch*, for example, comes from the Spanish word *rancho* meaning camp or small farm. Make a list of all the words you can think of that are connected with cowboys or cowboy life. Look in the dictionary to find how many of these words have Spanish origins.

RECOGNIZING ATTITUDES AND EMOTIONS

You have just finished reading about the relations between the Native Americans and the settlers as the westward movement took place. The two groups had such different attitudes toward the land. They did not agree about how it should be used and who it belonged to. These differing attitudes affected how they felt about each other.

Read each statement below. Some of these statements are exact quotes. Others have been rewritten to make them easier to understand. Decide if the statement is sympathetic or unsympathetic to the attitudes and emotions of the Native American.

On a separate sheet of paper write the numbers of the following statements. Write **S** for sympathetic statement or **U** for unsympathetic statement after each number.

1. They were the first to live on the land we now own. They have been driven from place to place. Many, if not most, of our Indian wars have had the beginnings in broken promises and acts of injustice.

2. The more we can kill this year, the less will have to be killed in the next war. They will all have to be killed or kept on as a type of pauper.

3. "The white man has been the chief obstacle in the way of Indian civilization."

4. It does not make a farmer out of an Indian to give him a piece of land. There are hundreds of thousands of white men who cannot be turned into farmers by any such gift.

5. "I have never in my life seen a good Indian (and I have seen thousands) except when I have seen a dead Indian."

6. The United States should give up the idea of a transcontinental railroad and give the Indian a department in the Cabinet to look out for his rights.

Those statements were made by the following people:
1. President Rutherford B. Hayes
2. William T. Sherman, Civil War General
3. Ely Parker, Bureau of Indian Affairs
4. Congressional Committee on Indian Affairs
5. James M. Cavanaugh, a settler in Montana
6. Wendell Phillips, an abolitionist

HOW WOULD YOU HAVE FELT IN THE 1870s?

Select one of the six statements given above. Pretend you are the person making that statement. Write an essay explaining how you would solve the problem of Native Americans. They wanted to hold their land and continue in their ways. Others wanted to take their land and have the Native American adopt a different way of life.

The Continuing Agricultural Revolution

┌─ VOCABULARY ─────────────────┐
combine	Grange
subsistence	Populist party
farmer	income tax
commercial	secret ballot
farmer	
└──────────────────────────────┘

An economic revolution How do Americans earn their living? What kind of work do they do? We were a nation of farmers during the first three centuries of this country's history. In 1850 most Americans lived on farms. In the 1980s only 4 out of every 100 Americans were living on a farm. Yet the United States today is one of the biggest producers of farm goods in the world. How is it possible for so few farmers to grow so much? This revolution in farming came with the use of machinery and science.

Farm machinery Before the Civil War farmers used more hand labor than machinery. But widespread use of farm machinery such as the reaper you read about in Chapter 8 began in the 1860s. Many farmhands were in the armies during the Civil War. Yet farmers had to grow more than before to feed both the large armies and the citizens at home.

Farm machinery such as threshers, binders, rotary plows, and disc harrows became widely used. Later the combined harvester-thresher, or **combine**, as it is usually called, replaced separate machines such as the reaper, harvester, and thresher. Farm machines, which were first pulled by horses, later were pulled by tractors or became self-powered with gasoline engines.

Science in farming Science helped farmers grow more. As you read in the last chapter, Congress set up land-grant colleges to help farmers. Scientists at these agricultural colleges carried on experiments to find better ways to farm. Teachers at these colleges taught these better methods of farming. Also at this time, Congress set up the Bureau of Agriculture. It became the Department of Agriculture in 1889. It, too, carried out scientific research to improve farming. The department spread this knowledge to farmers.

Farming as a business Before the Civil War, most small farmers in the South and most farmers in the North and West were **subsistence farmers.** They grew enough different crops to take care of the basic needs of the family: food and

A modern tractor can have a 400-horsepower motor. Have pupils try to imagine the machine shown in the top picture drawn by 400 horses. Some of your pupils might like to compute how long it would take the rig in the top picture to do the work that the one in the bottom could do in one day—assuming the machine has a 400-horsepower motor. (Approximately 12 days)

These two pictures show the changes that have taken place in large-scale farming. One gasoline-powered engine can do the work of 33 mules in far less time.

clothing. Since farming was done mainly by hand, a farm family, and sometimes one or two hired laborers, raised many different things on the farm. A farmer might raise potatoes, beans, corn, tomatoes, chickens, hogs, cows, and sheep. The farmer did not have to spend a lot to raise the crops since most of the work was hand or animal labor done with hoes and plows.

Farm machinery forced midwestern grain farmers to become **commercial farmers.** To make best use of the machines they had to buy much more land. To earn the money to pay for the land and machines they had to raise money-making crops. They had to grow just one or two crops. Farmers had to get enough money from these crops to buy all their family and farm needs. They had to depend on markets that were far away.

Most farmers could no longer take their crops to market themselves. They sold to dealers who would ship the farm goods to market and sell them. There was often a big difference between the price the farmers got and the prices the dealers got at the market. Farmers often had to borrow money to buy more land or machines. If prices dropped or the weather was bad, farmers would go deeper into debt. And prices did drop after the Civil War. Farmers grew even more. Prices kept going down. Yet people who bought the loaves of bread were not paying that much less. "Who is making all the money?" the farmers asked. Part of the answer, they felt, was the railroads and the bankers. One or two farmers alone could not fight these big businesses. <u>Farmers would have to organize into large groups.</u>

In what year was the Grange organized?

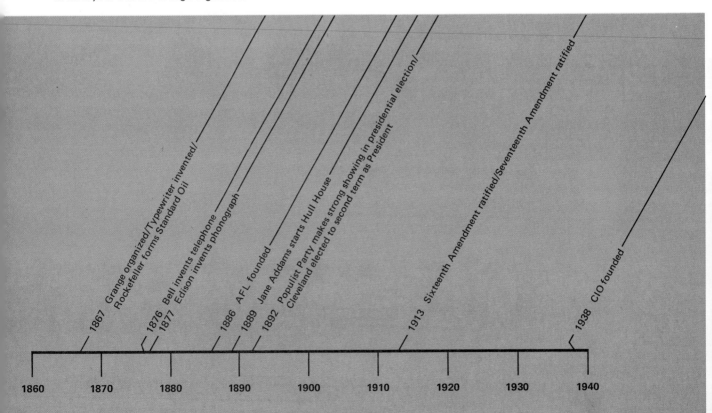

The Grange was both a social and a political group.

Have pupils study the Grange poster. Ask: What kinds of farm animals do you see? (Horses, cattle, sheep)

The Grange   The first major farmers' group was the **Grange.** It was organized to get better farm prices. It was also a way for farm families to get together and enjoy themselves. In time the Grange moved into politics. Grangers were able to get several states to pass laws that controlled the rates that railroads could charge. The Supreme Court said states could not make laws that affected transportation in other states. Such laws would have to be made by Congress and apply to all the states. In 1887 Congress finally passed the Interstate Commerce Act. This helped the farmers.

What tools do you see? (Plow, scythe, spade) What do you think the Grange motto "I Pay for All" means? (Answers will vary.)

The Populist party   There have always been two major parties in politics in the United States. Since 1860 these parties have been the Republican and Democratic parties. Sometimes a third party appears. One of the most important of these third parties was the **Populist party. Populist** means "people." The party was started in 1892. The membership was made up largely of farmers and working people. They felt that the government did not think their problems were very important. They wanted to make the government aware of how they felt.

In the election of 1892 the Populist party suggested a number of changes. These changes seemed very revolutionary at the time. People who were against the Populists said such changes would destroy the American way of life. But as you can see from the following list, these changes did, in time, become law. Populists wanted (1) an **income tax** that would rise as the amount of money a person had rose; (2) election of United States senators directly by the people; (3) the **secret ballot**—so no one could know how a person voted; and (4) a shorter working day for labor. The Constitution had to be changed because of two of these Populist ideas. Read about the Sixteenth and Seventeenth Amendments on page 123. Which Populist ideas became part of the Constitution of the United States?

CHECKUP

1. What is the difference between subsistence and commercial farming?
2. Why did the Civil War help the growth of large-scale farming?
3. Name two Populist party ideas that have become the law.

A Revolution in Industry

VOCABULARY

capital	patent
competition	monopoly
communicate	union

Industry expands   A revolution took place in industry as well as in farming. In the Industrial Revolution, factory machines driven by water power—and, eventually, steam power—replaced handwork, simple machines, and home crafts. As you read in Chapter 8, the revolution began with the textile mills started in New England by Samuel Slater. Other industries grew. The Civil War speeded up the growth of industry. It pushed the United States toward becoming the world's greatest industrial nation.

The United States changed as people moved from farms to cities and from hand labor to factory machines. There was an increase in the output of goods.

Causes of industrial growth   What made these changes possible? The United States was blessed with a large supply of the natural resources needed to become an industrial power, such as coal and iron ore. Americans had the **capital** or saved-up wealth, to invest in developing power machines and factories. There was a labor force on hand to work in industry. Inventions greatly changed ways of doing things. Bold, daring, and sometimes ruthless business leaders put together the resources, capital, labor, and inventions to build the United States into an industrial giant. As a result, the nation grew in ways hardly imagined 100 years earlier.

Steelmaking is one of our most important industries.

Giant industries appeared. These were huge businesses that had nearly all the power and made great fortunes for their owners. One reason for the growth of these companies was the desire to do away with **competition.** There is competition when there are many companies in an industry. Sometimes competition is a waste. It makes more sense to have just a few telephone companies rather than hundreds or thousands of them—all different—scattered across the country. Competition is also good. It keeps prices down. It also forces companies to be efficient. But in the years following the Civil War, a few business giants came to control the major industries. It was not until the beginning of this century that laws began to control the industrial giants.

The story of how Alexander Graham Bell almost lost his patent on the telephone is an exciting one. It would make an interesting extra-credit report.

Inventions The most important changes in American life during the Industrial Revolution came about because of inventions. The typewriter, telephone, electric light, phonograph, radio, and automobile all brought changes in American life during the first 30 years after the Civil War. Some American inventors, like Alexander Graham Bell and Thomas Alva Edison, became world famous for their inventions. Edison is often said to be the greatest inventor who ever lived.

Four inventions greatly speeded up the way we **communicate** with, or make things known to, each other. These were the typewriter in 1868, the telephone in 1876, the linotype for printed matter in 1884, and wireless telegraphy in 1895.

The table on this page lists many American inventors. Imagine what your life would be like without their inventions.

The earliest telephone operators were boys and young men. Men are returning to this occupation today.

IMPORTANT INVENTIONS

Lightning rod (1752)	Benjamin Franklin
First workable steamboat (1787)	John Fitch
Cotton gin (1793)	Eli Whitney
Cast-iron plow (1819)	Jethro Wood
Screw propeller for ships (1826)	John Ericsson
Revolver (1835)	Samuel Colt
Steel plow (1837)	John Deere
Morse code (1840)	Samuel Morse
Sewing machine (1846)	Elias Howe
Refrigeration (1851)	John Gorrie
Safety elevator (1852)	Elisha Otis
Typewriter (1868)	Christopher Sholes Samuel Soulé Carlos Glidden
Railroad air brake (1868)	George Westinghouse
Barbed wire (1873)	Joseph Glidden
Telephone (1876)	Alexander Graham Bell
Submarine (1881)	John Holland
Linotype (1884)	Ottmar Mergenthaler
Shorthand (1888)	John Gregg
Adding machine (1888)	William Burroughs
Machine gun (1890)	John M. Browning
Airplane (1903)	Wright Brothers
Vacuum tube for radio and television (1907)	Lee DeForest
Stoplight (1923)	Garrett Morgan
Computer (1930)	Vannevar Bush
Instant camera (1937)	Edwin Land
Transistor (1947)	John Bardeen Walter Brattain William Shockley

This was a telephone exchange in 1907. Most operators by this time were women.

Two Great Inventors

Two Americans, above many others, certainly deserve the title Genius of Invention. They are Thomas Alva Edison and George Washington Carver.

The pleasure of listening to recorded music is the result of Edison's invention of the phonograph in 1877. This alone would give him a place among the world's great inventors. But he also invented or improved upon the electric light, the mimeograph machine, the stock ticker, the typewriter, and a type of telephone transmitter. Another of his inventions has also brought entertainment to millions. In 1889 he developed the kinetoscope. This machine made pictures seem to move. *The Great Train Robbery,* made in the Edison studio, was the first movie that told a story. Edison held over one thousand **patents.** A patent is a right given by the government to an inventor to be the only one to use, make, or sell his or her invention.

George Washington Carver did not take out patents on his inventions. He wanted as many people as possible to make use of his ideas. Carver made things from plants. He found more than 300 uses for the peanut. Face cream, coffee, shoe polish, and ice cream are only a few of the peanut-based products he developed. He did the same for sweet potatoes and soybeans. His work freed many Southern farmers from having to depend on just one crop. During World War I he invented dehydrated foods. Dehydration takes the water out of food. Eggs, milk, and potatoes in powdered form are easy to ship and to store. Thomas Edison and Henry Ford wanted Carver to work for them. However, he stayed in his laboratory at Tuskegee Institute in Alabama.

Business leaders   Natural resources, capital, workers, and inventions were the base of the Industrial Revolution in the United States. Hard-working business people put them all together to form the giant businesses.

Three men stand out more than any others: Andrew Carnegie in steel; John D. Rockefeller in oil; John P. Morgan in banking.

Andrew Carnegie   Carnegie was born in Scotland in 1835. His family came to the United States when he was a boy. In Scotland they had been very poor. They hoped to find a better life here. Carnegie went to work full time even though he was only 12 years old. During the Civil War he put money into the iron ore business. After the war he became interested in the steel industry. It was here that he made his great fortune.

Carnegie built very up-to-date steel mills. He hired skilled workers. His mills turned out large numbers of steel rails for the growing railroads. Carnegie wanted as little competition as possible. He began to drive other steel mill owners out of business. By 1892, Carnegie ruled a giant steel empire. Less than 10 years later, he de-

Other business leaders were: Hanna and Frich in iron and steel; Hill and Pullman in railroading; Firestone and Goodrich in rubber; Guggenheim in copper; Cooke and Giannini in banking; Field in communications; Armour and Swift in meatpacking; Duke and Reynolds in tobacco; Field and Wanamaker in mer-

cided he had had enough of big business and sold his company to J. P. Morgan. Morgan used the Carnegie Company to put together an even larger steel company. This was the United States Steel Corporation.

Carnegie did feel that his money should be used for the good of the people. He spent the rest of his life giving away much of his fortune.

John D. Rockefeller   Rockefeller was born in western New York but he grew up in Cleveland, Ohio. He worked as a clerk and bookkeeper. He was noted for his careful handling of money. After oil was discovered at Titusville, Pennsylvania, in 1859, Rockefeller entered the oil industry. He joined an inventor who found a better way to refine oil. Rockefeller formed Standard Oil Company in 1867.

Under Rockefeller's leadership, Standard Oil drove out just about all competing firms. By 1877 Rockefeller controlled 95 percent of all the oil refineries in the United States. This was almost a complete **monopoly** (sole control) of the entire oil business in the country. Standard Oil made petroleum products for lighting and heating and for gasoline engines. In 1911, the Supreme Court ordered Standard Oil broken up into different competing companies. Many of today's oil companies were once part of Standard Oil, which by itself is still the nation's leading oil company. It is also one of the largest of all corporations in the world.

In 1911 Rockefeller, who lived to be nearly 98, turned over the business to his son. He devoted much of his billion-dollar fortune to good works.

Andrew Carnegie

John D. Rockefeller

John P. Morgan   J. P. Morgan was born into a wealthy family in Connecticut. His father, Junius S. Morgan, was an American who founded a banking house in London, England. The younger Morgan was educated in Boston, Switzerland, and Germany. After working in his father's bank in London he entered banking and railroad businesses in the United States.

chandising; Westinghouse in appliances; Sinclair and Getty in oil; Chrysler and Durant in automobiles; Du Pont in chemicals; Mellon and Reynolds in aluminum; Watson in business machines; Penny and Ward in retailing.

John Pierpont Morgan

Morgan's firm became one of the leading banking houses in the world. He controlled vast amounts of money. He believed in putting businesses together into larger, more efficient units. He organized many great corporations such as United States Steel, International Harvester, and the Southern Railroad.

Morgan collected great works of art. You can see them today in such places as the Metropolitan Museum and Pierpont Morgan Library in New York City.

Controlling big business Many Americans did not agree with Morgan about combining businesses into giant corporations. They felt that companies competing with each other would offer lower prices, better quality, and better service.

The state and federal governments tried to control business combinations that lessened competition. Congress set up the Interstate Commerce Commission to regulate railroads. This was the first federal law for controlling American business. In 1890 Congress passed the Sherman Antitrust Act. This law was used to break up big businesses that tried to do away with competition.

Labor The giant industries of the United States could not have grown without a large work force. Working conditions usually were not good. People worked long hours. Children often worked the same hours as men and women. There was very little concern about worker safety. Many people were killed in factory or mine accidents. Others were crippled for life. Workers could not do much about these conditions. They lost their jobs if they complained. Many workers felt that they had to act together in groups. Only in this way would they be powerful enough to make the owners of mines and factories listen to them. They would have to form **unions.**

There were many small unions started in the United States. None was really successful. In many cases, the membership was too small to have any power.

In 1886 Samuel Gompers founded the American Federation of Labor (AFL). This union worked for better wages, shorter working hours, and safer working conditions for its members. The members of this union were the skilled craftworkers.

210

This is a Labor Day parade in New York City in 1909. The women in the wagons are members of the International Ladies Garment Workers Union. The average pay for a garment worker at that time was $4.00 for an 80-hour work week.

The Triangle Shirtwaist Co. fire would make an interesting report.

Another important and successful labor union was the Congress of Industrial Organizations (CIO). This group was started in 1938. Most of the members of this union were workers in an industry rather than a craft. They could be unskilled as well as skilled. The CIO drew its members from industries such as the automobile and steel industries. By 1945 there were 6 million members in the CIO. The two groups—the AFL and the CIO— became one large union in 1955. The membership today is about 20 million.

The average worker in the United States today enjoys a high standard of living.

There are strict laws to see that working places are safe and clean. Child labor laws limit the amount of work a child may do. These laws also limit the kind of work children may do. Labor unions and the concern of most Americans for the way poeple live have brought about these changes.

CHECKUP

1. Name one invention and why you think it was important.
2. With what industry or business was each of the following men connected: Andrew Carnegie, John D. Rockefeller, J. P. Morgan?
3. What are the AFL and CIO?

The proper name for the Statue of Liberty is Liberty Enlightening the World. It was a gift from the people of France in 1884; formally dedicated by President Grover Cleveland in 1886. The statue stands 1 inch over 151 feet (46.05 m) high and weighs 450,000 pounds (204,000 kg). It is over 305 feet (92.99 m) from the base of the pedestal to the top of the torch.

Welcome to Our Shores!

┌── VOCABULARY ──────────────┐
│ immigrant   ghetto   │
│ emigrate   quota   │
│ naturalized   │
└────────────────────────────┘

Land of immigrants The United States is a land of **immigrants**—people born in other countries. More people have come here than to any other country. The original 13 colonies were settled mainly by people from England, Ireland, and Scotland.

Fewer than one million immigrants came here in the 50 years from 1790 to 1840. In the next 80 years, more than 35 million immigrants came.

Why they came Most people came because they believed that the United States was a land of opportunity—a land where they and their children would have a new start in life and a good chance to succeed. Those who had come first wrote back to tell of the vast land. They wrote of chances to get ahead or even get rich. What made the United States still more attractive were the bad conditions in their own countries. To live, many had to **emigrate,** to leave their native lands.

American citizens There are two kinds of American citizens. One is native-born. The other is naturalized. The native-born person is born in the United States or to parents who are American citizens. **Naturalized** citizens are people who were born in a foreign country and were citizens of that country. They come to the United States. They give up their foreign citizenship and state that they would like to become American citizens. After 5 years they take an oath of allegiance to the United States and become naturalized citizens. They have nearly all the rights and duties of a native-born citizen.

Ellis Island in New York harbor was the first stop for many immigrants from 1892–1954. It was called The Gateway to the New World.

Except, of course, becoming President or Vice President of the United States.

The Statue of Liberty has been a welcome sign to immigrants since 1886.

Have pupils observe the clothing on the people in this picture. Ask: What time period is shown here? (Late 19th Century)

New citizens are pledging allegiance to the United States.
A person can become a citizen after 5 years' residency in the United States and at least 6 months in the state in which he or she is applying. An alien, married to a U.S. citizen, can apply after 3 years.

Changes in immigration About 17 million immigrants came to the United States from 1840 to 1900. About 18 million more entered between 1900 and 1920.

From 1840 to the 1870s, the great bulk of immigration was from northern and western Europe, from such places as Great Britain, Germany, and Scandinavia. Most of these people settled on farms and homesteads in the western portions of the United States. Many Irish did settle in cities like Boston and New York. Some Germans settled in western cities like Cincinnati, St. Louis, and Milwaukee. More and more people were coming from southern and eastern Europe in the period from 1880 to 1920. Mostly they were from Italy, from Austria-Hungary and other parts of the Austro-Hungarian empire, from Russia and Poland, and from Greece. These new immigrants were lured here to work in factories and mines. Recruiters traveled all over Europe looking for people who would work for low pay in growing American industries.

These immigrants settled in cities for the most part. They tended to settle together in sections of the city where they could live among people from home. This kept their customs and native languages alive. They drew comfort from living near and taking care of one another. Such neighborhoods where people of similar ethnic, racial, or religious backgrounds live are often called **ghettoes.** Large cities like New York and Chicago had large immigrant neighborhoods, or ghettoes.

Closing the door The United States generally welcomed immigrants with open arms. The United States was used to many different people living here from colonial times onward. "Give me your tired, your poor, your huddled masses yearning to breathe free, the wretched refuse of your teeming shore" are the words of welcome in Emma Lazarus's poem inscribed on the Statue of Liberty.

Over 9 million immigrants entered the U.S. in 1905. This was the high point. It fell to less than 2 million in 1935 in the middle of the Depression.

Immigrants have given a great deal to this country. The architect I.M. Pei, born in China, designed this wing of the National Gallery in Washington, D.C.

Some Americans did not feel comfortable with these new immigrants. Their ways of living seemed so foreign and strange. Movements grew to close the doors of the United States and not let people come in as freely as before.

From 1776 when the United States declared independence until 1882, there were no laws dealing with immigration. All could come here to live and work. In 1882 a law stopped Chinese laborers from entering. That year there was also a law that banned criminals. Insane people, very poor people, and those who were sick were also banned. A law in 1917 kept out people who could not read. Under this law, all immigrants 16 years or older had to prove that they could read 30 to 80 everyday words in English or any other language. During the 1920s, immigration was limited still more. Only about 350,000 immigrants a year were allowed into the United States. By 1929 only 150,000 could enter each year. This number was divided among the countries of the world. Each country got a **quota**—a set number of

people who could come to the United States. Immigrants from northern and western Europe were favored. Asians were kept out completely. Later laws changed this. Today there are no longer any restrictions on the countries from which immigrants may come. There are, however, still very strong rules about the number who may enter each year.

CHECKUP

1. What was one reason why many immigrants came to the United States?
2. What is a quota?
3. What are two ways to become an American citizen?
4. What is a ghetto?

Growth of the Cities

VOCABULARY	
rural	zoning
urban	social work
suburb	

Country to city   After the Civil War there was a shift of the population of the United States. The country was changing from a **rural** to an **urban** nation.

Urban areas are city areas. These range from towns of at least 2,500 people to large cities of more than 1,000,000. A city has both an inner city area and the **suburbs** around it. Suburbs are small towns just beyond a city. Rural areas are country areas. These areas can be either farm or nonfarm. Of the 54,000,000 people living in rural areas in 1950, for example, only 23,000,000 lived on farms. The other 31,000,000 people lived in villages and other nonfarm places.

Famous immigrants are good subjects for oral reports: Joseph Pulitzer, Carl Schurz, Jacob Riis, Nikola Tesla, Louise Nevelson, Thomas Nast, Yasao Kuniyoshi, Enrico Fermi, Felix Frankfurter, Henry Kissinger.

In 1850, 85 percent of Americans lived in the country, mostly on farms. Only 15 percent lived in cities. See the chart on this page. By 1880, 72 percent of Americans were rural and 28 percent were urban. This change was a result mainly of three things. First, more and more of the immigrants coming here after 1870 were settling in cities. Machinery replaced some farm labor. So people were moving from farming areas to urban places. The building of factories in and near cities caused many country people to move to cities for the new jobs. Look at the chart again. What are the figures for 1920? Where did most Americans live—in the city or in the country? Look again at the percentages for 1880. Now look at the numbers for 1970. What happened in those 90 years?

Cities get larger   In 1790 only 28,000 people lived in Philadelphia. It was the second largest city in the United States. By 1850 Philadelphia had a population of over a hundred thousand. However, at that time it was only the fourth largest city.

The cities grew rapidly during the period from 1850 to 1900 without much

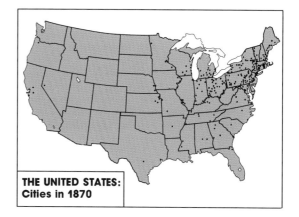

THE UNITED STATES: Cities in 1870

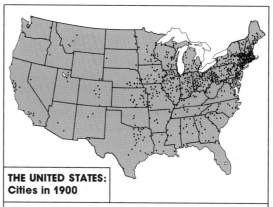

THE UNITED STATES: Cities in 1900

The number of cities more than doubled in 30 years. In what parts of the United States did most of the new cities appear? What caused this growth?

planning. This caused problems. Very little was done for health and recreation. Tenement houses were built quickly for the many people moving to the city. They had little air or light. The plumbing was

RURAL AND URBAN POPULATION, UNITED STATES, 1850–1980					
Year	Total	Urban	Percent	Rural	Percent
1850	23,192,000	3,544,000	15%	19,648,000	85%
1880	50,156,000	14,130,000	28%	36,026,000	72%
1900	75,995,000	30,160,000	40%	45,835,000	60%
1920	105,710,000	54,158,000	51%	51,552,000	49%
1950	150,697,000	96,468,000	64%	54,229,000	36%
1970	203,212,000	149,325,000	72%	53,887,000	28%
1980	226,505,000	167,614,000	74%	58,891,000	26%

poor and there was little proper sanitation. Factories polluted the water and air. Cities did little to control this. Very little land was set aside for parks, open spaces, and recreation areas. And there was little **zoning**, or dividing the city into parts. The result was that factories, stores, and homes were all jumbled together. Overcrowded housing, lack of recreation, and boredom led to more family problems and crime.

Making city life better   Efforts were made to reform cities, to change them for the better. One way was to build parks, to keep open spaces. Frederick Law Olmsted built Central Park in New York City in 1858. He also designed and built parks in other cities in the United States. He made up a name for his work—landscape architecture. He made American cities more beautiful and livable with the parks he built.

People crowded into the cities. Housing could not keep up with the numbers. Often whole families lived in one room. On the lower east side in New York City at the turn of the century over 5,000 people lived on one block.

Some cities value their old buildings. Quincy Market in Boston is a good example of how an old market area has been made useful once again.

Laws were passed to improve housing and sanitation. Buildings had to have a certain number of windows for better light and better air circulation. Sewers and waste disposal plants were built. Pigs no longer roamed in New York City to clean up the garbage in the streets.

In 1889 Jane Addams began Hull House in Chicago. It was the most famous settlement house in the United States. A settlement house provides services for the people who live in a crowded city neighborhood. At Hull House, workers ran a nursery for young children of working mothers. They taught English to recent immigrants. They helped people get jobs, aided them when they got in trouble. Hull House gave people in the neighborhood a place to come to play games from checkers to basketball. Milk and other foods were provided for poor families. Another famous settlement house was the Henry Street Settlement House in New York City. Settlement workers like Jane Addams were doing **social work**—helping people. The new profession of social work came from their efforts. Addams won the Nobel Peace Prize in 1931.

A changing nation   The United States was changing in many ways. There was the change from an agricultural to an industrial economy. There was the change from country to city living. The changes came very fast in the years from 1850 to 1900. Problems arose because of this. Americans went about the business of solving the problems and making the changes as they had always done, with energy and confidence.

CHECKUP

1. In 1850, what percent of Americans lived in rural areas? In urban areas? In 1970, what was the percent of rural people? Urban?
2. How does zoning help city growth?
3. What good did settlement houses do?

II/CHAPTER REVIEW

KEY FACTS

1. Improved farm machinery and scientific developments in crops and livestock changed farming in the United States.

2. A seemingly endless supply of raw materials, a growing population, new inventions, and leadership that believed in unrestricted growth turned the United States into an industrial giant.

3. More people have come to the United States to live than to any other country.

4. As the United States has changed from a rural to an urban nation, the growth of most cities has not been planned, which has resulted in many problems.

VOCABULARY QUIZ

On a separate piece of paper write the word or phrase that best completes each sentence.

1. Most farmers in the United States before the Civil War were **a**) commercial farmers, **b) subsistence farmers.**

2. Populist means **a) people**, **b**) well-liked.

3. Capital is **a) saved-up wealth**, **b**) natural resources.

4. The telephone and telegraph are inventions in **a**) transportation, **b) communication.**

5. Sole control of an industry is an example of **a) monopoly**, **b**) competition.

6. People coming together for a common purpose form a **a**) ghetto, **b) union.**

7. Naturalized citizens are born in **a**) the United States, **b) a foreign country.**

8. A quota is **a) a set number of people**, **b**) an immigrant.

9. Suburbs are **a**) country villages, **b) small towns just outside a city.**

10. Social work is **a) helping people**, **b**) planning a city.

REVIEW QUESTIONS

1. What two things brought about a change in farming after the Civil War?

2. How did inventions help American industry grow?

3. Why did working people want to form labor unions?

4. Where did most immigrants come from before 1880? Between 1880 and 1920?

5. In what year did the census show that more Americans lived in cities than in the country?

6. Give two reasons why zoning and city planning are important.

ACTIVITIES

1. Write a report on George Washington Carver, Luther Burbank, or some other agricultural scientist. Emphasize how their work has aided the commercial farmer.

2. Make a catalog of farm machines. Describe what each is used for.

3. Learn about the life of a famous immigrant to the United States. Make a report to the class.

4. Plan an ideal city. Draw a picture of what you think it would look like.

INTERPRETING A CARTOON

This cartoon was drawn in the late 1940s. Passenger cars were not manufactured during World War II. The factories were turning out tanks, trucks, and other war vehicles. In 1946, after the war ended, two million passenger cars were produced.

Study the cartoon carefully and answer these questions.

1. How many new cars will be produced in 1948?   5 million

2. How do you know that the cartoon is about the United States?

Shape of the country implied by Florida peninsula—sign

3. Who or what does the figure in the cartoon represent?   Police—traffic control officer

4. What feeling or emotion do you think he is showing?   Puzzlement, surprise

5. What, do you think, is the cartoonist's message?

There will be so many cars that the United States will turn into one big parking lot.

In 1980 American automobile manufacturers produced nearly seven million cars. In addition over three million foreign cars were imported.

Draw a cartoon of your own on this same theme.

4/UNIT REVIEW

1. Some Southern states seceded after the 1860 election fearing that President-elect Lincoln would try to abolish slavery. — *Was Lincoln really a threat to slavery? Would he have tried to end slavery in the South?*

2. The Union side had more people, ships, factories, and money than the Confederate side, yet the Union had a struggle to win the Civil War. — *Why was the war so hard to win? How did Emancipation help win the war?*

3. Black voting and carpetbag governments began in the South in 1867, two years after the war ended; the carpetbag governments stayed in power an average of only four years and did some good things such as starting public school systems. — *Why do you think these governments are criticized so harshly even today as a period of poor and corrupt government?*

4. As Americans crossed the Mississippi and moved westward, the main groups of pioneers were trappers, miners, cattle ranchers, sheepherders, and farmers. — *What did each group contribute? Why did ranchers and sheepherders fight each other and then unite to fight the homestead farmers? Why did open-range grazing come to an end?*

5. The transcontinental railroads helped to open up the West to more settlers, but at the same time aided in the destruction of the way of life of the Native Americans. — *How did the railroad play a role in both of these developments? How were the Native Americans treated unjustly?*

6. The use of machinery and science made big changes in agriculture. More farmers became commercial farmers. — *What problems did farmers have as commercial farmers? What solutions did they develop?*

7. Inventions played an important role in a revolution in industry that made great changes in life and labor in the United States. — *Name the three inventions that you think had the greatest effect on American life. How did they change the United States? How did workers respond to the rise of big business in American life?*

8. The United States has been blessed with the contributions of immigrants. — *Select any nation and try to find up to five persons from that land who have contributed to the United States and tell what they did.*   For extra credit

9. Cities in the United States grew so rapidly with so little planning in the period after the Civil War that many problems arose in regard to crowding, government, health, housing, play areas, and sanitation. — *In what ways did cities start to change from the 1890s onward?*

The United States in the Twentieth Century

Suffragette

Douglas MacArthur

Martin Luther King, Jr.

Astronaut

RIGHT TO VOTE

Expanding Beyond Our Shores

VOCABULARY

foreign policy   isthmus
public opinion
protectorate

Foreign policy before 1890 The people of the United States were busy at home. There were the western parts of the country to be settled. The population was growing. Industry was developing. All growth brought problems with it. National affairs seemed more important than foreign affairs.

What were the relationships to foreign countries, or the **foreign policy**, of the United States in the early history of our country? There were two wars with other countries—the War of 1812 with Great Britain and the Mexican War (1846–1848). You read about these wars in Chapters 7 and 8. During most of the 1800s, however, our foreign policy was to stay out of European affairs. We also wanted to discourage the countries of Europe from interfering in the affairs of the Western Hemisphere.

Expansion into the Pacific By the end of the Civil War the United States began to look more seriously at territory beyond its borders. Alaska was purchased from Russia in 1867. In the same year the flag of the United States was raised over the Midway Islands in the Pacific. By 1899 we also controlled the Samoan Islands. Find these places on the map on page 466.

Why were Americans so interested in expanding into the Pacific area? One important reason was trade. Merchants from the United States, especially from New England, were trading with China as early as the 1780s. The whaling ships were very active in the Pacific in the 1820s and 1830s. All these ships needed places where they could stop to get fresh water and food. And when steam replaced the sail, the ships needed places where they could take on more coal. It would be better, thought the merchants and sea captains, if these places were under American control. Then we could always be sure of getting the goods we need. The United States Navy could also use these places as naval bases. That way our ships could fight well in many parts of the world. By 1898 the United States had a very good navy.

Hawaii Another reason why Americans became interested in places in the Pacific was the desire to spread our way of life to other people. Missionaries went to the Pacific islands to bring Christianity to the people who lived there. This is the

The ships were painted white for their goodwill tour. That is how the group became known as the White Fleet.

President Theodore Roosevelt sent the United States fleet on a goodwill trip around the world in 1907. It showed foreign powers the strength of this country.

When the ship returned to the United States they were immediately repainted gray. This is a more suitable color for a naval vessel that would be used in time of war.

way Americans came to the Hawaiian Islands. The missionaries were the first permanent American settlers. As you will read later in Chapter 21, the soil of Hawaii is very good for growing sugarcane. Soon Americans were starting large sugar plantations. In time they began to grow pineapple, too.

Hawaii was a kingdom, under the control of native rulers. But Americans owned a good deal of the land and had influence. In 1893 the Americans organized a revolt against the Hawaiian queen. They set up a new government and asked to become part of the United States. Congress was in favor of this. President Grover Cleveland did not approve of how the new government came into being and would not agree to the annexation of Hawaii. In 1894 Hawaii declared itself an independent republic. Which states that you studied about earlier were also republics before they became part of the United States?

When the Spanish-American War started in 1898, Hawaii became important to the United States. Part of that war took place in the Philippine Islands. Hawaii was a halfway point. Troops and supplies could be sent from there. Interest in making Hawaii part of the United States grew. Congress and the President acted. In 1898, Hawaii became a United States territory. Find the Hawaiian Islands on the map on page 227.

"Remember the *Maine!*" Turn to the world map on page 466 in the Atlas. Find Cuba. It is an island not far from the southern tip of Florida. Now, find the Philippine Islands in the Pacific Ocean. These two places, so far apart, were the scene of fighting during the Spanish-American War.

The war started in Cuba. Cuba had been ruled by Spain since the time of Columbus. Many Americans had long been against this rule. Newspapers stirred up

In what year did the Spanish-American War start? Who was President at that time?

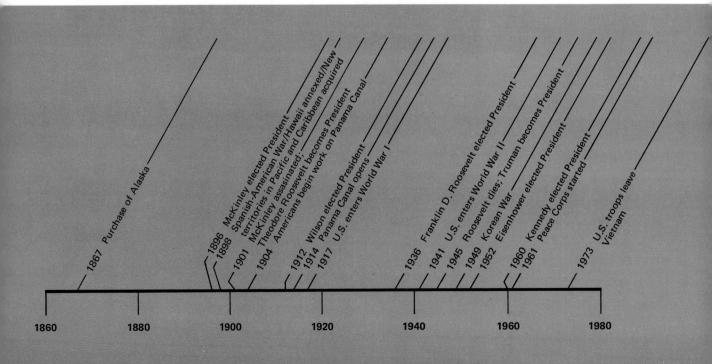

Black troops were very much a part of the fighting in Cuba. They still had white officers. In the regiment pictured here—the 9th and 10th Colored Cavalry—officers wore red sashes. The soldiers in red pants are Spanish. This action took place at the battle of Cuasimas, near Santiago, on June 24, 1898.

United States troops were not prepared to fight in a tropical climate. These soldiers fighting near Santiago, Cuba, are wearing woolen uniforms.
20°N/75°49′W

feelings by writing about the unjust and cruel treatment of the Cubans by Spanish rulers. Some of these stories were true, but many were not. Revolution and riot between Cubans and the Spanish were common.

The U.S. battleship *Maine* was sent to Cuba to protect Americans who lived there during this time of unrest. On February 15, 1898, the *Maine* was blown up in the harbor of Havana, Cuba. Two hundred sixty Americans were killed in the blast.

No one knows for sure who blew up the *Maine.* But Americans blamed Spain for the tragedy. Amerian **public opinion**, that is, the feelings of most of the people,

demanded war with Spain. By the end of April 1898, the Spanish-American War had begun. Its rallying cry was, "Remember the *Maine!*"

Fighting in the Philippines   Commodore George Dewey was in charge of the United States fleet in the Pacific. He had orders to attack the Philippine Islands, which belonged to Spain, if war broke out. Dewey sailed into the harbor of Manila at night. There were ten very old Spanish ships in the harbor. Nearly four hundred Spanish sailors were killed or wounded. There was only one American death.

Emilio Aguinaldo is a hero in Philippine history. His major interest was independence for his country. He lived to see the creation of the Republic of the Philippines.

When American troops got to the Philippines they were joined by Filipino freedom fighters. These were people who wanted freedom from Spanish rule. Their leader was Emilio Aguinaldo (a ge nal' dō). The Spanish soldiers were soon defeated by American and Filipino forces.

Fighting in Cuba   The United States was not ready for this war. The troops that landed in Cuba in June wore heavy woolen uniforms. The food supplies were not protected from the tropical heat and rain. A New York regiment known as the "Rough Riders" had to leave their horses in Florida because there was not room for them on the ship. The second in command of the Rough Riders was a young man from New York named Theodore Roosevelt. He had gathered together the cowboys, college athletes, and other adventure seekers who were members of the regiment.

The Rough Riders were part of the most famous battle of the war. This was the charge up San Juan Hill. The Americans lost many men in this battle but the hill was captured.

Results of the war   The Spanish-American War was over in 4 months. Far more Americans were killed by sickness than in battle. As a result of the war the United States gained the former Spanish territories of Guam, Puerto Rico, and the Philippine Islands.

A military government was set up in Cuba. Its purpose was to help the Cubans set up a government of their own. In 1901 the United States withdrew as a military government in Cuba. But Cuba was not completely independent. It was a **protectorate** of the United States. This meant that the United States would continue to get involved in Cuban affairs if we thought they needed help. The United States ended this policy toward Cuba in 1934.

Even though the war was over, fighting did not end in the Philippine Islands. The Filipinos, under Aguinaldo, did not want to exchange Spanish control for American control. They wanted independence. And they fought for it. Aguinaldo was captured and this put an end to the fighting, but not to the independence movement. As time passed, many Americans began to agree that the Philippines should be prepared for self-government and should become independent. This happened after World War II.

The Spanish-American War made the rest of the world take a good look at the United States. This country had defeated a European power. We had gained new land

226

disease. Walter Reed discovered that a certain type of mosquito transmitted the disease. William Gorgas initiated the changes in sanitation practices that

Have the pupils use the string technique to measure the distances between the west coast of the United States and the various possessions shown on the map. Have them use the same technique on the map

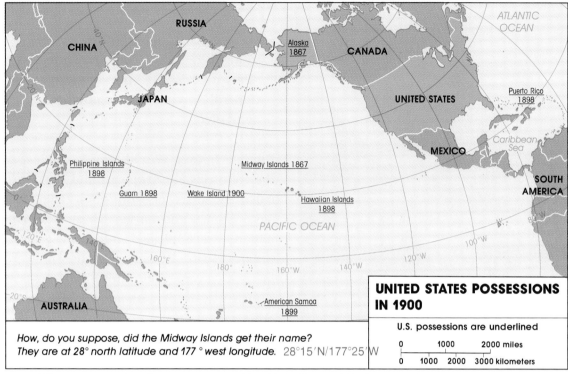

RUSSIA
ATLANTIC
OCEAN
CHINA
Alaska
1867
CANADA
Puerto Rico
1898
JAPAN
UNITED STATES
MEXICO
Caribbean
Sea
Philippine Islands
1898
Midway Islands 1867
SOUTH
AMERICA
Guam 1898
Wake Island 1900
Hawaiian Islands
1898
PACIFIC OCEAN
AUSTRALIA
American Samoa
1899

How, do you suppose, did the Midway Islands get their name?
They are at 28° north latitude and 177° west longitude. 28°15′N/177°25′W

UNITED STATES POSSESSIONS IN 1900

U.S. possessions are underlined

| 0 | 1000 | 2000 miles |
| 0 | 1000 | 2000 | 3000 kilometers |

on p. 466 to measure the distance between New York City and the Hawaiian Islands going around South America.

in the Pacific Ocean and the Caribbean Sea. The war did not make the United States a great power. It just made the rest of the world realize that we already were one.

Panama Canal Study the map on this page. Find all the overseas possessions of the United States in 1900. See how many there are in the Pacific Ocean. How was the United States going to protect these islands? Of course, the navy was the answer. But what would happen if most of the ships were in the Atlantic and something happened in Hawaii? It would take weeks and weeks for the ships to move down and around the South American continent. It became very clear that a faster way had to be found. The idea of building a canal, a waterway,

across Panama, was not a new one. The California gold rush showed the need for a canal across the **isthmus**. An isthmus is a narrow strip of land between two seas or oceans. Look at the map on page 466 in the Atlas. See how much time would be saved if a ship going from New York to San Francisco did not have to go all the way around South America.

A French company had started to build a canal across Panama. They were stopped by disease and a lack of money. The United States government offered to take over the task if the government of Panama would give the United States control of a zone 10 miles (16 km) wide around the canal.

Work began on the canal in 1904. Colonel George Goethals directed the work. President Roosevelt's orders "to make the

wiped out the mosquito's breeding places first in Havana and later in the Panama Canal Zone when he was appointed chief sanitary officer there.

227

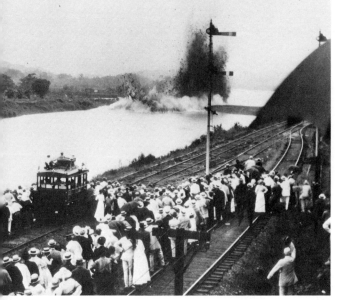

The Gamboa Dike had held the ocean waters apart.

The waters of the Atlantic and Pacific oceans merged after the explosion shown here. This was part of the ceremonies connected with opening the Panama Canal in 1914.

dirt fly" were closely followed. It cost over $375 million to build the Panama Canal and took over 10 years. But when the first ship went through in 1914, everyone thought money and time had been well spent.

The Canal Zone was under complete United States control until 1978. At that time this country and Panama signed a new treaty. Under its terms the government of Panama took over the Canal Zone. It will take control of the Panama Canal in 2000.

CHECKUP

1. What is one reason why the United States wanted territory in the Pacific Ocean?
2. What territory did the United States gain as a result of the Spanish-American War?
3. Why was it important to build the Panama Canal?

You may wish to play songs from this period such as "Over There."

The World Wars

┌─ VOCABULARY ──────────────────────┐

neutral	dictatorship
Allies	persecution
Central Powers	Axis powers
armistice	ration

└──────────────────────────────────┘

Europe before World War I   Most of the countries of Europe around 1900 were ruled by kings or emperors. They had large armies and navies. These powerful nations were divided into two groups. Great Britain, France, and Russia were in one group. Germany and Austria-Hungary were the major powers in the other group. These countries kept building their armies and navies. They became larger and larger. This was dangerous. Anything could start these countries fighting with each other and soon all of Europe would be in a war. This is what happened in 1914 when World War I started in Europe.

The United States before World War I   The United States was not very interested in what was going on in Europe. Americans were more concerned with what was happening in the Western Hemisphere and within the United States itself. Woodrow Wilson was President when the war began in Europe. He asked the American people not to take sides, to stay **neutral**. Most Americans were neutral. They did not think that the United States should take part in this European war.

The United States in World War I   As the years passed and the war in Europe went on, the United States found it harder

New weapons—Tank first used by the British in 1916; submarines in wide use for first time; airplanes and airships used first for observation and reconnaissance, later for bombing and air battles; poison gas.

and harder not to take sides. Most Americans favored the **Allies**—Great Britain, France, and Russia. German submarines were sinking British ships. Sometimes Americans were passengers on these ships and American lives were lost. The most famous of these incidents was the sinking of the *Lusitania* in 1915. There were 128 Americans among the 1,200 people who were killed. Strong feeling against the **Central Powers**—Germany, Austria-Hungary, and the Ottoman Empire (Turkey)—grew. But still people did not want American soldiers to fight in Europe. One of the reasons President Wilson was reelected in 1916 was because "he kept us out of war."

By 1917, however, Germany had started up submarine warfare again, and more American lives were lost. The United States decided at last to enter World War I on the side of the Allies. President Wilson asked Congress to declare war to make the world "safe for democracy."

The United States was not really ready for war. But lessons had been learned from the Civil War and the Spanish-American War. All young men had to sign up for the armed forces. Those who had special jobs, such as farmers, or those who were studying to be doctors did not have to join. Those young men who did go into the armed forces were sent overseas with the proper supplies. Money for the war was raised by the sale of Liberty Bonds. Farmers worked overtime to raise more crops. People at home had "wheatless Mondays" and "meatless Tuesdays" so that more food could go to the soldiers. Gasoline use was limited. Pleasure and business travel on railroads was also limited. Trains were used to move troops and supplies. People at home made sacrifices to help the soldiers in Europe.

The United States did not enter World War I until 1917. American troops, such as these pictured here, made a big difference to the Allied cause.

Women went to Europe as nurses and with the Red Cross. They replaced the men who had worked on farms and in factories. They worked in groups that made warm scarves, socks, and gloves for the soldiers who had to face the cold European winter. They kept their families fed on the wheatless and meatless days. Women were very active in the war effort during this time.

The Allies were helped enormously by the presence of the American soldiers. By May 1918 American soldiers were pouring into France at the rate of 10,000 a day. Americans took part in several big battles. They fought in the second battle of the Marne River, at Château-Thierry, and at St. Mihiel. The Central Powers were in retreat.

In November 1918, the Germans asked for an **armistice**, an end to the fighting. At eleven o'clock in the morning of November 11, 1918, fighting in World War I stopped.

Woodrow Wilson understood how tragic war is. He wanted World War I to be a "war to end all war." He thought no one should be a winner or a loser. Punishment would only cause a future war, he thought. But many people could not easily rid themselves of the feelings of hatred stirred up by the war. They had lost a great deal. Look at the chart on this page. See how many lives were lost. In the peace settlement, therefore, Germany was forced to give up land to the victorious allies. Germany also had to pay the victors for part of the cost of the war. In just 20 years, German feelings about "getting even" would result in an even bigger and more tragic war.

COMBAT CASUALTIES OF WORLD WAR I	
United States	49,000
Italy	460,000
Great Britain	1 million
Austria	1.2 million
France	1.4 million
Russia	1.7 million
Germany	1.8 million

Cost of the war: 337 billion dollars

The League of Nations   Woodrow Wilson had another idea on how to avoid war. This was the League of Nations. Instead of fighting, countries could meet together and talk about their problems. The powers of Europe accepted the idea. But the President could not convince the United States Congress of the importance of the League. Wilson lost his health in the bitter fight to see his dream come true. But Congress voted against joining the League of Nations. And without one of the most powerful nations in the world, the League was doomed to failure.

Another war   World events in the 1930s seemed to bring another war closer and closer. **Dictatorships**, or harsh rule by one person or group, were appearing. Several countries were beginning to prepare for war. They hoped to gain more land through war. Japan invaded China. Italy invaded Ethiopia. Find these countries on the world map in the Atlas. But Germany became the greatest threat to the world under the powerful leadership of Adolf Hitler.

Hitler wanted to restore the pride of the German people. The peace treaty ending World War I made them pay heavily. Many Germans saw war as the only way

The symbol on the armband and flag is a swastika (swāz′ tǐ kə). It is an ancient symbol in the form of a cross with the ends bent at right angles in one direction. The swastika appears in many cultures—Byzantine, Buddhist, Celtic and Greek. The Indians of North and South America used them as ornamentation. In 1920 the Nazi party adopted

The Nazis collected and burned books by Jewish authors and other books that contained what they thought were dangerous ideas. They wanted to control the minds of the people.

the swastika (turned once clockwise) as a symbol. It became a symbol of evil and was banned from Germany after the war.

of gaining back their national honor. Hitler blamed Germany's defeat in World War I on the Jews. Many Germans believed him. Even before the war started, a steady **persecution** of the Jews within Germany began. When people are persecuted they are made to suffer for their beliefs. The persecution continued as Germany conquered other European countries. The result was the horrible death of six million Jews.

Hitler built an army and marched on neighboring countries. The League of Nations did nothing as Hitler disobeyed the terms of the World War I treaty. Finally England and France declared war on Germany. By mid-1941, the Allies, led by Britain, France, Russia, and China were at war with the **Axis powers**, chiefly Germany, Italy, and Japan. The Axis powers controlled much of Europe at this time and were victorious in the Pacific.

The women in this photo are riveting the aluminum "skin" of an airplane to its frame. Most American planes in WWII had metal "skins" rather than fabric or wood.

Pearl Harbor Most Americans did not want to enter war again. The United States did supply a great deal of war materials to the Allies for several years. But war was avoided until December 7, 1941. President Franklin Roosevelt called this day "a day that shall live in infamy." On that day Japan, hoping to gain control of the Pacific Ocean, made a surprise attack on United States forces at Pearl Harbor, Hawaii. On December 8, 1941, Congress declared war.

United States industry rose to the challenges of wartime production. An enormous number of planes, tanks, and ships were produced. No other country ever made such a large amount of war materials in such a short time.

Many women worked in defense plants. These women are working on a B-17 bomber. It was called the Flying Fortress.

American planes in WWII were produced on large assembly lines where workers were trained to do specialized jobs.

Billions of dollars worth of weapons and other military equipment were made in factories across the United States. Millions of Americans were involved in war work.

The planes in the foreground are Curtis P-40 Warhawks, a plane that saw action in every front during the war. The "P" stood for Pursuit. P-40's were the planes used by the famous "Flying Tigers."

The United States was lucky to have such outstanding military leaders as Dwight D. Eisenhower, Douglas MacArthur, and Chester Nimitz. Eisenhower led all Allied troops to victory in Europe. A brilliant plan called *island hopping* led to victory in the Pacific. MacArthur was commander of the Allied forces in the southern Pacific. Nimitz was in charge of the naval and marine forces.

Over 15 million American men and women served in the armed forces in World War II. Well over a million were killed, wounded, or missing in action. But they and their allies fought boldly and bravely, and the Axis powers were defeated. The war ended first in Europe in the spring of 1945. Franklin Roosevelt had died suddenly, just weeks before the European victory. Hitler killed himself before being captured.

It would be the task of Roosevelt's Vice President, Harry Truman, to end the war in the Pacific. The Japanese refused to agree to a surrender. Then Harry Truman made one of the most difficult decisions any leader in history has had to make.

The United States, with the help of many scientists who had escaped Hitler's Germany, had developed a terrible weapon of destruction—the atomic bomb. Should it be used to save American lives and end the war more rapidly?

Truman's answer was "Yes!" On August 6, 1945, a plane dropped the first atomic bomb over Hiroshima, Japan. Three days later a second Japanese city—Nagasaki—was hit. More than a quarter of a million people were killed or injured. The cities were destroyed. Five days later the Pacific war was over.

The war at home   The American people made sacrifices in this war also. The use of many goods like gasoline, sugar, and meat was **rationed**, or limited. Millions of people went to work building needed war equipment. Many people spent part of their income to buy war bonds. War bonds raised money to pay for the war.

Six million women went to work during the war. Over two million women worked in the nation's defense plants. They also served in the armed forces.

Japanese Americans were not treated well during World War II. Other Americans feared them. After the attack on Pearl Harbor they were taken from their homes and brought to camps. They lived under very crowded conditions in the camps. They were kept under guard. Many sons and daughters of Japanese Americans fought honorably for the United States. No Japanese American was ever found guilty of spying. But their story shows how war brings out people's fears, suspicions, and anger.

Results   World War II was the most destructive war in history. More than 55 million people died. The cost is impossible to measure. It is just too large! Cities were destroyed. People were moved from their homelands.

It is hard to understand in the face of this enormous tragedy that some good things happened also. Many valuable inventions, such as sulfa drugs, resulted. Americans made friends in Europe and Japan after the war by helping to prevent starvation and to rebuild homes, cities, and countries.

The Japanese signed surrender terms on September 2, 1945, on board the battleship Missouri in Tokyo Bay. Foreign Minister Mamora Shigemitsu signed the surrender for Japan. Admiral Chester Nimitz signed

Another result of the war was the organization of the United Nations. This group of world nations would work together for peace and human rights. In an age of atomic bombs, war had to be avoided if at all possible. The United States would play an active role in the United Nations. The headquarters are even in New York City.

The Soviet Union and the United States became the two leading world powers. The differences between these two countries would influence United States foreign policy for years to come.

for the U.S. General Douglas MacArthur accepted Japan's surrender in the name of all of the Allies.

CHECKUP

1. How did the United States get into World War I?
2. What were the causes of World War II?
3. What was the difference in United States involvement in the League of Nations and in the United Nations?

The Cold War

---VOCABULARY---
communism
cold war
NATO
Peace Corps
isolated

Changing sides   The United States and the Soviet Union did not remain friends after World War II ended. The Soviet Union has a Communist government. People who live under **communism** have less freedom than people who live in democracies. One of the goals of communism, as stated by many of its leaders, is to spread the idea to as many countries as possible.

Many countries in Eastern Europe became Communist with Russian support after the war. What went on in these countries became a secret from the western countries, including the United States. Winston Churchill, the British leader, said that the Soviet Union was "pulling down an iron curtain." The United States and other western nations began to actively encourage democratic governments especially in those parts of Asia and Africa that were just becoming independent. Communists were also active in these countries. The United States sent large amounts of food and military supplies to countries around the world to stop the spread of communism. The competition between the western nations and the Communist countries under the leadership of the Soviet Union became known as the **cold war**. There are no battles in a cold war, no tanks, no bombs. There is no destruction. A cold war is a war of words. The United Nations has often served as a major battleground in the cold war.

The Soviet Union has been successful many times in gaining new followers. It was a great shock to many Americans when Cuba became Communist in 1959. Cuba is only 90 miles from Florida. Find Cuba on the map on page 470.

NATO   Relations between the iron curtain countries and the western democracies did not get better as the 1940s came to an end. The United States joined the

countries of Western Europe in a military treaty and formed the North Atlantic Treaty Organization—**NATO**. The first members of NATO were the United States, Canada, Great Britain, France, Norway, Denmark, Iceland, Belgium, the Netherlands, Luxembourg, Portugal, and Italy. Later other countries joined, making 15 member countries in all. Look at the map on this page. Find all the NATO members. These countries promised to help one another in case of attack from the Soviet Union. They formed an armed force made up of soldiers from each country. Dwight

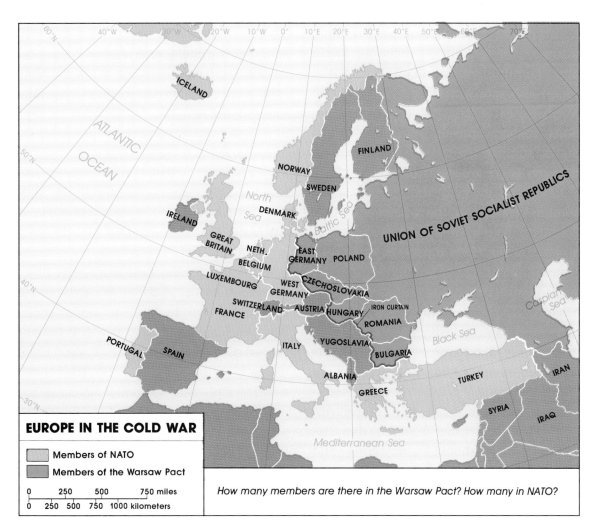

EUROPE IN THE COLD WAR

◻ Members of NATO

◼ Members of the Warsaw Pact

0   250   500   750 miles

0   250 500 750 1000 kilometers

How many members are there in the Warsaw Pact? How many in NATO?

D. Eisenhower became the first commander of the NATO forces.

The Soviet Union and other European Communist countries formed a similar group in 1955. They are known as the Warsaw Pact countries. The map on page 235 shows who they are. The Warsaw Pact membership is made up of all the Communist countries of Europe except Albania and Yugoslavia.

Small hot wars   World War II did not end all fighting all over the world. China became a Communist nation soon after World War II. Korea had been divided into two parts after the war. North Korea was a Communist country. China backed North Korea in an attempt to make all Korea one Communist country. The Soviet Union also sent weapons and supplies to North Korea. A large force of United Nations soldiers, mostly from the United States, stopped the takeover. No one won the war. There are still two Koreas today.

Just how involved the United States should become in the affairs of other countries has been a hard question to answer. In the 1960s and 1970s, the United States found itself defending South Vietnam from Communist takeover. Many Americans thought that it was wrong for the United States to be fighting in Vietnam. Some didn't like the way the war was being fought. Others believed that the South Vietnamese people should be fighting the Communist takeover themselves. Still other Americans believed that the United States should send guns and planes, but not troops. In the late 1960s the Vietnam war came close to splitting the American people into two camps, one group for fighting the war to a victory and the other group for getting out of Vietnam as quickly as possible. The last American soldiers finally left Vietnam in 1973. In 1975 the country fell to North Vietnam. Today there is only one Vietnam and it is under Communist rule.

Peace Corps   If people have enough to eat, live in good housing, and have clothes to wear, they are less likely to become involved in revolution. This was the idea behind the **Peace Corps**, which was started by President John F. Kennedy. This program has sent thousands of Americans to many developing countries. These Americans have helped build schools, hospitals, and roads. They have helped farmers plant better crops. They have taught school and helped train doctors and nurses. The Peace Corps believes in people helping people.

Peacemaker   The United States has acted to help ease the tension in the Middle East. The Arab countries did not like it when the United Nations formed the state of Israel in 1948. There have been many wars in the Middle East since that time. President Anwar el-Sadat of Egypt made the first move in 1977 to bring peace between his country and Israel. President Carter offered the services of the United States in helping the two countries make a treaty. Only time will tell if lasting peace will finally come to this part of the world.

In 1972 President Richard Nixon visited China. There had been no diplomatic relations between the two countries since 1949. This trip helped improve relations between the United States and China.

Peace Corps volunteers work in countries all over the world. This volunteer is teaching a Nigerian student how to operate a linotype machine.

Ask: In what trade is a linotype machine used? (Printing) Review inventions in ch. 10 if pupils could not answer the question.

Relations with the Soviet Union are sometimes good and sometimes bad. Among the good things have been agreements not to test atomic weapons above the ground where they could cause dangerous pollution. There is more trade now between the two countries. In 1975 Russian and American ships joined in space.

However, the Soviet Union still tries to spread communism to more countries. The policy of the United States has been to stay out of war if possible. That is why this country led the boycott of the 1980 Summer Olympics that were held in the Soviet Union. This act was a protest against the Russian takeover of Afghanistan in late 1979. Find Afghanistan on the map on page 466 in the Atlas.

The United States has changed its foreign policy since 1900. We no longer feel that we can be **isolated**, or standing apart, from what happens in the rest of the world. We know we have to work with the other countries of the world if we want peace.

CHECKUP

1. When did the cold war start?
2. Who did the United States support in Korea and Vietnam?
3. What is NATO?

237

KEY FACTS

1. During the nineteenth century the United States gradually acquired overseas territories.

2. The Spanish-American War added to United States overseas possessions and led to recognition of the United States as a world power.

3. The United States did not want to become involved in a European war but eventually joined the Allies in World War I.

4. The failure of the League of Nations, harsh treatment of Germany after World War I, and Japanese expansion in Asia all led to World War II.

5. The United States and its allies, the western democracies, oppose the Soviet Union and its allies, the eastern Communist countries, in the cold war.

VOCABULARY QUIZ

Choose the word or phrase that best completes each sentence.

1. The feelings of most of the people about a subject is called (**a**) majority rule, (**b**) public opinion, (**c**) voting, (**d**) campaigning.

2. A country that has been a protectorate of the United States is (**a**) Great Britain, (**b**) Soviet Union, (**c**) France, (**d**) Cuba.

3. A narrow strip of land between two large bodies of water is called (**a**) a canal, (**b**) an island, (**c**) a waterway, (**d**) an isthmus.

4. In World War I Great Britain, France, and Russia were known as the (**a**) League of Nations, (**b**) Allies, (**c**) Central Powers, (**d**) Rough Riders.

5. If a country is *neutral* it (**a**) has a Communist government, (**b**) has territory in many parts of the world, (**c**) does not want to take sides in war, (**d**) is a member of NATO.

6. An *armistice* is (**a**) an end to fighting, (**b**) a declaration of war, (**c**) a collection of guns, (**d**) a group of countries.

7. The Axis powers in World War II were (**a**) Russia, China, and Japan, (**b**) Germany, Italy, and Great Britain, (**c**) France, Russia, and Great Britain, (**d**) Germany, Italy, and Japan.

8. A group founded after World War II in which countries talk over the problems is (**a**) the United Nations, (**b**) the Central Powers, (**c**) the League of Nations, (**d**) the Allies.

9. Fighting with words, not bombs or guns, is called (**a**) a treaty, (**b**) a reform, (**c**) a cold war, (**d**) an armistice.

10. A group formed to help people help themselves is (**a**) NATO, (**b**) the Central Powers, (**c**) the Peace Corps, (**d**) the Warsaw Pact.

REVIEW QUESTIONS

1. What were two reasons why the United States wanted territory in the Pacific Ocean?

2. Why did President Wilson think the League of Nations was necessary?

3. What is the United Nations? NATO? The Peace Corps?

4. In what countries did the cold war become "hot"?

ACTIVITIES

1. Write a report on the history of either Hawaii or Alaska. For the one you choose, tell what life was like before it became part of the United States and how it came to be part of the United States.

2. Write a report about one of the following people: Theodore Roosevelt, Woodrow Wilson, Emilio Aguinaldo, George Dewey, John Pershing, Dwight Eisenhower, or Douglas MacArthur. You may use an encyclopedia as well as biographies for your source material.

READING A TABLE

Sometimes it is easier to present many facts in table or chart form. The table on this page tells you about land that belongs or belonged to the United States. Such land is called an overseas territory or possession. Use the information from the table to answer these questions.

1. In what area were most of the territories or possessions located? Pacific Ocean

2. What two possessions have become states? Hawaii   Alaska

3. In what year did the United States acquire Hawaii, Guam, and Puerto Rico? 1898

4. What did the United States acquire in 1903? Panama Canal Zone

5. Which is the smallest possession? Midway Islands

6. Which United States possession has the smallest population? Wake Island

7. Where are the Virgin Islands? Caribbean Sea

8. What is the present status of the Philippine Islands? Independent

9. Which is larger in size, Alaska or Hawaii? Alaska

10. Which has the larger population? Hawaii

UNITED STATES OVERSEAS TERRITORIES AND POSSESSIONS

Name	Location	Size	Population	Acquired	Present status
Alaska	Pacific	589,757 sq mi (1,527,464 sq km)	300,000	1867	State (1959)
Midway Islands	Pacific	2 sq mi (5 sq km)	2,200	1867	Possession
Hawaii	Pacific	6,450 sq mi (16,705 sq km)	865,000	1898	State (1959)
Guam	Pacific	212 sq mi (549 sq km)	107,000	1898	Territory
Philippines	Pacific	115,707 sq mi (300,000 sq km)	48,000,000	1898	Independent (1946)
Puerto Rico	Caribbean	3,435 sq mi (8,897 sq km)	2,900,000	1898	Commonwealth
Wake Island	Pacific	3 sq mi (8 sq km)	1,600	1899	Possession
American Samoa	Pacific	76 sq mi (197 sq km)	36,000	1899	Territory
Canal Zone	Panama	647 sq mi (1,676 sq km)	42,000	1903	U.S./Panama control
Virgin Islands	Caribbean	133 sq mi (344 sq km)	100,000	1916	Territory
Marshall, Caroline & Mariana Island groups	Pacific	717 sq mi (1,857 sq km)	115,000	1947	Pacific Islands Trust Territory (U.N.) (Northern Marianas Commonwealth 1981)

The United States Since 1900

VOCABULARY

bicentennial	aviation
naturalist	assembly line
muckraker	depression
conservation	income
synthetic	New Deal
Dust Bowl	

Bicentennial On July 4, 1976, the United States had a birthday party. We celebrated our **bicentennial**, or 200 years as a country. People from all 50 states celebrated by remembering our past. It was a celebration that helped us understand the many goods things that have taken place in American history. It gave us continued pride in our country and the things for which it stands. But it was also a time to take an honest look at our country's problems.

The United States was a greatly different place in 1976 than it was in 1876, when the country celebrated its one-hundredth birthday. A new United States, a modern United States, was born during this country's second hundred years.

In Chapter 12 you studied how the United States role in world affairs really grew during this time. In this chapter you will see how new ideas, inventions, and laws have made changes within the United States. People and events have come together to change the way our country thinks and acts.

Ask pupils to rearrange the vocabulary words in alphabetical order.

Theodore Roosevelt Theodore "Teddy" Roosevelt was an early leader of this new, modern United States. Roosevelt was born into a wealthy, upper-class Dutch family in New York. As a boy Teddy was weak and sickly. He suffered from a disease that made it hard to breathe. He also had poor eyesight and other problems. But through hard work and determination he built a strong and healthy body. He was able to enjoy rugged sports such as boxing, swimming, hiking, and hunting. "Teddy bears" originated during Teddy Roosevelt's administration.

In his early life he was a **naturalist** (a person who studies nature), a legislator, a rancher in the West, a historian, New York City police commissioner, and Assistant Secretary of the Navy. He quit this last job to become a colonel in the Spanish-American War. He was part of a group called the Rough Riders. He returned from the war a national hero. Soon he was elected governor of New York. This lead to his election as vice-president during William McKinley's second term. But 6 months later, McKinley

In the middle of the twentieth century, the United States turned its attention to space. Who knows what the twenty-first century will bring!

The shuttle holds 3 astronauts and 1 to 4 scientists. There are 3 main engines and 2 maneuvering engines at the base. The shuttle, covered with 30,761 tiles, can withstand the intense heat of re-entry. Show pupils a picture of the Wright brothers airplane. Discuss the changes in flight over the past 80 years.

Fuel tank

Rocket booster

Space shuttle

USA

You may want to assign mini-reports that pupils can present orally to the class on Teddy Roosevelt's childhood and youth; his years as a rancher and writer; his early political career; his experiences as Colonel of the Rough Rider's; his presidency; his family; and his later years.

was assassinated. At age 42, Theodore Roosevelt was the youngest person ever to take the office of President of the United States. In 1906 Roosevelt was the first American to receive the Nobel peace prize for the peace conference he mediated between the Russians and the Japanese.

Roosevelt and reform As President, Roosevelt worked hard to improve the standing of the United States in international affairs. He also worked hard to make this country a better place to live.

Roosevelt was greatly influenced by a group of writers he called **muckrakers.** These people wrote about wrongdoing in business and politics. Roosevelt hated injustice. Poor working conditions and mistreatment of Americans made him very angry. He was joined by many men and women who wanted to make things better.

Roosevelt moved to control business more closely. Then some of the worst wrongdoings could not occur. A major triumph was the passage of the Pure Food

and Drug Act. This law called for some government control over the contents of food items. It ended practices like leaving shredded bones in cans of meat. Certain drugs could be sold only with a doctor's prescription. These reforms were small but important beginnings.

Roosevelt, the naturalist, also developed a program of **conservation.** Conservation is saving important natural resources. The United States Forest Service was started. Millions of acres of forestland were set aside as national land in the West. New national parks, game preserves, and wild-bird refuges were established. In Chapter 1 you read about Yellowstone, which was our first national park.

These kinds of government activities were rare before Roosevelt's time. The two presidents who followed Roosevelt— William Howard Taft and Woodrow Wilson —continued the reforms he began. These reforms are still continued today.

Read passages from Upton Sinclair's novel *The Jungle* as an example of the influence of muckrakers.

Who was President when the twentieth century began? Who is President now? Who was President when you were born? When was the first airplane flight? When did Americans first land on the moon?

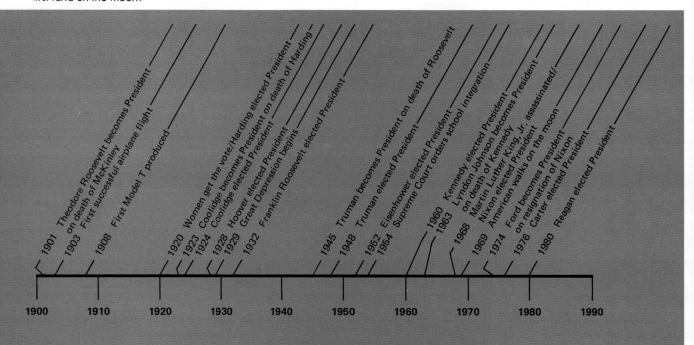

The people are walking along the shores of the Pacific Ocean in Olympic National Park in the state of Washington. Have you ever visited a national park?

In 1908 Roosevelt appointed the first National Conservation Commission to evaluate the natural resources in the United States.

New discoveries Many things that we take for granted today were unknown 100 years ago. These things would change the nation and the world. Among them were inventions that would lead to radio and to television. In 1903 the first movie that told a story, "The Great Train Robbery," appeared. **Synthetic** fibers made from chemicals were first produced in 1935. A giant industry was to grow from the discovery of oil near Spindletop, Texas, in 1901.

Transportation was changed in two ways. On December 17, 1903, on the windy beaches of Kitty Hawk, North Carolina, Orville Wright flew a "heavier than air" machine for 12 seconds. Later that day his brother, Wilbur, made a 59-second flight. Many people refused to believe a flight had really happened. It was too amazing! Humans could not fly! But they could fly, thanks to these two hard-working bicycle shop owners from Dayton, Ohio. Not even the Wrights could have dreamed of the many ways **aviation** would change our country. Can you think of some of the ways aviation has improved the United States?

The automobile In the same year that the Wright brothers made their flights, a young man in Detroit, Michigan—Henry Ford—was starting out in the automobile business. He was not the first person to build an automobile. Many Europeans and Americans were ahead of him. But all of these early cars were expensive. Only the rich could have them. Ford's first automobile can be seen at the Henry Ford Museum in Dearborn, Mich.

In 1908 Ford decided to build a lightweight, practical, cheap car that most people could afford. The car would be the Model T. To hold down costs, the Model T would be the only model built by the Ford Motor Company. As Ford said, "Any customer can have a car painted any color that he wants so long as it is black."

Ford combined ideas borrowed from others with ideas of his own. He used Eli Whitney's idea of interchangeable parts. In 1913 he applied the idea of the **assembly line.** Each worker does one small part of the job while the product rolls past.

The Ford Model T cost $895 in 1908, still too expensive for most people, but $600 less than any other car on the market. As more people bought it and as the assembly line was started, the price steadily dropped. By 1925 a new "tin lizzie," as the Model T was nicknamed, cost only $260. A total of 15 million of these cars were sold before they were replaced by the Model A late in 1927.

You may want to assign some pupils to build models and/or prepare special reports on the great inventions of the late 1800s through the mid-1900s.

Building Model-T automobiles on assembly lines and keeping the design simple made it possible for the Ford Motor Company to make cars that people could afford to buy.

And the United States changed like never before! In the early 1900s, roads were poor and almost impossible to drive on after rain or snow turned them to mud. Cars were open and dirty to ride in. Gas stations were few and far between. Speed limits were set at 6 to 10 miles per hour to protect horses. These conditions changed as more people bought cars. A new freedom developed. It was easier to travel longer distances. The suburbs were born. Suburbs are living areas outside the city. New businesses sprang up. The United States was on wheels.

The Great Depression Newspaper headlines of the 1930s might have read: *Millions Out of Work! Fortunes Lost Overnight! People Lose Homes—Live in Piano Crates and Junk Cars! Thousands of Americans Starving!*

After a long period of prosperity, the United States was entering the Great De-

pression. What causes a **depression**? In the 1930s it was because too many people were spending more money than they had. Their **income**, or money earned, did not keep up with the money they spent. They borrowed money from banks that they could not repay. Often people took their savings from banks. Soon many banks had to close because they had no more money. Over 4,000 banks closed between 1929 and 1932.

Without money people could not buy new things. If businesses could not sell goods, they would close. And if businesses closed, people lost jobs. By 1932, one out of four Americans did not have a job. Poor farming methods and dry weather had turned much of the farmland in the Great Plains to dust. Find the Great Plains on the map on page 263. Thousands of farming families were forced to move from the **Dust Bowl**, as this area came to be called.

Pupils may want to interview their grandparents about their experiences during the Great Depression and World War II and prepare reports for the class.

Many thousands of acres of farmland on the Great Plains were turned to dust by poor farming practices and many years of very little rain. Scenes such as this one were not unusual; many farms were buried under the dust.

During the Great Depression thousands of people were left with no money, no homes, no food. The country was in bad shape. "Brother, Can You Spare a Dime?" was a popular song of the time. The American people hoped that new leadership would solve this terrible problem. Franklin Delano Roosevelt was elected President in 1932.

FDR Franklin Delano Roosevelt was called FDR by the newspaper people. Roosevelt was born into a wealthy family in New York in 1882. He was a distant cousin of Theodore Roosevelt. Shortly after graduation from law school, FDR became involved in politics. He became a New York State senator in 1910. From 1913 through World War I he was Assistant Secretary of the Navy. He ran unsuccessfully for vice-president in 1920.

The home of FDR, located in Hyde Park, NY, is a national historic site.

Tragedy struck in 1921. He became a victim of polio. He could not move his legs. Many thought his career was over. But Roosevelt gamely fought back. He exercised hard to regain his strength. Although he would always need help to walk, his recovery was successful. Out of this experience Roosevelt started the Warm Springs Foundation, a place in Georgia to help other polio victims.

Roosevelt soon returned to national politics. In 1928 he was elected governor of New York. In 1932, he defeated Herbert Hoover for the office of President.

The New Deal Roosevelt had been elected because many voters felt he could lead them out of the Great Depression. The first task he had was to give the nation faith in itself again. "The only thing we have to fear is fear itself," declared the warm, confident voice of the new President. Often during his time in office, Roosevelt explained his programs and tried to make people feel better through a series of "fireside chats." These were broadcast to millions by radio.

Roosevelt saw the government as the solution to the country's problems. He caused the government to create jobs and grant other types of aid to people. This was known as a **New Deal** for the American people. Soon millions went back to work for the federal government on jobs such as forestry projects and the building of dams, parks, sewers, schools, airports, roads, and public buildings. Artists, writers, singers, and dancers were aided by money from the government. Farmers were given more help. The labor union movement was encouraged to grow.

Roosevelt's efforts were well thought of by most people. He was reelected three times, in 1936, 1940, and 1944. He is the only person ever to have been elected to more than two terms as President.

By 1940, the Depression was easing, but it was not over. Large numbers of Americans still did not have work. It would take another world war to put Americans back to work.

The post-war nation   The United States came out of World War II as the most powerful nation in the world. Two of its war heroes succeeded Harry Truman as President—Dwight Eisenhower in 1953 and John Kennedy in 1961. The country faced a promising future!

But the United States faced some very painful times as well. Assassination took the lives of John F. Kennedy, his brother, Robert, and Dr. Martin Luther King, Jr. The war in Vietnam bitterly divided our nation, especially the young and the old. President Richard Nixon and several top aides were forced to resign. Americans were held hostage by a foreign country. Energy was in short supply. Our air, land, and water became much more polluted. Prices for food, clothing, and shelter went higher.

Americans are concerned about these problems. Many people are willing to make sacrifices to control high prices. Steps have been taken to combat pollution so that our environment can become safer. Energy is being conserved. We have shown that no American, not even a President, is above our laws.

Space holds a promise of the future. Neil Armstrong was the first person to step on the moon, in 1969. As he did, he said, "That's one small step for a man, one giant leap for mankind." In one way, he expressed the desire of this country to do things for the good of all people all over the world.

A decade of change   The 1980s will surely prove to be another period of change. Ronald Reagan was elected President in 1980. He was faced with a number of serious problems. Inflation continued to be an economic problem. Inflation happens when prices go higher and higher because money has less and less value. Unemployment was another problem. The need to keep a strong army and navy was felt as war broke out in the Mideast in 1980. Helping to keep world peace would not be an easy task for the President.

The 1980 census showed that the United States is continuing to change. People are still moving to the western and southern parts of the country. State representation in Congress has changed between 1970

You may want to assign biographies of important historical figures of the 1950s, 60s, and 70s now.

On January 20, 1981, Ronald Reagan took his oath of office and became the fortieth President of the United States.

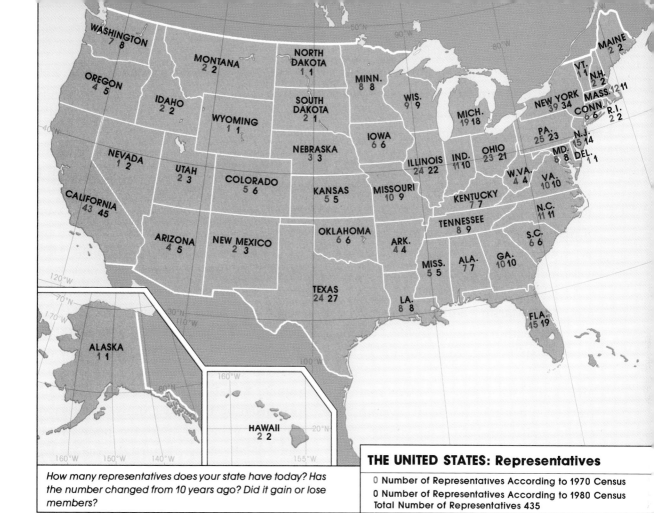

State	1970	1980
WASHINGTON	7	8
MONTANA	2	2
NORTH DAKOTA	1	1
MINN.	8	8
WIS.	9	9
MICH.	19	18
MAINE	2	2
VT.	1	1
N.H.	2	2
MASS.	12	11
NEW YORK	39	34
CONN.	6	6
R.I.	2	2
OREGON	4	5
IDAHO	2	2
WYOMING	1	1
SOUTH DAKOTA	2	1
IOWA	6	6
NEBRASKA	3	3
PA.	25	23
N.J.	15	14
NEVADA	1	2
UTAH	2	3
COLORADO	5	6
ILLINOIS	24	22
IND.	11	10
OHIO	23	21
MD.	8	8
DEL.	1	1
CALIFORNIA	43	45
KANSAS	5	5
MISSOURI	10	9
KENTUCKY	7	7
W.VA.	4	4
VA.	10	10
N.C.	11	11
ARIZONA	4	5
NEW MEXICO	2	3
OKLAHOMA	6	6
ARK.	4	4
TENNESSEE	8	9
S.C.	6	6
MISS.	5	5
ALA.	7	7
GA.	10	10
TEXAS	24	27
LA.	8	8
FLA.	15	19
ALASKA	1	1
HAWAII	2	2

How many representatives does your state have today? Has the number changed from 10 years ago? Did it gain or lose members?

THE UNITED STATES: Representatives

0 Number of Representatives According to 1970 Census
0 Number of Representatives According to 1980 Census
Total Number of Representatives 435

and 1980. Some states have lost representatives as their population has grown smaller. Other states have gained. There are other changes in the population, too. In the 1980s there will be more older people in this country than young people. There will also be more women than men. Isn't it interesting to think what the United States will be like in the 1990s?

CHECKUP

1. What changes did Theodore Roosevelt bring to the United States?
2. What new ideas and discoveries changed the country in the early 1900s?
3. What caused the Great Depression?
4. What things did Franklin Roosevelt do to try to end the Depression?

The Struggle for Human Rights

VOCABULARY

human rights   boycott
sit-in

Human rights Perhaps the great struggle for **human rights** since World War II best shows the pain and the promise of the United States. It is a painful thing when all people are not treated fairly and equally. The violence and misery of slums, poverty, and riots are painful examples of what can happen. But it is very promising when millions of Americans of all races join together to try to build a country that lives up to the promises of the Declaration of Independence and the Constitution. Black Americans have renewed their efforts to gain full freedom, dignity, and equality.

In 1954 the Supreme Court of the United States declared that public schools had to serve both black and white students equally. Through the brave efforts of many students, some of them as young as you are, educational opportunities were increased.

A leader in the human rights movement was Dr. Martin Luther King, Jr., a preacher with a mission in life. "I have a dream," spoke Dr. King stirringly. That dream was for the complete equality of all Americans. King was a patient man. He worked through the legal system. He challenged unjust laws, but always acted peacefully.

Dr. King gained nationwide fame in Montgomery, Alabama, in 1955. At that time blacks were required to sit in the back of the bus. But one day a quiet woman named Rosa Parks decided to sit in the "whites only" section of the bus. She was arrested. Dr. King led a **boycott** of Montgomery buses to protest her ar-

rest. People who supported Dr. King would not use the buses until anyone could sit wherever she or he pleased. The boycott was successful.

King's ideas were used widely. **Sit-ins** were held in which people refused to leave "whites only" lunch counters until they were served. Protest marches were staged. Many people, including King himself, were beaten and thrown in jail. Many people came to support laws and rights that would help blacks.

During the presidency of Lyndon Johnson, great progress was made. In 1964 a law was passed that gave blacks the right to use all businesses that serve the public. Equal chances for jobs were also promised by this law. Johnson's "War on Poverty" provided help for poor Americans of all races. Robert C. Weaver was appointed as Secretary of Housing and Urban Development and became the first black Cabinet member in 1966. A year later, Thurgood Marshall became the first black Supreme Court justice. The black middle class continued to grow.

Still there are wide differences in the way many black and white Americans live. Riots in the nation's large cities in the 1960s made this point clear. King's assassination pointed out the hatred that still exists. But the lives of millions of Americans are greatly improved because of the leadership of Dr. King.

Equality for all   Many other groups also demanded better treatment under the law. Native Americans demanded that treaties be honored. Some tribes received hunting and fishing rights that had been promised them. Farm workers, many of

Martin Luther King, Jr., walks children to school on the first day of integrated classes in Mississippi in 1966.

Point out that Dr. King's birthday, January 15, is celebrated as a legal holiday in many states to commemorate his contributions to human rights.

whom are Mexican Americans, gained rights under the leadership of Cesar Chavez. The United States government recognized that many Japanese-American citizens were treated badly during World War II.

You read in Chapter 7 how, in 1848, American women came together for the first time to demand rights equal to those of men. The movement grew. Gradually some states passed laws that gave women more control over their own lives. Wyoming gave women the vote in 1869. Women's colleges were started. Slowly, very slowly, women began to enter the professions. Elizabeth Blackwell was, in 1849, the first woman to graduate from medical school.

An amendment to the Constitution that would give women the right to vote was first proposed to Congress in 1878. It did not receive enough votes to pass. The amendment came before Congress nearly every year after that. Each time it was defeated. Finally in 1919—success! The Nineteenth Amendment giving all female citizens the right to vote was passed by Congress and became part of the Constitution of the United States in 1920.

Today 35 percent of American women hold full-time jobs. In 1970 only 18 percent worked full-time outside the home. Women are doing jobs today that once were thought suited only for men. There are women coal miners and telephone linepersons. Women are engineers and scientists. They are running big industries. Some women are still being paid less for doing the same work as men. There is still a way to go in the struggle for equal rights for women.

Decisions made in courts throughout the United States have affected human rights. Carlos Cadena is the senior judge for the Texas Court of Civil Appeals.

This movement toward equality is a process that has been carried on throughout history. It will not end until *all* Americans can say for themselves the words carved on Dr. King's tombstone: "Free at last, free at last, thank God Almighty, I'm free at last."

Promise for the future   Americans must realize what a wonderful place this is to live. We have goods and wealth beyond the dreams of much of the world. We have ways to be heard when we disagree with one another and the government. We have freedom. We have sharp minds and fresh ideas. We have people willing to work hard for themselves and for others. It is our responsibility to continue to build our country and fulfill the dreams of the brave men and women who have gone before us.

CHECKUP

1. What decision did the Supreme Court make in 1954 that affected human rights?
2. What was Martin Luther King, Jr.'s contribution to the struggle for human rights?
3. In what year did women citizens get the right to vote?

13/CHAPTER REVIEW

KEY FACTS

1. New ideas, inventions, and laws have greatly changed our nation since 1900.

2. Theodore Roosevelt is an example of the new American leadership that helped the country progress in its second hundred years.

3. Franklin Delano Roosevelt used the power of government to lift the United States out of the depression of the 1930s.

4. Americans have successfully survived the pain of assassination and scandal in the 1960s and 1970s and are constantly taking steps to make the United States better.

5. Due to the efforts of Dr. Martin Luther King and others, the goal of equal rights for all Americans is much closer to reality.

VOCABULARY QUIZ

Fill in the missing words or phrases in the following paragraphs. Write your answers on a separate sheet of paper.

The United States celebrated its (1) bicentennial, its two hundredth birthday, in 1976. The country had changed a great deal in that time.

Once people made most of the things they needed at home. Then the (2) industrial revolution took place. Goods manufactured in factories took the place of goods made at home. Industries grew. One of the most important was the automobile industry. (3) Henry Ford designed a car he called the Model T. The car was made on an (4) assembly line. When things do not go well for businesses and workers do not have jobs or money to buy goods, the country goes into an economic (5) depression. (6) Franklin D. Roosevelt was President during such a time in the 1930s. (7) Inflation is another economic problem. It affects the value of money.

People today are very interested in the environment. Theodore Roosevelt was interested in (8) conservation, saving natural resources. While he was President the (9) Forest Service was started. People are also interested in human welfare. Freedom and equality for all are (10) human rights.

REVIEW QUESTIONS

1. Why was a national forest system started?

2. Who were the muckrakers? What did they do?

3. How does an assembly line work?

4. Why was the Model T such a popular car?

5. How did New Deal policies help people during the Depression?

6. What was Dr. Martin Luther King's part in the battle for human rights?

ACTIVITIES

1. There are national parks of one kind or another all over the United States. Find out the name of a park near where you live. Investigate what the park offers. Plan a trip to the park. Describe what can be done there.

2. The idea behind the Model T was to design a car that could be built cheaply and in great numbers so that many people could afford to buy one. Do you think this was a good idea? What do you think the automobile of the future will look like? Will it run on gasoline? Design a car of the future. You can draw a picture, write a description, or do both.

3. The first person to step on the moon was an American. Make a list of the Americans who have flown in space. Tell what each did. Begin your list with Alan B. Shepard.

13/SKILLS DEVELOPMENT

READING A MAP: THE 1980 PRESIDENTIAL ELECTION

In 1980 Ronald Reagan was elected President of the United States. When people vote for President they do not vote directly for the candidate. They vote for electors. These electors are pledged to vote for one or the other of the candidates. Their votes are called electoral votes. In order to be elected President, a candidate must have more than half of the electoral votes. The person with the most votes in each state gets all that state's electoral votes.

The questions below are based on the map and the information on this page.

1. Which two states have the most electoral votes? California, New York

2. How many *states* did former President Carter win in the 1980 election? 6 and D.C.

3. How many electoral votes did he get? 49

4. How many *states* did President Reagan win? 44

5. How many electoral votes did President Reagan get? 489

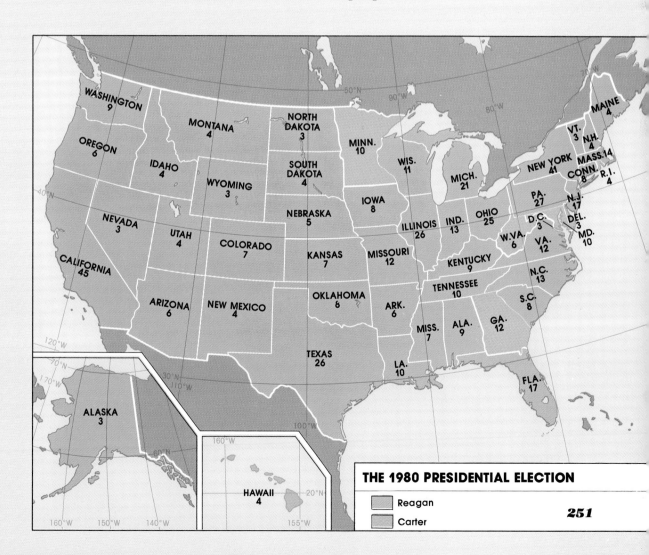

THE 1980 PRESIDENTIAL ELECTION

Reagan

Carter

251

5/UNIT REVIEW

1. The United States began to expand beyond its shores in the nineteenth century. — *List the territories acquired by 1900 and tell how or why each was acquired. Which of these are still part of the United States?*

2. The United States has fought in two world wars. — *What caused World War I and World War II? How did the United States get involved in each?*

3. Woodrow Wilson's dream of a League of Nations after World War I came true with the creation of the United Nations after World War II. — *Find more information about the League of Nations and the United Nations in an encyclopedia. Why did the United States join one but not the other?*

4. Since World War II the United States has been more involved in world affairs than ever before in its history. — *Give at least three examples of United States involvement in world affairs since 1945.*

5. The years around 1900 are often called the "birth of modern America." — *Why is this so?*

6. Theodore Roosevelt had strong ideas about the role of government. — *How did his activities in conservation and controlling big business show this?*

7. New inventions, the automobile, the airplane, and so on, changed the way of life in the United States. — *Imagine life without one of these important inventions. Write a story about how your life would be different without automobiles, or airplanes, or synthetic fabrics, or any other invention you think is important.*

For extra credit

8. The Great Depression occurred in the period between the two world wars. — *What causes a depression? Do you think it can happen again? Explain.*

9. The movement for human rights and equality is a process that has gone on throughout our history. — *Which groups have made the largest gains in the area of human rights in the last 35 years?*

The United States: A Land of Great Variety

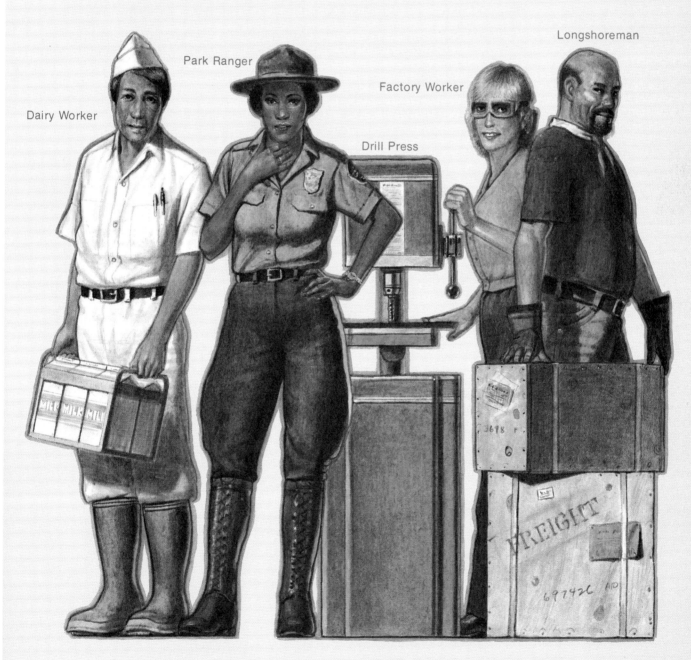

Dairy Worker

Park Ranger

Factory Worker

Drill Press

Longshoreman

Tools of Geography

VOCABULARY

region	boundary
political map	population
	density

The study of geography In the first chapter of this book you learned about reading maps. You also learned that being able to read maps will help you find out about the geography of our great country.

But what does learning geography really mean? Of course it means more than reading maps. Maps are just one of the tools we use to study geography. When we study geography, we learn about the earth's physical features. Mountains, plains, rivers, forests, and islands are just a few of the physical features found in our country.

When we study the geography of a place, we also learn something about its climate. If you know the climate of a place, you have a good idea of how hot or cold that place is at any time of the year. You also know the parts of the year in which rain or snow is expected.

The study of natural resources, such as oil, coal, and iron, is a part of geography. Geography also deals with cities and industries. But most of all, geography is the study of how people use the earth.

The United States: one nation, many regions Because our country is so big, you could not possibly study all of its geography at once. It helps to divide the country into parts, or **regions.** Then you can study one part at a time. In the next seven chapters of this book, you will be learning about the different parts of the United States—one at a time.

We could divide the United States in many different ways in order to study it. We could divide it into dry lands and wetlands, or highlands and lowlands. Or we could divide it into parts with many people and parts with few people. These are all perfectly good ways to divide the United States into regions.

Your book uses still another way of dividing the country. The map on page 255 shows the regions you will be studying this year. They are the New England, Middle Atlantic, Southeast, North Central, South Central, Mountain West, and Pacific regions.

Find your state on the map. In which of these seven parts is your state?

Maps Before studying the regions of the United States, let's learn something about the states that make up the whole country. One way of doing this is to look at maps.

Emphasize to pupils that a study of geography is not only a study of maps and the earth's physical features but also includes climate, natural resources, cities, industries and how people use the earth.

Distribute outline maps of the United States to the class. Have pupils label and color the seven regions they will be studying.

The map shows the seven regions you will study. The lighthouse in the picture is on the coast of Oregon on a piece of land called Devil's Elbow.

Ask pupils to name the physical features shown in the picture. Then ask: What evidence indicates that people have been here? Why did they build the lighthouse?

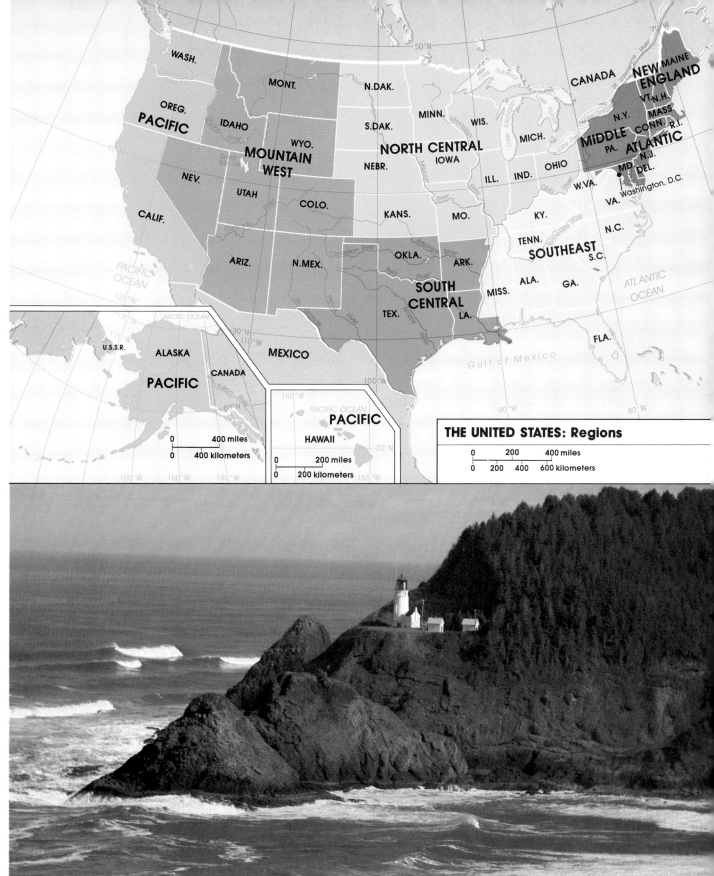

WASH.

MONT.

N.DAK.

CANADA

NEW MAINE
ENGLAND

OREG.

PACIFIC

IDAHO

MINN.

WIS.

VT. N.H.

N.Y.

MASS.

WYO.

S.DAK.

MICH.

MIDDLE

CONN. R.I.

NEV.

MOUNTAIN

NORTH CENTRAL

PA. ATLANTIC

WEST

NEBR.

IOWA

N.J.

UTAH

OHIO

MD. DEL.

CALIF.

COLO.

ILL. IND.

W.VA.

Washington, D.C.

KANS.

MO.

KY.

VA.

PACIFIC
OCEAN

ARIZ.

N.MEX.

OKLA.

ARK.

TENN.

N.C.

SOUTHEAST

S.C.

SOUTH
CENTRAL

ALA.

GA.

ATLANTIC
OCEAN

TEX.

LA.

MISS.

FLA.

Gulf of Mexico

U.S.S.R.

ALASKA

MEXICO

PACIFIC

CANADA

PACIFIC

0   400 miles

0   400 kilometers

PACIFIC OCEAN

PACIFIC

HAWAII

0   200 miles

0   200 kilometers

THE UNITED STATES: Regions

0   200   400 miles

0   200   400   600 kilometers

You have already learned about some of the facts that maps can tell you. When you found Yellowstone National Park at 45° north latitude and 110° west longitude, you used the map on pages 14 – 15. That map told you the name of each state. It showed you where each state is and gave you an idea of its size.

Turn to the map on pages 14 – 15 again. A map like this is called a **political map.** This one shows you the different states in our country. Another political map might show you the different countries in the world. In other words, a political map shows you the names and **boundaries**, or borders, of different countries or states. A boundary is a line that separates one state or country from another.

Find the boundaries of your own state on the map. Name the states that share these lines. Find the boundary between the United States and Canada. Do you see the boundary between the United States and Mexico?

A political map might also show you where the cities of a state or country are. How does the map key on page 15 help you find some important cities in the United States? The key also helps you find the state capitals. A state capital is the city in which the government of the state meets. Do you know the capital city of your state? Find it on the map. Can you find the capital of our country? How does the map key help you find it?

Tables   The map on pages 14 – 15 is a good tool for learning some facts about the United States. But as you know, there are other ways in which you can find information. The rows and columns of the table on page 257 give you, in another form, some of the same facts shown on the map. A table is a fast and handy way to learn what you want to know.

The table on page 257 gives you the area, or size, of each state. The table also gives you the rank in area of each state. Which is our biggest state? Our smallest? Is your state one of these two? If not, what is the rank of your state? What is the area of your state? You can see that it is easier and faster to find certain facts in a table than on a map.

For example, you can tell by looking at the map on pages 14 – 15 that Nevada is bigger than Delaware. However, the map can't tell you exactly how big each of those states is. For that kind of information, the table on page 257 is more useful.

Graphs   A third way to show the size of some of our states is to use a graph. A graph is any one of several different kinds of drawings. You have already used several graphs in this book. Some graphs, like the one on page 347, use symbols to give information. Some, like those on pages 258 and 271, use lines or bars. One kind of graph is shaped like a pie divided into parts. There is a pie graph on page 357.

A bar graph makes it easy to compare facts. Look at the top graph on page 258. It uses bars to show the sizes of our five largest and five smallest states. In this case, the graph gives you an idea of the great differences in sizes.

No one way of learning facts is better than another. You will need to be able to use maps, tables, and graphs to learn about the geography of the United States.

AREA AND POPULATION OF THE FIFTY STATES

State	Area in sq mi	Area in sq km	Rank in area	Population (in thousands)	Rank in population
Alabama	51,609	133,667	29	3,890	22
Alaska	586,400	1,518,776	1	400	50
Arizona	113,909	295,024	6	2,718	29
Arkansas	53,104	137,539	27	2,286	33
California	158,693	411,015	3	23,669	1
Colorado	104,247	270,000	8	2,888	28
Connecticut	5,009	12,973	48	3,108	25
Delaware	2,057	5,328	49	595	47
Florida	58,560	151,670	22	9,740	7
Georgia	58,876	152,489	21	5,464	13
Hawaii	6,424	16,638	47	965	39
Idaho	83,557	213,822	13	944	41
Illinois	56,400	146,076	24	11,418	5
Indiana	36,291	93,994	38	5,490	12
Iowa	56,290	145,791	25	2,913	27
Kansas	82,264	213,064	14	2,363	32
Kentucky	40,395	104,623	37	3,661	23
Louisiana	48,523	125,675	31	4,204	19
Maine	33,215	86,027	39	1,125	38
Maryland	10,577	27,394	42	4,216	18
Massachusetts	8,257	21,386	45	5,737	11
Michigan	58,216	150,779	23	9,258	8
Minnesota	84,068	217,736	12	4,077	21
Mississippi	47,716	123,584	32	2,521	31
Missouri	69,686	180,487	19	4,917	15
Montana	147,138	381,087	4	787	44
Nebraska	77,227	200,018	15	1,570	35
Nevada	110,540	286,299	7	799	43
New Hampshire	9,304	24,097	44	921	42
New Jersey	7,836	20,295	46	7,364	9
New Mexico	121,666	315,115	5	1,300	37
New York	49,576	128,402	30	17,557	2
North Carolina	52,719	136,542	28	5,874	10
North Dakota	70,665	183,022	17	653	46
Ohio	41,222	106,765	35	10,797	6
Oklahoma	69,919	181,090	18	3,025	26
Oregon	96,981	251,181	10	2,633	30
Pennsylvania	45,333	117,412	33	11,887	4
Rhode Island	1,214	3,144	50	947	40
South Carolina	31,055	80,432	40	3,119	24
South Dakota	77,047	199,552	16	690	45
Tennessee	42,244	109,412	34	4,591	17
Texas	267,339	692,408	2	14,228	3
Utah	84,916	219,932	11	1,461	36
Vermont	9,609	24,887	43	511	48
Virginia	40,815	105,711	36	5,346	14
Washington	68,192	176,617	20	4,130	20
West Virginia	24,181	62,629	41	1,950	34
Wisconsin	56,154	145,439	26	4,705	16
Wyoming	97,914	253,597	9	471	49

Pupils may find it easier to read the table with the aid of a ruler or the straight edge of a piece of paper.

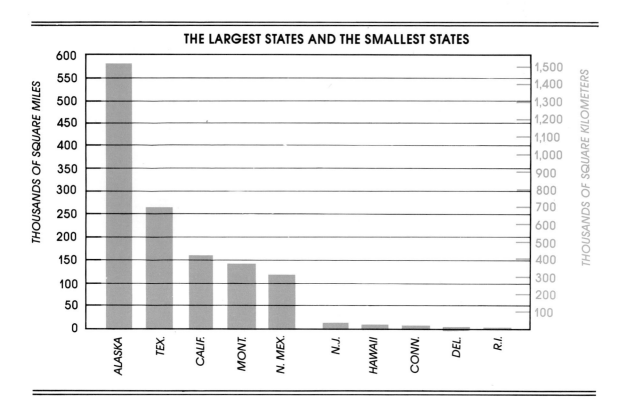

THE LARGEST STATES AND THE SMALLEST STATES

Which state is the largest in area? Which has the highest population density?

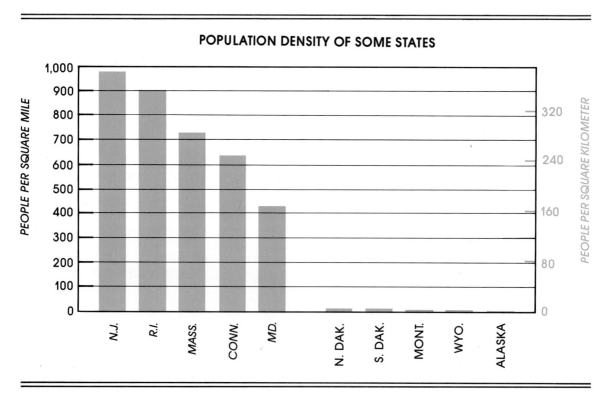

POPULATION DENSITY OF SOME STATES

Select another group of ten states from the table on p. 257. Have pupils draw a graph of the area and/or population of those states.

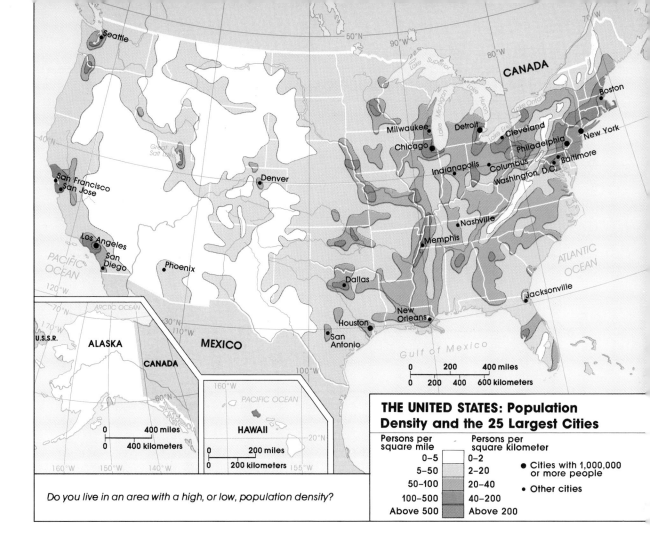

THE UNITED STATES: Population
Density and the 25 Largest Cities

Persons per square mile	Persons per square kilometer	
0–5	0–2	● Cities with 1,000,000 or more people
5–50	2–20	
50–100	20–40	● Other cities
100–500	40–200	
Above 500	Above 200	

Do you live in an area with a high, or low, population density?

Using the tools of geography to learn about people   The study of people is one of the most important parts of geography. There are more than 226 million people in the United States. Where do they all live? The map above shows you. It is called a population density map.

When we speak of **population density**, we are referring to the number of people per square mile or square kilometer in a certain area, such as a state or country. Of course, each square mile or kilometer in that area won't have exactly the same number of people. Population density means the average number of people per square mile or kilometer. The higher the average number of people to the square mile or kilometer, the higher the population density.

The map above shows you the population densities of the United States. It also shows you the 25 largest cities in the United States. Six of these cities have at least 1 million people living in them. They are New York, Chicago, Los Angeles, Philadelphia, Houston, and Detroit.

Population density, like size, can be shown on a graph. Look at the lower graph on page 258. It shows the population densities of ten of our states. Compare this graph with the top graph. You can see that some of our large states,

259

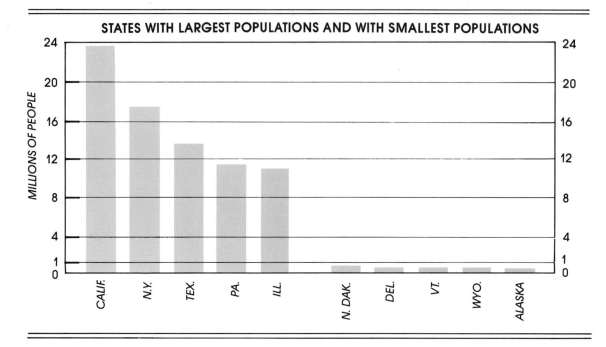

STATES WITH LARGEST POPULATIONS AND WITH SMALLEST POPULATIONS

MILLIONS OF PEOPLE

CALIF. | N.Y. | TEX. | PA. | ILL. | N. DAK. | DEL. | VT. | WYO. | ALASKA

Which state has the largest population? Which state has the smallest population? Which state has about 12 million people?

such as Alaska and Montana, have very low population densities. On the other hand, some of the small states, such as New Jersey, Connecticut, and Rhode Island, have very high population densities.

Remember, population density is the average number of people per square mile or kilometer. It is not the total

Direct pupils' attention to the picture. Ask: What are the characteristics of a densely populated area?

Chicago is one of our largest cities.

number of people in a state. The graph above shows the total number of people in ten of our states. For this graph, we picked the five states with the most people and the five with the fewest.

A table can give you a great many facts in a small space. Look again at the table on page 257. This table gives you the total number of people in every state.

The map on page 259, the graphs on pages 258 and 260, and the table on page 257 together give you a very good idea of where Americans live.

CHECKUP

1. What kind of information is usually given on a political map?
2. Which are the five largest and the five smallest states in our nation?
3. Which are the five most populated and the five least populated states in our nation?
4. What is population density?

41°53′N, 87°38′W

Landforms of the United States

VOCABULARY

relief map	peninsula
physical map	source
landform	mouth
plain	delta
coastal plain	channel
plateau	pollute
mountain	irrigate
island	hydroelectric power

The varied land   The surface of the earth is not the same all over. Some of the earth's surface is high, and some is low. Some of the earth's surface is land. A great deal more of the earth's surface is water. Some parts of the earth's surface are easier for people to live on than others. Some parts have many people. Some have very few.

Look at the map on page 263. This is a **relief map,** or **physical map.** It shows you the kinds of land surfaces, or **landforms,** the United States has. It tells you how high or low the land is. It also names the largest rivers and lakes.

Do you remember the words from "America, the Beautiful," which you read at the very beginning of your book?

For purple mountain majesties
Above the fruited plain!

Those words tell you something about two very important landforms.

Plains   Some of the more than 226 million people in the United States live on our country's **plains.** A plain is a wide area of flat or gently rolling land.

Crops such as wheat and corn cover thousands of acres in the Central Plains.

Pupils may want to gather pictures showing a variety of land features for a booklet or for the bulletin board. Be sure they label the land features shown in the pictures.

The peak of Mount McKinley is covered with snow all year round.

63°30'N, 151°W

The largest plain in the United States is in the middle of the nation. This is the Central Plains. Look again at the relief map on page 263. Find the Great Plains on the western edge of the Central Plains. See how the Great Plains stretches north and south from the Canadian border to the Mexican border, a distance of more than 1,000 miles (1,600 km). You will be learning more about the Great Plains when you study the North Central states.

A plain that is bordered by a large body of water is called a **coastal plain.** The Atlantic Coastal Plain and the Gulf Coastal Plain are two large coastal plains in the United States. Find them on the map.

Plateaus   Another landform is called a **plateau.** A plateau is a large, high area of land. It generally rises steeply from the land around it, at least on one side. The top, or surface, of a plateau is usually flat and level, like a plain.

The Colorado Plateau is a large plateau in the region called the Mountain West. Find it on the map on page 263. Is it higher or lower than the coastal plains? Than the Great Plains? How did the map key help you answer?   higher; higher
The key gives the elevation of each plains area.

Mountains   Some Americans live on or near high, steep lands called **mountains.** A mountain is a part of the earth's surface that rises sharply from the land around it. A mountain has a broad base and narrows to a small peak at the top. A group of mountains is called a chain or a range.

The highest mountains in the United States are in Alaska. Among them is Mount McKinley, the highest point in the United States. It is 20,320 feet (6,190 m) high. Find this towering mountain on the map on page 263.

The longest mountain chain in the United States is the Rocky Mountains. Like the Great Plains, these mountains stretch from Canada to within a few hundred miles of Mexico. The Rocky Mountains are very high. Some peaks rise more than 14,000 feet (4,300 m). Find these mountains on the same map.

262   Mount McKinley, named for William McKinley our 25th president, is sometimes called the "top of the continent" because it is the highest summit in all of North America. The Indians named it *Denali* which means "The Great One."

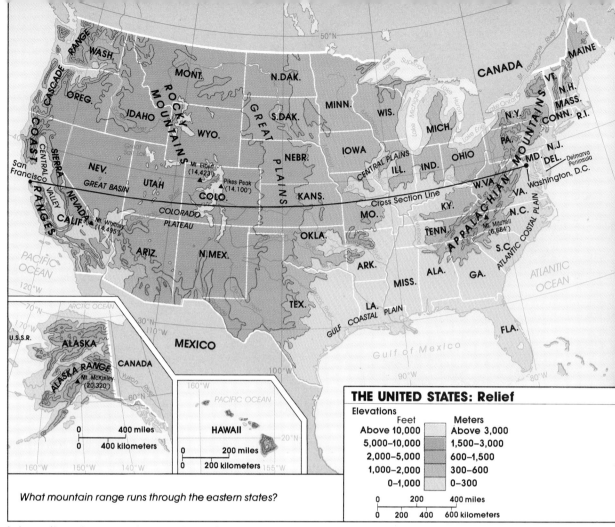

THE UNITED STATES: Relief

Elevations

Feet	Meters
Above 10,000	Above 3,000
5,000–10,000	1,500–3,000
2,000–5,000	600–1,500
1,000–2,000	300–600
0–1,000	0–300

0   200   400 miles

0   200   400   600 kilometers

What mountain range runs through the eastern states?

Ask pupils to locate and name the various physical features of the United States shown on this map.

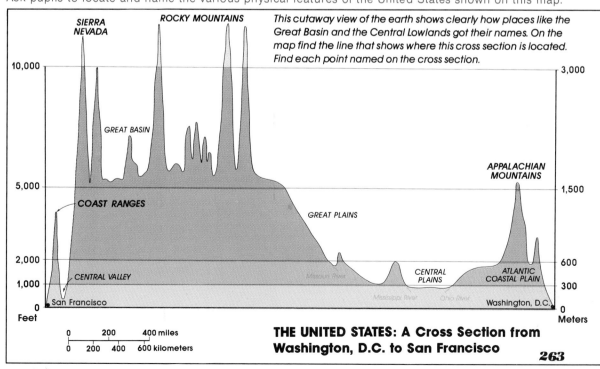

This cutaway view of the earth shows clearly how places like the Great Basin and the Central Lowlands got their names. On the map find the line that shows where this cross section is located. Find each point named on the cross section.

0   200   400 miles

0   200   400   600 kilometers

THE UNITED STATES: A Cross Section from Washington, D.C. to San Francisco

263

These islands are in a lake in the Tongass National Forest in southeastern Alaska.

Tongass is the largest national forest in the United States. Western hemlock, Sitka spruce, yellow and western red cedar, lodgepole pine, and alder all grow well in the mild temperatures and heavy rainfall of this rain forest.

Islands and peninsulas   Many people in our country live on **islands.** An island is a body of land completely surrounded by water. Turn to the map of the United States on pages 468 – 469. You can see that several states have islands off their shores. One state, Hawaii, is made up entirely of islands. The Hawaiian Islands are in the Pacific Ocean. More than 1 million people live on another island. It is a small island called Manhattan. Manhattan Island is in New York City.

In some states, people live on land called a **peninsula.** A peninsula is a piece of land almost surrounded by water. Most of one state—Florida—is a peninsula. Find the peninsula of Florida on the map on pages 468 – 469. What bodies of water touch this piece of land?

Another large peninsula is called the Delmarva Peninsula. It has this name because it is made up of parts of three different states. The *Del* stands for Delaware. The *mar* stands for Maryland. And the *va* stands for Virginia. The Delmarva Peninsula is on the east coast of the United States. See if you can find it on the map on page 263.

This peninsula is on the coast of Washington.

Point out to pupils that there are 4 kinds of islands: continental, volcanic, coral and barrier.

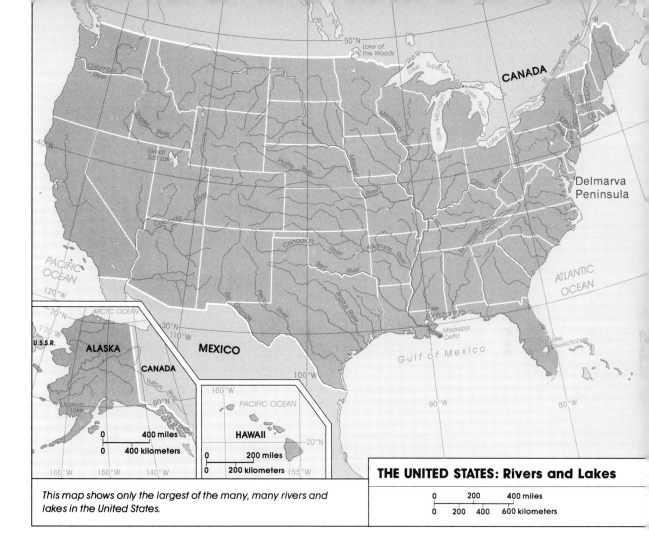

This map shows only the largest of the many, many rivers and lakes in the United States.

THE UNITED STATES: Rivers and Lakes

| 0 | 200 | 400 miles |
| 0 | 200 | 400 | 600 kilometers |

Missouri

Mississippi

Yukon

Rio Grande

Arkansas

Colorado

Columbia

Snake

Red

A wealth of water As you have learned, much of the earth's surface is water. From the beginning, great numbers of Americans, like people of all nations and ages, have chosen to live near oceans, lakes, and rivers. As you read this section and the next, you will find some of the reasons for this.

As you look at the map on page 263 and the map above, you will notice many rivers. Although there are hundreds and hundreds of beautiful rivers in the United States, only the largest are shown on these maps. Among those labeled are the nine rivers that are over 1,000 miles (1,600 km) in length.

The most important river in our country is the Mississippi. On the map above, trace the route of the Mississippi from its **source** in Minnesota to its **mouth** in Louisiana. A **delta** has formed here where the Mississippi empties into the Gulf of Mexico. A delta is a low, level piece of land at the mouth of a river. It is found where a river has formed more than one **channel.** Find the Mississippi Delta on the map above.

Our country also has a great many lakes. The largest of these are the Great Lakes. In fact, they are among the largest lakes in the world. These five huge lakes stretch from Minnesota to New York.

Sources differ as to the longest river in the United States. Some say the Mississippi; others the Missouri. Our source is *Webster's New Geographical Dictionary.*

The same source was used to determine the nine rivers that are over 1,000 miles (1,600 km) long.

Lead a class discussion on the importance of water, how people can conserve water, and ways to clean up our polluted rivers and lakes. You may want pupils to draw posters, compile a booklet or design a bulletin board that emphasizes the importance of this most valuable resource.

They are, in order of size from largest to smallest, Lakes Superior, Huron, Michigan, Erie, and Ontario. We share four of these lakes with Canada, our neighbor to the north. Only Lake Michigan lies entirely within the United States. Lake Michigan is larger than the states of Vermont, New Hampshire, Rhode Island, Massachusetts, Connecticut, New Jersey, Delaware, Maryland, and Hawaii.

We are fortunate to have so many freshwater rivers and lakes. We are also lucky enough to be bounded by three great oceans. They are the Atlantic, the Pacific, and the Arctic oceans. On the map on page 263, find the coasts of the United States that touch these three oceans.

Importance of water Our many sources of water are valuable for a great number of reasons. The rivers and lakes are most important as sources of drinking water. The waters of some of our rivers and lakes are too **polluted**, or dirty, to drink. But the waters of many others give us plenty of fresh drinking water.

Some parts of our country do not always have enough rain to grow crops. Here water from rivers and lakes is used to **irrigate** the fields.

Some of the larger lakes and rivers, such as Lake Michigan and the Mississippi River, serve as transportation routes. Ships use these water routes to carry all kinds of goods and materials from one part of the country to another.

The larger bodies of water are also important to the fishing business in the United States. Fish are very valuable as food for people all over the world.

Discuss major and/or minor bodies of water located in your area. Ask pupils how those bodies of water are important to the community.

Barges like this one on the Columbia River use our waterways to carry goods.

Hoover Dam: 726 ft (221 m) high; 1,244 ft (379 m) long; 660 ft (200 m) thick. Hoover Dam holds the water in Lake Mead, a large reservoir. The dam controls floods; provides electric power to Arizona, Nevada and southern California; provides water for irrigating farmland; and supplies water to several cities.

Some rivers, such as the Tennessee and the Niagara, provide electric power. The water from these rivers turns large generators. The generators change the power of moving water into electric power. Power from this source is known as **hydroelectric power.** The electricity can be used to light our homes. It can be used to run factory machines that make thousands of products.

Our lakes and rivers also give us beautiful places just to enjoy. Many people love to swim or boat. Others like to go fishing. People like to spend their vacations near many of our lakes and rivers.

Our oceans are also important for many reasons. The Atlantic, the Pacific, and the Arctic oceans are all sources of fish. Fine beaches along the Pacific and Atlantic attract thousands of visitors each year. The Atlantic and Pacific oceans also serve as major ocean highways to countries all over the world.

This hydroelectric plant is on the Colorado River.

36°N, 114°44′W

As you know, many Americans live near water. Look at the population map on page 259. You can see that many large cities have grown up near our ocean coasts and along our lakes and rivers. Now you know why that is so.

People of all ages enjoy the water.

CHECKUP

1. Name three important landforms in the United States.
2. What is the difference between an island and a peninsula?
3. What is the longest river in the United States? The largest lake?
4. Name at least four important ways people in the United States use their lakes, rivers, and oceans.

267

The Earth and the Sun

VOCABULARY

weather	seasons
climate	axis
temperature	rotation
precipitation	revolution

Weather Have you ever planned a picnic and had to call it off because it rained? Have you ever felt like flying a kite, only to discover that there was no wind? Have you ever wanted to go swimming but decided it was too cold? Has your school ever closed because of a snowstorm? If any of these things happened to you, your plans were changed because of the **weather.**

Weather is the condition of the air at a certain time. Rain, snow, wind, heat, and cold are all part of the weather. The weather may be hot or cold. It may be sunny or cloudy. It may be dry or wet. It may be raining or snowing. It may be windy or calm. Our big country has many different kinds of weather, just as it has many different kinds of land.

Climate The kind of weather a place has over a long period of time is its **climate.** The two most important parts of any place's climate are **temperature** and **precipitation.** Temperature refers to the amount of heat in the air. Precipitation is rain, snow, mist, sleet, or hail.

Which of these three places gets the most precipitation? The least?

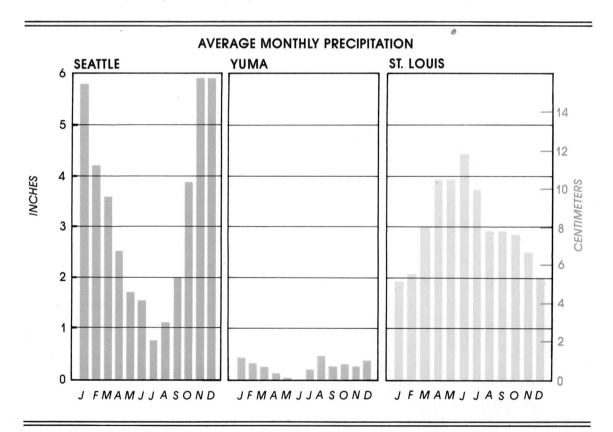

AVERAGE MONTHLY PRECIPITATION

SEATTLE   YUMA   ST. LOUIS

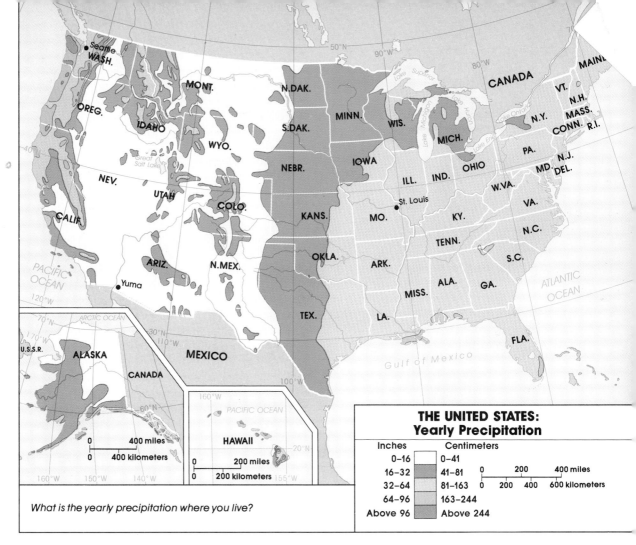

Inches	Centimeters
0–16	0–41
16–32	41–81
32–64	81–163
64–96	163–244
Above 96	Above 244

What is the yearly precipitation where you live?

Ask: What is the weather like today? How would you describe the climate of our area?

You probably know more about the climate where you live than you think you do. Of course, on some days it may rain when you don't expect it to. And a day that you expect to be hot and sunny may turn out to be chilly and windy. But most of the time you know the times of the year, or **seasons,** in which you can expect warm or cold weather. You know the months that have the most rain or snow.

Precipitation   Maps can help us learn a great deal about rain and snow in the United States. Look at the map of yearly precipitation above. Yearly precipitation is the total amount of precipitation that falls during a year. Find your state on the map. Now look in the key to discover how many inches or centimeters fall in your area. Which are the driest parts of our country? Which are the wettest?

You remember that graphs also help you learn important facts. You might want to know how much rain or snow falls from month to month in a certain place. You could look at a precipitation graph. On page 268 you will see precipitation graphs for Seattle, Washington; Yuma, Arizona; and St. Louis, Missouri. The graphs show the average amounts of rain or snow that fall in each of these cities each month of the year.

You may want to invite a local weather specialist to the class to discuss weather and climate and to demonstrate the use of weather instruments.

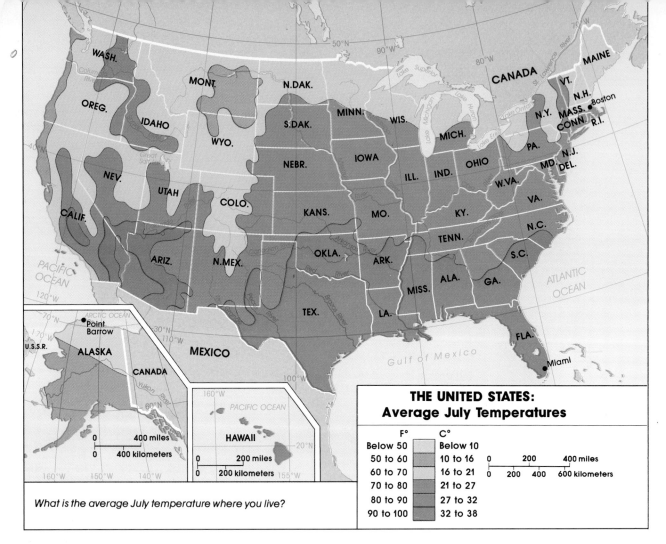

THE UNITED STATES: Average July Temperatures		
F°	C°	
Below 50	Below 10	
50 to 60	10 to 16	0 200 400 miles
60 to 70	16 to 21	0 200 400 600 kilometers
70 to 80	21 to 27	
80 to 90	27 to 32	
90 to 100	32 to 38	

What is the average July temperature where you live?

Temperature In most parts of our country one season is generally hotter than the others, and one is colder than the others. Look at the map above. This map shows the average July temperatures in the United States. Find your state. What is the average July temperature in your part of the state? How did the key help you find out?

Southeastern California and southwestern Arizona have the hottest Julys in the United States. Alaska has the coldest.

Now look at the map on page 271. This map shows the average January temperatures. What is the average January temperature where you live? This map shows that Hawaii and the southern tip of Florida are the hottest places in the United States in January. Northern Alaska is the coldest. It has an average January temperature of −10° Fahrenheit (−23°C).

A graph is helpful if you want to know average temperatures for each month of the year for any one place. The graphs on page 271 show the average monthly temperatures for Point Barrow, Alaska; Boston, Massachusetts; and Miami, Florida. Where is it warmest in May? Where is it coldest? In which of these three places does the temperature stay nearly the same all year long?

Miami

Point Barrow

Miami

Which place has the greatest difference between winter and summer temperatures? Point Barrow

270

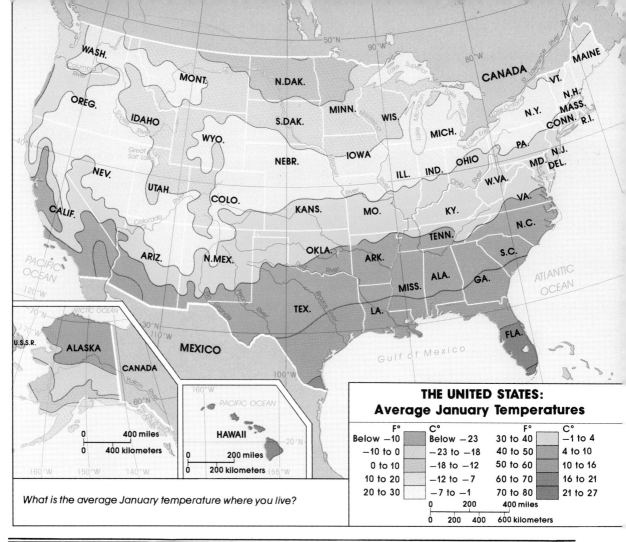

THE UNITED STATES:
Average January Temperatures

F°	C°		F°	C°
Below −10	Below −23		30 to 40	−1 to 4
−10 to 0	−23 to −18		40 to 50	4 to 10
0 to 10	−18 to −12		50 to 60	10 to 16
10 to 20	−12 to −7		60 to 70	16 to 21
20 to 30	−7 to −1		70 to 80	21 to 27

What is the average January temperature where you live?

AVERAGE MONTHLY TEMPERATURES

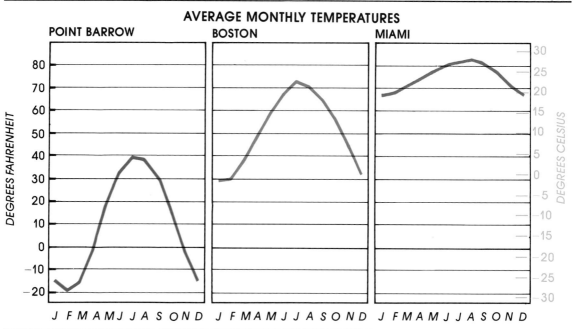

POINT BARROW   BOSTON   MIAMI

Ask: What is the average monthly temperature for Boston in December? (32° F; 0° C) in July? (72° F; 23° C) What is the average monthly temperature for Point Barrow in February? (−20° F; −28° C) What is the average monthly temperature for Miami in December? (65° F; 19° C)

In this picture taken from Apollo 8, *the earth seems to rise over the moon.*

The brownish spot in the lower right-hand view of the earth is northern Africa.

Spinning in space   When you ride on a highway, you might be moving along at a speed of about 55 miles (90 km) an hour. If you fly in a jet plane, you might be traveling 560 miles (900 km) an hour. What is the fastest speed you have ever reached? Do you think you have ever moved at a speed of 795 miles (1,280 km) an hour? How would you like to speed along at 67,000 miles (107,800 km) an hour?

You may never have known it, but every day you move at a speed of 795 miles an hour. You also travel 67,000 miles an hour. This may sound strange to you. But it is true.

The first speed, 795 miles an hour, is the speed at which the earth turns, or rotates, on its **axis** every day. The earth's axis is an imaginary line that goes through the earth from the North Pole to the South Pole.

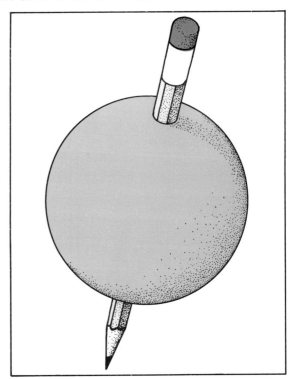

In this drawing the pencil acts as the axis for the ball. Our earth spins on its axis in the same way. It makes one complete turn every 24 hours.

Christmas week of 1968 Apollo 8, containing Astronauts James Lovell, Jr., William A. Anders, and Frank Borman, soared toward the moon. The astronauts were awe-struck as they looked back at Earth. The spacecraft circled the moon 230,000 miles away from Earth.

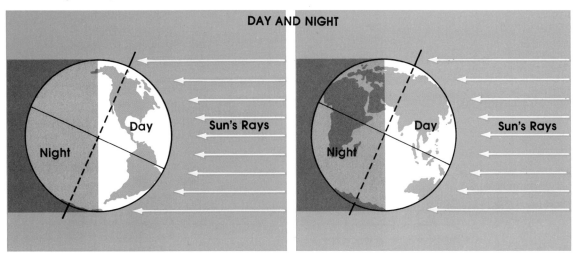

DAY AND NIGHT

The dotted line is the earth's axis. The solid line is the equator. When it is night on one side of the earth it is day on the other.

Suppose you were to push a pencil through the middle of a rubber ball. Then suppose you held the pencil steady while turning the ball around the pencil. Your ball would be doing the same thing that the earth does when it turns on its imaginary axis. The only difference would be that the ball had a pencil as an axis.

The earth's 24-hour **rotation** on its axis causes our day and night. Our heat and light come from the sun. Only about half the earth can receive the sun's rays at any given time. When our half of the earth receives the sun's rays, it is our daytime. When the other half of the earth is getting the heat and light of the sun's rays, it is our nighttime.

If the earth did not turn on its axis, the same side would always face the sun. The other half of the earth never would. If this happened, the side facing the sun would become too hot for people to live there. The side of the earth turned away from the sun would become too cold for people to live.

Journey around the sun   The earth takes 365 days to move once around the sun. So besides rotating on its axis once in every 24 hours, the earth also moves around the sun once in every year. This **revolution** is a journey of about 595 million miles (960 million km). The earth makes this journey at a speed of about 67,000 miles an hour. That means that in the past minute you have moved more than 1,000 miles (1,600 km)!

This yearly journey has a great deal to do with our climate. The revolution of the earth around the sun causes our seasons. Look carefully at the diagram on page 274. Notice that the axis of the earth is tilted. This tilt never changes. It stays the same throughout the earth's 365-day journey around the sun.

Now look at the position of the earth on June 22. June 22 is the beginning of summer in the Northern Hemisphere. You can see that the northern part of the earth is tilted toward the sun. That means the strongest, most direct rays of the sun

273

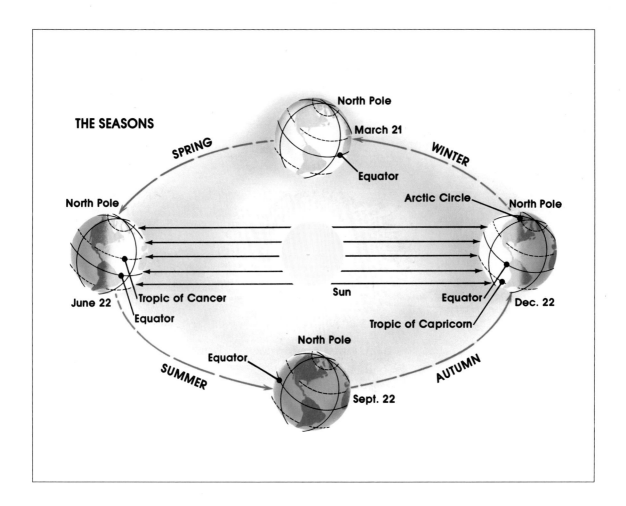

THE SEASONS

SPRING

WINTER

North Pole

March 21

Equator

Arctic Circle

North Pole

North Pole

Sun

Tropic of Cancer

Equator

Equator

June 22

Tropic of Capricorn

Dec. 22

Equator

North Pole

SUMMER

AUTUMN

Sept. 22

This diagram shows why there are seasons. The labels give the seasons for the Northern Hemisphere.

are shining on the Northern Hemisphere. When we receive the most direct rays of the sun, we have our summer.

The seasons in the Southern Hemisphere are just the opposite of those in the Northern Hemisphere. June 22 is the beginning of winter in the Southern Hemisphere. At that time the Southern Hemisphere is tilted as far away from the sun as it ever gets, so the sun's rays reach the Southern Hemisphere at a slant.

In December, January, and February, when it is winter in the Northern Hemisphere, it is summer in the Southern Hemisphere. At that time, the sun's rays reach the Northern Hemisphere at a slant while shining more directly on the Southern Hemisphere. December 22 is the first day of winter in the Northern Hemisphere. It is the first day of summer in the Southern Hemisphere. May is an autumn month in the Southern Hemisphere.

CHECKUP

1. What is weather? Climate?
2. What kinds of precipitation are there?
3. What causes day and night?
4. What causes the seasons?

Natural Resources

> **VOCABULARY**
>
> | | |
> |---|---|
> | natural | ore |
> | resource | smelting |
> | petroleum | atomic energy |
> | fuel | nuclear energy |
> | reserves | agricultural |
> | anthracite | milling |
> | bituminous | |

Riches of the earth   How long do you think you could live without fresh air or clean water? Without fertile soil, where would we grow our food crops? Air, water, and soil are **natural resources.** Natural resources are all the things found in and on the earth that are useful to people. They are not made by people. They are provided by nature. Without some of these resources we couldn't live.

You know that the United States is a rich and powerful country. One of the most important reasons for this is that we have so many natural resources. On pages 265 – 267, you read about how important water is to people in the United States. But there are many other valuable natural resources in our country.

Ask: What forest products are a part of your every day life?

Forests   Forests are a great natural resource. From trees come lumber and other products. Lumber is used for building houses, furniture, and many other things. The United States is the second largest lumber-producing country in the world.

A great deal of wood from our forests is made into pulp for paper products. The paper in this book is made from wood. We use more lumber and paper than any other country in the world.

Which nation produces the most lumber?   U.S.S.R.

Which state produces the most lumber?   Oregon

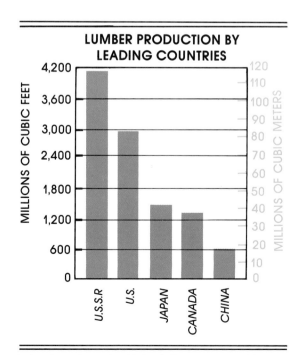

LUMBER PRODUCTION BY LEADING COUNTRIES

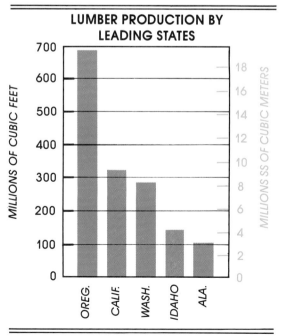

LUMBER PRODUCTION BY LEADING STATES

Ask: How much lumber does the United States produce yearly in millions of cubic feet? (2,900) in millions of cubic meters? (82)

How much more lumber does Oregon produce yearly than Alabama in millions of cubic feet? (581) in millions of cubic meters? (16)

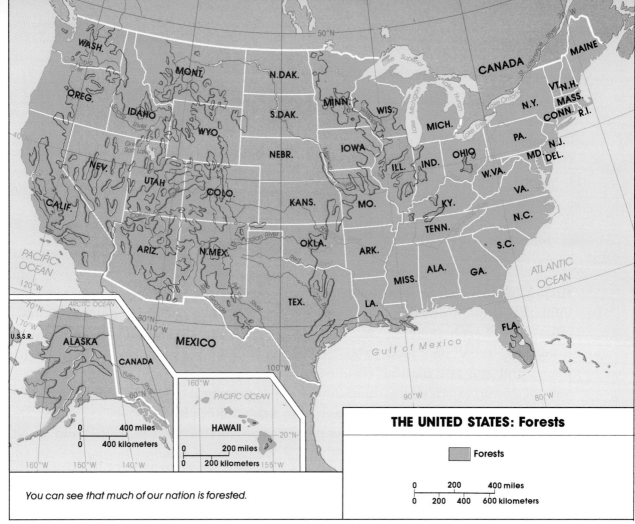

THE UNITED STATES: Forests

Forests

0   200   400 miles
0 200 400 600 kilometers

You can see that much of our nation is forested.

Ask: Which United States region has the fewest forests? (North Central)

Discuss with pupils the kinds of trees that are found in the forest regions of their state.

There are more than 750 million acres (300 million ha) of forests in the United States. Almost every part of our country has some forest land. Some large forests are found in all the regions of the United States. But the most important forests for lumbering are in the Pacific region. You will learn more about these great forests when you read about the Pacific region.

Fuels Natural gas, **petroleum**, and coal are **fuels.** Fuels are very important to all of us. They are necessary to the life of the United States. Fuels give us the energy that runs our cars, buses, trucks, trains,

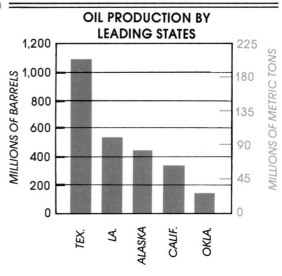

OIL PRODUCTION BY LEADING STATES

Which state produces about 500 million barrels of oil a year? About 1,100 million barrels?

Have pupils write to the National Wildlife Federation, 1412 16th St. N.W., Washington, D. C. 20036 for information concerning forest and water conservation practices.

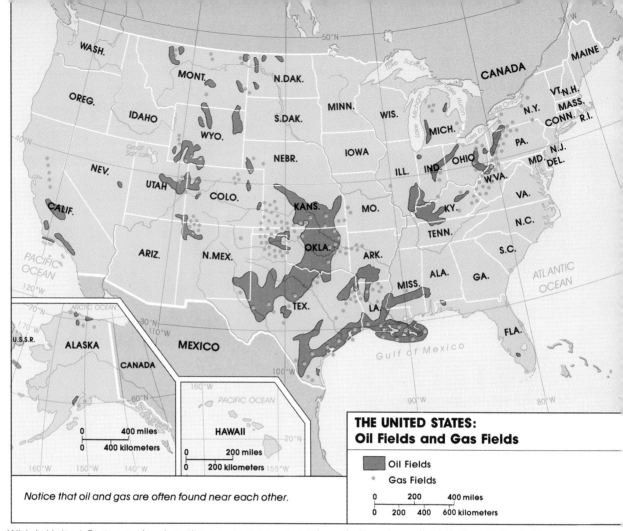

THE UNITED STATES:
Oil Fields and Gas Fields

Oil Fields
Gas Fields

Notice that oil and gas are often found near each other.

Which United States region has the greatest concentration of oil and gas fields? (South Central)

ships, and airplanes. Fuels are used to heat or cool our homes and factories. They also provide electricity to run machines in our factories.

The United States is the third largest oil-producing country in the world. Thirty-one of our states produce oil. Look at the graph on page 276. You can see that Texas, Louisiana, Alaska, California, and Oklahoma are the leading producers of oil in our country. Find these states on the map above.

Although oil was discovered in northern Alaska in 1968, it took a long time to solve the problems involved in getting the oil. It was not until the late 1970s that Alaska

became one of our five leading producers of oil.

The United States is rich in oil. But we use huge amounts of it. When trees are cut down in our forests, new trees can be planted. But once oil is taken from the earth, it cannot be put back. So our supplies are quickly running out. Today we must get almost half of our oil from other countries. We get a great deal of oil from the Middle East; from Nigeria, Libya, and Algeria in Africa; from Venezuela in South America; from Indonesia; and from Canada and Mexico.

Look at the map above. Find all the states that produce natural gas. This

Ask: How many miles per gallon does your family car consume? Why is it important to purchase fuel-efficient cars today?

The average price per gallon of regular gasoline in 1965 was 31 cents. Ask: What is the price per gallon of gasoline today?

277

UNITED STATES OIL PRODUCTION, 1955-1990

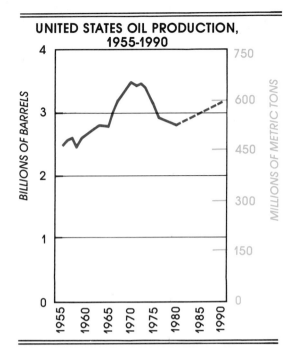

BILLIONS OF BARRELS

MILLIONS OF METRIC TONS

Oil production increased sharply in which years?

COAL PRODUCTION BY LEADING STATES

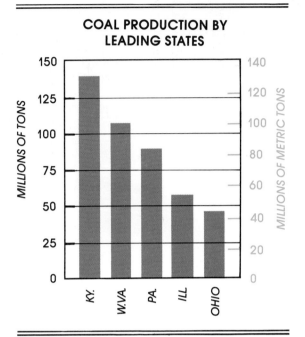

MILLIONS OF TONS

MILLIONS OF METRIC TONS

KY.   W.VA.   PA.   ILL   OHIO

Find these five states on the map at the right.

You can see how big this coal shovel is by comparing it to the bulldozer.

278 Big Muskie: 410 ft (125 m) long—1½ times the length of a football field; 151 ft (46 m) wide—the width of a football field; 27,000,000 lbs (12,258,000 kg). The bucket, used to move huge areas of earth in strip mining for coal, is big enough to hold a full battalion of marines (1,100 people).

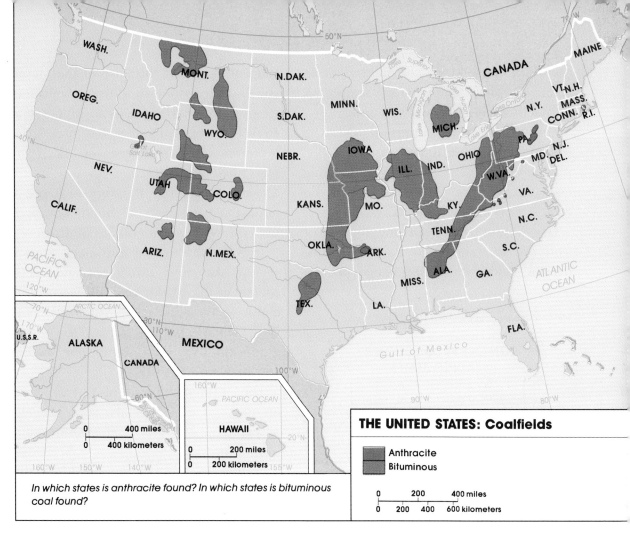

THE UNITED STATES: Coalfields

Anthracite

Bituminous

0   200   400 miles

0   200   400   600 kilometers

In which states is anthracite found? In which states is bituminous coal found?

country has huge supplies of natural gas. More are being found every year. However, Americans burn great amounts of gas every year. Millions of Americans use natural gas. We use it to heat our homes and cook our food. We are using up this natural resource faster than we can find new supplies. Once gone, natural gas, like oil, cannot be replaced.

Another natural resource that is an important source of energy is coal. This fuel is used to make half of all the electricity used in this country. The United States has the largest known **reserves** of coal in the world. Coal reserves are supplies of coal that have not been mined. But we know that they are in the earth and can

be used. The United States mines more coal than any other country. In 1975 about 170,000 people worked in our coal mines. By 1985 about 125,000 more people may be working in these mines.

Look at the map above. You can see that coal is found in many of our states. There is more than one kind of coal. **Anthracite** (an´ thrə sīt), or hard coal, is found in several states. Of these states, Pennsylvania produces the most. Mining of **bituminous** (bə tü´ mə nəs) coal, or soft coal, is also important in Pennsylvania. The map above shows you that soft coal is found in many states. The right-hand graph on page 278 shows the leading coal-mining states.

Metals   Metals are yet another great resource. The United States' supply of metals is one of the world's richest.

One of our most important metals is iron. It is found in a kind of rock called iron **ore.** By using heat from burning coal, the iron can be melted out of the rock. This is called **smelting.**

Our largest center for the mining of iron ore is the Mesabi Range in Minnesota. Find the Mesabi Range on the map on page 281. Because of the Mesabi mines, Minnesota produces about four times as much iron ore as any other state. However, the United States uses great amounts of this resource, too. There are still huge amounts of iron ore in the Mesabi Range. But the very best ore is almost all used up. Now much of our iron ore comes to us from other countries.

Iron can be turned into steel. Steel is one of the most important and useful metals in the world. You will learn more about steelmaking when you read about the Middle Atlantic states. The lower graph on this page shows our leading steelmaking states.

The United States also has large amounts of other metals, such as gold, silver, copper, lead, aluminum, and uranium.

Copper is one of our most valuable metals. Its most important use is in the making of electric wire. Most of the wires that carry the electricity that we use in our homes, factories, and offices are made of copper. You might not even be able to turn on a light in your home if it were not for copper wire. The map on page 281 shows where copper is found in the United States. Again, in spite of our great reserves of copper, we use more than we can mine. So we must buy copper from other countries.

Uranium is a metal that is our newest source of energy. For many years no one knew that it was a valuable resource. Then it was found to be the main source of a new kind of energy. It is called **atomic energy,** or **nuclear energy.** This kind of energy can produce electricity, just as oil and coal can.

Minnesota produces most of our iron ore.

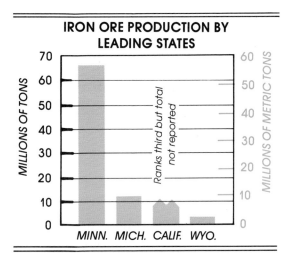

Which large lakes are these states near?

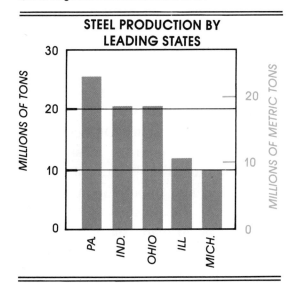

Have pupils bring to class current articles on the national concern over nuclear power plants. You may want to set up a classroom debate for and against nuclear energy.

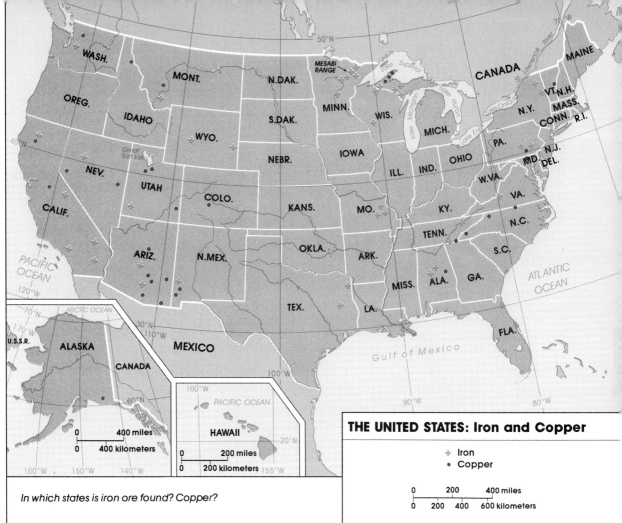

THE UNITED STATES: Iron and Copper

+ Iron
• Copper

| 0 | 200 | 400 miles |
| 0 | 200 | 400 | 600 kilometers |

In which states is iron ore found? Copper?

Ask: What important food products are grown in our state?

Soil and agriculture Without soil, we would have no crops. Without crops, we would not have enough food. The soil and climate in many parts of our country are very good for growing crops. The United States is the world's leading **agricultural**, or farming, country. We are one of the few countries in the world that grow more food than they can use. Much of our food is sent to other countries. Wheat in particular is shipped in huge amounts to other lands.

Look at the graph at the right. You can see that California is the leading farming state. Look at the graphs on pages 282 – 283. Name the five leading wheat states, corn states, and cotton states.

Ask: What is the value of farm production in California? ($9,800,000)

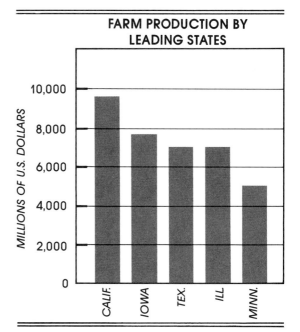

FARM PRODUCTION BY LEADING STATES

MILLIONS OF U.S. DOLLARS

What is the value of farm production in Iowa?

$7,900,000

281

This is the final assembly area of an airplane factory near Seattle, Washington.

Emphasize to pupils that natural resources are important to us not only because they provide us with food, clothing, and shelter but also because the products made from natural resources provide jobs for millions of Americans.

Industry One of the meanings of *industry* is the making, or manufacturing, of goods. Steelmaking is an industry. So is the making of copper wire. These industries grew because of our rich supplies of natural resources. Steelmaking uses coal and iron ore. To make copper wire, copper ore is needed.

The United States has a big textile, or cloth-making, industry. This developed because our rich soils grow fine cotton. The wheat-**milling** industry grew because of our rich wheat-growing lands. Wheat milling is the grinding of wheat into flour. Lumber milling, turning logs into lumber, grew because of our great forests. Oil refining, making oil and other products from raw petroleum, grew because of our rich oil reserves. The airplane and automobile industries also depend on many resources.

These industries and many others provide millions of jobs for Americans. The steel industry alone gives jobs to more than half a million people. You will learn more about these industries as you read about the different regions in our nation.

CHECKUP

1. Name at least four of our important natural resources.
2. What metal has recently been found to be a valuable source of energy?
3. Which is our most important farming state?
4. Name one industry that depends on iron ore, one that depends on forests, and one that depends on good soil.

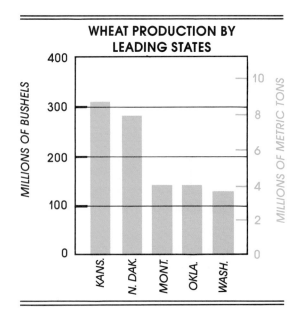

WHEAT PRODUCTION BY LEADING STATES

How much wheat does Kansas produce each year?

You may want to take the class on a field trip to a local industrial plant. 310 million bushels (8½ million metric tons)

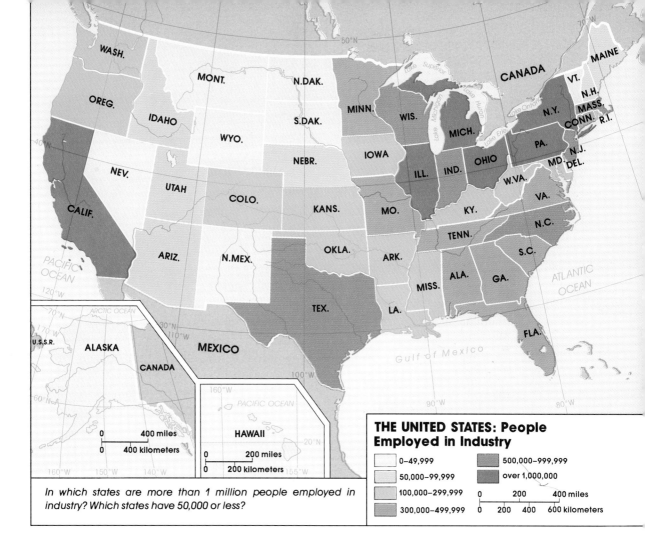

THE UNITED STATES: People Employed in Industry

0–49,999	500,000–999,999
50,000–99,999	over 1,000,000
100,000–299,999	
300,000–499,999	

0   200   400 miles
0   200   400   600 kilometers

In which states are more than 1 million people employed in industry? Which states have 50,000 or less?

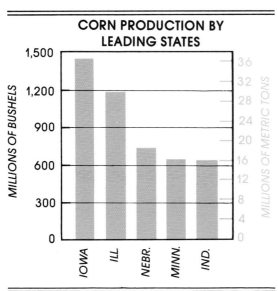

CORN PRODUCTION BY LEADING STATES

MILLIONS OF BUSHELS / MILLIONS OF METRIC TONS

IOWA · ILL. · NEBR. · MINN. · IND.

How much corn does Illinois produce each year?

1,200 million bushels (30 million metric tons)

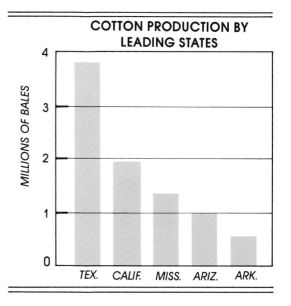

COTTON PRODUCTION BY LEADING STATES

MILLIONS OF BALES

TEX. · CALIF. · MISS. · ARIZ. · ARK.

How much cotton does California produce each year?

1.9 million bales

283

14/CHAPTER REVIEW

KEY FACTS

1. The most important part of geography is the study of the ways people use the earth.

2. Three important tools of geography are maps, tables, and graphs.

3. The United States has a huge variety of landforms and natural resources.

4. Two of the most important parts of both weather and climate are temperature and precipitation.

5. The rotation of the earth causes night and day.

6. The revolution of the tilted earth around the sun causes the seasons.

VOCABULARY QUIZ

Beside the number of each sentence, write the word or words that best completes the sentence. Write on a sheet of paper.

1. Two parts, or ___regions___, of the United States are the Mountain West and the Southeast.

2. The ___population density___ of most of Alaska is less than 5 people per square mile (2 per sq km).

3. At the mouth of the Mississippi River a ___delta___ has formed.

4. Electricity created by the force of moving water is called ___hydroelectric___ power.

5. Rain, sleet, and snow are all forms of ___precipitation___.

6. The earth rotates on its ___axis___.

7. It takes a year for the earth to complete one ___revolution___ around the sun.

8. Another name for oil is ___petroleum___.

9. Hard coal is called ___anthracite___.

10. Soft coal is called ___bituminous___ coal.

REVIEW QUESTIONS

1. What is the difference between a political map and a physical, or relief, map?

2. Which is the largest state in the United States? The smallest?

3. Name at least five landforms found in the United States.

4. Where are the highest mountains in the United States found?

5. Which state is made up entirely of islands?

6. What is the difference between weather and climate?

7. Why do we have night and day?

8. What causes the changing seasons?

ACTIVITIES

1. In an almanac, find the population of your state for the past ten censuses. Make a line graph to show how the population has changed. Show the number of people along the side and the years across the bottom of the graph. Give your graph a title. If you live in Alaska or Hawaii, use the United States population instead.

2. In an almanac, find the names of the world's ten largest lakes. Label the lakes on a world map. How many of the Great Lakes are labeled on your map?

3. Keep a record of the weather in your area for a few weeks. Record the temperature at the same time of day each morning and afternoon. Note whether it was raining, snowing, sunny, cloudy, or foggy. What was the highest morning temperature? The lowest? What was the highest afternoon temperature? The lowest? What were the average morning and afternoon temperatures? How often was there precipitation? Were most days sunny or cloudy?

14/SKILLS DEVELOPMENT

READING A MAP: WORLD POPULATION DENSITY

On page 259 of this chapter you saw a map of population density in the United States. That map also shows the 25 largest cities in the United States. The map below shows population density in the whole world. It also shows the world's 25 largest cities. Use the map below, as well as the map on page 259, to answer the following questions. You may need to refer to the Atlas maps, as well.

1. Are any of the 25 largest cities in the United States located in your state? How many?

2. Name the cities in the United States that have more than 1 million people.

3. Which state, Nevada or Massachusetts, has a higher population density?

4. Which of the 25 largest cities in the United States is located at 30° north latitude and 90° west longitude?

5. How many of the cities shown on the United States population map are within 100 miles (160 km) of a large body of water?

6. Two states each have three or more cities among the 25 largest cities in the United States. Name them.

7. Name the city in the United States that is one of the 25 largest cities in the world.

8. Which continent has the largest number of cities that are among the 25 largest cities in the world?

9. What is the southernmost city shown on the world population map?

10. What is the northernmost city shown on the world population map?

11. How many people per square mile are there in most of Australia? Per square kilometer?

12. What is the population density in most of central India?

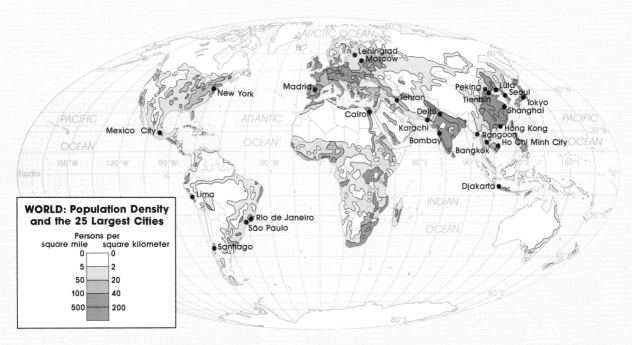

WORLD: Population Density and the 25 Largest Cities

Persons per	
square mile	square kilometer
0	0
5	2
50	20
100	40
500	200

15 The New England States Today

The Land and Climate

VOCABULARY
landscape	upland
promontory	sound
elevation	temperature
	extreme

The Atlantic Coast   The United States is a huge nation of about 3,615,000 square miles (9,372,850 sq km). It is divided into 50 states. As we said earlier, it would be hard to study all 50 states at once, so we will divide them into 7 regions.

The first region, New England, has six states. They are Maine, New Hampshire, Vermont, Massachusetts, Rhode Island, and Connecticut.

The two main features of the New England **landscape** are coastline and mountains. Five of the six states are along the Atlantic coast. Which New England state does not border on the ocean?   Vermont

Along Maine's northern coast are many bays and **promontories.** High, rocky land that juts out into the sea along a coastline is called a promontory. The highest point on the Atlantic coast is on Mount Desert Island in Acadia (ə kā′ dē a) National Park, Maine. Here is found Cadillac Mountain, which is 1,530 feet (467 m) high. Farther south, there are stretches of sandy beaches as well as jagged coastline. A famous feature of New England's Atlantic coast is Cape Cod in Massachusetts. Part of this peninsula is Cape Cod National Seashore.

The Appalachian Mountains   The second main feature is the mountain range known as the Appalachian Mountains. In the United States, this range extends from Mount Katahdin in Maine south through all the rest of the New England states except Rhode Island. In New Hampshire, the Appalachians are called the White Mountains. The highest peak in the White Mountains is Mount Washington. With an **elevation** of 6,288 feet (1,917 m), Mount Washington is also the highest point in New England. In Vermont, the Appalachians are called the Green Mountains. In Massachusetts, the Appalachians are called the Berkshires. The Appalachians continue south through Connecticut and the Middle Atlantic and southern states as far as northern Georgia.

The Appalachian Mountain system actually extends into New England from eastern Canada.

Other features   Rolling hills and **uplands** make up most of the countryside between the mountains and the coast. Most of the lowlands are along the coast. However, some are also found in the central areas and in the Connecticut River valley.

There are many rivers and lakes throughout New England. The largest lake

The English explorer, Captain John Smith, visited this northeastern region in 1614, and named it *New England* in honor of his native land.

The map shows you that much of New England is covered by the Appalachians. The photograph shows the rugged, rocky shores typical of the Maine coast.

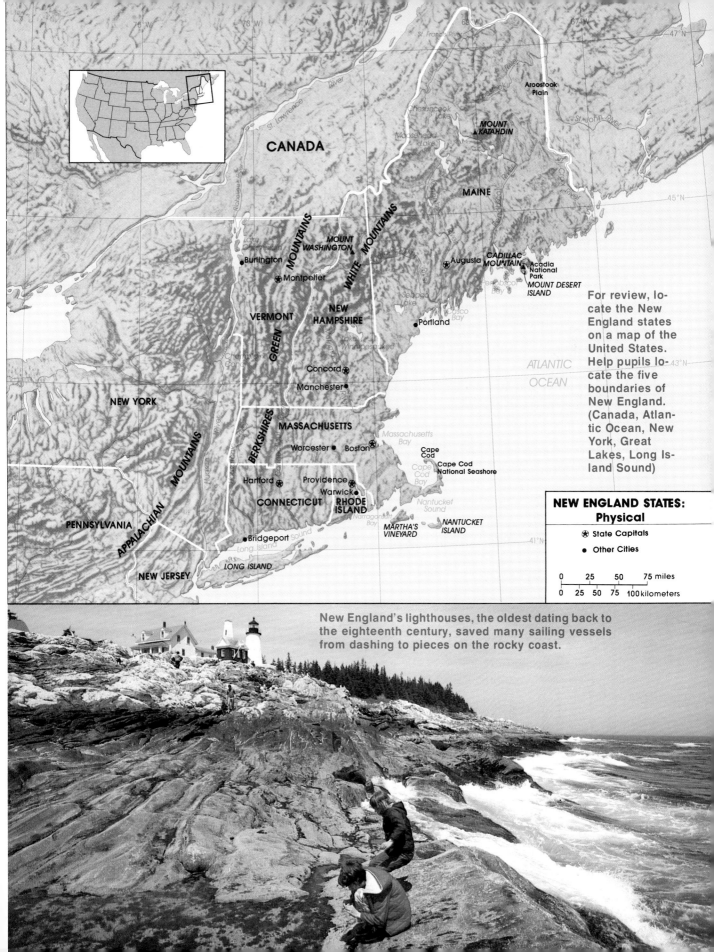

CANADA

MAINE

MOUNT KATAHDIN

Aroostook Plain

St. John River

Chesuncook Lake

Moosehead Lake

VERMONT

GREEN MOUNTAINS

Lake Champlain

• Burlington

⊛ Montpelier

WHITE MOUNTAINS

MOUNT WASHINGTON

NEW HAMPSHIRE

CADILLAC MOUNTAIN

⊛ Augusta

Acadia National Park

MOUNT DESERT ISLAND

Penobscot Bay

Sebago Lake

Casco Bay

• Portland

Lake Winnipesaukee

Concord ⊛

Manchester •

NEW YORK

BERKSHIRES

APPALACHIAN MOUNTAINS

Hudson River

MASSACHUSETTS

Worcester • Boston ⊛

Massachusetts Bay

Cape Cod

Cape Cod Bay

Cape Cod National Seashore

Hartford ⊛

Providence ⊛

Warwick •

CONNECTICUT

RHODE ISLAND

Nantucket Sound

Narragansett Bay

MARTHA'S VINEYARD

NANTUCKET ISLAND

PENNSYLVANIA

NEW JERSEY

• Bridgeport

Long Island Sound

LONG ISLAND

St. Lawrence River

ATLANTIC OCEAN

47°N
45°N
43°N
41°N

75°W 78°W 68°W 67°W

For review, locate the New England states on a map of the United States. Help pupils locate the five boundaries of New England. (Canada, Atlantic Ocean, New York, Great Lakes, Long Island Sound)

NEW ENGLAND STATES: Physical

⊛ State Capitals

• Other Cities

0   25   50   75 miles

0 25 50 75 100 kilometers

New England's lighthouses, the oldest dating back to the eighteenth century, saved many sailing vessels from dashing to pieces on the rocky coast.

is Lake Champlain, which is between Vermont and New York State and extends into Canada. The longest river is the Connecticut River. It begins in New Hampshire and flows along the New Hampshire–Vermont border, through Massachusetts, and empties into Long Island **Sound.** Among the other large rivers are the Penobscot (pə nob′ skot), Kennebec (ken ə bek′), and Merrimack.

Climate The mountains, the Atlantic Ocean, and the northern location all affect the climate of New England. The table and the graph will help you to better understand this region.

The mountains and the northern areas are the coldest parts of the region. These areas also have greater **temperature extremes.** Temperature extremes are the highest and lowest recorded temperatures. Along the coast, it is milder throughout the year.

Every month has some precipitation. Winters with 100 inches (254 cm) of snow are common in parts of Maine. Snowfall is heavy throughout the rest of New England as well. Cloudy and overcast skies are also common to this area.

Mount Washington is the windiest place in the United States. The average daily wind speed is 35 miles (56 km) per hour. Wind speeds greater than 230 miles (370 km) per hour have been recorded there.

You can see that some parts of New England have very severe winters. How-

For each city, the first bar shows total precipitation. The second bar shows snowfall alone. To find the total precipitation, scientists figure out how much rain the snow is equal to. Then they add that amount to the rainfall. From 6 to 30 inches (15–76 cm) of snow equals 1 inch (2.5 cm) of rain.

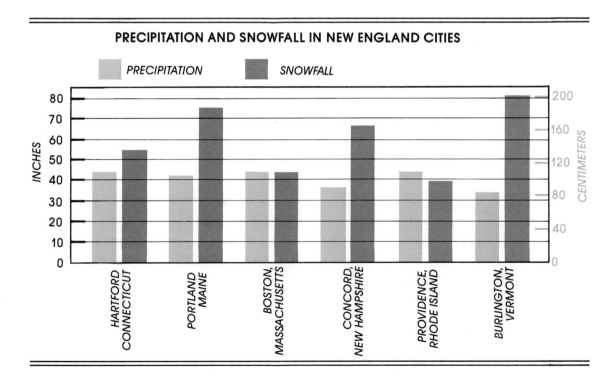

PRECIPITATION AND SNOWFALL IN NEW ENGLAND CITIES

TEMPERATURE, NEW ENGLAND CITIES

Weather station	Average January temperature		Average July temperature		Temperature extreme °F		Temperature extreme °C	
	°F	°C	°F	°C	High	Low	High	Low
Hartford, Conn.	25	−4	73	23	102	−26	39	−33
Portland, Maine	22	−6	68	20	103	−39	39	−39
Boston, Mass.	29	−2	73	23	102	−2	39	−24
Concord, N.H.	21	−6	70	21	102	−37	39	−38
Providence, R.I.	28	−2	72	22	104	−13	40	−25
Burlington, Vt.	17	−8	70	21	101	−30	38	−34

ever, winter is only one part of the New England climate. Fresh spring growth and autumn colors mark changing seasons. Coastal winds, though harsh in winter, are cooling and relaxing in the summer.

CHECKUP

1. What are the two main features of the New England landscape?
2. Name two factors that affect New England's climate.
3. What are the coldest parts of New England? The mildest?

Mining, Fishing, and Other Industries

┌─VOCABULARY─────────────────┐
mineral	spermaceti
quarry	synthetic
fleet	armory
quota	import
trawler	
└────────────────────────────┘

Minerals   The resources of New England, like the landscape and climate, are varied. Sand, gravel, and stone are found in all the states. These **mineral** resources

are needed for many types of construction. The mines and **quarries** of northern New England produce granite, slate, and marble used in buildings and monuments throughout the United States.

Vermont is the leading source of talc in the United States. Talc is a soft mineral that when ground into a powder is used in making crayons, paint, paper, soap, and talcum powder. In slab form it is used in electrical insulation and as furnace insulation.

Vermont ranks second in the United States in the production of asbestos and slate. Asbestos is a fire-resistant mineral used for purposes similar to those of slab talc. Slate is a hard, blue-gray, layered rock well known to students of earlier days. Their lessons were written on a slate chalkboard in the front of the classroom. Many students had smaller slates for use at their seats. Slate roofs are still found on some old buildings. Slate roofs are fireproof and don't wear out. However, they are brittle and break quite easily, which is one reason that slate is no longer in common use for roofs.

A huge slab of stone is lifted from a quarry by a motor-driven pulley.

The uses of minerals can be graphically presented. Ask pupils to bring in objects made of granite, slate, or marble. Display the objects and label them according to the minerals they contain.

Some craftworkers do the carving and sculpturing of granite and marble. Other artisans carve inscriptions on the polished surface of the stone.

Quarrying   It is difficult to get granite, marble, and slate from the ground and prepare these stones for use. Some stone is taken from underground mines and some from deep quarries or open pits. Workers use torches on the slabs of stone. The heat of the torch makes the stone expand and crack. A skillful worker can guide where and how a slab separates.

Stone cutters use special saws to cut the huge slabs of granite and marble into more manageable sizes and shapes. Some slabs are cut into smaller slabs for steps, blocks for buildings, or tiles for floors. Polishing machines are used to smooth the surface of the hard, heavy stone.

Fishing   Fishing is an industry that has a long tradition in New England. As the colonists settled along the New England coast, they found the tall pine, fir, and oak trees to be good resources for shipbuilding. Soon fishing **fleets** were sailing out of harbors from Maine to Connecticut. They searched far into the North Atlantic Ocean for cod, flounder, halibut, and haddock. Mackerel and herring were most often found swimming in large schools in the waters off the coast. Here also were found lobsters and other shellfish.

Fishing remains important to this day. However, there have been many changes. For many years fishing fleets from other countries had such good catches that they were using up the stock of fish in the rich fishing grounds of the Atlantic. The New England fish catch dropped from about 700 million pounds (320 million kg) in 1965 to less than 525 million pounds (240 million kg) in 1975.

In 1977 the United States extended its fishing zone from 12 nautical miles (22 km) to 200 nautical miles (370 km). (Nautical miles are longer than the miles we use on land.) This meant that foreign fishing fleets needed permits to fish within 200 nautical miles of our coast. Our own fleets have had to limit their catches. Some types of fish, like cod, flounder, and haddock, were becoming so scarce that **quotas** have been set up. Limiting catches will let the supply of fish grow.

1 nautical mile=6,076.115 feet (1,852 m). 1 statute mile=5,280 feet (1,609 m)

Changes have also been made in the fishing vessels themselves. Boats with sails are now used almost entirely for pleasure. Today's fishing **trawler** is likely to have a large diesel engine, a radio, radar, and refrigerated areas for storing the catch. The radio allows a captain to talk to other captains in the fleet, as well as to people on shore. Finding schools of fish is easier today because radar is used.

Diesel power, good quarters for the crew, and refrigeration make it possible to travel farther after the schools of fish. That in turn means the captain and the crew are away from their families longer. With the extension of the zone, better

A load of pollack and other kinds of fish has just been dumped into this fishing boat from Gloucester, Massachusetts.

Sea gulls follow fishing boats, hoping for their favorite food.

equipment, and quotas on the catches, perhaps the outlook for the fishing industry will change for the better.

Whaling   Once, New England ports sheltered many whaling ships, as well as fishing boats. Whales provided many valuable products. People burned whale oil in their lamps. From the whale oil, they used a waxlike solid called **spermaceti** (spėr mə set' ē) in making candles. They used whalebone in making fans and other articles.

In the early days, whales were caught in the coastal waters of New England. In time, however, whales became scarce there. As the years passed, whaling captains hunted the giant creatures in distant waters. New England whaling ships sailed around the southern tip of South America and then far north in the Pacific Ocean. Sometimes a whaling ship would be away from its home port for as long as 2 or 3 years.

Many sailors never returned from these long voyages. A whale could crush a whaleboat with one blow of its giant tail. Indeed, huge whales now and then sank the whaling ships themselves.

For more than 50 years after the Revolutionary War, whaling remained important. Then people learned how to get petroleum from the earth. When this happened, whale oil was no longer needed for lamps. The New England whalers turned to fishing or other jobs, and the old whaling ships slowly rotted in the harbors.

Textiles   For many years New England was the most important manufacturing center in America. Here were the neces-

Research project: Some pupils may like to find out what efforts are being made by private groups to save whales from extinction.

291

sary harbors, trading ships, skilled workers, and water power. Manufacturing is still important in New England but the products have changed somewhat.

One of the most important and earliest industries of New England was textile manufacturing. You read about Samuel Slater and the first textile mill in Chapter 8. You may remember that in the nineteenth century, northern mills made cloth from cotton grown on southern plantations.

During the first half of the twentieth century, most of New England's cotton mills either closed down or moved to the southeastern states. Here the mills were near the cotton supply. Also, wages were lower in the south. Some New England cotton mills closed because there was less demand for cotton. People wanted the new **synthetic** materials instead.

New England is still a leading producer of textiles. Today, however, most of the mills produce woolens. Most of the raw wool comes from New Zealand and Australia. It is carried by ship to Boston Harbor. From there it goes to spinning and weaving mills in nearby cities. Here, fine woolen cloth is made.

Shipbuilding   Although tall-masted trading ships are a part of history, shipbuilding is still important in New England. Some of today's shipbuilders make sailboats and yachts for recreational use. Others work in the shipyards that build modern vessels. Nuclear-powered submarines for the United States Navy are built at Groton, Connecticut, near New London. There are other shipyards along the New England coast.

Small, delicate, precise instruments are needed for modern ships. Skilled workers in New England make these instruments, as well as electronic equipment, computers, gauges, and other equipment.

Silverware and firearms   In a sense, precision manufacturing has long been a part of the story of New England. Silverware and firearms, both of which take great skill in manufacturing, have been made in New England since the colonial days. Paul Revere is famous for his midnight ride. He is almost as well known for his skill as a silversmith. Even today, a certain style of bowl is called the Revere bowl. Of course, Revere was not the only New England silversmith. There were others who made fine silver. And people today still look to New England for beautiful examples of the craft.

Many of our soldiers in the Revolutionary War were armed with guns produced at Springfield, Massachusetts. The **armory** here has made firearms for United States soldiers for most of our history. Now there is a museum at the Springfield armory. There the history of firearms can be studied. Hartford, Connecticut, was the home of one of the country's best-known guns: the Colt six-shooter revolver. Many high quality sporting guns are still made in Connecticut and Massachusetts.

Leather   The leather goods industry is another New England industry that is no longer as large as it once was. Leather goods, such as saddles, harnesses, and footwear, were made from colonial days to the early 1900s. Then came the auto-

Samuel Colt, inventor of the first repeating revolver uncomplicated and sturdy enough for long-term use, was born in Hartford, Conn., in 1814. The factory that he set up in Hartford manufactured arms used in both the Mexican and the Civil wars. The famous Colt six-shooter was widely used in the American West.

In this picture of the shipyard at Quincy, Massachusetts, you can see three tankers under construction. They will carry liquified natural gas.   42°20′N/71°05′W

mobile. You can guess what happened to the demand for saddles and harnesses then.

Shoe manufacturing has suffered for different reasons. A greater variety of materials are being used in the making of shoes. Leather is still important, but many shoes are made of synthetics. These shoes usually cost less than leather shoes, so there is less demand for leather shoes. A second reason is that much footwear is now **imported** from foreign countries. The value of imported footwear grew from $629 million in 1970 to over a billion dollars in 1975. By 1978 the value of imported footwear was more than $2.5 billion. The next time you buy a pair of shoes, look at either the shoes or the box they came in to see where they were made.

Shoes are still being made in New England, especially in Massachusetts. Maine has developed a reputation for moccasins and outdoor leather boots. Boots, moccasins, and other leather products have made leather a major industry in Maine today.

CHECKUP

1. Name two minerals found in New England and tell how each is used.
2. Why have quotas been set up for United States and foreign fishing fleets?
3. How have synthetic materials changed both the textile and the shoe industries?

Agriculture and Forests

---VOCABULARY---

livestock	renewable
fertile	resource
cash crop	tract
income	lumberjack
bog	saw timber
evergreen	recycle
deciduous	

Hay, livestock, and vegetables New England's soil is not suitable for all kinds of agriculture. In some places it is quite rocky and too thin for raising crops like wheat or oats. However, the cool, moist climate and thin soil is suited to raising hay. Some of the land can be used for the grazing of dairy cattle. Raising chickens is another important farming activity in each of the six states. Neither chickens nor cattle need level land, and there is a ready market for both nearby. New England does not grow enough feed for these farm animals. Farmers depend on farms in the North Central states for grain for their **livestock**. Small patches of level land are used to raise vegetables, which are sold at roadside stands or in nearby towns and cities.

Growing tobacco There is some level land along the coast and in the river valleys and in the central regions. Here the land is more **fertile** and suitable for raising crops. One crop that is raised in the fertile lands of Connecticut and Massachusetts is tobacco. From colonial times, farmers living in the Connecticut River Valley have grown tobacco. Not as many acres of land are set aside today for

raising tobacco as there were 30 or 40 years ago. However, tobacco is a good **cash crop** because it provides more **income** per acre than most other crops.

Growing potatoes In northeastern Maine's Aroostook (ə rüs' tək) River valley, the soil is rich and silty, or fine-grained. Summers are cool and moist. Even though the growing season is short, it is long enough to raise good potato crops. The Aroostook Valley has become famous for fine quality potatoes. The business of raising potatoes makes up nearly 80 percent of Maine's income from crops.

The Aroostook Valley is not very close to the major cities, but potatoes keep very well and are easy to transport. A cool dry place is suitable for storage. Maine potatoes are sold throughout the United States and Europe.

Blueberries and cranberries Two other important New England crops are grown in the eastern parts of Maine and Massachusetts. The two crops are blueberries and cranberries. You have probably enjoyed eating both fruits without knowing where they were grown. Maine is the leading producer of low-bush blueberries in the United States. The bushes, which are 6 to 18 inches (15 cm to 45 cm) high, grow wild in the fields and on the hillsides of Maine. The berries ripen in August. At that time, Indian families come from Maine's northern neighbor, New Brunswick, Canada, to help with the harvest. Most of the berries are shipped to other parts of the country. Some are shipped fresh. Others are frozen or canned.

The flooding and draining necessary to the cultivation and harvesting of cranberries are easily accomplished on Cape Cod's low land.

Workers on Cape Cod guide cranberries to a pipe that carries them into a truck.

The second crop, cranberries, is popular throughout the United States during the Thanksgiving and Christmas holidays. The **bogs** near Cape Cod, Massachusetts, are the major source of the nation's cranberries. Bogs are wet swampy lands. They are drained when the plants need to be cared for. Then the water is allowed to flood the bogs again. When the bogs are flooded, the water helps to keep weeds from growing. Flooding also helps to keep the plants from freezing in early spring and late fall. The ripe berries are harvested in the fall.

A forested region   Rhode Island is the only New England state in which the number of acres of farmland is about the same as the amount of wooded or forested land. In the other five states, there is more forested land than farmland. Overall, about 80 percent of New England is forested. Maine, New Hampshire, and Vermont have the highest percentages of forested land.

Several kinds of trees are found in New England forests. Pine and spruce are quite common. Both are **evergreens** and keep their needles all year. You may be familiar with the types of pine and spruce that are used as Christmas trees. New England forests also have **deciduous** (di sij′ ủ əs) trees, such as oak and chestnut, which lose their leaves in the fall.

To the Native Americans, and later to the Europeans who settled in New England, the forests played an important role. The forests sheltered the game that provided food and clothing. Both Indians and colonists used firewood in cooking and heating. Logs and lumber were used for homes and other buildings and for furniture. As you know, the lumber from coastal forests was used in shipbuilding. And as you will see, the sugar maple yielded yet another valuable product.

Pupils might contribute to a table display of typical New England products.

295

Maple syrup Have you ever had maple candy from Vermont? Perhaps you have had real maple syrup on pancakes or waffles. The flavor of real maple syrup is different from that of pancake syrup, which contains only a little maple syrup.

The history of Vermont maple syrup and candy goes back to pioneer days. For many early settlers, maple syrup and candy were the only sweets. To make the syrup and candy, the settlers collected sap from certain kinds of maple trees. This was done in early spring. Often the snow was still on the ground and the air was cold and wintry. However, within the tree, the sap had begun to rise. The settler bored a hole into the tree and placed a tap in the hole. The sap flowed slowly through the tap and into a container. Each day while the sap was rising, a collector went from tree to tree emptying the containers. The sap was taken to the sugarhouse where it was boiled for a long time to remove most of the water. Nearly 40 buckets of sap were needed to produce one bucket of syrup. Today, some farmers use the same methods to get the sap. Others use a system of plastic tubing to carry the sap from the taps to the sugarhouse. That way there is no need to go from tree to tree collecting buckets.

Trees, a renewable resource The Indians left the forests almost untouched. However, the colonists cleared huge areas of forests for their farms and towns. There was so much forest land that no one worried about how much wood was cut. Today, the demand for wood products is so high that we must keep track of the amount of wood that is cut. Fortunately, forests are a **renewable re-**

The boy in the picture (left) is emptying a bucket of sap into a pail. The horse-drawn wagon in the background will carry the sap to the sugarhouse. This system of plastic tubing (right) carries the sap directly to the sugarhouse.

Most of the maple syrup and maple sugar produced in the United States comes from Vermont, New Hampshire, and Maine.

source. In order to have a supply of wood in the future, people now treat trees as "crops." Only large, older trees that yield large amounts of good lumber are cut. New trees are planted to take their place. Sometimes the planting is done even before the old trees are harvested.

Many lumber and paper companies own large **tracts** of forested land. National and state governments also control large forested areas. Many farmers set aside parts of their land for growing trees.

Cutting timber   In the past, workers called **lumberjacks** cut down trees with axes and handsaws. Sometimes two people would work together with a two-man saw, but the lumberjack's job was still difficult and dangerous. For this reason, legends developed about the strength and daring of the lumberjack.

Today the colorful lumberjack, equipped only with a sharp axe and handsaw, lives only in legends. Hand tools are still used for some jobs, but most cutting is done with powerful chain saws. Power saws have made lumbering easier, although it is still hard work.

Hauling timber   After trees are felled and the branches trimmed off, the logs must be hauled out of the forest. Until about 60 years ago, this job was done by teams of horses or oxen. In the spring, when the snow melted, the ground was too muddy for the animals to get through. So the logs were cut in winter while the ground was still frozen. The oxen dragged the logs down the mountains and hills to rivers like the Kennebec and Penobscot. Then in the spring when the ice melted,

This crane is loading logs onto the truck that will take them to the papermill.

the lumberjacks would guide huge log drives down the swiftly flowing rivers to the sawmills.

Today trucks have replaced both the oxen and the log drives. Most woodcutting is still done in the winter, because the logging roads become seas of mud in the spring. It is as hard for the trucks to get through as it once was for the oxen. Very few logs are moved by water.

Uses of timber   Today, as in colonial times, timber has many uses. Some trees are cut for **saw timber**. Lumber used in the building trades comes from saw timber. Some trees are used for making plywood and furniture. A few are very carefully chosen for use in boatbuilding. Smaller trees are cut for pulpwood, which is used in making paper.

Pulpwood and paper are major industries in New England. Maine is a pulpwood leader not only in New England, but in the nation as a whole. New England is noted for fine paper. Some paper is sold nationally, and some is sent to foreign markets.

HOW PAPER IS MADE

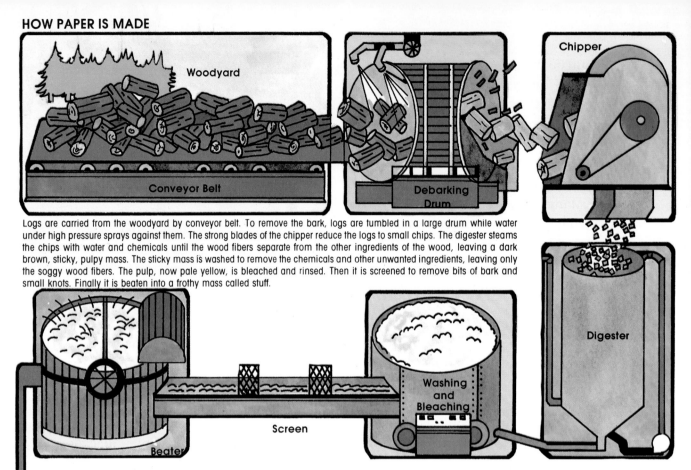

Logs are carried from the woodyard by conveyor belt. To remove the bark, logs are tumbled in a large drum while water under high pressure sprays against them. The strong blades of the chipper reduce the logs to small chips. The digester steams the chips with water and chemicals until the wood fibers separate from the other ingredients of the wood, leaving a dark brown, sticky, pulpy mass. The sticky mass is washed to remove the chemicals and other unwanted ingredients, leaving only the soggy wood fibers. The pulp, now pale yellow, is bleached and rinsed. Then it is screened to remove bits of bark and small knots. Finally it is beaten into a frothy mass called stuff.

On the Fourdrinier machine, the stuff flows from the head box onto a wire mesh belt. The belt moves rapidly away from the flow of stuff, shaking sideways as well. In a few seconds the stuff has lost most of its water and has become rough, thick soggy paper. The paper passes over suction boxes, which remove more water, then passes on to a belt of wool felt and

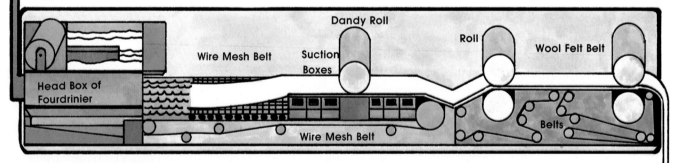

travels under the dandy roll and other rolls, which press the paper and remove more moisture. After steam-heated drums dry the damp paper, it is pressed between steel rollers called calenders, which give it a smooth finish. As the paper comes off the calenders, it is wound into huge rolls.

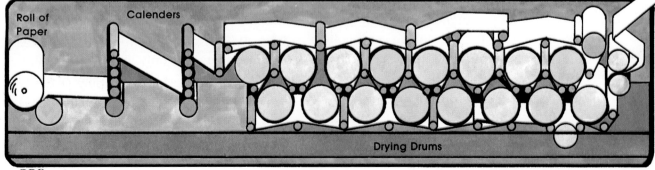

Making paper   The first step in supplying pulpwood for the mill is planting and caring for trees. Spruce and pine are commonly grown for pulpwood. When the trees are ready for harvesting, workers may clear an area by cutting all the trees. If the trees vary in size, the workers cut down only the older trees, leaving the younger trees to grow. The fallen trees are trimmed of their branches, and cut into logs about 4 feet (1 m) long. Machines load them on large trucks that haul the logs to the mill.

At the mill, the bark is removed and the logs are cut into chips or ground up. The chips (or ground wood) are mixed with water and chemicals to form the pulp. As you can see in the drawing, the pulp passes through a number of machines. After the last stage shown in the drawing, the processes differ according to the kind of paper being made.

Pulp, paper, and the environment
Pulp mills need a lot of water. Many mills are on freshwater streams and rivers. In the past, the water and chemicals used in making paper were dumped into the streams. The water became polluted. Now at most mills the chemicals are removed and the water is cooled before it goes into the streams. The animals and plants that need the streams again have fresh, clean water.

Not all paper is made from newly cut pulpwood. When you have time, look at your notebook or at other paper supplies in your room or at home. On some paper goods or their wrappers, you will see a stamp saying that the paper is **recycled**. That means it is made of paper that has been used before. The used paper was collected, perhaps in a paper drive. Then the collected paper went through processes like the ones described earlier.

CHECKUP

1. In what ways do the soil and climate affect the types of crops grown in New England?
2. What are four important crops grown in this region?
3. Name three ways the early colonists and Indians used the forests.
4. How are forests used today?

Tourism, People, and Communities

-VOCABULARY-

tourism	gristmill
broadleaf	urban
foliage	metropolitan
landmark	area

Tourism   In a way, **tourism** is one of New England's important industries. All kinds of businesses are helped by the tourists who come to New England throughout the year. Tourists need restaurants, motels, and gas stations. They buy many different things, from magazines to suntan oil to skis. Many businesses have opened just to take care of the needs and wants of tourists.

Camping   Some visitors come to New England to camp in the national and state forests and parks. Most camping grounds have picnic tables, places for cooking, and safe, clear, water. Nature trails allow hikers to enjoy the beauty of the woods and

299

This peaceful Connecticut village is typical of many New England villages.

to see the many living things found there. These forests and parks are a welcome change for people who spend most of the year in the city.

Beautiful foliage   The maple, oak, beech, and other **broadleaf** trees give New England a resource other than lumber and paper. Each autumn the leaves of these trees change from green to bright red, yellow, orange, and other colors. The brilliant **foliage** attracts tourists who plan fall trips just to see the wooded hills and valleys in full color.

Winter sports   The New England winter also brings visitors. These people come for winter sports, especially skiing. In the mountains of Vermont alone, there are more than 50 ski areas. In most winters there is plenty of snow. However, if nature does not provide snow, snowmaking machines are put to work.

Coastal attractions   Another tourist attraction is the seacoast. The Maine coast is dotted with small islands, about 2,000 of them between New Brunswick and New Hampshire. The bays and promontories make a rugged, rocky coast that many people enjoy. Acadia National Park, much of which is on Mount Desert Island, just to the northeast of Penobscot Bay, has more than 3 million visitors a year. There they enjoy fishing, boating, and just watching the sea. Southeastern Maine's Old Orchard Beach, near Portland, is one of the few sandy beaches in northern New England. It attracts tourists from up and down the coast.

Maine has about 3,000 miles (4,800 km) of beautiful, deeply indented coastline.

As we mentioned earlier, one of the nation's most famous landscape features is Cape Cod in Massachusetts. Cape Cod has the shape of a hook. The body of water within the hook is Cape Cod Bay. As you may know, the *Mayflower* anchored in Cape Cod Bay while some of the Pil-

Bulletin-board display: Attractive pictures of New England's tourist attractions are easily obtained. Pupils can write letters to the chambers of commerce of the various state capitals, or they might visit a local travel agency for pamphlets and other tourist literature.

Plimoth Plantation provides appropriate seasonal activities and exhibits. These may range from sail setting on the *Mayflower II* to a real wedding in the seventeenth-century manner. A visit to this site is a rewarding experience. There may be a historic site or museum in your area that would also be of great interest.

grims explored the coastline for a place to settle. Now Cape Cod is a national tourist attraction. It is crowded with visitors during the summer months. Some people return to Cape Cod year after year.

Historic sites   A different type of attraction found along the coast and elsewhere in New England is the restored village. Mystic, Connecticut, was a seaport in the nineteenth century. It has been restored so that you can see how people lived in a coastal village more than one hundred years ago. You can see how peo-

Years ago, when winter travel was often by sleigh, it was sometimes necessary to shovel snow onto the protected bridge in order to provide a surface for the runners.

These children have just skiied through a covered bridge near Franconia, New Hampshire.

Crew members work in the rigging of a sailing ship at Mystic Seaport in Connecticut.

ple dressed, the tools they used, and the homes and stores they built. Up the coast, in Maine, near the mouth of the Kennebec River, the Bath Iron Works and Marine Museum help one to understand old methods of shipbuilding and America's seafaring history. Both Plymouth Rock, where the Pilgrims came ashore from the *Mayflower,* and the reconstructed village, Plimoth Plantation, facing Cape Cod Bay, can be visited throughout the year. Docked nearby is a full-sized model of the *Mayflower.* As you explore the small ship, you get a feeling for the crowded conditions of the passengers and crew. At Sturbridge, in south central Massachusetts, is another reconstructed village. Here one can see how people lived in the early nineteenth century.

Throughout New England there are reminders of our nation's past. Tourists enjoy traveling through small rural villages that at first glance seem to have changed very little since they were first founded 200 or 300 years ago. It is still possible to find covered bridges that were built across small, clear streams more than 100 years ago. There are old farm and village homes that served as stops for runaway slaves using the underground railway. You read about that route to freedom earlier. Historic **landmarks** abound in New England towns. You could spend several days visiting those in Boston alone. In fact, one of the things that ties the New England states together is their historic flavor. Of course, much of New England is very up-to-date. But as one travels through the region, one gets a feeling for history that is found in few other parts of the United States.

301

A region of villages More than 12 million people live in the six New England states. Only about one of every four lives in either a small village or a rural setting, even though much of the region is dotted with small villages.

Many villages got their start at a crossroads for travelers more than a century ago. Many are found on a stream or river that provided a water supply and waterpower for a **gristmill** and sometimes a means of transportation. Some villages were once thriving communities that grew up around a textile mill, a leather factory, or a sawmill. When these small factories closed down, people began to move away. You can still find small communities based on one industry, such as a quarry or a papermill. Other communities vary in population depending on the season. A coastal village that swarms with people in the summer may be practically deserted in the winter. Discussion question: What might happen in a one-industry community if that industry should close up?

A region of cities The largest **urban** area in New England begins just north of Boston, Massachusetts. It extends southward through Connecticut. In fact, the eastern coast as far south as Washington, D.C., is one big urban area. In three of the six New England states—Connecticut,

Massachusetts, and Rhode Island—more than three of every four people live in an urban setting. In two of these states, the capital is also the largest city. Vermont, with the lowest portion of its people living in urban areas, also has the smallest capital. The table at the bottom of the page lists each New England state and names the capital and largest city and gives the population of each.

There are different ways of reporting the population of cities. The table below shows the population of the city itself. Sometimes you will see population figures for **metropolitan areas.** These figures are much larger. A city's metropolitan area includes the city and all the smaller towns and cities around the city. Look at the map on page 306. Find the cities of Cambridge, Newton, and Waltham. These are all part of Boston's metropolitan area. This area has a population of almost 3 million. The Hartford metropolitan area has over 700,000; that of Providence, more than 900,000.

Growth of cities The cities of New England have grown at different rates. We know this because every 10 years, beginning in 1790, the government has taken a census. The graph on page 303 shows the

Ask: Which capital cities are also the largest cities in their states?

NEW ENGLAND STATES: CAPITALS AND LARGEST CITIES

State	Capital	Population	Largest city	Population
Connecticut	Hartford	136,000	Bridgeport	142,000
Maine	Augusta	22,000	Portland	62,000
Massachusetts	Boston	563,000	Boston	563,000
New Hampshire	Concord	30,000	Manchester	91,000
Rhode Island	Providence	157,000	Providence	157,000
Vermont	Montpelier	8,000	Burlington	38,000

population changes that have taken place in six cities since 1800.

There are many different reasons for the changes. The graph does not show which nearby communities were within the city limits in one year and not in another. Industries may have closed down or moved away. There are probably many more reasons for the changes in population. Find each of these six cities on the map on page 306. Does location help to explain how any city grew? Help pupils locate these six cities on a large map and discuss possible reasons for their original growth.

Like many cities today, three of these cities are losing population. Which three are they?

POPULATION GROWTH, NEW ENGLAND CITIES

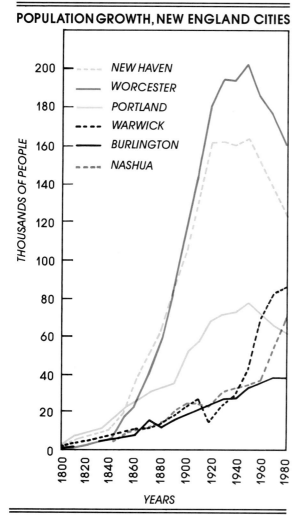

Six cities You have been introduced to a number of cities in this chapter. The table on page 302 listed the capital and largest city in each New England state. On the graph you saw how the population of six New England cities has changed over the years since 1800. You read about Mystic, an early port; the armory at Springfield; and the shipyard at Groton. Now let's look more closely at six New England cities.

Boston By far the largest city in New England, Boston is the capital of Massachusetts. It is one of the 20 largest cities in the United States. There are about 563,000 people in Boston. About 2,760,000 people live in the metropolitan area. This area takes in about 90 smaller cities, towns, and other communities.

Boston is an important port city. It is also a center of trade, transportation, banking, and insurance. Within the city, the major industries are electronics and publishing. Among the hundreds of industries in the Boston area are food processing and the manufacture of machinery, medical instruments, and optical instruments. Fishing fleets supply the large seafood markets in the city.

Cultural and educational opportunities abound in Boston. Lovers of music find hundreds of concerts to attend. There are many art galleries and museums, as well as a museum of natural science, a planetarium, and an aquarium. Boston and the Boston area are the home of many colleges and universities. Among them are the well-known schools of Harvard, M.I.T., Tufts, Wellesley, and Brandeis (bran' dīs).

303

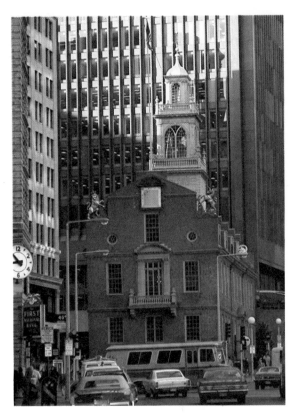

The Old State House in Boston sits in the midst of the hustle and bustle of a busy city. 42°20'N/71°05'W

Boston was founded in 1630 by Puritan colonists. In the Revolutionary period, it was the site of the Boston Massacre, the Boston Tea Party, and other important events. Today, one can relive Boston's history as one follows the Freedom Trail. This is a 1½-mile (2.4 km) route that takes one past Beacon Hill, the Boston Common, the Old North Church, and other sites of historic interest.

Burlington With a population of 38,000, Burlington is the largest city in Vermont. Burlington's location has helped to make it one of Vermont's resort centers. The city is built on a hillside overlooking Lake Champlain. The famous Green Mountains are just 20 miles (30 km) to the east. In the summer, tourists are attracted by the cool climate and by boating on Lake Champlain. Iceboat racing, skiing, and other outdoor sports bring tourists in the winter.

Burlington is a port city. Ships from the St. Lawrence River can reach Lake Champlain by way of a canal and the Richelieu (rish' ə lü) River in Canada. Ships traveling south from Lake Champlain use a canal and the Hudson River. Oil and gasoline are the major products carried by ships in the harbor. In addition to being a transportation and trade center, Burlington is Vermont's leading manufacturing center. Industries in the city make steel for building, electronics equipment, aircraft, appliances, and cereal. 42°28'N/73°14'W

Concord Concord is located on the Merrimack River in southern New Hampshire. It is the state's capital and third largest city. With a population of 30,000, it is the smallest of the six cities being described. When Concord was founded in 1659, it was called Penny Cook, after the Indian name *Penacook*, which means "a crooked place." The Indians gave it this name because of the many bends in the river. Later the name was changed to Rumford, after a local settler. Then in 1765 it was given the name Concord. The city became the state capital in 1808. The government offices in Concord are housed in several beautiful buildings. The State House, or capitol building, is made of granite from nearby quarries and marble from Vermont.

Printing is Concord's leading industry. More than 50 nationally sold magazines are printed in Concord. Electronic equipment, leather goods, and wood products are also made in Concord. The city is a center of retail trade. 43°13′N/71°34′W

New Haven   New Haven is on the north shore of Long Island Sound. The population of the city is 126,000. About 416,000 people live in the metropolitan area. This port city is the third largest city in Connecticut. Oil tankers outnumber other cargo ships in New Haven Harbor.

The New Haven area has about 1,000 industrial companies. These companies make such goods as guns, electrical appliances, machine tools, hardware, toys, and rubber goods.

Founded by the Puritans in 1638, New Haven is an educational and cultural center for southern Connecticut. It is well known for its fine museums and galleries. It is the home of Yale University, the third oldest school of higher learning in the United States. 41°52′N/72°58′W

Portland   Portland is the largest city in Maine. Its city population is 62,000. About 183,000 people live in the metropolitan area. Most of the city is on two hills overlooking Casco Bay. Portland's deepwater port is the Atlantic coast's second busiest oil shipping center. A pipeline carries oil from Portland to Montreal, Canada.

Much of the activity found in Portland has to do with the sea. Besides being an important oil port, the city is also busy with a growing fishing industry, seafood processing plants, and shipbuilding. Other industries include printing and the manufacture of metal products, clothing, and electronic parts.

Portland is the birthplace of Henry Wadsworth Longfellow, a well-known poet. There are many buildings of historic interest in the city. In what is now the city of South Portland stands the oldest lighthouse in the nation, the Portland Head Light. A branch of the University of Maine is located in Portland. 43°41′N/70°18′W

Providence   Providence is Rhode Island's capital and largest city. Its city population is 157,000. About 918,000 people live in the metropolitan area. The city was founded by Roger Williams in 1636. The port at Providence has been important since the early days of our nation. It has more than 10 miles (16 km) of waterfront, and is the third largest port in New England.

The manufacture of jewelry and of silverware are the city's leading industries. Other products include textiles, machinery, and rubber goods.

One of Providence's features is its fine collection of historic homes and buildings. People in the city have worked to restore and preserve many homes built before the Revolutionary War. Brown University, one of the oldest schools of higher learning in the United States, is found in Providence. 41°50′N/71°25′W

CHECKUP

1. Many different businesses depend upon tourists. Name as many of those businesses as you can.
2. What are some of the reasons tourists have for visiting New England?
3. Describe the difference between the population of a city and the population of a city's metropolitan area.
4. Choose two of the six cities described on the past few pages. How are they alike? Different?

305

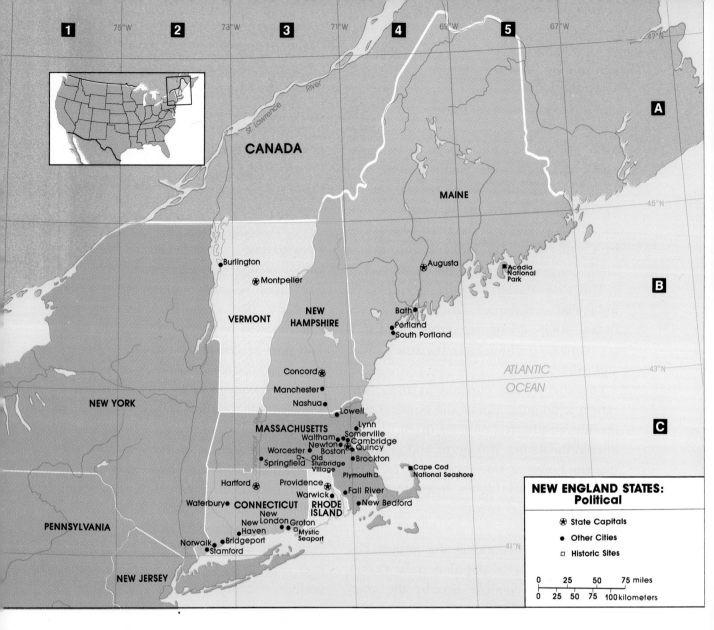

St. Lawrence River

CANADA

MAINE

A

47°N

45°N

•Burlington

⊛Montpelier

VERMONT

NEW HAMPSHIRE

Augusta
⊛

■Acadia National Park

B

Bath•

•Portland
•South Portland

ATLANTIC OCEAN

43°N

Concord⊛

Manchester•

Nashua•

NEW YORK

Lowell•

Lynn•

C

MASSACHUSETTS

Somerville•
Waltham• •Cambridge
Newton• Quincy•
Worcester• Boston•
Springfield• □Old •Brockton
    Sturbridge
    Village

■Cape Cod National Seashore

Connecticut River

Plymouth□

Hartford•⊛

Providence•⊛

Warwick•

•Fall River

Waterbury•

CONNECTICUT

RHODE ISLAND

•New Bedford

41°N

Norwalk•

New Haven•

New London•

Groton•

Bridgeport•

□Mystic Seaport

Stamford•

PENNSYLVANIA

NEW JERSEY

NEW ENGLAND STATES: Political

⊛ State Capitals

• Other Cities

□ Historic Sites

0   25   50   75 miles

0   25   50   75   100 kilometers

Cities with less than 100,000

Augusta (Maine) B-4
Bath (Maine) B-4
Brockton (Mass.) C-3
Burlington (Vt.) B-2
Cambridge (Mass.) C-3
Concord (N.H.) B-3
Fall River (Mass.) C-3
Groton (Conn.) C-3
Lowell (Mass.) C-3
Lynn (Mass.) C-4
Manchester (N.H.) C-3
Montpelier (Vt.) B-3
Nashua (N.H.) C-3
New Bedford (Mass.) C-4

New London (Conn.) C-3
Newton (Mass.) C-3
Norwalk (Conn.) C-2
Portland (Maine) B-4
Quincy (Mass.) C-3
Somerville (Mass.) C-3
South Portland (Maine) B-4
Waltham (Mass.) C-3
Warwick (R.I.) C-3

Cities with 100,000–499,000

Bridgeport (Conn.) C-2
Hartford (Conn.) C-3
New Haven (Conn.) C-3

Providence (R.I.) C-3
Springfield (Mass.) C-3
Stamford (Conn.) C-2
Waterbury (Conn.) C-2
Worcester (Mass.) C-3

City with 500,000–999,000

Boston (Mass.) C-3

City with 1,000,000 or more

None...............................

The cities shown on the political maps in Chapters 15–21 are the capital of each state, all cities with a population of 75,000 or more, and communities mentioned in the text. Population figures used were from the 1980 census.

In some cases the cities are not technically incorporated cities, but they are included anyway to give a truer picture of the distribution of urban areas within the region.

This map has a grid system like the one on the map of Wyoming on page 21. This time the lines of latitude and longitude form the grid. Find Stamford on the list above. The letters C-2 mean it is in box C-2. Find Stamford in box C-2 on the map.

THE NEW ENGLAND STATES	Connecticut	Maine	Massachusetts	New Hampshire	Rhode Island	Vermont
Source of Name	From an Indian word *Quinnehtukput*, meaning "beside the long tidal river"	First used to distinguish the mainland from the offshore islands. It has been considered a compliment to Henrietta Maria, queen of Charles I of England. She was said to have owned the province of Mayne in France.	From two Algonquin words, meaning "great mountain place"	From the English county of Hampshire	From the Greek island of Rhodes	From the French *vert mont*, meaning "green mountain"
Nickname(s)	Nutmeg State	Pine Tree State	Bay State; Old Colony State	Granite State	Ocean State	Green Mountain State
Capital	Hartford	Augusta	Boston	Concord	Providence	Montpelier
Largest Cities (1980 Census)	Bridgeport Hartford New Haven	Portland Lewiston Bangor	Boston Worcester Springfield	Manchester Nashua Concord	Providence Warwick Cranston	Burlington Rutland Bennington
Population Rank (1980 Census)	25	38	11	42	40	48
Population Density Rank	4	36	3	20	2	29
Area Rank	48	39	45	44	50	43
State Flag						
State Bird	American robin	Chickadee	Chickadee	Purple finch	Rhode Island Red	Hermit thrush
State Flower	Mountain laurel	White pine cone & tassel	Mayflower	Purple lilac	Violet (unofficial)	Red clover
State Tree	White oak	White pine	American elm	White birch	Red maple	Sugar maple
State Motto	*Qui transtulit sustinet* (He who transplanted still sustains)	*Dirigo* (I direct)	*Ense petit placidam sub libertate quietem* (By the sword we seek peace, but peace only under liberty)	Live free or die	Hope	Vermont, freedom and unity
Interesting Facts	In 1954 the world's first atomic-powered submarine, the *Nautilus*, was launched from Groton. *The Courant*, published in Hartford, is the oldest United States newspaper still being published.	Maine leads the nation in lobster production, and leads the world in the production of the flat tins of sardines. Eastport is farther east than any other city in the United States.	The first shots of the Revolutionary War were fired in Lexington and Concord. Harvard is the oldest university in the United States.	New Hampshire's vote was the deciding vote that ratified the United States Constitution.	Although it is the smallest state in the nation in physical size, it is the nation's leader in the production of costume jewelry and lace.	Vermont leads the nation in the production of maple syrup. It is also the birthplace of the Morgan horse.

307

KEY FACTS

1. Atlantic coastline and Appalachian Mountains are the two main landscape features of New England.

2. The climate of New England is affected by its northern location, the Appalachian Mountains, and the Atlantic Ocean.

3. New England's industries, such as fishing, lumbering, and the manufacture of textiles and other products, have undergone major changes since the colonial times.

4. The landscape and climate of New England affect the type of farming in the region.

5. The location of communities is influenced by such things as transportation, landscape, and water and other resources.

VOCABULARY QUIZ

Beside the number of each sentence write the letter of the word that best completes the sentence. Write on a sheet of paper.

a. renewable   **f.** synthetic

b. elevation   **g.** trawlers

c. landscape   **h.** quarries

d. foliage   **i.** bogs

e. promontory   **j.** metropolitan

1. Plains, mountains, and other physical features make up the ____c____ of a region.

2. Today, ____f____ materials are often used instead of natural materials.

3. Fishes and forests are ____a____ resources.

4. A ____j____ area includes a central city and the nearby communities.

5. Slate, marble, and other kinds of stone are dug from ____h____.

6. The ____b____ of Cadillac Mountain is 1,530 feet (467 m).

7. Today, fishing ____g____ are equipped with radar, radio, and refrigerated areas.

8. Each fall, the ____d____ of broadleaf trees turns to red, yellow, and other bright colors.

9. A ____e____ is high rocky land that juts out into the ocean.

10. Cranberries are grown in ____i____ .

REVIEW QUESTIONS

1. Describe the New England climate.

2. Name three important rivers of New England.

3. Name three industries of New England.

4. Name four New England farm products.

5. In which two New England states is the capital also the largest city? Which state capital is the smallest? The largest?

6. Name two New England cities. What is each noted for?

ACTIVITIES

1. Plan a route that you would follow if you were to spend a year in New England. On an outline map, show your route and the places you would visit. Label seasonal attractions, such as swimming and skiing, as well as points of interest. Be sure to make a map key. To go with your map, make a pamphlet in which you briefly describe each place you plan to visit.

2. Write a report about an imaginary New England village. In the report, name your village, tell where it is, why it was founded at this particular spot, and describe the area. Give the size of the population in the first year, 10 years later, 50 years ago, and today. Tell how the village has changed and describe some of the results of those changes. Make a map of the village.

Some pupils might like to construct a mural to go with Activity 2.

15/SKILLS DEVELOPMENT

READING A MAP: A NATIONAL PARK

Use what you have learned about map reading to answer the following questions.

1. On the map on this page, find the name of the island on which most of Acadia is located. What is the island's name? Mount Desert Island

2. What color is used for Acadia National Park? What color is used for other land? Green; Brown

3. In addition to the main island, several other islands are labeled on the map. What are their names? Great Cranberry, Little Cranberry, Baker, Bartlett

4. How many bodies of water are labeled on the map? What are they? 4: Frenchman Bay, Somes Sound, Long Pond, Atlantic O.

5. What route would you take to get from Southwest Harbor to Pretty Marsh? 102

6. How would you get from Bar Harbor to Seal Harbor? Rte. 3

As you may remember from Chapter 1, symbols as well as labels are used on many maps. The symbols are explained in the key.

7. Find the symbol for campgrounds in the key. How many campgrounds are shown on the map? 11

8. Find the symbol for lighthouses. How many are shown on the map? 3

9. Find the symbol for the national park headquarters. Find the headquarters on the map. What town is nearby? Hulls Cove

In Chapter 1, you learned how to use a grid system when you worked with a map of Wyoming. A grid system is made up of lines that form boxes where they cross one another. The rows and columns are labeled with letters and numbers.

10. Which town is in box A-3? B-2? C-1? Salisbury Cove, Somesville, Pretty Marsh

11. Which body of water is entirely within box C-2? Long Pond

As you learned, the part of map that helps you find distances is called the scale. Use the scale to answer questions 12 to 14.

12. About how far is it from Bar Harbor to Seal Harbor, measuring in a straight line? 7 miles (11 km)

13. About how far is it in a straight line from Salisbury Cove to the southernmost lighthouse? 15 miles (24 km)

14. About how long is the main island at its longest point? About how wide is it at its widest point? 16 miles (25 km); 12 miles (20 km)

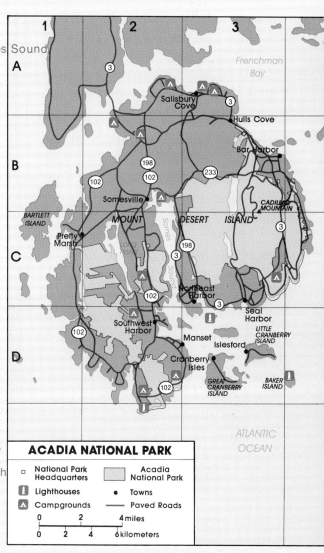

ACADIA NATIONAL PARK

□ National Park Headquarters
▮ Lighthouses
▲ Campgrounds

Acadia National Park
• Towns
— Paved Roads

0   2   4 miles
0 2 4   6 kilometers

309

CHAPTER
16 The Middle Atlantic States Today

The Land

┌─ VOCABULARY ─────────────┐
| bay   valley |
| harbor   foothill |
└──────────────────────────┘

Where is it? The Middle Atlantic region is just where its name tells us it is. Look at the map of the United States on pages 14–15. Find the states of New York, Pennsylvania, New Jersey, Delaware, and Maryland. These are the Middle Atlantic states. And they really are in the "middle." They are located between the New England states and the Southeastern states, which you will learn about in the next chapter. Notice that all except one of the Middle Atlantic states have some part that borders on the Atlantic Ocean. Which state does not? Pennsylvania

The Atlantic Coastal Plain One of the most important landforms of the Middle Atlantic region is the Atlantic Coastal Plain. You read about this plain in Chapter 14. Find this large area on the map on page 311. In which of the Middle Atlantic states is the plain the narrowest? Where is it the widest? New York; Delaware and Maryland

Along the eastern edge of the Atlantic Coastal Plain are many miles of **bays** and **harbors.** A bay is a part of a sea or ocean that cuts deep into the land. Harbors are

Ask: What are "protected waters"—what are they protected from?

protected waters where ships can anchor safely. On the map on page 311 find Chesapeake, Delaware, and New York bays. In which states do you find them? Did you name Maryland and Virginia for Chesapeake Bay? For Delaware Bay did you name New Jersey and Delaware? Did you also include Pennsylvania? For New York Bay did you name New York and New Jersey?

These three bays were also important in the history of our country. Ships carrying settlers and goods were able to enter the country by way of the deep, protected harbors formed by these great bays. The harbors are still important today. Ocean-going ships from many ports and even many nations travel in these bays on their way to and from the ports on the shores of the bays.

Also along the eastern edge of the Middle Atlantic region stretch mile after mile of find sandy beaches. Every summer thousands of families visit these beaches to swim and sail and enjoy the sun and the cool ocean breezes.

The Appalachian Mountain system From the Atlantic coast, the broad plain of flat or gently rolling lowland stretches westward and begins to change. The land becomes rougher. Slowly the plain gives

On the map you can see the two most important landforms of the Middle Atlantic states: the Atlantic Coastal Plain and the Appalachian Mountains. The picture shows people enjoying a beach on the Atlantic Ocean.

310
A bulletin-board display showing changes in water transportation from Native American canoes to modern ocean vessels would make an interesting project.

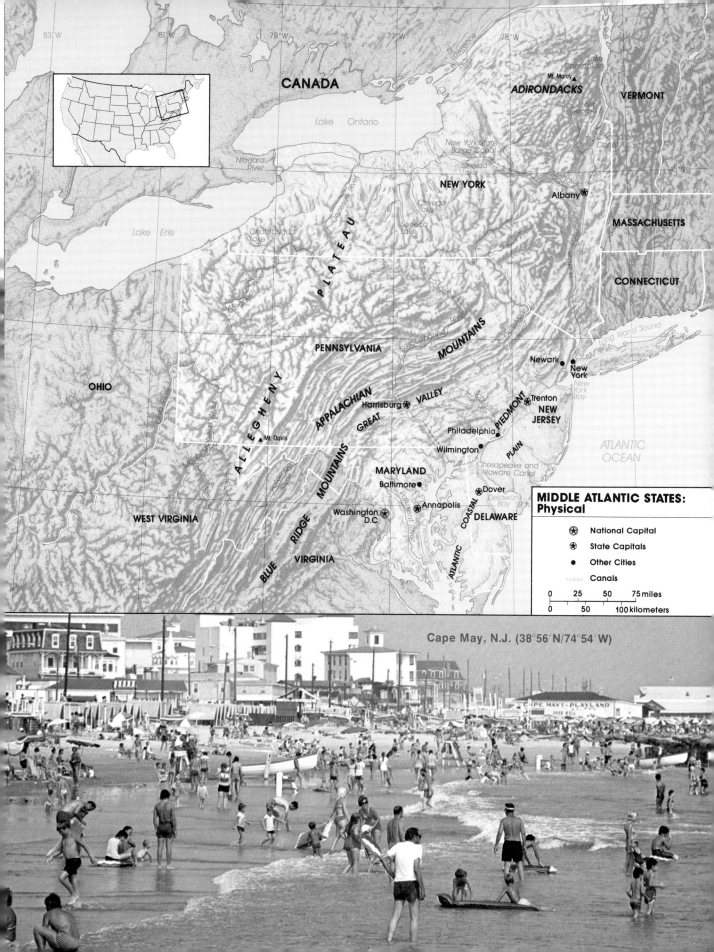

CANADA

St. Lawrence River

Mt. Marcy ▲

ADIRONDACKS

VERMONT

Lake Champlain

Lake Ontario

NEW YORK

New York State Barge Canal

Oneida Lake

Champlain Canal

Albany ⊛

MASSACHUSETTS

Niagara River

Genesee River

Cayuga Lake

Seneca Lake

CONNECTICUT

Lake Erie

Chautauqua Lake

P L A T E A U

Allegheny River

Delaware River

MOUNTAINS

Hudson River

Long Island Sound

OHIO

PENNSYLVANIA

Susquehanna River

Schuylkill River

Newark ●

New York ●

New York Bay

A L L E G H E N Y

APPALACHIAN

VALLEY

Harrisburg ⊛

GREAT

Trenton ⊛

PIEDMONT

NEW JERSEY

▲ Mt. Davis

Philadelphia ⊛

ATLANTIC OCEAN

Monongahela River

BLUE

RIDGE

MOUNTAINS

Wilmington ●

PLAIN

Chesapeake and Delaware Canal

WEST VIRGINIA

Potomac River

MARYLAND

Baltimore ●

Patuxent River

Annapolis ⊛

⊛ Dover

Delaware Bay

39°N

DELAWARE

Washington, D.C. ⊛

Chesapeake Bay

COASTAL

VIRGINIA

ATLANTIC

MIDDLE ATLANTIC STATES:
Physical

⊛ National Capital

⊛ State Capitals

● Other Cities

‧‧‧ Canals

0   25   50   75 miles

0   50   100 kilometers

Cape May, N.J. (38°56′N/74°54′W)

CAPE MAY PLAYLAND

way to a belt of low, tree-covered hills and rich green **valleys.** These are the **foothills** of the great Appalachian system.

The Appalachian Mountain system is a huge area of mountains, plateaus, and valleys. You remember from Chapter 15 that the Appalachian system in the United States starts in Maine and runs south through New England. This same system of mountain ranges continues southwest through the Middle Atlantic region. The Appalachian ranges include, among others, the high peaks of the Adirondacks in New York and the older, lower Blue Ridge Mountains that begin in the southern part of Pennsylvania.

Among the forested mountains of the Appalachians are many valleys. The most important of these is called the Great Valley. Find this valley on the map on page 311. The Great Valley is important because of its fine farmland. It also forms part of a route that leads through the mountains to the land west of the Appalachians.

Look at the map on page 311. What kind of landform do you find west of the Appalachians? In what states do you find the Allegheny Plateau? The Allegheny Plateau, which is west of the Appalachians, runs through New York, Pennsylvania, and West Virginia.

Rivers and lakes   Among the important physical features of the Middle Atlantic region are its many beautiful lakes and rivers. The rivers that flow through the Middle Atlantic states played an important part in our country's history. They were the routes by which explorers and settlers could most easily reach new lands from the Atlantic coast.

One of the most important of these rivers is the great Hudson. The Hudson River flows south through the Appalachian Mountains. On the map on page 311 trace the Hudson River from its mouth in New York Bay to the place where it meets the Mohawk River. What city grew up near this point?   Albany

Three other important rivers flow south and east through the Appalachians. Find the Delaware, Susquehanna (səs kwə han′ ə), and Potomac rivers on the map. Which two of these rivers form state boundaries? Which two rivers flow into Chesapeake Bay?   Delaware and Potomac; Susquehanna and Potomac

The Middle Atlantic region is well known for its fine lakes. The biggest by far are Lakes Ontario and Erie. These are two of the Great Lakes that form a boundary between the United States and Canada, our neighbor to the north. Find these two lakes on the map on page 311. Can you trace a water route by which people and goods can move from New York Bay to Lake Ontario and Lake Erie?

While Lakes Ontario and Erie are the two most important lakes in the Middle Atlantic states, there are hundreds of beautiful lakes scattered all through the Middle Atlantic states. These lakes draw thousands of visitors each year. People come not only in the summer to swim and sail, but also in the winter months to take part in winter sports such as ice-skating and iceboating.

CHECKUP

1. Name the states in the Middle Atlantic region.
2. Why were the rivers in this region important in our country's history?
3. The foothills to the west of the Atlantic Coastal Plain are the edge of what mountain system?
4. Which two Great Lakes are in this region?

Climate and Natural Resources

Temperature   The word *middle* in *Middle Atlantic region* also tells us something about the climate. The weather in most of this region is hardly ever extremely hot or cold for very long at a time. However, the winters are longer and colder in the northern parts and in the high mountains. The temperature in these areas often drops below 0°F (−18°C). In the Adirondacks, temperatures have been recorded well below −40°F (−40°C).

42°52′N/78°55′W

These children in Buffalo are enjoying the snow, but shoveling a path to the house must have been hard.

But the *average* winter temperatures of the Middle Atlantic region are not nearly so cold. Look at the map of average January temperatures on page 271 in Chapter 14. Find the average temperatures of the Middle Atlantic states. You can see that the word *middle* can be used to describe them.

In the summer also this area has "middle" temperatures. Sometimes July temperatures in the lower elevations and in the more southern parts may get as high as 100°F (38°C), or even higher. However, the average temperature is about 75°F (24°C) in the summer. Look at the map of average July temperatures on page 270 in Chapter 14. Find the average July temperatures for each of the Middle Atlantic states.

Precipitation   The amounts of rain and snow that fall in the Middle Atlantic region also vary. The mountain areas tend to have much more precipitation than some of the other parts. In some mountain areas, precipitation is more than 50 inches (127 cm) every year. In Wilmington, Delaware, there is an average of about 40 inches (102 cm).

Buffalo is a city on Lake Erie in New York state. During a recent winter, Buffalo had 175.6 inches (446 cm) of **sleet**, or frozen rain, and snow. If all that snow and sleet had been on the ground at one time, it would have been more than 14 feet (4 m) high. Of course, that was an unusual winter. But the yearly average is over 80 inches (203 cm). On the other hand, southern New Jersey, Delaware, and Maryland have only about 20 inches (51 cm) of snow a year.

Most of the Niagara River goes over Niagara Falls. The rest goes through the Welland Ship Canal, built by Canada as a shipping route around the falls.

Niagara Falls is split into two parts: American Falls (left) and Horseshoe Falls on the Canadian side of the river (center). (43°06'N/74°04'W)
The falls provide about 4 million kilowatts of electricity to Canada and the United States.

Soil and water   The Middle Atlantic states are rich in some of our most important resources. There is enough sunshine, rain, and good, fertile soil in these states to grow feed for herds of dairy cattle as well as fine crops of vegetables and fruit.

Beautiful woodlands cover many of the hills and slopes of the Middle Atlantic region. These woodlands supply very little lumber for building and making paper. But they do provide a home for the many birds and small animals that live in these states. And the woodlands also give people a place to enjoy the quiet beauty of trees, flowers, and small streams.

You have already learned something about how important water is for transportation and recreation in the Middle Atlantic states. This region also has a good supply of clean drinking water, although some of its rivers and streams have become too polluted, or dirty, for people to use or for fish to live in.

You read earlier that since colonial times New England's fast-moving rivers have made power to run machines. Some of the states in the Middle Atlantic region also have waterpower that can be changed into electricity. In the Middle Atlantic region, where the coastal plain meets the foothills of the Appalachians, there are many rivers and waterfalls. These gave waterpower that ran some of the country's earliest factories.

Turn to the map on page 311 and find the Niagara River between Lakes Erie and Ontario. Between these two lakes the river makes a huge drop. At this point are great waterfalls. About 200,000 tons (181,400 t) of water rush over the falls every min-ute. Much of this tremendous power is turned into electricity by large power plants. This electricity is used in homes and factories on both the Canadian and the American sides of the falls.

Drake built a wooden rig and used a steam engine to operate a drill.

Fuels   The first oil well in the United States was drilled in the Middle Atlantic region. In 1859, a man named Edwin Drake drilled this early well in western Pennsylvania. For a long time most of the oil produced in the United States came from this area.

Oil and natural gas still come from these fields. But Pennsylvania is no longer one of our leading oil states. The huge coalfields in the Appalachians of western Pennsylvania are a far more important source of fuel than Pennsylvania's oil fields. The map on page 279 of Chapter 14 shows you that these fields stretch from the Middle Atlantic region to Alabama.

CHECKUP

1. What parts of the Middle Atlantic region tend to have the coldest winters?
2. What word would you choose to describe the climate of the Middle Atlantic region?
3. Name at least three resources of the Middle Atlantic region.

Farming and Industry

VOCABULARY

poultry	Manufacturing
truck farm	Belt
	petrochemical

Food for the cities   The millions of people in the Middle Atlantic states need huge amounts of food. They need the products that are raised on farms. And although cities cover much of the land in the Middle Atlantic region, there are still farms in every one of the Middle Atlantic states. In fact half of Delaware and a third of Pennsylvania are farmland. There are fewer farms than there once were. And very few people work on the farms. But still the farms of the Middle Atlantic region are able to supply a great deal of the needed food. Modern methods and machinery make that possible.

New York and Pennsylvania are well known for their dairy farms. Pennsylvania is one of the leading milk-producing states in the country. These two states also raise cattle for meat. In every Middle Atlantic state, **poultry** farms supply eggs and chickens for the city markets. As you know, fine crops of fruits and vegetables abound in the Middle Atlantic states. Southern Delaware farms are well known for sweet, white corn. The soil and climate are also well suited for growing potatoes and strawberries. Maryland's farms grow rich crops of barley, wheat, and soybeans. Southwestern New Jersey is known for its fine **truck farms.** Truck farms are farms on which many different vegetables are grown in large amounts to be sold in markets.

Food from the sea   Some of the food produced in the Middle Atlantic states comes from the sea. Many harbors along the coasts of New Jersey, Delaware, and Maryland are fishing ports. Fishing boats leave from these ports every day for deeper waters. They return with fine catches of many kinds of fish. Much of the catch is frozen in nearby plants. Then the catch is sent to cities all over the United States.

The waters of Chesapeake and Delaware bays are noted for their valuable catches of shellfish, such as crabs, clams, lobsters, and oysters.

After picking up a load of milk, a truck driver stops to talk with a farmer in Pennsylvania. In the pasture are part of the farmer's herd of Holstein cows.

The Manufacturing Belt

The Middle Atlantic region is one of the greatest industrial areas in the Americas. Millions of dollars worth of goods are made and sold in the Middle Atlantic region. In fact, it has been called the **Manufacturing Belt** of the United States. About 24 out of every 100 workers in the Middle Atlantic region have jobs in factories and mills. They make machines, chemicals, clothes, ships, cameras, cloth, paper, and many, many more kinds of goods.

One of the important industries of this area is the manufacture of synthetics. This industry had its beginning in 1802 when gunpowder mills were first built along the Brandywine River in Delaware. With the discovery of nylon and other fabrics about 40 years ago, large **petrochemical** industries grew. It is quite likely that much of your clothing is made from synthetic fabrics, such as nylon or Dacron.   Remind pupils that a synthetic fabric is one made from materials produced by humans rather than from natural materials.

Iron

Industry has been important in the Middle Atlantic region since iron ore was first discovered in eastern Pennsylvania in the eighteenth century. The early settlers also found great amounts of limestone, another ingredient needed to make iron. The settlers burned wood from the great forests to make charcoal. Then they burned the charcoal to make the high heat needed to melt the iron from the ore. The charcoal, limestone, and iron ore were heated together in stone furnaces to make the liquid iron. Later, the iron cooled and hardened. From the iron the settlers made their own pots and kettles, tools and nails, and many other necessary goods.

Later, Pennsylvania's rich coal supplies were discovered. Then the ironmakers used coal instead of charcoal to heat their furnaces.

Pittsburgh and steel

As you read in Chapter 14, iron can be turned into steel. Steel can be used to make even more things than iron can. Steel is one of the most important products in the world today. Just think of all the cars, tall buildings, strong bridges, and hundreds of other things that are made at least partly of steel. Today more than 500,000 people in the United States have jobs that have something to do with making steel.

After the Civil War there was a need for more and more steel. Pennsylvania could not mine enough iron to meet this need. Steel mills had to get iron ore from other parts of the country. Mines as far away as the Mesabi mines in Minnesota began shipping ore to the city of Pittsburgh in western Pennsylvania. The ore from these mines could travel most of the way by water.

On the map on page 324 find the port city of Pittsburgh. It is located at the point where the Allegheny (al ə gā′ nē) and Monongahela (mə nän gə hē′ lə) rivers meet to form the Ohio River.

Now turn to the map of the United States on pages 14–15. Find the city of Duluth (də lüth′), Minnesota, on Lake Superior. Iron ore from the Mesabi mines was loaded on barges at Duluth. From Duluth, the barges went across Lakes Superior, Huron, and Erie to the port city of Erie, Pennsylvania. Trace the route of the iron ore barges on the map of the United States. From the port of Erie the

316

HOW STEEL IS MADE

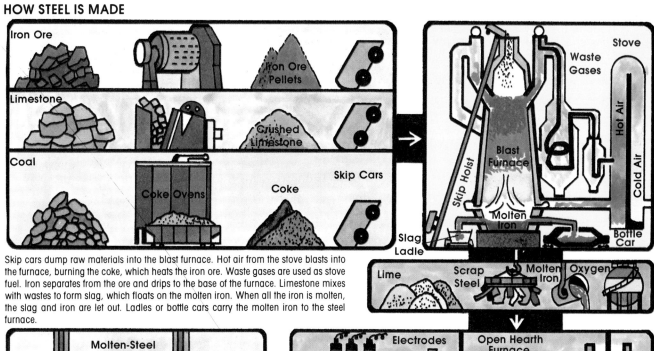

Skip cars dump raw materials into the blast furnace. Hot air from the stove blasts into the furnace, burning the coke, which heats the iron ore. Waste gases are used as stove fuel. Iron separates from the ore and drips to the base of the furnace. Limestone mixes with wastes to form slag, which floats on the molten iron. When all the iron is molten, the slag and iron are let out. Ladles or bottle cars carry the molten iron to the steel furnace.

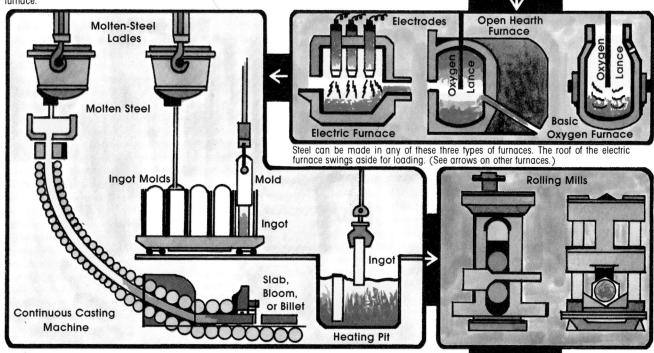

Steel can be made in any of these three types of furnaces. The roof of the electric furnace swings aside for loading. (See arrows on other furnaces.)

Molten steel is poured into ingot molds through a hole in the bottom of the ladle. When the ingots have cooled enough to solidify, the molds are stripped away. Heating pits bring the ingots to the same temperature throughout. At the rolling mill, large rollers press the red-hot ingots into slabs, blooms, or billets. From slabs come sheets of metal used in cans, autos, and other products. Blooms produce rails, beams, and other products. Rods, wire, nails, pipes, and many other products come from billets. In some modern mills, continuous casting machines turn molten steel directly into slabs, blooms, or billets.

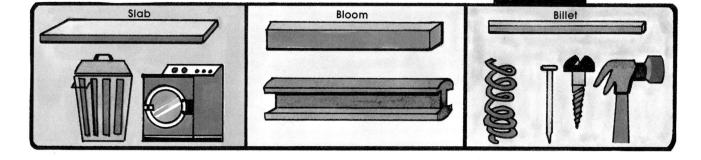

At one time Pittsburgh had so much air pollution that street lights were on at noon. City regulations stopped the burning of soft coal in homes in the 1940s, improving air quality. Since then, more regulations and a drop in steel production have further improved air quality.

iron continued its journey by way of rail-road and the Allegheny River to Pittsburgh. Iron is carried along the same route today.

River barges could also bring coal and limestone to Pittsburgh for the giant furnaces and steel mills. And the rivers could carry the products of Pittsburgh's mills and factories to markets in other parts of the country. Pittsburgh became the most important center of steelmaking in the Americas.

Today much of the iron ore used in the Middle Atlantic states comes from other countries. It is shipped by boat and rail from places as close as Canada and as far away as Venezuela (ven əz wā′ lə) in South America. Other important steelmaking centers have grown up in Pennsylvania, as well as in Illinois, Indiana, Ohio, New York, and Maryland. However, steelmaking is still Pittsburgh's most important industry. And the steel mills in and around the city make more than 26 million tons (24 million t) of steel each year.

This represents about 1/5 of the nation's steel production.

CHECKUP

1. Name four farm products of the Middle Atlantic region.
2. For what foods are the waters of Chesapeake and Delaware bays noted?
3. For what product is Pittsburgh most noted?

In this view of Pittsburgh, looking westward along the Allegheny River, you can see in the foreground some of the steel mills for which the city is famous.

Cities

Huge cargo containers are lined up on the dock ready to be loaded on this Australian ship at Port Elizabeth.

VOCABULARY

commerce   megalopolis
suburb

A region of great cities   Look at the population density map on page 259 in Chapter 14. You can see that some of the most densely populated areas in the United States are in the Middle Atlantic region. In fact, New Jersey is the most densely populated state in the country. There are an average of 979 people per square mile (378 people per sq km) living in New Jersey.

About 87 out of every 100 people in the Middle Atlantic region live in urban areas. The table below shows how many people live in each of the Middle Atlantic states. It also shows what percentage of those people live in urban areas.

Perhaps people know the Middle Atlantic region best for its cities. Cities are very important to the people of the Middle Atlantic states. Most of the factories and mills in this great industrial region are found in and around the cities. So are most of the banks and offices, stores and businesses of every kind.

URBAN POPULATION OF THE MIDDLE ATLANTIC STATES

State	Total population	Percent urban
New York	17,557,000	89
New Jersey	7,364,000	92
Pennsylvania	11,867,000	81
Delaware	595,000	69
Maryland	4,216,000	86

Importance of ports   Many of the great cities of the Middle Atlantic region are port cities. They are on harbors or bays, rivers or lakes, or even canals. The five largest cities in the Middle Atlantic states are New York, Philadelphia, Baltimore, Washington, D.C., and Pittsburgh. Find them on the map on page 324. You will see that all these cities, except Washington, are ports. On what bodies of water are the cities located?

One of the major reasons these cities grew big and important was ease of transportation. In the early days of our country, travel by water was easier and faster than travel over land. Explorers used the waterways to get into the wilderness. As settlers move westward, many of them used water routes. Waterways were important for shipping of goods and supplies to and from the different settlements. Water travel made trade with other countries possible.

The port cities of the Middle Atlantic region became centers of trade and

Have some pupils research the early development of these cities, relating major themes in the cities' histories to their access to the ocean.

319

commerce. *Commerce* means the buying and selling of goods. Many of these cities are still important commercial and shipping centers. Goods from other parts of the United States and from all over the world pass through these busy ports. The table below lists five of the largest ports in the Middle Atlantic region. It also shows how many tons of cargo, or goods, are loaded and unloaded at their busy docks each year. You can see that the port of New York is the busiest port in the Middle Atlantic region. It is also the busiest port in the whole country.

MAIN SEAPORTS OF THE MIDDLE ATLANTIC REGION (Figures are rounded)

Port	Short tons of cargo per year
New York, N.Y., and New Jersey	179,600,000
Baltimore	52,400,000
Philadelphia	50,600,000
Marcus Hook, Pa.	28,700,000
Paulsboro, N.J.	26,200,000

New York City New York is the most populated city in the United States. About 7 million people make their homes in this great city. And many more millions of people live in the New York metropolitan area. This area includes all the smaller cities and towns around New York City. Look at the map on page 324. Find the cities of Newark, Elizabeth, Paterson, and Jersey City in New Jersey and the city of Yonkers in New York State. These cities and more in Connecticut, New York, and New Jersey are all part of the New York metropolitan area. There would not be room on the map to show all the smaller towns and cities around New York City. Every day thousands of people from the communities around New York City travel into the city to their jobs.

New York is one of the most important business, banking, trading, and manufacturing centers in the world. Two of its largest industries are the manufacturing of clothing and publishing of books. You might be wearing something right now that was made in New York City. And some of your schoolbooks may have come from there also.

Welcome to America Since the Dutch settled in New Amsterdam in 1624, New York has welcomed millions of new Americans. Perhaps the Statue of Liberty in New York Harbor was the first thing your parents or grandparents or great-grandparents saw when they arrived in America.

For more than 350 years people from all over the world have poured into this country through New York Harbor. Most of them have come in search of more freedom and a better life. From New York, many of these immigrants have gone on to help build every corner of America. But many have stayed in New York to make it one of the world's most interesting and exciting cities.   Remind pupils that Ellis Island in New York harbor received more than 16 million prospective American citizens.

Philadelphia Philadelphia is the biggest city in Pennsylvania and the fourth largest city in the United States. It is one of the busiest ports and manufacturing centers in the Middle Atlantic region. Look at the map on page 324. Find

Philadelphia has approximately 2 million people. The Philadelphia metropolitan area covers almost 4,000 sq mi (10,400 sq km).

A $3.5 billion urban renewal program that will take 40 years to complete was begun in Philadelphia during the 1960s.

The first balloon in the United States to carry people took off from Philadelphia in 1793. That historic event and others are celebrated during the city's Freedom Week festival.

40°00′N/75°10′W

Philadelphia where the Delaware River meets the Schuylkill (skül′ kil) River. Huge oceangoing ships can travel from the Atlantic Ocean into Delaware Bay. From there they can move through deep channels in the Delaware River until they reach the busy docks of Philadelphia's waterfront.

Old and new Philadelphia was carefully planned and laid out by William Penn in 1682. Later, it was the scene of stirring events in our nation's history. Today, thousands of visitors come to Philadelphia to see Independence Hall where the Declaration of Independence was signed in 1776. They come to see the famous Liberty Bell that rang out the news that a new nation was born. They visit the fine old buildings where great leaders such as Thomas Jefferson and Benjamin Franklin planned a new kind of government.

Philadelphia is well known for its lovely old buildings and tree-shaded streets. But it is also a modern city with tall buildings and busy streets crowded with cars and buses. And like other important Middle Atlantic cities, its airports, railroad stations, and highways make it a transportation center as well.

Baltimore Baltimore, on Chesapeake Bay, is another of the great Middle Atlantic ports. Ships loaded with oil, wheat, coal, automobiles, iron, and steel move through its deep harbor.

Find Baltimore on the map on page 324. Move your finger past Baltimore northward on Chesapeake Bay. Do you see the waterway that connects Chesapeake Bay with the mouth of the Delaware River? This is the Chesapeake and Delaware Canal. It allows ships to travel from Baltimore to Philadelphia without having to go southward and around Virginia's Cape Charles to Delaware Bay. Ships taking this route pass the busy cities of Wilmington, Delaware, and Camden, New Jersey, as well as the ports of Marcus Hook, Pennsylvania, and Paulsboro, New Jersey.

Baltimore is the most southern city of the Middle Atlantic region's great Manufacturing Belt. Its factories make millions of dollars worth of goods. These include all kinds of products made of metal. One of the largest steel mills in the country is found in Baltimore. And from its earliest days, Baltimore has been famous as a shipbuilding city.

321

In the port is the ship *Constellation*, built in 1797. It may be the oldest ship still afloat in the world.

Regions Depend on One Another

Washington, D.C., as the nation's capital, connects the Middle Atlantic region with every other state. There are other ways in which these states are related to other parts of the nation.

Port cities, such as New York, Philadelphia, and Baltimore, provide for the entry of goods from other nations. These goods are then shipped to other parts of the United States. At the port of Wilmington, Delaware, you can see hundreds of cars that have been imported from Europe. They will be loaded on auto transport trailers and moved west, south, and north. At the same port, you will see American-made cars waiting to be exported to other countries.

The Middle Atlantic states depend upon the North Central states for grain. Can you think of other goods that might be exchanged between these two regions?

Have you ever listed all the things you use during just one day? If you do that and then find out where they come from, the interconnections begin to show up quickly. Pennsylvanians drink Florida orange juice and visit Florida in the winter to enjoy the sunshine. New Yorkers depend upon Texas and Mississippi for cotton, but create designs for clothing that is manufactured in the Southeast. Can you think of an example of how New Jersey is connected with other parts of the nation?

Washington, D.C. On the map on page 324 find the capital city of each state in the Middle Atlantic region. What tells you they are the capital cities? Each of these cities is the center of the state's government. Here the state leaders work at managing the affairs of the state.

The United States also has a capital city. It is the city of Washington in the District of Columbia—Washington, D.C., for short. Find Washington, D.C., on the map on page 324. It looks as though it is in the state of Maryland. But Washington is not part of any state. It is built on land given to the national government by Maryland when George Washington was President.

Washington is on the Potomac River. But Washington is not an important port city. Neither is it a city of factories and mills. There are few big business com-panies in Washington. But Washington, D.C., is the most important city in America to all of us. The main business of Washington is the government of the United States. More people in and around Washington work at government jobs than at any other kind.

The President of the United States lives and works in Washington. In this city, senators and representatives from every state of the Union make the laws that rule our land. In Washington the Supreme Court, the highest court of the land, makes decisions that affect every one of us every day of our lives.

An exciting visit Every year millions of people come to visit their country's capital. They walk down the broad avenues that were planned by a French en-

322

Remind pupils that Benjamin Banneker, a black mathematician of the Revolutionary period, helped to lay out the boundaries of the District of Columbia.

Congress meets in the Capitol building in Washington, D.C., our nation's capital. (38°55′N/77°00′W)

gineer, Pierre (pē är′) Charles L'Enfant (län′ fän′), before the city was built. They visit the White House, where the President lives, and the Capitol building, where the Senate and House of Representatives meet. They visit the Supreme Court building. Here they may even watch the nine judges of the Court at work. On the banks of the Potomac River, visitors admire the lovely buildings that were built to honor two of our country's great heroes— George Washington and Thomas Jefferson. From the top of the Washington Monument, people can look out over one of the most beautiful cities in the world.

Megalopolis   You have been learning about some of the cities of the Middle Atlantic region. And, of course, there are other important cities in the Middle Atlantic states, many more than we have room to tell about. Most of the cities are on the Atlantic Coastal Plain. Many of them have spread out far from their centers. Their metropolitan areas include many **suburbs.** Suburbs are the cities, towns, and villages that surround a large city.

The groups of cities and suburbs have spread so far into the countryside that they touch each other. Look at the map on pages 14–15. You can see that the area from Boston in New England to Washington, D.C., seems to be one huge city. This kind of city area is called a **megalopolis** (meg ə lop′ ə lis). mega = large polis = city

This is a very important area. It has millions of people, thousands of factories and businesses, many busy ports, and miles of highways and railroads. But many people feel that we must try to keep some green countryside and open spaces between the cities. Why do you think they feel that this is important?

This is a good question for class discussion.

CHECKUP

1. Which is our most densely populated state?
2. Name four large cities in the Middle Atlantic region.
3. What is a megalopolis?

323

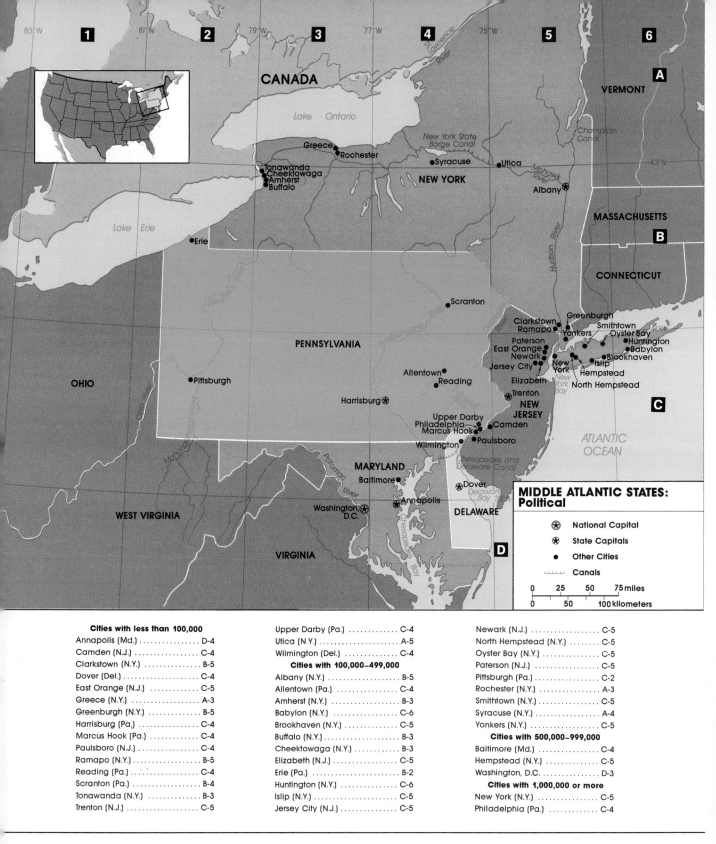

MIDDLE ATLANTIC STATES: Political

⊛	National Capital
✪	State Capitals
●	Other Cities
⌇	Canals

0 25 50 75 miles
0 50 100 kilometers

Cities with less than 100,000

Annapolis (Md.)	D-4
Camden (N.J.)	C-4
Clarkstown (N.Y.)	B-5
Dover (Del.)	C-4
East Orange (N.J.)	C-5
Greece (N.Y.)	A-3
Greenburgh (N.Y.)	B-5
Harrisburg (Pa.)	C-4
Marcus Hook (Pa.)	C-4
Paulsboro (N.J.)	C-4
Ramapo (N.Y.)	B-5
Reading (Pa.)	C-4
Scranton (Pa.)	B-4
Tonawanda (N.Y.)	B-3
Trenton (N.J.)	C-5
Upper Darby (Pa.)	C-4
Utica (N.Y.)	A-5
Wilmington (Del.)	C-4

Cities with 100,000–499,000

Albany (N.Y.)	B-5
Allentown (Pa.)	C-4
Amherst (N.Y.)	B-3
Babylon (N.Y.)	C-6
Brookhaven (N.Y.)	C-5
Buffalo (N.Y.)	B-3
Cheektowaga (N.Y.)	B-3
Elizabeth (N.J.)	C-5
Erie (Pa.)	B-2
Huntington (N.Y.)	C-6
Islip (N.Y.)	C-5
Jersey City (N.J.)	C-5

Newark (N.J.)	C-5
North Hempstead (N.Y.)	C-5
Oyster Bay (N.Y.)	C-5
Paterson (N.J.)	C-5
Pittsburgh (Pa.)	C-2
Rochester (N.Y.)	A-3
Smithtown (N.Y.)	C-5
Syracuse (N.Y.)	A-4
Yonkers (N.Y.)	C-5

Cities with 500,000–999,000

Baltimore (Md.)	C-4
Hempstead (N.Y.)	C-5
Washington, D.C.	D-3

Cities with 1,000,000 or more

New York (N.Y.)	C-5
Philadelphia (Pa.)	C-4

Look at the list of cities above. Then find on the map the two cities with 1 million or more people.

324

THE MIDDLE ATLANTIC STATES	Delaware	Maryland	New Jersey	New York	Pennsylvania
Source of Name	From Delaware River and Bay; named in turn for Sir Thomas West, Lord De La Warr	In honor of Henrietta Maria (queen of Charles I of England)	From the Channel Isle of Jersey	In honor of the English Duke of York, who later became King James II of England	In honor of Admiral Sir William Penn, father of William Penn. It means "Penn's Woodland."
Nickname(s)	Diamond State; First State	Free State; Old Line State	Garden State	Empire State	Keystone State
Capital	Dover	Annapolis	Trenton	Albany	Harrisburg
Largest Cities (1980 Census)	Wilmington Newark Dover	Baltimore Rockville Hagerstown	Newark Jersey City Paterson	New York Hempstead Brookhaven	Philadelphia Pittsburgh Erie
Population Rank (1980 Census)	47	18	9	2	4
Population Density Rank	7	5	1	6	8
Area Rank	49	42	46	30	33
State Flag					
State Bird	Blue hen chicken	Baltimore oriole	Eastern goldfinch	Bluebird	Ruffed grouse
State Flower	Peach blossom	Black-eyed Susan	Purple violet	Rose	Mountain laurel
State Tree	American holly	White oak	Red oak	Sugar maple	Hemlock
State Motto	Liberty and independence	*Fatti maschii, parole femine* (Manly deeds, womanly words)	Liberty and prosperity	*Excelsior* (Ever upward)	Virtue, liberty, and independence
Interesting Facts	Delaware was the first state to ratify the Constitution in 1787. It is the home of the largest chemical company in the world.	The land for Washington, D.C., our nation's capital, was given to the United States government by Maryland.	The first baseball game on record took place in Hoboken on June 19, 1846. West Orange is the home of Thomas Alva Edison.	West Point is the home of the United States Military Academy. New York City is the world's largest seaport and headquarters for the United Nations.	The Declaration of Independence was signed at Independence Hall in Philadelphia. The world's largest chocolate and cocoa factory is in Hershey. The first oil well in the United States was drilled in Titusville.

16/ CHAPTER REVIEW

KEY FACTS

1. Important features of the Middle Atlantic region include the bays and waterways, the Appalachians, and the Atlantic Coastal Plain.

2. The climate and soil of the Middle Atlantic region are suited to truck, dairy, and poultry farming.

3. Waterpower and coal are important energy resources of the Middle Atlantic region.

4. Important industries of the Middle Atlantic region include the manufacture of petrochemicals, iron, and steel.

5. Most of the Middle Atlantic region is heavily urban.

VOCABULARY QUIZ

Write the letter of the term next to the number of its description. Write on a sheet of paper.

a. foothills   f. truck farm
b. megalopolis   g. suburbs
c. sleet   h. petrochemical
d. commerce   i. temperature
e. harbor   j. Manufacturing Belt

g 1. The cities, towns, and villages that surround a large city

e 2. A protected place along a coast where ships load and unload goods

a 3. A landform often found between plains and mountains

i 4. The hotness or coldness of the air

c 5. Frozen rain

f 6. A vegetable farm

j 7. Term used to describe the huge industrial area of the Middle Atlantic region

h 8. A term used to describe industries that produce such materials as nylon or Dacron

b 9. A huge urban area made up of many cities and their suburbs

d 10. The buying and selling of goods

REVIEW QUESTIONS

1. Name the Middle Atlantic states.

2. Describe the physical features and climate of the Middle Atlantic region.

3. Name three important resources of the Middle Atlantic region.

4. Explain why the harbors and waterways of the Middle Atlantic region were important in the past and are still important today.

5. In which city is each of the following found: Liberty Bell, White House, Statue of Liberty?

6. Choose two of the cities described in the chapter and tell why each is important.

ACTIVITIES

1. Steel and petrochemicals are major products of the Middle Atlantic region. Look in an encyclopedia to find the kinds of products made from petrochemicals. Then label one sheet of paper *Steel Products* and another *Petrochemicals.* List as many items as you can find at home and in school that are made from these two products.

2. Choose two cities described in this chapter. (Do not choose a city in which you live.) For 2 weeks, look in your local newspaper for articles about the two cities.

First separate the articles by city. Then group the articles for each city. Put all the sports stories together, all the crime stories together, and so on. Then compare the two sets of articles. How do they show you that the two cities are alike? Different?

16/SKILLS DEVELOPMENT

USING CONTEXT CLUES

The following article is taken from *A Brief Course in Geography*, a book published in 1882. As you read the article, you will notice that some words are underlined. These are words whose meaning you may not know. However, you should be able to figure out what they mean by the way in which they are used.

NEW YORK is the richest and most populous of the United States, and has the greatest number of large towns.

Towns. New York City is one of the chief commercial ports in the world, and is the greatest city upon the Western Continent. Brooklyn is occupied mainly by people who transact business in New York. These two cities, with the populous towns around them, contain (1881) over two million inhabitants.

Buffalo and Albany and large commmercial towns. They are at opposite ends of the railroad and canal which cross the state from east to west. Albany is the capital.

The products of the Central States pass through these places, and are sent down the Hudson to New York City, or by railroad to Boston.

Rochester is situated at the beautiful falls of the Genesee River, which are nearly 100 feet high. The great water-power thus afforded is used for the numerous flour mills and other factories, which have made the place so prosperous.

Troy is an important manufacturing and commercial city. Saratoga is visited by invalids for its mineral-springs, and is a fashionable watering-place.

Syracuse is an important manufacturing place, and is in the midst of the greatest salt-producing region in the country.

Show that you understood the underlined words by matching each word with its meaning. Write your answers on a sheet of paper.

1. Populous   a. well-liked, b. heavily populated
2. Occupied   a. lived in, b. had a job
3. Transact   a. carry on, b. send out
4. Inhabitants   a. people who live in a given place, b. people who travel to a given place.
5. Situated   a. flooded, b. located
6. Afforded   a. bought, b. provided
7. Numerous   a. large number of, b. huge
8. Prosperous   a. beautiful, b. rich
9. Invalids   a. sickly people, b. thirsty people
10. Watering-place   a. resort with a waterfall that people like to visit, b. resort with water thought to be health-giving.

Show how well you understood the article by answering the following questions.

1. What title would you give the article? Answers will vary.
2. Which city was the capital? Albany
3. Which city was visited for its mineral-springs? Saratoga
4. Which cities were linked by railroad and canal? Buffalo and Albany
5. Which city used a waterfall to produce power? Rochester
6. Which city was the largest city and the most important port? New York
7. Which city was in an important salt-producing area? Syracuse

Since this article was written about 100 years ago, some of the information may no longer be true. Find out what is still true by looking up the cities in an encyclopedia or other reference book.

327

17 The Southeast States Today

The Land

```
VOCABULARY
temperate          barrier islands
tidewater          shoal
key                reef
coral
```

The region   The Southeast has ten states: Virginia, West Virginia, Kentucky, Tennessee, North Carolina, South Carolina, Georgia, Florida, Alabama, and Mississippi.

Much of the Southeast is covered by coastal plains. Of course, there are other kinds of landforms, too. They include mountains and inland plains. The climate of much of the Southeast is hot and wet. However, in the mountains it is more **temperate.** A temperate climate is one that is neither extremely hot or cold nor extremely wet or dry.

The coastal plains   The Atlantic Coastal Plain, which you learned about earlier, continues on from the Middle Atlantic states through Virginia, North and South Carolina, Georgia, and Florida. The Gulf Coastal Plain is the plain along the Gulf of Mexico. It stretches west from Florida into Alabama and Mississippi. Both coastal plains reach inland as much as 200 miles (320 km) in many areas.

The swamps   Here and there along both coastal plains are large swamps and **tidewater** areas. Tidewater is a name that is given to low-lying coastal land that is often flooded with seawater. When the land is covered with water, it is hard to tell where the sea ends and land begins. One way in which swamps differ from tidewater is that swamps are *always* under water.

Discussion question: Why is there a need for wildlife refuges?

The Everglades   From Lake Okeechobee south, much of Florida is swampland known as the Everglades. There are towns and cities along the seacoasts, but much of the inland area is given over to wildlife refuges and parks. A wildlife refuge is a place set aside for wild animals. Hunting is not allowed. People may not build on the land or make roads through it. The best known park is Everglades National Park in Florida.

Many kinds of plants grow in the Everglades. Sawgrass covers acre after acre, but shrubs and trees, such as cypress, palm, and mangrove, have taken over large areas, too. Because there is a warm, wet climate, plants grow rapidly.

The Everglades is home to an amazing number of birds—egrets, herons, pelicans, cranes, and others. Alligators, crocodiles, turtles, snakes, snails, and raccoons all make

Have pupils research these plants and animals and draw pictures of them. Make a bulletin-board display of the results of their research.

On the map find the Atlantic Coastal Plain and the Gulf Coastal Plain. The picture shows part of a chain of islands that stretches from Florida 150 miles (240 km) into the Gulf of Mexico.

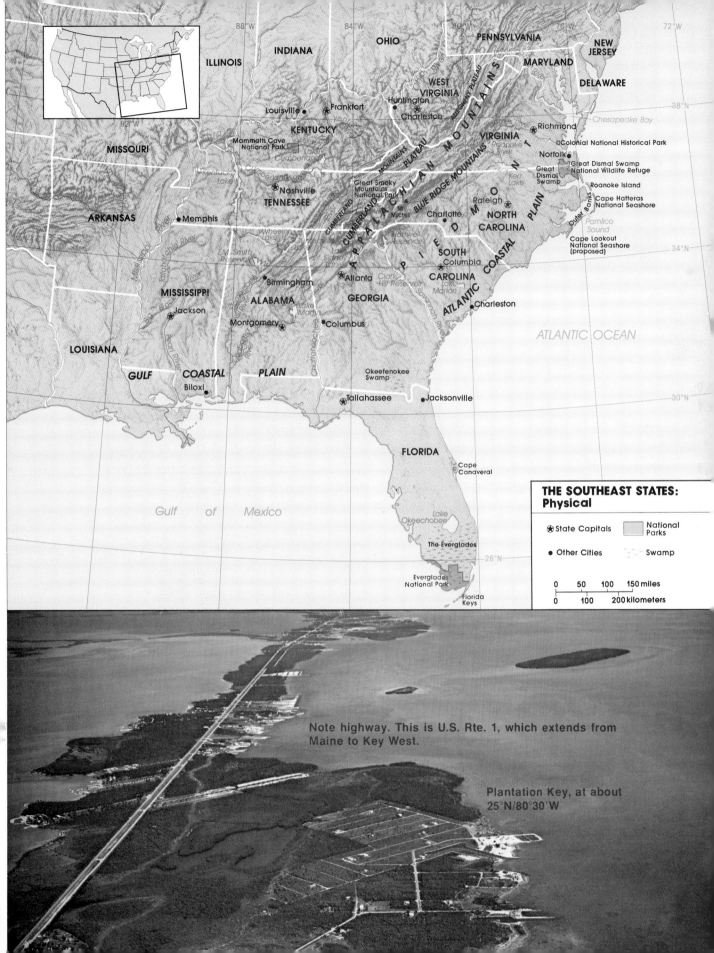

ILLINOIS
INDIANA
OHIO
PENNSYLVANIA
NEW JERSEY
MARYLAND
DELAWARE
WEST VIRGINIA
Huntington
Charleston
VIRGINIA
Richmond
Colonial National Historical Park
Norfolk
Great Dismal Swamp National Wildlife Refuge
Great Dismal Swamp
Roanoke Island
Cape Hatteras National Seashore
Pamlico Sound
Outer Banks
Cape Lookout National Seashore (proposed)
MISSOURI
Louisville
Frankfort
KENTUCKY
Mammoth Cave National Park
Kentucky Lake
Nashville
TENNESSEE
Great Smoky Mountains National Park
Mt. Mitchell
Charlotte
Raleigh
NORTH CAROLINA
A P P A L A C H I A N   M O U N T A I N S
CUMBERLAND
BLUE RIDGE MOUNTAINS
ALLEGHENY PLATEAU
PLATEAU
MOUNTAINS
ARKANSAS
Memphis
Wheeler Lake
Norwell Reservoir
SOUTH CAROLINA
Columbia
Clark Hill Reservoir
Lake Marion
Atlantic
Charleston
P I E D M O N T
A T L A N T I C   C O A S T A L   P L A I N
Mississippi River
Atchafalaya River
L.M. Smith Reservoir
Lake Sidney Lanier
Atlanta
GEORGIA
Birmingham
ALABAMA
Black River
MISSISSIPPI
Jackson
Montgomery
Lake Martin
Columbus
Savannah River
Chattahoochee River
Okeefenokee Swamp
Pearl River
LOUISIANA
Biloxi
GULF   COASTAL   PLAIN
Tallahassee
Jacksonville
ATLANTIC OCEAN
Gulf   of   Mexico
FLORIDA
Cape Canaveral
Lake Okeechobee
The Everglades
Everglades National Park
Florida Keys

THE SOUTHEAST STATES: Physical

✴ State Capitals   ▢ National Parks

● Other Cities   ⌇ Swamp

| 0 | 50 | 100 | 150 miles |
| 0 | 100 | 200 kilometers |

Note highway. This is U.S. Rte. 1, which extends from Maine to Key West.

Plantation Key, at about 25°N/80°30′W

A snowy egret looks for food while an alligator basks in the sun. These are just two of the many, many animals that make their home in the Everglades of Florida.

their home in the Everglades. The rare sea cow, or manatee, lives in the Everglades, as do thousands of insects.

The Florida Keys   A string of islands stretches southwest from the tip of Florida. These islands are the Florida **Keys**. They are little bits of land, barely above sea level, made of **coral** and limestone. The keys reach 150 miles (240 km) into the Gulf of Mexico. They are connected to one another by at least 40 bridges. A highway runs most of the length of the keys.

The Outer Banks   Another interesting group of islands is found along North Carolina's coast. The Outer Banks, as these islands are called, are a line of **barrier islands**. These sandy strips of land are called barrier islands because they form a barrier that protects the mainland.

The Outer Banks were once a part of a major disaster area for sailing vessels. The water is shallow here, and there are **shoals** and **reefs.** Shoals are underwater sand bars. The water above them is very shallow. Reefs are chains of rocks at or near the surface of the water. There have been hundreds of shipwrecks along the Outer Banks. Lighthouses now warn ships of the offshore danger.

Two large sections of the Outer Banks are taken up by Cape Hatteras National Seashore and the proposed Cape Lookout National Seashore. Another area is a wildlife refuge. One of the few villages is Kitty Hawk, where the Wright brothers made the first successful airplane flight. This flight took place on December 17, 1903. It covered a distance of 120 feet (37 m) and lasted 12 seconds.

The Piedmont   The Atlantic Coastal Plain rises gently to the Piedmont. The Piedmont is the upland area that lies between the Coastal Plain and the Appalachian Mountains. At the eastern edge of the Piedmont is the Fall Line, which begins in the north. It stretches south as far as Georgia. The Fall Line marks the point at which one finds waterfalls on the rivers flowing toward the coast. The waterfalls were a source of power in colonial days. Here too, the rivers change from swift-flowing streams into slow, gentle rivers that the ships of the time could use.

330

Ridges and plateaus To the west of the Piedmont are the Appalachians. These mountains cover a large part of the South-east. The Blue Ridge Mountains form the easternmost range of the Appalachians. This range begins in Pennsylvania and continues south through the Atlantic Coastal states to Georgia. The highest point of the Appalachian chain is Mount Mitchell in North Carolina.

West of the Blue Ridge Mountains in the north is the Allegheny Plateau. The Cumberland Mountains are south of this rugged plateau. The Cumberland Mountains are really a part of the Cumberland Plateau. The Cumberland Plateau stretches from West Virginia south through Kentucky, Virginia, and Tennessee to northern Alabama.

Hills and lowlands As you travel westward, the mountains and plateaus give way to rolling hills. In Kentucky, this area is known as Bluegrass country. The

Kentucky's Bluegrass country is noted for its horse farms, on which fine horses like this mare and foal are raised.

name comes from the blue flowers in the grass that carpets the hills. Finally, in western Kentucky and Tennessee, you find yourself in lowlands. These lowlands are the Ohio and Mississippi river valleys.

Rivers Throughout the southeastern states there are many rivers and streams. The Mississippi River forms the western border of Tennessee and most of that of Mississippi. You will learn more about this great river later. The Ohio River, another of our great rivers, borders West Virginia and Kentucky. The Cumberland River begins in Kentucky and loops down into Tennessee before flowing back through Kentucky to join the Ohio.

A fourth river, the Tennessee, is very important to the Southeast. At one time, the Tennessee and other nearby rivers flooded the land each spring. Then in 1933, Congress set up the Tennessee Valley Authority, or TVA, as it is called. The TVA built dams to help control the flooding. The TVA also provides water for irrigation, generates electricity, manufactures fertilizer, and has introduced soil conservation methods to many people in the area. In addition, the Tennessee River has been made navigable from Knoxville, Tennessee, to Paducah, Kentucky, where it joins the Ohio River.

CHECKUP

1. Describe one way in which a swamp differs from a tidewater.
2. What line marks the point at which waterfalls generally occur as rivers flow toward the coast?
3. Name at least four different landforms found in the Southeast.
4. What are shoals and reefs?

331

Climate

┌─ VOCABULARY ─────────────────────┐
│ frost-free   hurricane   │
│ humid   │
└───────────────────────────────────┘

Temperature   In some places in the Southeast, the temperature rarely goes below 60°F (16°C), even in January. At others, the average January temperature is about 32°F (0°C). In general, the warmest places are in the southern coastal plains and in the lowlands west of the mountains. In these low-lying areas, there are long periods of warm weather. **Frost-free** is used to describe the period when the temperature is always above freezing. The frost-free season lasts 6 months or more in most coastal areas. This makes for a long growing season throughout much of the Southeast.

The coolest parts of the Southeast are in the hills and mountains. In fact, elevation is one of the main reasons for temperature differences in the Southeast. But elevation is not the only reason for these differences. Otherwise Norfolk, Virginia, and Miami, Florida, would have the same climate. They are both on the Atlantic Coastal Plain, and both are less than 30 feet (9 m) in elevation. Yet Norfolk's average yearly temperature is 59°F (15°C), while Miami's is 76°F (24°C). The difference is that Miami is closer to the equator (0° latitude) than Norfolk is. Miami is at about 26° north latitude; Norfolk is at about 37° north latitude.

The table at the top of this page shows you how latitude affects temperature. Each city on the table is at about the same elevation, but the latitude is different.

TEMPERATURE AND LATITUDE

City	Latitude	Average yearly temperature
Norfolk, Va.	37°N	59°F (15°C)
Wilmington, N.C.	34°N	64°F (18°C)
Savannah, Ga.	32°N	66°F (19°C)
Tampa, Fla.	28°N	72°F (22°C)
Miami, Fla.	26°N	76°F (24°C)

Which city is farthest from the equator? Which is closest to the equator? What happens to the temperature as you move closer to the equator?

The table at the bottom of this page shows how elevation affects temperature. The places on the table are paired by latitude, but have different elevations. Which place in each pair has the warmer temperature: the place with the high elevation, or the one with the low elevation?

Precipitation   Most of the precipitation in the Southeast is rain. Snow is rare

TEMPERATURE AND ELEVATION

City	Elevation	Average yearly temperature
Charleston, S.C.	40 ft (12 m)	65°F (18°C)
Atlanta, Ga.	1,010 ft (308 m)	61°F (16°C)
Raleigh, N.C.	434 ft (132 m)	59°F (15°C)
Asheville, N.C.	2,140 ft (652 m)	56°F (13°C)
Norfolk, Va.	24 ft (7 m)	59°F (15°C)
Roanoke, Va.	1,149 ft (350 m)	56°F (13°C)
Richmond, Va.	164 ft (50 m)	58°F (14°C)
Beckley, W. Va.	2,504 ft (763 m)	51°F (11°C)

Each year the Weather Bureau prepares a list of names for hurricanes. Until 1978, only feminine names were used. Then in 1979, the bureau started using both masculine and feminine names. The name for the first hurricane of the year begins with the letter A, the second name with B, and so on through the alphabet.

except in the mountain and northernmost areas. Even in the northern areas, the amount of snow that falls in a whole year is about the same as the amount that falls in one good New England storm.

Rainfall varies in the Southeast from about 40 inches (100 cm) a year to almost 70 inches (180 cm). The rainiest places are along the coasts. In these places, the most rain falls during the summer, when the temperature is at its highest. This combination causes hot, **humid** summers.

Ask pupils to explain the meaning of *humid*. Remind them to use the Glossary when they do not know the meaning of a word.

Hurricanes   The coastal states may not get much snow, but they do have storms. **Hurricanes** often pass through the area. These storms have rapidly spinning walls of moist air around an inner area, or "eye," that is calm and cloudless. The "eye" alone may be several miles across, while the storm as a whole may be 100 to 300 miles (160 – 480 km) wide.

The hurricanes that affect the United States form over the Atlantic Ocean east of the Caribbean. They move west and northwest into the Caribbean and the Gulf of Mexico, striking the lands in their path. Many hurricanes leave their westward path and head north and northeast. Fortunately, some storms then blow out to sea. Others strike the Gulf or Atlantic coast, battering everything in their path with winds that reach 75 to 125 miles (120 – 200 km) an hour.

CHECKUP

1. In what parts of the Southeast would you be likely to find the coolest temperatures?
2. In this region, when does most rain occur? What part of the region gets the most rain?

The winds and waves of a hurricane are exciting, but they are very destructive.

Agriculture, Industry, and Resources

Agriculture   One of the major crops in the Southeast is **citrus fruit**. Florida leads the United States in citrus production. As you drive through the Florida peninsula, you can see orange, lemon, lime, and grapefruit groves along the highways. In the cities and suburbs, many homeowners have citrus trees.

Croplands in the Southeast are also used to raise cash crops of tomatoes, lettuce, and many other vegetables. Two or three crops can be grown in a year in many places.

In Virginia, along the sandy coastal plain, there are large fields of potatoes, tomatoes, and strawberries. Peaches are grown from Georgia through Delaware. South Carolina leads the United States in peach production. Peanuts are grown from Virginia through Georgia and Alabama. Georgia is the United States' leading producer of peanuts. Other food crops include apples, corn, pecans, and sweet potatoes.

Not all crops are used for food. Two important nonfood crops from the Southeast are tobacco and cotton. Tobacco is grown throughout much of the Southeast. The leading states in tobacco production are North Carolina, Kentucky, and Virginia.

In the 1800s, cotton was one of the most important crops in the South. It

The climate in many parts of the Southeast is good for cotton. This machine harvests the cotton balls.
Ask: Why is less cotton planted now? (Demand is lower because of competition from synthetics.)

is still an important crop, although not as much cotton is planted now. Today farmers in Mississippi, Alabama, and Tennessee are the Southeast's leading producers of cotton.

Cotton needs a growing season of at least 6 months. It also needs plenty of rain in the spring and summer, and fairly dry weather during the fall harvest season. For these reasons, most of the cotton is grown in the inland areas, which are drier than the coastal areas.

The Southeast is important for its livestock, too. Cattle are raised in all ten states. Georgia, Alabama, North Carolina, and Mississippi rank second through fifth in the production of meat chickens in the United States. Hogs are important in several states.

334

Research question: Why is the Brahman breed of cattle used extensively in the Southeast?

Tourism   One of the largest industries of the Southeast is tourism. Florida's income from tourism is about four times as large as that of any other state in the Southeast. The warm, sunny weather attracts many travelers. Walt Disney World, Gulf Coast and Atlantic beaches, the Florida Keys, the Everglades, the Kennedy Space Center at Cape Canaveral, and other interesting places bring many visitors.

There are historic sites throughout the Southeast. One of the best known is Williamsburg, Virginia. Williamsburg has been restored to show visitors what homes looked like, how people dressed, and the work people did when our country was very young.

See picture, p. 85.Near Williamsburg is the site of Jamestown. Here one can see ruins of the old settlement. Both Williamsburg and the Jamestown site are part of the Colonial National Historical Park. Near the Jamestown site is a state park in which you can see some reconstructed homes. These homes give you an idea of the way people of Jamestown lived. Also in this park are full-sized models of the ships that brought the colonists to Jamestown.

A visitor to Charleston, South Carolina, finds the nation's oldest museum and the Fort Sumter National Monument, where the first shots of the Civil War were fired.

Another interesting place to visit is St. Augustine, Florida. This town is the oldest existing European settlement in what is now the United States.

People who like camping, hiking, and other outdoor activities find much to enjoy in the Southeast. Wildlife abounds in the parks and elsewhere. Thousands of kinds of plants grow in the warm climate. Many lakes and streams offer freshwater fishing, and people can go deep-sea fishing in the waters off the coast. Throughout the area, tourists can observe the nesting areas of **migratory birds.** Migratory birds are birds that fly south for the winter.

The name of the state park is Jamestown Festival Park.

The first shots of the Civil War were fired at Fort Sumter in the harbor of Charleston, South Carolina. Confederate forces fired on the Union troops holding the fort.

32°48′N/79°57′W

A third national park in the Southeast is Shenandoah National Park. Have pupils find out where it is, when it was established, and how big it is. (Virginia; 1926; 190,591 acres [77,189 ha])

These boys and girls are backpacking in the Great Smoky Mountains. Judging by their faces, it's time to rest.

Ask: Have you ever gone backpacking? Where? What did you bring with you?

One park that offers many of these attractions is the Great Smoky Mountains National Park. This park is along the border between Tennessee and North Carolina. It draws more than 10 million visitors a year. Another well-known park is Mammoth Cave National Park in south-central Kentucky. People from all over the United States come to the park to explore the cave.

Fishing   Another important industry of the Southeast is fishing. From Chesapeake Bay come crabs, oysters, and menhaden (men hā′ dən). Menhaden is a kind of fish that is either used as bait or made into fertilizer and oil.

From the Atlantic Ocean and the Gulf of Mexico come oysters, scallops, crabs, lobsters, shrimp, menhaden, and red snappers. The red snapper is a food fish. Fish catches in Virginia and North Carolina are among the ten largest in the United States.

Tree farming   At one time almost all of the Southeast was forested. Now much of the land has been cleared so people can use it for other purposes. However, there is still a large demand for lumber. Hardwoods, such as maple and oak, are needed for furniture and for use in building. Papermills need softwoods, such as pine and poplar. Softwoods are also used for some kinds of furniture and for building. **Tree farming** has become important in meeting the demand for these different kinds of lumber. A tree farm may be a few acres of a farmer's land. Or it may be a huge tract owned by a lumber company. Scientists work on these large tree farms, developing new, fast-growing kinds of trees. There are more tree farms in Mississippi than in any other state.

The coniferous trees of the woodlands and tree farms of the coastal plains provide the raw materials for the paper industry. As in New England, many mills have polluted the air and water. Now state and national laws are helping to control pollution.

Textiles   Many industries of the Southeast are directly related to agriculture. One such industry is the textile industry. Mills from Virginia through Georgia make not only cotton but also rayon, nylon, and other synthetics. Good workers, well-run plants, and good transportation have helped to make southern mills our leading producers of textiles. South Carolina leads the nation in textile production.

Food processing   Citrus products from Florida reach all parts of the United States. Much of the fruit chosen to be

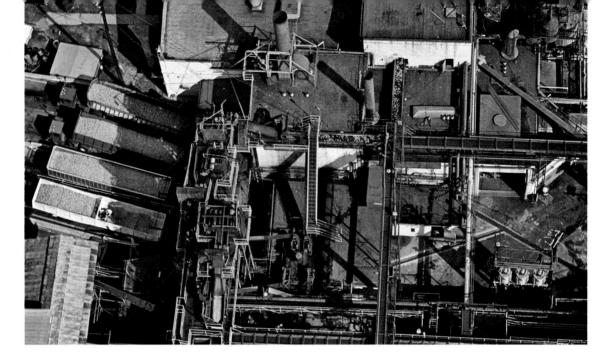

Several truckloads of fruit start their journey through this citrus-processing plant. Notice the fruit on the conveyor belt in the center of the picture.

This citrus-processing plant is in Apopka, Florida (28°40'N/81°30'W).

sent fresh is handpicked before it is fully ripe. The fruit is then cleaned, dyed, labeled, and sorted by size. Finally it is packed into crates and shipped to markets all across the country.

Fruit that is to be made into frozen or canned juice is loaded into large trucks after it is picked. These big tractor-trailer trucks hold tons of oranges or other fruits. At the food-processing plant, the load is weighed. Then it is emptied by raising the whole trailer up so the fruit rolls out. Almost the whole process, from emptying the truck to filling the cans with juice, is handled by machines. Workers operate the machines and make sure they are running properly.

Canning and freezing vegetables is another important food-processing industry. Most ripe vegetables, like fruits, spoil within a short time after picking. When these foods are canned, dried, or frozen, they can be enjoyed throughout the year.

Minerals Several important resources are found underground in the Southeast. There are large deposits of oil and gas. Mines in Alabama and Georgia are our leading sources of bauxite. Bauxite is used in making aluminum. Mines in Florida, Tennessee, and North Carolina lead the country in phosphate production. This mineral is used in fertilizers.

You might not think of stone, gravel, sand, and clay as important natural resources. After all, you can pick up a stone or a handful of gravel or sand in many places. However, these materials are important. Our highways and many construction projects could not be completed without them. The Southeast is an important source of these resources.

Coal Large amounts of coal are mined in the Southeast. More than half our coal comes from a huge coalfield that stretches from Pennsylvania into Alabama, a distance

337

of more than 700 miles (1,100 km). Kentucky ranks first in the United States in coal production; West Virginia, second.

At one time coal was the main fuel in use in the United States. Then more and more people began using oil and gas. As a result, many coal mines were closed. Now we have begun to run out of oil and gas. Both fuels have become very expensive. Coal is once again important.

Some coal is near the surface of the earth. It can be mined by a method called **strip mining**. Large earthmovers are used to clear away the **overburden**, or layers of earth that cover the coal. Once the overburden has been removed, machines like the one in the picture on page 278 dig the coal and load it into trucks to be hauled away.

Strip mining is safer and less costly than underground mining. However, strip mining destroys the land. Mining com-

From this picture, you can see why land that has been strip mined needs to be reclaimed.

panies must now restore the land after the coal has been mined. Restoring the land is costly. However, not restoring it is even more costly in the long run. If the land is left without its topsoil and plant cover, the remaining earth **erodes**. Few plants will grow in the poor soil. Large areas of land become both unsightly and of little value.

Another problem occurs when eroded soil chokes nearby streams, killing fish and thus upsetting the natural balance

Underground mines are used when the **seam** of coal is deep in the ground. Although today's miners use machines, underground mining is a difficult job. Each day the miners ride an elevator that takes them deep into the earth. When they leave the elevator, they find themselves in a system of tunnels and "rooms" that have been hollowed out of the earth. These rooms may be only about as high as the seam is thick. Often, this means that the ceiling is not high enough to allow miners to stand upright. The miners sit in long, low machines that dig out the coal.

Underground mining has always been a dangerous job. Sometimes there are cave-ins, and miners are crushed. Sometimes the digging releases poisonous or explosive gases. Coal dust presents further problems. When there is a lot of coal dust in the air, the dust may explode. Miners who breathe coal dust for many years often get a disease called black lung. Today there are laws to help protect the safety of the miners. There are fewer deaths and injuries than there once were, but mining can still be dangerous.

CHECKUP

1. Which state is the leading grower of citrus?
2. Name at least four tourist attractions found in the Southeast. Tell where each is found.
3. Which state is the leading coal producer?

This picture was taken in Tennessee, but at one time, scenes like it could be found in many strip-mined areas.

Population and Cities

SOUTHEASTERN STATES: POPULATION AND CITIES

States	Population	Percent urban	Cities of 100,000 or more people
Florida	9,740,000	86	8
North Carolina	5,874,000	45	5
Georgia	5,464,000	57	4
Virginia	5,346,000	66	9
Tennessee	4,591,000	63	4
Alabama	3,890,000	62	4
Kentucky	3,661,000	46	2
South Carolina	3,119,000	48	0
Mississippi	2,521,000	27	1
West Virginia	1,950,000	36	0

Population　Florida has the largest population of the southeastern states and the seventh largest population of the 50 states. It is one of the five fastest growing states in the United States. Most people in Florida live in cities.

West Virginia has the smallest population of the southeastern states. Less than half the people live in cities.

The table shows the population of each southeastern state, the number of cities with populations of 100,000 or more, and the percent of the population living in urban areas.

Cities　Only two southeastern cities have populations of more than 500,000. They are Memphis, Tennessee, and Jacksonville, Florida, two of the 25 largest cities in the United States.

At one time, the Southeast had few large cities. Today, however, much manufacturing has moved to the Southeast. New industries have developed. *Manufacturing cities* have grown with these industries. Cities have developed as *trade centers,* where the goods produced by industry are sold. Because the goods must be shipped to other places, *port cities* have increased in size. The increase in tourism has brought growth to another kind of city, the *resort city.* Of course, none of the cities is just a trade center, just a resort, or just a port. Miami, for example, started as a resort. Now the city is important in manufacturing and transportation, too. In the next few pages, we'll look at Miami and some other cities.

Atlanta　With a population of about 422,000 Atlanta is the largest city in Georgia. Atlanta has served as Georgia's capital since the time of the Civil War. The National Center for Disease Control is in Atlanta. At this center, people look for ways to control outbreaks of diseases that spread from one person to another.

Atlanta is a leading industrial center. Airplanes, automobiles, chemicals, textiles, and furniture and many other products are made in and around Atlanta.

Atlanta is the Southeast's center for foreign trade. Governments from about 11 countries have set up **consulates** in Atlanta. The people in the consulates help make trade agreements between business people from their countries and business people in and around Atlanta.

You may wish to introduce the words *communicable* and *epidemic* during discussion of the Atlanta Center for Disease Control.

Have pupils find out which governments have consulates in their city or in the nearest large city.

339

Fort Knox is only about 20 miles (32 km) from Louisville. Have pupils find out why Fort Knox is important.

Birmingham   Birmingham, Alabama, has been the Southeast's leading iron- and steel-producing center for over 100 years. The city is near the coal, limestone, and iron ore needed to make iron and steel. Railways provide transportation for these raw materials and for the finished products. Since the 1940s the city has tried to attract new industries so that it would not be dependent on just one industry. Now food-processing and chemical plants are among Birmingham's many industries.

Charleston, South Carolina   Charleston is a small city with a population of about 70,000, although the metropolitan area has about 412,000 people. Charleston is one of the oldest cities in the United States. At the time of the Revolutionary War, Charleston was the most important city and port south of Philadelphia. It served as the business and cultural center of the area. Charleston still serves as a port for both trade and military purposes.

Charleston, West Virginia   The resources near Charleston, West Virginia, have helped the city grow into the major trade and industrial center of the state. Coal, chemicals, limestone, lumber, salt, clay, and gas are leading products of the city's industries.

Charlotte   Charlotte is the largest city in North Carolina. With more than 670 manufacturing companies, it is a major industrial center. The chief products are chemicals, cloth, foods, and machinery. Charlotte is also a very important trucking center. Charlotte became a city before the Revolutionary War.

340

Jackson   Jackson is the capital and by far the largest city in Mississippi. Jackson has about 203,000 people, while the other cities in the state have less than 50,000 people each. Jackson's central location has helped it grow as a center of transportation. This in turn helped it grow as a trading and manufacturing center. A nearby supply of gas also helped the city bring in industry.

Louisville   Louisville (lü′ i vil) is the largest city in Kentucky. This important transportation center is on the banks of the Ohio River. Plastics, automobiles, meat packing, and tobacco are a few of the city's important industries. The world's largest publisher of Braille books and magazines is in Louisville. Braille books are books for blind people. The well-known Kentucky Derby horse race is held in Louisville.

Bring to class a copy of a Braille book and allow pupils to examine it. Such books are available in many public libraries.

A barge loaded with coal floats past Louisville on the Ohio River.

Have pupils find proof in the picture that Louisville is a transportation center.

Memphis   This Tennessee city serves as a trade center for much of the South Central region of the United States, as well as for western Tennessee. Cotton and livestock and many other agricultural products are marketed in Memphis.

Memphis is a transportation center for the area, too. Located on the Mississippi River, it is one of the major North American ports.

Miami   Miami, Florida, is one of the newer cities of the United States. It was founded in 1870 and officially became a city in 1896. This city is home to many thousands of Cuban **refugees.** People whose lives and property have been in danger have been fleeing from Cuba since the revolution there in 1959. Most of them have come first to Florida. Many of them have stayed there.

Tourism is Miami's leading industry, although the city is a transportation center because of its major air, sea, and rail connections. The city also is the nation's third largest center of the **garment,** or clothing, industry.

Norfolk   Norfolk, Virginia, is the largest of a group of cities around the Port of Hampton Roads. The other cities that share the port are Portsmouth, Newport News, and Hampton. More goods are **exported** from the Port of Hampton Roads than from any other Atlantic port. The Port of Hampton Roads is the biggest coal port in the world. The largest naval base in the United States is located in Norfolk. The harbor and the city's airlines, railroads, and highways have helped make Norfolk the largest city in Virginia.

Several ships are berthed at this Norfolk navy base. Among them are aircraft carriers and cargo ships.

Rural areas   Of course, not all of the Southeast is made up of cities. Many areas have few people living in them. Farming areas usually have a low population density. Certain physical features account for other areas of low population density.

Look at the population density map on page 259. What physical feature accounts for the low population density in most of southern Florida? If you can't remember, look at the map on page 329. What physical feature accounts for the area of low population density that runs northeast to southwest through the middle of the southeastern region? Let's see why this area has such a low population density.

Everglades

Appalachian Mountains

Appalachia   People settled in the many small valleys of the Appalachians as early as the seventeenth century. Here they built farms just big enough to meet their own needs. Travel was difficult in this hilly land. There wasn't enough good farmland for the large farms that

The old crafts have undergone a revival in Appalachia. (Left) An old woman teaches the art of making brooms. (Right) Fairgoers watch a potter demonstrate her craft.

need a market in which to sell crops. For these reasons, few towns grew up in Appalachia, as this region is called. Because there were so few ways of making a living, many young people left Appalachia as soon as they were old enough to look for work. During the 1800s, some coal-mining towns were built. However, many of these almost disappeared when the demand for coal fell off. For those who remained in Appalachia, life was hard. **Poverty** was widespread.

Even today, Appalachia remains a region of small farms and villages. However, some of the mining towns are again beginning to grow because of the renewed need for coal. Modern fertilizers and farming methods have helped farmers in the area to grow larger crops. This means

they have more money to spend in nearby towns and villages. The TVA brought electricity to some parts of Appalachia. This in turn allowed businesses to develop. Ski resorts and campgrounds in the area bring tourists who want the same kinds of services they find at home. New roads have made travel easier. Appalachia is becoming less isolated. For these reasons, there is less poverty in the area. More young people are staying in the region. Life in Appalachia is becoming more and more like life in the rest of the nation.

CHECKUP

1. What are the two largest cities of the Southeast?
2. Name three cities that serve as ports. Locate each city on a map.
3. What are three things that are happening to bring change to Appalachia?

342

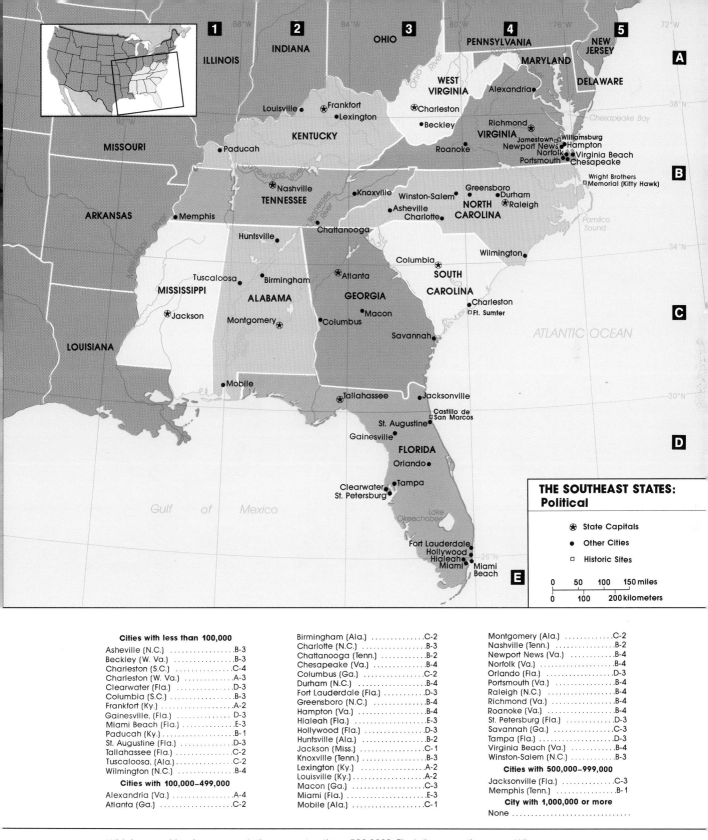

THE SOUTHEAST STATES: Political

⊛ State Capitals
● Other Cities
▫ Historic Sites

0   50   100   150 miles
0   100   200 kilometers

Cities with less than 100,000

Asheville (N.C.) B-3
Beckley (W. Va.) B-3
Charleston (S.C.) C-4
Charleston (W. Va.) A-3
Clearwater (Fla.) D-3
Columbia (S.C.) B-3
Frankfort (Ky.) A-2
Gainesville, (Fla.) D-3
Miami Beach (Fla.) E-3
Paducah (Ky.) B-1
St. Augustine (Fla.) D-3
Tallahassee (Fla.) C-2
Tuscaloosa, (Ala.) C-2
Wilmington (N.C.) B-4

Cities with 100,000–499,000

Alexandria (Va.) A-4
Atlanta (Ga.) C-2

Birmingham (Ala.) C-2
Charlotte (N.C.) B-3
Chattanooga (Tenn.) B-2
Chesapeake (Va.) B-4
Columbus (Ga.) C-2
Durham (N.C.) B-4
Fort Lauderdale (Fla.) D-3
Greensboro (N.C.) B-4
Hampton (Va.) B-4
Hialeah (Fla.) E-3
Hollywood (Fla.) D-3
Huntsville (Ala.) B-2
Jackson (Miss.) C-1
Knoxville (Tenn.) B-3
Lexington (Ky.) A-2
Louisville (Ky.) A-2
Macon (Ga.) C-3
Miami (Fla.) E-3
Mobile (Ala.) C-1

Montgomery (Ala.) C-2
Nashville (Tenn.) B-2
Newport News (Va.) B-4
Norfolk (Va.) B-4
Orlando (Fla.) D-3
Portsmouth (Va.) B-4
Raleigh (N.C.) B-4
Richmond (Va.) B-4
Roanoke (Va.) B-4
St. Petersburg (Fla.) D-3
Savannah (Ga.) C-3
Tampa (Fla.) D-3
Virginia Beach (Va.) B-4
Winston-Salem (N.C.) B-3

Cities with 500,000–999,000

Jacksonville (Fla.) C-3
Memphis (Tenn.) B-1

City with 1,000,000 or more

None ....

Which two cities have populations greater than 500,000? Find them on the map. What places shown on the map would you like to visit?

THE SOUTHEAST STATES	Alabama	Florida	Georgia	Kentucky	Mississippi
Source of Name	From the Alabamu Indian tribe meaning "I clear the thicket."	From the Spanish, (pascua florida) meaning "feast of flowers"	In honor of George II of England	From an Iroquoian word Ken-tah-ten meaning "land of tomorrow"	From an Indian word meaning "Father of Waters"
Nickname(s)	Yellowhammer State	Sunshine State	Peach State; Empire State of the South; Goober State	Bluegrass State	Magnolia State
Capital	Montgomery	Tallahassee	Atlanta	Frankfort	Jackson
Largest Cities (1980 Census)	Birmingham Mobile Montgomery	Jacksonville Miami Tampa	Atlanta Columbus Savannah	Louisville Lexington Owensboro	Jackson Biloxi Meridian
Population Rank (1980 Census)	22	7	13	23	31
Population Density Rank	26	11	21	23	31
Area Rank	29	22	21	37	32
State Flag					
State Bird	Yellowhammer	Mockingbird	Brown thrasher	Kentucky cardinal	Mockingbird
State Flower	Camellia	Orange blossom	Cherokee rose	Goldenrod	Magnolia
State Tree	Southern pine (longleaf)	Sabal palm	Live oak	Coffeetree	Magnolia
State Motto	Audemus jura nostra defendere (We dare defend our rights.)	In God we trust	Wisdom, justice, and moderation	United we stand, divided we fall	Virtute es armis (By valor and arms)
Interesting Facts	Montgomery was the first capital of the Confederacy. George Washington Carver did his famous research on the peanut at Tuskegee Institute.	Three fourths of the nation's oranges and grapefruit are produced here. The manned space flights are launched from the John F. Kennedy Space Center.	It is the largest state east of the Mississippi. It is called the "Goober State" because the state leads the nation in the production of goobers, or peanuts.	It is the nation's largest producer of coal. The federal government's huge gold supply is kept at Fort Knox.	The Petrified Forest near Flora has giant stone trees as old as 30 million years. There are more tree farms in Mississippi than in any other state.

344

THE SOUTHEAST STATES	North Carolina	South Carolina	Tennessee	Virginia	West Virginia
Source of Name	In honor of Charles I of England	In honor of Charles I of England	From the name of a Cherokee Indian village—Tanasie	In honor of Queen Elizabeth I of England	In honor of Queen Elizabeth I of England
Nickname(s)	Tar Heel State	Palmetto State	Volunteer State	The Old Dominion; Mother of Presidents	Mountain State
Capital	Raleigh	Columbia	Nashville	Richmond	Charleston
Largest Cities (1980 Census)	Charlotte Greensboro Raleigh	Columbia Charleston North Charleston	Memphis Nashville-Davidson Knoxville	Norfolk Virginia Beach Richmond	Huntington Charleston Wheeling
Population Rank (1980 Census)	10	24	17	14	34
Population Density Rank	17	19	18	16	25
Area Rank	28	40	34	36	41
State Flag					
State Bird	Cardinal	Carolina wren	Mockingbird	Cardinal	Cardinal
State Flower	Dogwood	Carolina yellow jessamine	Iris	American dogwood	Rhododendron
State Tree	Pine	Palmetto	Tulip poplar	Flowering dogwood	Sugar maple
State Motto	*Esse quam videri* (To be rather than to seem)	*Animis opibusque parati* (Prepared in mind and resources) *Dum spiro spero* (While I breathe, I hope)	Tennessee—America at its best	*Sic semper tyrannis* (Thus always to tyrants)	*Montani semper liberi* (Mountaineers are always free)
Interesting Facts	On December 17, 1903, the Wright brothers made their first flight from Kitty Hawk. The dangerous Cape Hatteras, off the coast, is known as the "Graveyard of the Atlantic."	It was the first state to withdraw from the Union before the Civil War. On April 12, 1861, Confederate troops fired the opening shots of the Civil War on Fort Sumter in Charleston Harbor.	It is called the Volunteer State because it is known for its tradition of excellent military service. Davy Crockett and President Andrew Jackson were natives of Tennessee.	Eight presidents of the United States were born in Virginia. They include Washington, Jefferson, Madison, Monroe, W. Harrison, Tyler, Taylor, and Wilson. The first permanent English settlement was in Jamestown, 1607.	Free delivery of mail in rural areas was started here in 1896. The first natural gas well to be discovered in the nation was found in Charleston.

345

17/CHAPTER REVIEW

KEY FACTS

1. Important landforms of the Southeast include swamps, the Piedmont, hills and plateaus, the Appalachian Mountains, and the Atlantic and Gulf coastal plains.

2. The Tennessee River system is used for shipping, recreation, irrigation, and power.

3. Climate is related to latitude and to elevation.

4. Much of the Southeast has a climate suited to growing a variety of important crops.

5. Major industries of the Southeast include tourism, textiles, food processing, fishing, lumbering, mining, and manufacturing.

6. The largest cities of the Southeast are Memphis and Jacksonville.

VOCABULARY QUIZ

Write the letter of the term next to the number of its description. Write on a sheet of paper.

a. barrier islands   **f.** tidewater

b. overburden   **g.** hurricane

c. temperate   **h.** consulate

d. humid   **i.** citrus

e. shoals   **j.** refugees

c **1.** Neither extremely hot nor extremely cold

e **2.** Underwater sand bars

a **3.** Islands along a coast that help protect the mainland

g **4.** A storm with winds that reach speeds of 75 to 125 miles (120 – 200 km) an hour

i **5.** A kind of fruit that includes lemons, oranges, and limes

f **6.** Low-lying coastal land that is often flooded with water

j **7.** People who flee from their homeland because their lives and property are in danger

b **8.** The earth covering a deposit of coal

h **9.** An office set up by the government of a foreign country to help business people work together

d **10.** Having much moisture.

REVIEW QUESTIONS

1. Where are the Atlantic and Gulf coastal plains located?

2. Describe the Everglades of Florida.

3. What is the Piedmont? Where is it located?

4. What do the letters TVA stand for? What does the TVA do?

5. How are temperature and latitude related? Temperature and elevation?

6. Name two important crops of the Southeast.

7. What is strip mining?

8. Give an example of each of the following kinds of cities: port city, manufacturing city, trade center, resort city.

9. What was life like in Appalachia at one time? How is it changing?

ACTIVITIES

1. Choose several of the places named in the section on tourism that you would like to visit. Look in magazines or write for information about those places. Plan how you would travel to the places. Tell what kind of transportation you would use (plane, bus, car, train), and show your route on a map.

2. On the left side of a sheet of paper make a list of agricultural products from the Southeast. Draw another line to make a column. For each product, name one state that produces the product. In a third column list some of the uses of the product. For example, for the product peanuts you might list candy, peanut butter, and cooking oil.

RESEARCH SKILLS: CAREER AWARENESS

In the next few years, there will be large numbers of job openings for the kinds of workers named on the graph below. Do you know what kinds of work all these people do? What does a stenographer do? A retail trade sales worker? A chef? If you don't know, look in a dictionary or an encyclopedia.

Look at the graph and answer the following questions.

1. Which workers should find a job most easily?   Secretaries and stenographers

2. Who would have more openings to choose from, a bookkeeper or a typist?   Bookkeeper

3. About how many openings will there be each year for custodians? For teachers?
160,000; 70,000

This graph is based on information found on tables in at least two almanacs. Find an almanac in your school library. Look in the index under "Jobs" or "Occupations" for the page on which the table is found. Find the number of openings for the job or jobs you might like to have. Are there several thousand openings, or only a few hundred? Why are there more openings for truck drivers than there are for astronomers? Why is it important to know how many openings there will be for a given kind of job?

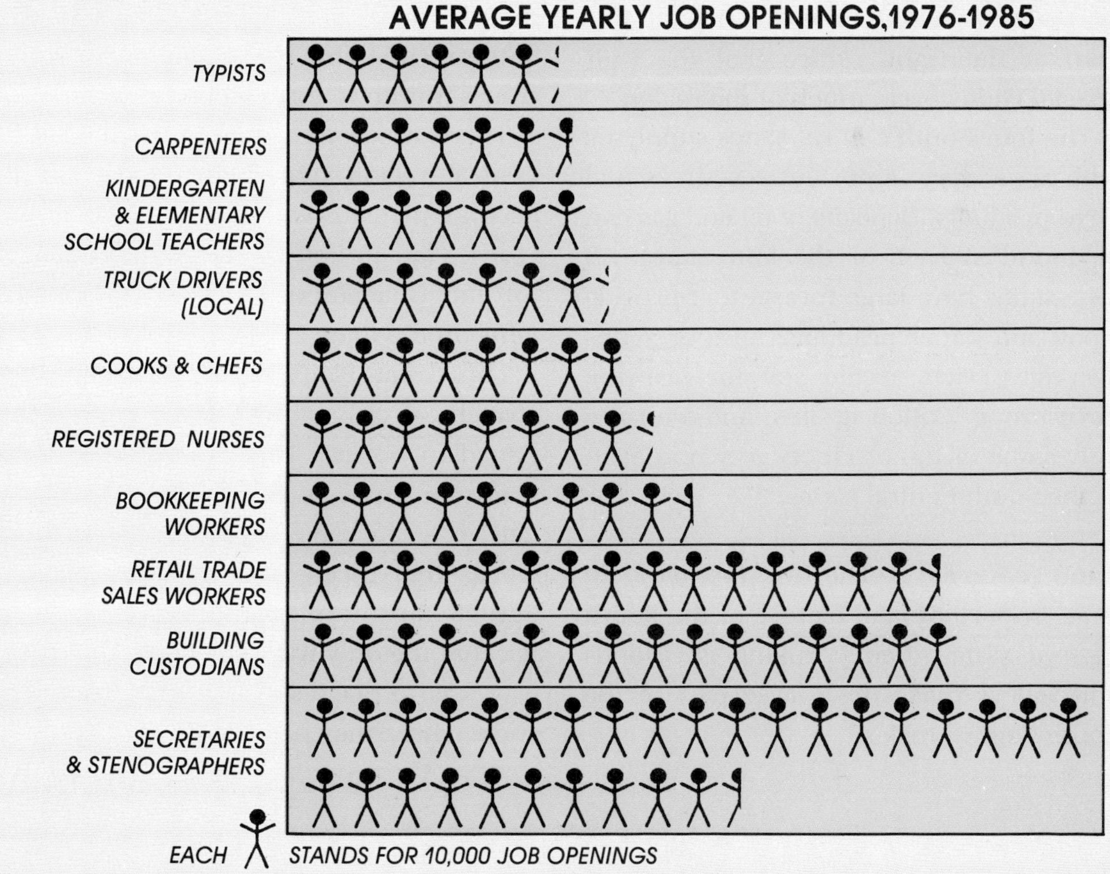

Have pupils graph the number of openings for other workers, find the educational requirements for the jobs they choose, and find average salaries for workers in those fields.

AVERAGE YEARLY JOB OPENINGS, 1976-1985

TYPISTS

CARPENTERS

KINDERGARTEN & ELEMENTARY SCHOOL TEACHERS

TRUCK DRIVERS (LOCAL)

COOKS & CHEFS

REGISTERED NURSES

BOOKKEEPING WORKERS

RETAIL TRADE SALES WORKERS

BUILDING CUSTODIANS

SECRETARIES & STENOGRAPHERS

EACH 人 STANDS FOR 10,000 JOB OPENINGS

The two almanacs referred to are *Information Please* (New York: Simon and Schuster) and *The Hammond Almanac* (Maplewood, N.J.: Hammond Almanac, Inc.)

CHAPTER
18 The South Central States Today

The Land and Climate

VOCABULARY

marshland	tornado
gulf	panhandle
silt	water vapor
levee	

Four similar states   The South Central region has the fewest states. There are only four states. They are Arkansas, Louisiana, Oklahoma, and Texas. The land features of the South Central states range from low **marshlands** along the coast, to high plains, to mountains. Look at the map at the right. Notice that the Gulf Coastal Plain covers much of the region.

The four South Central states supply us with some very important resources and farm products. Deposits of oil and gas can be found in each of the four states. All four states have large forests that provide wood and paper products. All four states also have rich, fertile soil for growing farm crops. Cotton, grains, and fruit are only some of the products grown in each of the South Central states.

Land features   The Gulf Coastal Plain is an important land feature of the South Central states. Gently rolling grasslands and valleys make up a large part of the South Central region.

The Mississippi River delta is in the Gulf Coastal Plain. The delta is in the low coastal marshland of Louisiana. The word *delta* comes from the Greek letter that looks like this Δ. River deltas often have a shape like the Greek letter.

The flow of a river causes deltas to form. Rivers usually flow into larger bodies of water, such as oceans or **gulfs**. A gulf is part of an ocean or sea that pushes into the land. **Silt**, or fine soil and ground stone, is carried by the flowing water. As the water slows down at the mouth of a river, the silt drops to the bottom. Over time the silt builds up at the river's mouth to form a delta.

There are several places in the South Central region where the land rises to become plateaus and mountains. Find the Ozark Plateau and the Ouachita (wäsh' ə tô) and Guadalupe (gwäd' əl üp) mountains on the map.

The Great Plains is a vast plain that stretches from southwestern Texas to the Canadian border. One part of the Great Plains in Texas is called *Llano Estacado* (län' ō es tə käd' ō). These are Spanish words that mean "staked (stākt) plains." Early Spanish explorers found the area so flat that the only way they could find their way was to place stakes in the ground to show where they had been.

An alternate pronunciation is gwad' əl üp' e, which is closer to the Spanish pronunciation.

Border rivers: Rio Grande, Mississippi, Pearl, Red, St. Francis

Can you find on the map all the rivers that form borders? Below the map is a photograph taken from a satellite showing part of the Mississippi delta area. The river is the bright blue line. The cloudy blue area is mud and silt in the water.

This photograph was produced from data relayed to earth by a Landsat satellite. For further information, see Supplementary Information in the Manual section for Chapter 18.

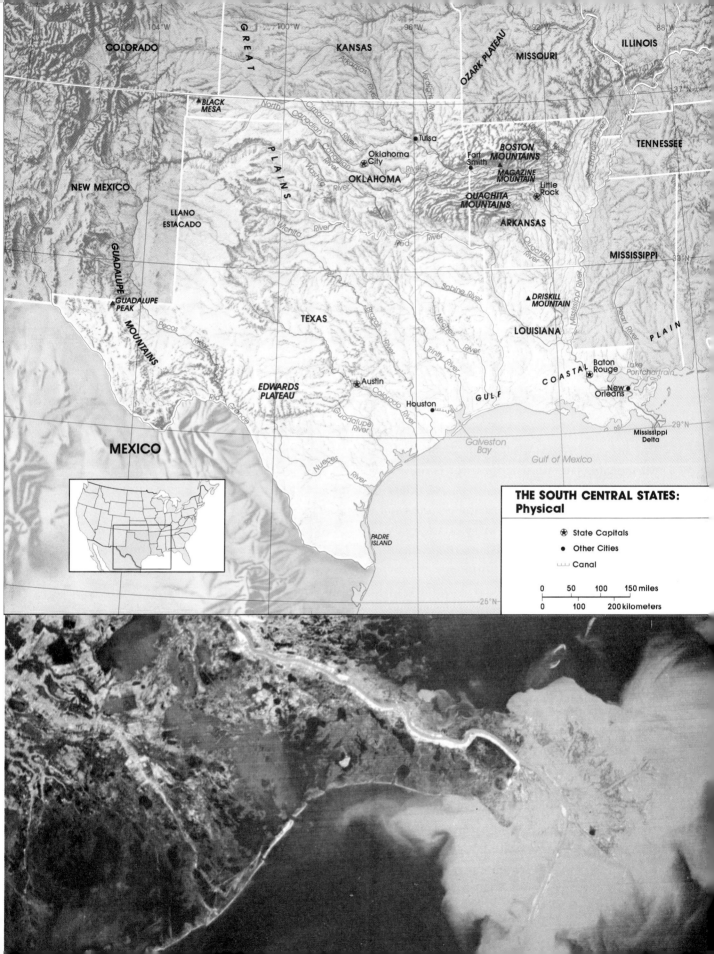

COLORADO

GREAT

104°W   100°W   96°W   92°W   88°W

KANSAS

ILLINOIS

OZARK PLATEAU

MISSOURI

37°N

BLACK MESA

Arkansas River

TENNESSEE

PLAINS

North Canadian River

Cimarron River

Verdigris River

Tulsa

BOSTON MOUNTAINS

Canadian River

Oklahoma City

Fort Smith

MAGAZINE MOUNTAIN

Little Rock

St. Francis River

NEW MEXICO

OKLAHOMA

OUACHITA MOUNTAINS

LLANO ESTACADO

Washita River

River

Ouachita River

ARKANSAS

Wichita River

MISSISSIPPI

33°N

Red River

Sabine River

GUADALUPE PEAK

GUADALUPE

Pecos River

TEXAS

Brazos River

Neches River

DRISKILL MOUNTAIN

Mississippi River

Pearl River

PLAIN

MOUNTAINS

Trinity River

LOUISIANA

Baton Rouge

Lake Pontchartrain

EDWARDS PLATEAU

Austin

Colorado River

COASTAL

New Orleans

Rio Grande

Houston

GULF

29°N

MEXICO

Guadalupe River

Mississippi Delta

Nueces River

Galveston Bay

Gulf of Mexico

THE SOUTH CENTRAL STATES: Physical

✪ State Capitals

● Other Cities

⊔⊔⊔ Canal

PADRE ISLAND

0   50   100   150 miles

0   100   200 kilometers

25°N

Mississippi levees may be as wide as 8 feet (2.4 m) at the top and 100 feet (30.5 m) at the base. They range from 15 to 30 feet (4.8–9.5 m) in height. Some experts disagree with the use of levees for flood control because of the increased danger should a levee break in an area where levees have raised the level of the river above that of the surrounding land.

This house remained standing in spite of the flood. Many others were swept away.

Sources differ on the length of the Mississippi. The source used here was *Webster's New Geographical Dictionary.*

Rivers   In Chapter 14 you learned that the source of the Mississippi River is in Minnesota. The Mississippi River is one of the nation's longest rivers. It is 2,348 miles (3,778 km) long. This major waterway serves as the eastern boundary of Arkansas and most of that of Louisiana. It forms a large part of the western boundary of Mississippi and all the western boundary of Tennessee. Look at the map of the United States in the Atlas, pages 468–469. What other states have the Mississippi River as a boundary?

The Mississippi has been a major transportation route throughout the history of the United States. Today it is still the busiest inland waterway in our country. Barges can travel on the Mississippi as far north as Minneapolis, Minnesota.

As you know, the river has left silt along the delta and coastal plain for hundreds of years. This has helped to make the land fertile and valuable for farming. However,

the river has also caused problems. There have been years when the river overflowed its banks and flooded the land. The flooding happened in the spring after the northern snows melted or after weeks of very heavy rain. The water flooded areas where the **levees** (lev' ēz) along the river were not strong enough or high enough to hold back the increased flow of the river. A levee is a wide wall built with earth.

One of the worst floods took place in 1927. It forced more than 300,000 people living in the Mississippi River plain to flee their homes. In 1973 high water flooded more than 13 million acres (5 million ha) of land in nine states from Illinois to Louisiana. The flooding destroyed millions of dollars worth of crops. It delayed the planting of other crops. It cost about $193 million to repair the damage. Only the very large levee system prevented more damage.

Answer to text question, col. 1, para. 1: Missouri, Kentucky, Illinois, Iowa, Wisconsin, Minnesota

Oceangoing ships can navigate the Mississippi as far as Baton Rouge, which has made that city an important port.

The Rio Grande, like the Mississippi River, serves as a boundary. It lies between Mexico and Texas. From its source high in the Rocky Mountains in Colorado, the river travels 1,885 miles (3,033 km) to reach the Gulf of Mexico. *Rio Grande* is a Spanish name. In English it means "Great River."

Other large rivers of the South Central region include the Arkansas River and the Red River. Barges can navigate the Arkansas River as far north as Tulsa, Oklahoma. Even though Tulsa is inland, it is a major port city.

In Kansas and Colorado, the Arkansas River is called the är kan′ zəs River.

The Red River flows through parts of each of the South Central states before it reaches the Mississippi River north of New Orleans. It is named the Red River because it carries red-colored silt. The land along the Arkansas and Red rivers has rich soil that is excellent for farming.

Ask: For which states does the Red River serve as a border? (Tex., Okla., Ark.)

Climate   Warm waters from the area around the equator flow into the Gulf of Mexico. These warm waters help control the climate of Louisiana and coastal Texas. Warm breezes blowing off the gulf help keep the summers warm and humid and the winters temperate. This means

SOUTH CENTRAL STATES: YEARLY PRECIPITATION

Weather station	Inches	Centimeters
Little Rock	49	124
Baton Rouge	54	137
Oklahoma City	31	79
Lubbock	18	46
Houston	48	122

Ask: Which city has the most precipitation? The least?

most winters are mild. Although the temperature does go below freezing, snow is rare. The mild winters give farmers a long growing season.

Western Texas has a cool, dry climate. Central Texas and most of Oklahoma have a warm, dry climate. The climate of Arkansas is warm and rainy. As you can see, there are different types of climates in this region. Look at the charts to find the temperature and precipitation of certain cities in the South Central region.

Tornadoes   During the months from March to June, the South Central states can have one of the most feared of all storms—the **tornado**. The South Central region is part of what is called "Tornado

Have pupils locate on the map on p. 362 each city on this table.

SOUTH CENTRAL STATES: TEMPERATURE

Weather station	Average January temperature		Average July temperature		Temperature extremes		Temperature extremes	
	°F	°C	°F	°C	High	Low	High	Low
					°F		°C	
Little Rock	40	4	81	27	108	−5	42	−21
Baton Rouge	51	11	82	28	103	10	39	−12
Oklahoma City	39	4	82	28	108	−4	42	−20
Lubbock	39	4	80	27	107	−16	42	−27
Houston	52	11	83	28	102	18	39	−8

The swirling winds of a tornado can cause nearly complete destruction. Yet right next to the storm track, there may be no damage at all.

Valley." This valley stretches from the Texas **panhandle** north to Nebraska and as far east as Ohio. A panhandle is a narrow strip of land.

Tornadoes often form in the late afternoon or early evening of a very hot, humid day. At such times, thick, dark clouds sometimes form into a cone-shaped cloud that becomes a high-powered, twisting windstorm. That storm is a tornado. Tornadoes make a roaring noise that sounds like a speeding train. **Water vapor** and dust picked up by the winds give the funnel its gray color.

In the center of the tornado, winds can swirl at speeds of 300 miles per hour (480 km per hr). The worst tornado on record was a mile (1.6 km) wide and traveled 220 miles (354 km) across three states at 60 miles (97 km) per hour.

CHECKUP

1. Why is the Gulf Coastal Plain an important land feature of the South Central states?
2. How was the Mississippi River delta formed?
3. What are the four kinds of climate found in the South Central region?

Agriculture

> **VOCABULARY**
>
> | | |
> |---|---|
> | sorghum grain | feedlot |
> | subtropical | overgraze |
> | erosion | rodeo |

A variety of crops The kinds of crops that are grown in the South Central region are closely connected to the rainfall, temperature, and land features you have just learned about. Many types of crops are produced in these four states. Soybeans, rice, sugarcane, cotton, sweet potatoes, and citrus fruits grow well in the warm, moist climate of Arkansas, Louisiana, and the coastal plains of Texas. Winter wheat and **sorghum** (sôr′ gəm) **grain** do well in the drier and more temperate areas of the region.

Along the Rio Grande in southern Texas and near the Gulf Coast, farmers grow citrus fruits and fresh vegetables. The long growing season, good rainfall, and irrigation from the river help to make citrus fruits and fresh vegetables important crops.

Cotton Texas is the leading cotton-producing state in the United States. Look at the table. How do the other three South Central states rank in the production of cotton? The combination of warm, wet climate and good soil helps to make cotton a very successful crop in this region. In Texas, a large part of the cotton crop is dependent on irrigation.

Sugarcane The **subtropical** climate of the lower delta area of Louisiana is very important for raising sugarcane. When sugarcane is harvested, the roots remain in the ground. As long as the roots do not

SOUTH CENTRAL STATES: RANK IN AGRICULTURAL PRODUCTION

Product	Ark.	La.	Okla.	Tex.
Sugarcane		3		4
Cotton	6	5	7	1
Soybeans	7	9		
Sweet potatoes		2		7
Rice	1	4		3
Citrus fruits				4
Winter wheat			2	7
Sorghum grain				1
Beef cattle			5	1

Ask: Which state is the leading producer of three of the agricultural products shown on this table? (Texas)

freeze, the plant will keep producing for several years. The lower delta area often has several years in a row without frost. This means that sugarcane does not have to be replanted very often.

Sugarcane farmers, like most other farmers, need machines to help them. Machines prepare the fields and plant the cane. Machines are also used for weeding, harvesting, and loading the cane onto trucks to ship to sugar-processing plants. Here the machines of the factory take over. The cane is cut, washed, and crushed. The workers run, repair, and clean the machines. Manufacturing the cane syrup and sugar is also done with machines. The syrup and sugar are then shipped to food-processing factories all over the United States.

Rice   Rice is another important crop grown in the South Central region. Arkansas, Louisiana, and Texas are three of the leading rice-growing states. To grow well, rice needs warm temperatures, from 70°F to 100°F (21°C − 38°C). Rice also needs lots of water. Even though most of the places where rice is grown get 40 or more inches (100 cm) of rain every year, more water is needed. Rice fields are irrigated to be sure there is plenty of water.

Rice is a very important food for many people all over the world. Sometimes rice is used in cereals.

Winter wheat   From central Texas through Oklahoma, winter wheat is an important crop. Winter wheat is planted in the fall. Its roots grow strong before winter's cold weather arrives. In the spring the wheat begins to grow rapidly. It is ready for harvest in early summer.

By planting winter wheat the farmers help to prevent soil **erosion**. In this area of little rainfall, plant roots are needed to help keep the soil from blowing away. The wheat plants help hold the soil during the long, dry winter season.

Raising cattle   Cattle ranching is one of the best known and most important agricultural activities in Oklahoma and Texas. In large parts of Oklahoma and Texas the soil is too dry and poor for growing crops. But this dry grassland is used for grazing. It is where the cattle and sheep ranches are found.

Because this area is so dry, many ranchers drill wells to get the water their cattle need. The wells cost a lot of money but without them the huge herds of cattle could not be raised.

Most cattle do not go directly from the grazing lands to the market place. The grasslands do not provide enough food to fatten cattle. Instead the cattle are sent to **feedlots**. Here the animals are fed special diets that add pounds every day. When the

An interesting economic activity of the South Central region, and one that is increasing in importance, is fish "farming." Have pupils prepare a report on the subject.

353

Today many of the largest ranches are controlled by corporations, rather than by individual ranchers.

cattle have gained enough weight they are sold for meat. The feedlot is then made ready for another herd.

Cattle ranching has been an important part of the history and growth of the United States. In Chapter 10 you read about the ranchers who were part of the fast growth of the Great Plains in the 1860s. In the early years of ranching, cattle were grazed on open land. But in the late 1800s, ranchers started fencing in their land. Ranches today are very large but they are not as large as in the frontier days. Mechanization does mean that fewer cowhands are needed.

The work of the cowhand hasn't changed much from the days of the Old West. Cowhands may ride in a jeep or even a helicopter instead of on a horse. However, they still watch over large herds of cattle all across the plains. Cattle must be moved from one grazing area to another to protect the grass from being **overgrazed**. Once a year, usually in the fall, there is a roundup. At the roundup, the young calves are branded with the letters of the ranch. The cattle are sorted. Some are sent to market and others are sent to feedlots.

The rodeo   Part of the colorful history of the West is the **rodeo**. The word *rodeo* is a Spanish word. In English it means "surround," or "round up." The rodeo started in the 1800s during the roundup. Along the trail to market, cowhands from different ranches would compete in riding and steer roping. Today, throughout Texas, Oklahoma, and other states in the West, the rodeo may be a monthly or yearly event. Rodeos are held on large ranches, in small towns, and in large

This cowhand is still on top of the bull, but how long will he last? If he falls, the clown will make sure the bull doesn't hurt him.

cities. In most small towns the prize is also small. Sometimes there are no prizes. Cowhands compete just for the fun of it. Only a few people earn their living by competing in the large rodeos. Whether large or small, rodeos are exciting. The cowhands eagerly try to see who can manage a bucking horse, ride a kicking bull, rope a speeding calf, or wrestle a steer to the ground. Just about everyone likes a rodeo. The stands are filled with young and old cheering for their favorite cowhand.

CHECKUP

1. Why do cotton, sugarcane, and rice grow well in this region?
2. How does winter wheat help the farmers?
3. Why are large areas of Oklahoma and Texas used for raising cattle?

Resources and Industry

Mineral resources   Each South Central state has valuable mineral resources. One resource is found in the Crater of Diamonds State Park near Murfreesboro, Arkansas. This park has the only diamond mine in the United States. If you find a diamond when you visit the park you can keep it!

Arkansas also has our most important bauxite mines. The bauxite mines are southwest of Little Rock. As you know, bauxite is used to make aluminum. However, the supply does not meet our need for aluminum. More bauxite must be imported from South America and Africa.

Texas and Louisiana are the leading producers of sulfur in the United States. Sulfur is a pale yellow mineral. It has many uses that are important to us. Sulfur is used to make rubber. It keeps the rubber from becoming sticky in the summer and too hard and brittle in cold weather. Sulfur is also used to make matches, gunpowder, and insect sprays.

Louisiana and Texas are also our leading producers of salt. Salt has over 14,000 uses! Some uses are making glass, preserving meat, and processing leather.

Energy resources   The South Central states have very large deposits of oil and gas. As you know, oil and gas are major sources of energy that people all over the world need. Texas, Louisiana, and Oklahoma rank among the leading states in the United States in supplying these very important energy resources.

One of the world's largest sources of oil—close to 10 billion barrels (1.3 trillion t)—lies under the plains of Texas. That equals almost one third of the country's known supply of oil. There is more oil off the coast of Texas, in the earth under the Gulf of Mexico. One of the world's largest underground areas of natural gas is also found in Texas—in the northwestern panhandle. Most of Louisiana's 1,000 gas and oil fields are found in the southern marshlands. Oil has also been found off the Louisiana coast in the Gulf of Mexico. There are deposits of oil and gas throughout most of Oklahoma. The state has about 70,000 oil wells. Arkansas also has supplies of oil in the southwestern part of the state and of gas in the Arkansas River valley.

Exploring for oil   Before oil can be used it must be brought up from inside the earth. **Geologists**, who study the earth's surface and the layers of rock below the surface, look for good places to drill oil and gas wells. These scientists know what to look for from studying other oil- and gas-producing regions. But even with the geologists' knowledge, very often only one in ten wells will have oil or gas. Wells that don't yield oil or gas are known as "dry wells" or "dry holes."

Geologists explore for new oil and gas reserves both on land and under the sea. In order to bring the oil and gas above the surface, many difficult problems have to be solved.

There is even a town in Louisiana named Sulpher.

Drilling an ocean well How do you drill a well when the ocean floor is 100 feet (30 m) or more below the surface of the water? And that is just the beginning! A well may have to be drilled another 20,000 feet (6,100 m) before oil or gas is found. Drilling platforms have been designed that float on the ocean surface. The **derrick**, or tall steel frame, is anchored to the ocean floor. The platforms and derricks are built to hold up in the strong winds and high waves of a storm.

Workers are taken to and from the drilling platform by boat or helicopter. They live on the platform. They can sleep, eat, bathe, and watch TV or movies, as well as work on the platform. The workers stay on the platform for two or three weeks at a time.

A well that is 20,000 feet (6,100 m) deep may take more than a year to drill. The drilling goes on every day, 24 hours a day.

The drill goes through the soil and into the rock layers of the earth. The drill must be hard and sharp to break through the rock layers. The cutting edges on the drill are made of diamonds. Diamonds are hard enough to cut away the rock.

Steel pipe casings are hollow tubes that are 16 to 34 feet (5–10 m) long. They are placed one on top of the other inside the part of the well that is drilled. The casings are sealed together. They are also sealed on the outside with concrete. The casings keep the well from caving in. They also keep dirt, salt water, and other materials from getting into fresh water lying inside the rock layers.

If a well produces oil, the workers put in a pump that pumps oil until the well runs dry. The oil is sent to a pipeline. The pipeline sends the oil to a storage tank. Then it is moved to a **refinery**. In the refinery the oil is made into many prod-

This drilling platform is in the Gulf of Mexico. The boat brings pipes and other supplies to the platform. The helicopter is used mostly to bring people.

On the graph, *Gasoline* includes auto and aviation fuels. *Fuel Oils* include oils used in home and industrial heating and diesel fuels for trucks, ships, and other heavy duty engines. *Other Fuels and Solvents* include ethane, liquefied gases, kerosene, naphtha, and other products. *Other* includes wax and other products that only a petroleum expert could describe.

ucts. The final products are sent by railroad, truck, ship, or pipeline all over the United States.

Uses of oil   Oil is used in many ways. When we think of oil, we usually think about running our cars or heating our homes. But oil and gas have many other uses. Look at the pie graph. You can see that most petroleum is made into gasoline and fuel oil. Gasoline is used for cars. Fuel oil is used to heat homes and other buildings. It is also burned to make power for factories. Fuel oil also includes **diesel fuel**, which is used in trucks, buses, and some cars. Jet fuels are a mixture of oil products that are specially made for jet airplanes. Oil is made into other fuels, as well. They are used in camp stoves and in many other ways. Some of these fuels are also **solvents**. That is, they are used for such purposes as thinning paints or dissolving grease. Asphalt and road oil are used to make smooth, longlasting road surfaces. Some oil is made into **lubricants**. These are oils and greases that are used to make a slippery coating between metal parts. The lubricants keep the metal parts from wearing out too fast.

As you read in Chapter 16, petroleum is also used to make petrochemicals. The products made from petrochemicals include medicine, fertilizer for growing food, plastics, and paint. Even some of the clothes you wear and the soap your clothes are washed in are made from petrochemicals.

Our country's demand for oil is very high. The United States has between 5 and 6 percent of the world's people. At the same time, we use 33 percent of the

PETROLEUM PRODUCTS

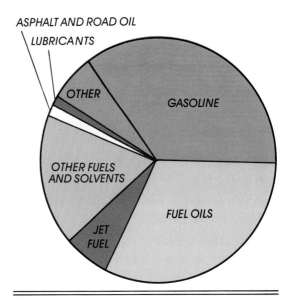

About 2/3 of our oil is used for what two products?

world's energy. Most of the energy we use comes from oil and gas. We have to import a lot of oil and gas to meet our needs. But every year there is less oil and gas in the earth. Therefore we must use our energy resources wisely. As you read in Chapter 17, coal has become an important energy resource again. Scientists are also trying to find other sources of energy. They are experimenting with heat from the sun and the ocean.

Oil spills   Oil spills are a danger that comes with shipping oil or drilling for it in the ocean. A spill may result from a problem with an offshore well or from an oil tanker that is broken up by a storm.

Oil spills can hurt people, beaches, plants, and wildlife. At sea or in a river the spilled oil is carried by the water's current. It may be carried up on a beach used by swimmers or sunbathers. It may also be carried into **tidal pools** and coastal marshlands. Tidal pools are pools of water left behind when the ocean moves away from the shore at low tide. Small forms of ocean life live in these pools. Marshlands are the home of many animals, especially water birds such as ducks, egrets, and gulls. Oil spills in areas near tidal pools and marshlands are likely to destroy or seriously hurt both animal and plant life. The feathers of water birds become covered with the thick oily substance. Globs of oil also sink to the bottom of the tidal pools and marshlands, polluting the water and killing the plants and animals.

Engineers, scientists, and government people are working together. They are trying to solve the problems of oil spills. They are learning how to control the spread of oil from spills.

Forests and lumber   Not all the South Central states' resources are underground. Forests cover almost half of Arkansas and Louisiana. In Arkansas this amounts to about 18 million acres (7 million ha) of land, and in Louisiana, about 15 million acres (6 million ha). Arkansas is among to top ten lumber-producing states in the United States. The lumber from both states is used for building materials and paper products. The paper in this book may have come from a tree grown in Arkansas or Louisiana.

Fishing   Fish are another resource that are important to this region. Fishing fleets work the waters of the Gulf of Mexico for shrimp, oysters, crabs, flounder, menhaden, and red snapper.

At present Louisiana and Texas are among the top ten states in the fishing industry. But the people in the fishing industry of these two states are worried. They do not yet know whether offshore drilling will harm the fish. Both the fishing industry and the oil industry provide jobs for many people. It is hoped that these two important industries can work side by side in the Gulf of Mexico without causing problems for either.

In at least one respect, offshore drilling has improved fishing: the rigs serve as reefs and attract fish.

Space exploration and electronics
Other industries of the South Central region include space exploration and travel, **electronics**, and tourism. The Lyndon B. Johnson Space Center in Houston, Texas, has played a very important role in the exploration of the moon, the planets, and outer space.

Electronics has become an important industry for Arkansas, Texas, and Oklahoma in the past few years. This industry needs highly skilled workers. People who

These children are visiting the Lyndon B. Johnson Space Center. Astronauts are trained at the center. The center keeps a constant watch over all its space flights.

People can camp right on the beach at Padre Island National Seashore, off the Texas coast. Padre Island is at about 97°W and between about 26°N and 28°N.

understand electronics have been able to improve televisions, radios, and other products. If you use a calculator or play video games, you are using electronic products that may have been made in one of these states. Our everyday lives are touched by the spacecraft and electronics industries of the South Central states.

Tourism　All the South Central states attract visitors. People visit each of the four states for different reasons. Some people want to learn about the Native Americans. Over 10 percent of the Indians of the United States live in Oklahoma. The Cherokees, the largest of the tribes in Oklahoma, have built a village to show what an ancient Indian village was like. Members of the tribe take visitors around the village.

The Cowboy Hall of Fame is in Oklahoma City. This museum attracts people of all ages. It teaches them about the way of life of the cowhand.

The Gulf Coast, from the Mississippi River delta to the southern end of Padre (päd' rē) Island in Texas, attracts many winter visitors. People want to escape from the cold North. They come to the Gulf Coast for boating, sight-seeing, sunbathing, and sport fishing.

Another place people like to visit is the Alamo in San Antonio, Texas. The Alamo is an old Spanish mission that was made into a fort. In Chapter 8, you read about the famous battle that took place at the Alamo.

National parklands and forests also attract visitors. Padre Island National Seashore has about 80 miles (130 km) of sandy beaches. National parks in the South Central region are Big Bend in Texas and (see p. 361) Hot Springs in Arkansas.

CHECKUP

1. Why are bauxite, sulfur, and salt important mineral resources?
2. Which South Central state has one of the world's largest sources of petroleum?
3. Name at least five ways people use petroleum products.

The French influence is particularly visible in the *Vieux Carre* (in French, vyə(r) ka rā; in local speech, vü cär), or "Old Square," better known as the French Quarter. The French Quarter is famous for its restaurants, night clubs, jazz, and historic buildings.

Population and Cities

Population and capital cities   Three of the nation's ten largest cities are in the South Central region. Houston, Dallas, and San Antonio, Texas, rank among the ten largest cities in the United States.

Little Rock, the capital of Arkansas, is on the Arkansas River. About 158,000 people live in Little Rock. It is the largest city in the state. Little Rock is Arkansas' center of transportation and trading.

Austin is the capital of Texas, but it is smaller than several other Texas cities. The city was named after Stephen F. Austin, an important leader in the American settlement of Texas.

Baton Rouge (bat' ən rüzh'), Louisiana's capital, is the second largest city in the state. The name *Baton Rouge* is French. In English it means "red stick." The city was named for a red pole that Indians raised in the 1700s to show the boundary between two of their nations.

Oklahoma City, the capital of Oklahoma, covers 649 square miles (1,681 sq km). It is the third largest city in land area in our nation. Almost one fourth of the people in the state live in or near Oklahoma City.   Like many cities of the South Central region, Oklahoma City has oil wells within the city. A major oil field surrounds the capitol building.

New Orleans   New Orleans is Louisiana's largest city. It lies on the Mississippi River. To the north of the city is the large, shallow Lake Pontchartrain.

The city's population of 557,000 is a mixture of people from many different cultures. The first people to live in the New Orleans area were American Indians. They were followed by French, Spanish, and African peoples. The mixing of these three groups has given New Orleans a culture that is rather different from most other American cities. New Orleans is like a European city in many ways.

New Orleans is also well-known for the Mardi Gras (mär' dē grä') festival. This exciting carnival lasts for several weeks. The main celebration takes place two weeks before Lent in the Christian calendar. Parades fill the streets and a holiday spirit takes over the city.

New Orleans is not just a tourist center. It is also an important center for shipping. The port of New Orleans is the second busiest port in our country.

Houston   Houston, like New Orleans, is a port city. It is the third largest port city in the United States. To reach the port of Houston, ships have to travel

This Mardi Gras float takes its theme from Around the World in Eighty Days, *a book by Jules Verne.*

New Orleans: 29°58'/90°07'W

through a deepwater channel. The channel connects Houston to the Gulf of Mexico 50 miles (80 km) away. With about 1,594,000 people, Houston is the largest city of the South Central region. Houston was founded in 1836. After the channel was built in 1914 the city of Houston grew very fast. It grew fast not only because of the port but also because of the rich oil deposits nearby.

Houston is a leader in oil refining, in petrochemical manufacturing, and in making parts for oil wells and pipelines. Oil refining is the city's most important industry. Houston: 29°46′N/95°22′W

San Antonio   San Antonio is a food-processing, industrial, and transportation center serving the farming and cattle-ranching country of western Texas. It is also a city with a rich culture. People in the city speak Spanish or English or both. Many shops display signs in both languages. About 789,000 people live in San Antonio.

Throughout the city there are many historic landmarks. These landmarks tell the story of the city's beginnings. They show the Spanish and Mexican influence. San Antonio: 29°28′N/98°31′W

Dallas/Fort Worth   Dallas and Fort Worth lie in north-central Texas. Only 30 miles (48 km) separate the two cities. Together they form the largest metropolitan area of the South Central states. Dallas is the second largest city of Texas. About 904,000 people live in Dallas, and about 385,000 people live in Fort Worth. Both cities are important in the aircraft industry. Fort Worth is one of our country's largest producers of airplanes.

The Dallas-Fort Worth area has a large amount of the known United States oil reserves. The area is also known as a very important transportation center. The Dallas-Fort Worth airport is one of the busiest airports in the United States. It lies between the two cities and in many ways is a city by itself. Seven interstate highways and a good railroad system also serve the area. Dallas: 32°47′N/96°48′W
Forth Worth: 32°45′N/97°20′W

Hot Springs   Hot Springs is in the Ouachita Mountains of Arkansas. The city was named for its 47 hot **mineral springs**. Most of Hot Springs National Park is in the city. It is the only city in the United States that has most of a national park inside its borders.

About 35,000 people live in Hot Springs, But more than a million people visit the city every year. These people come to relax and bathe in the hot mineral water. The average temperature of the water is 145°F (63°C). The water is cooled down by about 40°F (22°C) before it enters the bathhouses. Ask: How hot is it then? (105°F or 41°C)

The Native Americans were the first to enjoy the hot springs. In 1807 a permanent white settlement was founded here by a trapper. By 1832 the area had become the first national health and recreation center in the United States. Today most of the people who live in Hot Springs work at the hotels, bathhouses, racetracks, and restaurants built for the tourists. Hot Springs: 34°30′N/93°03′W

CHECKUP

1. What is the capital city of Arkansas? Louisiana? Oklahoma? Texas?
2. Why is the Dallas-Fort Worth area important?

361

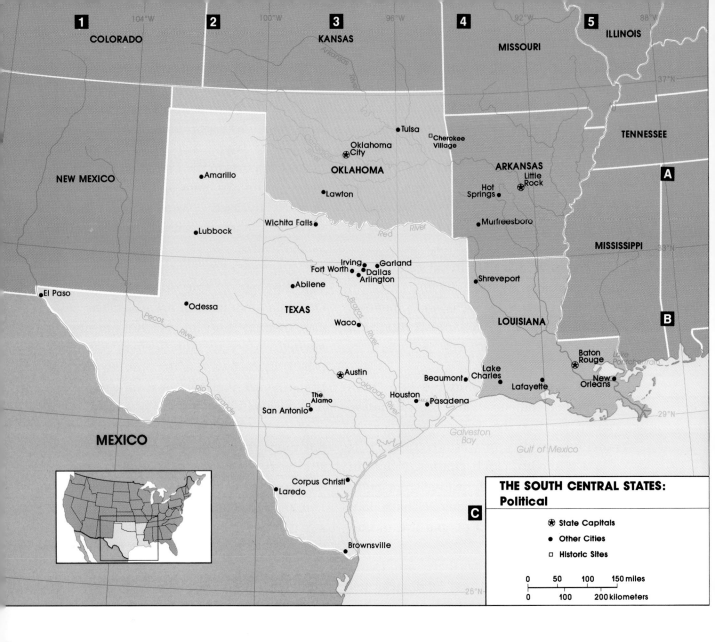

THE SOUTH CENTRAL STATES: Political

- ✹ State Capitals
- ● Other Cities
- ▫ Historic Sites

| 0 | 50 | 100 | 150 miles |
| 0 | 100 | 200 kilometers |

Cities with less than 100,000

Abilene (Tx.)	B-3
Brownsville (Tx.)	C-3
Hot Springs (Ark.)	A-4
Lafayette (La.)	B-4
Lake Charles (La.)	B-4
Laredo (Tx.)	C-3
Lawton (Ok.)	A-3
Murfreesboro (Ark.)	A-4
Odessa (Tx.)	B-2
Wichita Falls (Tx.)	A-3

Cities with 100,000–499,000

Amarillo (Tx.)	A-2
Arlington (Tx.)	B-3
Austin (Tx.)	B-3
Baton Rouge (La.)	B-5
Beaumont (Tx.)	B-4
Corpus Christi (Tx.)	C-3
El Paso (Tx.)	B-1
Fort Worth (Tx.)	B-3
Garland (Tx.)	B-3
Irving (Tx.)	B-3
Little Rock (Ark.)	A-4

Lubbock (Tx.)	A-2
Oklahoma City (Ok.)	A-3
Pasadena (Tx.)	B-4
Shreveport (La.)	B-4
Tulsa (Ok.)	A-4
Waco (Tx.)	B-3

Cities with 500,000–999,000

Dallas (Tx.)	B-3
New Orleans (La.)	B-5
San Antonio (Tx.)	B-3

City with 1,000,000 or more

| Houston (Tx.) | B-4 |

Which city has a million or more people? Find it on the map. Which city is at 30°N by 90°W?
Which city is at 30°N by 98°W? Houston; New Orleans; Austin

THE SOUTH CENTRAL STATES	Arkansas	Louisiana	Oklahoma	Texas
Source of Name	From a Quapaw Indian word meaning "downstream people"	In honor of Louis XIV of France	From two Choctaw Indian words meaning "red people"	From the Indian word *Tejas*, meaning "friends"
Nickname(s)	Land of Opportunity	Pelican State; Sportsman's Paradise; Creole State; Sugar State	Sooner State	Lone Star State
Capital	Little Rock	Baton Rouge	Oklahoma City	Austin
Largest Cities (1980 Census)	Little Rock Fort Smith North Little Rock	New Orleans Metropolitan Baton Rouge Shreveport	Oklahoma City Tulsa Lawton	Houston Dallas San Antonio
Population Rank (1980 Census)	33	19	26	3
Population Density Rank	34	22	35	30
Area Rank	27	31	18	2
State Flag				
State Bird	Mockingbird	Pelican	Scissortailed flycatcher	Mockingbird
State Flower	Apple blossom	Magnolia	Mistletoe	Bluebonnet
State Tree	Pine	Bald cypress	Redbud	Pecan
State Motto	*Regnat populus* (The people rule)	Union, justice, and confidence	*Labor omnia vincit* (Labor conquers all things)	Friendship
Interesting Facts	Mammoth Spring, in the northern part of the state, is one of the largest springs in the world.	About 5,000 miles (8,000 km) of rivers and waterways can be navigated. Almost half of North America's wild ducks and geese spend the winter in Louisiana's coastal marshes.	This state has the largest Indian population of any other state in the nation. Tulsa has been called the "oil capital of the world."	Texas is the only state in the United States that can be divided into two, three or four states by permission of Congress.

363

KEY FACTS

1. Important physical features of the South Central region include the Gulf Coastal Plain, the Mississippi delta, the Ozark Plateau, the Great Plains, and the Mississippi River.

2. The South Central region is important for its agriculture, which includes crops and livestock.

3. Resources of the South Central region include fish, lumber, and large deposits of oil and gas, as well as other minerals.

4. The oil in the Gulf of Mexico is very important, but drilling for it and transporting it present the danger of oil spills.

5. The largest cities of the South Central region are Houston, Dallas, and San Antonio.

VOCABULARY QUIZ

Next to the number of the sentence, write the term that best completes the sentence. Write on a sheet of paper.

silt	erosion
tornado	geologists
levees	refinery
feedlots	lubricants
overgrazed	deltas

1. __Levees__ along the Mississippi River help control flooding.

2. River __deltas__ often have the shape of the Greek letter Δ.

3. Plant roots help prevent __erosion__ of the soil.

4. A delta can be built up by deposits of __silt__ carried by a river.

5. __Geologists__ study the earth's surface and the layers of rock below the surface.

6. __Lubricants__ keep a machine's metal parts from wearing out too fast.

7. The swirling winds of a __tornado__ can cause nearly complete destruction.

8. If cattle are left too long in one grazing area, the land will become __overgrazed__.

9. Cattle are sent to __feedlots__ to be fattened for market.

10. At a __refinery__, oil is made into many products.

REVIEW QUESTIONS

1. How did the Llano Estacado, or staked plain, get its name?

2. Name three important rivers of the South Central region.

3. What effect do the warm breezes from the Gulf of Mexico have on the climate of Louisiana and coastal Texas?

4. Name at least four important agricultural products of the South Central states.

5. List one use for each of these minerals: bauxite, sulfur, and salt.

6. Why are the cutting edges on an oil drill made of diamonds?

7. Give an example of a petrochemical.

8. How does an oil spill harm plant and animal life?

9. Name the four South Central states and give the capital of each.

ACTIVITIES

1. Do some research on cattle raising and meat packing. Then make a chart on a large sheet of paper. Starting with cattle grazing on the range, show the main steps in getting beef to your table.

2. In an encyclopedia or other reference book, find out about the ways salt is obtained. Make drawings of the different processes. Make labels and captions for your drawings.

READING A MAP: UNITED STATES TIME ZONES

Earlier you learned that as the earth turns, one part of the earth gets lighter, while another gets darker. Because this is true, people have divided the earth into time zones.

There are 24 time zones. Seven of these time zones are used in the United States.

Each time zone is different by one hour from the zone next to it. New York City is in the Eastern Time Zone. Minneapolis is in the Central Time Zone. When it is 7 o'clock in New York, it is 6 o'clock in Minneapolis. In Denver, which is in the Mountain Time Zone, it is 5 o'clock. In San Diego, in the Pacific Time Zone, it is 4 o'clock. In the Yukon Time Zone, it is 3 o'clock; in the Alaska-Hawaii Time Zone, 2 o'clock; and in the Bering Time Zone, 1 o'clock.

At one time there were no standard time zones. Each town or city set its own times, based on the sun. You could ride 10 miles (16 km) down the road to the next town and arrive 20 minutes before you set out!

1. You live in Hawaii. Your grandmother lives in Georgia. You want to wish her a happy birthday before she leaves for work, which she does at 8 A.M. her time. At what time, your time, should you place the call? Before 3:00 A.M.

2. You live in New York. It is now 1 P.M. Eastern Standard Time. What time is it in Seattle? In Anchorage? In Phoenix?
10:00 A.M.; 9:00 A.M.; 11:00 A.M.

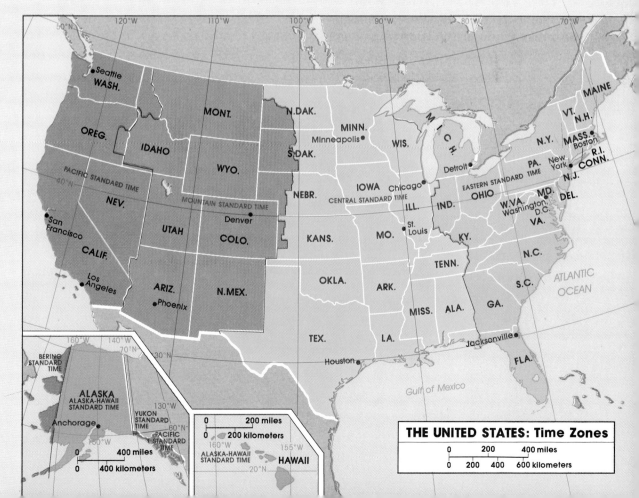

THE UNITED STATES: Time Zones

The Land

VOCABULARY

canyon	butte
Bad Lands	glacier
gully	inland sea
bluff	

The region   The North Central region is huge. It measures about 1,000 miles (1,600 km) from east to west and about 800 miles (1,300 km) from north to south. The 12 North Central states are Illinois, Indiana, Iowa, Kansas, Michigan, Minnesota, Missouri, Nebraska, North Dakota, Ohio, South Dakota, and Wisconsin.

What makes this group of states a region? The easiest answer to that question lies in the main physical feature: plains. Almost the whole region is covered by one kind of plain or another. Another answer lies in farming.

When people think of the Heartland, as this region is sometimes called, they think of the miles and miles of cropland that covers much of the area. They think, too, of the herds of beef cattle that graze in the western part of the region. Or they remember the Hay and Dairy Belt in the northeastern section.

Of course, there are differences from place to place. On one hand, you find thousands of acres of cropland. On the other, you find 8 of the 30 largest cities in the United States. You can drive for hundreds of miles and see nothing moving, other than a herd of cattle. You can also drive on streets clogged with the traffic of some of the most urbanized areas of the United States.

Landforms   In the eastern part of the region are the Central Lowlands. Along the western part of the North Central states is the Great Plains. The elevation of the region rises from east to west, until the plains meet the Rocky Mountains. However, the rise is so gradual that you do not notice it from the ground.

Most of the hills and mountains of the North Central states are fairly low. Even on the Ozark Plateau, the highest point is only 2,500 feet (762 m) high. One of the few places in which you find high mountains is in the Black Hills of South Dakota. This area is marked by steep **canyons** and high hills. Harney Peak in the Black Hills is the highest point of the North Central region. Elevation: 7,242 feet (2,209 m)

Bad Lands   Bad Lands are found in parts of South Dakota, Nebraska, and North Dakota. If you were to be suddenly dropped in the Bad Lands you might think you were on the moon. The Bad Lands are dry and rugged. There is little or no vegetation in the deep **gullies** and

(Lake Michigan)

On the map, find the only Great Lake that is entirely within the United States. The picture shows you the main physical feature of the North Central region: plains.

The checkerboard pattern in the photograph is the result of the practice of allowing fields to lie fallow in alternate years. This practice conserves moisture in the soil.

THE NORTH CENTRAL STATES: Physical

✪ State Capitals
● Other Cities

0   50   100   150   200 miles

0   100   200   300 kilometers

CANADA

MONTANA

NORTH DAKOTA
Bismarck ✪
WHITE BUTTE
Fargo ●

MINNESOTA

Lake of the Woods

Lake Itasca

MESABI RANGE

Lake Superior

MOUNT CURWOOD ▲

UPPER PENINSULA

MICHIGAN

GREAT

BLACK
HILLS

SOUTH DAKOTA
Pierre ✪
HARNEY PEAK ▲

Minneapolis ● ✪ St. Paul

WISCONSIN

Madison ✪ ● Milwaukee

Lansing ✪ ● Detroit

Lake Michigan

Lake Huron

Lake Ontario

Lake Erie

NEW YORK

WYOMING

BADLANDS

Sioux Falls ●

IOWA

Cedar Rapids ●

Des Moines ● ✪

Chicago ●

Fort Wayne ●

Cleveland ●

PENNSYLVANIA

PLAINS

NEBRASKA

North Platte River

Platte River

Omaha ●

Lincoln ✪

CENTRAL   LOWLANDS

INDIANA

ILLINOIS

Springfield ✪

Indianapolis ✪ ●

OHIO

Columbus ✪

WEST VIRGINIA

COLORADO

Kansas River

KANSAS

Topeka ✪

MISSOURI

Jefferson City ✪

St. Louis ●

Wichita ●

OZARK PLATEAU

KENTUCKY

VIRGINIA

NEW MEXICO

OKLAHOMA

ARKANSAS

TENNESSEE

ALABAMA

TEXAS

MISSISSIPPI

high, steep **bluffs** of the Bad Lands. North Dakota's highest peak, White **Butte** (byüt), is in the state's Bad Lands area.

Remind pupils to use the glossary for unfamiliar terms.

Lakes Thousands of years ago **glaciers** moved over much of the Northern Hemisphere. As they moved south, these large sheets of ice and packed snow helped to change the landscape. They carved out hollows and moved large masses of earth and huge boulders. After the ice ages passed, rivers and lakes were filled with water from the melted ice. These rivers and lakes have become an important part of the North Central states.

Four of the Great Lakes are part of the North Central region. The Great Lakes are so large that they are called **inland seas**. Their total area is greater than that of Indiana and Illinois.

THE GREAT LAKES: AREA

Name	Area (sq mi)	Area (sq km)
Superior	31,700	82,100
Huron	23,010	59,600
Michigan	22,300	57,760
Erie	9,910	25,770
Ontario	7,340	19,010

As you know, the lakes also serve as a part of an important water route—the St. Lawrence Seaway. Many cities, such as Detroit, Cleveland, Chicago, Milwaukee, and Duluth, have grown up along the shores of the lakes. Oceangoing ships travel between these cities and other ports in the United States and in other countries. The ships carry cargoes such as iron, grain, coal, and manufactured products.

The dry wastes of the Bad Lands are the result of years of wind erosion.

368 The soil of the Bad Lands is comprised of sand and gravel, with layers of clay, limestone, and sandstone. So exotic are some of the results of years of erosion that more than 240,000 acres (97,000 ha) in South Dakota have been set aside as the Badlands National Monument.

One river of this region, the Red River of the North, flows north into Canada. Most of the other North Central rivers flow generally southward.

Rivers

Three of our major rivers are found in the North Central States. These are the Ohio, Missouri, and Mississippi rivers. The Ohio River flows along the southern borders of Ohio and Indiana and the southeastern edge of Illinois. There it reaches the Mississippi. The Missouri River enters the North Central region in North Dakota. It flows through 6 of the 12 states. Near the port city of St. Louis, the Missouri River joins the Mississippi River.

The Missouri has touched the lives of many people. Its spring floods have taken lives and destroyed farms, homes, and businesses. Nearly 90 dams have been built to help control the Missouri and the many rivers and streams that flow into it.

The mighty Mississippi River starts as a tiny stream in northern Minnesota in the Lake Itasca (ī tas′ kə) area. As it flows south it forms parts of the borders of the North Central states of Wisconsin, Iowa, Illinois, and Missouri.

CHECKUP

1. Where is the highest point of the North Central states found?
2. Describe the Bad Lands.
3. Name the region's three major rivers.

In the second paragraph below, the word *usually* is important. Local condition saffect temperatures, too. Such is the case with Williston, which, although farther west than International Falls, has a slightly warmer winter average than International Falls.

Climate

Temperature

In northern Minnesota and North Dakota, winter temperatures have reached −40°F (−40°C) or lower. In these same states, temperatures higher than 100°F (38°C) have been recorded in the summer months of July and August. Of course, these are extremes. But in much of the region the usual range is quite large, too.

The table helps to show the temperature pattern. Notice that the places with average January temperatures higher than 25°F (−4°C) are in the south. Those places with average January temperatures lower than 25°F are in the north. You can also see that as one travels west, summer temperatures are usually hotter and winter temperatures colder.

Another thing that affects temperatures in the North Central region is the presence of the Great Lakes. The Great Lakes help keep the temperatures from getting as hot or as cold as they do farther west.

Weather station	Average January temperature °F	Average January temperature °C	Average July temperature °F	Average July temperature °C	Average yearly temperature °F	Average yearly temperature °C
Williston, N. Dak. 48°N/104°W	8	−13	70	21	41	5
International Falls, Minn. 49°N/93°W	2	−17	66	19	37	3
Sault Ste. Marie, Mich. 47°N/84°W	14	−10	64	18	40	4
Concordia, Kans. 40°N/98°W	26	−3	78	26	53	12
Columbia, Mo. 39°N/92°W	29	−2	77	25	54	12
Cincinnati, Ohio 39°N/85°W	32	0	76	24	55	13

NORTH CENTRAL STATES: AVERAGE TEMPERATURES

sü sant′ mə re′

Make sure pupils realize that the correlation of temperature with distance inland is a general pattern for the nation as a whole, not just for the North Central states. Ocean breezes help keep coastal winters milder and summers cooler than interior areas at the same latitudes.

The large bodies of water warm and cool more slowly than does the nearby land. Breezes coming across the lake warm the air in winter and cool it in summer. In Wisconsin, along the shore of Lake Michigan, the summer temperatures are lower and the winter temperatures higher than they are farther inland.

Precipitation   Like temperatures, precipitation varies with the seasons and from place to place. Generally the northern and western parts of the North Central region receive the least precipitation. The most precipitation falls in the southeastern part along the Ohio River valley.

The area around the Great Lakes lies between the two extremes. The rivers and the Great Lakes and the many other lakes affect the precipitation. The **water cycle** diagram helps to explain how water from the rivers, lakes, and plants **evaporates** to form rain-bearing clouds.

The average yearly precipitation in the North Central states ranges from 15 to 47 inches (50 – 119 cm). It comes in the form of rain, snow, sleet, and **hail.** In the winter months snow may blanket the northern parts of North Dakota through Michigan as early as November and stay on the ground until April. In some areas, the yearly average snowfall is more than 100 inches (250 cm).

CHECKUP

1. How do the Great Lakes affect the temperatures of the region?
2. What is the water cycle?

Water evaporates and forms clouds. Clouds contain many tiny droplets of water. These tiny drops combine to form larger drops, which fall as precipitation.

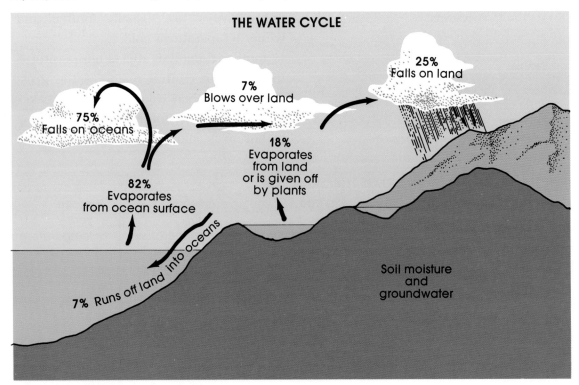

THE WATER CYCLE

25%
Falls on land

7%
Blows over land

75%
Falls on oceans

18%
Evaporates
from land
or is given off
by plants

82%
Evaporates
from ocean surface

7% Runs off land into oceans

Soil moisture
and
groundwater

Farmlands and Forests

┌─ VOCABULARY ─────────────────┐
wheat germ	gasohol
bran	vitamin
yield	market weight
└──────────────────────────────┘

Crops   Each of the 12 North Central states is part of our most important farming region. Much of the soil of the plains is fertile and deep. The frost-free season is long enough for many different kinds of crops. There is also enough rainfall for these crops.

The chief crops are corn and wheat. Soybeans, barley, oats, sorghum, rye, and hay are also very important. The table shows you how the North Central states rank in the United States in the production of these crops. Only ranks of one to ten are shown. Notice that the North Central region has the top ten corn-producing states, the top six soybean-producing states, and the top seven oat-producing states.

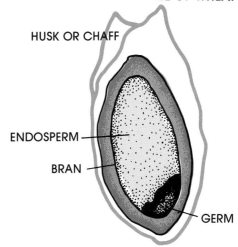

PARTS OF A KERNEL OF WHEAT

HUSK OR CHAFF

ENDOSPERM

BRAN

GERM

White flour is made from the endosperm of the wheat kernel. The whole kernel except the husk is used in making whole wheat flour.

Remind pupils that winter wheat is planted in the fall and harvested in early summer.

Wheat   Winter wheat is grown in the warmer southern areas from Ohio westward to Nebraska and Kansas. As you may remember, it is also grown in Oklahoma and Texas. If you look at the map on the next page, you will see that these areas form a belt across the middle of the United States. This is the Wheat Belt.

THE NORTH CENTRAL STATES: RANK IN CROP PRODUCTION

State	Wheat	Corn	Soybeans	Barley	Oats	Sorghum	Rye	Hay
Illinois	—	2	1	—	—	—	—	—
Indiana	—	4	5	—	—	—	—	—
Iowa	—	1	2	—	3	—	—	3
Kansas	1	—	—	—	—	2	—	10
Michigan	—	8	—	—	—	—	7	—
Minnesota	7	5	4	4	2	—	4	2
Missouri	10	9	3	—	—	4	—	8
Nebraska	8	3	—	—	7	3	5	5
North Dakota	2	—	—	1	5	—	2	9
Ohio	—	6	6	—	6	—	—	—
South Dakota	—	10	—	7	1	6	1	4
Wisconsin	—	7	—	—	4	—	—	1

Spring wheat is planted in the spring and harvested in the late summer.

Spring wheat is grown in the cooler and drier parts of the region. This includes western Minnesota and North and South Dakota.

Wheat is one of the few grains that is not used chiefly for animal feed. Wheat is used in breads and other baked goods, in cereals, and in other foods. **Wheat germ** and wheat germ oil are used mostly to enrich other foods. The **bran** is one part of the grain that is used mostly in animal feeds. A kind of alcohol made from wheat is used in several products. A wheat paste is used in insect sprays and in coffee substitutes. The wheat stalks are used to make fertilizer and boxes.

Refer pupils to the diagram of the wheat kernel on p. 371.

Corn   Part of the Corn Belt is in just about the same area as the Wheat Belt. Unless you live in the area, you are probably wondering how that is possible. The answer to this small riddle lies in the huge amount of farmland in the Corn Belt and Wheat Belt areas. There is plenty of room for the huge crops of both corn and wheat, not to mention all the other crops.

If you drive through the Corn Belt, you may notice that the corn plants are all almost exactly the same. They are all about the same height and all have several large ears of corn at about the same place on the plant. This is because scientists have worked to improve the quality of the corn and to get a bigger **yield** from each plant.

Plants that are alike make the work of the farmer easier and more productive. Harvesting machines have been designed so they can be carefully set to the height of the ears. The more alike the plants are,

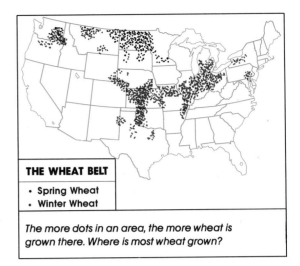

THE WHEAT BELT

• Spring Wheat
• Winter Wheat

The more dots in an area, the more wheat is grown there. Where is most wheat grown?

THE CORN BELT

The more dots in an area, the more corn is grown there. Where is most corn grown?

the more corn is harvested. This is also true of the harvesting machinery for other crops, such as wheat, oats, and soybeans.

Uses of corn   There are several kinds of corn. The two most important kinds are sweet corn and field corn. Sweet corn is the kind served as a vegetable with meals. Field corn is used mainly as animal feed, but it has many other important uses, too. You have probably eaten corn-

372

bread, which is made with corn flour or cornmeal. Many foods are sweetened with corn syrup. Corn oil is used in cooking and baking. It can be used in salad dressings and margarine. A kind of sugar called dextrose comes from corn. It is used as a sweetener and in the making of candy.

Many nonfood products are also made from corn. One that is becoming more and more important is alcohol. In some places it is now mixed with gasoline to make **gasohol**. Gasohol can be used instead of gasoline in automobiles and tractors. Other nonfood products made from corn are shellac, varnish, and plastics.

Cornstalks are also used. In some cases the stalks and even some ears of corn are left in the field. The stalks help keep the soil from blowing away. They also help to provide shelter or food for wild animals. Corncobs and cornstalks are used in making fiberboard and paper. Fiberboard is used in building.

Other crops   Most of the other large crops in the North Central states are used chiefly as animal feeds. Amost all sorghum and hay are used as feeds. Barley, rye, and oats are used largely for this purpose. Barley is also used in making malt. Barley grains, or "pearls," are used in soups, and barley flour is used in cereals and bread. Rye is used for bread and malt, also. The straw is used as a packing material and in making hats and other goods. Oats are used for cereals and baked goods. Soybeans are used in so many ways that we made a chart listing the main products made at least in part from soybeans.

Cattle and hogs   Cattle and hogs are also raised in the Corn Belt. Often cattle are raised in the dry grasslands of the Great Plains. Then they are sent to feedlots in the Corn Belt to be fattened before being shipped to market. Most hogs are not put out to graze, as cattle are. Rather, they spend their whole lives in pens.

A farmer knows how much of each kind of food and **vitamins** the animals need. He or she also knows how many weeks it will take for the animals to reach **market weight**. Market weight is the weight that an animal must reach before it is sent to market. If an animal is too light, the farmer doesn't make enough money. If the farmer lets the animals get too heavy, he or she will lose money on

If you have never heard of some of these products, look them up to find out what they are.

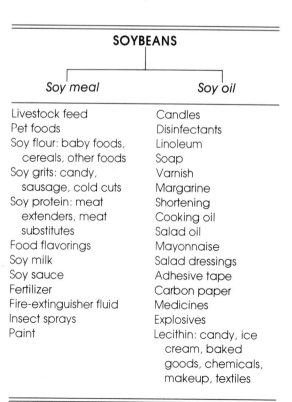

SOYBEANS	
Soy meal	*Soy oil*
Livestock feed	Candles
Pet foods	Disinfectants
Soy flour: baby foods, cereals, other foods	Linoleum
	Soap
Soy grits: candy, sausage, cold cuts	Varnish
	Margarine
Soy protein: meat extenders, meat substitutes	Shortening
	Cooking oil
	Salad oil
Food flavorings	Mayonnaise
Soy milk	Salad dressings
Soy sauce	Adhesive tape
Fertilizer	Carbon paper
Fire-extinguisher fluid	Medicines
Insect sprays	Explosives
Paint	Lecithin: candy, ice cream, baked goods, chemicals, makeup, textiles

Hogs spend all their lives in pens. When they are heavy enough, they are sent to slaughterhouses.

feed. That is why the quantity and quality of the food given to hogs in pens and cattle in feedlots is very carefully controlled. The proper amounts of each kind of food are mixed and given out automatically. That way a farmer can be sure the animals are being fed not only well, but as cheaply as possible.

Dairy farming   North of the Corn Belt is the Dairy Belt. Wisconsin is the leading dairy state. It has about twice as many dairy cows as each of the next two dairy states. Wisconsin and parts of Minnesota and Michigan are better for dairying than for other kinds of farming. The summers are a little cooler than they are in other parts of the North Central region. Often the countryside is hilly. This makes the land less suited to crops since most farm machinery is easier to use on level land. However, farmers in the Dairy Belt also raise some crops. Most of these crops, such as hay, oats, and corn, are raised for cattle feed. So much hay is raised that the name Hay and Dairy Belt is often used.

There are many ways in which milk can become unfit for use. For that reason the dairy farmer must meet high health

standards in order to sell milk. Barns, milking machines, and milk storage areas have to meet cleanliness standards. If they are not met, the farmer will not be able to sell the milk. Cattle are inspected to be sure they are not diseased. The milk itself is tested often.

The farmer must also keep careful records of the cost of feeding and caring for each animal. The amount of milk from each cow is also recorded. The value of the milk from each cow must be greater than the cost of the cow's feeding and care. Careful record-keeping helps everyone. Milk buyers know the product will be safe. Milk prices are kept as low as possible because the farmer knows which cows are the best producers. Those cows will be kept, while the ones that don't give much milk will be replaced.

Forests and wood products   Much of the North Central region is forested. The more heavily forested areas are in the north and the south. In the west, there isn't enough rainfall for trees. Much of the central area has been cleared of trees.

Some forests are used for recreation. Others supply wood for lumber, furniture, and paper. Trees also help control erosion and flooding. When large forests are cut down, melting snow and heavy rains wash soil away and flood streams. Tree roots help hold the soil and absorb water.

At this time, you may wish to have pupils do Activity 2 of the Chapter Review on p. 384.
CHECKUP

1. What are the two main crops of the North Central states?
2. Without looking back at the list of soybean products, how many can you name?
3. Why must a dairy farmer keep careful records?

The second and third dairy states are New York and California. The two states alternate frequently between second and third place.

Industry and Resources

The dairy industry   One of the many industries related to farming in the North Central states is the dairy industry. Milk from dairy farms is picked up by large milk trucks. Machines empty the farm's storage tanks and load the milk trucks.

The trucks deliver the milk to a processing plant. Here some of the milk is **pasteurized** and packaged in glass, plastic, or paper containers. Pasteurization is a process that makes milk safe to drink. Fresh milk is sent to markets, restaurants, and homes. Some milk is dried and packaged, and some is condensed and canned. Milk is also used to make cheese and butter.

Grain storage, transportation, and milling   A large business in the grain belt is grain storage and transportation. The highest building in many small farming communities is the **grain elevator**. At harvest time some farmers store grain on their farms. However, most farmers bring their truckloads of wheat and other crops to the local elevator. Here the crops are stored until they can be sold and shipped for processing.

Railroads are often used to move the grain from the elevators to the grain-processing plants. In the North Central states it is common to see a big diesel locomotive pulling a long line of railroad cars loaded with grain.

Duluth and Chicago are two important Great Lakes ports for shipping grain. Large barges loaded with grain can also be seen heading down the Mississippi and Missouri rivers on their way to New Orleans for shipment to other countries.

Grains are carried to different places depending on what they will be used for. Much of the wheat is taken to cities, such as Minneapolis, which has a large flour-milling industry. There the wheat is ground into flour and packaged. Some flour goes directly to large bakeries. Some is sent to a **wholesale market**. A wholesale market buys products in large quantities and sells them in smaller quantities to businesses. From the wholesale market, the flour goes to grocery stores and small bakeries.

Meat packing   The people of the United States eat a huge amount of beef and a large amount of pork. Much of the meat comes from the North Central states.

Omaha, St. Louis, and Kansas City, Kansas, are among the North Central region's major meat-packing centers. Animals are brought from the feedlots to these centers. Here, in meat-packing plants, they are slaughtered and made ready for shipping in refrigerated trucks and railroad cars.

There is very little waste in the meat-packing process. Most of the meat and several of the organs, such as the heart and liver, are used as food for people. Animal hides are sold to companies that make leather goods. Pet foods are made from scrap meats and bone meal, or powdered bone. The soap you used this

When crops are very good or when prices are low, the grain-belt region may run out of storage space. Abandoned schools and homes are sometimes used to supplement the elevators. Once in a while the grain is just piled on the ground and covered with a sheet of plastic or canvas.

morning and even medicines are **by-products** of the meat-packing process. The fertilizers used to feed your house plants and the glue used to mend the broken pot are some other by-products.

Economics lesson: The three basic necessities for an industrial economy

Farm machinery Another industry related to agriculture in the North Central states is the manufacture of farm machinery. More than half the country's farm machinery is made here. This industry has grown here for several reasons. First of all there is a good market. That is, there are people to buy the machinery. Farmers need plows and other farm machinery. Second, there are raw materials. The region has iron from which comes the steel to make the machinery. There is coal for power to run the factories and for making steel. Third, there is a good transportation network. Lakes, rivers, railroads, and highways are used to move both the raw materials and the finished products.

Minerals The North Central region is an important source of underground resources. Minnesota is our leading source of iron ore. Coal deposits are found in most of the 12 states. The major coal-producing states within the region are Illinois, Indiana, and Ohio. Oil and gas are found in several states.

Deep tunnels dug into the Black Hills near Lead (lēd), South Dakota, produce about one third of the gold in the United States. Mining gold is difficult work. Explosives must be used in the deep tunnels to blast the ore. The ore must be loaded and brought to mills. There the ore is further treated with chemicals. About 5 tons of rock must be mined to get 1 ounce of gold (4 t of rock to get 25 g of gold).

The United States is the world's largest producer of lead. Missouri produces more of this very heavy but soft metal than any other state. Lead is useful to us in many ways. A lead layer is used in hospitals and clinics to protect the doctors and technicians who run X-ray machines. Lead is also used in nuclear plants to prevent leaks of **radioactive** materials. Lead is used to make ammunition for guns, type for large printing machines, and some kinds of paint.

As you know, cement, stone, gravel, and sand are important for building construction and for highways. Each North Central state is a source of one or more of these products.

Iron ore Iron is found in Missouri, Michigan, Wisconsin, and Minnesota. As we said in Chapter 14, Minnesota's Mesabi Range is the leading source of iron ore in the United States. Although the richest ores have been used up, there are still large amounts of taconite. Taconite is a low-grade iron ore. This means it is more difficult and costly to separate the iron from the rest of the ore. Most mining in this area is done in **open-pit mines**. The world's largest open-pit mine is near Hibbing, Minnesota, in the Mesabi Range.

The iron is processed in plants near the mines. When the iron leaves the plant it is in the form of pellets that are about two-thirds iron. The pellets are then sent by rail to one of the ports on Lake Superior, such as Duluth or Superior. At these ports the iron pellets are emptied into storage bins. Conveyer belts move the pellets from the bins to ore carriers. The carriers move the iron to steel-manufacturing centers along the southern shores of Lake Michigan and Lake Erie. These centers produce about half the steel made in the United States. They include Gary, Cleveland, Toledo, Chicago, and Milwaukee, as well as several other cities in the area.

To reach these cities, the ore carriers travel on Lake Superior to Sault Ste. Marie (sü′ sānt′ mə rē′). From there the carriers use a canal to reach Lake Huron. To get from Lake Huron to Lake Erie, the carriers follow the St. Clair and Detroit rivers. These rivers and lakes and the canal, as well as other waterways, make up the St. Lawrence Seaway. Using the St. Lawrence Seaway, a ship can travel all the way from the Great Lakes to the Atlantic Ocean.

Discussion topic: Problem of boredom for assembly-line workers

Automobiles Factories in many cities of the North Central states make products from iron and steel. One of the most important of these cities is Detroit. Detroit is the auto and truck manufacturing center of the world.

Most cars and trucks are made in huge plants. These plants have thousands of workers, many of them highly skilled. Even so, much of the work is done by machines. Assembly lines play a big part in the making of cars. An assembly line is a moving belt on which part of the car is placed. Workers standing along the line add various pieces as the part passes them. Some plants may have several assembly lines. On one line, workers may build the frame of a car. On another line workers construct the body. Engines may be assembled on another. On the last assembly line the workers finish the auto with the parts from the other lines.

This is the world's largest open-pit iron mine, near Hibbing, Minnesota. The red color comes from the rust that forms in the iron ore.

Automobile makers need many other industries. Glass must be made for car windows. Car upholstery may be made from leather, cotton, wool, or synthetics. Other necessary products include paint, wiring, gasoline and oil, and tires. Of course, cars also need roads to drive on. So cement, asphalt, stone, and gravel are needed. You could name more materials. This list, though, shows how several industries can be involved in making one thing. The companies that make these products are found throughout the North Central states. Glass is made in Toledo, Ohio. Tires are made in Akron, Ohio. Other products are made in other cities.

CHECKUP

1. What is a grain elevator?
2. Name three nonfood products of the meat-packing industry.
3. What state is the leading producer of iron? Lead? Gold?
4. What kind of work might a person on an automobile assembly line do?

This assembly line worker in Flint, Michigan, is welding auto body parts together. Workers all up and down the line are doing the same thing.

Population and Cities

┌─ VOCABULARY ─────────────────────────┐
monument
└──────────────────────────────────────┘

Population   Nearly 60 million people live in the North Central states. The 12 states vary in population from less than 1 million to more than 11 million. The state with the largest population is Illinois. It has over 10 million more people than the state with fewest people, North Dakota.

Throughout most of the states you will find large metropolitan centers, such as Chicago, Detroit, and St. Louis. There are about 40 cities with more than 100,000 people. There are six cities with more than 500,000 people. Two, Chicago and Detroit, have more than 1 million people.

Chicago   Chicago is one of the three largest cities in the United States. About 3 million people live in the city. In the metropolitan area there are about 7 million people. Chicago is on Lake Michigan. This location has helped the city grow into a major center of business, industry, and transportation.   41°53′N/87°37′W

The port on Lake Michigan is one of the busiest in the United States. Ships carry grains, ores, and goods over Lake Michigan and along the St. Lawrence Seaway to the Atlantic Ocean. The Chicago Sanitary and Ship Canal connects Chicago with the Mississippi River.

The Chicago area is the home of more than 14,000 manufacturers. The largest of these make iron and steel, electrical equipment, and machinery. Other industries include publishing, foods, plastics, and construction.

Like other big cities, Chicago has many attractions. There is the Museum of Science and Industry, as well as several other museums. People can enjoy a symphony or an opera, a day at the zoo or the aquarium, an evening of ballet, or a picnic in one of the many parks. Several large libraries and many colleges and universities serve students in the area.

Downtown Chicago has hundreds of stores and office buildings. More than 300,000 people work in these stores and offices. Four of the ten largest skyscrapers in the world are in Chicago. In fact, the tallest building in the world, the Sears Tower, is in the city.

Cleveland · 1°29'N/81°42'W About 574,000 people live in Cleveland. The metropolitan area has about 2 million people. The city is the largest port on Lake Erie and the largest city in Ohio. It is one of the 20 largest cities in the United States.

Coal from Pennsylvania and Ohio and iron from Minnesota are the two major cargoes handled in the Cleveland harbor. These two resources have helped make the city an important iron- and steel-manufacturing center. Other manufacturing includes petroleum products, automobiles, chemicals, tools, and electrical equipment. Cleveland has several museums, a large library, several colleges and universities, and many parks. The Cleveland Orchestra is well known throughout the United States.

Detroit 2°20'N/83°03'W Detroit is the largest city in Michigan and the sixth largest city in the nation. More than 1 million people live in the city. More than 4 million people live in

Chicago's skyscrapers rise beside Lake Michigan. You can see the Chicago River near the center of the picture.

the metropolitan area. Detroit is on the Detroit River between Lake Huron and Lake Erie.

Important industries include the making of auto parts, machine tools, iron products, hardware, chemicals, drugs, paint, and wire products, as well as automobiles and trucks. Detroit also has one of the largest salt mines in the United States. The mine is under the city!

St. Louis With a population of about 453,000, St. Louis is the largest city in Missouri. It is one of the 30 largest cities in the United States and the nation's largest inland port.

St. Louis is second only to Detroit in the automobile industry. In fact, the area is important in the making of several kinds of transportation equipment. Airplanes,

Dearborn, which is near Detroit, is the site of the Henry Ford Museum and Greenfield Village. The museum houses a large collection of antique cars. Greenfield Village is made up of restored historic buildings that have been transplanted to the village. One of Edison's laboratories is on display there.

379

One pupil might do a report on the group of communities in Iowa known as the Amana Colonies. (See *Americana* magazine, pp. 30–35, September/October 1980.)

The famous Gateway Arch in St. Louis is a **monument** to remind us that St. Louis was the starting point, or gateway, for many pioneers heading west. 38°37'N/90°11'W

barges, railroad cars, and tugboats are all made here. Chemicals, foods, and metals are also important.

Like other large cities, St. Louis offers something for just about every interest. For sports fans there are several sports teams. For music lovers there is a symphony orchestra and an opera company. Several colleges and universities and a number of museums help people learn about their world.

Other cities   As we said earlier, there are many other large and important cities in the North Central states. Omaha is one of the nation's leading meat-packing centers. Minneapolis, Minnesota, is noted for electronics and precision instruments. Columbus is a center for the making of aircraft, appliances, and mining equipment. Kansas City, Missouri, is an important center for agricultural industries. It is also the country's leading maker of vending machines.

Indianapolis is the capital and largest city in Indiana. A major industrial, trans-

portation, and shipping center, Indianapolis is the eleventh largest city in the United States. One of the most famous auto races in the United States—the Indianapolis 500—is held here each year.

Milwaukee is the largest city in Wisconsin. It is one of the 20 largest cities in the United States. Its location on Lake Michigan has helped it grow into a major industrial and shipping center.

Cincinnati is one of the largest cities in Ohio. It is an industrial and trade center on the Ohio River.

Two other cities in the North Central region are Des Moines (di moin') and Wichita. Although they are smaller than the cities we've discussed so far, both are large cities. Wichita, with about 279,000 people, is the largest city in Kansas. It makes more than half of the world's small airplanes. Des Moines is the capital and chief center of trade in Iowa. Its population of about 191,000 makes it the state's largest city.

Although neither North Dakota nor South Dakota has very large cities, each state has several smaller cities. Sioux (sü) Falls, South Dakota, with a population of 81,000, is the largest city of the two states. It is South Dakota's leading livestock and trade center. Bismarck is the capital of North Dakota. The second largest city in the state, it is a shipping center for agricultural products.

Another North Central city, Rochester, Minnesota, is the home of the world famous Mayo Clinic.

CHECKUP

1. In which two states is the capital city also the largest city?
2. What are the major industries in Chicago? Detroit? St. Louis?
3. What are the major cargoes handled at the port of Cleveland? Where do they come from?

The Gateway Arch is made of steel and stands 630 feet (192 m) high. Special elevators carry visitors to an observation platform at the top for a view of the city. Below the arch is an underground museum with exhibits that tell America's history.

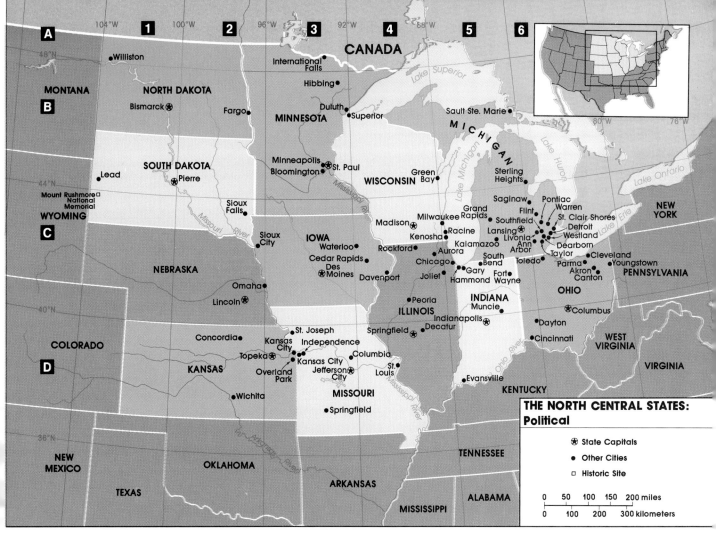

THE NORTH CENTRAL STATES: Political

✳ State Capitals
● Other Cities
□ Historic Site

| 0 | 50 | 100 | 150 | 200 miles |
| 0 | 100 | 200 | 300 kilometers |

Cities with less than 100,000

City	Ref
Aurora (Ill.)	C-4
Bismarck (N. Dak.)	B-1
Bloomington (Minn.)	B-3
Canton (Ohio)	C-6
Columbia (Mo.)	D-3
Concordia (Kans.)	D-2
Dearborn (Mich.)	C-6
Decatur (Ill.)	D-4
Duluth (Minn.)	B-3
Fargo (N. Dak.)	B-2
Green Bay (Wis.)	B-4
Hibbing (Minn.)	B-3
International Falls (Minn.)	A-3
Jefferson City (Mo.)	D-3
Joliet (Ill.)	C-4
Kalamazoo (Mich.)	C-5
Kenosha (Wis.)	C-5
Lead (S. Dak.)	B-1
Muncie (Ind.)	C-5
Overland Park (Kans.)	D-3
Parma (Ohio)	C-6
Pierre (S. Dak.)	B-1
Pontiac (Mich.)	C-6
Racine (Wis.)	C-5
Saginaw (Mich.)	C-6
St. Clair Shores (Mich.)	C-6

City	Ref
St. Joseph (Mo.)	D-3
Sault Ste. Marie (Mich.)	B-5
Sioux City (Iowa)	C-2
Sioux Falls (S. Dak.)	C-2
Southfield (Mich.)	C-6
Springfield (Ill.)	D-4
Superior (Wis.)	B-3
Taylor (Mich.)	C-6
Waterloo (Iowa)	C-4
Westland (Mich.)	C-6
Williston (N. Dak.)	A-1

Cities with 100,000–499,000

City	Ref
Akron (Ohio)	C-6
Ann Arbor (Mich.)	C-6
Cedar Rapids (Iowa)	C-4
Cincinnati (Ohio)	D-5
Davenport (Iowa)	C-4
Dayton (Ohio)	D-5
Des Moines (Iowa)	C-3
Evansville (Ind.)	D-5
Flint (Mich.)	C-6
Fort Wayne (Ind.)	C-5
Gary (Ind.)	C-5
Grand Rapids (Mich.)	C-5
Hammond (Ind.)	C-5
Independence (Mo.)	D-3
Kansas City (Kans.)	D-3

City	Ref
Kansas City (Mo.)	D-3
Lansing (Mich.)	C-5
Lincoln (Nebr.)	C-2
Livonia (Mich.)	C-6
Madison (Wis.)	C-4
Minneapolis (Minn.)	B-3
Omaha (Nebr.)	C-2
Peoria (Ill.)	C-4
Rockford (Ill.)	C-4
St. Louis (Mo.)	D-4
St. Paul (Minn.)	B-3
South Bend (Ind.)	C-5
Springfield (Mo.)	D-3
Sterling Heights (Mich.)	B-6
Toledo (Ohio)	C-6
Topeka (Kans.)	D-3
Warren (Mich.)	C-6
Wichita (Kans.)	D-2
Youngstown (Ohio)	C-6

Cities with 500,000–999,000

City	Ref
Cleveland (Ohio)	C-6
Columbus (Ohio)	D-6
Indianapolis (Ind.)	D-5
Milwaukee (Wis.)	C-5

Cities with 1,000,000 or more

City	Ref
Chicago (Ill.)	C-5
Detroit (Mich.)	C-6

How many state capitals have a population of less than 100,000 people? Between 100,000 and 499,000? Between 500,000 and 999,000?

Less than 100,000: four (Bismarck, Pierre, Jefferson City, Springfield). Between 100,000 and 499,000: six (Lincoln, Topeka, Des Moines, St. Paul, Madison, Lansing). Between 500,000 and 999,000: two (Indianapolis, Columbus).

THE NORTH CENTRAL STATES	Illinois	Indiana	Iowa	Kansas	Michigan	Minnesota
Source of Name	From the French version of an Indian tribe named the Illiniwek. It means "superior men."	Meaning "land of Indians"	From the Indian word *I-o-w-a* meaning "this is the place," or "The Beautiful Land"	From the Siouan word *Kansa*, meaning "people of the south wind"	From a Chippewa Indian word, *Michigama*, meaning "great lake"	From a Dakota Indian word meaning "sky-tinted water"
Nickname(s)	Prairie State	Hoosier State	Hawkeye State	Sunflower State; Jayhawk State	Wolverine State	North Star State; Gopher State; Land of 10,000 Lakes
Capital	Springfield	Indianapolis	Des Moines	Topeka	Lansing	St. Paul
Largest Cities (1980 Census)	Chicago Rockford Peoria	Indianapolis Fort Wayne Gary	Des Moines Cedar Rapids Davenport	Wichita Kansas City Topeka	Detroit Grand Rapids Warren	Minneapolis St. Paul Duluth
Population Rank (1980 Census)	5	12	27	32	8	21
Population Density Rank	10	13	32	37	12	33
Area Rank	24	38	25	14	23	12
State Flag						
State Bird	Cardinal	Cardinal	Eastern goldfinch	Western meadowlark	Robin	Common loon
State Flower	Violet	Peony	Wild rose	Sunflower	Apple blossom	Showy lady slipper
State Tree	White oak	Tulip	Oak	Cottonwood	White pine	Norway Pine
State Motto	State sovereignty, national union	The crossroads of America	Our liberties we prize and our rights we will maintain	*Ad astra per aspera* (To the stars through difficulties)	*Si quaeris peninsulam amoenam circumspice* (If you seek a pleasant peninsula, look around you)	L'Etoile du Nord (The North Star)
Interesting Facts	The first controlled chain reaction that created nuclear energy was produced by scientists at the University of Chicago. Scientists from around the world come to study the atom at the Fermi National Accelerator Laboratory, near Chicago.	The first international automobile race in the United States was held in Indianapolis in 1911. The Indianapolis 500 race is held every year on Memorial Day.	No other state uses as much land for farming as Iowa. 99% of Iowans can read and write. Sioux City has the largest popcorn processing plant in the United States.	Kansas lies midway between the Atlantic and Pacific Oceans. It is called the Sunflower State because the tall yellow prairie flower grows in most parts of the state.	Michigan has more than 11,000 inland lakes and about 150 waterfalls. Detroit is the "Automobile Capital of the World."	Minnesota produces three fifths of the nation's supply of iron ore —about 60 million tons a year. The Northwest Angle in the Lake of the Woods is the most northern part of the United States excluding Alaska.

382

		THE NORTH CENTRAL STATES				
	Missouri	Nebraska	North Dakota	Ohio	South Dakota	Wisconsin
Source of Name	Named after a tribe called Missouri Indians. *Missouri* means "town of the large canoes."	From an Oto Indian word *Nebrathka*, meaning "flat water"	From the Dakotah tribe, meaning "allies"	From an Iroquoian word meaning "great river"	From the Dakotah tribe, meaning "allies"	French version (Ouisconsin) of Indian name for a river (Miskonsing), meaning "gathering of the waters"
Nickname(s)	Show Me State	Cornhusker State; Beef State; Tree Planters State	Sioux State; Flickertail State	Buckeye State	Sunshine State; Coyote State	Badger State
Capital	Jefferson City	Lincoln	Bismark	Columbus	Pierre	Madison
Largest Cities (1980 Census)	St. Louis Kansas City Springfield	Omaha Lincoln Grand Island	Fargo Bismarck Grand Forks	Cleveland Columbus Cincinnati	Sioux Falls Rapid City Aberdeen	Milwaukee Madison Green Bay
Population Rank (1980 Census)	15	35	46	6	45	16
Population Density Rank	27	41	45	9	46	24
Area Rank	19	15	17	35	16	26
State Flag						
State Bird	Bluebird	Western meadowlark	Western meadowlark	Cardinal	Ring-necked pheasant	Robin
State Flower	Hawthorn	Goldenrod	Wild prairie rose	Scarlet carnation	American pasqueflower	Wood violet
State Tree	Flowering dogwood	Cottonwood	American elm	Buckeye	Black Hills spruce	Sugar maple
State Motto	*Salus populi suprema lex esto* (The welfare of the people shall be the supreme law)	Equality before the law	Liberty and union, now and forever: one and inseparable	With God, all things are possible	Under God the people rule	Forward
Interesting Facts	Missouri was one of the leading gateways to the West in pioneer days. St. Joseph was the eastern starting point of the Pony Express, and the Santa Fe and Oregon trails began in Independence.	The largest mammoth fossil ever found was discovered near North Platte. Nebraska's two national forests are the only national forests that have been planted by foresters.	The nation's largest coal reserves are here. Near Grenora there is a large glacial boulder covered with Indian picture writing. It is called Writing Rock.	Ohio is the birthplace of seven United States presidents: Grant, Hayes, Garfield, B. Harrison, McKinley, Taft, and Harding.	Carvings of the heads of George Washington, Thomas Jefferson, Theodore Roosevelt, and Abraham Lincoln were made on Mount Rushmore. It is one of the world's largest sculptures.	Wisconsin is the nation's leading producer of milk and cheese. More minks are raised in Wisconsin than in any other state.

383

19/CHAPTER REVIEW

KEY FACTS

1. Plains cover most of the North Central region.
2. The Great Lakes and the Mississippi and Missouri rivers, as well as the many other bodies of water, are important to the climate and industry of the North Central region.
3. The climate of the states in the North Central region varies with the location of the state.
4. Agricultural products from the North Central states help feed the entire nation.
5. Much of the North Central region's industry is closely related to its agriculture.
6. Mineral resources of the North Central region include lead, coal, gold, petroleum, and iron.
7. Detroit and St. Louis are two of the nation's leading cities in auto production.
8. The North Central region contains many of our largest cities, including Chicago, Detroit, and Indianapolis.

VOCABULARY QUIZ

Write the letter of the term next to the number of its description. Write on a sheet of paper.

a. grain elevator
b. wholesale market
c. bran
d. gasohol
e. radioactive
f. market weight
g. open-pit mine
h. vitamin
i. assembly line
j. Bad Lands

d 1. A fuel made from corn
j 2. A dry, rugged area with gullies and steep bluffs and little or no vegetation
a 3. A building in which wheat and other crops are stored
f 4. The weight that an animal must reach before it is sent to market
b 5. A market that buys products in large quantities and sells them in smaller quantities
i 6. A moving belt that carries a certain part of a product past workers who add pieces to the part
g 7. A large hole dug in order to reach the iron ore near the earth's surface
c 8. A part of the wheat kernel
e 9. Giving off harmful rays
h 10. A substance necessary for good health

REVIEW QUESTIONS

1. How did glaciers change the landscape of the North Central region?
2. Explain the water cycle either in words or by drawing a labeled diagram.
3. Name at least four important crops of the North Central region.
4. Where are most cattle raised?
5. Which state is our nation's leading dairy state?
6. Why is the making of farm machinery a leading industry of the North Central region?
7. Explain how one industry can lead to the growth of other industries.
8. Which two cities in the North Central region have more than 1 million people?

ACTIVITIES

1. Make a list of the products used in the manufacture of an automobile. Next, group the products according to the natural resources used in them. Third, make a map to show the location of those resources.
2. Paul Bunyan was a legendary logger. Read about Paul and Babe, his blue ox. Then write a report or draw a picture describing one of his adventures.

DESCRIPTIVE WRITING

In this passage from *The Adventures of Huckleberry Finn,* by Samuel Clemens, Huck and his friend Jim have run away. They are riding down the Mississippi on a raft. As you read, notice how the author gives a clear picture of the scene—the quiet peacefulness, the carefree mood. Clemens does not say that it is summer, that it is quiet and peaceful, and so forth, but his description lets you know these things.

Words in brackets [ ] have been put in by the editor to help you understand certain words.

Soon as it was night, out we shoved; when we got her [the raft] out to about the middle, we let her alone, and let her float wherever the current wanted her to; then we . . . dangled our legs in the water and talked about all kinds of things. . . .

Sometimes we'd have that whole river all to ourselves for the longest time. Yonder was the banks and the islands, across the water; and maybe a spark—which was a candle in a cabin window; and sometimes on the water you could see a spark or two—on a raft or a scow [flat-bottomed boat], you know; and maybe you could hear a fiddle or a song coming over from one of them crafts. It's lovely to live on a raft. We had the sky, up there, all speckled with stars, and we used to lay on our backs and look up at them, and discuss about whether they was made, or only just happened. Jim he allowed [thought] they was made, but I allowed they happened; I judged it would have took too long to *make* so many. Jim said the moon could 'a' *laid* them; well, that looked kind of reasonable, so I didn't say nothing against it, because I've seen a frog lay most as many, so of course it could be done. We used to watch the stars that fell, too, and see them streak down. Jim allowed they'd got spoiled and was hove [thrown] out of the nest.

Once or twice of a night we would see a steamboat slipping along in the dark, and now and then she would belch a whole world of sparks up out of her chimbleys [chimneys], and they would rain down in the river and look awful pretty; then she would turn a corner and her lights would wink out and her powwow shut off and leave the river still again; and by and by her waves would get to us, a long time after she was gone, and joggle the raft a bit, and after that you wouldn't hear nothing for you couldn't tell how long, except maybe frogs or something.

After midnight the people on shore went to bed, and then for two or three hours the shores was black—no more sparks in the cabin windows. These sparks was our clock—the first one that showed again meant morning was coming, so we hunted a place to hide and tie up right away.

Now answer these questions about the passage.

1. What did you read in the first and third paragraphs that let you know it was summer?

2. What descriptive word does the author use in place of the word *light?*

3. With what word does the author let you know that the sparks from the steamboat came out in bursts?

4. What words does the author use to tell you that the steamboat let out lots of sparks? What does he use instead of *fall down* to describe how they fell?

5. The discussion about the origin of the stars helps set the mood, too. Do you know why? What kinds of things would they talk about if they were worried or rushed or busy?

CHAPTER

20 The Mountain West States Today

The Land and Climate

VOCABULARY

timberline	arroyo
intermontane	desert
Continental	semidesert
Divide	rain shadow

The region What do you think of when you see the words *the West?* Do you think of mountains and deserts, buffalo and cacti, ghost towns and gold mines? Perhaps you think of skiing or hiking. If any of these things come to mind, you already have some idea of what the Mountain West region is like. Let's see what else we can learn about the region.

There are eight states in the Mountain West. In the north, next to Canada, are Idaho and Montana. In the south, next to Mexico, are Arizona and New Mexico. In between these four states are Wyoming, Nevada, Utah, and Colorado.

One look at the map on the next page will show you the landform that makes this region a region and gives it its name. You can see that the outstanding physical feature is the Rocky Mountains. Even the parts of the region not covered by the Rocky Mountains are high. In fact, just about the only lowlands are those along rivers. Look at the map on page 263 to find elevations in this region.

The Great Plains Along the eastern edge of the Mountain West is the high plain known as the Great Plains. You read about this important cattle and wheat area earlier. In the Mountain West, the Great Plains covers parts of Montana, Wyoming, Colorado, and New Mexico. The Great Plains slowly rises from east to west until it meets the Rocky Mountains.

The Rockies In the United States, the Rockies stretch from New Mexico to Canada. They continue north through Canada into the northern part of our largest state, Alaska.

These rugged mountains are much higher than the Appalachians to the east. The highest peak in the Rockies is Mount Elbert in Colorado. In fact all of the highest peaks of the Rockies—those over 14,000 feet (4,270 m)—are in Colorado.

The Rockies are beautiful mountains. At the base are meadows and broadleaf trees. As you climb higher, you find fewer broadleaf trees and more evergreens. As you climb still higher, you find fewer trees of any kind. Those that do cling to the rocky soil are short and often are bent and twisted by the wind.

If you climb high enough, you come to the **timberline.** Beyond this line no trees grow. If you stop here and look up, you

Mount Elbert is the highest peak in the Rocky Mountains. It is 14,433 feet (4,399 m) high. Find it on the map at the right. What state is it in?

The map on p. 387 shows all thirteen national parks in the Mountain West, including Yellowstone, which pupils studied in Chapter 1. Have pupils find the parks on the map.

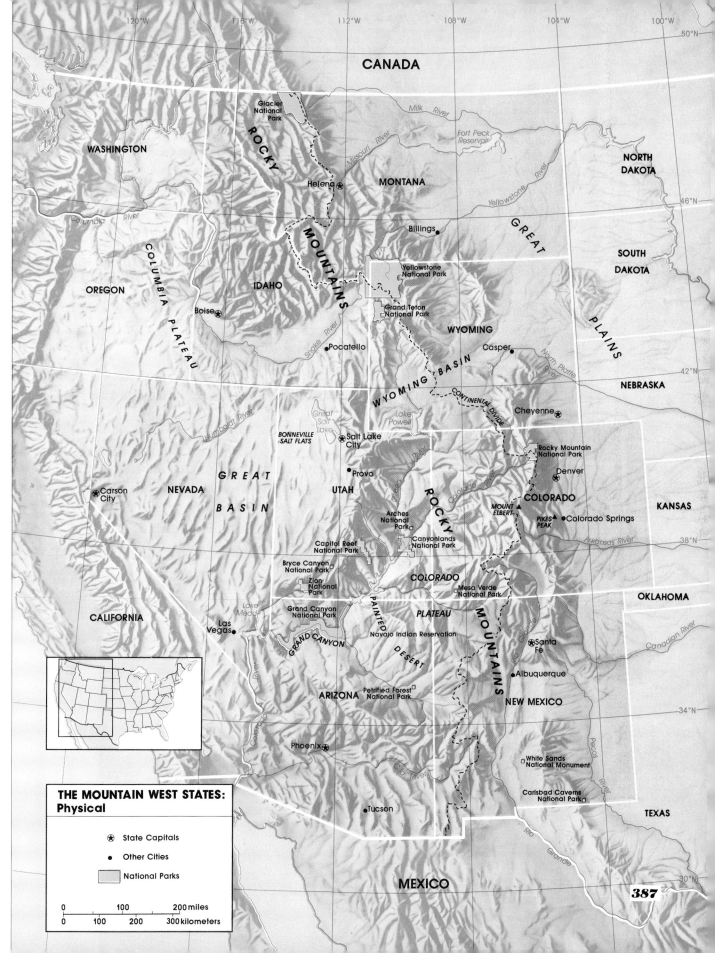

CANADA

120°W   116°W   112°W   108°W   104°W   100°W

50°N

WASHINGTON

ROCKY

Glacier
National
Park

Milk River

Fort Peck
Reservoir

NORTH
DAKOTA

Columbia River

Helena ✪

MONTANA

Missouri River

Yellowstone River

46°N

MOUNTAINS

Billings •

GREAT

SOUTH
DAKOTA

OREGON

IDAHO

Boise ✪

Snake River

Yellowstone
National Park

Grand Teton
National Park

WYOMING

Casper •

PLAINS

Pocatello •

WYOMING BASIN

North Platte River

42°N

NEBRASKA

COLUMBIA PLATEAU

CONTINENTAL DIVIDE

Cheyenne ✪

Humboldt River

Great
Salt
Lake

Lake
Powell

Rocky Mountain
National Park

BONNEVILLE
SALT FLATS

Salt Lake
City ✪

Denver ✪

CARSON
City ✪

GREAT

NEVADA

UTAH

Provo •

ROCKY

COLORADO

MOUNT
ELBERT ▲

KANSAS

BASIN

Green River

Arches
National
Park

Colorado River

PIKES
PEAK ▲

Colorado Springs •

Arkansas River

38°N

Capitol Reef
National Park

Canyonlands
National Park

Bryce Canyon
National Park

COLORADO

Zion
National
Park

Lake
Mead

Grand Canyon
National Park

PAINTED

PLATEAU

Mesa Verde
National Park

OKLAHOMA

MOUNTAINS

Las
Vegas •

GRAND CANYON

Navajo Indian Reservation

DESERT

Rio Grande

Santa
Fe ✪

Canadian River

CALIFORNIA

Colorado River

ARIZONA

Petrified Forest
National Park

NEW MEXICO

Albuquerque •

34°N

Phoenix ✪

Gila River

White Sands
National Monument

Pecos River

Carlsbad Caverns
National Park

TEXAS

Tucson •

Rio Grande

MEXICO

30°N

387

THE MOUNTAIN WEST STATES:
Physical

✪   State Capitals

•   Other Cities

National Parks

| 0 | 100 | 200 miles |

| 0 | 100 | 200 | 300 kilometers |

will see that even the grass and flowers do not grow on the highest peaks. Sunlight gleams on the snow that covers these rocky peaks all year long.

Have pupils find the Cascades and the Sierra Nevadas on the map on p. 468.

Intermontane region   You have probably noticed that there are mountain ranges along the Pacific Coast of the United States. The land between these mountains and the Rocky Mountains is known as the **intermontane** region. *Inter* means "between." You can guess what *montane* means. So the intermontane region is the land between the mountains.

The intermontane region has three major parts: the Columbia Plateau, the Colorado Plateau, and the Great Basin.

The landforms of the intermontane region range from rugged cliffs to steep-sided canyons to sandy desert. The Grand Canyon is in this region. It has been formed over millions of years by the Colorado River. The moving water has slowly worn away the soil and carried it

Have pupils find the Columbia and Colorado plateaus and the Great Basin on the map on p. 387.

downstream. Today thousands of people visit Grand Canyon National Park in Arizona to see the beautiful result of this slow process.

The Continental Divide   You may have noticed a line on the map on page 387 marked **Continental Divide.** This line runs along the high ridges of the Rocky Mountains. The Continental Divide is important in terms of the rivers of North America. The rivers to the east of the Continental Divide flow generally toward the east. Rivers to the west of the Divide flow generally west.

Have pupils find examples of westward-flowing rivers and eastward-flowing rivers on the map on p. 387.

Rivers and lakes   If we had to choose the most important river of the Mountain West, it would probably be the Colorado. This river and its tributaries supply water and hydroelectric power to people in seven states. Water from the Colorado system irrigates crops from Wyoming to southern California and New Mexico. Elec-

For millions of years the Colorado River has been forming the Grand Canyon.

tricity generated in power plants on the Colorado and its tributaries lights thousands of homes. People swim, fish, and go boating on lakes created by dams on the river.

In the northwest are the Snake River and the Salmon River, which flow into the Columbia River. The Columbia flows into the Pacific Ocean. These rivers are also used to supply water and power.

The streams and rivers that flow out of the Rockies into the Great Basin never reach the ocean. Instead they flow into lakes, such as the Great Salt Lake, or simply dry up in the dry, desertlike land. Many of the streams of the Great Basin and the Colorado Plateau have flowing water only following a heavy rainstorm or in spring when the snow melts in the mountains. Later they will slowly dry up until the next heavy rain or spring snow melt. The term **arroyo** is given to a dry streambed. An arroyo may be without flowing water for years.

Many rivers important to the North Central states and the South Central states start in the Rockies. Among these rivers are the Missouri and the Rio Grande. You can find others on a map.

Deserts   The intermontane lands south of the northern borders of Utah and Nevada   are   largely   **desert**   and **semidesert.** A desert is a dry land in which there is very little plant growth. You could describe a semidesert by saying that it is halfway between a desert and a grassland. A semidesert is not as dry and bare as a desert, yet it doesn't have as much rain or as much plant cover as a grassland.

Probably the best-known desert of the intermontane region is the Painted Desert in northern Arizona. This desert gets its name from its colorful soil and rock formations.

In New Mexico there are giant dunes of white "sand." The sand is not really sand but a mineral called gypsum. The gypsum comes from the bed of a lake that dries up each year, leaving behind large deposits of gypsum. The wind blows the gypsum into dunes. The White Sands National Monument is in this area.

In the area around Great Salt Lake in Utah one finds the Bonneville Salt Flats. The land here is covered with salt left behind by water that runs down off the mountains and dries up. Because the flats are so level, they are used for high-speed auto racing.

The desert and semidesert areas are by no means forgotten wastelands. In some places, thriving cities have grown up. Such cities include Las Vegas, Nevada; Salt Lake City, Utah; and Phoenix, Arizona. Irrigation has made fertile cropland out of other areas. Valuable minerals are mined here. In some places cattle and sheep can be grazed. Much of the area is a part of the national park system.

Have pupils find out what gypsum is used for.

Climate   The story of climate in the Mountain West is a tale told by mountains. Generally, the higher one goes, the cooler the air is. The temperature change is about $3\frac{1}{2}°F$ for every 1,000 feet of elevation ($2°C$ per 300 m). Pikes Peak is about 9,000 feet (2,700 m) higher than Denver. If the temperature in Denver is 72°F (22°C), the temperature on nearby Pikes Peak will be about 40°F (4°C).

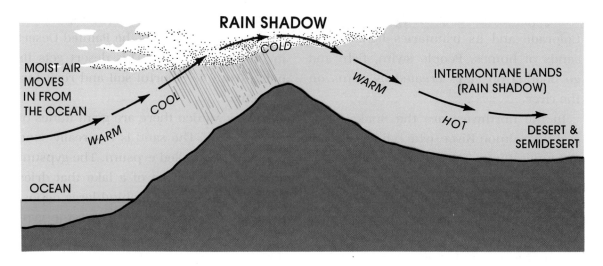

RAIN SHADOW

MOIST AIR MOVES IN FROM THE OCEAN

WARM

COOL

COLD

WARM

HOT

INTERMONTANE LANDS (RAIN SHADOW)

DESERT & SEMIDESERT

OCEAN

By the time the winds pass over the mountains, they have lost most of their moisture.

The mountains also affect precipitation. The winds that blow in off the Pacific Ocean are warm and wet. When they meet the mountains along the coast they are forced to rise. As they rise they are cooled. Cool air cannot hold as much moisture as warm air can.

The moisture in the air falls as rain or snow on the western slopes of the mountains along the coast. Meanwhile the winds continue on up and over the mountains. Now, however, the winds carry very little moisture. The air becomes warmer as it goes downhill and over the intermontane lands. This warm air can hold most of the moisture it does carry. It even absorbs moisture from the ground. As a result, <u>very little rain falls on the inter-</u> <u>montane lands. These lands are said to be</u> <u>in a **rain shadow.**</u> The whole rain shadow process repeats itself as the winds rise up and over the slopes of the Rockies. However, the Great Plains are not quite as dry as the intermontane lands. They receive some rain from winds coming in from the north and south.

The range in daily temperature in the Mountain West is quite large, both in summer and in winter. In Phoenix during a winter's day, you might be warm enough without a jacket. When night fell, however, you would be reaching for a warm coat.

The range in record temperature extremes is huge. Phoenix has a record high of 118°F (48°C) and a low of 17°F (-8°C). Alamosa, Colorado, has a record high of 93°F (34°C) and a low of -50°F (-46°C).

The greatest average yearly precipitation is only about 19 inches (48 cm). This is true even though large amounts of snow fall in some places. The snow is dry and powdery. It doesn't equal as much rainfall as do the wet and heavy snows of some other parts of the United States.

CHECKUP

1. What is the timberline? The Continental Divide?
2. What does *intermontane* mean? Where is the intermontane region?
3. Why is the Colorado River important?
4. What is a rain shadow?

See the Manual section for this chapter for more extensive climate statistics.

The Mountain States, Time-Life Books, contains on pp. 70–71 an easy-to-read map of the Colorado River system. This book is available in many libraries.

Agriculture, Resources, and Industry

> **VOCABULARY**
> shearing   fossil
> oil shale

Farming   Water is one of the most important resources in the Mountain West. It often determines how people use their land. Only a few parts of the Mountain West have enough water for crops. Wheat is grown in the Great Plains and along the Snake River. The Snake River area of Idaho is well known for another crop, potatoes. Idaho leads the United States in the production of potatoes.

Irrigation allows crops to be raised in other places. Irrigated land in Arizona and New Mexico produces large amounts of cotton. Fruits and vegetables grow well in the irrigated lands of Utah and Arizona.

Ranching   Cattle raising makes up a large part of the agriculture of the Mountain West. Cattle ranches here are very large. It takes about 20 to 25 acres (8–10 ha) of good grassland to feed one cow. In the drier areas where there is less grass, it takes even more land. Many ranchers in the Mountain West use national forest lands as well as their own lands for grazing cattle. Even so, ranches of 20,000 acres (8,100 ha) are common. Some are more than 60,000 acres (24,300 ha). The average size is about 4,000 acres (1,600 ha).

Because cows won't graze far from water, most ranchers in this dry land have to dig wells. The water is pumped into large troughs from which the cattle drink.

The Mountain West is well known for its sheep ranches, too. Seven of the ten leading sheep-raising states are in the Mountain West. Sheep are hardy enough to live on lands that cannot be used for other kinds of farming.

During the fall, winter, and spring, the sheep are kept on pastures near the ranch. During the hot summer when the grass dries up, the sheep are taken into the hills where the grazing is better. The herds are watched over by sheep herders, or shepherds, and their dogs. These dogs are trained to keep the sheep from straying.

Most lambs are born in the spring. They go with their mothers to the hill pastures for the summer. By the time the lambs return in the fall they are old enough to be sold for meat.

Some sheep are raised for wool. **Shearing**, or cutting off the wool, takes place in the spring, after the very cold weather is gone. By the time the cold weather returns, the sheep have grown another coat of wool.

Minerals   The Mountain West is rich in minerals. Large deposits of copper, lead, potassium, iron, and molybdenum (mə lib′ də nəm) are found here. Molybdenum is a silvery metal used to make blends of other metals stronger. Although the gold rush days are long gone, gold and silver are still mined in the Mountain West. Fuel resources include natural gas, oil, oil shale, coal, and uranium.

Oil shale   Shale is a kind of rock made of hardened clay, mud, or silt. **Oil shale** is shale that contains oil. There are rich deposits of oil shale in Colorado, Utah, and Wyoming. Unfortunately, many problems must be solved before we can remove the oil from the shale.

Shale may contain from 5 to 100 gallons of oil per ton (20 to 400 L per ton) of rocks. At the present time it takes 5 gallons of fuel to mine, transport, and refine the oil in 1 ton (20 L per ton) of shale. Does that make sense if only 5 gallons of petroleum could be taken from a ton (20 L per ton) of rock?

Another problem is the waste shale. A plant that would produce 50,000 barrels (7,905 kl) of oil per day would also leave enough waste shale to cover 20 acres (8 ha) of land a foot (30 cm) deep. The waste shale is made up of fine grains that are easily moved by the wind. This makes it difficult to get seeds to grow so that the land can be reclaimed for grazing or crops.

A large amount of water is needed to remove the oil from the shale. The areas of Colorado, Utah, and Wyoming in which the oil shale is found do not have enough water. Water would need to be carried from the Colorado, Missouri, Snake, and other rivers. However, the water from those rivers is needed for drinking, irrigation, and other purposes.

Because of these problems, oil shale is not yet an important source of fuel. However, the cost of oil is going up. Other sources are starting to run out. Oil companies may soon start looking more closely at shale. It is hoped that new ways of removing the oil will be found. Then perhaps the problems of getting enough water and of reclaiming waste shale will be solved.

Coal   Most coal mines in the Mountain West region are strip mines. Sometimes an entire mountaintop is removed to expose the coal beneath. When this is done, the land can never be completely restored. Some of the coal is found under land used for grazing or crops. A choice has to be made as to how the land will be used. On one hand is our growing need for coal as a fuel. On the other is the need for the products of agriculture. The choice is not easy.

Uranium   Uranium is used to produce nuclear energy. New Mexico, Wyoming, Colorado, and Utah are the leading sources of pitchblende, the ore from which we get uranium. This ore, like other nonrenewable resources, is limited. Processing the ore to get uranium that is pure enough to be used for nuclear energy is difficult and costly.

Less than 5 percent of the electrical energy used in the United States comes from nuclear power plants. About half of the states have nuclear power plants. Because of problems with such plants in the early 1980s, plans for new plants were stopped. If they can be made safe, perhaps more plants will be built.

Very strict laws govern the building and operation of nuclear power plants. These laws are needed because one of the by-products of producing nuclear energy is radioactivity. When something is radioactive, it sends out rays that are very harmful. These rays can cause disease and death. Many people feel that the laws controlling nuclear power are not strong enough. In fact, they think that nuclear energy is too dangerous to use.

Tourism and national parks   In 1872 our Congress set up the first national park. This was Yellowstone National Park. Today there are about 40 national parks and more than 250 monuments, memorials, and other areas under the care of the National Park Service. Nearly a quarter of them are in the Mountain West. Besides the areas under the care of the Park Service, there are many acres of land given over to national forests and wildlife refuges. In fact, the federal government owns almost half of the land in the Mountain West states.

There are also many state parks in the Mountain West. With all this land set aside for the public, it makes sense that tourism is an important business in the Mountain West. Visitors come to camp, hike, boat, fish, ski, and enjoy the scenery.

In some places you can study the geologic history from **fossils**, rocks, and canyon walls. The remains of Indian villages nearly a thousand years old may be seen. Pueblos and cliff houses of long ago interest many people. Landmarks left by the Spaniards can be found in many places in the southwest.

Places that show the history of our country's westward expansion during the 1800s can also be found. Old ranches, trading posts, and forts help to show how people lived here a hundred years ago. Near Ogden, Utah, a marker shows the spot where the first transcontinental railroad was finished in 1869.

Other industries   The Mountain West is not as heavily industrialized as other parts of the United States. However, there is some manufacturing. Factories produce aircraft, electronics equipment, machinery, transportation equipment, wood products, foods, and chemicals. Sports clothing and equipment are two new products of the area. Printing and publishing have become well established in some of the cities.

Ski resorts are a major industry in the Mountain West. Resorts such as Vail and Aspen in Colorado and Sun Valley in Idaho attract many visitors.

CHECKUP

1. Why must cattle ranches in the Mountain West be so large?
2. Why is the land of the Mountain West good for raising sheep?
3. Name five important mineral resources of the Mountain West.
4. What is one problem that must be solved if we are to get oil from oil shale?

Population and Cities

┌─ VOCABULARY ─────────────────────┐
│ oasis   │
└──────────────────────────────────┘

Population   The Mountain West is growing more rapidly than other regions. Of the ten states whose population is growing most rapidly, seven are in this region. It is not the region with the largest population. In fact four of the states are among the ten states with the smallest number of people. Throughout the eight states there are large areas of land where very few people live. *Have pupils look at the population density map on p. 259.*

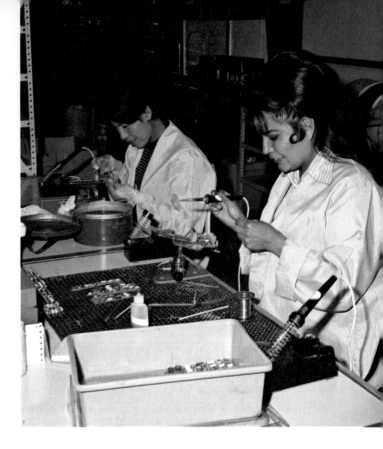

These women are working in the electronics factory on the Navajo reservation in Arizona.

MOUNTAIN WEST, INCREASE IN POPULATION, 1970 to 1980 (Figures rounded to nearer percent)	
State	*Percent of increase*
Nevada	64
Arizona	53
Wyoming	42
Utah	38
Idaho	32
Colorado	31
New Mexico	28
Montana	13

The Navajo   The Navajo is one of several tribes of Indians living in the Mountain West. The ancestors of the Navajo people moved from Alaska and Canada to the southwestern part of the United States about 500 years before Columbus landed in the West Indies. Of course this took place before any of those places had their present names. Today most of the Navajo people live on a reservation. The Navajo reservation is the largest one in the United States. Most of it is in the northeastern corner of Arizona. Parts of the reservation are in New Mexico and Utah as well.

The Navajo have undergone the same kinds of problems that have faced other Native American peoples. Some of these troubles are discussed in Chapter 10. However, life on the reservation is slowly improving. Many Navajo raise sheep or grow crops. Because the soil is so dry and poor, most of these people work very hard for very little return.

However, the Navajo people now own a lumber mill and an electronics company. These businesses give a good income to many Navajo workers. Skilled Navajo craftworkers make turquoise and silver jewelry and weave blankets. These beautiful articles are sold throughout the United States.

Have pupils check the chart on p. 397 to find out which four states are among the ten states with the smallest populations. (Wyo., Nev., Mont., Idaho)

Another major change on the reservation is the opening of coal mines. While the mines are a source of income to the Navajo, they are also a source of conflict. The money from the mines helps the Navajo to buy food and clothing and to give their children a better education. But Navajo tradition and culture always preserved the natural landscape. Coal mining changes it.

Ask: How does coal mining change the landscape?

Cities The two largest cities in the Mountain West are Phoenix and Denver. These two cities are among the 25 largest in the United States. Three of the nation's ten fastest growing cities are in the Mountain West. They are Aurora, Colorado Springs, and Albuquerque.

Phoenix The capital of Arizona, Phoenix is also the state's largest city. Phoenix got its start in 1870, when a few pioneers settled on the ruins of an ancient Indian village. Since then Phoenix has been growing rapidly, both in population and in area. In 1940 its population was about 65,000. By the late 1970s, the population of the city alone was more than ten times that large. The metropolitan area had about 1½ million people. In the 1870s, Phoenix was a few homes. Phoenix today sprawls over more than 250 square miles (650 sq km). 33°27′N/112°05′W

Phoenix has grown for many reasons. Irrigation of the desert has made it possible to grow vegetables and citrus fruits. The dry, clear air brings people for health reasons. With people come industries. Thousands of people have found jobs with the new electronics, aircraft, chemical, and other industries.

Denver Because Denver is 5,280 feet (1,609 m) above sea level, it is often given the nickname of "The Mile-High City." (One mile [1.6 km] equals 5,280 feet.) Denver lies on the western edge of the Great Plains. From many places in the city you can see the Rocky Mountains rising in the distance. 39°41′N/104°57′W

Denver is Colorado's capital and largest city. It got its start as a mining town. When the mining boom was over, Denver did not become a ghost town. The city was in the middle of a large agricultural area. Denver became a center of trade for the cattle, wheat, and other such products of the area.

Today the city is an important manufacturing and distributing center as well. Aerospace, food processing, luggage, and rubber goods are among Denver's many industries. The federal government has so many offices in the city that Denver is often called the "Washington of the West." A mint, an air force base, an arsenal, an army medical center, and a nuclear energy plant are among the many federal installations in the Denver area.

Ask: What is a mint? An arsenal? (Have pupils use a dictionary to find out if they do not know.)

Salt Lake City Salt Lake City is Utah's capital and largest city. About two thirds of the state's people live in or near Salt Lake City. The city was founded on the Great Salt Lake in 1847 by a religious group called the Mormons. This group had been persecuted first in New York State and then in Illinois. The Mormons moved to the Utah desert because they hoped to be far enough away from other people to be safe from persecution.

It took much hard work to build the farms and homes of the Mormon settle-

The phoenix is a bird connected with sun worship in Greek and Egyptian mythology. After a lifespan of 500 years or more, the phoenix sets fire to itself. From the ashes of its pyre, a new phoenix arises. The city of Phoenix got its name by analogy—it rose upon the ruins of an ancient village.

40°46′N/111°53′W

At this plant near Salt Lake City, coal is crushed and mixed with water to form a soupy mass called slurry. The slurry can then be piped to its destination.

ment. Irrigation was needed before even the smallest of gardens would produce.

Today this **oasis** in the desert is still largely Mormon. In fact about 70 percent of Utah's population is Mormon. In the heart of the city is the huge Mormon Temple, which took 40 years to build. Nearby is the Tabernacle, a large domed building. The Tabernacle is used for meetings and for concerts given by the famous Mormon Tabernacle Choir.

Salt Lake City is not just a religious center. It is a center for tourists who come to see the Great Salt Lake and the Temple and Tabernacle, and for skiers who visit the many ski resorts in the nearby mountains. Salt Lake City has many thriving businesses, including oil refining, electronics and clothing manufacturing, copper smelting, and printing. It is a trade center for agricultural and mining products.

CHECKUP

1. Which Mountain West state is growing most rapidly?
2. Why is coal mining a source of conflict among the Navajo?
3. What are the two largest cities in the Mountain West?
4. What group founded Salt Lake City?

Cities with less than 100,000		
Alamosa (Colo.) D-4	Scottsdale (Ariz.) E-3	Pueblo (Colo.) C-4
Arvada (Colo.) C-4	**Cities with 100,000–499,000**	Reno (Nev.) C-1
Boulder (Colo.) C-4	Albuquerque (N.Mex.) D-4	Salt Lake City (Utah) C-3
Carson City (Nev.) C-1	Aurora (Colo.) C-4	Tempe (Ariz.) E-3
Cheyenne (Wyo.) C-4	Boise (Idaho) B-1	Tucson (Ariz.) E-3
Glendale (Ariz.) E-2	Colorado Springs (Colo.) C-4	**City with 500,000–999,000**
Helena (Mont.) A-2	Denver (Colo.) C-4	Phoenix (Ariz.) E-2
Ogden (Utah) C-3	Lakewood (Colo.) C-4	**City with 1,000,000 or more**
Santa Fe (N.Mex.) D-4	Las Vegas (Nev.) D-2	None ....
	Mesa (Ariz.) E-3	

Despite its great size, the Mountain West is a region with few large cities. Which two states have no cities with a population of 100,000 or more? (Wyo., Mont.)

396

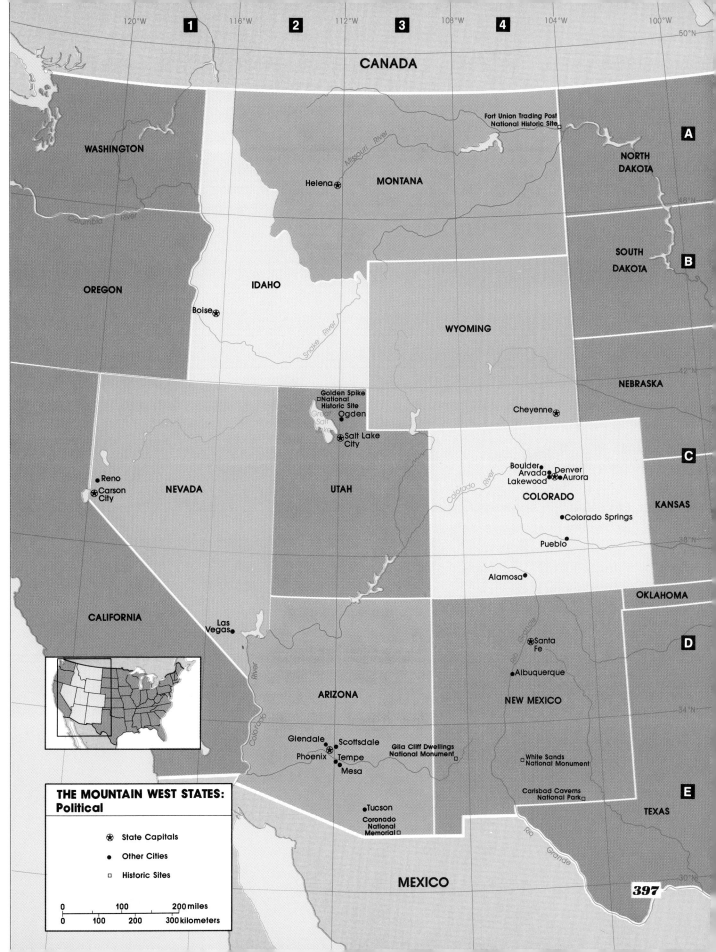

THE MOUNTAIN WEST STATES:
Political

⊛ State Capitals

● Other Cities

□ Historic Sites

| 0 | | 100 | | 200 miles |
| 0 | 100 | | 200 | 300 kilometers |

397

THE MOUNTAIN WEST STATES	Arizona	Colorado	Idaho	Montana
Source of Name	From Indian *Arizonac*, meaning "little spring"	From the Spanish, meaning "ruddy" or "red"	Means "gem of the mountains"	A Latinized Spanish word meaning "mountainous region"
Nickname(s)	Grand Canyon State	Centennial State	Gem State; Spud State; Panhandle State	Treasure State
Capital	Phoenix	Denver	Boise	Helena
Largest Cities (1980 Census)	Phoenix Tucson Mesa	Denver Colorado Springs Aurora	Boise Pocatello Idaho Falls	Billings Great Falls Butte-Silver Bow
Population Rank (1980 Census)	29	28	41	44
Population Density Rank	40	38	44	48
Area Rank	6	8	13	4
State Flag				
State Bird	Cactus wren	Lark bunting	Mountain bluebird	Western meadowlark
State Flower	Flower of saguaro cactus	Rocky Mountain columbine	Syringa	Bitterroot
State Tree	Paloverde	Colorado blue spruce	White pine	Ponderosa pine
State Motto	*Ditat Deus* (God enriches)	*Nil sine Numine* (Nothing without Providence)	*Esto perpetua* (May you last forever)	*Oro y plata* (Gold and silver)
Interesting Facts	Millions of tourists visit the Grand Canyon, the Painted Desert, and the Petrified Forest each year. London Bridge, at Lake Havasu City, is a stone bridge that was brought here from London, England.	Colorado is the highest state in the nation with an elevation of 6,800 feet (818 m). Eisenhower Memorial Tunnel is the world's highest tunnel for vehicles. It is 11,000 feet (3,400 m) above sea level.	In 1955, Arco was the first town to receive its power supply from nuclear energy. Hells Canyon is the deepest canyon in the United States.	More than 50 glaciers can be found on the rugged mountain slopes of Glacier National Park.

THE MOUNTAIN WEST STATES	Nevada	New Mexico	Utah	Wyoming
Source of Name	Spanish "snowcapped"	From the country of Mexico	From the Ute tribe, meaning "people of the mountains"	From a Delaware Indian word meaning "upon the great plain"
Nickname(s)	Sagebrush State; Silver State; Battle-born State	Land of Enchantment; Sunshine State	Beehive State	Equality State
Capital	Carson City	Santa Fe	Salt Lake City	Cheyenne
Largest Cities (1980 Census)	Las Vegas Reno North Las Vegas	Albuquerque Santa Fe Las Cruces	Salt Lake City Provo Ogden	Casper Cheyenne Laramie
Population Rank (1980 Census)	43	37	36	49
Population Density Rank	47	43	42	49
Area Rank	7	5	11	9
State Flag				
State Bird	Mountain bluebird	Roadrunner	Sea gull	Meadowlark
State Flower	Sagebrush	Yucca	Sego lily	Indian paintbrush
State Tree	Single-leaf piñon	Piñon	Blue spruce	Cottonwood
State Motto	All for our country	*Crescit eundo* (It grows as it goes)	Industry	Equal rights
Interesting Facts	This state has less rainfall than any other state in the United States. One of the world's largest dams, the Hoover Dam, is located near Las Vegas.	The world's first atomic bomb was exploded in the desert near Alamogordo on July 16, 1945. El Camino Real, Spanish for the Royal Road, is the oldest road in the United States.	Great Salt Lake is the largest natural lake west of the Mississippi River and is almost five times as salty as the ocean.	In 1872, Yellowstone became the first national park in the United States. In 1906, Devil's Tower became the first national monument.

KEY FACTS

1. Mountains, high plateaus, steep canyons, and deserts are the major land features of the Mountain West.

2. The Colorado River is used for irrigation, water supply, water power, and recreation.

3. The intermontane lands are dry because they are in a rain shadow.

4. Cattle and sheep raising make up a large part of the agriculture of the Mountain West.

5. The Mountain West has many important mineral resources.

6. The population of the Mountain West is growing rapidly.

VOCABULARY QUIZ

Next to the number of the sentence write the term that best completes the sentence. Write on a sheet of paper.

reservation	Continental Divide
desert	oil shale
arroyo	timberline
oasis	shearing
intermontane	fossil

1. The land between the Rockies and the mountains near the Pacific Coast is known as the _intermontane_ region.

2. Rivers to the west of the _Continental Divide_ flow generally west.

3. You can tell you are crossing an _arroyo_ when you see the stones polished by the water that sometimes flows there.

4. Most Navajo live on the _reservation_ in north-eastern Arizona.

5. When you find a rock that shows the imprint of a plant leaf or that of an animal's skeleton, you have found a _fossil_ .

6. The green trees and lawns of Salt Lake City create an _oasis_ in the desert.

7. No trees grow above the _timberline_ on a mountain slope.

8. A _desert_ is a land with very little rainfall and very few plants.

9. Clipping wool from sheep is called _shearing_ .

10. It is difficult to get oil from the kind of rock known as _oil shale_ .

REVIEW QUESTIONS

1. Describe how the vegetation changes as you climb the high mountains of the Rockies.

2. What are the three major parts of the intermontane region?

3. Why is the Colorado River system important to the people of the Mountain West?

4. What is a rain shadow?

5. Which state produces the most potatoes?

6. Name at least four mineral resources of the Mountain West.

7. What problems must be solved before oil shale is widely used?

8. Why do some people object to the use of nuclear energy?

9. Which park was the first national park?

10. Why is coal mining a source of conflict for the Navajo?

11. What are the two largest cities of the Mountain West?

ACTIVITIES

1. Make a booklet of national parks found in the Mountain West. In the booklet tell where the park is located, its size, and when it was founded. Then give a description of its most important features.

2. Read about life on a Navajo reservation. List the things a Navajo boy or girl might do during one day. Which activities are like your own? Which are different?

20/SKILLS DEVELOPMENT

LEARNING WORD ORIGINS

Words, like people and nations, have histories. There are people who study the history of words, just as there are people who study the history of nations. There is a lot to study, because languages have been growing and changing since the first word was spoken.

There are many reasons why this is true. Every time people make or discover something new, they need a new word. Also, people do not remain in one place. When they move, they take their language with them. Some of their words are adopted into the language of the people in the new land. Or if the immigrants are also the conquerors, they adopt some of the words of the original inhabitants. English, especially American English, is full of such words. *Arroyo, mesa, pueblo,* and *lariat* are a few of the words of Spanish origin that have become part of our vocabulary. From Native Americans, we borrowed *moccasin, canoe, succotash, kayak,* and a number of other words. The French, Dutch, and other settlers gave us still more words.

American place-names have many different origins. Here again we find words from several different languages. We also find places named after places in the homeland of the first settlers of an area. In addition there are places named after local people or after saints, presidents, royalty, or other famous people. Many place-names describe a physical feature, a plant, an animal, or an event. Place-names can come from the Bible or other works of literature. Some place-names are made-up words. A large number of names are borrowed from Indian words.

The list in the next column gives the origin of some place-names in the Mountain West.

Name	Source
Humboldt River	After Alexander von Humboldt, a German traveler and explorer
Bitterroot Mountains	After the bitterroot plant
Big Horn Mountains	After the mountain sheep
Gila River	After an Indian tribe
Boise	From the French word *bois*, "wooded"
Ogden	After a local man
Pueblo	Spanish word meaning "town." (It was the only settlement in the area, so it was just called "the town.")
Cheyenne	From an Indian tribal name
Nevada	Spanish word meaning "snowy"
Moscow	After the Russian city of that name

Now look at the following place-names. Try to guess the origin of each. Check your guesses in an encyclopedia, a dictionary, or a book of place-name origins, such as *American Place-Names,* by George R. Steward (New York: Oxford University Press, 1970).

1. Phoenix
2. Boulder
3. Carson City
4. Havre
5. Moab
6. Trinidad
7. Yellowstone
8. Rio Grande
9. Pocatello
10. Utah
11. Aurora
12. Mesa
13. Alamosa
14. Cody
15. Theodore Roosevelt Lake
16. Arizona
17. Tucson
18. Helena
19. Santa Fe
20. Lewis Range

401

The Land and Climate

┌─ VOCABULARY ────────────────────┐
earthquake   **permafrost**

volcano   **tundra**

ocean current
└─────────────────────────────────┘

Ka Lae is a cape on the island of Hawaii.

The region The Pacific region stretches from the northernmost point in the United States—Point Barrow, Alaska, at about 71°N—to the southernmost point in the United States—Ka Lae (kä lä' ā), Hawaii, at about 19°N. The Pacific region has five states: Alaska, California, Hawaii, Oregon, and Washington. Unlike the states in the other regions, these five states are not all together in one part of our nation. California, Oregon, and Washington are next to one another along the Pacific coast. Alaska and Hawaii, however, are both far away. Neither state borders any other state.

The Pacific region is one of great contrasts. At 20,320 feet (6,194 m), Mount McKinley in Alaska is the highest point in all of North America. The lowest point in North America is Death Valley in California at 282 feet (86 m) below sea level. On the coasts you find beaches of bright white sand and beaches with deep black sand. You also find places with steep, rocky cliffs at the water's edge. There are barren deserts and lush jungles. The vari-

Ask: What is the difference between the two elevation extremes? (20,602 feet [6,280 m] If necessary, draw a number line to illustrate why we *add* the elevations in this case.

ety of climates ranges from the cold, dry Arctic of Alaska to the hot, wet tropics of Hawaii.

Landforms Mountains and valleys are important landforms of the Pacific region. Look at the map on the next page. Notice the mountain system called the Coast Ranges, which stretches from southern California to northern Washington. Inland from these mountains are the Cascades and the Sierra Nevadas. Find these mountains on the map, too.

Between the Coast Ranges and these inland mountains are some of the most fertile valleys in our nation. The largest of these is the Central Valley of California. In Alaska the two major mountain ranges are the Brooks Range in the north and the Alaska Range in the south. Between the two is the Yukon River valley. Hawaii is also mountainous. In fact, the islands are the tops of submerged mountains.

The Brooks Range is actually the northernmost extension of the Rockies.

Waterways The Pacific Ocean washes the shores of all five states. There are many important harbors along the coast, including Washington's Puget (pyü' jət) Sound and California's San Francisco Bay. In the Gulf of Alaska there are several ports, and of course Hawaii has a number of ports, too.

Name the islands that make up the state of Hawaii. Notice the Alaska panhandle—the narrow strip of the state that extends south along Canada's western border.

There is a movement in Alaska to rename Mount Whitney. The proposed name is Denali, which is the mountain's original Indian name. The Department of the Interior has discussed this proposition but has not yet reached a decision.

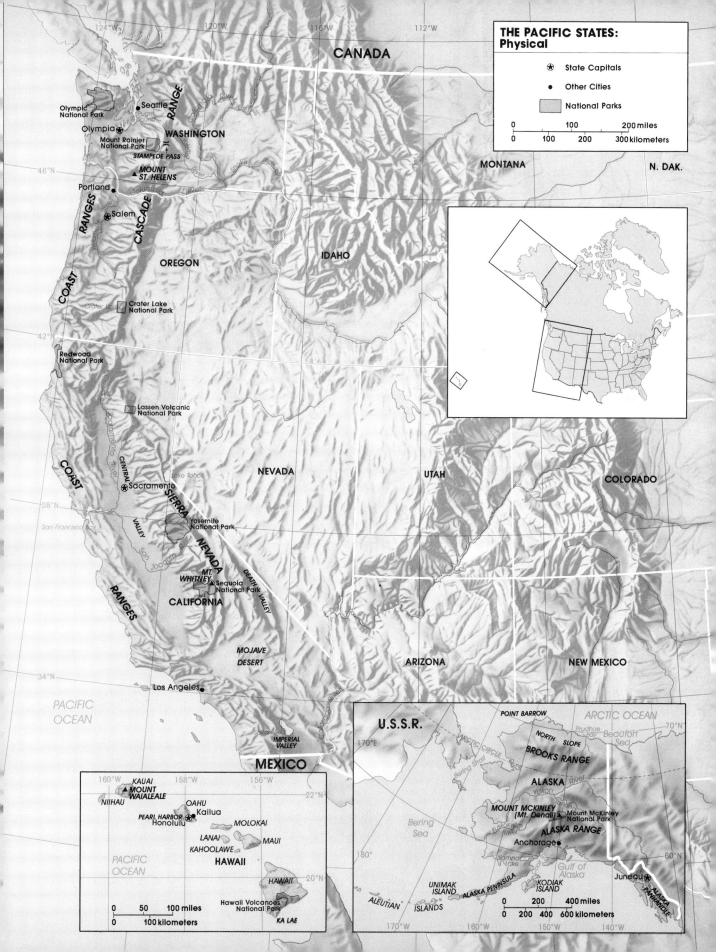

THE PACIFIC STATES: Physical

⊛ State Capitals
• Other Cities
▢ National Parks

0   100   200 miles
0   100   200   300 kilometers

CANADA

Olympic National Park
Seattle
Olympia
WASHINGTON
Mount Rainier National Park
STAMPEDE PASS
MOUNT ST. HELENS
Portland
Salem
OREGON
CASCADE RANGE
COAST RANGES
Crater Lake National Park
Redwood National Park
Lassen Volcanic National Park
Sacramento River
CENTRAL VALLEY
Sacramento
San Francisco Bay
Yosemite National Park
SIERRA NEVADA
San Joaquin
MT. WHITNEY
Sequoia National Park
DEATH VALLEY
CALIFORNIA
COAST RANGES
MOJAVE DESERT
Los Angeles
Salton Sea
IMPERIAL VALLEY
Colorado River

MONTANA
N. DAK.

IDAHO

NEVADA
UTAH
COLORADO

ARIZONA
NEW MEXICO

PACIFIC OCEAN

MEXICO

KAUAI
MOUNT WAIALEALE
NIIHAU
OAHU
Kailua
PEARL HARBOR
Honolulu
MOLOKAI
LANAI
MAUI
KAHOOLAWE
HAWAII
PACIFIC OCEAN
HAWAII
Hawaii Volcanoes National Park
KA LAE

0   50   100 miles
0   100 kilometers

U.S.S.R.
POINT BARROW
ARCTIC OCEAN
NORTH SLOPE
Prudhoe Bay
Beaufort Sea
ARCTIC CIRCLE
BROOKS RANGE
ALASKA
Yukon River
MOUNT MCKINLEY (Mt. Denali)
Mount McKinley National Park
ALASKA RANGE
Bering Sea
Anchorage
Illiamna Lake
Bering Strait
Gulf of Alaska
UNIMAK ISLAND
ALASKA PENINSULA
KODIAK ISLAND
Juneau
ALASKA PANHANDLE
ALEUTIAN ISLANDS

0   200   400 miles
0   200   400   600 kilometers

The longest river in the Pacific states is the Yukon River, which begins in Canada and flows through Alaska to the Bering Sea. The Yukon is the third longest river in North America.

Another important waterway is the Columbia River. This river is important for shipping, irrigation, waterpower, and fishing. It ranks as one of the world's most important salmon (sam′ ən) streams.

In California, the San Joaquin (san wä kēn′) and Sacramento rivers are a part of a statewide water plan. Rivers, canals, and aqueducts bring water from northern rivers and lakes to the dry parts of the state. California also uses water from the Colorado River.

The Pacific region contains two of the world's deepest lakes: Crater Lake in Oregon and Lake Tahoe on the border between California and Nevada. In the Western Hemisphere, only Canada's Great Slave Lake is deeper than these two lakes.

Lake Tahoe's greatest depth is 1,600 feet (500 m). Great Slave Lake's greatest depth is 2,015 feet (614 m).

Another interesting lake is the Salton Sea in southern California. It is actually a lake, but is called a sea because it has salt water. The Salton sea formed in an area that is about 280 feet (85 m) below sea level. Most of the water that created the lake came from the Colorado River when it flooded and left its course in the early 1900s. Since the Salton Sea now has no rivers flowing out of it, the water is saltier than ocean water.

You may wish to review with pupils the process by which lakes that have no outlets become salty.

Climate   Three main factors affect the climates of the Pacific states: mountains, ocean currents, and latitude. Hawaii is the warmest of the five states. It lies in the tropics, near the equator. Hawaii also has one of the wettest spots on earth. The north slope of Mount Waialeale (wī äl ā äl′ ā) on the island of Kauai (kaù′ ī) gets about 450 inches (1,125 cm) of rain a year. Warm, moist winds come in from the ocean, dropping most of their moisture

Crater Lake formed in the cone of a volcanic mountain. Wizard Island, shown in the picture, is also a volcanic formation. The lake's greatest depth is 1,932 feet (589 m).

42°56′N/122°06′W

People in the Pacific region experience two of nature's most violent forces: **earthquakes** and **volcanoes.**

An earthquake is a movement of the ground. A small earthquake can be just a gentle shaking or a sharp jolt. Although the motion usually lasts no more than a few minutes, a large earthquake can cause great damage. Large cracks form in the earth's surface. Roads buckle, bridges collapse, and buildings tumble to the ground. The side effects can include fires, floods, landslides, and tidal waves. In the Pacific states, earthquakes occur most often in California and Alaska.

A volcano is an opening in the ground through which melted rock and other materials pour. These materials are deep inside the earth. From time to time they push up through a weak spot in the earth's surface, and a volcano is born. A volcanic eruption may send clouds of ash, gases, and water vapor shooting into the air. Lava, or melted rock, may flow from a volcano for days.

Many of the mountains in the Pacific states were formed by volcanoes. Several of the Hawaiian Islands are themselves the tops of volcanic mountains. A recent volcanic eruption in the United States was that of Mount St. Helens in 1980. The eruption blew off the peak, sending tons of mud sliding down the mountainside. The mudslide swept away houses and bridges. A blast of hot gases shot out of the side of the mountain, burning everything in a path 15 miles (24 km) wide and 8 miles (13 km) long. A rain of ash fell over many square miles, damaging forests and crops, choking streams, lakes, and roadways, and sending thousands of people to shelter.

on the northern and eastern slopes of Waialeale and the other mountains of the Hawaiian Islands. The southern and western sides are in a rain shadow and get much less rain.

The rain shadow effect is at work in other parts of the Pacific states, too. The Central Valley and the lands to the east of the Cascades and the Sierra Nevadas are all quite dry.

In fact, most of California has a dry climate. Winds bearing rain blow off the ocean only in winter. Rainfall in summer is very rare. The yearly average precipitation is less than 20 inches (50 cm) in most places. Summers are hot, and winters are warm in most of central and southern California.

The lands along the coast from northern California to the Alaskan peninsula and the Aleutian Islands are affected by a **warm ocean current.** (An ocean current is a movement of the surface water in a regular path.) These lands have plenty of rainfall and milder temperatures than do the inland areas at the same latitudes.

Snowfall is heavy in southern Alaska and in the high mountains of Washington, Oregon, and northern California. One weather station in Washington, Stampede Pass, has an average yearly snowfall of 442 inches (1,123 cm).

This picture was taken during the midnight sun in Kotzebue (kät′ sə byü), Alaska, a town in northwestern Alaska, just above the Arctic Circle. 66°54′N/162°35′W

Kotzebue is on Seward Peninsula.

Northern Alaska is very cold and quite dry. The weather station at Barrow has an average yearly temperature of 9°F (−23°C). It has an average yearly precipitation of only 5 inches (13 cm). It is so cold here that only the top few inches of the ground ever thaw. Below that is **permafrost**, or ground that stays frozen all year long. Barrow is in the **tundra.** The tundra is a treeless plain. It is so dry and cold that very few kinds of plants can live there.

Central Alaska receives more rainfall than the tundra area. Along the Yukon River valley winters are cold and harsh. Summers are short and cool. The growing season may last only 100 days. However, it is possible to grow some vegetables and grains.

Midnight sun In the Arctic region of Alaska and in other Arctic lands, day and night are different from our day and night. At the North Pole, the sun does not set at all from the end of March to the end of September. From September to March the sun doesn't rise. Night lasts for 6 months and day lasts for 6 months. As you move away from the Pole, you find that the sun does rise and set during each 24-hour period.

Even so, from March to September, daylight lasts for a long time in the Arctic. The sun is still out at midnight in some places. In winter, the opposite is true. Then the sun is only out for a short time during each 24-hour period. At the Arctic Circle there is one 24-hour period of darkness in the winter and one 24-hour period of sunlight in the summer.

CHECKUP

1. What is the highest point in North America? The lowest?
2. What are the two main physical features of the Pacific region?
3. What three main factors affect the Pacific climates? How do they do so?

The midnight sun phenomenon is caused by the tilt of the earth in relationship to the sun.

Agriculture, Resources, and Industry

VOCABULARY

fish hatchery

Agriculture California's farmlands are among the richest in the world. The warm, sunny climate and rich soil are ideal for many crops. Water, the missing ingredient, is supplied by irrigation. It is

not surprising, then that California leads the nation in farm production and in the amount of land used for farming. (The graph on page 281 in Chapter 14 shows you which five states lead the nation in farm production.) California's two most important farming areas are the Central Valley and the Imperial Valley. The Imperial Valley is in southern California near the Salton Sea.

This orange grove near Bakersfield, California, gives you an idea of the vastness of California's agriculture. Bakersfield is at latitude 35°N and longitude 119°W. It is near the southern end of the Central Valley. Note how brown and dry the hills are. 35°22'N/119°01'W

Many crops are grown in these fertile valleys. There are citrus fruits, grapes, apricots, dates, and figs. There are vegetables, such as lettuce, tomatoes, and artichokes. Among the other important crops are rice and cotton. Cattle and other livestock are also raised. The chief farmlands of Washington and Oregon are found in the Willamette (wə lam′ ət), Yakima (yak′ ə mô), and Columbia river valleys and in the lowlands south of Puget Sound. Many different types of crops are grown in these areas. Washington apples are sold throughout the nation. There are many vegetable farms and dairy farms. This area has become famous for farms that grow roses and other flowers. Large wheat crops are grown on the dry plateau of eastern Washington.

Most of Alaska's farmlands are near Anchorage and Fairbanks. Potatoes, vegetables, and hay are among the most important crops. Blueberries and strawberries are harvested during the short growing season. Cattle and poultry are also raised. Most of the products are used locally.

Sugarcane and pineapple are Hawaii's two most important crops. Both crops are grown on large plantations. Hawaii is one of the world's leaders in pineapple production. Both fresh and canned pineapple are exported.

A third important export crop is coffee. Coffee is grown on the cooler mountain slopes rather than on the level land used for fields of sugarcane and pineapple.

On the islands of Maui (maü′ ē) and Hawaii cattle ranching is big business. Most of the beef raised on the islands is sold in Hawaiian markets.

Forests   Four of the five Pacific states have important lumbering industries. About half of Washington and Oregon, about one-third of Alaska, and about two-fifths of California are forested. Oregon is our leading lumber state. It produces about one-fourth of the nation's lumber and nearly three-fourths of the plywood. The graph on page 275 in Chapter 14 shows you that Oregon produces about twice as much lumber as California, the state with the second highest lumber production. Which state is third? Washington

Between the Cascades and the Coast Ranges in Washington and Oregon are huge forests of pine and other evergreens. The mild temperatures and plentiful rainfall are ideal for growing trees. Lumbering has been going on in this area for over 100 years. Sawmills, pulp and paper mills, and furniture factories make wood processing a leading industry of the area. Most of the lumber and wood products are shipped from Portland and ports along Puget Sound.

Timber is one of Alaska's leading products. Most of it comes from the southern coastal area and from the Yukon River valley. The growth of Alaska's industry and population has increased the local demand for wood products. Much lumber is also shipped to other markets.

California is famous for its huge redwood trees. One kind of redwood, the coast redwood, grows near the ocean, where it receives moisture from winds coming in off the Pacific. The other kind, the giant redwood, grows on the western slopes of the Sierra Nevadas. Both kinds of redwoods can grow to enormous size, although the coast redwood is the taller of

These two girls must feel like ants next to these huge redwoods. Redwoods grow to such great heights that their tops are often broken off by lightning.

the two. One coast redwood was reported to be 385 feet (117 m) high, and one giant redwood measured 325 feet (99 m). Redwoods can be as much as 30 feet (9 m) in diameter. Redwoods live for hundreds of years. Some of the largest redwoods are thought to be about 3,500 years old.

People do not agree on what should be done with the redwoods. Some people think they should be cut for lumber. The lumber is valuable for building, furniture, and other things. A single coast redwood can provide more than enough lumber for several houses. Other people feel that the remaining redwoods should be preserved for future generations to enjoy.

Fishing The Pacific states have an important fishing industry. Salmon play a large role in that industry. Salmon hatch in freshwater streams. They live in the

streams until they are at least 2 years old. Then they swim downstream and head far out to sea. After 2 or more years there, they return to the streams where they were hatched to lay their eggs. Soon after the eggs are laid, the salmon die.

Not all the salmon make it upstream to lay their eggs. Gulls and bears feed on the returning salmon. And when the salmon are running, fish canneries are busy 24 hours a day processing the catch.

Some streams and rivers are no longer available to salmon. Some streams are too polluted. On others, dams have been built. Unless fish ladders are built, the dams keep the fish from making their journey. A fish ladder is a series of pools, set up like steps, that fish can use to get past a dam. From Alaska to northern

Low walls called weirs separate the pools of a fish ladder. The raised section of the weir makes a backwater where fish can rest. Fish either jump the weirs or swim through holes near the weir's bottom.

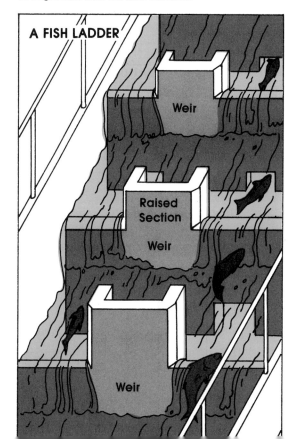

A FISH LADDER

Weir

Raised Section

Weir

Weir

California, **fish hatcheries** have been developed to offset the loss. Millions of eggs are hatched. When the young salmon have grown large enough, they are released in the streams and head out to sea.

Shellfish, especially crabs, are also important along the coast from northern California to Alaska. California port cities have fishing fleets that bring in catches of tuna and halibut.

Other products of the sea include otters, seals, and whales. All three were hunted for years until very few were left. Now some countries are trying to work together to control the numbers taken. Seals and otters have become tourist attractions at several places along the rocky Pacific coast. Tourists also come to watch the whales that migrate seasonally along the coast from the Arctic Ocean and the North Pacific Ocean to southern waters and back again.

Minerals   California leads the five Pacific states in the production of minerals. It ranks first in the nation in the production of several of those minerals. It is the third largest producer of iron ore. The state has been one of our leading producers of oil for many years. However, the known reserves are being used up. California's oil production has been going down since about 1970.

The discovery of gold near Sacramento in 1848 brought thousands of people to California. Gold is still mined but is no longer a leading mineral resource of California.

Like California, Alaska had a gold rush. Some gold is still mined along the Yukon River, but more interest is now given to the large oil and gas deposits near Prudhoe Bay on Alaska's North Slope. The North Slope is a broad, frozen tundra between the Brooks Range and the Beaufort Sea. In area it is about the size of the state of Washington. Geologists believe the North Slope has one of the largest oil reserves in North America.

The oil cannot be shipped out by tanker, because Prudhoe Bay is blocked with ice for much of the year. To get the oil from Prudhoe Bay to the places where it is needed, a large pipeline was built. The pipeline goes to Valdez, a port in southern Alaska. The 48-inch (122-cm) pipeline crosses three mountain ranges and 350 rivers and streams on its 800-mile (1,300-km) course. From Valdez the oil is taken by tanker to refineries in Washington and California. Much oil is exported to Japan and other nations.

Not everyone wanted the Alaskan pipeline to be built. Many people were worried about the danger of oil spills if the pipe were to break. Others worried that the warm oil carried by the pipe would melt the top layers of the permafrost and upset the natural balance. Our nation's demand for oil was so great that the pipeline was built in spite of these dangers. However, great care was taken in planning the pipeline so that the natural world would be hurt as little as possible. So far it seems to have done little damage.

Other industries   Tourism is a leading industry in each of the five Pacific states. People hike and camp in the breathtakingly beautiful mountains. They hunt and fish in the forests and streams. In California and Hawaii, they enjoy the surf and

410   California ranks first in the United States in the production of asbestos, boron, cement, gypsum, mercury, and tungsten.

As you can see, the pipeline crosses some pretty rugged country. This picture was taken 80 miles (130 km) north of Valdez. Notice the mountains in the background.

sunny beaches. People come to visit the twelve national parks in the Pacific states. These parks include Yosemite in California, Olympic in Washington, Crater Lake in Oregon, Mount McKinley in Alaska, and Hawaii Volcanoes in Hawaii.

The nation's largest aerospace manufacturing center is in southern California. Another large center is in Washington. Both passenger planes and military planes are built in these two centers.

Food processing is important in the cities near the farming centers. Most of the other industries of California, Washington, and Oregon make products that are the result of modern scientific developments. Among them are televisions, radios, and other electronic products. Southern California's dry, sunny climate made it an ideal place for the growth of the entertainment industry. Many movies and television programs are produced here.

CHECKUP

1. Which is our leading farming state? Lumbering state?
2. What is unusual about redwoods? Salmon?
3. What is Alaska's most important mineral resource?

411

Hawaii has a population made up entirely of minority groups: there is no ethnic majority. The percentages for each group are Caucasian, 26; Japanese, 25; Filipino, 10; Hawaiian and part-Hawaiian, 20; Chinese, 4; Korean, 1; black, 1; Samoan, 1; Puerto Rican, 1; mixed (except part-Hawaiian), 10; and other groups, 1.

Population and Cities

Population   The Pacific region has the state with the largest number of people (California) and the state with the smallest number (Alaska). Alaska not only has the fewest people, but also the fewest people per square mile of the fifty states. It is the largest state in area and smallest in number of people.

The region's largest population centers are on or near the coast. They include five of the 25 largest cities in the United States: Los Angeles, San Diego, San Francisco, and San Jose (san ə zā′) in California, and Seattle on Puget Sound in Washington.

During the 1970s, Alaska's population grew rapidly. Many people moved into the state from other parts of the United States. Among those who moved in were people who worked on building the Alaskan pipeline and a smaller number who came to set up **homesteads** in the Alas-

kan wilderness. The older residents include whites, Eskimos, Indians, and Aleuts (ə lüts′). Aleuts are the native people of the Aleutian Islands. The Eskimos, Indians, and Aleuts combined make up about 15 percent of Alaska's population.

Of Hawaii's more than 900,000 residents, only about 9 percent have Hawaiian ancestors. The population is made up of the descendants of immigrants from many parts of the world. People from Japan, the Philippines, China, Polynesia, Portugal, and the United States were among the early settlers. Their descendants have stayed on the islands.

Mexican Americans   There are at least 6 or 7 million Mexican Americans in the United States. More Mexican Americans live in California than in any other state. The roots of Mexican Americans can be traced back to the great Indian civilizations of Mexico and to the Spanish settlers of that nation. By the mid-1800s, over 75,000 Spanish-speaking persons lived in

Cities with less than 100,000	Cities with 100,000–499,000	
Barrow (Alaska) G-8	Anaheim (Calif.) E-2	Portland (Oreg.) B-1
Eugene (Oreg.) B-1	Anchorage (Alaska) H-9	Riverside (Calif.) E-2
Fairbanks (Alaska) H-9	Bakersfield (Calif.) D-2	Sacramento (Calif.) C-1
Hayward (Calif.) D-1	Berkeley (Calif.) D-1	San Bernardino (Calif.) D-2
Inglewood (Calif.) E-2	Concord (Calif.) D-1	Santa Ana (Calif.) E-2
Juneau (Alaska) I-10	Fremont (Calif.) D-1	Seattle (Wash.) A-1
Kailua (Hawaii) F-6	Fresno (Calif.) D-2	Spokane (Wash.) A-2
Norwalk (Calif.) E-2	Fullerton (Calif.) E-2	Stockton (Calif.) D-1
Olympia (Wash.) A-1	Glendale (Calif.) D-2	Sunnyvale (Calif.) D-1
Ontario (Calif.) D-2	Garden Grove (Calif.) E-2	Tacoma (Wash.) A-1
Orange (Calif.) E-2	Honolulu (Hawaii) F-6	Torrance (Calif.) E-2
Pomona (Calif.) D-2	Huntington Beach (Calif.) .. E-2	**Cities with 500,000–999,000**
Salem (Oreg.) B-1	Long Beach (Calif.) E-2	San Diego (Calif.) E-2
Santa Clara (Calif.) D-1	Modesto (Calif.) D-1	San Francisco (Calif.) D-1
Santa Monica (Calif.) D-2	Oakland (Calif.) D-1	San Jose (Calif.) D-1
Valdez (Alaska) H-9	Oxnard (Calif.) D-2	**City with 1,000,000 or more**
	Pasadena (Calif.) D-2	Los Angeles (Calif.) D-2

Compare this list of cities with the lists on pages 306, 324, 343, 362, 381, and 396. Which region has the most cities with a population of 500,000 to 999,000? (North Central)

412   "Hawaiians" are people descended from the Polynesians who first settled the islands. These Polynesians arrived at least by A.D. 1000 and possibly as early as the sixth century A.D.

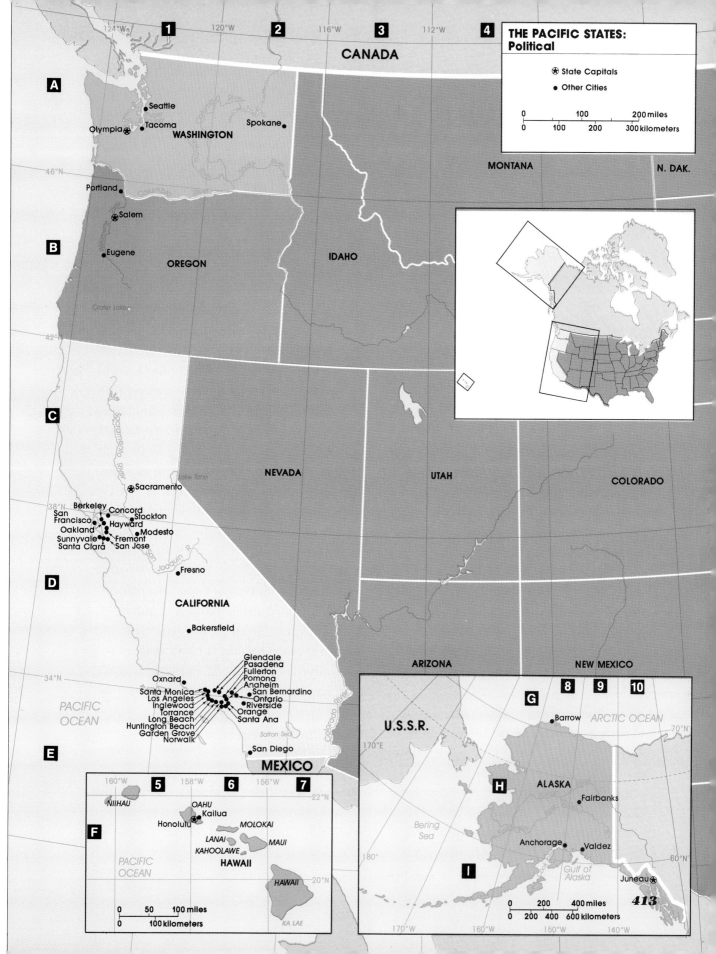

THE PACIFIC STATES:
Political

✳ State Capitals
• Other Cities

0   100   200 miles
0   100   200   300 kilometers

CANADA

MONTANA   N. DAK.

1 **2** **3** **4**

A

Seattle
Tacoma
Olympia ✳
Spokane
WASHINGTON

Columbia River
Snake River

46°N

Portland
Salem ✳
B
Eugene
OREGON
Willamette River
IDAHO

42°N

Crater Lake

C
Sacramento ✳
Lake Tahoe
NEVADA   **UTAH**   **COLORADO**
Sacramento River
38°N
Berkeley Concord
San Francisco Stockton
Oakland Hayward Modesto
Sunnyvale Fremont
Santa Clara San Jose
San Joaquin R.
Fresno

D
CALIFORNIA
Bakersfield

Glendale
Pasadena
Fullerton
Pomona
Anaheim
Oxnard   San Bernardino
34°N Santa Monica   Ontario
Los Angeles   Riverside
Inglewood   Orange
Torrance   Santa Ana
Long Beach
Huntington Beach
Garden Grove
Norwalk
Salton Sea
Colorado River

ARIZONA   **NEW MEXICO**

8 **9** **10**

G
Barrow   ARCTIC OCEAN
U.S.S.R.
170°E   70°N

H   **ALASKA**

PACIFIC OCEAN
San Diego
MEXICO

Fairbanks

Bering Sea

180°

Anchorage Valdez

Gulf of Alaska

60°N

Juneau ✳

E

160°W   158°W   156°W

5   **6**   **7**

22°N

NIIHAU   OAHU Kailua
Honolulu ✳ MOLOKAI
F LANAI   MAUI
KAHOOLAWE
HAWAII

PACIFIC OCEAN
20°N

HAWAII

KA LAE

0   50   100 miles
0   100 kilometers

I

0   200   400 miles
0   200 400 600 kilometers

413

170°W   160°W   150°W   140°W

the West before it became part of the United States. The gold rush in 1849, however, brought so many English-speaking settlers to the West that Mexican Americans were outnumbered.

The Mexican Americans shared their knowledge of farming, ranching, and mining with the newcomers. They taught them methods of mining gold and silver. They also taught them how to tame wild horses, brand cattle, and irrigate the land.

In spite of this, there was conflict between the two groups. Each had its own language, religion, and customs. Many English-speaking settlers thought of the Mexican Americans as "foreign."

As the new settlers came into power, they discriminated against Mexican Americans. Many Mexican Americans had to settle for poorer jobs, education, and housing. In spite of this, many people have moved from Mexico to the United States. They continue to do so today.

In recent years, many Mexican Americans have organized into groups to gain more opportunities for themselves. These groups draw attention to the problems of Mexican Americans throughout the country. They also encourage Mexican Americans to take pride in themselves and in their history, both Mexican and American.

Asian Americans   Like most other immigrant groups, Asian Americans have suffered from unfair and even cruel treatment. Asian Americans include people from China, Japan, the Philippines, Korea, and other nations of Asia. Often these people were allowed only the hardest and lowest paid jobs. Chinese Americans, for example, were hired to lay the track for the transcontinental railroad. Thousands of Japanese Americans were forced to give up their jobs and homes and to live in camps during World War II. Despite these and other hardships, Asian Americans have made good lives for themselves in the United States. They have been able to keep a sense of pride in their Asian heritage. At the same time, they have made important contributions to American life.

Alaskan cities   There are few cities in our largest state. Anchorage, the largest city, has about 44 percent of the state's population. Anchorage was badly hurt by an earthquake in 1964. It recovered fully and was one of the fastest growing cities of the nation during the 1970s. Anchorage is the headquarters for many large businesses. It is also a center for many government offices even though it is not the state capital. The mountains around Cook Inlet on the Gulf of Alaska form a beautiful backdrop for the city of Anchorage.

Many of Alaska's cities are near waterways or along the coast. Juneau, the capital, is on the Alaskan panhandle. Ketchikan and Sitka in the southeast are lumbering and fishing centers. Valdez is a port city. On the Arctic coast is Barrow, our nation's northernmost community. Fairbanks, in the interior, was a supply center during Alaska's gold rush. It is still a commercial and mining supply center.

Hawaiian cities   Hawaii's few cities include Kailua (kī lü′ ə), Kaneohe (kän′ ē ō′ē), Hilo (hē′ lō), and Honolulu. Honolulu is the capital and largest city. It is also the state's industrial and commercial

These men are using an outrigger canoe near Honolulu. The first Hawaiians came from Polynesia in outriggers.

center. Honolulu's leading industry is tourism. Each year about three million people visit the city's famous Waikiki Beach.

Tourists and residents alike are interested in the history of Hawaii's rulers. Iolani Palace near Honolulu is the nation's only royal palace. Here you can see robes and other treasures of the monarchs who ruled the islands during the 1800s.

Portland Oregon's largest city, Portland, is near the junction of the Columbia and Willamette rivers. Even though it is 100 miles (160 km) inland, it is a major deep-water port. At the port, ships are loaded with lumber, grain, wool, and bauxite. Waterpower has also helped the city grow as a manufacturing and trading center.

Seattle In the 1890s Seattle was the nation's chief link to the Alaskan gold fields. During the building of the big Alaskan pipeline the city was again the chief link. Aircraft manufacturing and shipbuilding are the major industries today. Other industries include lumbering; fishing; and the manufacture of chemicals, food products, and metals.

Seattle is built on several hills. Within the city borders are four lakes and many small parks that help to make the city a pleasant place to live in.

Los Angeles Los Angeles is by far the largest city of the Pacific region. It is one of the nation's three largest cities. The rich farmland in the area and nearby oil deposits have helped Los Angeles become the region's most important trade and manufacturing center.

Los Angeles is one of our nation's largest metropolitan areas. It stretches east about 100 miles (160 km) and includes Pasadena, Anaheim, and about 100 other cities.

After the eruption of Mount St. Helens in May 1980, the Columbia River was so clogged with volcanic ash that many oceangoing vessels were stranded in Portland until the channel could be dredged. Portland is about 50 miles (80 km) from Mount St. Helens.

Los Angeles has two major problems. One is water. Like the rest of southern and central California, the Los Angeles area is very dry. With such a large population, the demand for water is very large. About three quarters of the city's water must be carried by aqueduct from several different sources. These sources are streams in the Sierra Nevada, the Owens River in eastern California, the Colorado River, and the Feather River in northern California. As more people move into the Los Angeles area, the problem of providing water is becoming very serious.

The second problem is a result of the great number of industries in and around Los Angeles and of the huge number of automobiles that fill the highways of the area. Industrial fumes and auto exhaust sometimes combine to form a low-hanging cloud of polluted air called **smog.** Because the mountains around the city form a sort of pocket, the smog often remains over the city for days and even weeks at a time. Los Angeles is working on this problem, but has not completely solved it.

San Diego   San Diego is one of the nation's ten largest cities. San Diego's natural harbor is the home of a large fishing fleet and a United States Navy base. A center for oceanic studies has also been set up in San Diego. Aircraft, food processing, and electronic industries all help the city's growth.

San Francisco   San Francisco is built along the waterfront on San Francisco Bay and on steep hillsides. Many people think it is one of our most beautiful cities.

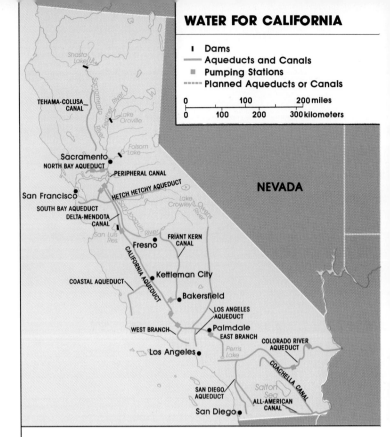

You can see that getting water to the cities and farms of central and southern California is a major project.

The city was nearly destroyed by an earthquake and fire in 1906. Food processing, oil refineries, chemical plants, and electronics are among the industries of the Bay area. The port of San Francisco is the largest on the Pacific Coast.

San Francisco also has one of the country's largest Chinese American populations. You can see signs written in Chinese, hear people speaking the language, and shop in markets or eat in restaurants specializing in Chinese foods.

CHECKUP

1. People of many different races and nations have settled in the Pacific states. How would this make the Pacific states an interesting place to live?
2. Which two Pacific cities would you most like to visit? Why?

THE PACIFIC STATES	Alaska	California	Hawaii	Oregon	Washington
Source of Name	Change of Aleut word meaning "great land" or "that which the sea breaks against"	From a book *Las Sergas de Esplandián* by Garcia Ordóñez de Montalvo (c 1500)	Uncertain; maybe named by traditional discoverer: Hawaii Loa; or named after Hawaii (Hawaiki) traditional Polynesian home	Named for a river the French called the Ouragon, which means "hurricane"	In honor of George Washington
Nickname(s)	The Last Frontier; Land of the Midnight Sun	Golden State	Aloha State	Beaver State	Evergreen State; Chinook State
Capital	Juneau	Sacramento	Honolulu	Salem	Olympia
Largest Cities (1980 Census)	Anchorage Fairbanks Juneau	Los Angeles San Diego San Francisco	Honolulu Kailua Hilo	Portland Eugene Salem	Seattle Spokane Tacoma
Population Rank (1980 Census)	50	1	39	30	20
Population Density Rank	50	14	15	39	28
Area Rank	1	3	47	10	20
State Flag				STATE OF OREGON 1859	
State Bird	Willow ptarmigan	California valley quail	Nene (Hawaiian goose)	Western meadowlark	Willow goldfinch
State Flower	Forget-me-not	Golden poppy	Hibiscus	Oregon grape	Rhododendron
State Tree	Sitka spruce	California redwood	Kukui	Douglas fir	Western hemlock
State Motto	North to the future	*Eureka* (I have found it)	*Ua mau ke ea o ka aina i ka pono* (The life of the land is perpetuated in righteousness)	The Union	*Al-Ki* (Indian word meaning "by and by")
Interesting Facts	The United States purchased the territory of Alaska from Russia in 1867 for about 2¢ an acre. Mt. McKinley (20,320 ft; 6,190 m) is the highest peak in the United States.	The highest temperature in the United States and the lowest point below sea level are both found in Death Valley. The coast redwoods are the tallest living things in the world.	One fifth of all the pineapples grown in the world are produced in Hawaii. Hilo is the wettest city in the United States with 133.57 in. (3,393 mm) annual rainfall.	Oregon is a leader in the production of nuts, lumber, and orchard fruits. Crater Lake is the deepest (1,932 ft; 589 m) natural lake in the United States.	Grand Coulee Dam, across the Columbia River, is the largest concrete dam and the greatest single source of water power in the United States. The eruption of Mount St. Helens on March 27, 1980, was the first volcanic eruption in the continental United States since 1914.

417

21 /CHAPTER REVIEW

KEY FACTS

1. The Pacific region has the northernmost and southernmost points in the United States, as well as the highest and lowest points.

2. Mountains and valleys are important landforms of the Pacific region.

3. Mountains, ocean currents, and latitude affect the climates of the Pacific states.

4. Agriculture is important in several parts of the Pacific region, but California is our leading state in farm production.

5. The Pacific region's resources include lumber, fish, and oil and other minerals.

6. Five of our 25 largest cities are in the Pacific region.

VOCABULARY QUIZ

Write the letter of the term next to the number of its description. Write on a sheet of paper.

a. tundra   **f.** smog
b. volcano   **g.** Aleutian
c. heritage   **h.** current
d. permafrost   **i.** earthquake
e. fish ladder   **j.** fish hatchery

h **1.** Movement of water in a regular path

b **2.** An eruption of gases, ash, and molten rock through a weak spot in the earth's surface

j **3.** A place where fish are raised

c **4.** Ideas, values, and customs passed on by one's ancestors

a **5.** A treeless plain that is so dry and cold that only a few kinds of plants can live there

g **6.** One of the islands that form an arc extending out from the Alaskan peninsula

e **7.** A series of pools that make it possible for fish to travel past a dam in a river

f **8.** A low-lying, cloudlike layer in the air formed by a mixture of pollutants

i **9.** A movement of the ground that makes cracks in the earth's surface

d **10.** A layer of earth that remains frozen

REVIEW QUESTIONS

1. What are the highest and lowest points in North America?

2. Why is the Salton Sea salty?

3. What effects do mountains, ocean currents, and latitude have on the climates of the Pacific region?

4. What are California's two most important farming areas?

5. Which state is our leading lumber state?

6. What is unusual about redwood trees? What is the disagreement concerning redwoods?

7. What mineral resource do we get from the North Slope? How does the resource get to the places where it is needed?

8. Why is life so often difficult for immigrant groups, such as Mexican Americans and Asian Americans?

9. Name five of the large cities of the Pacific states.

ACTIVITIES

1. You want to travel along the coast from San Diego to Anchorage. How many miles will you travel? What are the major cities that you will see along the route? Describe the weather that you might find.

2. For one week collect newspaper articles dealing with the Pacific states. How many different topics are included in your articles? (Climate, jobs, resources, industries, etc.) Which state is mentioned most often? How many articles deal with problems? Is one problem mentioned more often than others?

READING CLIMOGRAPHS

On this page there are two special kinds of graphs. They are called climographs because they show temperature and precipitation, two important parts of climate. Each climograph has temperature scales on the left side. They are printed in red. The scale on the outside is for Fahrenheit temperatures. The scale on the inside is for Celsius temperatures. The months of the year are given along the bottom of the graph. The average temperature for each month is shown by a red dot. The dots are connected to make it easier to see the temperature pattern for the year.

Now use the temperature information on the climographs to answer these questions.

1. Which place is warmer? Los Angeles

2. Is the average January temperature above or below freezing (32°F or 0°C) in Juneau? Below

3. Which three months have the same temperature in Los Angeles? July, Aug., Sept.

On the right side of the graph are the scales for precipitation. They are printed in blue. Centimeters are given on the inside; inches, on the outside. The blue bars show the average monthly precipitation.

Now use the blue bars to answer the following questions.

1. Which place is wetter? Juneau

2. Which place has no precipitation from May through October? Los Angeles

3. What is the greatest amount of precipitation for any one month in Juneau? In Los Angeles? 8 inches (20 cm); 3 inches (8 cm)

Think about both temperature and precipitation. How would you describe the climate of these two places? Los Angeles: Warm and dry
Juneau: Cold and wet

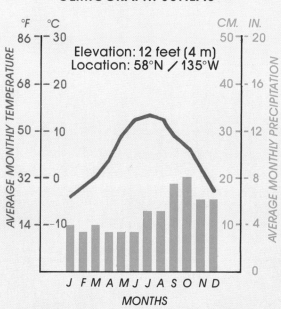

CLIMOGRAPH: JUNEAU

Elevation: 12 feet (4 m)
Location: 58°N / 135°W

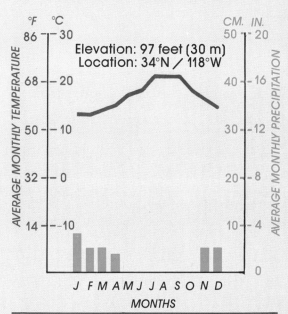

CLIMOGRAPH: LOS ANGELES

Elevation: 97 feet (30 m)
Location: 34°N / 118°W

6/UNIT REVIEW

1. The United States may be divided into seven regions. — *Name the seven regions. Be ready to point out on a map the states in each region.*

2. The major landforms in the United States include mountains and plains. — *What are two major mountain ranges? What is the high, dry, inland plain that stretches from Texas to North Dakota? Name the two plains along the southern and eastern coasts of the United States.*

3. The oceans and other bodies of water are extremely important to the United States. — *What three oceans form parts of the United States border? Name the five Great Lakes. Name at least three of our major rivers. In what ways are waterways important to us?*

4. Climate in the United States depends on many things, including distance from the ocean or other major body of water; latitude; elevation; and location in relation to mountains. — *What effect does elevation have on temperature? Why is the Great Basin so dry? Which would be warmer and wetter, a place near the Atlantic Coast, or a place in the interior at the same latitude?*

5. Agriculture is important in many parts of the United States, including much of the North Central region, California, Texas, and the Southeast. — *What are some of the important agricultural products of each of these areas?*

6. Each region of the United States has important resources. — *Where are our major forests? Major deposits of petroleum, natural gas, and coal? Name some of the important metal resources of the United States.*

7. Manufacturing is important throughout our nation, although some parts of the country have more industry than others. — *Where is the Manufacturing Belt? What are some of our major industries? How do industries depend on one another and upon natural resources?*

8. Population density in the United States varies from near 0 to more than 500 people per square mile (200 per sq km). — *Where do you find the areas of greatest population density? Of least density?*

9. The population of the United States is made up of people of varying ancestry. — *Why, do you think, have some groups been accepted and others not? Read about one group that has suffered discrimination. Make a report on what is being done to improve the situation.*

Canada And Latin America

Royal Canadian
Mounted Policeman

Canadian Lumberjack

Peruvian Indian spinning yarn

Latin American
Oil Worker

22 Canada

History and Government

```
┌─VOCABULARY───────────────────┐
│                               │
│  banks          Commonwealth  │
│  province       official language │
│  descent        Separatist    │
│                               │
└───────────────────────────────┘
```

Indians and Eskimos In Chapter 3 you learned that the first people who came to live in North America came from Asia. They probably came by way of Alaska. Those people were the ancestors of the Indians and Eskimos of Canada. The Eskimos settled in the Arctic area of Canada. They lived by hunting and fishing. The Indians who came to Canada went farther south than the Eskimos. They lived in central and southern Canada.

Of the 24 million people in Canada today, fewer than 20,000 are Eskimos. Some Eskimos still live in northern Canada. Some of them still hunt and fish for a living. Others work in industry, especially mining and transportation. There are about 300,000 Indians in Canada today. Many of them live on reserves, or reservations.

Ask: Where do many Indians in the United States live?

The first Europeans The first Europeans who came to Canada were explorers. They explored the eastern coast of what is now Canada and the United States. They caught fish on the Grand

Banks. **Banks** are a part of the seafloor that rise above the floor around them. Banks do not rise high enough to be a danger to ships, however. The Grand Banks are just off the island of Newfoundland (nü′ fənd lənd). The explorers came ashore to dry their fish and repair their boats. But few of these people made their homes here.

One French explorer, Jacques Cartier, sailed his ship up the St. Lawrence River as far as the present city of Montreal (mon trē ôl′). On his return to France, he described the rich soil in the valley of the St. Lawrence River. This land was very different from the rugged coast of eastern Canada. Here people could settle and till the soil.

French and British settlers French settlers began coming to Canada in the early 1600s. These early settlers built farms and villages in the St. Lawrence Valley. Most of them lived in what is now the **province** of Quebec (kwi bek′). A province is somewhat like a state in the United States. This French colony was called New France.

People also came to Canada from Great Britain. They settled in what is now New Brunswick, Prince Edward Island, and Nova Scotia (nō′ və skō′ shə). They also settled on Newfoundland.

Nova Scotia means "New Scotland."

On the map find landforms that are shared by Canada and the United States. The women in the picture show their Scots heritage in dress and in dance (a sword dance).

The name *Canada* comes from an Iroquois word that means "village, community, or group of huts."

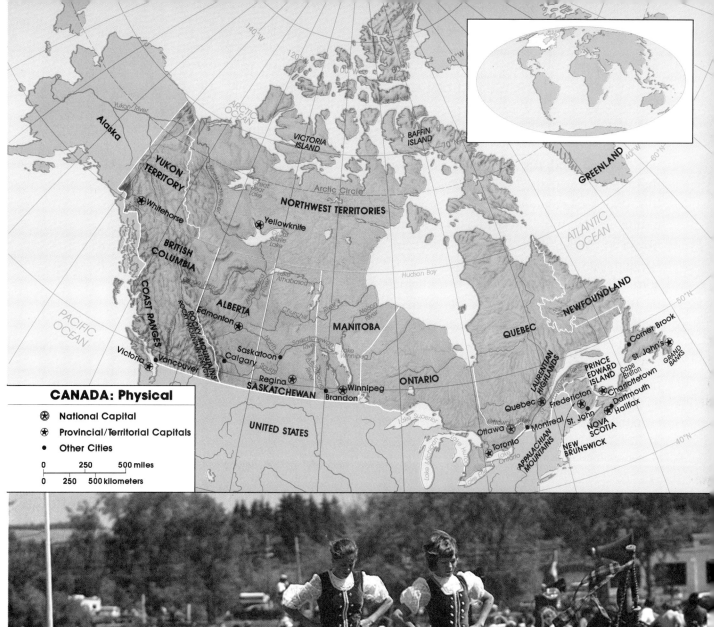

CANADA: Physical

⊛ National Capital

✪ Provincial/Territorial Capitals

• Other Cities

| 0 | 250 | 500 miles |
| 0 | 250 | 500 kilometers |

Alaska

YUKON TERRITORY

Whitehorse

ARCTIC OCEAN

VICTORIA ISLAND

BAFFIN ISLAND

GREENLAND

Arctic Circle

NORTHWEST TERRITORIES

Yellowknife

Great Slave Lake

Great Bear Lake

BRITISH COLUMBIA

COAST RANGES

ROCKY MOUNTAINS
ROCKY MOUNTAIN TRENCH

Victoria

Vancouver

ALBERTA

Edmonton

Calgary

Saskatoon

Lake Athabasca

Churchill River

MANITOBA

Lake Winnipeg

Hudson Bay

ATLANTIC OCEAN

NEWFOUNDLAND

QUEBEC

Corner Brook

St. John's

GRAND BANKS

PACIFIC OCEAN

Regina

SASKATCHEWAN

Brandon

Winnipeg

ONTARIO

LAURENTIAN HIGHLANDS

PRINCE EDWARD ISLAND

Cape Breton

Charlottetown

Quebec

Fredericton

Dartmouth

UNITED STATES

Lake Superior

Lake Michigan

Lake Huron

Ottawa

Toronto

Lake Ontario

Montreal

St. John

NOVA SCOTIA

Halifax

NEW BRUNSWICK

APPALACHIAN MOUNTAINS

Have pupils locate Canada's ten provinces and two territories on the map on p. 423. You may also wish to use the chart on p. 435 at this point.

New France remained a colony of France until 1759. France and Great Britain were at war in the mid 1700s. At the end of the war, France had to turn over New France to Britain. Great Britain then had Canada and the American colonies that later became the United States. When the American colonies gained their independence in the American Revolution, however, Great Britain kept control of Canada. After the American Revolution, some British settlers who had been living in the United States wanted to remain British citizens. Many of these people moved to Canada.

Today, about 45 percent of Canada's people are of British **descent**. Another 26 percent are of French descent. Most of Canada's more than 6 million French Canadians still live in the province of Quebec.

Ask: What other country can you think of that is made up of people from many ethnic groups?

Other peoples Through the 1800s, English, Irish, and Scots people continued to settle in Canada. Beginning in the late 1800s, people began moving to Canada from other European countries. There was a great wave of immigration from that time until World War I began in 1914. The people who came in that period settled mostly in the new industrial cities and on the farmlands of the prairies.

The next great period of immigration came in the 15 years after World War II. Between 1946 and 1961 about 2 million people came to Canada from Europe. These people were German, Dutch, Italian, Polish, and Scandinavian. Their descendants and about 35,000 black people and over 150,000 Japanese, Chinese, and other Asians make up most of the rest of Canada's population today.

Provinces and territories In 1867, Great Britain passed the British North America Act. It created a new government for Canada, which became known as the Dominion (də min' yən) of Canada. Under this act, Canada was divided into provinces. In 1867 there were four provinces—New Brunswick, Nova Scotia, Ontario, and Quebec. By 1905 five more provinces had been added—Manitoba, British Columbia, Prince Edward Island, Alberta, and Saskatchewan (sə skach' ə wən). In 1949 Newfoundland became Canada's tenth province. This province is made up of the island of Newfoundland plus part of northeastern Canada.

In addition to the ten provinces, Canada also has two territories. The Yukon Territory was formed in 1898, the Northwest Territories in 1912. Find each of Canada's provinces and territories on the map on page 434.

Canada never fought a war for independence. Instead, Great Britain slowly allowed Canadians more and more power in running their country. In 1931 Canada became an independent country.

Canada's national holiday, Dominion Day, is celebrated on July 1.

A Commonwealth nation If you have ever visited Canada, you probably noticed many photographs of Queen Elizabeth II of Great Britain. That is because Queen Elizabeth II is also queen of Canada. Canada is a member of the **Commonwealth**. The Commonwealth is made up of independent countries that were once ruled by Great Britain. The countries in the Commonwealth include, among others, Australia, New Zealand, and India. The countries of the Commonwealth share their ideas on many things, such as edu-

Benjamin Franklin, who was postmaster general of the British colonies in North America, helped establish Canada's postal system in 1763.

cation, food production, and health. Government leaders from the Commonwealth countries meet to discuss such matters as trade between countries. The Commonwealth countries work together as much as possible. They share a bond as members of the Commonwealth. The queen is a symbol of that bond.

Canada's government Canada, like the United States, has a federal form of government. The federation is made up of the ten provinces and the two territories. Each province has its own government.

A member of the Royal Canadian Mounted Police stands guard before the Parliament building in Ottawa.

42°25'N/75°42'W

The territories are run mainly by the federal government, although they do have some self-government.

The head of the government of Canada is the prime minister. Canada also has a governor-general who is appointed by Queen Elizabeth II on the recommendation of the prime minister. The lawmaking body of Canada is called Parliament. It has two houses—the Senate and the House of Commons. The people of Canada vote for the members of the House of Commons. The members of the Senate are appointed by the governor-general. The House is the more powerful of the two bodies.

The capital of Canada is Ottawa, in Ontario. Like Washington, D.C., Ottawa is chiefly a government city. Its major purpose is to carry on the business of government.

Ask: What are the official languages of Canada? What is the official language of the United States?

Two languages There are two **official languages** in Canada—English and French. English is the language of most Canadians. In the province of Quebec, where most French Canadians live, French is the chief language. Some French Canadians, called **Separatists**, want the province of Quebec to separate from Canada and become an independent country. In 1980 the people of Quebec voted against doing that.

Ask: Would you have voted to make the province of Quebec an independent country? Why?

CHECKUP

1. How did Canada come to be part of Great Britain?
2. What is the Commonwealth?
3. What is the head of the government of Canada called?
4. What are the two official languages of Canada?

425

The Land and Climate

VOCABULARY

maritime	pitchblende
conifer	tungsten
lock	

Canada's national motto is "From sea to sea."

A vast country   Canada is the second largest country in the world. Only the Soviet Union is larger in area. The country of Canada covers most of the northern half of North America. Canada, like the United States, spreads "from sea to shining sea." The Atlantic Ocean is on the east; the Pacific Ocean is on the west. Now look at the map on page 427. Trace the boundary between Canada and the United States.

There are many ways in which Canada and the United States are alike. They are almost the same size, although Canada is a little larger. You can see the same kinds of gas stations. You can buy United States newspapers and even pay for them with United States money. And most people speak English. But there is at least one important difference. Canada is much less densely populated. There are large areas of the country in which no people live. Let us see why this is so.

Canada is a little larger in area than the United States, but has only one tenth as many people.

Climate and vegetation   Large parts of Canada are too cold for most people. In many places the growing season is too short for crops. Often the land is too mountainous or rocky for farming.

Generally speaking, the farther north one travels in the United States, the colder the climate becomes. Canada is even farther north than the United States, excluding Alaska. In most of Canada, the winters are long and cold. January temperatures average below 0°F (−18°C) in more than two thirds of Canada. In the islands in the Arctic Ocean, January temperatures average below −40°F (−40°C).

Northern Canada has short, cool summers. These summers are not warm enough or long enough for crops to be grown. In the far northern areas the summer may last only a few weeks. In southern Canada the summers are warmer and longer. Crops can be raised in southern Canada. Most of Canada's farmland is in the south.

Much of Canada is covered by forests. These forests are one of Canada's most important resources. To the north of the forest areas is the tundra. Trees do not grow in the tundra because of the shortage of rain and the long, cold winters. Some plants, however, do grow here.

Ask: What is a physical region?

The Appalachian region   In Chapter 14 you learned that it is helpful to divide a large country into regions in order to study it. A physical region is one in which the land features are like one another. Canada has five such regions. They are (1) the Appalachian region, (2) the St. Lawrence Valley and Lakes Peninsula, (3) the Canadian Shield, (4) the plains region, and (5) the western mountain region. Find these five regions on the map.

The Appalachian Mountains are found in both the United States and Canada. In the United States these mountains stretch from Alabama to Maine. In Canada the Appalachian region is made up of the three **Maritime** Provinces of New Brunswick, Nova Scotia, and Prince Edward Island plus the island of Newfoundland. *Maritime* means "having to do with

426

Ask: Why is it that there are large areas of Canada in which no people live?

Have pupils locate Canada's five physical regions on the map on p. 427.

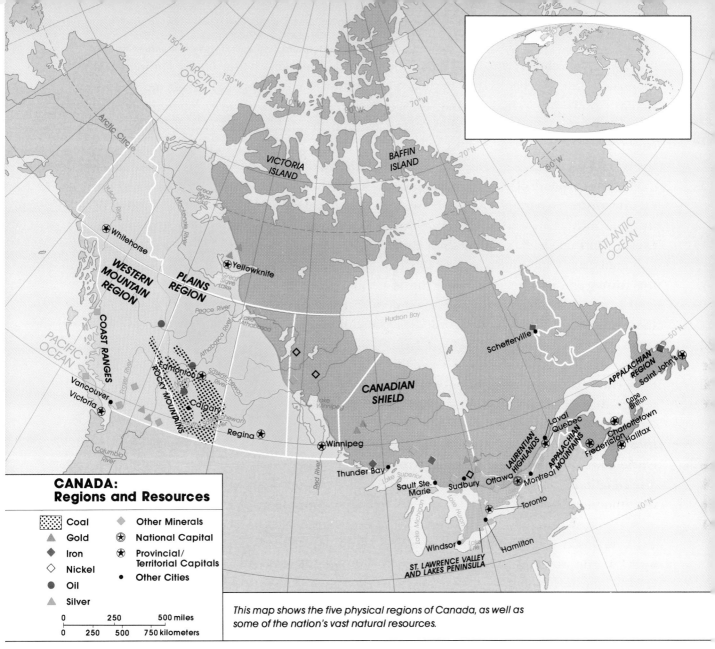

CANADA:
Regions and Resources

Coal

Gold

Iron

Nickel

Oil

Silver

Other Minerals

National Capital

Provincial/
Territorial Capitals

Other Cities

| 0 | 250 | 500 miles |
| 0 | 250 500 | 750 kilometers |

This map shows the five physical regions of Canada, as well as some of the nation's vast natural resources.

Have pupils identify which resources are found in each of Canada's provinces.

the sea." The region also includes a small part of Quebec southeast of the St. Lawrence River valley. As you can see on the map, this region borders on the Atlantic Ocean.

Most of the Appalachian region is made up of low hills. The hills have a mixture of hardwood trees and **conifers**. The summers here are cool. The winters are long, and there is a great deal of snow.

Most people in the Maritime Provinces live close to the coast, where the soil is better than in the hills. Farming is the chief occupation. Farmers raise dairy cattle and beef cattle. They grow potatoes, fruits, cereals, and feed crops.

There are no large cities in the Maritime Provinces. The chief city is Halifax, Nova Scotia. In winter the St. Lawrence River is frozen. Ships cannot

Canada has one the longest coastlines of any country in the world. Including island coasts, it has over 150,000 miles (240,000 km) of coastline.

reach such other Canadian cities as Montreal and Quebec. The harbor at Halifax, however, remains free of ice throughout the winter. Large ships carry cargo and passengers to Halifax through the winter months.

The large island of Newfoundland lies off the eastern coast of Canada between the Gulf of St. Lawrence and the Atlantic Ocean. On the island, summers are short and cool. The winters are severe. During the winter the only way to reach the island is by air. Ice blocks the seas around the island.

Forests cover much of Newfoundland. The land is rocky, and there is little soil to till. The riches of Newfoundland are found off its eastern coast on the Grand Banks. The Grand Banks is one of the most important fishing grounds in the world. Each year thousands of tons of fish are caught on the Grand Banks and off the other coasts of the Maritimes.

Ask: What is Canada's smallest land region? Why is this region so important?

St. Lawrence Valley and Lakes Peninsula   The next region you are going to study is made up of the valley of the St. Lawrence River and the peninsula that borders on three of the Great Lakes—Lake Ontario, Lake Huron, and Lake Erie. This is the smallest land region in Canada. Yet it is one of the most important regions in the country. In fact, about one half of Canada's people live here. Canada's two largest cities—Montreal and Toronto—are in this region. Ottawa, the capital of Canada, is also in this region.

This area is made up of lowlands. The relief is gentle. It goes from flatland to rolling hills. Farming is important here even though the winters are long and hard. The soil of the Lakes Peninsula is fertile. Large crops of fruits and vegetables are grown here. Farming is also important in the St. Lawrence Valley.

This region is also important because of the St. Lawrence Seaway. This water route between the Atlantic Ocean and the Great Lakes was built by a joint effort of the United States and Canada. The Seaway was opened in 1959. The Great Lakes, the St. Lawrence River, and several canals are all part of the Seaway.

The Atlantic Ocean is at sea level. Lake Superior is 600 feet (180 m) above sea level. To make up for the changing water level, the Seaway has a series of **locks**. A lock raises or lowers ships from one level to another.

Ask: How were the many lakes in the Canadian Shield formed?

The Canadian Shield   The largest region of Canada is the Canadian Shield. It covers about half the country. The Shield is shaped like a horseshoe. It curves around Hudson Bay and includes the Arctic Islands north of Hudson Bay.

Low hills cover much of the Canadian Shield. Toward the east and southeast the land rises to the Laurentian (lô ren′ chən) Highlands, which border the St. Lawrence River. The land becomes even more mountainous along the rugged coast in the east.

The Shield is made up of very old and very hard rocks. Many thousands of years ago, during the Ice Age, great sheets of ice covered this region. They scraped away the soil. Then they dug out hollows in the land. The ice has long since gone. The hollows are now filled with water. Lakes and swamps have formed in these hollows. New soil forms very slowly. So there

Forecasters use information from Arctic weather stations to help predict the weather for Canada, the United States, and Europe.

HOW A CANAL LOCK WORKS

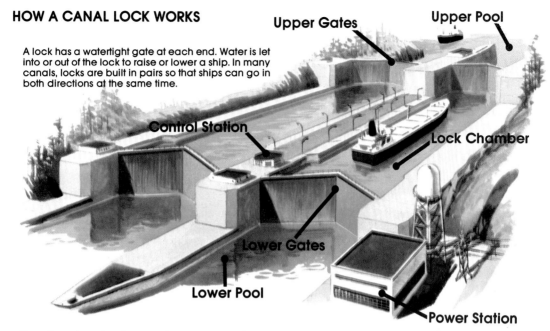

A lock has a watertight gate at each end. Water is let into or out of the lock to raise or lower a ship. In many canals, locks are built in pairs so that ships can go in both directions at the same time.

Upper Gates

Upper Pool

Control Station

Lock Chamber

Lower Gates

Lower Pool

Power Station

From *The World Book Encyclopedia.* © 1980. World Book–Childcraft International, Inc.

Passing from a Lower Level to a Higher Level

Water has been let out of the lock chamber, bringing it to the level of the lower pool. The lower gates have been opened to let the ship in the lock.

The lower gates are closed and the lock is filling with water from the upper pool.

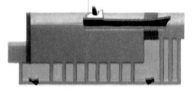

The water in the lock has reached the level of the upper pool. The upper gates are open to let the ship pass into the upper pool and continue upstream.

Passing from a Higher Level to a Lower Level

The lock chamber has been filled to the level of the upper pool. The upper gates are open and the ship is passing into the lock.

The upper gates are closed and water is draining from the lock into the lower pool.

The water in the lock has reached the level of the lower pool. The lower gates are open to let the ship pass into the lower pool and continue downstream.

is little soil over much of the Shield. As a result, crops cannot be grown. Few people live in the Canadian Shield because of its poor soil and cold climate.

Great forests spread across the southern half of the Canadian Shield. Lumbering has developed in places that can be reached by land or by water. Logs are floated down the many rivers in the Shield. The logging industry and industries related to it are very important to Canada. Canada exports a great deal of lumber. It also makes wood pulp and paper. Paper companies in the United

Ask: Why do few people live in the Canadian Shield?

Copper is smelted at this plant near Sudbury. Copper is just one of the Shield's many mineral resources.
46°30'N/81°0'W

Ask: Why is the Canadian Shield one of Canada's most important regions?

States and in many European countries buy large amounts of Canadian pulp. The forests also shelter fur-bearing animals. Some animals are trapped for their furs.

To the north of the forests is the tundra. This part of the Canadian Shield stretches to the Arctic Ocean. It spreads over the thousands of islands in the Canadian Arctic. Few people live in the tundra. During the summer, Eskimo people live near the coast where they can catch fish. But in the winter the sea is frozen. Many Eskimos then find shelter within the forests to the south.

The Shield has large deposits of copper, lead, and zinc. The world's largest deposit of nickel is near Sudbury, Ontario. Nickel is used to make certain kinds of steel. About one third of the world's nickel comes from Sudbury. **Pitchblende** is found in the northern part of the Shield. Uranium comes from pitchblende. Large amounts of gold are also mined in the Shield.

Iron is one of the most important resources found in the Shield. This ore has long been mined along the southwestern edge of the Shield. Large amounts of iron have been discovered in the interior of the Shield. Find Schefferville on the map on page 427. Ore mined at Schefferville is brought by railroad to ports on the St. Lawrence River. From these ports ships carry the ore to ironworks on the Great Lakes. There are major ironworks at Hamilton in Canada and at Buffalo, Cleveland, Detroit, and Chicago in the United States.

There are a great many lakes in the Shield. The lakes are the source of many rivers. Within the Shield and at its edge, these rivers break into waterfalls and rapids. These waterfalls and rapids are used to produce hydroelectric power for many of Canada's industries.

Ask: Do you think hydroelectric power is safer than nuclear power? Why?

The plains The Canadian plains are part of the same landform as the Great Plains in the United States. Canada's plains stretch from the border with the United States in the south to the Arctic Ocean in the north. In the south, where the Canadian plains meet those of North Dakota and Montana, the plains are several hundred miles wide. They narrow in the north.

The plains are not level. They rise slowly toward the Rocky Mountains on the west. The plains are also broken by hilly ridges that form a series of giant steps.

The northern plains are very much like the Canadian Shield. There are forests and then, farther north, tundra. Some of the forests have been cleared for farming. The climate in the northern plains is wetter than that of the southern plains.

Nickel is added to steel to make it stronger and to help prevent corrosion.

The plains of southern Canada are the nation's breadbasket. Here combines are harvesting wheat.

The combine cuts and threshes the wheat in one operation. Threshing separates the kernels of the wheat from the stalk.

The southern part of the plains is covered with prairies. Toward the east, these grasslands have been plowed, and wheat, corn, and feedstuffs are grown. Canada is one of the world's leading producers of wheat. Most of that wheat is grown on the prairies. In the western part of the prairies the climate is drier. Fewer crops can be grown, but ranching is important.

The plains region is a very important part of Canada. Much of the country's farmland is in the plains. In addition, there are large deposits of oil, coal, and gas. Many people have moved to the plains. Manufacturing has developed in the cities. A number of Canada's largest cities are in the plains. They include Winnipeg, Calgary, and Edmonton. These cities are shown on the map on page 434.

Western mountain region The Appalachian Mountains and the plains are found in both Canada and the United States. Two western mountain ranges also stretch north and south through Canada and the United States. These two ranges

The Japanese Current warms the coast of British Columbia. The coast of Newfoundland, in the same latitude, is icebound in winter because of the cold Labrador Current.

In Canada the Rocky Mountains and the Coast Ranges are separated by a narrow valley called the Rocky Mountain Trench. Have pupils locate in on the map on p. 427
are the Rocky Mountains and the Coast Ranges. Together they form Canada's fifth region, the western mountain region.

The Coast Ranges rise steeply from the Pacific Ocean. There is little flat land between the ocean and the mountains. Warm ocean currents make the climate along the coast milder than that of any other part of Canada. Moist winds from the ocean blow onto the mountains. This results in a very heavy rainfall. Many areas of Canada's west coast have more than 100 inches (250 cm) of rain in a year. Hundreds of rivers also rush down to the sea from the mountains.

The Canadian Rockies are among the highest mountains in the world. They rise steeply from the plains. Transportation across the mountains is difficult. However, there are a number of passes. Some roads and railroads have been built through these passes.

The Canadian Rockies are noted for their beauty. Shown here is Lake Moraine in Banff National Park in Alberta.

49°16'N/123°07'W

Lumbering is important in several parts of Canada. This sawmill is on the Fraser River near Vancouver.

Ask: In what ways are the Canadian Shield and the western mountain region alike?

The western mountains are rich in resources. There are deposits of coal, copper, gold, silver, iron, zinc, and **tungsten**. Mining is a major industry in this region.

The rivers of the western mountains are used to produce hydroelectric power. Much of this power is used to refine the ores mined in the mountains. Three of the major rivers of this region are the Fraser, the Columbia, and the Yukon. The Fraser flows from the Canadian Rockies to the Pacific Ocean. The Columbia flows from the mountains southward into the United States. The Yukon River flows into Alaska from northwestern Canada.

The western mountains are important for their resources. Because of their rivers, lakes, and beauty, the mountains also attract thousands of visitors every year.

CHECKUP

1. Name the five regions of Canada and tell why each is important.
2. Why is the St. Lawrence Seaway important?
3. Name two major mountain ranges of western Canada.

Tungsten, which has the highest melting point of any metal, is used to make filaments for electric lights. It also makes steel stronger and more elastic.

Canada has a population density of 6 people per square mile (2 per sq km). About 76 percent of Canada's people live in cities.

Cities

Ask: What is an economic activity?

Cities   Look at the map on page 434. You can see that most of Canada's cities are in Ontario, Quebec, and the southern parts of Manitoba, Saskatchewan, Alberta, and British Columbia.

Most cities in Canada began as trading centers for the areas around them. They are still important trading centers. Today they are also important centers for manufacturing. Manufacturing is Canada's most important **economic activity**. (Mining and agriculture are the second and third most important activities.) An economic activity is one that has to do with the production or selling of goods or services.

The table shows Canada's ten largest cities and their populations. Find each of these cities on the map on page 434.

CANADA'S TEN LARGEST CITIES
(Figures are rounded)

City and Province	Population
Montreal, Quebec	1,081,000
Toronto, Ontario	611,000
Winnipeg, Manitoba	592,000
Edmonton, Alberta	478,000
Calgary, Alberta	470,000
Vancouver, British Columbia	461,000
Hamilton, Ontario	410,000
Ottawa (Ontario)	304,000
Mississauga, Ontario	250,000
Laval, Quebec	246,000

CHECKUP

1. What are Canada's three most important economic activities?
2. Name five of Canada's ten largest cities.

Canada has one city, Montreal, with more than 1 million people. The United States has six: New York, Chicago, Los Angeles, Philadelphia, Houston, and Detroit.

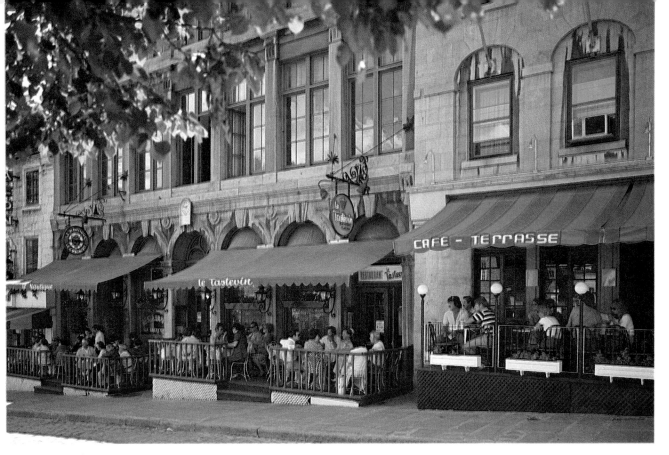

46°44′N/90°25′W

(Top) The names of these sidewalk cafes in Montreal reveal the French heritage of many Canadians. (Left) Toronto, the capital of Ontario, has a very modern city hall. (Right) Vancouver's protected harbor and its location on the Fraser River have helped the city become one of Canada's largest cities.

43°39′N/79°23′W

49°16′N/123°07′W

433

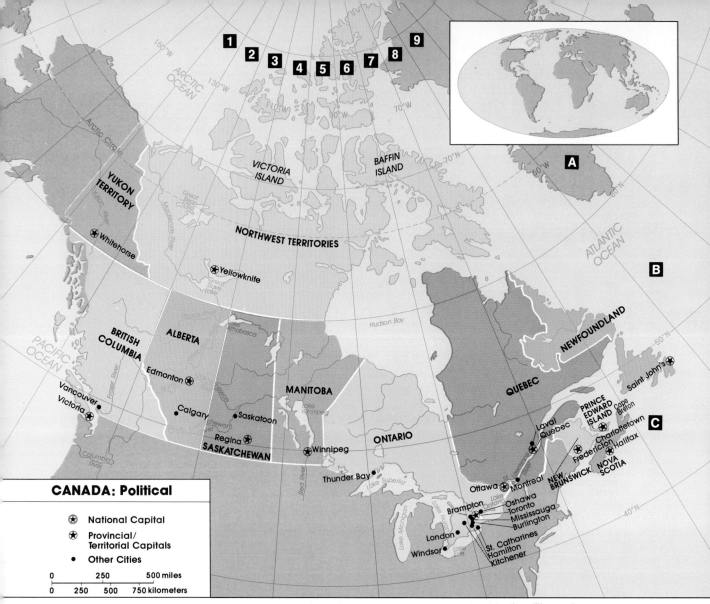

CANADA: Political

⊛ National Capital

⊛ Provincial/
   Territorial Capitals

• Other Cities

0		250		500 miles
0	250	500	750 kilometers	

All cities with 100,000 or more people are indicated on the map and in this list. The only cities of less than 100,000 people that are shown are provincial and territorial capitals.

Cities with less than 100,000

Charlottetown, P.E.I. C-8
Fredericton, N.B. C-8
St. John's, Newf. C-9
Victoria, B.C. C-2
Whitehorse, Y.T. A-1
Yellowknife, N.W.T. A-3

Cities with 100,000–499,000

Brampton, Ont. C-7
Burlington, Ont. C-7
Calgary, Alta. B-3
Edmonton, Alta. B-3

Halifax, N.S. C-8
Hamilton, Ont. C-7
Kitchener, Ont. C-6
Laval, Que. C-7
London, Ont. C-6
Mississauga, Ont. C-7
Oshawa, Ont. C-7
Ottawa C-7
Quebec, Que. C-7
Regina, Sask. B-4
St. Catharines, Ont. C-7
Saskatoon, Sask. B-4

Thunder Bay, Ont. C-6
Vancouver, B.C. C-2
Windsor, Ont. C-6

Cities with 500,000–999,000

Toronto, Ont. C-7
Winnipeg, Man. B-5

City with 1,000,000 or more

Montreal, Que. C-7

*Most of Canada's cities and most of the people are in the southern part of the nation.
Which city has 1 million or more people? Which capitals have less than 100,000 people?*

Montreal has more than 1 million people. Six capitals have less than 100,000 people: Charlottetown, Fredericton, St. John's, Victoria, Whitehorse, and Yellowknife.

CANADA

COUNTRY	TOTAL AREA	POPULATION AND POPULATION DENSITY	CAPITAL CITY AND POPULATION	LANGUAGES	OTHER FACTS
Canada	3,852,000 sq mi (9,976,000 sq km)	23,940,600 6 per sq mi (2 per sq km)	Ottawa 304,000	English*, French*	The United States and Canada together guard North America through the North American Air Defense Command.

PROVINCES	TOTAL AREA	POPULATION AND POPULATION DENSITY	CAPITAL CITY AND POPULATION	LANGUAGE(S)	OTHER FACTS
Alberta	255,285 sq mi (661,185 sq km)	2,086,400 8 per sq mi (3 per sq km)	Edmonton 478,066	English	Columbia Ice Field, consisting of huge glaciers formed during the Ice Age, is found in Alberta.
British Columbia	366,255 sq mi (948,596 sq km)	2,642,400 7 per sq mi (3 per sq km)	Victoria 70,000	English	Gold found near the Fraser River caused rapid settlement of interior sections of B.C. from 1850 to 1860.
Manitoba	251,000 sq mi (650,087 sq km)	1,028,700 4 per sq mi (2 per sq km)	Winnipeg 592,482	English, French, German, Ukrainian	The International Peace Garden found in Manitoba honors friendship between the United States and Canada.
New Brunswick	28,354 sq mi (73,437 sq km)	707,600 25 per sq mi (10 per sq km)	Fredericton 45,248	English, French	The waters of Reversing Falls are pushed back up the falls by the force of water at high tide.
Newfoundland	156,185 sq mi (404,517 sq km)	580,900 4 per sq mi (1 per sq km)	St. John's 88,000	English, French	In 1901 Marconi received the first transatlantic wireless signal at Cabot Tower on Signal Hill, St. John's.
Nova Scotia	21,425 sq mi (55,490 sq km)	853,100 40 per sq mi (15 per sq km)	Halifax 118,000	English, French	*Nova Scotia* (Latin for New Scotland) is almost completely surrounded by water.
Ontario	412,582 sq mi (1,068,582 sq km)	8,576,000 21 per sq mi (8 per sq km)	Toronto 611,171	English, French, German, Italian	Ontario was a refuge for southern slaves in the 1850's. It has about ¼ of the world's nickel ore.
Prince Edward Island	2,184 sq mi (5,657 sq km)	124,500 57 per sq mi (22 per sq km)	Charlottetown 17,063	English, French	The smallest province, P.E.I. is known for its long white and red sandy beaches and its fertile red soil.
Quebec	594,860 sq mi (1,540,680 sq km)	6,306,500 11 per sq mi (4 per sq km)	Quebec City 177,082	French, English	Chubb Crater, one of the world's largest meteor craters, is located in northwestern Quebec.
Saskatchewan	251,700 sq mi (651,900 sq km)	970,100 4 per sq mi (1 per sq km)	Regina 150,610	English, French, German	This province, called Canada's Breadbasket, is the greatest wheat-growing region in North America.

TERRITORIES	TOTAL AREA	POPULATION AND POPULATION DENSITY	CAPITAL CITY AND POPULATION	LANGUAGE(S)	OTHER FACTS
Northwest Territories	1,304,903 sq mi (3,379,683 sq km)	43,000 0.03 per sq mi (0.01 per sq km)	Yellowknife 8,256	English	This region covers almost 1/3 of Canada. The source of the Mackenzie River, Canada's longest river, is here.
Yukon Territory	207,076 sq mi (536,324 sq km)	21,400 0.1 per sq mi (0.04 per sq km)	Whitehorse 13,311	English	Mount Logan, in the St. Elias Mountains, rises 19,520 ft (5,950 m) and is the highest point in Canada.

*Official language(s)

KEY FACTS

1. The earliest Canadians were Indians and Eskimos.

2. Canada has two official languages—English and French.

3. Canada is larger than the United States, but has about one-tenth as many people.

4. Canada has many natural resources.

5. The main economic activities of Canada are manufacturing, mining, and agriculture.

VOCABULARY QUIZ

Write the letter of the term next to the number of its description. Write on a separate sheet of paper.

a. St. Lawrence Seaway   **f.** province

b. tundra   **g.** federal

c. hydroelectric power   **h.** Ice Age

d. Grand Banks   **i.** pitchblende

e. prime minister   **j.** plains

b **1.** A treeless region in northern Canada

i **2.** A source of uranium

c **3.** Waterpower

a **4.** Links the Atlantic Ocean and the Great Lakes

d **5.** A rich fishing ground

j **6.** An important farming area

g **7.** Canada's form of government

f **8.** A political division similar to a state

h **9.** A time when sheets of ice spread outward from the Arctic

e **10.** The head of Canada's government

REVIEW QUESTIONS

1. From which two groups of European settlers are most Canadians descended?

2. Where do most French Canadians live?

3. How is Canada's government organized?

4. What is the Commonwealth?

5. Name the five physical regions of Canada.

6. In which two regions do most of Canada's people live?

7. Why is the Canadian Shield an important region even though few people live there?

ACTIVITIES

1. In an encyclopedia or other reference book, find out about these four explorers: John Cabot, Henry Hudson, Jacques Cartier, and Samuel de Champlain. Write a report telling the following: (**a**) What country did each explorer work for? (**b**) What area of Canada did he explore? (**c**) When did he explore this area?

2. Prepare a report on the Separatist movement in Canada. Your report should tell why some French Canadians think the province of Quebec should become an independent country. You can find this information in an encyclopedia.

3. Prepare an oral report on people who explored the Arctic. This information can be found in an encyclopedia.

4. Make a chart that lists Canada's prime ministers and governors-general from 1867 to the present. Tell the years in which each person served. The information for this chart can be found in an encyclopedia.

5. Imagine that you have moved from the island of Newfoundland to the prairies of southern Saskatchewan. Write a letter to a friend describing the differences you find.

6. Plan a summer vacation for someone who will visit Canada for 2 weeks. Plan the trip so the visitor will learn about the great variety in Canada's land and vegetation.

22/SKILLS DEVELOPMENT

READING A MAP: CONTOURS

To measure your height, you would measure the distance from the bottom of your feet to the top of your head. The bottom of your feet would be your *base*. The earth's hills and mountains are also measured from base to top. The base for all hills and mountains is sea level. Find sea level (0 feet) on the drawing of the mountain (**A**). The lines on the drawing are contour lines.

Contour lines are a good way to show elevation. All points along one contour line are the same distance above sea level. Find the 500-foot contour line on the drawing (**A**). Now find it on the contour map of the mountain (**B**). What is the highest contour line shown on the drawing? What is the highest contour line shown on the map?   7,000 feet; 7,000 feet

Sometimes color is added between contour lines (**C**). What does the yellow stand for? 1,000–2,000 feet What is the elevation of the orange part? Can 2,000–4,000 you find the same part on the drawing (**A**)? feet

Elevation can be shown in this same way on maps of any part of the world. Map D shows part of Canada. What is the elevation of the land near the mouth of the Fraser River? What is the elevation of the highest places in this part of British Columbia? Where are the lowest places found?   0–500 feet, or 0–150 m; Over 7,000 feet, or 2,000 m; Along the coast.

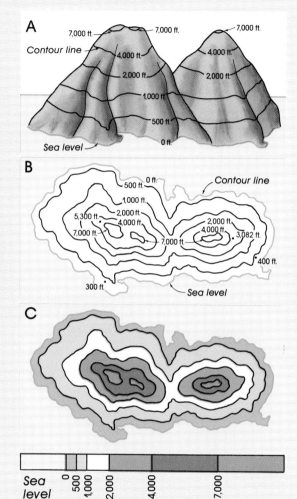

Feet above sea level

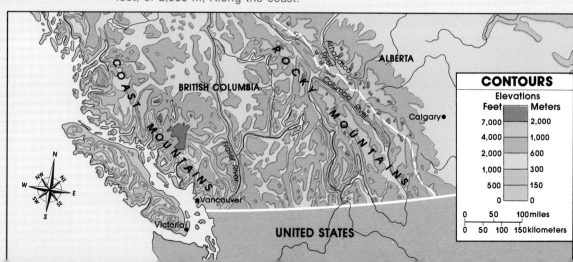

Latin America Yesterday and Today

┌─VOCABULARY─────────────────┐
developed   mestizo
  country
developing
  country
└────────────────────────────┘

From exploration to colonization   In Chapter 3 you learned what the terms *Latin America, Middle America,* and *Central America* mean. You also learned about such Indian peoples as the Mayas, the Aztecs, and the Incas. These Indian peoples lived in Latin America before any Europeans came to the Americas. The first Europeans to come to Latin America were explorers. You learned about some of them in Chapter 4.

After the explorers came, several European countries set up colonies in Latin America. Most of Latin America was colonized by two countries—Spain and Portugal. Portugal set up the colony of Brazil in South America. Spain made settlements in most of the rest of South America and in Middle America. Great Britain, France, and the Netherlands also set up colonies in Latin America. They colonized many of the islands in the Caribbean Sea. They also had colonies in the northern part of South America— British Guiana, French Guiana, and Dutch

Point out the pronunciation guide on p. 458.
Guiana. (If you need help pronouncing Latin American place names, see page 458.) British Guiana later became the country of Guyana. Dutch Guiana became Surinam. French Guiana is still a colony of France.

Ask: Which two nations colonized most of Latin America?

Spanish and Portuguese colonies Beginning about 1500, people from Spain and Portugal began settling in Latin America. Some of them planned to stay only a short time. They hoped to become rich quickly. So they looked for such riches as gold and silver. Others set up plantations. On these large farms, crops such as sugarcane, cotton, or fruit were grown.

The Europeans made slaves of many Indians. These Indians did much of the hard work in the mines and on the plantations. Also, black people were brought from Africa as slaves.

Independence   Most of Latin America remained under Spanish or Portuguese rule for about 300 years. Between 1791 and 1824, however, most of the Spanish colonies in Latin America fought wars to gain their independence. Brazil gained its independence from Portugal in 1822 without having to fight a war.

Though Spain lost most of its colonies in Latin America, it kept two important

Mexico's two mountain ranges are the Sierra Madre Oriental and the Sierra Madre Occidental. Oriental means eastern; occidental means western.
What are Mexico's two mountain ranges? Find the meaning of oriental and occidental in a dictionary. What mountain range runs almost the entire length of South America?

The Andes run almost the entire length of South America.

120°W   110°W   100°W   90°W   80°W   70°W   60°W   50°W   40°W   30°W

UNITED STATES

Hamilton ● BERMUDA (U.K.)

30°N

SIERRA MADRE OCCIDENTAL
SIERRA MADRE ORIENTAL

Gulf of Mexico

ATLANTIC OCEAN

Rio Grande

MEXICO
Guadalajara ●

Mexico City ✪
Citlaltépetl ▲
18,700 ft (5700 m)

Yucatán Peninsula

Nassau ●
BAHAMAS

GREATER ANTILLES

Tropic of Cancer

20°N

Havana ✪
CUBA

DOMINICAN REPUBLIC

Belmopan ●
GUATEMALA
BELIZE (U.K.)
HONDURAS
Guatemala ✪
San Salvador ✪
EL SALVADOR   NICARAGUA
Managua ✪
San José ✪
COSTA RICA
PANAMA ✪ Panama

JAMAICA
Kingston ●
Port-au-Prince ✪
HAITI
Santo Domingo ✪
PUERTO RICO (U.S.)
San Juan ✪
ANTIGUA (U.K.)
DOMINICA
ST. LUCIA
ST. VINCENT AND THE GRENADINES
BARBADOS
GRENADA
TRINIDAD AND TOBAGO

Caribbean Sea

ARUBA (NETH.)   CURAÇAO (NETH.)
LESSER ANTILLES

10°N

Barranquilla ●
Maracaibo ●
Caracas ✪
Lake Maracaibo

GUYANA
Georgetown ✪
Paramaribo ✪
SURINAME   Cayenne ✪
FRENCH GUIANA

PACIFIC OCEAN

Medellín ●
LLANOS
Bogotá ✪
Tolima ▲
18,425 ft (5616 m)

Orinoco River

VENEZUELA

GUIANA HIGHLANDS

Magdalena River

COLOMBIA

Equator   0°

Quito ✪
Cotopaxi ▲ 19,347 ft (5897 m)
ECUADOR
Guayaquil ●
Chimborazo ▲
20,561 ft (6168 m)

Amazon River

ANDES

PERU

Huascarán ▲
22,205 ft (6768 m)

BRAZIL

10°S

Callao ●
Lima ✪

Lake Titicaca

BOLIVIA
La Paz ✪
Santa Cruz ●
Sucre ✪
Lake Poopó

BRAZILIAN HIGHLANDS

São Francisco River

Brasília ●

20°S

Tropic of Capricorn

Atacama Desert

CHACO
PARAGUAY
Asunción ✪

Paraguay River
Pilcomayo River
Salado River

São Paulo ●

CHILE

ARGENTINA
Córdoba ●
Aconcagua ▲
22,834 ft (6960 m)
Valparaíso ●
Santiago ✪

URUGUAY
Buenos Aires ✪
Montevideo ✪

30°S

Paraná River
Uruguay River
Río de la Plata

PAMPAS

Colorado River

ANDES

40°S

PATAGONIA

LATIN AMERICA: Physical

✪ Capitals
● Other Cities

0   500   1,000 miles
0   500   1,000   1,500 kilometers

50°S

TIERRA DEL FUEGO
FALKLAND IS. (U.K.)

60°S

LATIN AMERICA: Political

⊛ Capitals

● Other Cities

1	**2**	**3**	**4**	**5**	**6**	**7**	**8**	**9**

A
B
C
D
E
F
G
H
I

120°W 110°W 100°W 90°W 80°W 70°W 60°W 50°W 40°W 30°W

UNITED STATES

Mexicali
Tijuana
Ciudad Juárez
Chihuahua
SIERRA MADRE OCCIDENTAL
SIERRA MADRE ORIENTAL
Monterrey
Mazatlán
MEXICO
León
Guadalajara
Mexico City
Puebla
Cuernavaca
Acapulco
Yucatán Peninsula
BELIZE (U.K.)
Belmopan
GUATEMALA
Guatemala
HONDURAS
Tegucigalpa
San Salvador
EL SALVADOR
NICARAGUA
Managua
San José
COSTA RICA
PANAMA
Panama

Gulf of Mexico
ATLANTIC OCEAN
Tropic of Cancer
Hamilton ● BERMUDA (U.K.)
Nassau
BAHAMAS
Havana
CUBA
GREATER ANTILLES
Guantánamo
Santiago de Cuba
HAITI
Port-au-Prince
JAMAICA
Kingston
DOMINICAN REPUBLIC
Santo Domingo
PUERTO RICO (U.S.)
VIRGIN ISLANDS (U.S.)
VIRGIN ISLANDS (U.K.)
San Juan
Road Town
St. Thomas
Ponce
Basseterre
St. Johns
ANTIGUA (U.K.)
Plymouth
Basse-Terre
ST. CHRISTOPHER-NEVIS (U.K.)
MONTSERRAT (U.K.)
GUADELOUPE (FR.)
Roseau
Fort-de-France
DOMINICA
MARTINIQUE (FR.)
ST. LUCIA
Castries
BARBADOS
Bridgetown
Kingstown
ST. VINCENT AND THE GRENADINES
St. George's
GRENADA
LESSER ANTILLES
TRINIDAD AND TOBAGO
Port of Spain
NETHERLANDS ANTILLES
Willemstad
CURAÇAO (NETH.)
ARUBA (NETH.)
Caribbean Sea

PACIFIC OCEAN
Barranquilla
Maracaibo
Caracas
Lake Maracaibo
Medellín
Bogotá
Cali
COLOMBIA
VENEZUELA
Orinoco River
Cauca River
Magdalena River
GUYANA
Georgetown
Paramaribo
SURINAME
Cayenne
FRENCH GUIANA
GUIANA HIGHLANDS

Equator

Quito
ECUADOR
Guayaquil
PERU
ANDES
Manaus
Amazon River
BRAZIL
Belém
Fortaleza
Recife

Callao
Lima
Lake Titicaca
BOLIVIA
La Paz
Lake Poopó
Santa Cruz
Sucre
BRAZILIAN HIGHLANDS
São Francisco River
Brasília
Salvador
Belo Horizonte

Tropic of Capricorn
Atacama Desert
CHACO
PARAGUAY
Asunción
Salado River
Nova Iguaçu
São Paulo
Santos
Curitiba
Rio de Janeiro
Paraná River
CHILE
ANDES
ARGENTINA
Córdoba
Salto
Rosario
URUGUAY
Porto Alegre
Valparaíso
Santiago
PAMPAS
San Justo
Buenos Aires
Montevideo
Colorado River
Río de la Plata

Equator 0°
10°S
20°S
30°S
40°S
50°S
60°S

PATAGONIA

TIERRA DEL FUEGO
FALKLAND IS. (U.K.)

0 500 1,000 miles
0 500 1,000 1,500 kilometers

440

The chart below lists all Latin American cities with a population of 500,000 or more as well as all capital cities. Selected cities with a population of less than 500,000 are also listed.

Cities with less than 100,000

Basse-Terre, Guad.	....	C-6
Basseterre, St. Chr. I.	.....	C-6
Belmopan, Bel.	....	C-4
Bridgetown, Barb.	....	C-7
Castries, St. L.	....	C-6
Cayenne, Fr. G.	....	D-7
Fort-de-France, Mart.	.....	C-6
Hamilton, Ber.	....	A-6
Kingstown, St. V.	....	C-6
Plymouth, Monts.	....	C-6
Port of Spain, T.T.	....	D-6
Road Town, Br. V.I.	....	C-6
Roseau, Dom.	....	D-5
St. George's, Gren.	......	C-6
St. John's, Ant.	....	C-6
St. Thomas, V.I.	....	C-6
Salto, Ura.	....	H-7
Sucre, Bol.	....	F-6
Willemstad, Neth. Ant.	....	C-6

Cities with 100,000–499,000

Acapulco, Mex.	....	C-3
Asunción, Para.	....	G-7

Brasília, Brazil	....	F-8
Callao, Peru	....	F-5
Chihuahua, Mex.	....	B-2
Cuernavaca, Mex.	....	C-3
Georgetown, Guy.	....	D-7
Guantánamo, Cuba	......	C-5
Kingston, Jam.	....	C-5
Managua, Nic.	....	C-4
Manaus, Brazil	....	E-6
Mazatlán, Mex.	....	B-2
Mexicali, Mex.	....	A-1
Nassau, Bah.	....	B-5
Panama, Pan.	....	D-5
Paramaribo, Sur.	....	D-7
Ponce, P.R.	....	C-6
Port-au-Prince, Haiti	......	C-5
San José, C.R.	....	D-4
San Juan, P.R.	....	C-6
San Salvador, El. Sal.	....	C-4
Santa Cruz, Bol.	....	F-6
Santiago, Dom. Rep.	.....	C-5
Santiago de Cuba, Cuba	....	C-5
Santos, Brazil	....	G-8

Tegucigalpa, Hond.	....	C-4
Tijuana, Mex.	....	A-1
Valparaíso, Chile	....	H-5

Cities with 500,000–999,000

Barranquilla, Col.	....	C-5
Belém, Brazil	....	E-8
Cali, Col.	....	D-5
Ciudad Juárez	....	A-2
Córdoba, Arg.	....	H-6
Curitiba, Brazil	....	G-8
Fortaleza, Brazil	....	E-9
Guatemala, Guat.	....	C-3
Guayaquil, Ecuad.	....	E-5
La Paz, Bol.	....	F-6
León, Mex.	....	B-2
Maracaibo, Ven.	....	C-5
Medellín, Col.	....	D-5
Nova Iguaçu, Brazil	.....	G-8
Pôrto Alegre, Brazil	......	G-7
Puebla, Mex.	....	C-3
Quito, Ecuad.	....	E-5

Rosario, Arg.	....	H-6
San Justo, Arg.	....	H-7
Santo Domingo, Dom. Rep.	....	C-6

Cities with 1,000,000 or more

Belo Horizonte, Brazil	.....	F-8
Bogotá, Col.	....	D-5
Buenos Aires, Arg.	....	H-7
Caracas, Ven.	....	C-6
Guadalajara, Mex.	....	B-2
Havana, Cuba	....	B-4
Lima, Peru	....	F-5
Mexico City, Mex.	....	C-3
Monterrey, Mex.	....	B-2
Montevideo, Ura.	....	H-7
Recife, Brazil	....	E-9
Rio de Janeiro, Brazil	....	G-8
Salvador, Brazil	....	F-9
Santiago, Chile	....	H-5
São Paulo, Brazil	....	G-8

Which nation has five cities with 1 million or more people? How many cities of 1 million or more people are capital cities?

Brazil has 5 cities with over 1 million people. Eight capital cities have over 1 million people: Bogotá, Buenos Aires, Caracas, Havana, Lima, Mexico City, and Santiago.

islands in the Caribbean Sea—Puerto Rico and Cuba—until 1898. Then after the Spanish-American War, Cuba became independent and Puerto Rico was given to the United States.

Before the Spanish colonies became independent, there were boundaries between the colonies. These boundaries ran across mountains and through forests. It was not certain just where the boundaries were. After the colonies became independent, each new country wanted to have as much land as it could. Since the boundaries were not certain, this caused problems. Often different countries claimed the same land. These claims led to wars. Some of these boundary problems remain today.

Latin America today One way to divide the world is into "**developed countries**" and "**developing countries.**" Developed countries are highly industrialized.

Developing countries are becoming industrialized. Developed countries are richer, developing countries are poorer. Most of Latin America is a developing area.

There are parts of Latin America, however, that are highly developed. There are large cities that are much like cities in the United States, Canada, and Europe. There are industries. There is great wealth. In developed countries, many people share in the wealth of the country. That is not true in much of Latin America. Although there are people with wealth, there are a great many more people who are very poor. They have poor food, clothing, and shelter. Many of them have not had much education.

In much of Latin America, workers produce a great deal less than workers in developed countries. There are fewer goods from the factories. There are smaller harvests from the land. In many

Ask: What are two differences between developed countries and developing countries?

The per capita gross national product of Latin America is $1,380. It is $9,700 in the United States and $9,170 in Canada.

areas, there is subsistence farming. That means a farm family grows enough food to meet its own needs, but there is little, if any, left to sell. Workers in Latin America work as hard as workers in developed countries. But in much of Latin America, workers have fewer machines and tools than workers in developed countries. The tools they have are simpler than the tools of workers in developed countries.

People of Latin America   There are more than 350 million people living in Latin America. About three fifths of those people live in urban areas. The other two fifths live in rural areas.

Most Latin Americans are of European descent. However, more than 20 million people of Latin America are Indians. They make up a large part of the population of Bolivia, Ecuador, and Peru. Some of the people of Latin America are **mestizos** (mes tē′ zōz). That means they have a mixed heritage—white and Indian. Mestizos make up a large part of the population in Chile, Colombia, El Salvador, Honduras, Mexico, Nicaragua, Paraguay, and Venezuela. Many of the people in Barbados, Haiti, and Jamaica are black. Cuba, the Dominican Republic, Panama, and Trinidad and Tobago have many people with mixed black and white ancestry.

CHECKUP

1. Name three Indian peoples who lived in Latin America before any Europeans came to the Americas.
2. Which two European countries colonized most of Latin America?
3. Define *subsistence farming* and *mestizo*.

Mexico

```
┌─ VOCABULARY ──────────────────────┐
│  henequen                         │
│                                   │
└───────────────────────────────────┘
```

The land   Mexico is the Latin American country that is nearest to the United States. Look at the map on page 440. You can see that Mexico is south of the United States. The boundary between the two countries is 1,934 miles (3,112 km) long. It begins in the west at the Pacific Ocean. It then runs across the mountains and desert until it reaches the Rio Grande. This river forms the rest of the boundary.

Mexico is the largest country of Middle America. From the border of the United States, it stretches 1,600 miles (2,600 km) to the border of Guatemala. Look again at the map on page 440. You can see that Mexico narrows toward the south. Then it juts to the north at the Yucatán Peninsula.

Most of Mexico is a high plateau. This plateau is bordered on the east and west by mountain ranges. To the east is the Sierra Madre Oriental. To the west is the Sierra Madre Occidental. These two ranges come together in the rugged mountains that lie to the south of Mexico City. Southeast of these mountains the land drops suddenly to the lowlands of the Yucatán.

Climate   There are few countries in the world with as much variety in climate as Mexico has. The mountains are cool most of the year. The plateau is very hot in summer, and warm in winter. It is also very dry. The lowlands in the south, including the Yucatán Peninsula, are hot and wet. Part of the lowlands is covered with dense forest. The rainfall varies from one part of the country to another.

Ask: Why is only one eighth of Mexico's land used for farming?

Agriculture   Only about one eighth of the land in Mexico is used for farming. The rest of the land is too mountainous or too dry. Much of the land that is farmed is of poor quality. Also, large parts of Mexico have very little rainfall. The best cropland is in the southern part of the plateau in central Mexico. Cattle are grazed in the northern part of the plateau because it is too dry for crops.

Corn is the most widely grown crop. More farmland is used for corn than for any other crop. Corn is the basic food of the Mexican people. Beans, wheat, cotton, sugarcane, and coffee are also major crops. Rice and **henequen** (hen' ə kin), which is used to make rope, are also grown. Fruits and vegetables are important crops, too. In fact, many of the fruits and vegetables eaten in the United States come from Mexico.

The growing of crops to be sold is called commercial agriculture. This kind of farming has increased in Mexico in recent years. But much of Mexico's agriculture is still subsistence farming. Most farms are small family farms.

Ask: What is the difference between subsistence farming and commercial agriculture?

Manufacturing and cities   Most of Mexico's factories are in or near Mexico City. Motor vehicles are made in Mexico City. There are also smelters to process silver, lead, and zinc ores. Mexico City also has chemical and engineering industries, as well as steel plants. Mexico City is also Mexico's capital and largest city. It has nearly 9 million people.

Mexico City is the largest city in the Western Hemisphere. It is built on the site of the Aztec city of Tenochtitlán.

There are other important cities in Mexico. Guadalajara, Mexico's second largest city, has many industries. Puebla is an important center for making textiles. Motor vehicles are made in Monterrey and Mazatlán. Monterrey and Monclova have blast furnaces and steelworks.

Mineral resources   The map on page 444 shows natural resources in Middle America and the Caribbean. Mexico is rich in mineral resources. It is one of the world's leading producers of silver. It is a major source of lead, zinc, and sulphur. It

More people live in Mexico City than in any other city in the Western Hemisphere.

19°N/99°W

443

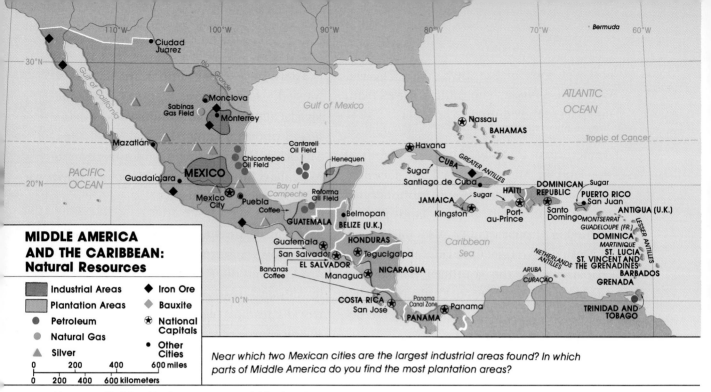

MIDDLE AMERICA
AND THE CARIBBEAN:
Natural Resources

- ■ Industrial Areas
- ■ Plantation Areas
- ● Petroleum
- ● Natural Gas
- ▲ Silver
- ◆ Iron Ore
- ◆ Bauxite
- ✪ National Capitals
- ● Other Cities

0   200   400   600 miles
0   200   400   600 kilometers

Near which two Mexican cities are the largest industrial areas found? In which parts of Middle America do you find the most plantation areas?

Have pupils identify the resources of Mexico that are indicated on the map above.

produces copper and gold as well. Most of these ores are taken from mines in the Sierra Madre and the plateau of northern Mexico.

Mexico's major resource, though, may be oil. For a long time, wells in the lowlands near the Gulf of Mexico have produced oil. In recent years, large amounts of oil have been discovered in the southern part of the country. Today Mexico produces only a small amount of the world's oil. It is possible, however, that with its large reserves, <u>Mexico may become one of the world's leading producers of oil.</u>

Ask: In recent years, large reserves of what resource have been found in Mexico?

CHECKUP

1. How does Mexico compare in size with the other countries of Middle America?
2. About how much of Mexico's land is used for farming?
3. What is Mexico's capital?
4. Name five of Mexico's important mineral resources.

Central America and the Caribbean

┌─ VOCABULARY ─────────────────┐
│ **tropical rain**   **cacao** │
│ **forest**   │
└──────────────────────────────┘

Central America   The area between Mexico and South America is Central America. Mountains cover most of Central America. Between the mountains and the sea are narrow coastal plains. Central America is a hot region with a heavy rainfall.

Much of Central America is covered with **tropical rain forests**. These are forests that grow in hot, wet lands. Trees and vines grow thickly in such forests. The rain forests of Central America were once a major source of mahogany and other kinds of hardwood lumber. Now large parts of the forest have been cleared to make room for plantations. Such crops as bananas, coconuts, coffee, and **cacao**

Refer to the material on Mexico, Central America, and the Caribbean in the charts on pp. 455–456.

Cacao is used to make chocolate. Indians once used cacao seeds for money.

(kə kā′ ō) are grown on these plantations. Many of these crops are exported to the United States.

There are six countries and one colony in Central America. The countries are Guatemala, El Salvador, Honduras, Nicaragua, Costa Rica, and Panama. The British colony, Belize, is also in this area.

Central America is also the site of the Panama Canal, which joins the Atlantic and Pacific oceans and divides the Republic of Panama into two parts. In 1903, the United States gained the rights to the narrow strip of land through which the canal was to be built. This strip was called the Canal Zone. The canal, which took ten years to build, was completed in 1914. In 1978, the United States Senate voted to return the Canal Zone to the Republic of

Panama but keep the rights to the actual canal. On December 31, 1999, we will turn over the rights to the canal as well.

Ask: How were the Caribbean islands formed?

The Caribbean   Have you ever wondered what the floor of an ocean looks like? The floors of the Atlantic and Pacific oceans are vast, wavy plains. From the floor, mountain ranges rise to great heights. Most of these ranges, of course, are covered by water. Some, however, are high enough to reach the surface of the oceans. Their peaks form islands. There are hundreds of such islands in the Caribbean Sea.

The islands of the Caribbean form an arc. It begins near the Yucatán Peninsula in Mexico and reaches almost to South America. The three main groups of islands in this region are the Greater Antilles, the Lesser Antilles, and the Bahamas. The Greater Antilles is made up of the islands of Cuba, Jamaica, Puerto Rico, and Hispaniola. Hispaniola is divided into two countries—Haiti and the Dominican Republic. The Lesser Antilles and the Bahamas are both made up of a number of smaller islands.

Most of the Caribbean islands are mountainous. The climate is warm in winter and hot and wet in summer. Sugarcane is the most important crop in these islands. Coconuts, bananas, and other tropical fruits are also grown. Tourism is important to many of the larger islands.

Cuba   Cuba is the largest island in the Caribbean. Its population is over 10 million. Cuba is a long, narrow island. Much of it is low and flat with fertile soil. The

It takes six electric mules to get a large ship through the canal. Four are used to pull the ship; two for braking.

Electric "mules" help an Egyptian ship move through the Panama Canal. It takes 15 hours for a ship to travel the entire length of the canal.

There is a United States naval base on Guantánamo Bay in Cuba.

most important crop of Cuba is sugarcane. Much of the sugar from this crop is exported. Tobacco, pineapples, citrus fruits, and coffee are also grown for export. A range of hills in the southeast contains deposits of iron, manganese, and copper.

Cuba was once a colony of Spain. Its capital, Havana, was founded by the Spaniards soon after they came to the Americas. Havana is Cuba's largest city. It has a population of more than 1 million. Havana has industries that process the farm products of the island. The city also handles most of Cuba's export trade.

Ask: What is Cuba's most important crop?

Jamaica   The island of Jamaica was once a British colony. It is now an independent country. Jamaica has about 2 million people.

Jamaica is a mountainous island. Sugarcane and bananas are the chief crops. Tobacco, coffee, cacao, spices, and citrus fruits are also grown. Jamaica is also an important source of bauxite. Much of this bauxite is shipped to the United States to be refined into aluminum.

The chief city of Jamaica is Kingston, on the south coast of the island. Most of Jamaica's trade passes through this city.

Haiti and the Dominican Republic
Since Haiti and the Dominican Republic share the island of Hispaniola, their geographic features are very much alike. In other ways the two countries are very different. Haiti's culture is French, although the people are of African descent. The culture of the Dominican Republic is Spanish. The country has a mixed Spanish and African population. Haiti is more densely populated than the Dominican Republic. Both countries produce sugar and coffee for export.

Port-au-Prince is the capital and chief city of Haiti. Santo Domingo is the capital and chief city of the Dominican Republic.

Puerto Rico   Christopher Columbus landed in Puerto Rico in 1493. He claimed the island for Spain. Spain controlled Puerto Rico until 1898. In that year Spain turned the island over to the United States.

The people of Puerto Rico are United States citizens, but Puerto Rico is self-governing. The United States gives aid and protection to the island. The Puerto Rican government, however, has control in all local matters. Some Puerto Ricans would like the island to become one of the states of the United States. Other Puerto Ricans want the island to be an independent country.

More than half of Puerto Rico is farmland. Most of the farms are small. Sugarcane is the chief crop. Coffee, tobacco, bananas, and other fruit are also grown. Puerto Rico has more than 2,600 factories. They turn out chemicals, food, and metal products, as well as clothing. Tourism is also an important industry in Puerto Rico.

San Juan is Puerto Rico's capital and largest city.

Ask: Do you think Puerto Rico should remain as it is, become a state, or become an independent country?

CHECKUP

1. When will the Panama Canal be returned to the Republic of Panama?
2. Name the six countries and the one colony that make up Central America.
3. What is the largest island in the Caribbean?

446 Ask: How are the cultures of Haiti and the Dominican Republic different?

At left center is Huascarán (wäs kə rän'), the highest peak in the Peruvian Andes.

South America

The land   South of Middle America and the Caribbean lies the huge continent of South America. Much of South America's coastline is straight and even. There are few bays and openings into the interior of the continent. For that reason it was difficult for early explorers to go very far inland from the coast. Even today little is known about some parts of the interior.

The chief physical features of South America are easy to understand. A range of giant mountains, the Andes, runs along the west coast. There is a narrow plain between the Pacific Ocean and the Andes.

To the east of the mountains there are the wide plains and plateaus that make up most of South America.

Let us look more closely at these physical features. The Andes run along the west coast of South America for almost 5,000 miles (8,000 km). The Andes are among the highest mountains in the world. There are several peaks in this range that are higher than any in the United States. Very few roads and railroads cross the Andes.

To the east of the Andes there are two high plateaus. The largest and highest of the two is the plateau known as the Brazilian Highlands. The Brazilian Highlands are on the east side of the continent. The other plateau is known as the Guiana Highlands. The Guiana Highlands are in the northern part of the continent.

On the map on p. 439 point out these physical features: the Andes, the coastal plain between the Andes and the Pacific, the two plateaus (Brazilian Highlands and Guiana Highlands).

The plains of South America have been built by the great rivers of the continent. The plain of the Orinoco River lies between the Guiana Highlands and the northern Andes. It is called the **Llanos**. *Llanos* is Spanish for "plains."

Between the Guiana Highlands and the Brazilian Highlands is the plain of the Amazon River. This vast plain is very flat and stretches for thousands of miles. It is known as the Amazon Basin.

Between the Brazilian Highlands and the southern Andes lie the plains of the Paraná and Paraguay rivers. This area is called the **Chaco**. Farther south, in Uruguay and Argentina, the plains are called the **Pampas**. The plains become narrower toward the southern end of the continent. That area is called **Patagonia**.

Climate and vegetation   The Amazon River flows very close to the equator. The Amazon Basin is always hot and humid. The heavy rainfall helps trees to grow. Most of the basin is covered with thick rain forest. It is very difficult to travel in this area. There are no railroads and very few roads. Most travel is by boat. Few people live in the forests of the Amazon Basin.

If you were to travel either north or south, away from the Amazon, you would find that the climate and vegetation change. It is still hot for most of the year. But the rainfall is less. It comes mostly in the summers. The winters are fairly dry.

When the climate changes so does the vegetation. Rain forests grow only where it is wet throughout the year, as in the Amazon Basin. Where the rainfall comes in one or two seasons, the vegetation is more open. It is made up of grassland with scattered trees. This kind of vegetation is called **savanna**. The Guiana Highlands and the Brazilian Highlands are covered mostly with savanna.

The Chaco has both savanna and forests. There are large swampy areas, too. The summers are hot and wet, and the winters warm and dry.

The Pampas are much drier than the Amazon lowlands. Summers are hot, but winters are cool. This leads to another change in vegetation. There are almost no trees. The land is a grassland like the Great Plains in the United States.

Patagonia, south of the Pampas, has a cool dry climate. Summers are cool, and winters cold. Some parts of Patagonia are as dry as a desert.

West of the Andes, along the narrow coastal plain, there are a number of climates. Near the equator it is hot and humid throughout the year. Rain forests grow on this part of the plain. North and south of the equator, there are savannas. The southern savanna is small. It soon gives way to desert. The plains along the coast of southern Peru and northern Chile are desert. Rainfall is less than 10 inches (25 cm) a year. On much of the land there is little or no plant life. South of the desert, in central Chile, there is a small area with hot, dry summers and warm, rainy winters.

As you travel from central Chile to southern Chile, the climate becomes cooler and wetter. Southern Chile is cool in summer and cold in winter.

CHECKUP

1. Describe South America's main landforms.
2. Describe the climates of South America.

448   *Patagonia* comes from a Spanish word meaning "big feet." The navigator Ferdinand Magellan gave this name to the Indians of this region because they wrapped their feet in furs.

Have pupils locate the 12 South American countries, French Guiana, and the Falkland Islands on the map on p. 440.

Brazil's rubber industry declined as a result of the growth of rubber plantations in Southeast Asia, especially in Malaysia, and the development of synthetic rubber.

The Countries of South America

┌─**VOCABULARY**─────────────────┐
nitrate   altiplano
landlocked
└────────────────────────────────┘

Twelve countries   South America has 12 countries. There are also two other political units that are not independent countries. French Guiana is controlled by France. The Falkland Islands, off the coast of southern Argentina, are a colony of the United Kingdom. These islands are also claimed by Argentina. Find French Guiana, the Falkland Islands, and the 12 countries of South America on the map on page 440.

Brazil   Brazil is the largest country of Latin America. It is only a little smaller in area than the United States. But it has about half as many people. The people of Brazil speak Portuguese.

Brazil has two giant regions: the Amazon Basin in the north and the Brazilian Highlands in the south. At one time the Amazon Basin was the world's main source of rubber. As a result a number of towns grew up along the rivers in this area. The city of Manaus grew as a result of the rubber industry. Now Brazil produces less than one percent of the world's rubber. When the rubber industry died out, so did many of the towns and cities.

Brazil has very large reserves of iron ore. Most of the iron that is mined here is exported to other countries. Brazil also has rich deposits of manganese and other important minerals.

Brazil is becoming an important manufacturing country. The meat-packing industry is very large. The textile industry is growing. Clothing, paper, hardware, chemicals, paints, and rubber are also manufactured.

The growth of manufacturing has led to the rapid growth of cities in Brazil. There are over 30 cities with populations of over 100,000. Rio de Janeiro is a great port and a leading industrial center of Brazil. It has

Refer pupils to the resource map and the charts on pp. 454–456.

Rio de Janeiro, on the coast of Brazil, has one of the world's largest harbors.   23°S/43°W

over 4 million people. São Paulo, Brazil's largest city, has 6 million people. São Paulo is an industrial and commercial center. There are many ports and industrial cities along the Atlantic coast. They include Pôrto Alegre, Salvador, Recife, and Fortaleza. Belém and Manaus are important river ports.

Until 1960 Rio de Janeiro was the capital of Brazil. Then the capital was changed to Brasília. You can see on the map on page 440 that most of Brazil's cities are along the coast. That is where most of Brazil's people live. Brasília was built farther inland. The government did this to encourage people to move to the vast interior of the country.

Brazil is the world's largest coffee producer. People began growing coffee about 100 years ago in the hills behind Rio de Janeiro. Today Brazil produces about one third of the world's coffee. The port of Santos handles most of the coffee export. Sugarcane, cotton, tobacco, cacao, and bananas are also important crops. The raising of cattle, horses, sheep, goats, and hogs is becoming more important. Brazil is trying to develop agriculture in the interior of the country. Most of the interior is in the Amazon Basin. Until now most of Brazil's farms and ranches have been within 500 miles (800 km) of the Atlantic coast. What do you know about the land and climate of the Amazon Basin that tells you why this is so?

Ask: Why was the capital of Brazil changed from Rio de Janeiro to Brasília?

Guyana, Surinam, and French Guiana
Guyana, Surinam, and French Guiana are on the northern coast, between Venezuela and Brazil. They all have damp, forested lowlands. Sugarcane is the major crop in all three lands. Rice, cacao, and coconuts are also grown. Guyana and Surinam are both sources of bauxite.

Georgetown is the chief city and port of Guyana. Paramaribo is Surinam's capital and largest city. The capital and chief port of French Guiana is Cayenne.

Ask: What is the center of Venezuela's oil industry?

Venezuela   Venezuela has three regions. In the northern part of the country there is the Andes region. South of the Andes is the Llanos in the valley of the Orinoco River. The third region is made up of part of the Guiana Highlands.

Mining is Venezuela's most important industry. Venezuela is one of the world's leading producers of oil. Most of the oil produced in South America comes from Venezuela. Lake Maracaibo, in northern Venezuela, is the center of the oil industry. Find Lake Maracaibo on the resources map on page 454. Venezuela also has some of the world's largest iron deposits. Iron is mined in the Guiana Highlands.

Two of Venezuela's major crops, coffee and sugarcane, are grown in the valleys of the Andes. Cattle are raised in the lowlands of the Orinoco River.

Caracas is Venezuela's capital and chief city. This large modern city is in the mountains of northern Venezuela.

Paraguay   Paraguay is a small inland country on the northern part of the Chaco. It is made up of savanna-covered plains and low plateaus that rise gently westward toward the Andes. Paraguay is mainly an agricultural country. Livestock is raised on the savanna for meat, wool, and hides. Crops include corn, sugarcane, and tobacco.

Most of the people live in the eastern part of the country, between the Paraguay and the Paraná rivers. Paraguay's only large city is its capital, Asunción.

Uruguay   Uruguay lies farther south than Paraguay, and is bordered on the east by the Atlantic Ocean. Uruguay has very good grazing land. Cattle and sheep are raised on the cool, dry grasslands. Uruguay's chief exports are animal products—meats, hides, and wool.

Uruguay has one large city, Montevideo. It is the country's capital and chief port. Montevideo is on the Río de la Plata.

Río de la Plata is a very wide, very short river formed by the Paraná and Uruguay rivers.

Argentina   Argentina lies between the Andes and the Atlantic Ocean. Most of Argentina is a vast, grass-covered plain. In northern Argentina is the Chaco. Because of the swamps and forests, much of the Chaco is difficult to cultivate. But agriculture is developing slowly in the Chaco.

South of the Chaco are the Pampas. Most of Argentina's crops are grown in the rich soil of the Pampas. Wheat, corn, flax, sunflower seeds, and feed crops are the chief agricultural products. Cattle raising is also important on the Pampas.

South of the Pampas is Patagonia. This cold, dry area has very few people and very little agriculture. Some sheep are raised for their wool. There are deposits of coal, iron, and oil in Patagonia.

Agriculture is the chief occupation of the people of Argentina. However, people do other kinds of work, too. Argentina's three main industries are meat packing, food processing, and textiles. The major manufacturing cities are the capital, Buenos Aires, and Córdoba and Rosario.

Ask: What are Argentina's three main industries?

Locate the Atacama Desert on the map on p. 454.

Chile   Chile is a strangely shaped country. It lies between the Pacific Ocean and the Andes. Chile is nearly 2,400 miles (3,900 km) long. Yet it is only about 200 miles (320 km) at its widest point.

In northern Chile is the Atacama Desert. This is one of the driest areas on earth. Yet it is very important because of its mineral resources. Chile is one of the world's leading copper producers. Much of its copper comes from this area. Also, **nitrate** salts have formed over the surface of the Atacama Desert. Nitrates are used to make fertilizers. Chile exports large amounts of nitrates.

In central Chile, wheat is the chief food crop. Corn, fruits, vegetables, and feed crops are also grown. Cattle raising is also important.

Most of Chile's people live in this region. Chile's two largest cities are in cen-

This copper mine in Chile is the world's largest.

451

tral Chile. Santiago, the capital, has over 3 million people. It is the largest city on the west coast of South America. Valparaíso is Chile's largest seaport.

In southern Chile, the land is rugged and mountainous. There are no cities in this cold, wet land. Some sheep are raised and there is also some lumbering.

Have pupils locate Bolivia, Peru, Ecuador, and Colombia on the map on p. 454.

The Andean countries   There are four more countries in South America— Bolivia, Peru, Ecuador, and Colombia. All four lie partly in the Andes and partly in the great forested plain that is drained by the Amazon River. There is little good farmland in any of these countries. Transportation is poorly developed. It is very difficult to reach the plains in the Amazon Basin from the coast of the Pacific Ocean. These four countries all have small populations. Many of the people in these four countries are Indians or mestizos.

Ask: What does landlocked mean? Which two countries of South America are landlocked?

Bolivia   Bolivia has no coastline. Like Paraguay, it is a **landlocked** country. Most of Bolivia lies on a very high plateau called the **altiplano**. The altiplano is surrounded by mountains. To the east there are forested lowlands.

Most of Bolivia's people live on the altiplano. The major cities are there. The capital of Bolivia is Sucre, but most of the government offices are in La Paz. La Paz is Bolivia's largest city.

The people of Bolivia use their crops themselves. Crops are not exported. Mining is Bolivia's major industry. Bolivia is one of the world's leading producers of tin. Silver, lead, and zinc are also mined. Bolivia does export some of these metals.

Peru   Peru borders on the Pacific Ocean. The country has three regions, the narrow coastal plain on the west, then the high mountains, and the Amazon plains on the east.

Peru was the home of the Inca Indians. Most of the descendants of the Incas, like many other South American Indians, live in the mountains. The descendants of the Spanish settlers live mostly on the lower western slopes of the mountains and along the coast. Most of Peru's cities are on the coastal plain. Lima, the capital, has about 3 million people.

Coffee, sugarcane, and tropical fruits are grown along the coastal plain. In the mountains some grain crops and potatoes are grown. In recent years the waters off the coast of Peru have become one of the great fishing areas of the world.

There are rich mineral resources in the Andes. Copper, silver, gold, lead, zinc, and iron are mined in the mountains.

Ecuador   The equator crosses the country of Ecuador. That is how the country gets its name, for the Spanish word for *equator* is *ecuador*. Quito, the capital, is almost on the equator. However, because Quito is 9,350 feet (2,850 m) above sea level, it has one of the most pleasant climates in the world.

Many of Ecuador's people grow corn, wheat, and potatoes for their own needs. The chief cash crops are bananas, cacao, and coffee.

The mountains of Ecuador are said to contain great mineral wealth. A little gold and silver have been mined, but mining is not a major industry in the country. Ecuador does produce some oil, however.

452   La Paz, Bolivia, is more than twice as high above sea level as Denver (the "mile-high city"), which is the highest major city in the United States.

Workers in Santo Domingo pack coffee beans. Coffee is one of Ecuador's major crops.

18°28'N/69°54'W

Colombia   Colombia is bordered by the Pacific Ocean and the Caribbean Sea. It stretches across the Andes to the plains of the Orinoco and Amazon rivers. Colombia is made up of three regions. There are hot, wet coastal lowlands in the northwest and west. The second region is in the northern Andes. Most of Colombia's people live in the valleys of the Andes. Bogotá, Colombia's capital and largest city, is in this region. The third region of Colombia is the Llanos. This plain makes up about three fifths of the country, but has only a small part of the people.

Commercial farming is important only in the second region—the Andes. Coffee, cotton, cacao, sugarcane, and bananas are Colombia's important cash crops. Some oil and small amounts of iron and coal are produced. There is a small but growing steel industry.

The future   South America is rich in resources. It has great amounts of many different minerals. It has rich farmland and huge forests. Making use of these resources will take time. There has been quite a lot of development of resources in South America in the past 25 years. The governments and people of South America are working to continue that development.

CHECKUP

1. List the 12 countries of South America. Which is the largest?
2. Which country produces the most oil?
3. Name the capitals of Argentina, Brazil, and Venezuela.

On the map on p. 454 point out the Strait of Magellan and Tierra del Fuego near the southern tip of the continent. Ferdinand Magellan, who sailed through the strait in 1520, named the archipelago Tierra del Fuego ("land of fire") because he saw so many Indian campfires burning on top of high cliffs.

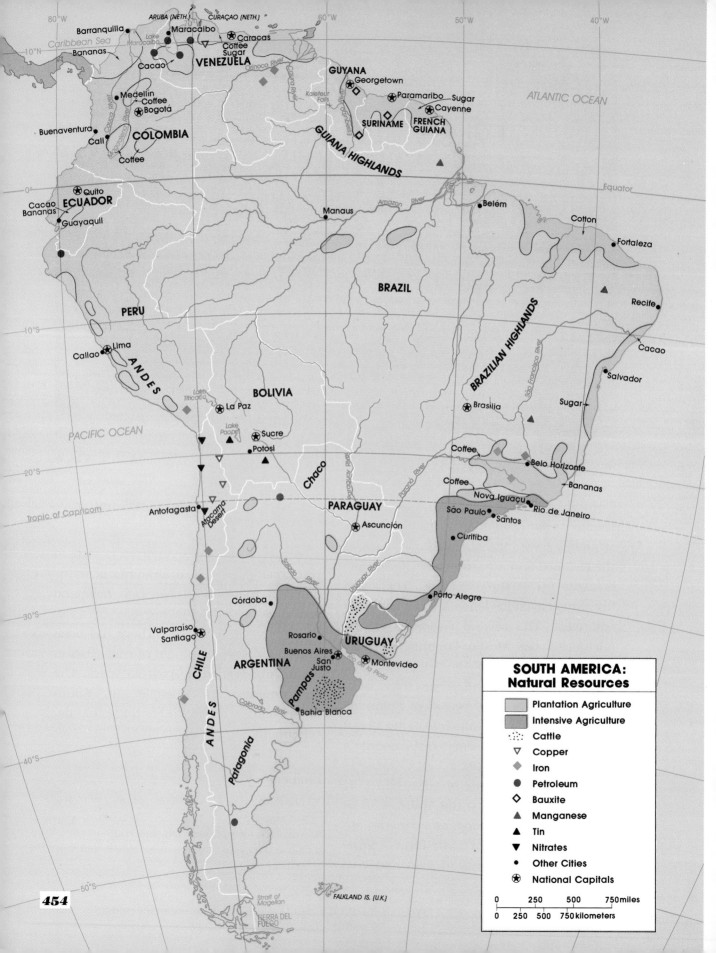

SOUTH AMERICA:
Natural Resources

Caribbean Sea
ARUBA (NETH.) CURAÇAO (NETH.)
Barranquilla
Maracaibo
Lake Maracaibo
Caracas
Coffee
Sugar
Bananas
Cacao
VENEZUELA
Medellin
Coffee
Bogotá
Buenaventura
Cali
COLOMBIA
Coffee
Cauca River
Orinoco River
Caura River
Kaieteur Falls
GUYANA
Georgetown
Paramaribo
SURINAME
FRENCH GUIANA
Cayenne
Sugar
GUIANA HIGHLANDS
ATLANTIC OCEAN
Equator
Quito
Cacao
Bananas
ECUADOR
Guayaquil
Manaus
Amazon River
Belém
Cotton
Fortaleza
BRAZIL
PERU
Callao
Lima
ANDES
Recife
Cacao
Salvador
São Francisco River
BRAZILIAN HIGHLANDS
BOLIVIA
Lake Titicaca
La Paz
Lake Poopó
Sucre
Potosí
PACIFIC OCEAN
Brasília
Sugar
Chaco
Coffee
Belo Horizonte
Bananas
Coffee
Nova Iguaçu
São Paulo
Rio de Janeiro
Santos
Tropic of Capricorn
Antofagasta
Atacama Desert
PARAGUAY
Ascunción
Paraná River
Uruguay River
Curitiba
Pôrto Alegre
Salado River
Córdoba
Rosario
Buenos Aires
San Justo
Pampas
Bahia Blanca
Uruguay River
Montevideo
URUGUAY
Colorado River
ARGENTINA
CHILE
Valparaíso
Santiago
ANDES
Patagonia
Tropic of Capricorn
Rio de la Plata
Strait of Magellan
FALKLAND IS. (U.K.)
TIERRA DEL FUEGO

SOUTH AMERICA:
Natural Resources

Plantation Agriculture
Intensive Agriculture
Cattle
Copper
Iron
Petroleum
Bauxite
Manganese
Tin
Nitrates
Other Cities
National Capitals

0   250   500   750 miles
0 250 500 750 kilometers

**MEXICO, CENTRAL AMERICA,
AND THE CARIBBEAN**

COUNTRY	TOTAL AREA	POPULATION AND POPULATION DENSITY	CAPITAL CITY AND POPULATION	LANGUAGE(S)	OTHER FACTS
Mexico	761,607 sq mi (1,972,552 sq km)	68,200,000 90 per sq mi (35 per sq km)	Mexico City 8,988,200	Spanish*, Maya, Mixtec, Nahuatl, Otomi, Tarascan, Zapotec	Mexico is a world leader in silver production. Mexico City is on the site of the ancient Aztec capital.
Bahamas	5,380 sq mi (13,935 sq km)	200,000 37 per sq mi (14 per sq km)	Nassau 125,500	English*	Christopher Columbus first sighted land at San Salvador in the Bahamas on October 12, 1492.
Barbados	166 sq mi (431 sq km)	300,000 1,807 per sq mi (696 per sq km)	Bridgetown 8,900	English*	Barbados is an island country that lies about 250 miles (402 km) north of Venezuela.
Costa Rica	19,575 sq mi (50,700 sq km)	2,200,000 112 per sq mi (43 per sq km)	San José 534,400	Spanish*	The Spanish words *costa rica* mean "rich coast." Columbus explored Costa Rica in 1502 looking for gold.
Cuba	44,218 sq mi (114,524 sq km)	10,000,000 226 per sq mi (87 per sq km)	Havana 1,981,300	Spanish*	Cuba is an island nation located 90 mi (140 km) south of Key West, Florida.
Dominica	290 sq mi (751 sq km)	100,000 345 per sq mi (133 per sq km)	Roseau 12,000	English*, French patois	Dominica, an island republic, gained full independence on November 3, 1978.
Dominican Republic	18,816 sq mi (48,734 sq km)	5,400,000 287 per sq mi (111 per sq km)	Santo Domingo 1,000,000	Spanish*	Santo Domingo was the first city to be founded by Europeans in the Western Hemisphere.
El Salvador	8,124 sq mi (21,041 sq km)	4,800,000 591 per sq mi (228 per sq km)	San Salvador 500,000	Spanish*, Nahua	El Salvador is the smallest mainland country in the Western Hemisphere.
Grenada	133 sq mi (344 sq km)	100,000 752 per sq mi (291 per sq km)	St. George's 6,600	English*, French dialect	An island nation in the Caribbean Sea, Grenada is one of the world's leading producers of nutmeg.
Guatemala	42,042 sq mi (108,889 sq km)	7,000,000 162 per sq mi (62 per sq km)	Guatemala City 1,227,800	Spanish*, Maya Indian dialects	Guatemala's Volcán Tajumulco, rising 13,845 ft (4,220 m), is the highest mountain in Central America.
Haiti	10,714 sq mi (27,750 sq km)	5,800,000 541 per sq mi (209 per sq km)	Port-au-Prince 703,100	French*, Haitian Creole	Haiti is the oldest Black republic in the world. The Indian word *haiti* means "high ground."
Honduras	43,277 sq mi (112,088 sq km)	3,800,000 88 per sq mi (34 per sq km)	Tegucigalpa 316,800	Spanish*	Honduras is among the world's top ten leading producers of bananas.
Jamaica	4,244 sq mi (10,991 sq km)	2,200,000 518 per sq mi (200 per sq km)	Kingston 169,800	English*	The name *Jamaica* comes from the Arawak Indian word *xaymaca*, which means "island of springs."
Nicaragua	50,193 sq mi (130,000 sq km)	2,600,000 52 per sq mi (20 per sq km)	Managua 400,000	Spanish*	Nicaragua is the largest Central American country. Cotton is this nation's most important product.
Panama	29,209 sq mi (75,650 sq km)	1,900,000 65 per sq mi (25 per sq km)	Panama City 439,900	Spanish*, English, Indian dialects	Panama is sometimes called "the Crossroads of the World" because of the Panama Canal.
Puerto Rico	3,435 sq mi (8,897 sq km)	3,186,000 1,019 per sq mi (393 per sq km)	San Juan 422,701	Spanish*, English*	Puerto Rico is an outlying area of the United States with its own commonwealth government.
St. Lucia	238 sq mi (616 sq km)	100,000 420 per sq mi (162 per sq km)	Castries 45,000	English*, French patois	St. Lucia is an island with thick tropical forests. Bananas are the chief crop.
St. Vincent and the Grenadines	150 sq mi (388 sq km)	94,000 627 per sq mi (242 per sq km)	Kingstown 21,000	English*, French patois	Soufrière is an active volcano and the highest point (4,048 ft; 1,234 m) on St. Vincent.
Trinidad and Tobago	1,980 sq mi (5,128 sq km)	1,200,000 606 per sq mi (234 per sq km)	Port of Spain 60,400	English*, French, Spanish, Hindi	Calypso music and the limbo dance originated on this two-island nation.

*Official language(s)

Land under intensive agriculture is always in use. This is possible because crops are rotated and fertilizers are used.

SOUTH AMERICA

COUNTRY	TOTAL AREA	POPULATION AND POPULATION DENSITY	CAPITAL CITY AND POPULATION	LANGUAGE(S)	OTHER FACTS
Argentina	1,072,067 sq mi (2,776,654 sq km)	27,100,000 25 per sq mi (10 per sq km)	Buenos Aires 2,975,000	Spanish*	Nine out of ten people in Argentina can read and write. This nation has the world's largest beef exports.
Bolivia	424,162 sq mi (1,098,581 sq km)	5,300,000 12 per sq mi (5 per sq km)	La Paz 655,000 and Sucre 62,000	Spanish*, Quéchua, Aymara	Bolivian forests have more than 2,000 kinds of trees. Mount Chacaltaya has the world's highest ski run.
Brazil	3,286,487 sq mi (8,511,965 sq km)	122,000,000 37 per sq mi (14 per sq km)	Brasilia 763,000	Portuguese*	Brazil leads the world in coffee production and is the largest and most populous Latin American country.
Chile	292,135 sq mi (756,626 sq km)	11,300,000 39 per sq mi (15 per sq km)	Santiago 3,186,000	Spanish*	The Chuquicamata copper mine in Chile produces more copper than any other mine in the world.
Colombia	439,735 sq mi (1,138,914 sq km)	26,700,000 61 per sq mi (23 per sq km)	Bogotá 3,102,000	Spanish*	Colombia's Pacific coast is the rainiest spot in the Americas with an annual rainfall of 350 in. (889 cm).
Ecuador	108,624 sq mi (281,334 sq km)	8,000,000 74 per sq mi (28 per sq km)	Quito 600,000	Spanish*, Quéchua, Jibaro	The world's highest active volcano, Cotopaxi, 19,347 ft (5,897 m), is in northern Ecuador.
French Guiana	35,135 sq mi (91,000 sq km)	62,000 2 per sq mi (1 per sq km)	Cayenne 30,000	French*	The French started using Devil's Island as a prison colony during the French Revolution, 1789-1799.
Guyana	83,000 sq mi (214,969 sq km)	900,000 11 per sq mi (4 per sq km)	Georgetown 66,000	English, Hindi, Urdu	Guyana is one of the world's leading producers of bauxite. King George VI waterfall drops 1,600 ft (488 m).
Paraguay	157,047 sq mi (406,752 sq km)	3,300,000 21 per sq mi (8 per sq km)	Asunción 442,000	Spanish*, Guarani	Paraguay's flag is the only national flag with one design on the front and another on the back.
Peru	496,222 sq mi (1,285,216 sq km)	17,600,000 35 per sq mi (14 per sq km)	Lima 3,303,000	Spanish*, Quéchua*, Aymara	The world's second largest river, the Amazon, begins in the Andes Mountains of northern Peru.
Surinam	70,060 sq mi (181,455 sq km)	400,000 6 per sq mi (2 per sq km)	Paramaribo 102,000	Dutch*, Taki-taki	About 80% of Surinam is covered by mountainous rain forests. The nation is a leading producer of bauxite.
Uruguay	68,037 sq mi (176,215 sq km)	2,900,000 43 per sq mi (16 per sq km)	Montevideo 1,230,000	Spanish*	Uruguay is the smallest country in South America. Pasturelands cover 4/5 of the land area.
Venezuela	352,143 sq mi (912,050 sq km)	13,900,000 39 per sq mi (15 per sq km)	Caracas 1,035,000	Spanish*	Angel Falls in the Guiana Highlands is the world's highest waterfall, plunging 3,212 ft (979 m).

*Official language(s)

23 / CHAPTER REVIEW

KEY FACTS

1. There were various Indian groups living in Latin America before any Europeans came to the Americas.

2. Most of Latin America was colonized by Spain and Portugal.

3. Although parts of it are highly developed, Latin America is considered a "developing area."

4. Many countries in Latin America are rich in mineral resources.

VOCABULARY QUIZ

Beside the number of the sentence, write the word that best completes the sentence. Write on a sheet of paper.

subsistence	bauxite
developed	cacao
plantation	developing
mestizo	Pampas
commercial	savanna

1. A large farm on which such crops as sugarcane and cotton are grown is a <u>plantation</u>.

2. A <u>mestizo</u> is a person of mixed white and Indian ancestry.

3. Aluminum is obtained from the mineral <u>bauxite</u>.

4. The raising of crops to be sold is called <u>commercial</u> agriculture.

5. A <u>developed</u> country is one that is highly industrialized.

6. The raising of only enough crops and livestock to meet the needs of a farm family is called <u>subsistence</u> farming.

7. A country that is becoming industrialized is called a <u>developing</u> country.

8. The chocolate in your candy bar comes from a crop called <u>cacao</u>.

9. <u>Savanna</u> is a kind of vegetation with grassland and scattered trees.

10. A plains area in South America that is similar to the Great Plains is the <u>Pampas</u>.

REVIEW QUESTIONS

1. Which two European countries colonized most of Latin America?

2. Explain three ways in which developed and developing countries are different.

3. What is the difference between subsistence farming and commercial agriculture?

4. What is the largest country in Middle America and what is its capital?

5. List the 12 countries of South America.

ACTIVITIES

1. Make a report on one of the following topics: "Animals of the Galapagos Islands," "The Pan American Highway," "Llamas of the Andes," or "The Deadly Piranha."

2. Look in an encyclopedia to find information on Simón Bolívar, José de San Martin, Francisco Miranda, Bernardo O'Higgins, Miguel Hidalgo y Costilla or Toussaint L'Ouverture. Write a report on how any two of these men helped Latin American colonies become independent.

3. Prepare an oral report on the Amazon River. In an encyclopedia or other reference book find out these facts about the river: (**a**) How long is it? (**b**) How wide is it at its widest point? (**c**) How many tributaries does it have? (**d**) What are some of the major ports on the river?

457

USING PRONUNCIATION SYMBOLS

In this book, words that may be hard to pronounce are respelled in parentheses, using a system of pronunciation symbols. Such a system is needed because so many letters have more than one sound. The letter *a* for example, can be pronounced with the sound you hear in *map, page, mare,* or *harm.* A pronunciation symbol stands for only one sound. The vowel sounds in the four words above have these four symbols: a, ā, â, and ä.

An accent, or stress mark, is used after one of the syllables in each respelling used in this book. The accent tells you that that syllable gets the most stress. Which syllable is stressed in the word *Cayenne* in the list below? Second

One important symbol is called a schwa(ə). This is the sound heard in many unstressed syllables. The schwa sound can be spelled with any of the vowels. What vowel is used to spell the schwa in LaPaz? a in La

The Key to Pronunciation for this book is on page 495. Use it to help you pronounce the names below. Which country rhymes with *hilly?* With *Katie?* Write your name and a friend's name using pronunciation symbols. Don't forget the accent.

Chile rhymes with hilly. Haiti rhymes with Katie.

Altiplano äl ti plä′ nō	Fortaleza fôrt əl ä′ zə	Port-au-Prince pôrt ō prins′
Amazon am′ ə zän	(French) Guiana gē an′ ə	Pôrto Alegre pôrt ü ə leg′ rə
Antigua an tēg′ ə	Grenada grə näd′ ə	Puebla pü eb′ lə
Antilles an til′ ēz	Guadalajara gwäd ə lə här′ ə	Puerto Rico pwert ə rē′ kō
Argentina är jən tē′ nə	Guatemala gwät ə mäl′ ə	Quito kē′ tō
Asunción ə sün sē ōn′	Guiana gē an′ ə	Recife rə sē′ fə
Atacama ät ə käm′ ə	Guyana gī an′ ə	Rio de Janeiro
Bahamas bə häm′ əz	Haiti hāt′ ē	rē′ ō dä zhə ner′ ō
Barbados bär bād′ əs	Havana hə van′ ə	Río de la Plata
Belém bə lem′	Hispaniola his pən yō′ lə	rē′ ō də lə plät ə
Belize bə lēz′	Honduras hän dùr′ əs	Rosario rō zär′ ē ō
Bogotá bō gə tô′	Jamaica jə mā′ kə	St. Lucia sānt lü′ shə
Bolivia bə liv′ ē ə	La Paz lə paz′	Salvador sal′ və dôr
Brasília brə zil′ yə	Lima lī′ mə	San Juan san wän′
Brazil brə zil′	Llanos lan′ ōz	Santiago sant ē äg′ ō
Buenos Aires	Manaus mə naùs′	Santo Domingo
bwā nə sar′ ēz	Maracaibo mar ə kī′ bō	sant əd ə min′ gō
Caracas kə rak′ əs	Mazatlán mäs ə tlän′	Santos sant′ əs
Cayenne kī en′	Mexico mek′ si kō	São Paulo sou pou′ lü
Chaco chäk′ o	Monclova mông klō′ və	Sierra Madre Occidental
Chile chil′ ē	Monterrey mänt ə rā′	sē er′ ə mäd′ rē äk sə den täl′
Colombia kə lum′ bē ə	Montevideo mänt ə və dā′ ō	Sierra Madre Oriental
Córdoba kôrd′ ə bə	Nicaragua nik ə räg′ wə	sē er′ ə mäd′ rē ôr ē en täl′
Costa Rica käs tə rē′ kə	Orinoco ôr ə nō′ kō	Sucre sü′ krä
Cuba kyü′ bə	Pampas pam′ pəz	Surinam sùr′ ə nam
Dominica däm ə nē′ kə	Panama pan′ ə mä	Tobago tə bā′ gō
Dominican (Republic)	Paraguay par′ ə gwī	Trinidad trin′ ə dad
də min′ i kən	Paramaribo par ə mar′ ə bō	Uruguay ùr′ ə gwī
Ecuador ek′ wə dôr	Paraná par ə nä′	Valparaíso väl pä rä ē′ sō
El Salvador el sal′ və dôr	Patagonia pat ə gō′ nyə	Venezuela ven əz wā′ lə
Falkland fô′ klənd	Peru pə rü′	Yucatán yü kə tan′

7/UNIT REVIEW

1. Two of the world's largest forest areas are in Canada and in South America. — *What are the chief differences between them?*

2. The United States imports a great deal of lumber. — *Which of these two forest regions, do you think, is the more valuable to us, that of Canada or that of South America?*

3. Imagine that you are traveling from Ecuador on the equator (a) southward to Cape Horn, and (b) northward to Alaska. — *List the kinds of climate that you would experience in each journey. What similarities would you find?*

4. The Panama Canal links the Atlantic Ocean with the Pacific. — *Which countries of the Western Hemisphere, do you think, benefit most from the canal? Why?*

5. Both Canada and Latin America are very rich in minerals. — *List some that are obtained from both.*

6. Canada is more developed than most of Latin America. — *List facts that show that this is so.*

7. Climate exerts a great influence on human activity. The Canadian northlands and the Amazon forest are both difficult environments. — *Explain how each limits human activity and development.*

8. North America, Central America, and South America are linked by a chain of mountains. — *Describe the changes of name and of form that these mountains undergo between Alaska and southern Chile.*

For extra credit

9. Two countries make up North America, while there are over 20 in Latin America. — *If Latin America had been made up of only two or three countries, how would its development have been different?*

10. Both Canada and Latin America contain very large areas in which very few people live. — *Name some of them, and explain why their population is so small.*

11. The Canadian Shield and the Brazilian plateau are both plateau regions made up of old, hard rock, yet they differ greatly in the ways in which they have been developed. — *What are the chief differences between them?*

The following books will be helpful in preparing to teach this material: *Teaching Social Studies in the Elementary and Middle Schools*, William Joyce & Janet Alleman. Holt, Rinehart and Winston (Contains excellent information on the concept of life roles.); *Future Shock*, Alvin Toffler. Random House.

You may also wish to use a series of four captioned filmstrips—*The Near Future* produced by Pomfret House.

Epilogue: Looking Forward

Responsibilities and roles   "And so, my fellow Americans, ask not what your country can do for you—ask what you can do for your country." It was with these words that President John F. Kennedy challenged Americans in his first moments as President. The challenge remains for each of us today.

You have learned a lot this year about the rights and freedoms Americans enjoy. But rights always involve responsibilities. This is true for young people as well as adults. It is true for you today.

You will have many different life roles—parts you will play in relation to others, to your work, and so on. These roles have already begun for you. They will expand as you get older. They can help you carry out your responsibilities to our nation.

Have pupils name rights they have as Americans. Ask: What responsibilities do we have to our country?

Role 1: Family membership   Each of you belongs to some type of family. You will remain a family member all your life. Right now you are a son or daughter, and perhaps a sister or brother. One day you might be in charge of your own family.

Have you ever stopped to think about your responsibilities as a family member? What jobs do you have that help your family throughout the week? What feelings do you share? What things do you learn? Your family is a very important training ground for life. You are learning to get along and work closely with others. You are learning you cannot always do things the way you want. You are learning to share joys and sorrows.

Do you remember reading in Chapter 2 about United States history being a family history? Your family helps you learn how to live in a much larger family—the United States of America!

460

Ask: In what sense is going to school your job? How is it like your parents' jobs? How is it different?

Have pupils make montages in which they show their understanding of the four life roles described in the reading.

Role 2: Your job Every job done cheerfully and to the best of your ability helps the United States become a better place. All jobs are important and worthwhile. The person who keeps the country clean, who makes the goods we buy, who works in an office, is as important as the person who runs the country.

Even if you do not have a paper route, mow lawns, babysit, or shovel snow, all of you have a job right now. It is studying and working hard in school. It is following the rules of the school. It is listening carefully to your teacher. It is cooperating with other students. It is coming to school every day unless you are sick.

True, you will not be paid in money for your school job. But you can be proud of a job well done. You can learn a great deal about rights and responsibilities. And you can become prepared for a paying job later on that will be suited to your abilities and that you will enjoy.

Role 3: Your spare time Americans have more and more leisure, or spare time. What is done with that time is an important measure of our future as a nation. This is as true for you as it is for adults.

It is fun to watch television. Many shows are interesting and educational. But many of us watch too much TV. Many times we do not think about what we watch. And, sadly, many of us cannot think of anything else to do besides watch TV.

You can do things to help build your body. Walking, biking, rollerskating, and playing ball are good activities. Can you think of others?

You can do things to build your mind. Stamp collecting, reading, and writing poetry are great hobbies. Can you think of other hobbies that are fun and make you think?

Are there people in your neighborhood who could use some help and friendship? Is there a walk-a-thon or some other event you could enter to raise money for others? Do you take time to look around you or to just sit and think? What are some other things that you rarely do that you could use your free time for?

Of all the great people you have read about in this book, there are none who were not driven to use their time in many different ways to make our country a better place. This country will be a better place if you use your time wisely.

Role 4: As citizen All of the things we have said add up to your very important role as a citizen of this nation and the world. In the future that will mean voting and being involved in community, national, and world events. But you are a citizen *now*.

You have learned how your country was born and what shaped it. You have to take those same ideas of freedom and equality to heart. You have to be willing to stand up for them.

You have to be willing to do things *now* to make the United States and the world better. You can encourage adults to vote. You can try to understand important events and people so you will be able to vote one day. You can complain if you are treated unfairly when buying things. You can help your family recycle papers, bottles, and cans. You can save energy. You

461

Ask: How do you like to spend your spare time? What do you gain from your spare time activities?

Have pupils list specific forms of energy they can conserve and ways in which they can conserve each.

Have pupils demonstrate their dictionary and writing skills by paraphrasing President Kennedy's words.

can decide *now* to stay away from crime, drugs, and other harmful things. You can try to influence friends who want to do things you know are not right. You can get involved in scout groups, church groups, or community groups that can help you find ways to make things better.

The right of citizenship is given to you. Whether you are a *good* citizen or a *bad* citizen is up to you.

President Kennedy also spoke these words: "Now the trumpet summons us again— . . . [a call to] struggle against the common enemies of man: tyranny, poverty, disease, and war itself." In thousands of ways you can answer that trumpet call for your nation and your world!

You in the twenty-first century   No one knows exactly what will happen in the future. But we do know one thing from our study of history—the future will be very different from the past or present. History is a record of change.

Think about this example. My grandfather came to the United States as a baby in the early 1890s. He came to a country that was hardly involved in world affairs. There were no cars or airplanes, no television, no computers. Most homes did not have electricity. The list of differences between then and now could go on and on. Does it make sense to expect that the United States will be the same 90 years from now as it is today? Of course not! In

462

Have pupils create and exhibit serviceable items using materials that would ordinarily be discarded.

Have pupils draw or build a model of a future community in space, underground, or underwater.

Have pupils write about possibilities for the future that they would like to see become realities by the year 2000.

Have pupils write one-minute commercials that suggest ways in which people can achieve a better world.

fact, it will probably change at a faster rate than it did for my grandfather.

We must understand that almost anything can happen in the future. Imagine telling my grandfather back in the 1890s that the United States would fight in two world wars; that people could sit at home and see pictures of events happening on the other side of the world. Imagine telling him that he would be able to fly across the country in hours; that the United States would send people to the moon. He would not have believed it. Yet he has seen it all happen. And we are being told some things just as unbelievable. Colonies in space! Average age of over 100 years! Robots to do housework! We must understand that the future is full of exciting possibilities.

The future involves choice But do we want just anything to happen? Are there some things that should not happen even though they are possible? What would we like to have happen in the future? Can we choose our future by working for certain goals?

One choice Imagine a world 90 years from now. Four people share one tiny room. The smell from the outside is hard to bear. People allow garbage to just lie there in the streets.

When did people stop caring? Perhaps it was when the nuclear war destroyed cities, crops, and much of the world population. Perhaps it was when industries stopped due to lack of needed energy to run them. Perhaps it was when there was no more drinkable water in the pollution-choked lakes and streams.

You think of the masses of people starving around the world. There are four times as many people as 100 years ago. You think of the way things were when you were a child. There was still time then to make this a better world. . . .

Ask: Why, do you think, did people stop caring? How can each one of us show a caring attitude every day?

Have pupils consider how the efforts of both individuals and the community are needed to eliminate th sources of pollution pictured here.

Ask: Why are efforts being made to develop solar energy as a practical power source? (Shortage of oil and natural gas)

Have pupils note the special collectors on the roof. Ask: Why are they set at an angle? (To best absorb sunlight)

Another choice   Imagine a different world 90 years from now. You may be about 100 years old. You have just finished playing a round of space tennis. You have a great deal of leisure time. You have retired from an active business life, but you still receive computer calls to give advice and help. Your many friends live all over the world—in domed cities or underwater cities. They may even live out of this world—in the lunar space colony where you once lived.

You live in a safe world. There has not been the least hint of war in 50 years. Nations finally realized that their abilities and resources were better used to provide food and shelter for their people than to make war. Nations cooperate with one another. The awful threat of nuclear war turns the thoughts of most people to peace.

Solar energy storage cells store the sun's power and provide all the energy anyone needs. It is cheap and easy to drive your plane-mobile and power all the appliances in your home.

Pollution is something your great-grandchildren study about in history books. You cannot remember the last time you saw trash and waste on the ground. The air is clean, the streams are pure.

You think of how happy you are to have helped to make this a better world. . . .

The choice is yours   Neither of these stories will ever come entirely true. Maybe the truth lies somewhere in the middle. But will we do our part to make a better country? A better world? Remember, not to decide is to decide. To take no action will result in a poorer world. We must choose what kind of world we want, and work for it.

Have pupils find out how homes are heated by solar heat and report to the class illustrating their talk.

A fable   There was once a wise old woman who lived back in the hills. All the children used to come and ask her questions. She always gave the right answers.

There was a naughty little troublemaker among the children. One day he caught a tiny bird and held it in his cupped hands. Then he gathered his friends around. He said, "Let's trick the old woman. I'll ask her what I'm holding in my hands. Of course, she'll answer that I have a bird. Then I'll ask her if the bird is living or dead. If she says the bird is dead, I'll open my hands and let the bird

Have pupils list the technological advances and the attitudes of individuals and society that they think are needed to create the world of "Another choice."

fly away. If she says the bird is alive, I'll quickly crush it and show her the dead bird. Either way, she'll be wrong."

The children agreed that this was a clever plan. Up the hill they went to the old woman's hut.

"Old woman, we have a question for you," they all shouted.

"What's in my hands?" asked the little boy.

"Why, it must be a bird," replied the old woman.

"But is it living or dead?" demanded the excited boy.

The old woman thought for a second and then replied, "It is as you will, my child."

So it is with the United States. Our country's future is in *your* hands. "It is as you will, my child."

Ask: Do you agree or disagree that "our country's future is in *your* hands"? What evidence can you give to support your opinion? How does your opinion affect how you live at the present time?

Atlas

THE WORLD
(Political)

0   1500 miles
0 2000 kilometers

North

ARCTIC

GREENLAND (Den.)

Arctic Circle

ICELAND

ALASKA (U.S.)

80°

CANADA

NORTH

60°

ATLANTIC OCEAN

Aleutian Is.

AMERICA

40°

UNITED STATES OF AMERICA

Azores (Port.)

Madeira (Port.)

MOR.

PACIFIC OCEAN

Bermuda Is. (U.K.)

Canary Is. (Sp.)

Midway Is.(U.S.)

Tropic of Cancer

HAWAII (U.S.)

MEXICO

MAURITANIA

20°

(U.K.)
BELIZE

WEST INDIES (see inset below)

CAPE VERDE IS.

SENEGAL

MALI

GUATEMALA
EL SAL.

GAMBIA
GUINEA-BISSAU
GUINEA

U. VOL.

Clipperton (Fr.)

VEN.

COLOMBIA

GUYANA

SURINAME

SIERRA LEONE
LIBERIA

GHA.

IVORY COAST

FR.GUIANA

180°   160°   140°   Equator   120°   100°   80°   60°   40°   20°

(U.S.&U.K.)

Galapagos Is. (Ec.)

ECUADOR

St. Paul's Rocks (Braz.)

P
O
L
Y
N
E
S
I
A

Phoenix Is. (U.K.)

Tokelau Is. (N.Z.)

PERU

SOUTH

Ascension

W. SAMOA (Fr.)

American Samoa (U.S.)

French Polynesia (Fr.)

BOLIVIA

BRAZIL

AMERICA

St.Helena

Tonga Is.

Cook Is. (N.Z.)

(U.K.)

PARA.

Tropic of Capricorn

(U.K.)

Easter I. (Chile)

CHILE

URU.

Tristan da Cunha Is.

Kermadec Is. (N.Z.)

ARGENTINA

ATLANTIC

PACIFIC OCEAN

OCEAN

40°

Chatham Is. (N.Z.)

Falkland Is. (U.K.)

South Georgia

South Sandwich Is.

60°

Antarctic Circle

80°

ANT

South

WEST INDIES

0   300 mi.
0   500 km

FLORIDA

Grand Bahama

Miami

Great Abaco I.

Nassau

Eleuthera

Andros I.

Cat I.

BAHAMAS

Great Exuma I.

Long I.

Tropic of Cancer

Havana

CUBA

Acklins I.

Mayaguana I.

Santiago-de-Cuba

Great Inagua I.

20°

Hispaniola

JAMAICA

HAITI

DOMINICAN REP.

Virgin Is. (U.K.)

Anguilla
St.Martin (Fr.&Neth.)

Kingston

Port-au-Prince

Santo Domingo

San Juan

PUERTO RICO (U.S.)

Barbuda

St.Christopher
Antigua

Guadeloupe (Fr.)

G R E A T E R   A N T I L L E S

L E S S E R   A N T I L L E S

Leeward Is.

Windward Is.

DOMINICA

Martinique (Fr.)

ST. LUCIA

HONDURAS

CARIBBEAN SEA

BARBADOS

ST. VINCENT AND THE GRENADINES

NICARAGUA

NETHERLANDS ANTILLES

Aruba

Curaçao

Bonaire

GRENADA

Tobago

TRINIDAD AND TOBAGO

Port-of-Spain

Trinidad

COSTA RICA

Barranquilla

Panama Canal

Caracas

PANAMA

Panamá

COLOMBIA

70°

VENEZUELA

60°

AFG.	—AFGHANISTAN	CZECH.	—CZECHOSLOVAKIA
ALB.	—ALBANIA	DJI.	—DJIBOUTI
ALG.	—ALGERIA	EL SAL.	—EL SALVADOR
AND.	—ANDORRA	EQ.GUI.	—EQUATORIAL GUINEA
AUST.	—AUSTRIA	GHA.	—GHANA
BAN.	—BANGLADESH	GIB.	—GIBRALTAR (U.K.)
BEL.	—BELGIUM	HUN.	—HUNGARY
BHU.	—BHUTAN	KAM.	—KAMPUCHEA
BOTS.	—BOTSWANA	LEB.	—LEBANON
BUR.	—BURUNDI	LIECH.	—LIECHTENSTEIN
CAM.	—CAMEROON	LUX.	—LUXEMBOURG
C.A.R.	—CENTRAL AFRICAN REP.	MAL.	—MALAWI
		MON.	—MONACO

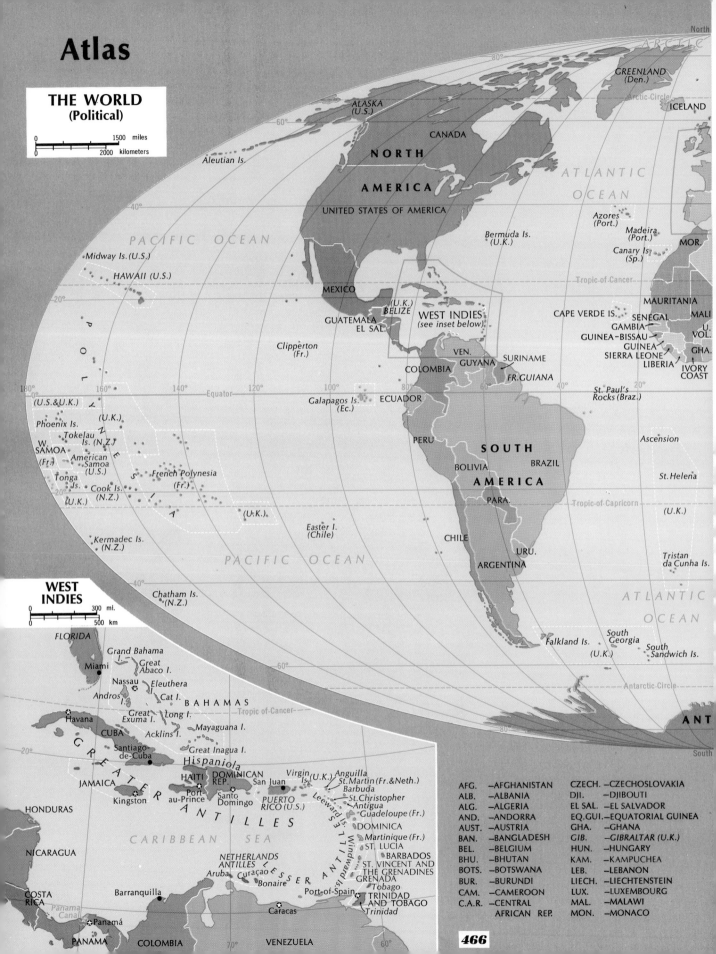

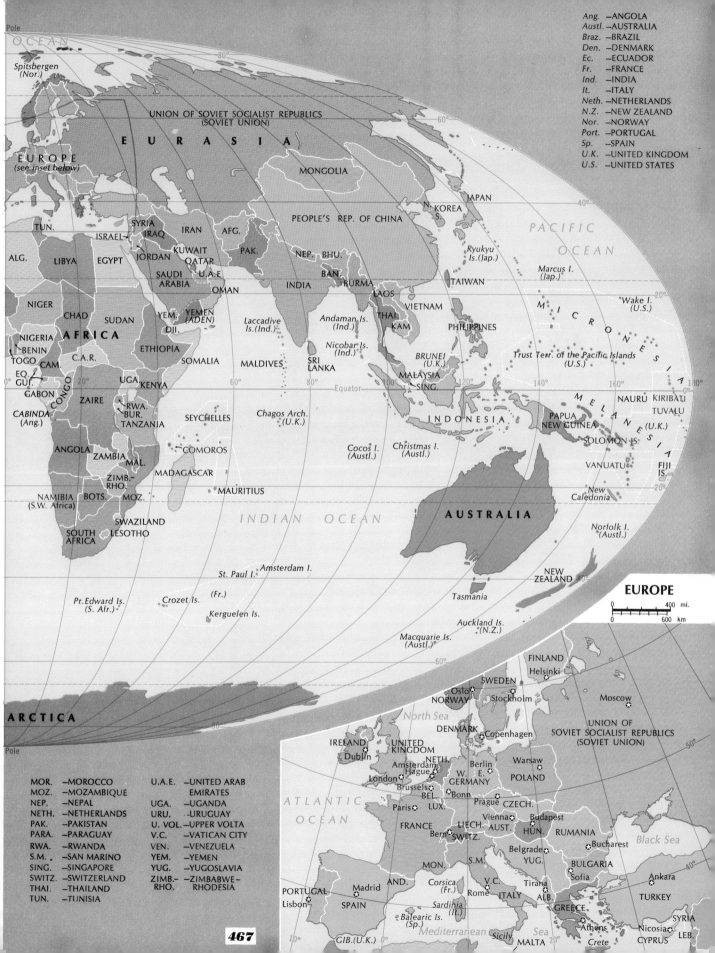

Ang. —ANGOLA
Austl. —AUSTRALIA
Braz. —BRAZIL
Den. —DENMARK
Ec. —ECUADOR
Fr. —FRANCE
Ind. —INDIA
It. —ITALY
Neth. —NETHERLANDS
N.Z. —NEW ZEALAND
Nor. —NORWAY
Port. —PORTUGAL
Sp. —SPAIN
U.K. —UNITED KINGDOM
U.S. —UNITED STATES

Pole
OCEAN
Spitsbergen
(Nor.)

UNION OF SOVIET SOCIALIST REPUBLICS
(SOVIET UNION)
E U R A S I A
EUROPE
(see inset below)
MONGOLIA
PEOPLE'S REP. OF CHINA
JAPAN
N. KOREA
S.
PACIFIC
OCEAN
TUN.
SYRIA
ISRAEL
IRAQ
IRAN
AFG.
JORDAN
KUWAIT
QATAR
U.A.E.
SAUDI
ARABIA
OMAN
PAK.
NEP. BHU.
INDIA
BAN.
BURMA
LAOS
THAI.
KAM.
VIETNAM
Ryukyu
Is.(Jap.)
TAIWAN
Marcus I.
(Jap.)
M I C R O N E S I A
Wake I.
(U.S.)
ALG.
LIBYA
EGYPT
NIGER
CHAD
SUDAN
YEM.
YEMEN
(ADEN)
DJI.
Laccadive
Is.(Ind.)
Andaman Is.
(Ind.)
PHILIPPINES
Trust Terr. of the Pacific Islands
(U.S.)
NIGERIA
BENIN
TOGO
CAM.
EQ.
GUI.
GABON
CONGO
C.A.R.
AFRICA
ETHIOPIA
SOMALIA
MALDIVES
SRI
LANKA
Nicobar Is.
(Ind.)
BRUNEI
(U.K.)
MALAYSIA
SING.
Equator
NAURU KIRIBATI
TUVALU
(U.K.)
ZAIRE
UGA. KENYA
RWA.
BUR.
TANZANIA
SEYCHELLES
Chagos Arch.
(U.K.)
INDONESIA
M E L A N E S I A
PAPUA
NEW GUINEA
SOLOMON IS.
CABINDA
(Ang.)
ANGOLA
ZAMBIA
MAL.
ZIMB.-
RHO.
MADAGASCAR
COMOROS
Cocos I.
(Austl.)
Christmas I.
(Austl.)
VANUATU
FIJI
IS.
NAMIBIA
(S.W. Africa)
BOTS.
MOZ.
MAURITIUS
New
Caledonia
Norfolk I.
(Austl.)
SOUTH
AFRICA
SWAZILAND
LESOTHO
INDIAN OCEAN
AUSTRALIA
Pr.Edward Is.
(S. Afr.)
Crozet Is.
Amsterdam I.
St. Paul I.
(Fr.)
Kerguelen Is.
Tasmania
NEW
ZEALAND
Auckland Is.
(N.Z.)
Macquarie Is.
(Austl.)
ARCTICA
Pole

EUROPE
400 mi.
600 km

FINLAND
Helsinki
SWEDEN
Oslo
NORWAY
Stockholm
Moscow
North Sea
DENMARK
Copenhagen
UNION OF
SOVIET SOCIALIST REPUBLICS
(SOVIET UNION)
IRELAND
Dublin
UNITED
KINGDOM
NETH.
Berlin
Warsaw
Amsterdam
Hague
W. E.
GERMANY
POLAND
London
Brussels
Bonn
Prague CZECH.
ATLANTIC
BEL.
LUX.
Paris
Vienna
LIECH. AUST.
Budapest
OCEAN
FRANCE
Bern
SWITZ.
HUN.
RUMANIA
Black Sea
Belgrade
YUG.
Bucharest
MON.
S.M.
BULGARIA
Sofia
Ankara
PORTUGAL
AND.
Corsica
(Fr.)
V.C.
Rome ITALY
Tirana
ALB.
Madrid
Lisbon
SPAIN
Sardinia
(It.)
GREECE
Athens
TURKEY
SYRIA
Nicosia
CYPRUS LEB.
Balearic Is.
(Sp.)
GIB.(U.K.)
Sicily
MALTA
Mediterranean Sea
Crete

MOR. —MOROCCO
MOZ. —MOZAMBIQUE
NEP. —NEPAL
NETH. —NETHERLANDS
PAK. —PAKISTAN
PARA. —PARAGUAY
RWA. —RWANDA
S.M. —SAN MARINO
SING. —SINGAPORE
SWITZ. —SWITZERLAND
THAI. —THAILAND
TUN. —TUNISIA

U.A.E. —UNITED ARAB
EMIRATES
UGA. —UGANDA
URU. —URUGUAY
U. VOL. —UPPER VOLTA
V.C. —VATICAN CITY
VEN. —VENEZUELA
YEM. —YEMEN
YUG. —YUGOSLAVIA
ZIMB.- —ZIMBABWE-
RHO. RHODESIA

467

C A N

Vancouver

C. Flattery

125° 120° 115° 110° 105° 100°

50° Vancouver

WASHINGTON
Olympia • Seattle • Tacoma
Mt. Rainier • Spokane
14,410 ft.
Portland • Columbia R.
Salem
Eugene **OREGON**

45°

C. Blanco

C. Mendocino

CASCADE RANGE

Great Falls • Missouri R.
Helena • **MONTANA**
Yellowstone R.
Billings

IDAHO
Salmon R.
Boise
Grand Teton
13,766 ft.
Idaho
Falls

Snake R.

WYOMING

NORTH DAKOTA
• Bismarck
Fargo •
MINN

**BLACK
HILLS**
Pierre ★
SOUTH DAKOTA
Cheyenne R.
Sioux Falls •

40°

SIERRA NEVADA
Reno • Carson City
Sacramento R.
San Francisco • Berkeley • Oakland
San Jose •
Central Valley
San Joaquin R.
Fresno •
Mt. Whitney
14,495 ft.

NEVADA
Humboldt R.
Great

Great
Salt Lake
Salt
Lake City • Ogden

Green R.

UTAH
Basin

Longs Pk.
14,256 ft.
Cheyenne ★
N. Platte R.
Denver •
COLORADO
Mt.
Elbert
14,433 ft.
Pikes Pk.
14,110 ft.
Pueblo •
Blanca Pk.
14,317 ft.
Arkansas R.

S. Platte R.
NEBRASKA
Omaha •
Platte R.
Lincoln •

GREAT

KANSAS
Topeka ★
Wichita •

Sioux
City •

35°

Pt. Conception

CALIFORNIA
Bakersfield •
Mojave Desert
Glendale • Pasadena
Los Angeles •
Long Beach • San Bernardino
Anaheim • Riverside
San Diego •

Las
Vegas •
Death
Valley

Colorado Plateau

Colorado R.

ARIZONA

Phoenix •

Santa Fe ★
Albuquerque •
NEW MEXICO

Amarillo •

Lubbock •

ROCKY MOUNTAINS

OKLAHOMA
Oklahoma ★
City
Tulsa •

30°

**PACIFIC
OCEAN**

Tucson •

El Paso •

Llano
Estacado

Fort
Worth • Dallas •

TEXAS
Waco •
Brazos R.

Red R.

Austin ★

GREAT PLAINS

Rio Grande

San
Antonio •

Houston •

170° 180° 170° 160° 150° 140° 70°

ASIA
SOVIET UNION

Arctic Circle
Bering Strait
Nome •
St.
Lawrence I.
St.
Matthew I.

Barrow •

BROOKS RANGE

ALASKA
Yukon R.
Fairbanks •
ALASKA RANGE
Mt. McKinley (Mt. Denali)
20,320 ft.
Anchorage •

CANADA

MEXICO

60°

Rio Grande

Laredo •
Corpus
Christi •

Monday
International Date Line
Sunday

**BERING
SEA**

Nunivak I.

Kenai
Pen.
Kodiak I.

Juneau •
Alexander Arch.

Gulf of
Alaska

60°

Coastal

ALEUTIAN ISLANDS
Near
Is.
Rat Is.
Andreanof
Is.

Unimak I.
Fox Is.

468

50° 170° 160° 150°

0   300 mi.
0   500 km

West longitude

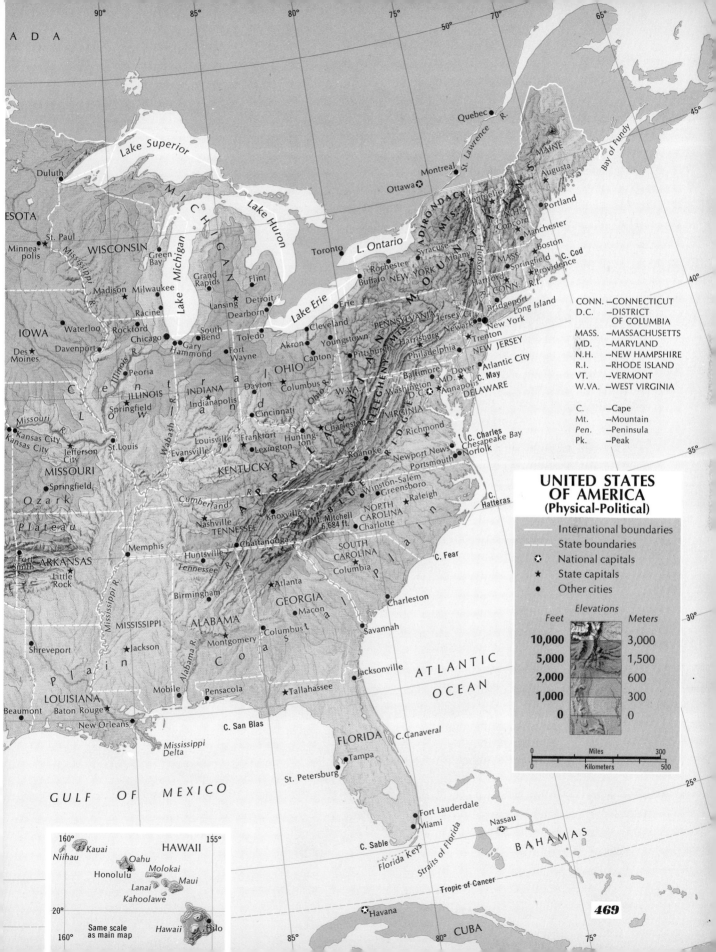

UNITED STATES OF AMERICA
(Physical-Political)

⎯⎯⎯	International boundaries
- - -	State boundaries
✪	National capitals
★	State capitals
●	Other cities

Elevations

Feet		Meters
10,000		3,000
5,000		1,500
2,000		600
1,000		300
0		0

Miles 0 — 300
Kilometers 0 — 500

CONN. — CONNECTICUT
D.C. — DISTRICT OF COLUMBIA
MASS. — MASSACHUSETTS
MD. — MARYLAND
N.H. — NEW HAMPSHIRE
R.I. — RHODE ISLAND
VT. — VERMONT
W.VA. — WEST VIRGINIA

C. — Cape
Mt. — Mountain
Pen. — Peninsula
Pk. — Peak

469

CANADA

ATLANTIC OCEAN

GULF OF MEXICO

BAHAMAS

CUBA

Tropic of Cancer

HAWAII
160° 155°
Niihau Kauai
Oahu Molokai
Honolulu Maui
Lanai
Kahoolawe
20°
Same scale as main map Hawaii Hilo
160°

ASIA
Bering Str.

ARCTIC OCEAN

Queen Elisabeth Is.

Greenland

Iceland

Bering Sea

St. Lawrence I.

Nunivak I.

60°

70°

160°

150°

140°

130°

120°

100°

80°

60°

40°

30°

20°

10°

Pt. Barrow

Beaufort Sea

Prince Patrick I.

Knud Rasmussen Land

80°

Alaska Pen.

ALASKA

BROOKS RANGE

Mt. McKinley 20,300 ft.

Yukon R.

Mackenzie R.

Victoria I.

Barrow Str.

Baffin Bay

Kodiak I.

Gulf of Alaska

Yukon

Plateau

COAST

Great Bear Lake

Southampton I.

Davis Str.

C. Farewell

Alexander Arch.

50°

Queen Charlotte Is.

ROCKY

Great Slave Lake

Peace R.

Athabasca R.

Arctic Circle

Hudson Bay

Labrador Sea

Labrador

60°

PACIFIC OCEAN

Vancouver I.

Mt. Rainier 14,410 ft.

Columbia R.

North

Saskatchewan R.

South

Great Plains

Missouri

Lake Winnipeg

Canadian Shield

St. Lawrence R.

Newfoundland

50°

40°

C. Mendocino

MOUNTAINS

Black Hills

North Platte R.

Lake Superior

LAURENTIAN HIGHLANDS

Montreal

Nova Scotia

San Francisco

Great Salt Lake

Great Basin

SIERRA NEVADA

Mt. Whitney 14,495 ft.

South

Mt. Elbert 14,431 ft.

Colorado R.

Colorado Plateau

Central Lowlands

L. Michigan

L. Huron

Detroit

Chicago

L. Ontario

L. Erie

APPALACHIAN MTS.

Long I.

New York

Philadelphia

Washington

C. Cod

40°

30°

Pt. Conception

Los Angeles

Ozark Plateau

Ohio R.

Mt. Mitchell 6,684 ft.

Chesapeake Bay

Guadalupe I.

Red R.

Mississippi R.

Coastal Plains

C. Hatteras

Eugenia Pt.

G. of California

Rio Grande

Bermuda Is.

30°

Arch. —Archipelago
C. —Cape
G. —Gulf
Mt. —Mountain
Pen. —Peninsula
Pt. —Point
RA. —Range
Str. —Strait

SIERRA MADRE OCCIDENTAL

SIERRA MADRE ORIENTAL

Houston

C. Canaveral

ATLANTIC OCEAN

Lower California

False Cape

GULF OF MEXICO

Florida Pen.

Florida Keys

Bahama Islands

Tropic of Cancer

NORTH AMERICA
(Physical)

Guadalajara

Mexico City

Citlaltepetl 18,700 ft.

Yucatan Pen.

Cuba

WEST INDIES

Greater Antilles

Hispaniola

Leeward Is.

Lesser Antilles

Windward Is.

20°

Elevations

Feet		Meters
10,000		3,000
5,000		1,500
2,000		600
1,000		300
0		0

Miles
0   500

Kilometers
0   800

CENTRAL AMERICA

CARIBBEAN SEA

SOUTH AMERICA

470

0°

100°

West longitude

90°

80°

70°

CARIBBEAN
SEA

Guajira
Pen.
Margarita I.   Tobago
Caracas   Trinidad
                 Orinoco R.
Orinoco R.   Delta
10°

G. of
Panama

Angel
Falls
GUIANA HIGHLANDS   Devils I.
                          C. Orange

Mt. Tolima
19,049 ft.
Meta R.
Bogotá
Magdalena R.
Cauca R.
Llanos

Malpelo I.   Amazon R.
                                              Delta
Caqueta R.   Rio Negro
Mt. Chimborazo   A M A Z O N   Marajó
20,561 ft.   Japura   Amazon   R.   I.   Equator   0°
0°
Gulf of   C. São Rog
Guayaquil   Marañón R.   Tapajóz R. Xingú R. Tocantins R.
Aguja Pt.   Juruá   B A S I N   Madeira   Parnaíba R.
                 Purus R.   Tocantins R.
                          Madeira   São Francisco R.
Mt. Huascarán   Beni R.   10°
22,205 ft.   Mamoré R.   Mato
10°   Grosso   Brasília
Lima   Ucayali R.   Mt. Ancohuma   Plateau   BRAZILIAN
                              21,490 ft.   HIGHLANDS
                 Lake Titicaca
                 L. Poopó   Gran   São Francisco R.
PACIFIC   Chaco   Paraguay R.
OCEAN   Pilcomayo R.   Mt. Bandeira
                                                                          9,462 ft.
20°   Paraná R.   São Paulo   C. Frio
                 Salado R.   Rio de Janeiro Tropic of Capricorn
San Felix I. San Ambrosio I.   Paraná R.   ATLANTIC
                                          Uruguay R.   OCEAN
Juan Fernández Is.
                 Mt. Aconcagua   Colorado R.
30°   22,834 ft.   Buenos Montevideo   30°
                 Santiago   Pampas   Aires   Río de la Plata
                                  Colorado R.
                                  Blanca Bay
                 Chiloé I.   San Matías Gulf
                 Chonos   Valdés Pen.
40°   Arch.   Gulf of
                 Taitao Pen.   San Jorge
                 Patagonia   C. Tres Puntas

Grande
Bay
Strait of   Strait of   Falkland Is.
Magellan   Magellan
50°
                 Tierra del Fuego
Cape Horn

Arch. —Archipelago
C.   —Cape
G.   —Gulf
Mt. —Mountain
Pen. —Peninsula
Pt. —Point

SOUTH AMERICA
(Physical)

Elevations
Feet   Meters

10,000   3,000

5,000   1,500

2,000   600

1,000   300

0   0

Miles
0   500
Kilometers
0   800

471

West longitude

ATLANTIC
OCEAN

20°

Madeira

Str. of Gibraltar

IBERIAN
PENINSULA

PYRENEES

Madrid
Ebro R.

Tagus R.

London

Paris

Loire R.

BRITISH ISLES

North
Sea

Hamburg

Elbe
Berlin
R.

ALPS

Po R.

Rhine

Danube R.

Corsica

Balearic
Is.

Tyrrhenian
Sea

Sardinia

Sicily

Maltese
Is.

Ionian
Sea

Adriatic Sea

Apennines

Budapest

CARPATHIAN

North
European
Plain

SCANDINAVIA

Stockholm

Baltic Sea

Baltic Plains

Leningrad

Moscow

Spitsbergen

Novaya Zemlya

ARCTIC OCEAN

North
Land

Kara Sea

Taymir

Barents
Sea

Kola pen.

N. Dvina R.

URAL MOUNTAINS

Kama R.

Volga R.

Ob R.

Yamal Pen.

Yenisei R.

West

Siberian

Plain

Mediterranean Sea

Crete

Aegean
Sea

Istanbul

Black Sea

ANATOLIA
Asia Minor

Cyprus

CAUCASUS Mts.

Dnieper R.

Don R.

Volga R.

Ural R.

Caspian
Sea

Aral
Sea

Kirgiz Steppe

Kazakh
Uplands

Ishim R.

Irtysh R.

Ob R.

Turan Lowland

Lake
Balkhash

Syr Darya

TIEN SHAN

Tarim Basin

Tropic of Cancer

AFRICA

Sinai Pen.

Red
Sea

HEJAZ

Syrian
Desert

Baghdad

Euphrates R.

Mesopotamia

Tigris R.

ZAGROS MOUNTAINS

Tehran

Plateau
of
Iran

Amu Darya

KUN LUN

HINDU
KUSH

H
I
M
A
L
A
Y
A

Plateau
of
Tibet

Mt. Everest
29,028 ft.

ARABIAN
PENINSULA

NEJD

Persian Gulf

Gulf of Oman

Indus R.

Indian
Desert

Delhi

Sutlej R.

Ganges R.

Ganges
Plain

Karachi

Hadhramaut

Gulf of Aden

Socotra

Arabian Sea

Bombay

WESTERN GHATS

Deccan
Plateau

Godavari R.

EASTERN GHATS

Madras

Equator

Laccadive Is.

Sri Lanka

Maldives

INDIAN

472

30°   40°   10°   50°   East longitude   60°   70°   80°

Laptev Sea

New Siberian Is.

120° 130° 80° 140° 150°

CHERSKI RA.

YERKHOYANSK RANGE

KOLYMA RANGE

Lena R.

Aldan R.

Amur R.

CENTRAL RA.

Kamtchatka Peninsula

Aleutian Is.

Bering Sea

50°

Sunday Monday

International Date Line

170°

Central Siberian Plateau

Lower Tunguska R.

Angara R.

SIBERIA

Sea of Okhotsk

Sakhalin

Kuril Islands

Sapulsk Is.

Tropic of Cancer 180°

20°

170°

Lake Baikal

Shilka R.

GREAT KHINGAN MTS.

Amur R.

Hokkaido

Sea of Japan

Honshu

Mt. —Mountain
Pen. —Peninsula
RA. —Range
Str. —Strait

EURASIA (Physical)

Elevations

Feet		Meters
10,000		3,000
5,000		1,500
2,000		600
1,000		300
0		0

Miles
0 — 800
Kilometers
0 — 1200

Mongolian Plateau

The Gobi

Manchuria Plain

Harbin

Shenyang

Tokyo

Kyoto Fujiyama 12,388 ft.

NAN SHAN

Great Wall

Hwang Ho R.

Peking

Yellow R.

Tientsin

Dairen

North China Plain

Yellow Sea

Korea Strait

Shikoku

Kyushu

Shanghai

East China Sea

Okinawa

Ryukyu Islands

Philippine Sea

PACIFIC OCEAN

10°

Chungking

Yangtze

BOHEA HILLS

Canton

Si R.

Hong Kong

Formosa

Luzon Strait

Philippine Is.

Hainan

Luzon

Manila

Samar

0°

Calcutta

Brahmaputra

Irrawaddy

South China Sea

Mindoro

Palawa

Panay

Negros

Mindanao

Equator

Bay of Bengal

INDOCHINA

PENINSULA

Ho Chi Minh City

Celebes Sea

Moluccas

Halmahera

Admiralty Is.

New Ireland

New Britain

Andaman Is.

Andaman Sea

Gulf of Siam

SNOW MTS.

New Guinea

10°

Nicobar Is.

Str. of Malacca

Malay Pen.

Natuna Is.

Borneo

Buru

Ceram

Aru Is.

Coral Sea

OCEAN

Mentawai Is.

Sumatra

Bangka

SUNDA ISLANDS

Java Sea

Celebes

Arafura Sea

20°

Jakarta

Java

Bali

Lombok

Sumbawa

Flores

Sumba

Timor

AUSTRALIA

90° 100° 110° 120° 130° 140°

473

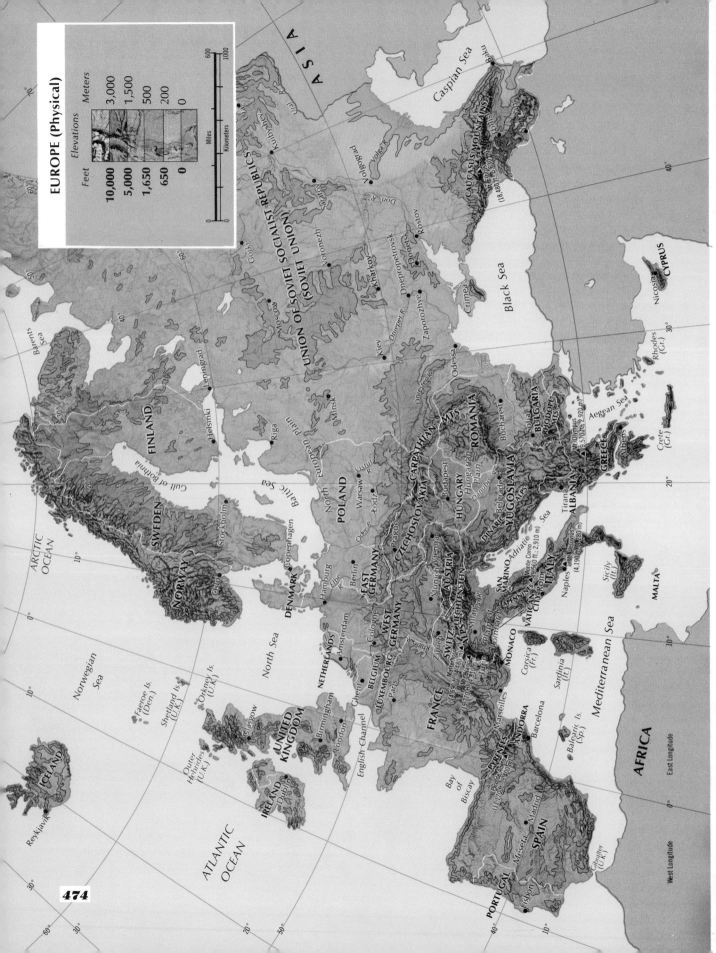

EUROPE (Physical)

Elevations

Feet	Meters
10,000	3,000
5,000	1,500
1,650	500
650	200
0	0

ASIA

ARCTIC OCEAN

Barents Sea

Ural Mts.

Ural R.

Kuybyshev

Volga R.

Vologograd

Don R.

Caspian Sea

Baku

CAUCASUS MOUNTAINS

Mt. El'brus
(18,480 ft.; 5,633 m)

UNION OF SOVIET SOCIALIST REPUBLICS
(SOVIET UNION)

Gorki

Voronezh

Rostov

Donets R.

Dnepropetrovsk

Zaporozhye

Kharkov

Moscow

Dnieper R.

Kiev

Odessa

Crimea

Black Sea

CYPRUS

Nicosia

Rhodes (Gr.)

Leningrad

Helsinki

Riga

Minsk

FINLAND

Gulf of Bothnia

North European Plain

Dniester R.

Bucharest

ROMANIA

CARPATHIAN MTS.

Budapest

Hungarian Plain

Danube R.

Sofia

BULGARIA

RHODOPE MTS.

Aegean Sea

Crete (Gr.)

SWEDEN

Baltic Sea

Stockholm

Copenhagen

DENMARK

POLAND

Warsaw

Vistula R.

Łódź

Oder R.

North Plain

Prague

CZECHOSLOVAKIA

HUNGARY

YUGOSLAVIA

Belgrade

DINARIC ALPS

Adriatic Sea

Tirana

ALBANIA

GREECE

Mt. Olympus
(9,570 ft.; 2,920 m)

Athens

NORWAY

Oslo

Hamburg

Elbe R.

Berlin

EAST GERMANY

WEST GERMANY

Cologne

Rhine R.

Munich

Vienna

AUSTRIA

LIECHTENSTEIN

ALPS

SAN MARINO

Milan

Po R.

Lombardy Plain

Monte Corno
(9,560 ft.; 2,910 m)

APENNINES

VATICAN CITY

Rome

ITALY

Naples

Mt. Vesuvius
(4,190 ft.; 1,280 m)

Sicily (It.)

MALTA

Mediterranean Sea

NETHERLANDS

Amsterdam

Ghent

BELGIUM

LUXEMBOURG

Paris

FRANCE

SWITZ.

Zürich

Matterhorn
(14,690 ft.; 4,480 m)

Mt. Blanc
(15,771 ft.; 4,810 m)

MONACO

Marseilles

Corsica (Fr.)

Sardinia (It.)

ANDORRA

Barcelona

PYRENEES

Pico de Aneto
(11,168 ft.; 3,404 m)

Balearic Is. (Sp.)

North Sea

English Channel

Bay of Biscay

UNITED KINGDOM

Birmingham

London

Glasgow

Outer Hebrides (U.K.)

Shetland Is. (U.K.)

Orkney Is. (U.K.)

Faeroe Is. (Den.)

IRELAND

Dublin

ICELAND

Reykjavík

ATLANTIC OCEAN

Norwegian Sea

SPAIN

Madrid

Meseta

PORTUGAL

Lisbon

Gibraltar (U.K.)

AFRICA

East Longitude

West Longitude

Miles

Kilometers

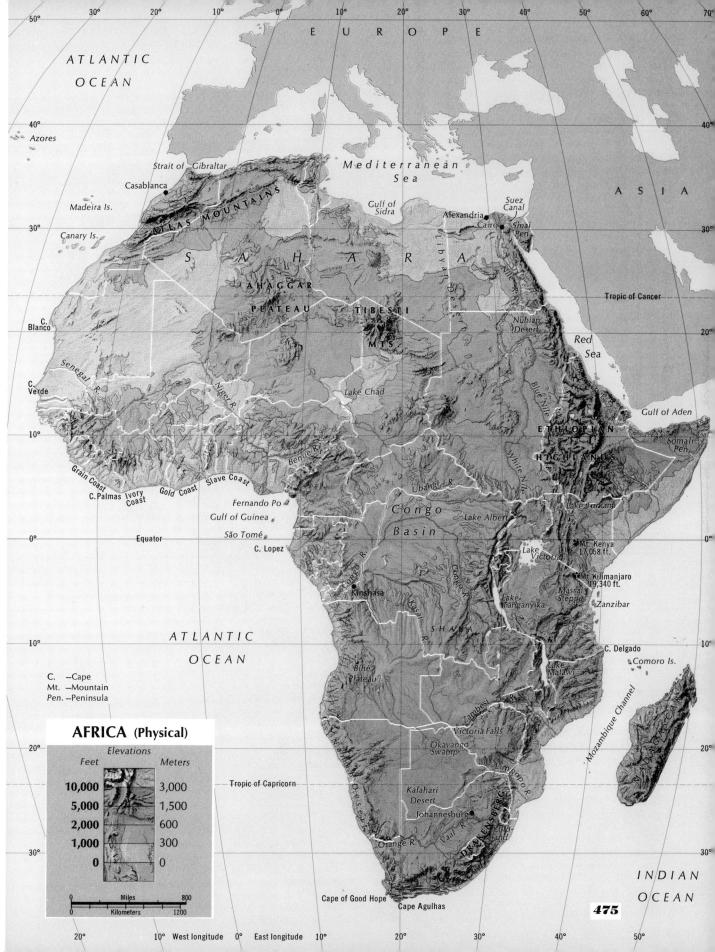

ATLANTIC
OCEAN

EUROPE

30°   20°   10°   0°   10°   20°   30°   40°   50°   60°   70°

MEDITERRANEAN
Sea

ASIA

Azores

Strait of Gibraltar

Casablanca

Madeira Is.

Canary Is.

ATLAS MOUNTAINS

Gulf of
Sidra

Alexandria

Suez
Canal

Cairo

Sinai
Pen.

Tropic of Cancer

S   A   H   A   R   A

AHAGGAR

PLATEAU

TIBESTI

MTS.

Libyan   Desert

Nubian
Desert

Nile R.

Red
Sea

C.
Blanco

C.
Verde

Senegal R.

Niger R.

Lake Chad

Benue R.

Blue Nile

ETHIOPIAN

HIGHLANDS

Gulf of Aden

Somali
Pen.

Grain Coast

C. Palmas   Ivory
Coast

Gold Coast

Slave Coast

Fernando Po

Gulf of Guinea

São Tomé

C. Lopez

Equator

Ubangi R.

White Nile

Congo
Basin

Lake Albert

Lake Turkana

Mt. Kenya
17,058 ft.

Lake
Victoria

Mt. Kilimanjaro
19,340 ft.

Congo R.

Kasai R.

Kwango R.

SHABA

Lake
Tanganyika

Massai
Steppe

Zanzibar

Kinshasa

ATLANTIC

OCEAN

C. Delgado

Comoro Is.

C. —Cape
Mt. —Mountain
Pen. —Peninsula

Bihé
Plateau

Lake
Malawi

Mozambique Channel

MADAGASCAR

AFRICA (Physical)

Elevations

Feet		Meters
10,000		3,000
5,000		1,500
2,000		600
1,000		300
0		0

Zambesi R.

Victoria Falls

Okavango
Swamp

Limpopo R.

Tropic of Capricorn

Kalahari
Desert

Namib Desert

Johannesburg

DRAKENSBERG

Zulu-
land

Orange R.

Vaal R.

Miles   0   800

Kilometers   0   1200

Cape of Good Hope

Cape Agulhas

INDIAN

OCEAN

475

20°   10°   West longitude   0°   East longitude   10°   20°   30°   40°   50°

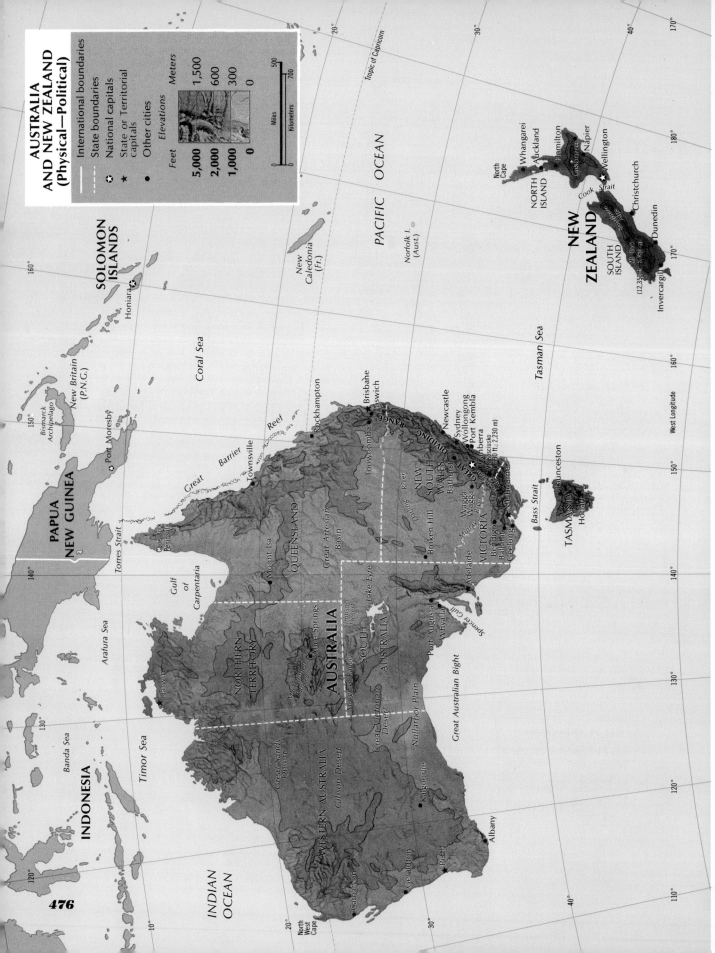

AUSTRALIA AND NEW ZEALAND (Physical—Political)

International boundaries
State boundaries
National capitals ☆
State or Territorial capitals ★
Other cities ●

Elevations

Feet	Meters
5,000	1,500
2,000	600
1,000	300
0	0

Miles
Kilometers

INDONESIA

Banda Sea

Timor Sea

Arafura Sea

Bismarck Archipelago

New Britain (P.N.G.)

PAPUA NEW GUINEA

Port Moresby ☆

Torres Strait

SOLOMON ISLANDS

Honiara ☆

Coral Sea

New Caledonia (Fr.)

PACIFIC OCEAN

Norfolk I. (Aust.)

Tropic of Capricorn

Gulf of Carpentaria

Cape York Peninsula

Great Barrier Reef

Townsville

Rockhampton

Brisbane
Ipswich

Toowoomba

QUEENSLAND

Great Artesian Basin

Mount Isa

NORTHERN TERRITORY

Alice Springs

Darwin ★

Macdonnell Ranges

Simpson Desert

SOUTH AUSTRALIA

Lake Eyre

Musgrave Ranges

AUSTRALIA

NEW SOUTH WALES

Darling River

Murray River

Broken Hill

Bathurst

Wagga Wagga

Newcastle
Sydney
Wollongong
Port Kembla

GREAT DIVIDING RANGE

Canberra ☆
Mt. Kosciusko
(7,310 ft.; 2,230 m)

VICTORIA

Bendigo
Ballarat
Geelong
Melbourne ★

Bass Strait

TASMANIA

Launceston

Hobart ★

Adelaide ★
Whyalla
Port Augusta
Spencer Gulf

Great Australian Bight

Nullarbor Plain

Great Victoria Desert

Gibson Desert

Great Sandy Desert

WESTERN AUSTRALIA

Kalgoorlie

Albany

Perth ★

Geraldton

Carnarvon

North West Cape

INDIAN OCEAN

Tasman Sea

NEW ZEALAND

North Cape

NORTH ISLAND

Whangarei
Auckland
Hamilton
Gisborne
Napier
Wellington ☆

Cook Strait

SOUTH ISLAND

Christchurch
Dunedin

Southern Alps

Mt. Cook
(12,350 ft.; 3,760 m)

Invercargill

West Longitude

GAZETTEER

The page references tell where each entry may be found on a map.

Abilene (39°N/97°W). Important railroad center at the end of the Chisholm Trail in the 1860s. Today, a city in Kansas on the Smoky Hill River. p. 191.

Acadia National Park. 116-acre (46-ha) national park in Maine. p. 309.

Adirondack Mountains. Mountains in northeast corner of New York. Highest peak is Mt. Marcy, with an elevation of 5,344 ft (1,629 m). p. 311.

Africa. The earth's second largest continent. p. 6.

Akron (41°N/82°W). Large industrial city on the Cuyahoga River in Ohio. p. 381.

Alaska Peninsula. Peninsula in Alaska separating the Bering Sea from the Pacific Ocean. p. 470.

Alaska Range. Mountains in south central Alaska. Mt. McKinley (Mt. Denali), the highest peak in North America, is in this range. Its elevation is 20,320 ft (6,194 m). p. 403.

Albany (43°N/74°W). Capital of New York. Located on the Hudson River. p. 324.

Albuquerque (35°N/107°W). Most populated city in New Mexico. Located on the Rio Grande. p. 397.

Aleutian Islands. Chain of islands extending west from the Alaska Peninsula. p. 468.

Allegheny Plateau. Part of the Appalachian system west of the Blue Ridge. p. 329.

Allegheny River. River in north central Pennsylvania, flows northward into New York, then south back into Pennsylvania. At Pittsburgh, it joins the Monongahela River to form the Ohio River. p. 311.

Amazon River. Second longest river in the world. Tributaries rise in the Andes Mountains and Guiana Highlands. Flows into the Atlantic Ocean near Belém, Brazil. p. 439.

Anchorage (61°N/150°W). Most populated city in Alaska. Located on Cook Inlet, an arm of the Pacific Ocean. p. 413.

Andes Mountains. High mountains that stretch north to south along the western side of South America. Highest peak, with an elevation of 22,840 ft (6,690 m), is Mt. Aconcagua. p. 439.

Annapolis (39°N/77°W). Capital of Maryland. Located on Chesapeake Bay. Site of the United States Naval Academy. p. 324.

Antarctica. The earth's third smallest continent. p. 6.

Antarctic Circle. A line of latitude located at 66½° south latitude. p. 9.

Antietam (39°N/78°W). Site, in Maryland, of a battle fought as a result of General Lee's first invasion of the North. His army retreated south following this battle. p. 175.

Appalachian Mountains. Chain of mountains stretching from Canada to Alabama. Highest peak is Mt. Mitchell, at 6,684 ft (2,037 m). p. 263.

Appomattox (37°N/79°W). Site, in Virginia, where General Lee surrendered his army to General Grant. p. 175.

Arctic Circle. A line of latitude located at 66½° north latitude. p. 9.

Arkansas River. Rises in central Colorado and flows into the Mississippi River in southeast Arkansas. p. 265.

Aroostook River. Rises in northern Maine and flows northeast into the St. John River in Canada. p. 287.

Asheville (36°N/83°W). City in North Carolina. Located near eastern entrance to Great Smoky Mountains National Park. p. 343.

Asia. The earth's largest continent. p. 6.

Asunción (25°S/58°W). Capital of Paraguay. Located on Paraguay River. p. 440.

Atacama Desert. Dry area in Chile. Major source of nitrates. p. 439.

Atlanta (34°N/84°W). Capital of and most populated city in Georgia. p. 343.

Atlantic Coastal Plain. Large plain located along the Atlantic coast from Maine to Florida. p. 263.

Atlantic Ocean. Large body of water separating North and South America from Europe and Africa. p. 6.

Augusta (44°N/70°W). Capital of Maine. Located on the Kennebec River. p. 306.

Austin (30°N/98°W). Capital of Texas. Located near the western edge of the Gulf Coastal Plain. p. 362.

Australia. The earth's smallest continent. p. 6.

Bad Lands. Dry, rugged areas with little or no vegetation. Located in South Dakota, in North Dakota, and in Montana. p. 367.

Baja California. A peninsula that separates the Pacific Ocean and the Gulf of California. Also called Lower California. p. 470.

Bakersfield (35°N/119°W). City in southern California. Located at the southern end of the Central Valley. p. 413.

Baltimore (39°N/77°W). The most populated city in Maryland. Located on Chesapeake Bay. One of the busiest seaports in the nation. p. 324.

Barrow (71°N/157°W). Small town in northern Alaska. p. 413.

Baton Rouge (30°N/91°W). Capital of Louisiana. Located on the Mississippi River. p. 362.

Beaufort Sea. Part of the Arctic Ocean northeast of Alaska. p. 403.

Belém (1°S/48°W). Seaport city on the Atlantic coast of Brazil. p. 440.

477

Bering Sea. Part of the North Pacific Ocean bounded on the east by mainland of Alaska and on the south and southeast by the Aleutian Islands. p. 468.

Bering Strait. Narrow body of water connecting the Arctic Ocean and Bering Sea. Separates Asia from North America. p. 470.

Berkshires. Low mountains or hills in Massachusetts. They are part of the Appalachian system. Highest peak is Mt. Greylock, with an elevation of 3,491 ft (1,064 m). p. 287.

Birmingham (34°N/87°W). Most populated city in Alabama. One of the nation's leading iron- and steel-producing centers. p. 343.

Bismarck (47°N/101°W). Capital of North Dakota. Located on the Missouri River. p. 381.

Black Hills. Mountainous area with steep canyons. Located in South Dakota and Wyoming. Harney Peak, South Dakota, the highest point in the North Central region, is in the Black Hills. Its elevation is 7,242 ft (2,209 m). p. 367.

Blue Ridge Mountains. Eastern part of the Appalachian system. They stretch from Pennsylvania to Georgia. p. 469.

Bogotá (5°N/74°W). Capital of Colombia. Located in the Andes Mountains. p. 440.

Boise (44°N/116°W). Capital of and most populated city in Idaho. p. 397.

Boston (42°N/71°W). Capital of and most populated city in Massachusetts. Located on Massachusetts Bay. p. 306.

Brasilia (16°S/48°W). Capital of Brazil. p. 440.

Brazilian Highlands. Highland area located in southeast Brazil. p. 439.

Brooks Range. Northernmost part of the Rocky Mountains. Located in northern Alaska. Mt. Michelson is the highest peak. Its elevation is 9,239 ft (2,816 m). p. 403.

Buenos Aires (35°S/58°W). Capital of and most populated city in Argentina. Located on the Río de la Plata. p. 440.

Buffalo (43°N/79°W). City in New York. Located on Lake Erie and the Niagara River. p. 324.

Bull Run (39°N/77°W). Stream that gave its name to the first big battle of the Civil War. Fought in Manassas, Virginia, the battle was won by the South. p. 175.

Burlington (44°N/73°W). Port city in Vermont located on Lake Champlain. p. 306.

Cadillac Mountain (44°N/68°W). Located on Mount Desert Island in Maine. It is the highest point on the Atlantic coast. It has an elevation of 1,530 ft (466 m). p. 309.

Calgary (51°N/114°W). City in Alberta, Canada. p. 434.

Camden (40°N/75°W). City in New Jersey. Located on the east side of the Delaware River, across from Philadelphia, Pennsylvania. p. 324.

Canadian Shield. Upland region extending in a horseshoe shape from the Labrador coast to the Arctic Ocean west of Victoria Island. p. 427.

Cape Canaveral (28°N/81°W). National Space Center. Site of launching for space flights. Located on the east coast of Florida. p. 329.

Cape Cod. Sandy peninsula in Massachusetts, known for its many beautiful beaches on the Atlantic Ocean. p. 287.

Caracas (11°N/67°W). Capital of and most populated city in Venezuela. p. 440.

Caribbean Sea. Part of the Atlantic Ocean bounded by South America on the south, Central America on the west, and Cuba, Puerto Rico, and other islands on the north and east. p. 7.

Carson City (39°N/120°W). Capital of Nevada. Located near Lake Tahoe. p. 397.

Cascade Range. Mountains that extend from northern California to Washington and into Canada. Highest peak, with an elevation of 14,408 ft (4,392 m), is Mt. Rainier. p. 468.

Cayenne (5°N/52°W). Capital of French Guiana. p. 440.

Central America. Made up of Guatemala, El Salvador, Honduras, Nicaragua, Costa Rica, Panama, and Belize. p. 7.

Central Lowlands. Large plain area located in the eastern part of the Central Plains. p. 263.

Central Plains. Located in the middle of the United States. Largest plain in the nation. p. 263.

Central Valley. Located in California between the Sierra Nevada and the Coast Ranges. Made up of the Sacramento Valley in the north and the San Joaquin Valley in the south. p. 468.

Chaco. Plains of the Paraná and Paraguay rivers. p. 439.

Charleston (33°N/80°W). Port in South Carolina. Founded in 1670. p. 343.

Charleston (38°N/82°W). Capital of West Virginia. Located at point where the Elk and Kanawha rivers join. p. 343.

Charlottetown (46°N/63°W). Capital of Prince Edward Island, Canada. p. 434.

Chesapeake Bay. Inlet of the Atlantic Ocean in Virginia and Maryland. It is about 190 miles (306 km) long. p. 311.

Cheyenne (41°N/105°W). Capital of Wyoming. p. 397.

Chicago (42°N/88°W). One of six cities in the United States with a population of more than 1,000,000. Located in Illinois, on the southern tip of Lake Michigan. p. 381.

Cincinnati (39°N/85°W). Large city in Ohio. Located on the Ohio River. p. 381.

Cleveland (42°N/82°W). Most populated city in Ohio. Located on Lake Erie at the mouth of the Cuyahoga River. p. 381.

Coast Ranges. Mountains along the Pacific coast of North America. They stretch from Alaska to California. p. 468.

Colorado Plateau. Large, high area of land located in the southern part of the Mountain West. p. 263.

Colorado River. Rises at the Continental Divide in Rocky Mountain National Park in northern Colorado and flows into the Gulf of California in Mexico. Very important source of irrigation water in southwest United States. p. 265.

Colorado Springs (39°N/105°W). City in Colorado. The United States Air Force Academy is located here. p. 397.

Columbia (39°N/92°W). City in Missouri. p. 381.

Columbia (34°N/81°W). Capital of South Carolina. Located on the Congaree River. p. 343.

Columbia Plateau. High area of land located in the northern part of the Mountain West. p. 468.

Columbia River. Rises in Rocky Mountains in Canada, and flows into the Pacific Ocean along the Washington-Oregon boundary. p. 265.

Columbus (40°N/83°W). Capital of Ohio. Located on the Scioto River. p. 381.

Concord (42°N/71°W). Massachusetts town where the American patriots met the British redcoats in a skirmish at the beginning of the American Revolution. p. 115.

Concord (43°N/72°W). Capital of New Hampshire. Located on the Merrimack River. p. 306.

Connecticut River. Longest river in New England. Rises in northern New Hampshire and flows into Long Island Sound at Old Saybrook, Connecticut. p. 265.

Córdoba (31°S/64°W). Large city in Argentina. p. 440.

Crater Lake (43°N/122°W). Located in Oregon in the Cascade Mountains. It is the deepest lake in the United States, with a depth of 1,932 ft (589 m). p. 403.

Cumberland Plateau. Part of the Appalachian system. Extends from West Virginia to Alabama. p. 329.

Cumberland River. Starts in Kentucky, flows into Tennessee and then back into Kentucky, where it joins the Ohio River. p. 329.

Dallas (33°N/97°W). The second most populated city in Texas. Located on the Trinity River. p. 362.

Deadwood (44°N/104°W). City in Black Hills of South Dakota. Was a busy gold mining community in the late nineteenth century. p. 191.

Death Valley. Very low valley, located at the northern edge of the Mojave Desert. It is 282 ft (86 m) below sea level. p. 468.

Delaware Bay. Arm of the Atlantic Ocean between New Jersey and Delaware. p. 311.

Delaware River. Rises in the Catskill Mountains in New York. Flows into the Atlantic Ocean at Delaware Bay. p. 265.

Delmarva Peninsula. Located on the east coast of the United States. Parts of Delaware, Maryland, and Virginia are on this peninsula. p. 263.

Denver (40°N/105°W). Capital of and most populated city in Colorado. Located at the base of the Rocky Mountains where they join the Great Plains. Has an elevation of 5,280 ft (1,609 m). p. 397.

Des Moines (42°N/94°W). Capital of Iowa. Located on Des Moines River. p. 381.

Detroit (42°N/83°W). One of six cities in the United States with a population of more than 1,000,000. Located on the Detroit River, in Michigan, near Lake Erie. p. 381.

Dodge City (38°N/100°W). City in Kansas on the Arkansas River. In 1860s it was an important railroad center on the Santa Fe Trail. p. 191.

Dover (39°N/75°W). Capital of Delaware. p. 324.

Duluth (47°N/92°W). Port city in Minnesota. Located at the western end of Lake Superior. p. 381.

Eastern Hemisphere. The half of the earth east of the prime meridian. p. 5.

Edmonton (54°N/113°W). Capital of Alberta, Canada. Located on the North Saskatchewan River. p. 434.

equator. A line drawn on maps that circles the earth halfway between the two poles. It is labeled 0° latitude. p. 5.

Erie (42°N/80°W). Port city located on the south shore of Lake Erie in the northwest corner of Pennsylvania. p. 324.

Erie Canal. Canal that connects Albany, New York, on the Hudson River, with Buffalo, New York, on Lake Erie. Original canal completed in 1825. p. 148.

Eurasia. The name often given to the total area covered by Europe and Asia. p. 472.

Europe. The earth's second smallest continent. p. 6.

Everglades. Large swamp located in southern Florida. p. 329.

Fairbanks (65°N/148°W). Town in central Alaska. Located on the Tanana River. p. 413.

Falkland Islands. Located in the South Atlantic Ocean, east of the southern tip of South America. p. 439.

Feather River. Located in California. Flows into the Sacramento River near Sacramento, California. p. 416.

Florida Keys. Chain of islands about 150 miles (241 km) long. They stretch southwest around the tip of Florida from Virginia Key, near Miami, to Key West. p. 329.

Fortaleza (4°S/39°W). Port city in northeast Brazil. p. 440.

Fort McHenry (39°N/77°W). Fort in Baltimore, which was attacked by British warships during the War of 1812. During the attack Francis Scott Key wrote the lyrics for the "Star-Spangled Banner." p. 137.

Fort Sumter (33°N/80°W). Fort on south side of the entrance to the harbor at Charleston, South Carolina. The first shots of the Civil War were fired here in 1861. p. 343.

Fort Ticonderoga (44°N/73°W). Fort on Lake Champlain. Captured in the first year of the American Revolution by Ethan Allen's soldiers but later retaken by the British. p. 115.

Fort Worth (33°N/97°W). City in Texas. Located on the Trinity River. p. 362.

Frankfort (38°N/85°W). Capital of Kentucky. Located on the Kentucky River. p. 343.

Fraser River. Rises in Canadian Rockies and flows into Pacific Ocean near Vancouver, British Columbia. p. 423.

Fredericton (46°N/67°W). Capital of New Brunswick, Canada. p. 434.

Gary (42°N/87°W). City in Indiana on the southern end of Lake Michigan. One of the most important steelmaking centers in the United States. p. 381.

Georgetown (7°N/58°W). Capital and chief port of Guyana. p. 440.

Gettysburg (40°N/77°W). Town in Pennsylvania. Site of a battle fought as a result of General Lee's second and last invasion of the North. His invasion was turned back. p. 175.

Grand Banks. Rich fishing area in Atlantic Ocean south of Newfoundland. p. 423.

Grand Canyon. (36°N/113°W). Famous canyon in Arizona formed by the Colorado River. p. 387.

Great Basin. Upland region. Located in the United States between the Rocky Mountains on the east and the Cascade Range and Sierra Nevada on the west. p. 468.

Greater Antilles. Group of islands in the West Indies. They include the islands of Cuba, Jamaica, Puerto Rico, and Hispaniola. p. 439.

Great Lakes. Five large lakes located in North America mostly along the border between Canada and the United States. p. 265.

Great Plains. Large plain area located in the western part of the Central Plains. p. 263.

Great Salt Lake (41°N/112°W). Located in the Great Basin. An inland lake with no streams flowing out of it. p. 387.

Great Slave Lake (62°N/114°W). The deepest lake in the Western Hemisphere. It is 2,015 ft (614 m) deep. It is in the Northwest Territories, Canada. p. 423.

Great Smoky Mountains. Part of the Appalachian system that extends along the North Carolina-Tennessee boundary. Highest peak is Clingmans Dome, with an elevation of 6,643 ft (2,024 m). p. 329.

Greenland. Large island belonging to Denmark, off the coast of northeast North America. Excluding the continent of Australia, it is the largest island in the world. p. 470.

Green Mountains. Located in Vermont. Part of the Appalachians. Highest point is Mt. Mansfield, with an elevation of 4,393 ft (1,339 m). p. 287.

Greenwich. A place in London, England, designated as 0° longitude. p. 11.

Groton (41°N/72°W). City in Connecticut. Located on Long Island Sound at the mouth of the Thames River. Site of large submarine shipbuilding base. p. 306.

Guadalajara (21°N/103°W). Second most populated city in Mexico. p. 440.

Guadalupe Mountains. Located in New Mexico and Texas. Highest peak is Guadalupe Peak, with an elevation of 8,751 ft (2,667 m). p. 349.

Gulf Coastal Plain. Large plain located along the Gulf of Mexico from Florida to Texas. p. 263.

Gulf of Alaska. Part of the Pacific Ocean east of Kodiak Island. p. 468.

Gulf of Mexico. Body of water surrounded by the United States, Mexico, and Cuba. p. 265.

Guiana Highlands. Located in northern South America from Venezuela through French Guiana. p. 439.

Halifax (45°N/64°W). Capital of Nova Scotia, Canada. Located on the Atlantic Ocean. p. 434.

Hamilton (43°N/80°W). Industrial city in Ontario, Canada. p. 434.

Hampton (37°N/76°W). City in Virginia. Located on Hampton Roads channel. p. 343.

Harrisburg (40°N/77°W). Capital of Pennsylvania. Located on the Susquehanna River. p. 324.

Hartford (42°N/73°W). Capital of Connecticut. Located on the Connecticut River. p. 306.

Havana (23°N/82°W). Capital of Cuba and the most populated city in the West Indies. p. 444.

Helena (47°N/112°W). Capital of Montana. p. 397.

Hibbing (47°N/93°W). Town located in Mesabi Range in Minnesota. It is near the world's largest open-pit iron mine. p. 381.

Hispaniola. Second largest island in the West Indies. p. 470.

Honolulu (21°N/158°W). Capital of and most populated city in Hawaii. Located on the island of Oahu. p. 413.

Hot Springs (35°N/93°W). City in Arkansas located in the Ouachita Mountains. p. 362.

Houston (30°N/95°W). City near Galveston Bay in Texas. One of the six cities in the United States with a population of more than 1,000,000. p. 362.

Hudson Bay. Large body of water in Canada. Connected with Atlantic by Hudson Strait. p. 423.

Hudson River. Rises in Adirondack Mountains and flows into New York harbor at New York City. p. 265.

Imperial Valley. Located in southeastern California and Baja California. Mostly below sea level. The Salton Sea is in this valley. p. 403.

Indianapolis (40°N/86°W). Capital of and most populated city in Indiana. p. 381.

International Falls (49°N/93°W). City in Minnesota on the Rainy River. p. 381.

Jackson (32°N/90°W). Capital of Mississippi. Located on the Pearl River. p. 343.

Jamestown (37°N/77°W). First permanent English settlement in America. Founded in 1607. p. 89.

Jefferson City (39°N/92°W). Capital of Missouri. Located on the Missouri River. p. 381.

Jersey City (41°N/74°W). Second most populated city in New Jersey. Located on the Hudson River across from New York City. p. 324.

Juneau (58°N/134°W). Capital of Alaska. Located on the Alaskan panhandle. p. 413.

Ka Lae (19°N/156°W). A cape on the southern tip of the island of Hawaii. The most southern point in the United States. p. 403.

Kansas City (39°N/95°W). City in Kansas. Located on the western side of the Missouri River. On the eastern side of the Missouri River is Kansas City, Kansas. p. 381.

Kansas City (39°N/95°W). City in Missouri. Located on the eastern side of the Missouri River across from Kansas City, Kansas. p. 381.

Kauai. Fourth largest of the Hawaiian Islands. p. 403.

Kennebec River. River in Maine. Flows south from Moosehead Lake to Atlantic Ocean. p. 287.

Kingston (18°N/77°W). Capital and chief seaport of Jamaica. p. 444.

Knoxville (36°N/84°W). City in Tennessee. Located on the Tennessee River. p. 343.

Lake Champlain. Located between New York and Vermont. Named after its discoverer, Samuel de Champlain. p. 287.

Lake Erie. Located along the border between Canada and the United States. Second smallest of the five Great Lakes. Has coastline in Michigan, Ohio, Pennsylvania, and New York. p. 265.

Lake Huron. Located along the boundary between Canada and the United States. Second largest of the five Great Lakes. United States portion of the lake is in Michigan. p. 265.

Lake Itasca. Source of Mississippi River. Located in Minnesota. p. 367.

Lake Maracaibo. An extension of the Caribbean Sea. Located in northwest Venezuela. Surrounded by rich oil fields. p. 439.

Lake Michigan. Located in the United States. Third largest of the five Great Lakes. Has coastline in Michigan, Wisconsin, Illinois, and Indiana. p. 265.

Lake Okeechobee. Large lake in Florida. Located at northern edge of the Everglades. p. 329.

Lake Ontario. Located along the border between Canada and the United States. Smallest of the five Great Lakes. United States portion of the lake is in New York. The only one of the Great Lakes that does not have a coastline in Michigan. p. 265.

Lake Pontchartrain. Lake near the southern end of the Mississippi River. p. 349.

Lake Superior. Located along the boundary between Canada and the United States. Largest of the five Great Lakes. Has coastline in Minnesota, Wisconsin, and Michigan. p. 265.

Lake Tahoe. Located on the border between California and Nevada. p. 403.

Lansing (43°N/85°W). Capital of Michigan. Located on Grand River. p. 381.

La Paz (17°S/68°W). Most populated city in Bolivia. The third highest city in the world. Its elevation is 11,736 ft (3,577 m). p. 440.

Las Vegas (36°N/115°W). Resort city in Nevada. p. 397.

Laurentian Highlands. Highland area in Quebec province, Canada, north of St. Lawrence River. Also called Laurentide Hills. p. 423.

Lead (44°N/104°W). City in South Dakota. Site of famous Homestake Mine, the largest gold mine in the United States. p. 381.

Lesser Antilles. Group of islands in the West Indies. Included in this island group are Virgin Is., Leeward Is., and Windward Is. p. 439.

Lexington (43°N/71°W). Massachusetts town where, in April 1775, a group of minutemen (militia) resisted British troops in the first battle of the American Revolution. p. 115.

Lima (12°S/77°W). Capital of and most populated city in Peru. p. 440.

Lincoln (41°N/97°W). Capital of Nebraska. Located on a tributary of the Platte River. p. 381.

Little Rock (35°N/92°W). Capital of Arkansas. Located on the Arkansas River. p. 362.

Llano Estacado. High plain in New Mexico, Oklahoma, and Texas. Also called the Staked Plains. p. 349.

Llanos. Large plain in northern South America. Drained by the Orinoco River. p. 439.

London (52°N/0° long). Capital and most populated city in the United Kingdom. Located along the Thames River. p. 10.

Long Island Sound. Body of water between south shore of Connecticut and north shore of Long Island. p. 287.

Los Angeles (34°N/118°W). City in southern California on the Pacific Ocean. One of six cities in the United States with a population of more than 1,000,000. p. 413.

Louisville (38°N/86°W). Most populated city in Kentucky. Located on the Ohio River. p. 343.

Lubbock (34°N/102°W). City in Texas. Located in the Llano Estacado. p. 362.

Madison (43°N/89°W). Capital of Wisconsin. Located on an isthmus between Lakes Monona and Mendota. p. 381.

Manaus (3°S/60°W). City in rain forest of Brazil. Located on the Negro River, a branch of the Amazon River. p. 440.

Maui. Second largest of the Hawaiian Islands. p. 403.

Memphis (35°N/90°W). Large city in Tennessee. Located on the Mississippi River. p. 343.

Merrimack River. Begins at Franklin, New Hampshire, and flows into the Atlantic Ocean at Newburyport, Massachusetts. p. 287.

Mesabi Range. Range of low hills located in northeast Minnesota. Most important source of iron ore in the United States. p. 281.

Mexico City (19°N/99°W). Capital of Mexico. The most populated city in North America. p. 440.

Miami (26°N/80°W). Large city in Florida. Located on Biscayne Bay. p. 343.

Middle America. The area from Mexico to Panama. It also includes the islands in the Caribbean. p. 7.

Milwaukee (43°N/88°W). Most populated city in Wisconsin. Located on Lake Michigan. p. 381.

Minneapolis (45°N/93°W). Most populated city in Minnesota. Located on the Mississippi River. p. 381.

Mississippi River. Second longest river in the United States. Rises in northern Minnesota and flows into the Gulf of Mexico near New Orleans, Louisiana. p. 265.

Missouri River. Longest river in the United States. Rises in western Montana and flows into Mississippi River near St. Louis, Missouri. p. 265.

Mohawk River. Largest tributary of the Hudson River. Joins the Hudson near Troy, New York. Part of the New York State Barge Canal. p. 311.

Monongahela River. Rises in West Virginia and flows into the Allegheny River at Pittsburgh to form the Ohio River. p. 311.

Monterrey (26°N/100°W). Industrial city in Mexico. p. 440.

Montevideo (35°S/56°W). Capital of and most populated city in Uruguay. Located on the Río de la Plata. p. 440.

Montgomery (32°N/86°W). Capital of Alabama. Located on the Alabama River. p. 343.

Montpelier (44°N/73°W). Capital of Vermont. Located on the Winooski River. p. 306.

Montreal (47°N/90°W). Most populated city in Canada. Located on an island in the St. Lawrence River. p. 434.

Mount Desert Island. Located off the northeast coast of Maine. It is about 14 miles (23 km) long and about 8 miles (13 km) wide. Part of Acadia National Park is on this island. p. 309.

Mount Elbert (39°N/106°W). Highest peak in the Rocky Mountains. Located in Colorado. It has an elevation of 14,433 ft (4,399 m). p. 387.

Mount McKinley or Mt. Denali (64°N/150°W). Located in Alaska Range in Alaska. Highest mountain peak in North America. Its elevation is 20,320 ft (6,194 m). p. 263.

Mount Mitchell (36°N/82°W). Has an elevation of 6,684 ft (2,037 m). Located in North Carolina. Highest peak in the Appalachians. p. 329.

Mount Waialeale (22°N/160°W). Peak with an elevation of 5,080 ft (1,569 m). Located in Hawaii on the island of Kauai. One of the rainiest places in the world. p. 403.

Mount Washington (44°N/71°W). Peak located in the White Mountains of New Hampshire. It is the highest point in New England. It has an elevation of 6,288 ft (1,917 m). It is also the windiest place in the United States. p. 287.

Mystic (41°N/72°W). Restored nineteenth century whaling seaport located on Long Island Sound in Connecticut. p. 306.

Nashville (36°N/87°W). Capital of Tennessee. Located on the Cumberland River. p. 343.

Newark (41°N/74°W). Most populated city in New Jersey. Located on the Passaic River and Newark Bay. p. 324.

New Haven (41°N/73°W). Large city in Connecticut. Located on Long Island Sound. At one time it was one of two capitals of Connecticut. p. 306.

New London (41°N/72°W). City in Connecticut. Located on Long Island Sound at the mouth of the Thames River. The United States Coast Guard Academy and a large United States Naval Submarine base are located here. p. 306.

New Orleans (30°N/90°W). Most populated city in Louisiana. Located on the Mississippi River. One of the busiest ports in the United States. p. 362.

Newport News (37°N/76°W). City in Virginia. Located at entrance to Hampton Roads channel. p. 343.

New York City (41°N/74°W). Most populated city in the United States. Located at mouth of the Hudson River in the state of New York. p. 324.

Niagara River. Short river that flows north connecting Lake Erie on the south with Lake Ontario to the north. The river passes over the famous Niagara Falls. p. 311.

Norfolk (37°N/76°W). City in Virginia. Located on Hampton Roads channel. p. 343.

North America. The earth's third largest continent. p. 6.

Northern Hemisphere. Half of the earth that is north of the equator. p. 5.

North Pole. Most northern place on the earth. p. 5.

North Slope. Area of Alaska located between the Brooks Range and the Beaufort Sea. One of our nation's largest oil fields was discovered here in 1968. p. 403.

Ogden (41°N/112°W). City in Utah. The transcontinental railroad was completed near here in 1869. p. 397.

Ohio River. Formed at Pittsburgh, Pennsylvania by the joining of the Allegheny and Monongahela rivers. Flows into the Mississippi River at Cairo, Illinois. Forms part of the boundary of five states. p. 265.

Oklahoma City (35°N/98°W). Capital of Oklahoma. p. 362.

Olympia (47°N/123°W). Capital of Washington. Located on Puget Sound. p. 413.

Omaha (41°N/96°W). City in Nebraska. Located on the Missouri River. p. 381.

Orinoco River. Located in Venezuela. Rises in the Guiana Highlands and flows into the Atlantic Ocean near Trinidad and Tobago. p. 439.

Ottawa (45°N/76°W). Capital of Canada. p. 434.

Ouachita Mountains. Located in Arkansas and Oklahoma. Part of the Ozark Plateau. p. 349.

Outer Banks. Group of islands located along the coast of North Carolina. p. 329.

Owens River. Located in California. Supplies water to Los Angeles through the Los Angeles Aqueduct. p. 416.

Ozark Plateau. Elevated area extending from Missouri through Arkansas into Oklahoma. p. 349.

Pacific Ocean. Large body of water stretching from the Arctic Circle to Antarctica and from the western coast of North America to the eastern coast of Asia. p. 6.

Padre Island. Sand reef off the coast of southern Texas in the Gulf of Mexico. A national seashore is located here. p. 349.

Paducah (37°N/89°W). City in Kentucky. Located on Ohio River near the point where the Tennessee River joins the Ohio River. p. 343.

Painted Desert. Small desert located mostly in northeastern Arizona. p. 387.

Pampas. Fertile agricultural plains area in Argentina and Uruguay. p. 439.

Paraguay River. Rises in Brazil and flows into the Paraná River at the southwest corner of Paraguay. p. 439.

Paramaribo (6°N/55°W). Seaport city and capital of Surinam. p. 440.

Paraná River. Formed in Brazil; flows into the Río de la Plata. p. 439.

Pasadena (34°N/118°W). City in southern California. Site of the annual Rose Bowl parade and football game. p. 413.

Patagonia. Barren plains area in southern Argentina. p. 439.

Paterson (41°N/74°W). City in New Jersey on the edge of the Atlantic Coastal Plain. p. 324.

Pearl Harbor (21°N/158°W). Inlet on the island of Oahu in Hawaii. Site of a U.S. naval base attacked by the Japanese on December 7, 1941. The next day, the United States declared war on Japan. p. 403.

Penobscot Bay. Inlet of the Atlantic Ocean. Located on the Maine coast. p. 287.

Penobscot River. River in Maine. Formed near Howland, Maine. Flows into Penobscot Bay. p. 287.

Philadelphia (40°N/75°W). City at the point where Delaware and Schuylkill rivers join. One of six cities in the United States with a population of more than 1,000,000. p. 324.

Phoenix (33°N/112°W). Capital of and most populated city in Arizona. Located on the Salt River. p. 397.

Pierre (44°N/100°W). Capital of South Dakota. Located on the Missouri River. p. 381.

Pikes Peak (39°N/105°W). Mountain peak in the Rocky Mountains. Has an elevation of 14,110 ft (4,304 m). p. 191.

Pittsburgh (40°N/80°W). Second most populated city in Pennsylvania. Located at point where the Allegheny and Monongahela rivers join. p. 324.

Point Barrow (71°N/157°W). Located in Alaska. The most northern place in the United States. p. 403.

Port-au-Prince (19°N/72°W). Capital of and chief seaport in Haiti. p. 444.

Portland (44°N/70°W). Seaport city in southern Maine. Located on Casco Bay, which is part of the Atlantic Ocean. p. 306.

Portland (46°N/123°W). Most populated city in Oregon. Located on the Willamette River near the point where it joins the Columbia River. p. 413.

Pôrto Alegre (30°S/51°W). Seaport city in southern Brazil on an inlet of the Pacific Ocean. p. 440.

Portsmouth (37°N/76°W). City in Virginia. Located on Hampton Roads channel. p. 343.

Potomac River. Rises in West Virginia and flows into Chesapeake Bay. Washington, D.C., is located on this river. p. 311.

Prime Meridian. 0° line of longitude that passes through Greenwich, England. It divides the earth into Eastern and Western hemispheres. p. 11.

Promontory Point (41°N/112°W). Place near Ogden, Utah, where tracks for the Central Pacific and the Union Pacific railroads were joined in 1869. p. 191.

Providence (42°N/71°W). Capital of Rhode Island. Located at the head of the Providence River. p. 306.

Prudhoe Bay. Small bay on Beaufort Sea. Located in northern Alaska near the mouth of the Sagavanirktok River. p. 403.

Puget Sound. Inlet of the Pacific Ocean in Washington stretching from Juan de Fuca Strait to Olympia. p. 403.

Quebec (52°N/72°W). City in Canada, on the north side of the St. Lawrence River. It was founded in 1608 by Samuel de Champlain. Today it is the capital of the province of Quebec. p. 434.

Quincy (42°N/71°W). Shipbuilding city in eastern Massachusetts. Birthplace of John, and John Quincy, Adams, the second and the sixth Presidents of the United States. p. 306.

Quito (0°lat/79°W). Capital of and most populated city in Ecuador. p. 440.

Raleigh (36°N/79°W). Capital of North Carolina. p. 343.

Recife (8°S/35°W). Seaport city located on the Atlantic coast on the eastern bulge of Brazil. p. 440.

Red River. Rises in New Mexico. Flows across the Texas panhandle and then forms boundary between Texas and Oklahoma. There are two other Red Rivers in the United States, one in Tennessee and another in Minnesota. p. 349.

Richelieu River. Flows out of the northern end of Lake Champlain and into the St. Lawrence in Canada. p. 287.

Richmond (38°N/77°W). Capital of Virginia. Located on the James River. p. 343.

Rio de Janeiro (23°S/43°W). The second most populated city in South America. Major port of Brazil. Located on the Atlantic coast. p. 440.

Río de la Plata. Body of water at the point where the Paraná and Uruguay rivers flow into the Atlantic Ocean. p. 439.

Rio Grande. Rises in the Rocky Mountains in Colorado. It empties into the Gulf of Mexico near Brownsville, Texas. It forms the boundary between Texas and Mexico. p. 265.

Roanoke (37°N/80°W). City in Virginia. Located on the Roanoke River. p. 343.

Rocky Mountains. Longest mountain chain in the United States. Stretches from Alaska to Mexico. Highest peak is Mt. Elbert, with an elevation of 14,433 ft (4,399 m). p. 468.

Rosario (33°S/61°W). City in Argentina. Located on the Paraná River. p. 440.

Sacramento (38°N/122°W). Capital of California. Located on the Sacramento River. p. 413.

Sacramento River. River in California that flows into San Francisco Bay. p. 416.

St. Augustine (30°N/81°W). City in Florida. Founded in 1565 by explorers from Spain. Oldest city in the United States. p. 74.

St. John's (48°N/53°W). Capital of Newfoundland, Canada. Located on southeast coast of Newfoundland Island. p. 434.

St. Lawrence River. Forms part of the boundary between Canada and the United States. Flows northeast from Lake Ontario to the Atlantic Ocean at the Gulf of St. Lawrence. p. 423.

St. Louis (39°N/90°W). Most populated city in Missouri. Located on Mississippi River near the point where it is joined by the Missouri River. p. 381.

St. Paul (45°N/93°W). Capital of Minnesota. Located on the Mississippi River. p. 381.

Salem (45°N/123°W). Capital of Oregon. Located on the Willamette River. p. 413.

Salt Lake City (41°N/112°W). Capital of and most populated city in Utah. Located near Great Salt Lake. p. 397.

Salton Sea. Salty, below-sea-level lake located in southern California. p. 403.

Salvador (13°S/39°W). Seaport city on east coast of Brazil. p. 440.

San Antonio (30°N/98°W). Large city in Texas. Located on the San Antonio River. Site of the Alamo. p. 362.

San Diego (33°N/117°W). First of 21 Spanish missions was built here. Today it is a large city located in southern California along the Pacific Ocean. p. 413.

San Francisco (38°N/122°W). Third most populated city in California. Located on San Francisco Bay. p. 413.

San Joaquin River. Located in California. Flows into the Sacramento River near San Francisco Bay. p. 416.

San Jose (37°N/122°W). City in California. p. 413.

San Juan (18°N/66°W). Capital of and most populated city in Puerto Rico. p. 444.

San Salvador. One of a group of islands called the Bahamas. Columbus landed on this island in 1492. p. 71.

Santa Fe (35°N/106°W). Spanish settlement started in 1609. Today the capital of New Mexico. p. 397.

Santiago (33°S/71°W). Capital of and most populated city in Chile. p. 440.

Santo Domingo (18°N/70°W). Capital of and chief seaport of the Dominican Republic. p. 444.

Santos (24°S/46°W). Seaport city on southeast coast of Brazil. p. 440.

São Paulo (24°S/47°W). The most populated city in South America. Located in Brazil. p. 440.

Saratoga (43°N/74°W). The British lost a very important battle to the Americans here during the Revolutionary War. This battlesite is located in the present-day city of Schuylerville, New York. p. 115.

Sault Ste. Marie (47°N/84°W). City in Michigan. Located at falls between Lakes Huron and Superior. p. 381.

Savannah (32°N/81°W). City in Georgia. Georgia colony was founded here in 1733 by a group led by James Oglethorpe. p. 343.

Schefferville (55°N/67°W). Iron-mining town in Quebec. p. 427.

Seattle (48°N/122°W). Most populated city in Washington. Located on east shore of Puget Sound. p. 397.

Sierra Madre Occidental. North-south mountain range in western Mexico. p. 439.

Sierra Madre Oriental. North-south mountain range in eastern Mexico. p. 439.

Sierra Nevada. High mountain range located mostly in eastern California. Mount Whitney, with an elevation of 14,495 ft (4,418 m), is located in this range. It is the highest peak in the United States outside of Alaska. p. 263.

Snake River. Rises in Yellowstone National Park in Wyoming. Flows into the Columbia River in Washington. p. 265.

South America. The earth's fourth largest continent. p. 6.

Southern Hemisphere. The half of the earth that is south of the equator. p. 5.

South Pole. The most southern place on the earth. p. 5.

Springfield (40°N/90°W). Capital of Illinois. Located on the Sangamon River. p. 381.

Springfield (42°N/73°W). Large city in Massachusetts. Located on the Connecticut River. p. 306.

Sucre (19°S/65°W). Capital of Bolivia. Located in the Andes Mountains. p. 440.

Sudbury (47°N/81°W). Nickel-mining town in Ontario, Canada. World's largest supply of nickel is in the area. p. 427.

Superior (47°N/92°W). City in Wisconsin. Located at western end of Lake Superior. p. 381.

Susquehanna River. Rises in Otsego Lake in New York. Flows into northern end of Chesapeake Bay. p. 311.

Tallahassee (30°N/84°W). Capital of Florida. Located in northern Florida. p. 343.

Tampa (28°N/82°W). City in Florida. Located on Tampa Bay. p. 343.

Tennessee River. Formed near Knoxville, Tennessee, by the joining of the Holston and French Broad rivers. Flows into the Ohio River at Paducah, Kentucky. p. 265.

Toledo (42°N/84°W). City in Ohio. Located on Lake Erie. p. 381.

Toronto (44°N/79°W). Capital of Ontario, Canada. Located on northeast end of Lake Ontario. p. 434.

Trenton (40°N/75°W). Capital of New Jersey. Located on the east side of the Delaware River. p. 324.

Tropic of Cancer. A line of latitude located at 23½° north latitude. p. 9.

Tropic of Capricorn. A line of latitude located at 23½° south latitude. p. 9.

Tulsa (36°N/96°W). Large city in Oklahoma. An important oil industry center. p. 362.

Valdez (61°N/146°W). Port town in southern Alaska. Oil from Alaska's North Slope is transported by pipeline to Valdez, where it is then put into oil tankers. p. 413.

Valparaíso (33°S/72°W). Major seaport of Chile. Located on Pacific Ocean. p. 440.

Vancouver (49°N/123°W). City in British Columbia, Canada. Located on an inlet of the Pacific Ocean. Canada's most important Pacific seaport. p. 434.

Vicksburg (32°N/91°W). General Grant's victory over the South at this battle split the South into two parts. Located on the Mississippi River in Mississippi. p. 175.

Victoria (48°N/123°W). Capital of British Columbia, Canada. Located on Vancouver Island. p. 434.

Virginia City (39°N/120°W). Once a booming mining town in Nevada. Today it is a very small village. p. 191.

Washington, D.C. (39°N/77°W). Capital of the United States. Located on the Potomac River. p. 324.

Western Hemisphere. The hemisphere in which all of South America and North America is located. The half of the earth west of the prime meridian. p. 5.

West Indies. Group of islands stretching about 2,500 mi (4,023 km) from near Florida to near Venezuela. p. 470.

White Butte (46°N/103°W). The highest peak in North Dakota. It has an elevation of 3,506 ft (1,069 m). p. 367.

Whitehorse (61°N/135°W). Capital of Yukon Territory, Canada. p. 434.

White Mountains. Part of the Appalachian system. Located in New Hampshire. Highest peak is Mt. Washington, with an elevation of 6,288 ft (1,917 m). p. 287.

Wichita (38°N/97°W). City in Kansas. Located on the Arkansas River. p. 381.

Willamette River. Located in Oregon. Flows into the Columbia River near Portland. p. 403.

Williamsburg (37°N/77°W). Colonial capital of Virginia. p. 26.

Wilmington (40°N/76°W). City in Delaware. Located on the Delaware River. p. 324.

Winnipeg (50°N/97°W). Capital of Manitoba, Canada. Located on the Red River. p. 434.

Yakima River. Located in Washington. Flows into the Columbia River near Richland. p. 403.

Yellowknife (62°N/114°W). Capital of Northwest Territories, Canada. Located on Great Slave Lake at the mouth of Yellowknife River. p. 434.

Yellowstone National Park (45°N/110°W). Oldest and largest national park in the United States. Most of it is in Wyoming. p. 7.

Yonkers (41°N/74°W). City in New York. Located on the Hudson River. p. 324.

Yorktown (37°N/77°W). The Americans won a decisive victory over the British here during the Revolutionary War. Following this loss the British were ready to make peace. p. 115.

Yucatán Peninsula. Located in Central America. Separates the Gulf of Mexico and the Caribbean Sea. p. 439.

Yukon River. The third longest river in North America. Formed in Yukon Territory, Canada, and flows into the Bering Sea. p. 470.

Yuma (33°N/115°W). City in southwest Arizona. Located where the Gila River joins the Colorado River. p. 269.

GLOSSARY

abolitionist. A person opposed to slavery and in favor of ending it. p. 142.

agricultural. Having to do with farming of crops or animals. p. 281.

Alamo. An old Spanish mission in San Antonio. The *Alamo* was the scene of a famous battle between Texas and Mexico in 1836. p. 153.

Allies. The name given to those countries supported by and later joined by the United States in World War I and World War II. p. 229.

altiplano. A very high plateau in the Andes of Bolivia. p. 452.

amendment. A formal correction or change. p. 120.

Antarctic Circle. A line of latitude that circles the earth at 66½° south latitude. p. 9.

anthem. A song in praise of one's country or religion. p. 136.

anthracite. Hard coal. p. 279.

apprentice. A person learning a trade or craft. p. 93.

archaeologist. A scientist who studies objects, ruins, and other evidence of human life in the past. p. 36.

architect. A person who designs and draws plans for buildings and makes sure the plans are carried out by the builders. p. 132.

architecture. The designing of buildings. The style of buildings. p. 154.

Arctic Circle. A line of latitude that circles the earth at 66½° north latitude. p. 9.

armada. The Spanish word for a fleet of armed ships. p. 76.

armistice. A halt to fighting by agreement between the warring nations. p. 230.

armory. A place where firearms are manufactured or stored. p. 292.

arroyo. The name given to a dry streambed. p. 389.

Articles of Confederation. The document that listed the powers of the central government and the powers of the states in the period before the Constitution was written. p. 118.

artifact. An object left by people who lived long ago. p. 36.

assembly line. A moving belt that carries a certain part of a product past workers who add pieces to the part. p. 243.

atomic energy. The power that is derived from making changes in atoms. Atoms are small bits of matter. p. 280.

aviation. The art or science of operating and navigating aircraft. Also, the designing, development, and manufacture of aircraft. p. 243.

axis. An imaginary line that goes through the earth from the North Pole to the South Pole. p. 272.

Axis Powers. The name given to Italy, Japan, and Germany, the countries that fought against the Allies in World War II. p. 231.

Bad Lands. Areas in South Dakota, North Dakota, and Nebraska that are dry and rugged and have little or no vegetation. p. 366.

bank. A part of the ocean floor that rises above the rest of the surrounding ocean floor. p. 422.

barrier island. One of a group of islands that are just off the mainland and act as a protective obstruction, or barrier. p. 330.

bay. A part of a lake or ocean extending into the land. p. 310.

bicentennial. A two-hundredth anniversary. p. 240.

Bill of Rights. The first ten amendments to the Constitution. p. 120.

bituminous. Having to do with a type of coal. *Bituminous* coal is also called soft coal. p. 279.

blockade. To stop (block) a particular group from moving goods or people. During the Civil War, the North used its navy to *blockade* ports in the South. p. 173.

bluff. A high, steep bank or cliff. p. 368.

bog. Wet, swampy land. p. 295.

bonanza. A mine producing rich ores. Something extremely profitable. p. 189.

Boston Tea Party. An incident staged by the Sons of Liberty to protest a tea tax imposed by Britain on the American colonies. On this occasion, 342 cases of tea, carried on British ships, were dumped into the Boston Harbor. p. 109.

boundary. The border of a state or country. p. 256.

boycott. An organized campaign in which people refuse to have any dealings with a particular group or business. p. 248.

bran. The cracked outer coating of cereal grains separated from flour by sifting. *Bran* is used mostly in animal feed. It is high in fiber content. p. 372.

broadleaf. Having a leaf that is broad (unlike a needle leaf). Examples of *broadleaf* trees are maple, oak, and beech. p. 300.

Bureau of Indian Affairs. A federal agency given the duties of controlling Native Americans and looking out for their interests. p. 198.

burgess. A representative in a branch of the legislature of colonial Virginia. p. 87.

butte. A small, flat-topped hill with steep sides. p. 368.

by-product. Something that is made or produced while the main product is being made. p. 376.

Cabinet. A group of advisers to the President of the United States. p. 128.

cacao. A South American plant whose seeds are used in the making of chocolate, cocoa, and cocoa butter. p. 444.

canal. A waterway made by people. *Canals* are dug to carry water for crops and people, for boats, and to drain swampy lands. p. 59.

canyon. A very deep valley with steep sides. p. 366.

capital. Money invested in factories, machines, or any other business. p. 206.

carpetbagger. The name given to the Northern whites who moved to the South after the Civil War. p. 180.

cartographer. A person who makes maps. p. 18.

cash crop. A crop grown for sale rather than for the use of the farmer. p. 294.

causeway. A bridge made by building up earth in narrow strips until it is above the water. p. 58.

cede. To give up or surrender something to someone. p. 154.

census. A government count of the number of people in a country. p. 121.

centimeter. A measure of distance in the metric system. A *centimeter* (cm) is a little less than half an inch. p. 13.

Central Powers. The name given to Germany, Austria-Hungary, and the Ottoman Empire (Turkey) during World War I. p. 229.

Chaco. The plains of the Paraná and Paraguay rivers. p. 448.

channel. **1.** The path of a river. **2.** Another name for a canal. **3.** A strait, or narrow body of water, between two parts of land. p. 265.

Chief Justice. The leader of the Supreme Court. p. 128.

chronological order. The listing or discussing of events in the order in which they took place. p. 30.

citizen. A person who by birth or choice becomes a member of a country. p. 41.

citrus fruit. An edible fruit, with a firm thick skin and a pulpy flesh with a sweet-sour taste. Oranges, lemons, limes, and grapefruits are *citrus fruits.* p. 334.

civilization. The stage of cultural development marked by the presence of cities, trade, government, art, writing, and science. p. 57.

climate. The pattern of weather that a place has over a period of years. Temperature and precipitation are two important parts of *climate.* p. 268.

coastal plain. A wide area of flat or gently rolling land that is bordered by a large area of water. p. 262.

cold war. A war of words that runs the risk of resulting in a real war. p. 234.

colony. A place that is settled at a distance from the country that governs it. p. 70.

combine. A farm machine, developed in the late 1800s, that combines the work of the reaper, the harvester, and the thresher. p. 202.

commerce. The buying and selling of goods. p. 320.

commercial farmer. A farmer who uses machinery to farm, and who raises crops and animals for sale. p. 204.

Committees of Correspondence. Colonial groups that maintained contact with and sent news to each other through letters. p. 108.

common. The name given to the center of most colonial New England towns. The *common* was land that belonged to everyone who lived in the town. p. 92.

Commonwealth. An association of countries that were once part of the British Empire. p. 424.

communicate. To exchange or give information in any way, such as by talking or writing. p. 207.

communism. A social and economic system in which most property is owned by the government and shared by the governed. p. 234.

compass rose. A small drawing on a map, used to show directions. p. 8.

competition. The effort made by businesses of the same type or within the same industry to gain a bigger share of the market for themselves. p. 206.

conifer. A cone-bearing, evergreen tree. p. 427.

conservation. The management of natural resources in such a way as to prevent their waste or complete destruction. p. 242.

constitution. A set of laws by which a country is governed. p. 118.

consulate. The building or office in which a consul lives. A consul is an official sent to a foreign nation by his or her government to represent it. p. 339.

continent. A huge area of land. There are seven *continents:* North America, South America, Europe, Africa, Asia, Australia, and Antarctica. p. 6.

Continental Congress. The name given to the meeting of the group of representatives from the American colonies. p. 109.

Continental Divide. A high ridge dividing rivers or streams that flow to opposite sides of a continent. p. 388.

coral. A limestone-like hard substance made up of the skeletons of certain types of tiny sea animals. p. 330.

cotton gin. A machine used to separate cotton from its seeds. p. 150.

crop lien. A first claim on the profit of a crop. p. 178.

culture. The way of life of a group of people, including their customs, traditions, and values. p. 50.

custom. A long-established way of doing things. p. 50.

debt. Something, usually money, that is owed to someone. p. 94.

deciduous. Losing leaves at the end of a season. p. 295.

Declaration of Independence. The document that stated the reasons for the desire of the American colonies to be independent of British control. p. 112.

delta. Land built up by silt deposits at the mouth of a river. p. 265.

democracy. Rule or government of, for, and by the people. p. 92.

depression. An economic condition in which business is very bad and large numbers of people are unemployed. p. 244.

derrick. A tall, steel frame, over an oil well, that holds the equipment used for drilling and hoisting. p. 356.

descendant. One who comes from a specific ancestor. p. 46.

descent. Ancestral background. p. 424.

desert. A very dry place, with little rainfall and few plants. p. 55.

developed country. A country that has a high level of industrialization and technology. p. 441.

developing country. A country that is trying to increase its level of industrialization and technology. p. 441.

dictatorship. Harsh rule by one person or group. p. 230.

diesel fuel. A fuel used in trucks, buses, cars, and ships that have a specific type of engine. p. 357.

diplomat. One who represents his or her government in important dealings with other nations. p. 132.

District of Columbia. A part of the United States—not part of any state—set aside as the capital of the United States of America. p. 129.

dry farming. Farming techniques, used in areas of little rainfall and no irrigation, that are designed to keep moisture in the soil. p. 188.

Dust Bowl. The area in the Great Plains in which soil erosion caused by poor farming methods and a long period of little rainfall resulted in severe dust storms. p. 244.

earthquake. A shaking, or trembling, of the earth, often leaving cracks in the earth's surface, that is caused by the shifting of layers of the earth far beneath the surface. p. 405.

economic activity. Any activity that has to do with the production or selling of goods and services. p. 432.

electronics. An area of scientific study from which television, radio, computers, and other electrical devices have developed. p. 358.

elevation. The height of something. The *elevation* of land is its distance above or below sea level, usually measured in feet or meters. p. 286.

emancipate. To set free. p. 174.

emigrate. To leave one's native land. p. 212.

empire. The territories and peoples under the control of a powerful nation. p. 58.

equator. A line, drawn on maps and globes, that circles the earth exactly halfway between the North Pole and the South Pole. It is labeled 0° latitude. p. 4.

Era of Good Feelings. The period following the War of 1812 (during the presidency of James Monroe) when the United States experienced peace and unity. p. 139.

erode. To wear away the earth's surface. Wind and water can *erode* the earth. p. 338.

erosion. The wearing away of the earth's surface by wind, running water, waves, or ice. p. 353.

evaporate. To change from a liquid into gas (vapor). p. 370.

event. An important happening. p. 27.

evergreen. Having green leaves (either broadleaf or needle) all year round. p. 295.

executive branch. The part of government responsible for carrying out the laws that Congress passes. The President is the head of the *executive branch.* p. 119.

expedition. A journey undertaken for a specific purpose, such as exploration. p. 72.

explore. To search for new things and places. p. 64.

export. Something that is sent to another country, usually for sale there. Also, to send something to another country for sale. p. 341.

express. Traveling with very few or no stops between places. p. 24.

factory. A building in which goods are made by machine. p. 33.

federal. Having to do with a form of political organization in which power is divided between national government and the governments of the states. p. 119.

feedlot. A plot of land where livestock are fed and fattened for sale. p. 353.

fertile. Able to produce plentifully. p. 294.

fish hatchery. A place where fish eggs are hatched and the young fish raised until they are old enough to be released in streams. p. 410.

fleet. A group of ships sailing together for a given purpose. p. 290.

foliage. The leaves of trees. p. 300.

foothill. A hill at the foot or near the bottom of mountains or higher hills. p. 312.

foreign policy. The way in which one country deals with another. p. 232.

fossil. The hardened remains or traces of an ancient plant or animal. p. 393.

Freedman's Bureau. A governmental agency set up at the end of the Civil War to help the freed slaves and others who were poor and homeless. p. 178.

free state. A state, before the Civil War, in which slavery was not permitted. p. 166.

frost-free. A term used to describe the period when the temperature is always above freezing. p. 332.

fuel. A substance burned to produce power or heat. p. 276.

garment. An article of clothing. p. 341.

gasohol. A fuel produced by mixing grain alcohol with gasoline. p. 373.

geologist. A scientist who studies rocks and rock formations. p. 355.

ghetto. A neighborhood where people of similar ethnic, racial, or religious backgrounds live. p. 213.

glacier. A large body of slowly moving ice. p. 368.

grain elevator. A large building for storing grain. p. 375.

grandfather clause. Laws passed in the South in the 1890s that allowed only those persons to vote whose father or grandfather had voted on or before January 1867. p. 183.

Grange. The first major farmers group, organized to get better prices for farm products and as a social club. p. 205.

gristmill. A place where grain is ground into flour. p. 302.

gulf. A part of the ocean that extends into the land. p. 348.

gully. A ditch or small valley dug in the earth by running water. p. 366.

hail. Precipitation in the form of pieces of compacted ice and snow. p. 370.

harbor. A protected body of water, safe for ships and other vessels. p. 310.

hemisphere. The name given to any half of the earth. p. 2.

henequen. The fiber of a plant grown mainly in Yucatán, used for making rope and other coarse materials. p. 443.

hessian. A German soldier hired to fight for the British in the Revolutionary War. p. 115.

historian. A person who studies the past and often writes about it. p. 37.

homestead. A house and the land surrounding it. Often, land given to a family or sold to them at a low rate to encourage settlement. p. 191.

House of Burgesses. The representative assembly in colonial Virginia. p. 87.

human rights. The basic civil, economic, political, and social rights of all people. p. 247.

human sacrifice. The killing of one or more people as offerings to a god. p. 58.

humid. Damp or wet. Humidity is measured by the amount of water vapor in the air at a given time. p. 333.

hurricane. A tropical storm with strong winds and heavy rains. p. 333.

hydroelectric power. Electricity produced from moving water. p. 267.

immigrant. A person from one country who comes into another country to live there. p. 151.

impeachment. The charging of a public official with having done something illegal while in office. p. 180.

import. To bring in goods from a foreign country, usually for the purpose of selling those goods. Also, the goods themselves. p. 293.

inauguration. A ceremony to put someone in office. p. 126.

income. Money earned. p. 244.

income tax. A tax based on the amount of money earned. p. 205.

indentured servant. A person who sold his or her services for a certain period of time in exchange for free passage to a foreign land. p. 86.

independence. Freedom from the control of another country or person. p. 106.

indigo. A plant from which blue dye is made. p. 94.

Industrial Revolution. The period of great change in the way people worked and lived, brought about by the invention of power-driven machines. p. 149.

inflation. An economic condition in which the value of money decreases and the price of goods increases. p. 158.

initiative. A procedure that allows voters to introduce a bill they would like to see become a law. p. 193.

inland sea. A body of water, surrounded by land, that is too large to be considered a lake. p. 368.

interchangeable parts. Identical parts that can be used in place of each other in making a product. p. 150.

intermontane. Having to do with a land or region that lies between mountain ranges. p. 388.

irrigate. To bring water to crops, usually through canals, ditches, or pipes. p. 266.

island. A body of land completely surrounded by water. p. 264

isolate. To set apart and alone from others. p. 237.

isthmus. A narrow strip of land joining two larger bodies of land. p. 73.

Jacksonian democracy. The increased participation in government by the people. Occurred during the presidency of Andrew Jackson. p. 141.

journal. A diary-like record of events, experiences, and thoughts kept on a regular basis. p. 84.

judicial branch. The part of government that is in charge of deciding the meaning of laws. p. 119.

key. **1.** A device on a map used to tell what real things or places the symbols on the map stand for. p. 16. **2.** A small piece of land, barely above sea level, usually made of coral and limestone. For example, the Florida Keys. p. 330.

kilometer. A measure of distance in the metric system. A *kilometer* (km) is a little more than half a mile. p. 13.

landform. A feature of the earth's surface created by nature. p. 261.

land grant. The distribution of land to settlers, railroads, and farming (agricultural) colleges by the government in the late 1800s. Also, the land so distributed. p. 191.

landlocked. Having no coastline. A *landlocked* country is surrounded on all sides by other countries. p. 452.

landmark. An easily recognizable or famous object that marks or identifies an area. p. 301.

landscape. The landforms of an area. p. 286.

latitude. Distance, measured in degrees, north and south of the equator. Lines of *latitude* are used to locate places on the earth. p. 9.

league. A group of people joined together for a common purpose. p. 53.

legislative branch. The part of government responsible for making laws. p. 119

levee. A wide wall built with earth and used for flood control. p. 350.

livestock. Farm animals raised for home use or profit. p. 294.

Llanos. A large plain in northern South America that is drained by the Orinoco River. *Llanos* is the Spanish word for "plains." p. 448.

lock. An enclosed area on a canal, with gates on both sides, used for raising or lowering ships as they go from one water level to another. p. 428.

London Company. A group formed for the purpose of establishing an English colony in Virginia. Members of the group were to share in the costs and the profits. p. 84.

Lone Star Republic. The independent nation of Texas (1836–1845), so called because its flag had only one star. p. 153.

longhouse. A shelter built by Native Americans, especially the Iroquois. p. 52.

longitude. Distance, measured in degrees, east and west of the prime meridian. Lines of *longitude* are used to locate places on the earth. All *longitude* lines pass through the North Pole and the South Pole. p. 9.

Loyalist. A colonist who was a supporter of Great Britain and King George III. p. 114.

lubricant. A substance used to make a slippery coating between two surfaces to prevent wear on those surfaces. p. 357.

lumberjack. One whose work involves cutting down trees for commercial use. p. 297.

Manufacturing Belt. The Middle Atlantic region of the United States, so called for its large number of factories and mills that manufacture a wide variety of goods. p. 316.

maritime. Having to do with the sea. p. 426.

market weight. The weight that an animal must reach before it is sent to be sold. p. 373.

marshland. Soft, wet land that is usually soaked with water. p. 348.

massacre. The killing of a large group of people who have little or no defense. p. 108.

mass production. The making of goods in large quantities, usually by machine. p. 150.

mass transit. A way of moving a great number of people from one place to another at the same time. Trains, subways, buses, and airplanes are types of *mass transit*. p. 23.

Mayflower Compact. A document signed by the Pilgrims by which they agreed to make laws as needed for the colony's good and to obey these laws. p. 88.

megalopolis. A group of cities so close to one another that they seem to form a continuous urban area. p. 323.

meridian. Another name for a line of longitude. p. 10.

mestizo. A person of mixed European and Native American ancestry. p. 442.

metropolitan area. An area made up of a large city or several large cities and the surrounding towns, cities, and other communities. p. 302.

Middle Passage. The name given to the trip from Africa to America on a slave ship. p. 96.

migratory bird. A type of bird that flies south (to a warmer area) for the winter. At the end of winter, *migratory birds* return to their northern homes. p. 335.

mileage chart. A table used to show the number of road miles between places. p. 22.

militia. An organized military force usually called upon during emergencies. p. 114.

milling. The grinding of grain into flour. Also, the processing of steel and other products. p. 282.

mineral. A substance, found in the earth, that is neither plant nor animal. p. 289.

mineral spring. Water, rising from the ground, that is thought to cure illness and relieve pain because of its high mineral content. p. 361.

Minuteman. A member of an army of citizens, at the time of the Revolutionary War, who claimed to be ready to fight the British at "a minute's notice." p. 110.

missionary. A person sent to teach a religion to people of a different faith and to provide them with any help they might need. p. 78.

monopoly. Sole control of an entire industry. p. 209.

monument. Something, such as a building, tower, or sculpture, built in remembrance of a person or an event. p. 380.

mound. A pile of earth used as the platform for an important building or, by groups of Native Americans, as a burial site. p. 48.

mountain. A part of the earth's surface that rises sharply from the land around it. A *mountain* has a broad base and narrows to a peak. p. 262.

mountain men. Fur trappers who played an important part in the expansion of the United States in the 1800s. p. 159.

mouth. A place where a stream or river enters a larger body of water. p. 265.

muckraker. A person who writes about wrongdoing in business and politics. p. 242.

Native American. One of any group of American Indians; people whose ancestors came to America long before anyone else. p. 39.

NATO. (Stands for North Atlantic Treaty Organization.) A military alliance between the United States and some countries in Europe. p. 235.

naturalist. A person who studies nature. p. 240.

naturalize. To become a citizen of a country other than the one in which one was born. p. 212.

natural resource. Something that is provided by nature and is useful to people. p. 275.

naval stores. Supplies made from pine trees, such as ships' masts, tar, and turpentine, produced and shipped by the Carolina settlers to England for use in England's navy. p. 94.

neutral. Standing apart in an argument or fight and not taking sides. p. 228.

New Deal. A term used to describe policies put forward by President Franklin Roosevelt to fight the Great Depression. In the *New Deal,* the government created jobs and granted other types of aid to people. p. 245.

nitrate. A mineral used in the manufacture of fertilizers. p. 451.

North Pole. The most northern place in the world. The *North Pole* is located in the Arctic Ocean. p. 4.

Northwest Passage. A nonexistent water route, sought by early explorers, that would provide a shortcut from Europe to Asia and the East Indies via North America. p. 77.

nuclear energy. The power released from the nucleus, or core, of an atom. p. 280.

oasis. A place in a desert where there is water; a fertile place in a dry area. p. 396.

oath. A solemn promise. p. 126.

ocean current. A regular movement of the surface water of an ocean or a river, caused mostly by winds and differences of water temperature. p. 405.

official language. The language authorized by a nation's government as the language of that nation, but not necessarily the language of the majority of the people. Government documents are written in the *official language.* Some countries have several *official languages.* p. 425.

oil shale. Rock containing a substance from which an oil-like product can be made. p. 391.

"Old Ironsides." The nickname given to the *Constitution,* a ship that became famous for its role in defeating the British in the War of 1812. p. 138.

open-pit mine. A mine in the form of a large hole dug in the earth's surface, rather than in the form of underground tunnels. p. 376.

open-range grazing. The unrestricted grazing of cattle. *Open-range grazing* ended with the use of barbed-wire fences by farmers in the late 1800s. p. 190.

oral history. The history or tradition of a people handed down from one generation to another by word of mouth. p. 35.

ore. A material containing the mineral for which it is mined. Examples are iron *ore* and copper *ore.* p. 280.

Oregon Trail. The route from Missouri to Oregon used by settlers moving to the northwest in the 1800s. p. 158.

overburden. The layers of earth that cover a bed of coal. In strip mining, the *overburden* is removed by machines, loaded into trucks, and dumped elsewhere. p. 338.

overgraze. To allow animals to graze, or feed upon grass, for so long that the grass dies or is pulled up by the roots, allowing erosion to take place. p. 354.

Pampas. The name given to the large grass-covered plains of Uruguay and Argentina, in South America. p. 448.

panhandle. A narrow strip of land. p. 352.

Parliament. The lawmaking body of England. Also, the lawmaking body of Canada. p. 106.

pasteurize. To heat a liquid to a high temperature and then rapidly chill it. This is a process used to kill harmful bacteria in liquids such as milk. p. 375.

Patagonia. A barren plain in southern Argentina. p. 448.

patent. An official paper giving an inventor the right to be the only person to make or sell his or her invention for a certain time. p. 208.

patriot. A person who loves and loyally supports his or her country. In the struggle against the British, a person who fought for the independence of the American colonies. p. 115.

Peace Corps. A program started by President John F. Kennedy to help people in the developing world. p. 236.

peninsula. A piece of land extending into the water from a larger body of land. p. 84.

permafrost. A permanently frozen layer of the soil, sometimes extending to great depths below the earth's surface in very cold regions. p. 406.

persecution. The harsh treatment of a person or group. p. 231.

petrochemical. A chemical or synthetic material produced from petroleum or natural gas. p. 316.

petroleum. The oily liquid, found in the earth, from which gasoline, kerosene, and many other things are made. p. 276.

physical map. A map that shows the kinds of land surfaces on the earth. p. 261.

pilgrim. A person who travels for religious reasons. p. 87.

pioneer. A person who does something first, preparing the way for others. The first settlers were *pioneers.* p. 159.

pitchblende. The brownish black mineral that is the chief source of uranium. p. 430.

plain. A wide area of flat or gently rolling land. p. 261.

plantation. A large farm on which one main crop is grown. p. 95.

plateau. A large, high, rather level area that is raised above the surrounding land. p. 262.

political map. A map that shows the different countries in the world or the different states in a country. p. 256.

poll tax. A tax a person had to pay in order to be allowed to vote. p. 183.

pollute. To make the earth's soil, water, and air unclean by putting waste materials into them. p. 266.

population. The number of people living in an area. p. 20.

population density. The average number of people per given unit of area (such as a square mile or square kilometer) in a state, country, or other area. p. 259.

Populist party. A political party that showed its greatest strength in the election of 1892. p. 205.

poultry. Chickens, turkeys, and other birds raised for eggs or meat. p. 315.

poverty. The condition of being poor. p. 342.

preamble. An introduction. p. 113.

precipitation. Moisture that falls on the earth's surface in the form of rain, snow, sleet, hail, fog, or mist. p. 268.

presidio. A Spanish word meaning "military fort." p. 155.

prime meridian. A line of longitude that passes through the Royal Observatory in Greenwich, England. It is the 0° line of longitude, from which distances east and west are measured in degrees of longitude. p. 10.

privateer. A privately owned, armed ship having the government's permission to attack enemy ships. In the Revolutionary War, *privateers* joined the United States in fighting the British. p. 116.

proclamation. An official announcement. p. 174.

promontory. High rocky land that juts out into the sea along a coastline. p. 286.

protectorate. A place or country under the protection of another country. p. 226.

province. A district or division of a country. In Canada, a *province* is similar to one of our states. p. 422.

public opinion The way most people feel about something. p. 225.

Puritan. A member of certain Protestant groups in sixteenth- and seventeenth-century England or New England. p. 90.

Quaker. A member of a religious group. *Quakers* also call themselves "Friends." p. 98.

quarry. A place from which materials such as marble, stone, slate, or limestone are cut, dug, or blasted. p. 289.

quota. A fixed, and usually limited, number. p. 214.

radioactive. Giving off harmful rays. p. 376.

rain shadow. An area that does not get much rain because it is on the protected side of high mountains. p. 390.

ratify. To give formal approval to. p. 122.

ration. To put a limit on the amount of something that someone can buy or use. p. 233.

recall. The removal, by the voters, of a person from elected office before the end of his or her term. p. 193.

Reconstruction. The name given to the period (1865–1877) following the Civil War. p. 177.

recycle. To process used or discarded goods in order to create materials or goods that can be used again. p. 299.

reef. A chain of rocks or coral at or near the surface of the water. p. 330.

referendum. A procedure that allows the people, rather than elected representatives, to vote on a law. p. 193.

refinery. A building with machines that change a natural resource to make it pure or to make different products from it. p. 356.

refugee. A person who flees to another place for protection or safety. p. 178.

region. A part of the earth's surface that has common characteristics. p. 254.

relief map. A map that shows the elevation of land on the earth's surface. p. 261.

renewable resource. A resource that can be replaced by nature or by people. p. 296.

representative. One who is elected to decide matters for others. A *representative* is usually in a lawmaking group. p. 87.

republic. The political system in which the people elect representatives to manage their country. p. 119.

reservation. A piece of public land set aside, or reserved, by the government for the use of a particular group of people. p. 198.

reserves. Supplies of fuel or other things available or set aside for future use. p. 279.

resort. A place providing recreational and other facilities for people on vacation. p. 27.

revolution. **1.** Complete, often violent, change in government. p. 106. **2.** One complete turn of the earth around the sun. The earth takes one year to complete one *revolution.* p. 273.

rodeo. A Spanish word meaning "to surround" or "to round up." A *rodeo* is a public show or contest in which those taking part may ride a bronco or a bull, rope a calf, or wrestle a steer. p. 354.

rotation. One complete turn of the earth on its axis. The earth takes 24 hours to complete one *rotation.* p. 273.

rural. Having to do with the countryside; non-urban. p. 214.

savanna. A treeless grassland, or a grassland with scattered trees and bushes, especially in tropical lands that have seasonal rains. p. 448.

saw timber. Lumber used for building. p. 297.

scalawag. A term used in the South after the Civil War to describe white Southerners who sided with the new state governments. p. 180.

scale. The relationship between real size and size used on a map or model. Also, the line, drawn on maps, that shows this relationship. p. 12.

schedule. A printed timetable, such as a *schedule* listing the exact times of the coming and goings of trains, buses, and planes. Also, a timetable giving the days and times of events, such as baseball games. p. 24.

seam. A layer of coal or other mineral. p. 338.

season. A period of the year. There are four *seasons* in most areas of this country—spring, summer, autumn, and winter. p. 269.

secede. To withdraw from an organization or nation. p. 171.

secretary. An officer of state who heads a governmental administrative department. p. 128.

secret ballot. A term used to describe a way of voting in which only the voter knows how he or she has voted. p. 205.

sectionalism. The attaching of great importance to the beliefs or interests of a region. p. 171.

semidesert. An area that has little rainfall or plant cover. A *semidesert* area is not quite as dry as a desert, nor does it have as much plant cover as a grassland. p. 389.

Seneca Falls convention. A meeting in 1848 led by Elizabeth Stanton and Lucretia Mott to outline the goals of a women's rights movement. p. 143.

separation of powers. The division of governmental power into three parts, or branches: legislative, executive, and judiciary. p. 119.

Separatist. **1.** A person wishing to separate from the Church of England; a Pilgrim. p. 87. **2.** One who wants political independence for a part of a country. p. 425.

sharecropping. Farming land for the owner in return for a share of the crops. p. 178.

shearing. Cutting the wool off sheep or other animals. p. 391.

shoal. An underwater sandbar. *Shoals* make the water above them shallow. p. 330.

silt. Very fine pieces of soil and ground stone carried by moving water. p. 348.

sit-in. A form of group protest in which the group sits in a public place for a long period of time. p. 248.

sleet. Frozen rain. p. 313.

smelting. The process of separating metals from other materials in their ores. p. 280.

smog. A mixture of smoke and fog. p. 416.

social work. A profession in which the worker helps people with their problems. p. 217.

solvent. A substance, usually in liquid form, that is capable of thinning or dissolving another substance p. 357.

sorghum grain. Grain from any of a group of tall grassy plants that look somewhat like corn plants. *Sorghum grain* is an important crop worldwide and is used in the making of syrup, as feed for livestock, and in the manufacture of brushes and brooms. p. 352.

sound. A long, wide stretch of water connecting two larger bodies of water or separating a main body of land from an island. p. 288.

source. The place where a stream or river begins. p. 265.

South Pole. The most southern place in the world. The *South Pole* is located on the continent of Antarctica. p. 4.

spermaceti. A waxlike substance obtained from the oil of the sperm whale. p. 291.

spiritual. A type of religious song, originally composed and sung by slaves on Southern plantations. p. 98.

strait. A narrow body of water connecting two larger bodies of water. p. 46.

strip mining. A type of mining in which large machines strip off the overlying material and dump it to one side to expose the mineral. *Strip mining* is often used when minerals are near the earth's surface. p. 338.

subsistence farmer. A farmer who grows just enough crops to take care of his or her family's needs with little, if any, left over for sale. p. 202.

subtropical. Having to do with the regions bordering the tropics. p. 352.

suburb. A smaller community on the outskirts of a large city. p. 214.

subway. An underground train used to transport a great number of people from one place to another, usually within a city. p. 23.

survey. To measure the size, shape, length, and width of a piece of land. p. 186.

swamp. Wet, spongy land. p. 34.

symbol. Something that stands for, or suggests, something else. p. 16.

synthetic. Something that is not made directly from natural materials, such as nylon, which is made from chemicals produced from coal and other natural materials. Also, artificial. p. 243.

telegraph. A message sent electrically by wire. p. 150.

temperate. Not extreme. A *temperate* climate is neither extremely hot or cold nor extremely wet or dry. p. 328.

temperature. The amount of heat or cold as measured on a given scale, such as the Fahrenheit scale or the Celsius scale. p. 268.

temperature extreme. The highest or lowest recorded temperature. p. 288.

tepee. The tentlike shelter used by certain tribes of Native Americans. The *tepee* was made of buffalo skins stitched together, draped over poles, and secured to the ground. p. 54.

term. The time during which an official may hold office. p. 129.

terraces. A series of flat, wide ledges cut into the side of a hill or mountain to make places where crops can be grown. p. 61.

textile. Having to do with cloth. Also, woven fabric. p. 149.

tidal pools. Pools of water left behind when the ocean changes from high tide to low tide. p. 358.

tidewater. A low-lying coastal area often flooded by seawater. p. 328.

timberline. The elevation above which trees, or timber, cannot grow. p. 386.

tornado. A violent, high-powered windstorm that can cause much destruction. A *tornado* is nicknamed "twister" because of the storm's swirling winds that form a cone-shaped cloud. p. 351.

tourism. The industry made up of the businesses that encourage tourists to come to an area and those that take care of tourists' needs once they have arrived. p. 299.

town meeting. A meeting of the inhabitants of a town to discuss or vote on town affairs. p.92.

tract. An area of land. p. 297.

Trail of Tears. The name given by the Cherokees to their journey from Georgia to Oklahoma after they had been forced off their land by the United States government. p. 142.

transcontinental. Going across a continent. p. 193.

transportation. The moving of people and goods from one place to another. p. 33.

trawler. A boat used for commercial fishing. p. 291.

tree farming. The use of scientific methods to grow trees for the sale and commercial use of their lumber. p. 336.

tribe. A group held together by family and social ties, geography, or custom. p. 46.

tropical rain forest. A very thick forest, usually of broad-leaved trees and vines, in an area where rainfall is very heavy and temperatures are warm all year long. p. 444.

Tropic of Cancer. A line of latitude that circles the earth at 23½° north latitude. p. 9.

Tropic of Capricorn. A line of latitude that circles the earth at 23½° south latitude. p. 9.

truck farm. A farm on which large amounts of many types of vegetables are grown for sale. p. 315.

tundra. A rolling or nearly level, treeless plain found in Arctic regions. p. 406.

tungsten. A hard, heavy metal that is often mixed with steel to create a material hard enough to use in the making of machine tools. *Tungsten* is also used in electric light bulbs. p. 432.

turnpike. In early America, a toll road. Today, any high-speed highway. p. 146.

Underground Railroad. The secret routes by which abolitionists helped runaway slaves to escape to free states or to Canada where they could build new lives as free people. p. 169.

union. 1. A group of people or states. p. 129. **2.** In industry, a group formed for the purpose of protecting the interests of its members. p. 210.

upland. High land. p. 286.

urban. Having to do with a town or city. p. 214.

valley. A long, low area, usually between hills or mountains or along a river. p. 312.

vitamin. Any of a group of substances, found in foods, that are needed for health and for the working of the body and its parts but that do not directly give energy or aid growth. p. 373.

volcano. An opening in the earth, usually at the top of a cone-shaped hill, out of which gases, rock, ashes, and/or lava may pour from time to time. Also, the hill around such an opening. p. 405.

War Hawk. A person, especially in Congress, who supported the War of 1812. In modern times, one who favors declaring war on another country. p. 137.

water cycle. The process by which water evaporates from the earth's surface, forms clouds, condenses, and returns to the earth in the form of precipitation. p. 370.

water vapor. Water in its gaseous form. *Water vapor* is not visible. p. 352.

weather. The condition of the air at a certain time, in terms of precipitation, temperature, and other factors. p. 268.

wheat germ. The innermost part of the wheat kernel. *Wheat germ* is high in vitamin content. p. 372.

White House. The residence of the President of the United States. The *White House* is located in Washington, D.C. p. 131.

wholesale market. A place where products are bought in large quantities and then sold in smaller quantities to businesses. p. 375.

yield. The total amount produced. p. 372.

zoning. The division of a city into parts reserved for specific purposes. *Zoning* provides for residential, business, and other areas. p. 216.

INDEX

Key to Pronunciation

a	hat, cap	i	it, pin	ou	house, out	zh	measure, seizure
ā	age, face	ī	ice, five	sh	she, rush	ə	represents:
ã	care, air	ng	long, bring	th	thin, both		a in about
ä	father, far	o	hot, rock	ŦH	then, smooth		e in taken
ch	child, much	ō	open, go	u	cup, butter		i in pencil
e	let, best	ô	order, all	ù	full, put		o in lemon
ē	equal, see	oi	oil, voice	ü	rule, move		u in circus
ėr	term, learn						

The Key to Pronunciation above is from *The World Book Dictionary,* © 1979 World Book-Childcraft International, Inc.

J

Jackson, Andrew, 139 – 142
Jackson, Miss., 340
Jacksonian democracy, 141
Jamaica, 446
Jamestown Colony, 84 – 87
Japanese Americans, 233, 249
Jay, John, 111, 118, 128
Jefferson, Thomas, 108, 111, 128
  and Declaration of Independence, 112, 113
  as President, 132 – 133, 135
  talents of, 132
Jews persecuted by Hitler, 231
Johnson, Andrew, 177, 179 – 180
Johnson, Lyndon, 248
Jolliet, Louis, 79
Jones, John Paul, 116
Judicial branch, 119

K

Kachinas, Pueblo, 56
Kansas, 366
Kansas City, Mo., 380
Kennedy, John F., 236, 246
Kentucky, 129, 328
Key, Francis Scott, 136
Key on maps, 16 – 17, 20
Keys, Florida, 330
King, Martin Luther, Jr., 246, 248
Kino, Eusebio, 154 – 155
Kivas, Pueblo, 56
Knox, Henry, 128
Korean war, 236
Ku Klux Klan, 182

L

La Salle, Robert de, 79
Labor unions, 210 – 211
Lakes, 265 – 267, 312, 368, 404
Lakes Peninsula, 428
Landforms
  of Mexico, 442
  of Middle Atlantic region, 310, 312
  of Mountain West, 386, 388 – 389
  of New England, 286, 288
  of North Central region, 366, 368 – 369
  of Pacific region, 402, 404
  of South America, 447 – 448
  of South Central region, 348, 350 – 351
  of Southeast region, 328, 330 – 331
  of United States, 261 – 267
Land-grant colleges, 191, 202
Latin America
  colonies in, 438, 441
  developed parts of, 441
  as developing area, 441 – 442
  meaning of term, 60
  people of, 442
Latitude, 9 – 11
  temperature and, 332
Laurens, Henry, 118
Lead, 376
League of Iroquois, 53
League of Nations, 230, 231
Lee, Robert E., 154, 173, 174, 176 – 177
Legislative branch, 119
L'Enfant, Pierre, 130, 323
Lesser Antilles, 445
Levees, 350
Lewis and Clark expedition, 133 – 135
Liberia, 169
Lima, Peru, 452
Lincoln, Abraham, 170 – 175, 177
Little Rock, Ark., 360
Livestock, 294, 334
  See also Cattle; Hogs; Poultry; Sheep.
Livingston, Robert, 133
Llanos, 448
London Company, 84
Lone Star Republic, 153
Long drives, 189 – 190
Longhouse, Iroquois, 52
Longitude, 10 – 11
Los Angeles, Calif., 415 – 416
Lost Colony of Roanoke, 81
Louisiana, 277, 348
Louisiana Purchase, 133
Louisiana Territory, 133
Louisville, Ky., 340
Lowell factories, 149

Loyalists, 114
Lumber, 275, 297, 336, 358, 408 – 409

M

MacArthur, Douglas, 233
McClellan, George B., 174
McKinley, Mount, 262, 402
McKinley, William, 240, 242
Madison, Dolley, 138 – 139
Madison, James, 119, 120, 138
Magellan, Ferdinand, 73 – 75
Magellan, Strait of, 73
Maine, 91, 286, 294
Maine, 225
Manhattan Island, 99, 264
Manufacturing Belt, 316
Maps
  drawing, 18
  importance of, 27
  key on, 16 – 17, 20
  locating places on, 4 – 11
  physical, 261
  political, 256
  relief, 261
  of roads, 20 – 22
  scale on, 12 – 13
  symbols on, 16 – 17, 20
  of world, 4 – 6, 9 – 11
Marion, Francis, 34, 116
Maritime Provinces, 426 – 427
Marquette, Jacques, 78 – 79
Marshall, James, 157
Marshall, Thurgood, 248
Marshlands, 348
Maryland, 94, 310
Mass production, 150
Mass transit, 23 – 25
Massachusetts, 286
  Pilgrims in, 88
  Puritans in, 90 – 91
Massachusetts Bay Colony, 90 – 91
Massasoit, 89
Mayas, 57 – 58
Mayflower, 88
Mayflower Compact, 88
Meat packing, 375 – 376
Megalopolis, 323
Memphis, Tenn., 341
Meridians, 10

Merrimac, 176
Mesabi Range, 280, 316, 376
Mestizos, 442
Metals in United States, 280
Metric system, 13
Metropolitan areas, 302
Mexican Americans, 154 – 155, 249, 412, 414
Mexican Cession, 154
Mexican War, 153 – 154
Mexico, 75, 442 – 444
Mexico City, Mexico, 443
Miami, Fla., 341
Michigan, 366
Michigan, Lake, 266
Middle America, 60
Middle Atlantic region, 310 – 323
Middle colonies, 98 – 100
Middle East, 236
Middle Passage, 96 – 97
Midnight sun, 406
Midway Islands, 222
Mileage chart, 22
Militia, state, 114
Milling, 282, 375
Milwaukee, Wis., 380
Minerals
  in Andes countries, 452
  in Canada, 430, 432
  in Chile, 451
  in Mexico, 443 – 444
  in Mountain West, 391 – 392
  in New England, 289 – 290
  in North Central region, 376
  in Pacific region, 410
  in South Central region, 355
  in Southeast, 337 – 338
Mining, 189, 289 – 290, 338
  See also Minerals.
Minneapolis, Minn., 380
Minnesota, 366
  iron ore in, 280, 316, 376
Minuit, Peter, 99
Minutemen, 110, 111
Mississippi, 328
Mississippi River, 79, 265, 350, 369
Missouri, 366
Missouri River, 369, 389
Mitchell, Mount, 331
Monitor, 176
Monroe, James, 133, 139

CREDITS

Cover: Gregory Hergert
Unit openers: Gregory Hergert
Graphs and charts: Joe LeMonnier/Craven Design Studio, Inc.
Maps: R. R. Donnelley Cartographic Services
State table art: Kathy Hendrickson

Chapter 1 3: © Earl Roberge/Photo Researchers, Inc. 16: Robert Lee II. 18: Doug Bates. 19: Silver Burdett, courtesy Northeast Airways. 20: © Barry Hennings/Photo Researchers, Inc. 23: © Tom McHugh/Photo Researchers, Inc. 24: W. McKinney/Shostal Associates. 25: Lakeland Bus Lines. 26: Colonial Williamsburg. 27: New York Yankees and the New York City Department of Parks and Recreation.

Chapter 2 31: © George Holton/Photo Researchers, Inc. 32: *t.* © 1982 William Hubbell/Woodfin Camp & Associates; *b.* Crazy Horse Foundation/Photo by Robb DeWall. 33: © Jack Spratt/Picture Group. 34: Culver Pictures. 35: Elizabeth Crews/Stock, Boston. 36: Museum of the City of New York. 37: William Franklin McMahon. 38: Wide World Photos. 39: Victoria Beller-Smith for Silver Burdett. 40: Harry T. Peters Collection, Museum of the City of New York. 41: Mimi Forsyth/Monkmeyer Press.

Chapter 3 47: Natural History Museum of Los Angeles County. 48: Courtesy of the American Museum of Natural History. 49: © Georg Gerster/Photo Researchers, Inc. 50: E. R. Degginger. 51: Silver Burdett. 52: Kyuzo Tsugami. 53: J. R. Eyerman/Black Star. 54: James Jerome Hill Reference Library, St. Paul, Minnesota. 55: © 1982 Jeffrey Jay Foxx/Woodfin Camp & Associates. 56: Museum of the American Indian. 57: © George Holton/Photo Researchers, Inc. 59: © Robert Frerck. 61: Courtesy of the American Museum of Natural History.

Chapter 4 65: Courtesy of the U. S. Naval Academy Museum/Photo by M.E. Warren for Silver Burdett. 66: Ted Spiegel/Black Star. 67: Don Pulver. 69, 70, 73: The Bettmann Archive. 76: From the art collection of Business Men's Assurance Company, Kansas City, Missouri. 79: © 1979 Imagery. 80, 81: Culver Pictures.

Chapter 5 85: © Farrell Grehan/Photo Researchers, Inc. 87: Colonial Williamsburg. 88: Joseph LeMonnier/Craven Design Studio, Inc. 90: Culver Pictures. 91: The Bettmann Archive. 92: Greg Derr for Silver Burdett. 93: *Paul Revere,* by John Singleton Copley, Gift of Joseph W., William B., and Edward H. R. Revere, Courtesy, Museum of Fine Arts, Boston. 94: Enoch Pratt Free Library, Baltimore. 95: Taylor Oughton. 96: The Schomburg Center, The New York Public Library, Astor, Lenox and Tilden Foundations. 97: Kyuzo Tsugami. 99: Parker Galleries, London. 100: The Title Guarantee Company. 103: Culver Pictures.

Chapter 6 107: Selectmen's Room, Abbot Hall, Marblehead, Massachusetts. 109: The Bettmann Archive. 111: J. Clarence Davies Collection, Museum of the City of New York. 112: Architect of the Capitol. 114: The Valley Forge Historical Society. 116: Harry T. Peters Collection, Museum of the City of New York. 117: The Bettmann Archive. 119: Nebraska State Building Division. 123: Les Moore/UNIPHOTO.

Chapter 7 127: Private Collection of John and Lillian Harney. 130: White House Historical Association. 132: *t.* Eric Carle/Shostal Associates; *b.* © Lee Battaglia/Photo Researchers, Inc. 133: Barry Morgan/UNIPHOTO. 136: Les Moore/UNIPHOTO. 138: Courtesy of the U.S. Naval Academy Museum. 139: White House Historical Association. 140: Library of Congress. 142: *l.* U. S. Mint; *r.* U.S. Postal Service. 143: The Bettmann Archive.

Chapter 8 147: *t.* C. R. Smith Collection, University of Texas, Austin, Texas; *b.* Prints Division, The New York Public Library, Stokes Collection. 149: Yale University Art Gallery, Mabel Brady Garvan Collection. 150: State Historical Society of Wisconsin. 152: Library of Congress. 153: San Jacinto Museum of History Association. 154: © 1979 Michal Heron. 155: Kyuzo Tsugami. 156: The Bettmann Archive. 158: The Schomburg Center, The New York Public Library, Astor, Lenox and Tilden Foundations. 160: Taylor Oughton. 161: Pat O'Hara/Visualeyes.

Chapter 9 167: U.S. Department of the Interior, National Park Service, Gettysburg National Military Park. 170: The Cincinnati Art Museum. 171: Culver Pictures. 173: National Archives. 174: Harry T. Peters Collection, Museum of the City of New York. 175: Library of Congress. 177: U.S. Department of the Interior, National Park Service, Appomattox Court House National Historical Park. 178: Library of Congress. 180: The Bettmann Archive. 181: Library of Congress. 182: Culver Pictures.

Chapter 10 187: Harry T. Peters Collection, Museum of the City of New York. 188: The Nebraska State Historical Society. 189: California State Library. 193: Brown Brothers. 194: Utah State Historical Society. 195: Manuscripts and Archives Department, Baker Library, Harvard University. 197: *l.* The Denver Public Library, Western History Department; *r.* National Archives. 199: Library of Congress.

Chapter 11 203: *t.* National Archives; *b.* © Harald Sund. 205: Library of Congress. 206: © M. E. Warren/Photo Researchers, Inc. 207, 209, 210: Culver Pictures. 211: The Bettmann Archive. 212: Culver Pictures. 213: Andrew Sacks/Black Star. 214: Jim Howard/Alpha. 216: Jacob Riis Collection, Museum of the City of New York. 217: *l.* Laurence R. Lowry; *r.* The Bettmann Archive. 219: The Des Moines Register.

Chapter 12: 223: Courtesy of the U.S. Naval Academy Museum. 225: © Gemini Smith, Inc./Photo Researchers, Inc., from a lithograph in the Library of Congress. 226: Culver Pictures. 228: Brown Brothers. 229, 231, 232: Culver Pictures. 234: National Archives. 237: Leon V. Kofod.

Chapter 13 241: Susan Greenwood/Liaison. 243: © Harald Sund. 244: Ford Archives/Henry Ford Museum, Dearborn, Michigan. 245: Culver Pictures. 246: © 1982 Dilip Mehta/Woodfin Camp & Associates. 247: United Press International. 248: Wide World Photos. 249: San Antonio Light.

Chapter 14 255: © Stephen J. Krasemann/Photo Researchers, Inc. 260: Arnold Zann/Black Star. 261: © Harald Sund. 262: © Kent and Donna Dannen/Photo Researches, Inc. 264, 266: © Harald Sund. 267: *t.* © 1982 Chuck O'Rear/Woodfin Camp & Associates; *b.* Hanson Carroll/Peter Arnold, Inc. 272: NASA. 278: Bucyrus Erie. 282: © Harald Sund.

Chapter 15 287: Laurence R. Lowry. 290: Barre Granite Association. 291: Bohdan Hrynewych/Stock, Boston. 293: Laurence R. Lowry. 295: © Dick Hanley/Photo Researchers, Inc. 296: *l.* © 1978 Michael Philip Manheim; *r.* G. H. Coffman/Taurus Photos. 297: International Paper Company. 298: Ric Del Rossi. 300: © Robert Perron/Photo Researchers, Inc. 301: *t.* Clyde Smith/Peter Arnold, Inc.; *b.* © Farrell Grehan/Photo Researchers, Inc. 304: Ivan Massar/Black Star.

Chapter 16 311: E. R. Degginger. 313: Paul Pasquarello/Gamma-Liaison. 314: © Thomas D. W. Friedmann/Photo Researchers, Inc. 315: John Colwell/Grant Heilman Photography. 317: Ric Del Rossi. 318: H. Edelman/UNIPHOTO. 319: D. Brewster/Bruce Coleman. 321: Cary Wolinsky/Stock, Boston. 323: © Porterfield-Chickering/Photo Researchers, Inc.

Chapter 17 329: Laurence R. Lowry. 330: © Robert C. Hermes/Photo Researchers, Inc. 331: © Jerry Cooke/Photo Researchers, Inc. 333: National Oceanic and Atmospheric Administration. 334: © Bruce Roberts/Photo Researchers, Inc. 335: © Russ Kinne/Photo Researchers, Inc. 336: E. R. Degginger. 337: © Steve Proehl/Photo Researchers, Inc. 338: © Farrell Grehan/Photo Researchers, Inc. 340, 341: © Van Bucher/Photo Researchers, Inc. 342: *l.* © 1982 Michal Heron/Woodfin Camp & Associates; *r.* West Virginia Department of Commerce/Photo by Gerald S. Ratliff.

Chapter 18 349: NASA. 350, 352: E. R. Degginger. 354: Silver Burdett. 356: Christopher Harris/Shostal Associates. 358: © 1982 Craig Aurness/Woodfin Camp & Associates. 359: F. Muth/Shostal Associates. 360: C. Harris/Shostal Associates.

Chapter 19 367: © Harald Sund. 368: © Phil Degginger. 370, 371: Joseph LeMonnier/Craven Design Studio, Inc. 374: © Phil Degginger. 377: J. Fire/Shostal Associates. 378: Michael Hayman/Stock, Boston. 379: F. Boler/Shostal Associates. 380: W. Plaster/Shostal Associates.

Chapter 20 388: D. Dietrich/Shostal Associates. 390: Joseph LeMonnier/Craven Design Studio, Inc. 393: Sol Israel/Shostal Associates. 394: S. Voynick/Shostal Associates. 396: © Phil Degginger.

Chapter 21 404, 406: © Harald Sund. 407: E. R. Degginger. 409: *t.* David Forbert/Shostal Associates; *b.* Ric Del Rossi. 411: Pro Pix/Monkmeyer Press. 415: *t.* Mitchell Barosh/Shostal Associates; *b.* Cary Wolinsky/Stock, Boston.

Chapter 22 423: G. Baer/Shostal Associates. 425: A. Williams/Shostal Associates. 429: Ted Hankey. 430: © G. R. Roberts/Photo Researchers, Inc. 431: *t.* Malek/Shostal Associates; *b.* Lillian N. Bolstad/Peter Arnold, Inc. 432: Eric Carle/Shostal Associates. 433: *t.* K. Scholz/Shostal Associates; *b.l.* Eric Carle/Shostal Associates; *b.r.* Eric Carle/Shostal Associates.

Chapter 23 443: Eric Carle/Shostal Associates. 445: © Gianni Tortoli/Photo Researchers, Inc. 447: G. Ziesler/Peter Arnold, Inc. 449: Joan Kramer & Associates. 451: R. Rosene/Shostal Associates. 453: G. Ricatto/Shostal Associates.

Epilogue 460, 462, 463, 464, 465: Tim Lundgren.

1 2 3 4 5 6 7 8 9 10—RRD—88 87 86 85 84 83 82 81

Tools for Learning About Your Country

UNIT 1

TOOLS FOR LEARNING ABOUT YOUR COUNTRY

Dear Parent,

Your child is beginning a very exciting study in which we will learn a lot about our country and ourselves. I would like to keep you informed about this study throughout the year by means of parent letters. I would also like to encourage you to show an interest in your child's social studies by asking questions often. Perhaps when there are television programs about history or geography, you can watch them together as a family.

In Unit 1 your child will first learn some basic map reading skills. You can help with this study by playing road map games with your child, and by asking your child to help plot the route and figure the distance for a vacation trip. Involving your child in these ways makes the skills practical and therefore easier to learn.

Also in Unit 1 we will be learning about the meaning and the importance of history. You might like to explore your own family history with your child. Where did your family originally come from? Did members of your family ever fight for our country? Did any of your family come in contact with famous people? Do you have any famous ancestors? These kinds of questions help your child understand that United States history is about US!

I am looking forward to an enjoyable year working with your child on some important social studies skills and concepts. With your help the year can be even more meaningful.

Sincerely,

TOOLS FOR LEARNING ABOUT YOUR COUNTRY

BULLETIN-BOARD DISPLAYS

1. Collect and display different kinds of maps, such as a United States map, a map of the world, and a road map. Place a list of four or five questions next to each kind of map.

2. Display a grid and number it by tens. Place pictures at different points on the grid. Next to the grid write a list of the pictures. As an introduction to learning about latitude and longitude, ask pupils to write the coordinate numbers that tell the location of each picture.

GETTING STARTED

1. If you have just distributed the books to the pupils, take them on a guided tour through the book. Have pupils locate and discuss the purpose of each part of the book from the Acknowledgment to the Index.

2. Ask pupils to turn to the unit opening art for Unit 1 on p. 1. Tell them that this montage gives a clue to what they will study in Unit 1. Then pose these questions:

a. *What is each person doing?*

b. *Why do you think the woman is reading the map?*

c. *Why is the boy holding the globe?*

d. *Why are the grandfather and his granddaughter pointing to the photo album?*

e. *Why do we call maps, globes, and photographs "Tools for Learning About Your Country"?*

CHAPTER 1 PAGES 2–29

READING MAPS

THEME

Maps provide a wealth of information. They help us to understand the world around us and to cope with everyday life.

PROJECTS

1. Have pupils look through old magazines for maps of various types. Have them mount and display the maps.
2. Have pupils collect or draw pictures showing the various modes of transportation that people use or have used. Have them write captions for the pictures and display them.
3. Ask pupils to collect pictures from old magazines that illustrate the theme, "What America Means to Me." Have them make a booklet in which to place the pictures along with their comments about why they chose each picture.

LESSON 1 PAGES 2–11

WHERE IS IT?

GOALS

1. To understand the patriotic and geographic meaning of the words to "America, the Beautiful." 2. To locate on a map or globe the earth's hemispheres, the North and South Poles, the equator, the prime meridian, the Tropic of Cancer, Tropic of Capricorn, Arctic Circle, and Antarctic Circle. 3. To name and locate on a map the earth's seven continents and the countries of North America. 4. To understand the use of a compass rose. 5. To use cardinal and intermediate directions, and latitude and longitude to locate places on a map. 6. To know the size relationship of cities, states, countries, continents, and hemispheres. 7. To identify the 50 states of the United States and each state capital.

TEACHING SUGGESTIONS

1. **Reading Lyrics.** The lyrics of "America, the Beautiful" describe some of the geography of our nation. After pupils have read the lyrics on p. 2, ask them to give examples from their own community or state of some of the key geographic terms in the lyrics. Pose these questions.

a. *Are grains, such as corn or wheat, grown in our community? In our state?*
b. *Are there any mountains nearby?*
c. After explaining that *fruited plain* means "an abundance of crops," ask if there are any crops other than grains grown in the area.
d. *Is our community located near the sea or any other body of water?*
e. *Do we live in a city? What is the largest city in our state? How far are we from it?*

2. **Discussion.** Encourage pupils to tell about places in the United States they have visited. You may wish to show these places on an outline map of the nation.

Ask whether any of your pupils have visited a national park. If necessary, explain that a national park is land put aside by the government for the enjoyment of the people.

Tell pupils that in this chapter they will be taking an imaginary trip to one of those parks—Yellowstone National Park. Ask each pupil to make a list of five to ten questions that need to be answered before the trip to Yellowstone. Make a composite list of the questions on the chalkboard. Be sure the following questions are included.

a. *Where is Yellowstone?*
b. *What is the climate (weather) like there?*
c. *What kinds of clothes should I pack?*
d. *What kinds of activities will I find there?*
e. *How far away is it?*
f. *What kind of transportation will I use to get there?*

The above questions can all be answered by looking at maps. Many of these questions will be addressed in this chapter.

3. Demonstration. After the class has read pp. 3–6, cut in half, along what would be the equator, either a tennis ball, a sponge rubber ball, an orange, or some other round object. Push two pins or thumbtacks into the ball to represent the Poles. Hold the two pieces together and tell the class that this represents the earth and that each half is a hemisphere.

Then show pupils a globe and ask them to find the earth's hemispheres. Point out to them that the globe is a model of the earth and have them locate the continents and oceans.

4. Using a Globe. A globe is an essential tool for teaching the cardinal directions. Do the following activities with a globe.
a. Point out the location of the North Pole and of the South Pole.
b. Have a pupil place a finger on the North Pole and then move it away from that point. Ask: *In what direction have you moved your finger?* Guide pupils to the realization that when starting at the North Pole, all directions are south.
c. Repeat this activity using the South Pole as a starting point.

5. Reading a Diagram. Ask pupils to study the diagram on p. 4.
a. Write *N* (for north) on the chalkboard.

b. Ask a pupil to come to the board and write *S* in the appropriate place (opposite *N*).
c. Ask another pupil to write *E* in the correct position. If necessary remind this pupil that when you face north, east is the direction to your right.
d. Have a third pupil mark *W*.

Repeat this same exercise with *N* at various locations on the board. Finally, use a compass to find out where north really is in your classroom, and put a placard up on the north wall. Then have pupils place placards for south, east, and west on the appropriate walls.

6. Place Geography. Using the map on p. 6, ask pupils the following questions.
a. *Through which continents does the equator pass?* (South America, Africa, Asia)
b. *Which continents are entirely north of the equator?* (North America, Europe) *Which are entirely south of the equator?* (Australia, Antarctica)
c. *Which continents border on both the Pacific and Atlantic oceans?* (North America, South America, Antarctica)
d. *Which continents are west of Africa and Europe?* (North America, South America)
e. *Which continent is north of Australia?* (Asia)
f. *Which continent is south of Africa?* (Antarctica)
g. *On which continent do we live?* (North America)

7. Reading a Map. Using the map on p. 7, ask pupils the following questions.
a. *This is a map of which continent?* (North America)
b. *Which two countries in North America are the largest in land area?* (Canada and United States)
c. *What large bodies of water surround North America?* (Pacific, Arctic, and Atlantic oceans, Gulf of Mexico, Caribbean Sea, Bering Sea)

d. *Name the national capitals of the following countries: United States* (Washington, D.C.); *Canada* (Ottawa); *Mexico* (Mexico City); *and Guatemala* (Guatemala City).

e. *What does* (*DEN.*) *mean under Greenland?* (Denmark) (*U.K.*) *under Belize?* (United Kingdom) (*U.S.*) *under Puerto Rico?* (United States) Lead pupils to the understanding that the parentheses contain the name of the country to which the territory belongs.

f. *Which country borders Panama to the north?* (Costa Rica)

g. *Which countries are islands in the Caribbean Sea?* (Cuba, Jamaica, Haiti, Dominican Republic, Puerto Rico, Trinidad and Tobago)

h. *Which country is north of the United States?* (Canada)

i. *Which country is west of Belize and Honduras?* (Guatemala)

8. Place Geography. Have pupils turn to the map of the United States on p. 8. You may wish to ask pupils to respond to the following exercises either orally or in writing.

a. *Name five states that border on the Pacific Ocean.* (Alaska, Hawaii, Washington, Oregon, California)

b. *Name the states that border on the Great Lakes.* (Minnesota, Wisconsin, Michigan, Illinois, Indiana, Ohio, Pennsylvania, and New York)

c. *Name the states that share a boundary with Canada.* (Alaska, Washington, Idaho, Montana, North Dakota, Minnesota, Michigan, Ohio, Pennsylvania, New York, Vermont, New Hampshire, Maine) *With Mexico.* (California, Arizona, New Mexico, Texas)

d. *Find the spot where the borders of four states meet.* (Utah, Colorado, Arizona, New Mexico)

e. *Which states have the most neighbors?* (Tennessee and Missouri each have eight neighbors.)

f. *Name the states along the Mississippi River.* (Louisiana, Mississippi, Arkansas, Tennessee, Kentucky, Missouri, Illinois, Iowa, Wisconsin, Minnesota)

9. Reading Latitude. Have pupils turn to the map showing latitude lines on p. 9. Ask them the following questions about the map.

a. *Why do we use latitude lines?* (To locate places exactly)

b. *Is the United States in the northern or southern latitudes?* (Northern)

c. *Which continent is in both the northern and southern latitudes?* (South America)

d. *Are the Tropic of Cancer and the Arctic Circle latitude lines in the northern or southern latitudes?* (Northern)

e. *Are the Tropic of Capricorn and the Antarctic Circle latitude lines in the northern or southern latitudes?* (Southern)

f. *How are the labels on the north latitude lines different from the labels on the south latitude lines?* (North latitude lines have the letter N next to the degrees, south latitude lines have the letter S.)

g. *Is the equator in the north or south latitudes?* (Neither; it is the dividing line between the north and south latitudes.)

h. *Which latitude line runs through Central America?* (15°N)

i. *Which latitude line runs through the southern tip of South America?* (45°S)

● **10. Using Latitude and Longitude.** Have pupils turn to the world map on pp. 10–11. Instruct them to place the right or left index finger on New Orleans. Ask them to move their finger along the latitude line to find the number of degrees north latitude for New Orleans. Write *30°N* on the chalkboard.

Have pupils place their index finger on New Orleans again. Ask them to move their finger along the longitude line to the equator to find the number of degrees west longitude. Write *90°W* on the chalkboard.

Follow the same procedure for Mexico City and Tokyo. Discuss with the pupils how to find the number of degrees when a city falls between the grid lines shown. Then ask pupils to find the latitude and longitude of each city, write the coordinates on the chalkboard; or assign this activity as seatwork and correct it orally with the class.

Minneapolis	(45°N/94°W)
Ottawa	(45°N/76°W)
Alexandria	(31°N/30°E)
Nanking	(32°N/119°E)
Durban	(30°S/31°E)
Melbourne	(38°S/145°E)
Kinshasa	(5°S/15°E)
Leningrad	(60°N/30°E)
Manaus	(3°S/60°W)
Bombay	(19°N/74°E)

For those pupils who do not grasp the concept of latitude and longitude easily, do the following activity. On the chalkboard, draw five parallel vertical lines approximately 2 inches apart. Cross these lines with five parallel horizontal lines. Now trace over the middle vertical line and the middle horizontal line, making them heavier than the others. From left to right, label the vertical lines 2, 1, 0, 1, and 2. From top to bottom, label the horizontal lines 2, 1, 0, 1, and 2. Now write North at the top of the diagram, South at the bottom, East at the right, and West at the left. Explain that North refers to everything above the heavy horizontal line; South, to everything below it. East refers to everything to the right of the heavy vertical line; West, to everything to the left of it. Ask several pupils in turn to come and place an X at the intersection of various coordinates, such as North 2 and West 1.

Place the degree sign (°) beside each numeral on the diagram. Explain that a degree is a unit of measure of latitude and longitude and that we can exactly locate any place if we know its latitude and longitude. Next, using the map on pp. 14–15, have pupils give the approximate coordinates of the following cities.

Denver, Colorado	(39°N/105°W)
Memphis, Tennessee	(35°N/86°W)

Then have pupils name the cities located by the following coordinates.

39°N/120°W	(Reno, Nevada)
30°N/90°W	(New Orleans, Louisiana)
40°N/83°W	(Columbus, Ohio)
44°N/69°W	(Augusta, Maine)

For pupils who require a challenge, you may wish to divide them into pairs and have them take turns finding the names of places for the following coordinates on the map on pp. 14–15.

58°N/135°W	(Juneau)
36°N/87°W	(Nashville)
31°N/84°W	(Tallahassee)
35°N/107°W	(Albuquerque)
47°N/123°W	(Seattle)
43°N/72°W	(Concord)

Then ask them to find the coordinates for the following places.

Madison, Wis.	(43°N/89°W)
Kansas City, Mo.	(39°N/94°W)
Austin, Tex.	(31°N/98°W)
San Francisco, Cal.	(37°N/123°W)
Salt Lake City, Utah	(41°N/113°W)
Oklahoma City, Okla.	(36°N/97°W)
Boston, Mass.	(43°N/72°W)

SUPPLEMENTARY INFORMATION

International Date Line. The International Date Line roughly follows the line of longitude labeled 180°, which is the line that forms half of the great circle that divides the world into the Eastern Hemisphere and Western Hemisphere. (The other half of this circle is the prime meridian.)

When one crosses the International Date Line, the date changes by exactly 1 day. A traveler moving from west to east would gain a day; one traveling in the opposite direction would lose a day. This change is necessary because the local times gradually change east and west of the prime meridian, so that by the time one reaches the International Date Line, there is a difference of 12 hours in either direction. In some cases the lines (including the International Date Line) that divide the earth into time zones vary from the meridians of longitude in order to allow certain geographic and political divisions to fall within the same zone.

LESSON 2 PAGES 12–15

HOW FAR IS IT?

GOALS
1. To use a map scale to determine distance between two points. **2.** To know that scale is the ratio between map distance and real earth distance. **3.** To draw a map to scale.

TEACHING SUGGESTIONS
1. Understanding Scale. Have pupils bring in toy airplanes, dolls, trains, cars, and so on. Ask what each toy has in common with the thing it represents. Lead pupils to discover that the models, while they look like the real things, are smaller than the things they represent. Pose this question: *Why is it necessary for these models to be smaller than the real things?*

Note that maps, too, are drawn smaller than the areas they represent. On the chalkboard, draw a 1-foot square. Next to it draw a 3-inch square. Then draw a rectangle that is 3 inches by 5 inches. (If you are using the metric system, draw a 30-cm square, followed by a 10-cm square and a 10-cm by 20-cm rectangle.) Ask pupils which of the smaller shapes better represents the large square. Point out that a scale must be consistent. If a scale is 1 inch to 1 mile, it must be 1 inch to 1 mile in every direction.

● **2. Drawing Scale.** Have pupils measure the length and width of your classroom. Round off the dimensions to the nearer foot or meter and write them on the chalkboard. Ask pupils how they would show the size and shape of their classroom on a sheet of notebook paper. Obviously, they would have to make a scale drawing. Let us assume that your classroom is 32 feet (10 m) by 24 feet (7 m). Ask the following questions if you use customary measure. (The questions do not work with metric measure, since a drawing with a scale of 1 cm to 1 m would fit easily on notebook paper.) *Our room is 32 feet long. If we let 1 inch stand for 1 foot, how long a line would we need to show this length?* (32 in.) *That's too long for our notebook paper. What if we let 1 inch stand for 2 feet? How many inches long would our line be?* (16 in.) *That's still too long. Let's say that 1 inch stands for 4 feet. How long will our line be?* (8 in.) *How long a line will we need to represent the 24-foot width of our room?* (6 in.)

Now have pupils draw on their paper a rectangle that is 8 inches long and 6 inches wide. (For metric scale: 10 cm by 7 cm) Beneath the rectangle, have them draw a line 1 inch (1 cm) long. Under the line, have them write "1 inch stands for 4 feet." ("1 centimeter stands for 1 meter.") Keeping this scale in mind, help pupils indicate the location of your desk on their maps. Then have each pupil indicate the location of his or her own desk. Continue that procedure with other items in the classroom.

Guide pupils who have difficulty grasping the concept of scale through another drawing to scale using graph paper. If the dimensions of the school, playground, and parking lot are available, you may want to have pupils draw those areas to scale.

Ask pupils who require a challenge to draw to scale an area such as their bedroom or a local park.

3. Diagraming. Some of your pupils may wish to draw a map of a professional football field or a major-league baseball infield. The dimensions of both are given below. Professional football field:
a. Goal line to goal line—100 yards (91.4 m)
b. Goal line to end line—10 yards (9.1 m)
c. Width of the field—160 feet (48.8 m)

Major-league baseball infield:

a. Home plate to first base—90 feet (27.4 m)

b. First base to second base—90 feet (27.4 m)

c. Second base to third base—90 feet (27.4 m)

d. Third base to home plate—90 feet (27.4 m)

e. Pitcher's rubber to home plate—60.5 feet (18.4 m)

4. Using Scale. To give pupils practice in working with scale, have them do the following activity. First have them place a large dot at the center of a blank sheet of paper and label it *Washington, D.C.* Then, without concern for the actual location of the cities, have pupils draw (to scale) lines between this dot and each city on the list below, which gives approximate air distances from Washington, D.C. For example, if the scale used is 1 inch to 1,000 miles, pupils should draw a 4.5-inch line from the dot to represent the air distance to Rome. (If the scale is 1 cm to 1,000 km, the line would be 7.2 cm.) Have pupils put a dot at the end of the line and label it *Rome*. Have them continue in the same manner for each of the following cities.

a. Mexico City—1,900 miles (3,000 km)

b. London—3,600 miles (5,900 km)

c. Paris—3,900 miles (6,200 km)

d. Rome—4,500 miles (7,200 km)

e. Moscow—4,900 miles (7,800 km)

f. Cairo—6,000 miles (9,400 km)

g. Tokyo—6,000 miles (10,900 km)

h. Peking—7,000 miles (11,200 km)

i. Bangkok—8,800 miles (14,200 km)

5. Reading a Map. Ask pupils the following questions about the map on pp. 14–15.

a. *Find the state we live in. Which states border our state?*

b. *What is the capital of our state?*

c. *Name the other cities in our state shown on the map.*

d. *How many miles is the capital of our state from Washington, D.C.?*

e. *Name the capitals of the states that border our state.*

f. *Name the state capitals that are located along the Missouri River.* (Helena, Montana; Bismarck, North Dakota; Pierre, South Dakota; Jefferson City, Missouri)

g. *Which states have the Ohio River along a border?* (Ohio, West Virginia, Kentucky, Indiana, Illinois)

The proximity of water was very influential in the growth of cities in the United States. Ask pupils to name all the cities along the Mississippi River and its tributaries. Then ask them to name all the cities along the Atlantic and Pacific oceans, the Gulf of Mexico, the Great Lakes, the Gulf of Alaska, and the Bering Sea. Lead pupils to an understanding of why so many cities developed near water.

LESSON 3 PAGES 16–22

THE LANGUAGE OF MAPS

GOALS

1. To use a map key to determine the meaning of map symbols. **2.** To know that map symbols stand for real things and places. **3.** To know that maps use labels as well as symbols. **4.** To identify a specific map feature by its map label. **5.** To use a road map and a mileage chart.

TEACHING SUGGESTIONS

● **1. Reading a Map Key.** Have pupils study the map on p. 17. Then pose the following questions.

a. *Describe the symbol used for hospitals.* (A cross inside a square)

b. *How many campgrounds are shown on this map?* (Eight)

c. *How many entrances are there?* (Five)

d. *Describe the locations of the entrances.* (N, S, E, W, NE)

e. *Find Shoshone Lake on the map and describe its location.* (SW section)

f. *How far is it from Old Faithful to the West Entrance?* (About 18 mi or 28 km straight-line distance)

g. *How far is it from the East Entrance to the first picnic area?* (About 7 mi or about 11 km straight-line distance)

For pupils who have difficulty grasping the concept of reading a map key, you may wish to try the following activity. Ask pupils to draw the outline of an imaginary country, state, or park. Discuss the kinds of symbols that they should include on their maps. Help them develop a map key to explain their symbols. Then ask them to place the symbols on their maps. Also help the pupils to develop a scale of miles for their maps.

Pupils who require a challenge may develop an imaginary country, symbols, and a map key on their own. Or you may want to select a photograph from the text for which these pupils can make a map, symbols, and a map key.

2. Reading a Road Map. Have pupils study the road map on p. 21 and respond to the following questions.

a. *What interstate highway would you use if you wanted to go from Sheridan to Casper?* (Rt. 87)

b. *How many people live in Cody?* (5,000 to 9,999)

c. *If you went from Worland to Thermopolis on Route 20, in which direction would you be traveling?* (South or southeast)

d. *Name all the cities and towns you would pass if you traveled on Route 80 from Evanston to Cheyenne.* (Mountain View, Lyman, Green River, Rock Springs, Thayer Junction, Tipton, Wamsutter, Rawlins, Walcott, Laramie)

e. *What is the symbol for an Interstate highway? A U.S. highway? A state highway? An elevation point?* (See map key)

3. Using a Map. Obtain road maps of your state or region. Have pupils use the map index to find their city or town on the map. Then read or hand out mimeographed copies of directions that take pupils on a tour in their state.

4. Scale. To reinforce the idea of scale you may wish to do the following activity.

a. Ask pupils to look at the mileage chart on p. 22 to find the distances from Los Angeles to Yellowstone (1,105 mi) and from Yellowstone to Washington, D.C. (2,065 mi).

b. Have pupils add the two distances to find the mileage from Los Angeles to Washington, D.C., via Yellowstone. (3,170 mi)

c. Have pupils round the three distances to the nearer thousand. (1,000; 2,000; 3,000)

d. Ask pupils to draw a 6-inch line on a sheet of paper. Tell them that the line represents the approximate distance from Los Angeles to Washington, D.C., via Yellowstone, which is 3,000 miles.

e. Have pupils place a dot at either end of the line and label one dot *Los Angeles* and the other *Washington, D.C.*

f. Ask: *What is the scale of this line if 6 inches stands for 3,000 miles?* (1 in. to 500 mi)

g. Have pupils place a dot on the line to represent the approximate distance to Yellowstone. (This dot should be about 2 inches from the dot for Los Angeles.)

5. Reading a Mileage Chart. Ask pupils to turn to the mileage chart on p. 22. Ask them to find the following distances.

a. *Chicago to St. Louis.* (285 mi)

b. *New Orleans to Boston.* (1,550 mi)

c. *New York to Yellowstone.* (2,135 mi)

d. *Kansas City to Miami.* (1,530 mi)

e. *The greatest distance shown on the chart.* (3,425 mi from Seattle to Miami)

LESSON 4   PAGES 23–25

MASS TRANSIT

GOALS

1. To know the meaning of *mass transit*.
2. To appreciate America's highly developed transportation system. **3.** To read a transportation schedule.

TEACHING SUGGESTIONS

1. Graphing. The following is a list of approximate average speeds for various means of transportation. Have pupils show the information on a graph.

a. Walking—3 miles (5 km) per hour
b. Bicycling—10 miles (15 km) per hour
c. Ship—30 miles (50 km) per hour
d. Automobile—55 miles (90 km) per hour
e. Train—75 miles (120 km) per hour
f. Airplane—560 miles (900 km) per hour

2. Reading a Bus Schedule. Have pupils turn to the bus schedule on p. 25. Go over the various elements of the schedule. Ask pupils the following questions:

a. *What time would you have to catch the bus in Dover to arrive in New York by 8:50 A.M.?* (7:30 A.M.)
b. *What time would your friend in Boonton have to catch the same bus?* (7:55 A.M.)
c. *Which bus stop has the least amount of bus service to and from New York City?* (Hackettstown)
d. *Which bus stop would give you the greatest number of choices for bus service to and from New York City?* (Mt. View Circle)
e. *If you left New York City at 5:30 P.M., what time would you arrive in Pine Brook?* (6:00 or 6:05 P.M.)
f. *Which trip would take a longer time: the 5:40 P.M. bus from New York City to Denville or the 7:00 P.M. bus from New York City to Denville?* (5:40 P.M. bus) *How much longer?* (15 min. longer)
g. *If you went to New York City for dinner and a show, what is the latest bus you could catch to get home to Boonton?* (1:00 A.M.)
h. *If you missed the 9:55 A.M. bus from Mine Hill/Kenvil to New York City, how long would you have to wait for the next bus?* (4½ hr)
i. *If you missed the 3:25 P.M. bus from Boonton to New York City, how long would you have to wait for the next bus?* (½ hr)

MAPS ARE IMPORTANT

GOALS

1. To appreciate the functions and importance of maps. **2.** To use a variety of maps and map-like diagrams, such as a stylized town map and a seating plan. **3.** To use a standard grid system consisting of numbers and letters. **4.** To review the parts of a business letter.

TEACHING SUGGESTIONS

1. Reading a Seating Plan. While pupils are looking at the seating plan of Yankee Stadium on p. 27, ask them to respond to the following questions.

a. *Which gate is closest to the Club Boxes?* (Gate 4)
b. *Are the odd-numbered sections on the first-base side or the third-base side of the stadium?* (First-base)
c. *Where would you like to sit if you were in Yankee Stadium? Why?*

2. Map Reading. Have pupils study the map of Colonial Williamsburg on p. 26. Ask: *In which direction and on what streets would you travel if you were going from the Williamsburg Theater to the Guardhouse? From the Guardhouse to the Governor's Palace? From the Governor's Palace to the Windmill? From the Windmill to the Boatmaker? Where could you have dinner?* (Answers will vary.)

3. Using Coordinates. Tell pupils to make believe they work at the Information Center in Colonial Williamsburg, and that they want to help visitors to easily locate places to visit in Williamsburg. To do this they need to make a Colonial Williamsburg Directory. Direct pupils' attention to the letters at the top and bottom of the map on p. 26 and the numbers to the left and right of the map. Explain that the letters and numbers, or coordinates, help pinpoint a place on the map.

Ask pupils to locate the windmill on the map without using the coordinates. Now have the pupils place one forefinger on the *E* and the other forefinger on the *3*. Ask them to move the fingers along the map from *E* and from *3* until their fingers meet. Tell them that knowing these coordinates (*E,3*) makes it easier to locate the windmill. Ask the pupils to follow the coordinates *E,4* until their fingers meet. They should be able to tell you that they are at the Prentis Store.

Assign pupils to make a Colonial Williamsburg Directory listing the coordinates on the map for the following places.

a. *Governor's Palace* (D,3)
b. *Musical Instrument Maker* (E,4)
c. *Baker* (F,4)
d. *Wigmaker* (F,4)
e. *Gunsmith* (G,5)
f. *Printer, Book Binder* (E,4)
g. *Boot Maker* (D,4)
h. *Blacksmith and Harnessmaker* (C,4)

4. Writing a Business Letter. Have pupils write to various organizations asking for maps, schedules, diagrams, and tables. Review with pupils the parts of a business letter. Encourage pupils to explain why they are asking for this information, and to be specific, polite, and neat.

1/CHAPTER REVIEW   PAGE 28
Answers for Review Questions
1. The four hemispheres are Northern, Southern, Eastern, and Western.
2. The United States is found in the Northern and Western hemispheres.
3. The North Pole is the most northern place on earth. The South Pole is the most southern place on earth.
4. A continent is one of the seven large areas of land on the earth.
5. The United States is found on the North American continent.
6. A map scale tells you the relationship between distance on the earth and distance on a map.
7. A map key tells you the meaning of the symbols used on a map.
8. Mass transit is any way of moving a great many people at one time.
9. Possible answers include bus, subway, train, airplane, ferry, and ship.
10. Answers will vary.

1/SKILLS DEVELOPMENT   PAGE 29
Answers for Skills Development
1. c. South Pole: most southern place
2. 3. Continents
3. B. How Far Is It?
4. II. Our History

CHAPTER 2 PAGES 30–43

OUR HISTORY

THEME

History is a telling of what happened in the past. Geography and archaeology are important to history. Pupils should study United States history in order to understand their country and be productive citizens.

PROJECTS

1. Organize a field trip to a local museum to find out about the history of your community. In preparation for the trip, pupils should consider the following questions: *Who were the first settlers in your community? When did they settle? Why did they select your community? Did Native Americans live in the community? What were the early industries? Did any famous people come from your community?* You may also wish to invite someone from a local historical organization to your class to talk about local history.

2. Have pupils write a paragraph or two on what citizenship in the United States means to them. If you have pupils in your class who are not United States citizens, ask them to name the country they would prefer to be a citizen of and explain why. You may want some pupils to research and prepare an oral report on the responsibilities of a citizen in the United States and another oral report on the naturalization process.

LESSON 1 PAGES 30–34

WHAT IS HISTORY?

GOALS

1. To understand what history is. 2. To explain what chronological order is. 3. To know that people, events, and geography affect history.

TEACHING SUGGESTIONS

1. **Discussion.** Prior to having the pupils read the lesson, ask the following questions:
a. *What is history?*
b. *Who has a history?*
c. *Why is it important to know about history?*
   After pupils have read pp. 30–34 pose these questions:
d. *If you wrote your family's history in chronological order, where do you think you would start? Who would be the most recent family member in your family's history?*
e. *Can you name other famous people who have affected history besides those mentioned in the text?*
f. *Can you give an example of "people making events happen that cause other people to make other events happen"?* (p. 33)
g. *What is the geography of your community like? Does it help explain why people do certain things in your community?*

2. **Reading a Map.** Ask pupils to turn to the physical map of the United States in the Atlas on pp. 468–469. Have them locate their state and identify the physical features shown on the map. Ask them to explain how those physical features may have influenced their state's history.

3. **Current Events.** Find an article about a national issue from a current magazine.

After you have read the article to the class, ask pupils to describe the events in the article in chronological order. List the events on the chalkboard. Then ask pupils:

a. *Who are the people who may affect the outcome of the events in this article?*

b. *Has geography affected the events? If so, how?*

Change one aspect of the circumstances surrounding the event(s) and ask pupils how that change would affect the outcome of the event(s).

4. **Creative Writing.** Tell pupils to imagine that the United States space program has just discovered that people can live on Mars. Ask them to write several paragraphs on how they think the discovery will affect their own futures and the future development of the United States.

LESSON 2   PAGES 35–37

HOW DO WE LEARN ABOUT THE PAST?

GOALS

1. To distinguish between oral history and written records. 2. To understand how pictures help us learn about the past. 3. To describe the work of an archaeologist. 4. To explain how artifacts help us learn about the past.

TEACHING SUGGESTIONS

1. **Discussion.** After pupils have read pp. 35–37, pose the following questions:

a. *How is our way of living different from the time when your parents and grandparents were children?*

b. *What might be some of the problems in relying on oral history?*

c. *How do you think archaeologists know where to dig?*

d. *If you were a historian, how would you choose which events to write about?*

2. **Picture Reading.** Draw the class's attention to the picture on p. 36. On the chalkboard draw two columns and write *Then* and *Now* at the top of each column. Ask pupils to name things in the picture that are no longer found in an American city. Write their responses under the *Then* column. Ask them to state what has replaced the items in the *Then* column and write the replacements in the *Now* column.

3. **Community Resources.** You may want to invite a local archaeologist or archaeology professor to speak to your class about archaeology. Find out if he/she can bring samples of archaeological tools and artifacts to the class.

4. **Community Resources.** You may want to invite a senior citizen to share oral history with the class. It would be especially interesting to find someone who was actively involved in World War II or who remembers the Depression. Ask pupils to plan and write down their questions prior to the visit.

SUPPLEMENTARY INFORMATION

Alex Haley and Oral History. Perhaps one of the best-known stories based on oral history in America is the book *Roots* by Alex Haley. *Roots*, which was also presented on television, is a historical account of Haley's family going back to the time when the author's ancestor, Kunta Kinte, was taken from Africa as a slave.

Haley's inspiration for the story dates back to his childhood visits to his grandmother's house in Henning, Tennessee. As a boy he used to listen to his older relatives tell stories of "the African" whose name was passed down through generations along with a few other African words. His family's oral tradition inspired Haley to set out on a quest to learn more about his ancestors and his homeland. His years of research finally led him to his ancestral village of Juffure in Africa where an oral historian, the village "griot," recounted the long history of the village.

Haley was very excited when the griot told the tale of Omoro Kinte's oldest son, Kunta, who went out to cut wood and was never heard from again. The two oral traditions matched! He had accomplished what many Americans—especially black Americans—had considered an almost impossible task, and a task that certainly would have been impossible without oral history. In fact, the oral history was so accurate on both sides of the Atlantic that Haley found much of it could be substantiated by written records from the old slave ships and plantations.

LESSON 3   PAGES 38–41

WHY STUDY UNITED STATES HISTORY?

GOALS
1. To understand how present freedoms in the United States were influenced by past history. 2. To understand the importance of learning from the past. 3. To explain why good citizens need to know their country's history.

TEACHING SUGGESTIONS
1. **Discussion.** Before pupils read pp. 38–41, write this question on the chalkboard: *Why do we study United States history?* On the chalkboard, make a list of responses to the question. Then have pupils read the lesson and answer the following questions:
a. *How does our list compare to the reasons given in the lesson for studying United States history?*
b. *How does understanding your family's past help you to understand more about yourself?*
c. *Why do you think people decided long ago that it was important for young people to go to school?*

d. *In what sense is United States history a "family history"?* (p. 39)
e. *Why is it "necessary for you to be a good citizen"?* (p. 41)
2. **Creative Writing.** Ask pupils to write a story or essay on the topic, "Life Without the Telephone" (or airplanes, cars, electricity, engines, computers or other inventions which have changed the world). Emphasize to pupils the fact that the past has strongly influenced the present.
3. **Drawing a Cartoon.** Draw pupils' attention to the author's statement in the first column on p. 39 that says "You are like a bridge between the past and the future." Ask pupils to show that they understand the meaning of this statement by drawing a cartoon or sketch which illustrates this idea.
4. **Citizenship.** Distribute paper to pupils. Have them write the Pledge of Allegiance, leaving a space between each line of the pledge. Then ask them to rewrite each line of the pledge explaining its meaning in their own words. Encourage them to use the dictionary if necessary. When they have finished the assignment, discuss with them their interpretations of the pledge.
● 5. **Integrating Concepts.** Read a section of a historical biography to the class. Ask pupils to write a short essay that describes the important people, events, and geographical factors in the life of the historical figure. In another paragraph ask them to explain what they think are the ways historians learned about the life of this individual. In a concluding paragraph have them explain why they think it is important for Americans to learn about the actions and beliefs of the individual.

You may want to lead pupils who have difficulty grasping concepts in a discussion of the biography after reading it to them. In the discussion cover the points mentioned above. If during the discussion these pupils seem to understand the concepts, you may want to have them write a short essay on the most important points discussed or draw a picture-essay emphasizing the important events in the person's life.

You may want to assign those pupils who require a challenge to read a biography on their own. When they have completed their reading, have them write essays stressing what our nation has learned from the actions and beliefs of that biographical figure.

2/CHAPTER REVIEW PAGE 42
Answers for Review Questions

1. Suggested answers: A historian might interview people who lived during a certain time period, read primary and secondary source documents, study old paintings or photographs, study archaeological finds, or write a book that describes his or her findings. A geographer might study landforms, weather, climate, bodies of water, plants and animals that live in a certain area, natural resources, and how people affect and use their natural environment. An archaeologist would spend his or her working day studying the remains of plants and animals, digging through ruins of buildings, and piecing together the story that artifacts, found within or outside the ruins, might tell.

2. The four ways historians learn about the past are through **a.** pictures, **b.** oral history, **c.** the discoveries of archaeologists, and **d.** written records.

3. Answers will vary but should include these points: It is important to study United States history because it helps us to understand the present, it helps us learn from past mistakes and successes, and it helps us to become better citizens.

1/UNIT REVIEW PAGE 44
Answers for Unit Review

1. The four hemispheres are the northern, southern, eastern and western hemispheres. (You may want to ask pupils to locate them on a globe.)

2. The earth's seven continents are Asia, Africa, Australia, Antarctica, North America, South America, and Europe. (You may want to have pupils label the continents on an outline map.)

3. This is a map activity on lines of latitude. You may want pupils to use the map on p. 9 to check their work.

4. The name given to 0° longitude is the prime meridian.

5. You can find the city of San Diego, California, using latitude and longitude if you find the number of degrees latitude on the map and then find the number of degrees longitude. The city is located where those two numbers meet.

6. The four in-between directions are northeast, northwest, southeast, and southwest.

7. Some pupils may need guidance on making a map of the classroom. You may want to distribute graph paper for this activity.

8. Pupils' answers will vary but should include at least three of these kinds of mass transit in the United States: bus, train, airplane, and ferry.

9. Pupils' answers will vary.

10. Answers will vary, based on pupils' reactions to the information in Chapter 2.

11. Good citizens know the history of their country, participate in the voting process, and obey the laws of their country. Pupils may have additional answers. You may want to display pupils' artwork showing people being good citizens.

UNIT 2

An Age of Adventure

UNIT 2

AN AGE OF ADVENTURE

Dear Parent,

Your child is beginning a new unit in Social Studies. It is called An Age of Adventure. It is a study of the early history of the United States. The three chapters in the unit deal with Native Americans; exploration and settlement by the Vikings, Columbus, the Spanish, French, Portuguese, Dutch, and English; and the beginnings of the original thirteen colonies.

Please encourage your child to share with you the new information and understandings learned in class. Since this is the first full history unit of the year, you may want to explore the history of your community with your child. This unit will come alive for your child particularly if your ancestors were Native Americans, early explorers, or colonists in the original thirteen colonies. Also if you live near a Native American village or a site of early exploration and settlement, now would be an excellent time to plan a family trip to one of these places.

This interest and involvement on your part can add greatly to your child's understanding of our nation's beginnings.

Sincerely,

AN AGE OF ADVENTURE

BULLETIN-BOARD DISPLAY

Display a large outline map of the world on the bulletin board. Using different colored markers, record the paths of the different groups of Native Americans as they arrived in the New World. Use the map on p. 48 as a guide. The map can also illustrate the exploration routes of the Vikings, Spanish, Portuguese, French, Dutch, and English through the use of different colors. Add these routes to the display as they are introduced in the unit. Make sure a map key is provided to explain the colors.

GETTING STARTED

1. Ask pupils the following question: *If the first Americans arrived before history was recorded in written form, how do we know what they looked like, and how and where they lived?* (Artifacts, oral history, art work, ruins) Have pupils pretend that all writing will be destroyed over the next 5,000 years; have them draw or cut out from magazines picture "artifacts" that would give archaeologists 5,000 years from now clues to what life was like in America during the 1980s. Share the pictures as a group and discuss the conclusions archaeologists of the 6980s could come to about life in America in the 1980s.
2. Have pupils turn to the unit opening art. Ask them the following questions.
a. *Who do you think these people are?* (North American Indian, Columbus, a Pilgrim, and a Conquistador)
b. *Why is the clothing so different on each person shown?* (Cultural differences, different sources of cloth, different methods of weaving, different living habits, knowledge of uses for metal)

CHAPTER 3 PAGES 46–63

THE FIRST AMERICANS

THEME

Native Americans arrived in America and established a wide variety of cultures throughout North and South America long before Columbus's discovery of America in 1492.

PROJECTS

1. Information on local Native American groups can often be obtained from an Intertribal Council or historical society in your area. They may be able to provide speakers, craft and dance demonstrations, and opportunities for pupils to meet Native Americans.

2. Divide pupils into groups of three or four and assign each group to build models of the temporary camps, permanent villages, or large cities of the Native Americans on a cardboard or wood base. Give pupils the choice of selecting a tribe or empire described in Chapter 3 or one they find in an outside source. Have pupils gather building materials such as pipe cleaners, straws, clay, grass, twigs, stones, and construction paper. Encourage them to make their selected camp, village, or city as accurate as possible.

LESSON 1 PAGES 46–50

NATIVE AMERICANS

GOALS

1. To understand how and why Native Americans came to America. 2. To read The Routes of Early American Indians map. 3. To understand that the migration of Native Americans throughout North and South America took place over thousands of years. 4. To know what a strait is and to locate other straits in the world. 5. To list five things later settlers learned from the Native Americans.

TEACHING SUGGESTIONS

1. **Map Reading.** Ask pupils to turn to the map on p. 48. Pose the following questions:
a. *Where is Asia located on this map?* (Northwest corner)
b. *What is the name of the narrow strip of water between Asia and North America?* (Bering Strait)
c. *How did the first Americans cross from Asia to North America thousands and thousands of years ago?* (What is now the Bering Strait was a narrow strip of land then.)
d. *On which continent did the Native Americans spread out first?* (North America)
e. *What is the distance from the Bering Strait to the southern tip of South America?* (More than 11,000 miles, or about 18,000 km)

Make sure pupils understand that the migration was gradual, taking place over thousands of years. Point out that groups of people probably settled in various spots along the routes and that the descendants of the members of those groups probably moved on from time to time. Make sure pupils realize that it is highly unlikely that any one group of people started out at the beginning of the arrow in Asia and traveled all the way to the southern tip of South America.

2. Making a Time Line. To illustrate the relationship between the number of years Native Americans have been on the North American continent and the number of years since the arrival of the first Europeans here, draw a 42-inch time line on the chalkboard. Each inch should represent 1,000 years. The first date should be marked 40,000 B.C., when some experts believe that Native Americans first arrived in North America. The last date on the time line should be the present. A third date, 1492, should be marked on the time line at 41½ inches. Darken the area between 1492 and the present (½ inch). Darken the other 41½ inches with another color chalk to indicate the presence of Native Americans prior to the arrival of Europeans. (Metric: 126 cm total length, 1492 at 124½ cm)

3. Research Report. Some pupils may want to research and prepare an oral or written report on one of the big game animals hunted by Native Americans. Among the big game animals were the bison, moose, mammoth, caribou, musk-ox, horse, mastodon, camel, and great ground sloth. Encourage pupils to describe the animal and its habits and to include how the animal was hunted and used by Native Americans, and how archaeologists learned of the existence of the animal. Be sure they research the ancient animals rather than the modern-day species.

4. Map Reading. Have pupils turn to the Atlas, pp. 466–476. Using the physical maps in the Atlas and the definition of strait on p. 46, ask them to locate other straits in the world and name the bodies of water they connect.

5. Becoming an Archaeologist. Ask pupils to collect up to ten artifacts from home or school that tell something about them without revealing their names. Have them discreetly place the artifacts in a box or paper bag and place the box or bag in a designated location in the classroom. Ask pupils to select a box or bag that is not their own and study the artifacts carefully, as an archaeologist would. When all the pupils think they know whose artifacts they have selected, have them state the person's name and explain the clues that helped them to make that choice. If some pupils guess incorrectly the first time, you may want to give them a second chance.

LESSON 2   PAGES 50–56

IROQUOIS, SIOUX, AND PUEBLO

GOALS

1. To compare the homes, food, and customs of the Iroquois, Sioux, and Pueblo. **2.** To evaluate how the environment of the Iroquois, Sioux, and Pueblo affected their life-style. **3.** To locate on a map the land regions where the Iroquois, Sioux, and Pueblo lived.

TEACHING SUGGESTIONS

1. Reading Recall. After pupils have read about the Iroquois pp. 50–53, pose the following questions.

a. *In what region were the Iroquois tribes located?* (The northeastern part of the Eastern Woodlands area)

b. *Describe the education of Two Rivers.* (He trained to be a warrior; practiced long-distance running and lacrosse; learned to move quietly through the woods, to use a tomahawk and bow and arrows and to hide his feelings.) *Would you prefer your present-day education or Two Rivers's education?*

c. *How did the Iroquois replace their dead warriors?* (With captives who survived running the gauntlet)

d. *What were the "Three Sisters"?* (Corn, beans, squash)

e. *Who was Hiawatha?* (A great Iroquois leader who believed in peace) *Why was he important to the Iroquois nation?* (He convinced all five Iroquois tribes to live in peace. He organized the League of Iroquois, which held a peace council each year.)

f. *What was the role of women in the Iroquois government?* (They chose and, if necessary, replaced the tribe's sachems and Pine Trees.)

g. *Two Rivers wanted to be a Pine Tree or a sachem when he grew up. What would he do as a Pine Tree?* (He would be part of a group of warriors who would decide when the League of Iroquois would fight.) *As a sachem?* (He would be a leader and ruler of his people and would be a member of the League of Iroquois.)

2. Place Geography. Have pupils turn to the physical map of the United States in the Atlas, pp. 468–469. Using the description on p. 50 as a guide, ask them to locate the area of the United States where the Iroquois lived. Follow the same procedure for locating the lands of the Sioux, p. 53, and the Pueblo, pp. 54–55.

Once pupils have found the general location of each tribe, point out to them that the Eastern Woodlands Indians were found from the Canadian border to the Gulf Coast and from the East Coast to the Mississippi River; the Iroquois nation was located in upper New York state. The Plains Indians settled in the region from the Mississippi River west to the Rocky Mountains and from Canada to Mexico; the Sioux tribes were located in what is today Minnesota and North and South Dakota. The Southwest Indians settled in the area of present-day Arizona, New Mexico, southern Utah, and northern Mexico; the Pueblos were found in New Mexico and Arizona.

● **3. Reading Recall.** After pupils have read pp. 53–54, ask the following questions.

a. *What was the land like where the Sioux lived?* (Wide, open land covered with short, tough grass; hard, dry ground; few trees; difficult to farm)

b. *Why were the buffalo so important to the Sioux?* (Source of food, clothing, blankets, covering for their homes, glue, cooking pots)

c. *How were buffalo hunted by the Sioux?* (Bow and arrows, driving them over cliffs or into deep snow or icy lakes)

d. *Why did the Sioux need lightweight, easy-to-pack homes?* (So that they could quickly break camp and follow the herds of buffalo)

e. *How were Sioux boys trained to be good warriors?* (They learned to be good runners, wrestle, swim in ice-cold water, do without food for a long time, and endure pain without complaining.)

After pupils have read pp. 54–56, have them ask questions about the Pueblos for other pupils in the class to answer. Or ask pupils the following questions.

a. *Where did the name Pueblo come from, and what does it mean?* (The Spanish word for "village")

b. *Describe the land where the Pueblos live.* (Very dry, hot desert land with very few trees)

c. *How did the Pueblos protect themselves from the Navajo?* (Both by fighting and by pulling up the ladders that led to their homes)

d. *Why did the Navajo frequently raid the Pueblo villages?* (To take food and other supplies)

e. *What was the Pueblos' main source of food?* (Maize) *Why was it so difficult to grow?* (Because the soil was so dry)

f. *Who were the kachinas, and why were they important to the Pueblos?* (Good spirits who protected the Pueblos and their crops; they prayed to the spirits to bring rain and good crops)

g. *What was a kiva?* (An underground room that the Pueblo men used for religious ceremonies. They also used kivas in the winter to tell stories, weave blankets, and teach the young Pueblo boys.)

For pupils who have difficulty grasping concepts, write the following across the top of the chalkboard: *Iroquois*, *Sioux*, and *Pueblo*. Write the following down the left side of the chalkboard: *Land*, *Homes*, *Food*, *Education*, and *Protection*. Either through oral discussion or written activity, ask the pupils to fill in the chart with words that describe each category for each Indian group.

For pupils who require a challenge, you may wish to have them, individually or in small groups, research and prepare a presentation for the class on another Native American group. Encourage them to use their library skills to research information about the tribe's homes, food, clothing, beliefs, laws, education, and special traditions. Possible choices include the Algonquian, Cheyenne, Apache, Nez Percé, Alaskan, Cherokee, Chinook, Paiute, or Cree tribes.

4. Interpreting the Facts. After comparing the life-styles of the Iroquois, Sioux, and Pueblo, pupils should come to the realization that environment affects the life-style of a given group of people. Point out to the pupils that in order to survive, the Pueblos and the Sioux had to use a great deal of ingenuity. The Iroquois, by contrast, lived in an environment with more plentiful and varied sources of food and clothing. Help pupils arrive at the generalizations that a group's life-style and level of technological development are in part determined by their natural environment. Then ask pupils how their own natural environment affects their life-style and level of technological development.

SUPPLEMENTARY INFORMATION

Horses. When the first Native Americans arrived in America, there were a variety of large animals to "greet" them. Among those animals was the horse, which was native to America. These ancestors of the modern horse traveled in great herds. There is evidence that the early Native Americans hunted the horse for food rather than using the horse for transportation. For unknown reasons, the horse became extinct in the Americas in those ancient times. Fortunately, however, groups of North American horses had migrated over the land bridge into Asia, spread throughout that continent, and survived.

In 1519 the Spanish conquistador Hernando Cortes brought ten stallions and six mares to Mexico. These horses were the first known to be in the Americas in hundreds of thousands of years. Subsequent Spanish explorers who settled in northern Mexico and the southeastern United States brought more horses to the Americas. The Spanish were aware of the importance of the horse for transportation and power. They forced the Pueblo Indians to work for them and care for their horses, but the Pueblos could not use or own the horses.

In 1680 the Pueblos rose up against their Spanish oppressors, gained their freedom, and gained possession of several thousand horses. The Pueblos traded the horses with other tribes. As a result the horse spread once again through North and South America and radically changed the Indian way of life. Suddenly the Indians were able to travel to places they had never been before, they had contact with tribes they had never seen before, and they had a way of hunting they had never known before.

LESSON 3 PAGES 57–61

MAYAS, AZTECS, AND INCAS

GOALS

1. To explain and give examples of specialization of labor. **2.** To know the marks of a civilization. **3.** To describe the marks of civilization in the Maya, Aztec and Inca empires. **4.** To locate the Maya, Aztec, and Inca empires on a map. **5.** To identify on a map North America, South America, Central America, Middle America, and Latin America.

TEACHING SUGGESTIONS

1. Preparing for Reading. Ask pupils to raise their hands if they had cereal for breakfast. Introduce the concept of specialization of labor by asking them to name all the jobs connected with bringing cereal from the fields to their breakfast tables. List the jobs on the chalkboard. Responses may include farmers; manufacturers and sellers of fertilizer, farm machinery, cereal, gasoline, boxes and paper; grain purchasers; grocers; checkout cashiers; baggers; government regulators; artists; and advertising production people. Pupils should see that literally hundreds of people had important roles related to the processing and transportation of that box of cereal.

Point out that this was not always the way food was processed and transported in the past, nor is it the way food is processed in some countries today. In ancient times people used to raise and prepare food by themselves and only for themselves. The Mayas were one early group of people who changed this method of growing and preparing food. Ask pupils to read about the Mayas and find out how they came to have jobs other than just raising food. Explain to pupils that this is, in the broadest sense, what makes a civilization—people exchanging goods and services with other people through specialization of labor. Ask pupils to find the marks of Maya civilization as they read pp. 57–58.

2. Discussion. After pupils have read about the Maya empire, pp. 58–59, ask them to name the kinds of jobs that developed for those people who were not farmers. List the jobs on the chalkboard.

Then ask pupils to explain how each job was important to the development of the Maya civilization.

3. Map Reading. Have pupils turn to the map on p. 58. Ask them the following questions.

a. *Which continents are shown on the map?* (Part of North America, South America)

b. *Look at the key. What color represents the area where the Maya civilization was located?* (Yellow-green) *Find that area on the map.*

c. *Using the map in the Atlas on p. 471 (or a large display map in the classroom), name the present-day countries whose land was part of the Maya empire long ago.* (Belize, most of Guatemala, parts of Mexico, western El Salvador, Honduras) Follow the same procedure for the Aztec empire (Mexico) and the Inca empire (Peru, parts of Ecuador, Chile, and Bolivia). You may want to distribute outline maps of Latin America; then have pupils make their own color keys and color the areas of each empire according to their keys.

4. Reading Recall. After pupils have read about the Aztecs, pp. 58–59, ask the following questions.

a. *How were the Maya and Aztec civilizations alike?* (They had similar homes, clothing, and farming methods; they studied the arts and sciences; they both had a form of writing; they both practiced human sacrifice.)

b. *Why did the Aztecs practice human sacrifice?* (They were offerings to their gods.) You may want to share the following with your pupils: Huitzilopochtli (wē-tsē lō pōch′ tlē), the god of sun and war, was an important and favorite god of the Aztecs. The Aztecs believed that this god needed the sacrifice of human blood and hearts so that the sun would rise each morning.

c. *Would you rather be a prisoner of war of the Iroquois (p. 51) or of the Aztecs? Why?*

d. *The Aztecs were very skilled people. How does our knowledge of Tenochtitlán support this fact?* Encourage pupils to study the mural of Tenochtitlán, p. 59, for answers in addition to the reading. (They built causeways, wooden bridges, roads, canals, huge pyramids, and temples; it was a well-planned and well-protected city.)

● **5. Skimming for Facts/Taking Notes.** After pupils have read pp. 59 and 61, distribute paper to them. Ask them to write *The Power of the Inca Government* at the top of the paper, and number 1 through 7 down the left side. Have them skim pp. 59 and 61 looking for examples of the power of the Inca government to write down. Discuss their selections orally and make a master list on the chalkboard from their responses. (The seven points should include a large empire in physical size and population, great armies, an excellent road system, great wealth, ownership of all land, ownership of all but daily survival food, and power to determine who received education.)

You may wish to have pupils who have difficulty grasping concepts skim and take notes on all of Lesson 3. Check their work.

You may wish to have pupils who require a challenge answer the following questions, which require them to think about what they have read.

a. *How do you think we know that the Incas were great road builders?* (Some of the roads still exist today; they wind through the very steep Andean mountains.)

b. *How do you think that we know that the Inca rulers were very successful?* (By the vastness of their empire, the huge stone palaces, the great wealth)

c. *How do we know so much about the Inca civilization if the Incas had no system of writing?* (Archaeological artifacts, ruins of the ancient cities and roads, art, oral his-tory, and written records of explorers who found and took their great wealth)

d. *How were the Incas different from the Mayas and Aztecs?* (Terrace farming; sacrifice of animals rather than people; no form of writing; the government, not the people, owned the land; ate guinea pig and llama meat)

e. *Would you rather have been a Maya, an Aztec, or an Inca? Why?*

6. Making a Map. After pupils have read and studied p. 60, distribute or have pupils trace outline maps of the North and South American continents. Ask them to make a map key that will identify the areas of North America, South America, Central America, and Middle America on their maps. Because these land areas overlap, you may want to suggest the following symbols for the map key: diagonal lines for North America; a light, solid color for South America; small dots for Central America; and a dark outline for Middle America. Also have them draw a dark blue horizontal line separating Latin America from the United States and Canada.

3/CHAPTER REVIEW   PAGE 62
Answers for Review Questions

1. The land bridge was important because this narrow strip of land enabled the first people to reach the Americas.

2. Answers will vary.

3. The Mayas, Aztecs, and Incas were great civilizations because they had these marks of a civilization:

Mayas—a form of writing; varied jobs such as weavers, traders, and builders; a scientific knowledge of the stars and weather

Aztecs—a form of writing; a strong government that lasted over 300 years; the great city of Tenochtitlán

Incas—excellent builders of great roads and pyramids; a strong government; fine arts and crafts

EXPLORATION

THEME

Christopher Columbus, though not the first to reach America, blazed the trail for future European exploration and settlement in the New World. He exemplified the courage, skill, and sense of adventure exhibited by many of the early explorers. After Columbus's initial explorations, Portugal, England, France, and the Netherlands joined Spain in discovering and claiming areas of the New World.

PROJECTS

1. Before the compass was invented, sailors used the sun and stars to determine direction. When the sky was overcast they obviously could lose their direction very easily. Navigators probably developed a very simple form of the compass around the 1000s to 1100s. The compass was an extremely important invention for the explorers of the 1400–1600s.

Have pupils duplicate the first magnetic compass by following these directions:
a. Materials: a steel needle, a bar magnet, a cork, a nonmetal bowl, and water.

b. Magnetize the needle by rubbing the sharp end in *one direction* along the north side of a bar magnet. Rub the needle in one direction at least 15 times. Emphasize to pupils that they must not rub it back and forth. Correctly rubbing the needle arranges all the molecules in a north-south pattern.
c. Float the piece of cork in a nonmetal bowl filled with water. The cork should be approximately 1 inch (4 cm) in diameter and ¼ inch (1 cm) thick.
d. Have pupils lay the magnetized needle on the floating cork. After some movement the needle should point steadily toward the magnetic North Pole.
e. Pupils can check the accuracy of their ancient compass by comparing its reading with that of a modern compass.
2. Pupils may like to choose a theme from this chapter to develop a storyboard. A storyboard has pictures across the top and captions at the bottom describing the pictures in detail. The pictures should be presented in appropriate sequence. Pupils should restrict themselves to four to six frames. Sample themes include:
a. The Vikings Come to America
b. Columbus's Four Voyages
c. Spanish, French, or English Explorers
d. Spaniards Conquer the Aztecs

LESSON 1 PAGES 64–67

EARLY EXPLORERS

GOALS

1. To know what an explorer is. 2. To explain how we know that the Vikings were the first explorers in the Americas. 3. To read a time line of the age of exploration.

TEACHING SUGGESTIONS

1. **Discussion.** Direct pupils to read the first three sections on p. 64. Through discussion be sure that pupils understand what an explorer is and that exploration can take place as close as the classroom or as far as outer space.

Point out to pupils that the question "Who discovered America?" has been one of the most controversial questions in history. They will probably be able to tell you that Columbus is usually given the credit for discovering America. Remind them that the Native Americans had lived in the Americas for thousands of years before Columbus ever set sail from Spain. Tell them that the more proper question should be "Which European nation discovered America first?" Allow pupils time to think about the question and give answers. Then direct them to read the rest of the lesson through column one on p. 67.

2. Reading a Map. Have pupils turn to the map of Europe in the Atlas on p. 474. Ask them to locate the Scandinavian countries. Then have them turn to the world map on pp. 466–467 and ask them to estimate the route the Vikings probably sailed to eventually reach North America. It is important for pupils to note that the Vikings settled in Iceland and Greenland before reaching Newfoundland in Canada. This route of travel is a good indication of why the Vikings were the first to reach North America. By "island hopping" the trip was not as long, dangerous, and laborious as it might have been if they had made the trip directly.

3. Distinguishing Fact from Opinion. After pupils have completed reading Lesson 1, ask them to tell whether each of the following statements is based on known facts or on someone's opinion about the facts.
a. *Our stories about Vikings were passed down by the Vikings themselves.* (Fact)
b. *The house found by archaeologists is Leif Ericson's.* (Opinion)
c. *Viking settlements died out because of fights with the Native Americans.* (Opinion)
d. *The Vikings were the first Europeans in America.* (Opinion)
e. *Archaeological proof has been found that Vikings visited "Vinland" about the year 1000.* (Fact)

4. Using a Time Line. Have pupils turn to the time line on p. 66. Ask the following questions:
a. *Which group of European explorers were the first to come to the New World?* (The Vikings)
b. *How many years passed from the time the Vikings were known to be in the New World until Columbus rediscovered the New World?* (492)
c. *During which century did the greatest number of explorations take place?* (The 1500s)
d. *Verrazano was the first explorer from France. How many years passed from the time Columbus rediscovered the New World until the French decided to join in the explorations?* (32)

SUPPLEMENTARY INFORMATION
Viking Ships. The Vikings were considered excellent shipbuilders. The keel, which they added to their ships, not only stabilized the vessels but also made them swift and easy to steer. A square woolen sail on a 40 foot (12 m) mast gathered the wind to power the ship. When there was no wind or when they had to maneuver through shallow river waters, there were from 16 to 30 oarsmen on each side of the ship ready to row. The prow of the Viking ships curved gracefully into the head of a dragon or snake. It was an honor for Viking lords to be buried in their ships. Our knowledge of Viking ships was gained through the archaeological discoveries of these seaworthy shrines.

LESSON 2   PAGES 67–71

CHRISTOPHER COLUMBUS

GOALS
1. To explain Columbus's idea for a new route to the Indies. **2.** To know what Col-

umbus's important discovery was and to understand why it was so important. **3.** To use a map key and scale to read a map of Columbus's voyages.

TEACHING SUGGESTIONS

1. Reading Recall. After pupils have read pp. 67–71, ask them to answer the following questions in oral or written form:

a. *How did Columbus's experiences in his youth spark his interest in the sea?* (Growing up in a major seaport city; watching ships in the port; going to sea and learning about sailing as a teenager)

b. *Why did the Europeans consider the Indies to be so attractive and important?* (They could acquire valuable and unusual items for trade, such as jewels, ivory, silks, and spices.)

c. *Why were the trade routes to and from the Indies so difficult?* (A large part of the trip was over deserts, mountains, and valleys. The traders needed pack animals as well as ships. Both the animals and the ships, laden with the valuable goods, were victims of robbers.)

d. *Why did Portugal refuse to support Columbus's voyage?* (The king of Portugal thought that Columbus was asking for too much money and power. Also, his geographers did not agree with Columbus's calculations of distance to Asia.)

e. *What did Spain hope to gain from supporting Columbus's voyage?* (Gold and a faster route to the Indies)

f. *Where did Columbus first sight land in the New World?* (San Salvador)

2. Reading a Map. Have pupils turn to the map on p. 71. Ask the following questions:

a. *How many voyages did Columbus make to the New World?* (Four)

b. Look at the map key. *Which color represents his first trip?* (Gray) *Second trip?* (Red) *Third trip?* (Blue) *Fourth trip?* (Green)

c. *Which voyage took the most northern route?* (The first)

d. *On which voyage did he set foot in South America?* (The third)

e. *How long was the first voyage?* (11,200 mi, or 18,000 km)

f. *Name at least three modern island countries that Columbus visited.* (Bahamas, Cuba, Trinidad, Jamaica, and Haiti and the Dominican Republic)

● **3. Discussion.** Before they read the lesson, encourage pupils to think about Columbus as a person. After they have completed reading the lesson, ask pupils to describe Columbus. Compile their responses in a list on the board. Then ask pupils what characteristics they think make a person great. Write those responses on the board also. Finally ask pupils if they think Columbus should be considered a great person and ask them to explain their answers.

You may want to ask pupils who have difficulty grasping concepts to skim the lesson and write down the words that describe the kind of person Columbus was. When they complete their lists, ask them to tell you in written or verbal form if they think Columbus should have been disgraced in his later years.

You may wish to have pupils who require a challenge write an essay entitled Why Christopher Columbus Was (or Was Not) a Great Person.

LESSON 3   PAGES 72–76

EXPLORERS FOR SPAIN AND PORTUGAL

GOALS

1. To understand why so many explorers set sail for the New World. **2.** To outline the experiences of the Portuguese and Spanish explorers. **3.** To explain the reason why Spanish explorations of the Americas and Spanish power in the world declined after 1588.

TEACHING SUGGESTIONS

1. Reading for Thinking. Introduce the lesson by discussing the concept of "First come, first served." Ask pupils what the expression means and tie it into the concept that the first explorer to find a territory could claim it for his country.

After pupils have read pp. 72–76 pose the following interpretive questions:

a. *Why do you think some discoveries were made by accident?*

b. *Have you ever been really hungry? What have you done about it? Do you think you could ever be hungry enough to eat rats, sawdust, and leather as Magellan's crew did?*

c. *Why is Magellan given credit for being the first to sail around the world if he died before he completed the journey?*

d. *What were some of the advantages of the Spanish explorations? What were some of the disadvantages, particularly for the Native Americans who were "discovered"?*

● **2. Outlining.** Have pupils review the steps in making an outline on Skills Development p. 29. Ask them to make an outline of the Portuguese and Spanish explorers mentioned in this lesson and include at least two or three important points about each explorer. Ask them to make a title for their outline. Be sure pupils make their outlines neat. Save the outlines so that pupils can add the French, Dutch, and English explorers to it in Lesson 4.

You may want to guide pupils who have difficulty grasping concepts through part of the outline and have them finish it on their own. For example, you might do this much of the outline together.

I. Portuguese explorers
   A. Vasco da Gama
      1. Set sail in 1497
      2. Sought a route to the Indies
      3. Was the first to sail around the tip of Africa to reach the Indies

   B. Pedro Cabral
      1. Set sail in 1500
      2. Was looking for Asia by way of Africa
      3. Landed in Brazil instead and claimed it for Portugal
II. Spanish explorers
   A. Ponce de León
      1. Set sail in 1513
      2. Looked for the Fountain of Youth
      3. Found Florida and claimed it for Spain
   B. Balboa

You may want to have pupils who require a challenge write a few paragraphs in which they pretend that they are on Pizarro's or Cortés's expedition and that they have discovered the Aztec or Inca empire. Ask them to describe the trip across the ocean, the Aztec or Inca civilization (they may refer back to Chapter 3 for a review), and their treatment of these Native Americans and their possessions. This may be done when they have completed the outline.

3. Using Map Skills. Distribute outline maps of North and South America to pupils. Ask them to develop a key and show on their maps the land areas discovered by the Portuguese and Spanish explorers. Also ask them to show the approximate route Magellan sailed. Be sure they label the places mentioned in the lesson. Have them use the Atlas maps on pp. 470 and 471 as guides. Have pupils save the maps to use in Lesson 4.

SUPPLEMENTARY INFORMATION

Cortés. Moctezuma (or Montezuma), Emperor of the Aztecs, had an elaborate spy system. Therefore, it was not long before he knew of the arrival of Cortés, the size of his army, and of how the Spaniards used firearms. Moctezuma sent messengers bearing gifts and a request for Cortés to leave, which Cortés rejected.

Cortés entered Tenochtitlán in the autumn of 1519, avoiding an ambush on the way. He made a prisoner of Moctezuma and used him to rule the country.

Cortés left the city on another expedition. When he returned, he found the Indians on the point of rebellion, angered by Moctezuma's submission to Cortés. In the summer of 1520, fighting broke out. Although the Spaniards had superior weapons and killed thousands of Aztecs, they were driven from the city because they were outnumbered.

Cortés remained undaunted. Taking refuge with friendly tribes, he rebuilt his army, replenished his supplies, and made plans for the siege of Tenochtitlán.

In 1521 Cortés was ready to attack. He had reinforcements from the West Indies in addition to many Indians from tribes who hated the Aztecs. Cortés did not want to enter Tenochtitlán by means of the causeways where so many of his followers had been slaughtered. He used European-style ships to carry his troops throughout the city. The ships gave the Spaniards control of the lake; this prevented the Aztecs from getting supplies. Great parts of the city were leveled so that the Spaniards could use their horses to better advantage. Thousands of Aztecs were killed as they tried to escape across the lake. Many others were taken as prisoners.

LESSON 4   PAGES 77–81

FRENCH, DUTCH, AND ENGLISH IN AMERICA

GOALS

1. To understand why the French, Dutch, and English started exploring the Americas. 2. To outline the experiences of the French, Dutch, and English explorers. 3. To show on a map the territories opened up by the French, Dutch, and English.

TEACHING SUGGESTIONS

1. **Reading for Thinking.** Ask pupils to read the "Northwest Passage" section on p. 77. Have them turn to the map in the Atlas on p. 470 and discuss why a Northwest Passage would have been an excellent discovery. Also discuss why, from looking at the map, it was impossible to find that Northwest Passage.

Direct pupils to complete reading Lesson 4 through p. 81. Ask the following questions:

a. *What did the French, Dutch, and English find instead of a Northwest Passage?* (What is today Canada and the United States)

b. *How did the French treatment of the Native Americans compare to the Spanish treatment of them?* (The French learned from them and traded with them rather than conquering them as the Spanish had done.)

c. *Who was more important to the development of the New World: Champlain or Hudson? Why?* (Answers will vary.)

d. *What do you think happened to the colonists on Roanoke Island?* (Answers will vary.)

2. **Outlining.** Have pupils review their outline of the Portuguese and Spanish explorers from Lesson 3. Then ask them to follow the same format for outlining what they have learned about the French, Dutch, and English explorers.

3. **Using Map Skills.** Have pupils add the land areas discovered by the French, Dutch, and English to their outline maps of North and South America used in Lesson 3. Again remind them to add to their map key, label the places mentioned in Lesson 4, and use the Atlas maps on pp. 470 and 471 as guides. You may want to display the completed maps on the bulletin board.

4. **Community Resources.** If you live in an area where any of the explorations mentioned in the chapter have taken place, you may want to have the class visit a local

museum or historical site that has information about the exploration. Also, note if there is Portuguese, Spanish, French, Dutch, or English influence in local place-names, crafts, cuisine, and architecture.

5. Reviewing the Chapter. To review the many explorers introduced in the chapter, you may want to make flash cards with clues that tell about each of the explorers. Flash the clues in front of the class and ask if they can guess the explorer that matches the clues.

6. Career Awareness. Ask pupils what jobs are available today in the field of exploration and discovery. (Space, new resources, science) Have them look for articles describing new discoveries and explorations in current magazines and newspapers.

All the early explorers were men. Ask: *Are jobs in exploration and discovery open to women as well as men today?*

4/CHAPTER REVIEW PAGE 82

Answers for Review Questions

1. Columbus's discovery of America was so important because he opened up a whole new world to the Europeans.
2. The Spanish had the greatest and earliest claims to the New World because they were the first nation to become involved in and finance extensive explorations.
3. The Spanish conquered the Native Americans and took their lands and possessions. The French learned from the Native Americans and traded with them. They also tried to teach them Christianity.
4. Some of the difficulties in starting a settlement or colony include getting along with the people of the area, finding a healthy climate, locating good land for farming that is also near an ocean port, having enough supplies to last until the homes are built and the first crops are harvested, and having settlers who are dedicated to the effort.

CHAPTER 5 PAGES 84–104

COLONIZATION

THEME

Each English colony in the New World had a distinctive start and each colony contributed to the American way of life today. By 1760 characteristics had developed in New England, the Middle Colonies, and the Southern Colonies which made each region unique.

PROJECTS

1. Have pupils do individual or group reports on some of the interesting and well-known people of the early colonial period. Some suggestions include Captain John Smith, Chief Powhatan, John Rolfe, Pocahontas, William Bradford, John Winthrop, William Penn, Roger Williams, Anne Hutchinson, Cecilius Calvert, James Oglethorpe, Robert "King" Carter, Squanto, and Peter Stuyvesant. Ask pupils to share their reports with the class.
2. Have pupils do research on colonial crafts. Ask them to describe the crafts or actually make some of the colonial crafts. You may want to work with the art teacher on this project, or invite a craftsperson from the community to demonstrate a colonial craft to the class. If there is a local museum that displays colonial crafts, encourage pupils to visit the museum.
3. Ask pupils to draw a mural showing a typical New England colonial town, a Southern colonial plantation, and a city, such as Philadelphia, from the Middle Colonies.

THE FIRST COLONIES

GOALS
1. To know the names and dates of the first two English settlements in North America. 2. To understand the geographical importance of the location of the first settlements. 3. To identify Captain John Smith, the London Company, the Pilgrims, and Squanto. 4. To appreciate the significance of the Mayflower Compact and the House of Burgesses as early forms of government.

TEACHING SUGGESTIONS
1. Preparing for Reading. Before pupils read Lesson 1, divide them into four or five groups. Tell each group to pretend that a new, undeveloped continent has been discovered and that their group has decided to settle on the new continent. Have each group plan in writing what they should bring with them, how they should govern themselves, and what six activities they should start immediately upon arriving in the new land.

When they have completed the assignment ask each group to share and discuss their plans with the rest of the class. Allow each group to question the choices made by the other groups. Then ask pupils to think about their own plans as they read about the plans and experiences of the Jamestown and Plymouth colonists.

● **2. Making Comparisons.** When the class has finished reading Lesson 1, draw their attention to the chalkboard where you have made a chart with two columns; one titled *Jamestown*, the other *Plymouth*. Ask pupils to recall and compare the experiences the settlers had in establishing each colony. Write their responses on the chart. Points pupils should note include **a.** reasons for sailing to America, **b.** reasons for selecting the site for the colony, **c.** the laws established, **d.** first activities, **e.** experiences with the Native Americans, **f.** problems the colonists faced, and **g.** reasons for eventual success.

You may want to have pupils who have difficulty grasping concepts make an outline of the events at Jamestown and at Plymouth.

You may wish to have pupils who require a challenge write a journal for a week or two as the early Jamestown colonists did. Pupils should date each entry, tell the events that happened that day, and express their opinions of the events.

3. Reading a Time Line. Have pupils turn to the time line on p. 86. Ask them to use the time line in answering the following questions:

a. *Which colony was established first: Plymouth or Jamestown?* (Jamestown) *New Amsterdam or New York?* (New Amsterdam) *Connecticut or Maryland?* (Connecticut)

b. *How many years were there between the establishment of Jamestown and of Georgia?* (126) *Massachusetts Bay Colony and Rhode Island?* (16) *The Carolinas and Pennsylvania?* (12)

c. *In which century were most of the colonies begun?* (Seventeenth) *Which decade?* (1630s)

4. Reading a Chart. Have pupils turn to the "Population of Jamestown, 1619–1624" chart. Ask them the following questions:

a. *What was the population of Jamestown in 1619?* (1,000)

b. *How many people arrived in 1620?* (About 100)

c. *How many people arrived after 1620?* (5,051)

d. *At least how many people settled in the colonies between 1619–1624?* (Hint: Add 1619 population to total number known to have arrived since 1619.) (6,151)

e. *What is the difference between the actual population in 1624 and the total*

number of known people possible? (4,874)
f. *What do you think might have happened to all those people who are not part of the population in 1624?* (Returned to England, died of disease, killed in 1622 Indian raid)

SUPPLEMENTARY INFORMATION

Pocahontas. According to Captain John Smith, who had been captured by the Indians, an Indian girl named Pocahontas saved his life. When he returned to Jamestown after being a captive, Captain Smith explained to the anxious settlers that he was on the ground with his head on a rock. Just as Chief Powhatan was about to club him, Pocahontas, Powhatan's daughter, knelt down and placed her head over Smith's head. She begged her father to spare his life. She was 12 years old at the time.

Pocahontas helped maintain peaceful relations between the Indians and the colonists. In 1614 she married an English settler named John Rolfe. She was converted to Christianity and was baptized Rebecca. In 1616 she went to England with John and their son, Thomas. The English treated her like a princess.

Just before she was to return to America, Pocahontas died of smallpox. Her son returned to Jamestown after being educated in England. He became an important member of the Virginia colony.

LESSON 2 PAGES 90–93

NEW ENGLAND COLONIES

GOALS

1. To understand why the New England colonies were established. **2.** To explain how New England geography affected the occupations of the settlers there. **3.** To describe the influence of New England

settlers on democracy and education. **4.** To locate the New England colonies on a map.

TEACHING SUGGESTIONS

1. Reading a Map. Before pupils read Lesson 2, ask them to turn to the map of the English colonies on p. 89. Pose the following questions:
a. *Which colonies are part of New England?* (New Hampshire, Massachusetts Bay, Rhode Island, and Connecticut)
b. *Why do you think this group of colonies was collectively named New England?* (The colonists were English, from England, settling a new land.)
c. *Where are most of the early colonial capitals located?* (Along the coast) *What does that tell you about the early settlers?* (Most settlers came by boat from England and remained near the coast for harbors and supplies.)
d. *The Massachusetts Bay Colony included the land area of two present-day states. What are those states?* (Massachusetts and Maine)
2. Reading a Time Line. Direct pupils' attention to the time line on p. 86. Ask them to find the date of the New England colony that was settled first (1620). Then have them find the date when the last of the New England colonies was settled (1636). Have them calculate that the New England colonies were established in 16 years. Ask them why they think New England was settled so rapidly. Then direct pupils to read Lesson 2.
● **3. Reading Recall.** When pupils have finished reading the lesson, pose the following questions:
a. *What were two major reasons why the Puritans moved from England to New England?* (Religious freedom, a chance to make better lives)
b. *Why did colonists moved from Massachusetts Bay Colony to settle in Connecticut?* (The rich fertile valleys) *To settle in*

Rhode Island? (Religious freedom)

c. *There were many dangers in coming to the New World, but people came anyway. If you had lived in the 1630s would you have left England to come to the New World? Why or why not?*

d. *How did these early settlers establish laws?* (The property owners could participate in town meetings where they discussed and voted on town business.) Point out to pupils that some New England towns still have town meetings today.

e. *How was the dame school different from school today?* (Met in a house rather than in a school building; children in most schools today do not wear duncecaps and they cannot be beaten for misbehaving; girls and boys did not receive equal education as they do today; formal education in school was completed for girls by the age of 8 and boys by the age of 13, then they learned a craft or trade.)

You may want to have pupils who have difficulty grasping concepts make a chart that describes the start of each New England colony. Have them give the following information in the chart: the name of the colony, the date it was started, the person or group who started it, and the reason it was started.

You may wish to have pupils who require a challenge either write a letter to a friend in England telling about their daily life in New England in 1650, or write an opinion essay expressing whether they think it was worth it for the colonists to come to New England and why.

LESSON 3   PAGES 93–98

THE SOUTHERN COLONIES

GOALS

1. To name and locate the original Southern colonies. **2.** To understand the reasons for both white and black people settling in these Southern colonies. **3.** To explain how geography influenced the occupations of the Southern colonists. **4.** To compare the life of a plantation owner with that of a slave.

TEACHING SUGGESTIONS

● **1. Discussion.** Ask pupils to read Lesson 3 to the top of p. 95. Lead a discussion on why each Southern colony was established and ask pupils to locate each colony on the map on p. 89. Have pupils note the role of the English kings in each settlement. One pupil might want to research each of the English kings mentioned and share with the class the years each king reigned. Also, be sure pupils are aware of the products that were developed or grown in this region. Have them compare the products to those developed or grown by the colonists in New England and be sure they understand the geographical reasons for the differences and similarities.

You may wish to have pupils who have difficulty grasping concepts continue to build on the charts they developed in Lesson 2, Teaching Suggestion 3.

You may wish to have pupils who require a challenge use their library skills to research the growth of one or all of the Southern colonies in greater detail. Have them prepare oral reports to present to the class.

2. Making Comparisons. After pupils have read pp. 95–98, have them compare the life of a plantation owner with that of a slave. This activity may be done through discussion and a chart of pupils' responses on the chalkboard or as a written exercise with a follow-up discussion.

3. Reading a Table. Have pupils turn to the "Colonial Population by Race" table on p. 96. Ask them to use the table to answer the following questions. Be sure to point out that the numbers do not represent the population for the same year for all the colonies listed.

a. *Which colony had the largest black population?* (Virginia) *The largest white population?* (Massachusetts)

b. *Which colony had more than twice as large a black population compared to the white population?* (South Carolina)

c. *Which non-Southern colony had the largest black population?* (New York)

d. *Which region had the smallest black population?* (New England)

LESSON 4 PAGES 98–101

THE MIDDLE COLONIES

GOALS

1. To name and locate the original Middle colonies and explain why they are "middle" colonies. **2.** To understand why Pennsylvania was an attractive colony for settlers to choose. **3.** To understand how the English claimed land originally settled by Dutch and Swedish colonists.

TEACHING SUGGESTIONS

● **1. Discussion.** After pupils have read Lesson 4, ask them to turn to the map on p. 89, locate the Middle colonies and explain why they were called the "middle" colonies. Be sure pupils understand who came to the Middle colonies, why they came, and what their occupations were. Also be sure pupils understand why Delaware and New York were considered English colonies even though they had originally been settled by the Swedish and Dutch.

You may want pupils who have difficulty grasping concepts to add the facts about the Middle colonies to the charts that they started for the New England and Southern colonies in Lessons 2 and 3.

You may want to have pupils who require a challenge research one or all of the Middle colonies in greater detail and present their findings orally to the class.

2. Research Report. Have pupils reread the paragraph about Philadelphia in column 1 on p. 99. Point out to them that a very well-known man in American history named Benjamin Franklin was very influential in the development of Philadelphia as a leading colonial city. He formed the group that organized the first lending library, which became the model for lending libraries throughout North America. Not only did he help to establish the first fire department in 1736, but he also helped found the first fire insurance company in 1752. He worked on the development of the hospital and helped start a school that later became the University of Pennsylvania. As postmaster of Philadelphia, he also improved the city's postal system and eventually provided the same service for a postal system throughout the colonies.

Franklin is such an important and interesting figure in American history that you may want pupils to research and prepare oral reports and illustrations about his life and his contributions to America. The reports can be divided to cover the following topics: the child and youth, the Philadelphia printer, the self-educator, the inventor, the diplomat, and the delegate to the Second Continental Congress and to the Constitutional Convention of 1787.

3. Film/Filmstrip. Show a film or filmstrip depicting life in colonial America. Coronet Instructional Films of Chicago, Illinois, has a series of short films covering colonial life in New England, the Middle colonies, and the Southern colonies. Multi-Media Corporation of Dayton, Ohio, has a sound filmstrip titled *Slavery in the U.S.*

4. Reading a Chart. As a review of Chapter 5, have pupils turn to the chart on p. 101. Ask them a variety of questions about the chart. Be sure they note that the chart is arranged in order according to the date of settlement. You may want to ask each pupil to write ten questions about the English colonies. Have each pupil exchange questions with a partner and answer the partner's questions.

5/CHAPTER REVIEW PAGE 102
Answers for Review Questions
1. The Native Americans helped the people of Jamestown and the Pilgrims by providing food, showing them the best places to fish, and teaching them how to plant corn.

2. The Mayflower Compact is important to United States history because it was a set of laws established by the people for the good of the people in the settlement. Our government today is based on the same principle of laws made by the citizens for the good of the citizens of our nation.

3. The geography of New England influenced the jobs of the colonists because the natural harbors along the coast were excellent for shipping, trading, and fishing and the rocky soil was not good for large farms.

4. The Middle colonies were so-called because they were located between the New England and Southern colonies.

5. Answers will vary.

2/UNIT REVIEW PAGE 104
Answers for Unit Review
1. One theory about the way Native Americans came to the Americas is that they crossed a strip of land connecting Asia to the Americas that is today a body of water called the Bering Strait.

2. Answers will vary depending on which Native Americans settled in your area.

3. Pupils' answers will vary for the kinds of foods they have eaten recently that were developed by Native Americans. Some Native American words that have become part of our language are *moccasin*, *succotash*, *skunk*, *canoe*, *chipmunk*, and *toboggan*.

4. Answers will vary.

5. Have pupils use the maps on pp. 71, 74, and 78 as guides to showing the claims made by various explorers on their own outline maps. Be sure they make a key for their maps.

6. You may want to make a display of pupils' montages of "Americans All" on the bulletin board.

7. Reasons early settlers came to the Americas
a. Desire for riches
b. Religious freedom
c. A chance to make a new life
d. By force
Group(s) that match(es) the reason:
a. Spanish
b. Puritans, Pilgrims, Catholics, Quakers
c. Indentured servants, London Company, Puritans, debtors
d. Africans

8. New England Colonies:
a. Massachusetts Bay, settled by the English (Puritans and Pilgrims)
b. New Hampshire, settled by Massachusetts Bay colonists
c. Rhode Island, settled by Massachusetts Bay colonists (Roger Williams, Anne Hutchinson, and their followers)
d. Connecticut, settled by Massachusetts Bay colonists
Southern Colonies:
a. Virginia, settled by the English (London Company)
b. Maryland, settled by the English (Lord Baltimore and the Catholics)
c. North Carolina, settled by Virginia colonists
d. South Carolina, settled by the English
e. Georgia, settled by the English (James Oglethorpe and the debtors)
Middle Colonies:
a. New York, settled first by the Dutch
b. Delaware, settled first by the Swedes
c. New Jersey, settled first by the Dutch
d. Pennsylvania, settled first by the Swedes and then by William Penn and the Quakers

UNIT 3

A New and Growing Nation

UNIT 3

A NEW AND GROWING NATION

Dear Parent,

Your child is starting a new unit in the United States and Its Neighbors called "A New and Growing Nation." That unit looks at the history of the United States from approximately 1760 to 1860. The topics in the unit include the struggle of the colonists to gain freedom and independence during the Revolutionary War; a growing nation under Washington Jefferson, Madison, and Jackson; the influences of industry, labor, and reform on life in America; and the growth of the West.

It is important that your child be encouraged to share with you the main ideas in this unit. How people value freedom and have always valued freedom might make a good topic for family discussion. What freedoms are important to your family? Would your life be different without the constitutional guarantees of freedom? What might your lives be like if you did not enjoy freedom of speech? Freedom of worship? Freedom of the press? Freedom of a fair trial when accused of doing something wrong?

Perhaps someone you know has come to the United States in search of freedom. Or you may have become acquainted with such a person through reading or through television. You might talk with your child about that person to help him or her see how people desire and prize freedom.

Thank you for helping your child understand more fully ideas that are so important to each one of us.

Sincerely,

UNIT 3 PAGES 105–163

A NEW AND GROWING NATION

BULLETIN-BOARD DISPLAY

To help pupils follow the territorial expansion of the United States from the 13 original colonies to the settlement of the Pacific coast, display a large outline map of the United States. Or use an opaque projector to project the map on p. 157 on a large sheet of paper and trace the outline it casts on the paper. Fill in the 13 original colonies with a colored marker. As pupils study the territories added to the original colonies by purchase, war, or treaty, have them place each on the outline map. Remember to make a key to identify each acquisition. Or write on the map the name of each acquisition. Have pupils title the map.

GETTING STARTED

1. Ask pupils to look at the unit opener on p. 105 and pose these questions:
a. *Have you ever seen pictures of these four people before? What do you know about them?*
b. *Why, do you think, are they in the same drawing?*
c. *What do these people say to you about the new unit? What do you think you will be studying in the unit?*
2. Have pupils turn to the map on p. 474 of the Atlas. Have them locate England. Have them situate the 13 original colonies. Ask them to use the scale to find the distance between England and the colonies. Ask how they think England and the colonies communicated. Help pupils talk about the difficulties that can arise when people cannot communicate easily because of the distance between them. Have them consider what might result as a consequence of those difficulties.

BIRTH OF A NATION

THEME

The American Revolution was fought for the cause of liberty by many different Americans. The nation and government that resulted from that war were designed by people who wanted to "secure the blessings of liberty to ourselves and our posterity."

PROJECTS

1. Have pupils start a "Hall of Fame of Great Americans" by choosing and reporting on persons who contributed to the development of the United States when it was "a new and growing nation."

2. Have pupils work in small groups to set up laws governing the conduct and management of the class. Tell them that after they have voted on the laws they want to accept, those laws will be posted and become the standard by which the class will be governed. Pupils will soon see that simply making laws is not enough.

LESSON 1   PAGES 106–109

BAD FEELINGS GROW BETWEEN BRITAIN AND THE COLONIES

GOALS

1. To know the meaning of the words "No taxation without representation." **2.** To describe how the colonists reacted to the British tax laws. **3.** To appreciate the purpose of the first Continental Congress. **4.** To find specific information about a period of history from a time line.

TEACHING SUGGESTIONS

1. Picture Reading. After pupils have read "The French and Indian War" on p. 106 and understand the concepts *independence* and *revolution*, have them study the reproduction of Archibald Willard's painting on p. 107. Then ask the following:

a. *How old do the three main figures in the painting appear to be? What does that tell you about the people who were willing to fight for freedom?* (Answers will vary.)

b. *Note the bandage on the main figure at the right. What does that tell you about the freedom fighters?* (Answers will vary.)

c. *What does the background seem to suggest is going on?* (Answers will vary.)

d. *This painting is called "The Spirit of '76." How is the artist using the word spirit in the title of his painting?* (Influence that stirs up and rouses)

2. Discussion. Help pupils appreciate the colonists' desire for freedom from Great Britain's rule by asking them how they think they would feel if the government suddenly began to pass laws limiting their freedom.

3. Role-Playing. After pupils have read "No taxation without representation" on p. 106, have several assume the role of tax collectors representing the British Parliament and develop an argument for taxing the colonists. Have a group of pupils assume that they are Sons of Liberty and develop an argument against taxation by Britain. After both groups have presented their arguments, have a third group of pupils, acting as concerned citizens, weigh the arguments presented and decide on a course of action.

4. Doing Research. After pupils have read "No taxation without representation" on p. 106, have them use encyclopedias and other available reference works to find what articles were subject to taxation by the British Parliament between 1764 and 1770. Have them list the principal articles taxed by the Sugar Act of 1764 (Refined sugar, molasses, and wine); the Stamp Act of 1765 (Colonial newspapers, legal documents, business papers, diplomas, pamphlets, almanacs, playing cards, and dice); Townshend Act of 1767 (Tea, paper, lead, glass, and paint imported into the colonies).

5. Debating. Resolved, That the colonists were right to disobey the laws imposed upon them by Great Britain. Have pupils base their arguments on information given in the text and in reference material available to them.

6. Creative Writing. After pupils have read "The Intolerable Acts" on p. 109, have them imagine that they are members of the Committees of Correspondence living in Boston in 1774. Have them write letters to friends in Virginia describing the restrictions placed upon them by the Intolerable Acts and the implications the restrictions have upon their lives.

7. Reading a Time Line. Have pupils use the time line on p. 108 to answer the following questions:

a. *What laws were passed right after the Boston Tea Party?* (Intolerable Acts)

b. *How many years after the first shots of the American Revolution were fired at Lexington and Concord was the peace treaty signed in Paris?* (8)

c. *Which came first: Shots fired that started the American Revolution or the Declaration of Independence?* (Shots fired)

d. *Which came first: The Constitution became the law of the land or the Declaration of Independence was signed?* (The Declaration of Independence)

● **8. Vocabulary Building.** After pupils have read pp. 106–109, write the following words on the chalkboard: *independence, revolution, Parliament, massacre, Commit-* *tees of Correspondence, Boston Tea Party, Continental Congress.* Ask pupils to copy each word, write its meaning, and use it in a sentence.

For those pupils who have difficulty grasping the concepts, you may wish to review the words and definitions orally, and check their sentences. As a memory aid show these pupils that they can combine their vocabulary words into a brief paragraph that summarizes the basic concepts of the lesson: When the British *Parliament* would not give the colonists their *independence*, they decided to get it by *revolution*. There was a *massacre* in Boston in 1770. *Committees of Correspondence* were formed to let the colonists know what was happening. After the *Boston Tea Party* and the closing of Boston harbor by the British, the colonists called a *Continental Congress.*

You may wish to have pupils who require a challenge start writing clues for a word-find or crossword puzzle that will include vocabulary and concepts throughout Chapter 6. Upon completion of Chapter 6, the pupils may exchange their puzzles.

LESSON 2   PAGES 110–113

THE MOVE TO INDEPENDENCE

GOALS

1. To understand the significance of the events at Lexington and Concord. **2.** To identify the role of Paul Revere, Ethan Allen, George Washington, Peter Salem, Thomas Paine, and Thomas Jefferson in the struggle for independence. **3.** To appreciate the Declaration of Independence as a document that ensures the freedom of all Americans.

TEACHING SUGGESTIONS

1. Reading Poetry. Read to the pupils "Paul Revere's Ride" by Henry Wadsworth

Longfellow. To help them understand the poem ask the following:

a. *When did Paul Revere start his midnight ride?* (April 18, 1775)

b. *What signal was Revere's friend to give him?* (Hang one lantern from Old North Church if the British were coming by land; two, if by sea.)

c. *What message was Revere to spread?* (People were to get up and to arm.)

2. Making a Chart. Have pupils make a class chart on which they record when and where the Second Continental Congress met, the colonies represented, its most distinguished delegates, and its chief accomplishments.

3. Interviewing. Set up this imaginary situation. Paul Revere, Ethan Allen, George Washington, and Peter Salem have been invited to appear on a news program in Boston in 1775. Have half the pupils prepare questions to ask the four men about their role in the struggle for independence. Have the remaining pupils review the contributions of those men to the colonists' cause. Select different pupils to act as interviewers and interviewees.

● **4. Writing Résumés.** Have pupils write résumés in which they state why George Washington would make a good Commander in Chief of the Continental Army, why Thomas Paine would make a good spokesperson for the cause of independence, or why Thomas Jefferson would make a good author of a declaration of independence. If possible obtain a job application form and study it with your pupils. Have them create and fill out a job application for one of the people mentioned in this activity.

You may wish to review "George Washington" on p. 111 with those pupils who have difficulty grasping the idea of a résumé. Help them see that Washington's experiences and attitudes prepared him to serve as commander in chief.

You may wish to have pupils who require a challenge give oral reports on delegates to the Second Continental Congress who especially distinguished themselves in the cause of freedom both before and during the Congress.

5. Reading for Appreciation. Have pupils read "The Declaration of Independence" on p. 113 to answer these questions:

a. *What basic rights do all people have?* (Right to life, to liberty, to be happy)

b, *What is the purpose of government?* (To help people keep their basic rights)

c. *When can people get rid of their government?* (When it does not protect people's rights)

d. *How does the Declaration of Independence help us today?* (Answers will vary.)

SUPPLEMENTARY INFORMATION

The Sources of the Declaration of Independence. A major source of inspiration for Thomas Jefferson as he prepared the Declaration of Independence was an Englishman! From John Locke, an English philosopher who wrote in the late 1600s, Jefferson borrowed the contract theory of government which argued that government would be unnecessary in a perfect society. But since there is no such thing as a perfect society, individuals are appointed to govern and to guarantee the natural rights that all citizens possess. Locke stated that if a government ceased to carry out that function, it should be eliminated. The people control the government, not vice versa.

John Locke supplied the philosophy for revolution; Thomas Paine supplied the practical application of that philosophy to the colonists' situation. In his pamphlet *Common Sense,* which appeared in January 1776, Paine wrote, "I offer nothing more than simple facts, plain arguments, and common sense." Paine's work was widely read by hundreds of thousands of Americans and by all the colonial leaders, notably Jefferson. Paine pointed out the practical advantages of independence: a captured patriot would be treated as a prisoner of war rather than being shot as a rebel, property of Loyalists could be seized, and there would be a better chance of getting foreign aid. Paine's rhetoric really spurred the independence movement. ". . . The period of debate is closed," he wrote. "Arms . . . must decide the contest. . . . The blood of the slain, the weeping voice of nature cries, 'TIS TIME TO PART!'"

LESSON 3   PAGES 114–118

WAR!

GOALS
1. To identify at least three disadvantages the Americans faced at the outset of the Revolutionary War. **2.** To name and locate the major battles of the Revolutionary War. **3.** To name the terms of the Treaty of Paris.

TEACHING SUGGESTIONS
1. Interpreting Data. Have pupils read "Outlook bad" on pp. 114–115. Ask them to predict strictly on the basis of that reading who would win the American Revolution.

● **2. Locating Battle Sites.** Provide pupils with outline maps of the eastern United States. After they have read pp. 115–116, have them locate on their maps the principal battles of the American Revolution.

You may wish to have pupils who have difficulty grasping the concepts scan the text to find information about the following battles:

a. New York City
b. Trenton
c. Philadelphia
d. Saratoga
e. Charleston
f. Yorktown

Ask pupils to locate the battles by states and then, using the map on p. 115 as a guide, locate those battle sites on their own maps.

You may wish to have pupils who require a challenge prepare diagrams of battle campaigns, such as the campaigns of upper New York State, campaigns in Pennsylvania and New Jersey, the war on the frontier, and the southern campaigns.

3. Dramatizing. Have pupils choose events in the American Revolution that they would like to dramatize. Have them prepare scripts using their texts, encyclopedias, and other available resource materials. Have some pupils make props. The following events readily lend themselves to dramatization:

a. Christmas Night, 1776, in Trenton, New Jersey
b. The winter of 1777–1778 at Valley Forge
c. The encounter between the *Bonhomme Richard* and the *Serapis*

4. Making Diary Entries. Ask pupils to imagine that they lived during the American Revolution and were deeply involved in the war either by rendering military service or by living as civilians in an area of intense warfare. Have them write a series of diary entries in which they record that period in their lives. Suggest that they might write about their part in military maneuvers, their feelings about a victory or a defeat for the Americans, the effect of the war on their everyday lives, ways in which they coped with wartime living.

5. Making Charts. After pupils have read "Why the Americans won" on p. 117, have them title sheets of paper The American Revolution, divide their papers into two columns, and label one column British Advantages and the other column American Advantages. Have them find in the text at least five assets for each side and list them in the proper columns.

SUPPLEMENTARY INFORMATION

Blacks in the American Revolution. One embarrassing question faced by colonial leaders was what to do about black soldiers fighting for independence. Because it seemed awkward to have slaves fight for freedom while they themselves were not free, the first position taken was that only free blacks could fight. But many blacks, slave and free, had already fought side by side with white soldiers at Lexington, Concord, and Bunker Hill.

When Washington took command of the Continental army, he issued a ban on all blacks in the service. This command was quickly reversed when the British welcomed and promised freedom for blacks who would fight for them. With the exception of Georgia and South Carolina, all the states accepted blacks in their armies by the end of the war. Most blacks who served received their freedom.

There were only a few all-black regiments. Those that did exist fought bravely and received many accolades. Several blacks distinguished themselves in the line of duty. At the battle of Bunker Hill, Peter Salem was not the only black hero. Salem Poor was later commended before Congress for being "a brave and gallant soldier." Prince Whipple and Oliver Cromwell crossed the Delaware with Washington. Lemmuel Haynes assisted on the Ticonderoga expedition. Spying done by a black named Pompey Lamb made possible "Mad Anthony" Wayne's victory at Stony Point. Henri Christophe, one of 700 free Haitians fighting with the French, was wounded at the siege of Savannah. He went on to help free and rule Haiti.

All together 5,000 of America's 300,000 fighting soldiers were black. As an indication of attitudes already formed, the majority of black participants were from the North.

THE CONSTITUTION OF THE UNITED STATES

GOALS

1. To identify powers given to the federal government by the Continental Congress and powers reserved to the states. **2.** To understand the purpose of the separation of powers among the three branches of government. **3.** To appreciate the Bill of Rights.

TEACHING SUGGESTIONS

1. Role-Playing. After pupils have read "Articles of Confederation" on p. 118, have one group of pupils acting as spokespersons for the national government and another group acting as spokespersons for the states meet to discuss their grievances under the Articles of Confederation. Have a third group of pupils act as impartial judges who identify the problems that burden each side and recommend how they might be remedied.

2. Working in Groups. Have pupils prepare a display summarizing the accomplishments of the Constitutional Convention. Have some pupils find in their texts, encyclopedias, and other available reference works the major obstacles faced by members of the Constitutional Convention (strong central government versus states' rights; fears smaller states had about the larger states; the question of slaves and free persons) and how those obstacles were overcome. Have other pupils consider the ideas proposed or advocated by such leaders as Hamilton, Gouverneur Morris, Roger Sherman, Elbridge Gerry, Edmund Randolph, and William Paterson.

3. Reading for Information. After pupils have read "A new plan of government" on p. 119, have them determine whether the following powers belong to the national or state governments:

a. To declare war (National)

b. To print or coin money (National)

c. To provide schools (State)

d. To control trade with foreign countries (National)

e. To issue hunting licenses (State)

f. To enforce traffic laws (State)

4. Making Charts. After pupils have read "Separation of powers" on p. 119, have them make charts on which they identify the three branches of the federal government, the composition of each, and the function of each.

5. Applying Current Events. Have pupils gather pictures of members of the present legislative, executive, and judicial branches of the government. Have them find or draw pictures of the Capitol in Washington, D.C., the White House, and the Supreme Court. Have them display their pictures associating the legislative branch with the Capitol; the executive branch with the White House; and the judicial branch with the Supreme Court.

6. Finding Information. Help pupils consider ways to find out who represents them in the Senate and House of Representatives. Have them consider how the following might be helpful:

a. family

b. newspapers

c. news magazines

d. telephone directory for number of the District Board of Elections

e. district headquarters of major political parties

f. library

Describe the *Legislative Manual* published annually by the state legislature and the *Washington Information Directory* published by Congressional Quarterly Inc., which lists all the members of Congress and their committee assignments.

Ask pupils to volunteer to find out who represents the state in the Senate and who represents the district in the House of Representatives and report back to the class.

7. Reading and Interpreting. Have pupils refer to pp. 122–123 to answer the following questions about the Bill of Rights:

a. *What five freedoms are guaranteed under the First Amendment to the Constitution?* (Religion, speech, press, assembly, petition the government)

b. *Why, do you think, was the Third Amendment written into the Constitution?* (Pupils may say colonists remembered the Intolerable Acts.)

c. *What are the Fifth, Sixth, Seventh, and Eighth Amendments about?* (People's rights when accused of serious crimes)

d. *Why, do you think, was the right to a jury trial an important concern of the framers of the Constitution?* (It had been denied under British rule.)

e. *Which of the first ten amendments to the Constitution is most important to you? Why?* (Answers will vary.)

6/CHAPTER REVIEW PAGE 124

Answers for Review Questions

1. Answers will vary. Pupils may mention freedom to make the laws that would apply to them, freedom to choose their own leaders, and so on.

2. The Declaration of Independence is such an important writing because it has served as a guide to freedom-loving people throughout the world.

3. Answers will vary.

4. The war discussed in this chapter is called both the Revolutionary War and the War for Independence because in this war the colonists fought the British for independence, or freedom from Great Britain's rule.

5. The results of the Revolutionary War were the following: The United States was an independent nation bounded by the Mississippi River, the Great Lakes and Canada, and Florida. The United States would have fishing rights off Canada's coast. All war debts had to be paid by both sides.

6. The Thirteenth Amendment ended slavery. The First Amendment guaranteed freedom of speech and press. The Nineteenth Amendment allows both men and women to vote. The Twenty-first Amendment repealed the Eighteenth Amendment.

CHAPTER 7 PAGES 126–145

A NATION GROWS: WASHINGTON THROUGH JACKSON

THEME

In the first 50 years under the Constitution our government was launched through the skillful leadership of great people. Washington's presidency defined what powers the President would have; Jefferson's expanded our nation's territory; Madison's finally resolved the threat of British intervention in our nation; and Jackson's extended the nation's democratic character.

PROJECTS

1. Have pupils find pictures of the Presidents studied in this chapter. After they have mounted and displayed their pictures, have them indicate when each President assumed office and completed his term of office. When each presidency has been studied, have the pupils find ways to record its major accomplishments.

2. Have pupils draw or collect pictures of flags that are part of our nation's history. They might use the following years to study changes in the design of the flag: 1775, 1776, 1777, 1795, 1818, 1908, 1912, 1959, 1960. They might include state flags and armed forces flags in their study as well as facts about displaying and caring for the flag.

LESSON 1 PAGES 126–131

OUR FIRST PRESIDENT

GOALS

1. To understand why George Washington was the unanimous choice for President in 1789. **2.** To name the three departments in Washington's Cabinet and the first secretary of each. **3.** To identify at least three precedents set by Washington's presidency. **4.** To appreciate the growth of the presidency since 1789.

TEACHING SUGGESTIONS

1. Interpreting a Quotation. After pupils have read "Everyone's choice" on p. 126,

write these words on the chalkboard, "*first in war, first in peace, and first in the hearts of his countrymen.*" Ask:

a. *What is meant in saying Washington was "first in war"?* (As Commander in Chief of the Continental Army, he brilliantly led the American troops to victory in the Revolution.)

b. *What does "first in peace" mean?* (He was the first President of the United States after peace had been won in the Revolution.)

c. *What does "and first in the hearts of his countrymen" mean?* (He was widely admired and honored.)

d. *What were some of the ways in which Washington continued to be honored after* he *left public life?* (The nation's capital was named in his honor. A monument was erected to him in Washington, D.C. A state was named in his honor. Cities, bridges, and streets have been named for him. His birthday is a federal holiday.)

2. **Making Charts.** Have pupils read "Starting a government" on p. 128 to find the three departments that made up Washington's Cabinet in 1789. Have pupils make charts listing the departments, describing the work of each, and naming the department's secretary.

3. **Research.** Explain that when the Supreme Court, called for by the Constitution, was established by congressional action in September 1789, Washington appointed John Jay as first Chief Justice. Samuel Osgood of Massachusetts, a man who had served in the Continental Congress, became the first Postmaster General when that department was formed.

Have pupils refer to almanacs to find the names of the departments in the Cabinet today. (Interior; Agriculture; Defense; Commerce and Labor; Education; Health and Human Services; Housing and Urban Development; Transportation; Energy)

4. **Current Events.** Have pupils make a bulletin-board display of the President's Cabinet using pictures from newspapers and magazines. Have them identify each Cabinet member.

5. **Questions and Answers.** To help pupils understand that while Washington was President he set precedents that continue to be honored today, ask:

a. *Why was a Cabinet created when Washington was President?* (To advise him)

b. *Who chose the secretary of each department of the Cabinet?* (Washington)

c. *Does the President chose his own Cabinet today?* (Yes)

d. *What happened when Congress passed a tax law in 1791?* (Some people refused to pay.)

e. *What did Washington do?* (Formed an army to stop them)

f. *What power was Washington showing by that action?* (That he headed the executive branch of the government, which enforces laws)

g. *What was Washington showing future Presidents by his action?* (How to be strong leaders)

h. *How many terms did Washington serve as President?* (Two)

i. *What tradition did Washington establish by serving his country as President for two terms?* (Two-term tradition)

6. **Making Cartoons.** Have pupils depict differences between Washington's presidency and the modern presidency by making cartoons based on the information on p. 131.

●7. **Vocabulary Building.** After pupils have read pp. 126–131, write the following words on the chalkboard: *inauguration, oath, Secretary, Cabinet, Chief Justice, term, Union, District of Columbia, White House.* Ask pupils to copy each word, write its meaning, and use it in a sentence.

For those pupils who have difficulty grasping the concepts, you may wish to review the words and definitions and check their sentences. Show these pupils that they can combine their vocabulary words into a paragraph that serves as a memory aid and summarizes the basic concepts of the lesson. For example: At his *inauguration* Washington took an *oath* to serve his country as President. In his first *term*, Congress formed a *Cabinet* and he chose a *secretary* of each. He also chose a *Chief Justice* of the Supreme Court. Three states entered the *Union* while he was *President*; the *District of Columbia* was planned but the *White House* was not yet built.

You may wish to have pupils who require a challenge start writing clues for a word-find or crossword puzzle that will include vocabulary and concepts throughout

Chapter 7. Upon completion of Chapter 7 the pupils may exchange their puzzles.

SUPPLEMENTARY INFORMATION

Benjamin Banneker (1731–1806). One of the truly remarkable persons in our young nation was Benjamin Banneker. As a free black living in Maryland, Banneker attended an integrated school, something of a rarity for the times. At that school he became interested in mathematics and science. While still a young man, Banneker built a clock carved completely out of wood. The only models he had were a picture of a clock and a pocket watch. The clock worked well for over 50 years.

When Banneker was 40 years old, he met George Ellicott, a Quaker, who had moved to Maryland to establish a flour mill. Ellicott recognized Banneker's mechanical genius and began to lend him books on mathematics and astronomy. Banneker became keenly interested in astronomy and soon was finding errors in the leading astronomical texts. In 1789 he predicted a solar eclipse with remarkable accuracy. Out of that interest Banneker became the "Black Poor Richard" and began to issue almanacs. When Thomas Jefferson received a copy of Banneker's first almanac, he was so impressed that he sent it to the Academy of Sciences in Paris as proof of the abilities of blacks.

It was Jefferson who recommended Benjamin Banneker to President George Washington for a position on the commission that was to survey and plan the city of Washington, D.C. That was a virtually unheard of honor for a black person at the time; it helped to secure Banneker's reputation as the best-known black person in the early years of our nation.

Banneker carried out his work for two years. In 1791 he returned to his farm in Maryland and resumed writing his almanac and continued his astronomical studies. Banneker went on to become an active proponent of world peace, using his almanac as a convenient forum. He wrote *A Plan of Peace—Office for the United States* in which he recommended that a Secretary of Peace be appointed to the Cabinet. He suggested that militia laws, military titles, parades, and uniforms be done away with. His life was a search for freedom and independence. Directed by such ideals, he contributed to the development of the whole nation.

LESSON 2   PAGES 132–135

THOMAS JEFFERSON, A REMARKABLE MAN

GOALS

1. To appreciate the scope of Thomas Jefferson's genius. **2.** To understand why the Louisiana Purchase was so important to our nation's development. **3.** To identify the results of the expedition of Lewis and Clark.

TEACHING SUGGESTIONS

1. Reading for Information. Tell pupils that at a White House dinner in May 1962, at which 49 winners of the Nobel Prize were honored, President John F. Kennedy said, "I think this is the most extraordinary collection of talent, of human knowledge . . . ever gathered at the White House, with the possible exception of when Thomas Jefferson dined alone." Have pupils read "A man of many talents" on p. 132 before asking:

a. *How did Jefferson serve our country before it became a nation?* (Wrote the Declaration of Independence)

b. *How did he serve our country after it became a nation?* (Was a minister to France; was first secretary of state, second Vice-President, third President)

c. *What were some of his inventions?* (The swivel chair and "dumbwaiter")

d. *How did he help education?* (Started

the University of Virginia)

e. *Of which of his accomplishments was he most proud?* (Declaration of Independence, Statute of Virginia for religious freedom, and University of Virginia)

f. *Which accomplishments of Jefferson do you think were most important? Why?* (Answers will vary.)

● 2. **Career Awareness.** After pupils realize that Thomas Jefferson was a lawyer, writer, diplomat, politician, architect, scientist, inventor, farmer, and educator, explain that those careers are still important today. Have them gather information about those careers by considering the following points:

a. Preparation required or desirable
b. Kind of work involved
c. Average pay scale
d. Employment opportunities
e. Satisfactions inherent in the work

You may wish to have pupils who have difficulty grasping the concepts use a dictionary to find the meaning of the unfamiliar words. Ask them to name people they may know who are presently in those careers. Have them compare the kind of knowledge needed by a lawyer with that needed by a farmer, that needed by an architect with that needed by an educator, and so on. Have them describe what they consider to be the inherent satisfactions in the careers.

You may wish to have pupils who require a challenge prepare a series of questions prior to interviewing people pursuing the careers discussed, write up their answers, and report their findings to the class.

3. **Map Reading.** Have pupils refer to the map on p. 135 to answer the following questions:

a. *Locate St. Louis by determining its approximate latitude and longitude.* (39°N/ 90° W)

b. *On what river is St. Louis located?* (Mississippi)

c. *What two rivers meet just north of St. Louis?* (Mississippi and Missouri)

d. *In what direction did Lewis and Clark go as they followed the Missouri River?* (Northwest)

e. *What two rivers did Lewis and Clark follow much of the way to the Pacific Ocean?* (Missouri and Columbia)

f. *What river makes up the eastern boundary of the Louisiana Territory?* (Mississippi)

g. *What made up much of the western boundary?* (Rocky Mountains)

h. *What important city on the Gulf of Mexico was gained by the Louisiana Purchase?* (New Orleans)

i. *What is the distance between St. Louis and New Orleans?* (The distance is 673 miles, or 1,083 km. Pupils may estimate between 650 and 700 miles, or 1,046 and 1,125 km.)

j. *Why was New Orleans an important addition to the United States?* (A port city, it enabled goods to travel as far northeast as Pennsylvania and as far west as the Pacific Ocean.)

4. **Answering Checkup Questions.** Divide the class into three groups; assign each group one of the Checkup questions on p. 135. Allow time for the class to discuss the answers given by each group.

LESSON 3   PAGES 136–139

OUR NATIONAL ANTHEM

GOALS

1. To know the background of our national anthem. 2. To identify the causes of the War of 1812. 3. To understand the effects of the War of 1812 on our nation.

TEACHING SUGGESTIONS

1. **Picture Reading.** Have pupils look at the picture of "The Star-Spangled Banner" on p. 136. Ask:

a. *How many stars are on the flag?* (15)

b. *How many stripes are on the flag?* (15)

c. *Why did the flag have 15 stars and 15 stripes?* (Originally a star and a stripe were added for each new state. This was later changed so there would be a stripe for each of the first 13 states and a star for every state.)

d. *What is the condition of the flag?* (Tattered and torn, a part is missing)

2. Paraphrasing. After pupils have read the first verse of "The Star-Spangled Banner" on p. 136 and have become familiar with the circumstances under which it was written, ask them to rewrite the first verse in their own words. They need not write poetry, but are to concern themselves with conveying the ideas expressed by Francis Scott Key, using correct grammar, spelling, and punctuation.

3. Map Reading. Have pupils refer to the map on p. 137 to answer these questions:

a. *In what general areas were the battles of the War of 1812 fought?* (Great Lakes region, Chesapeake Bay area, Gulf of Mexico)

b. *What did the battle sites in the war have in common?* (Located on or near bodies of water)

c. *What river joins Lake Erie and Lake Ontario?* (Niagara)

d. *Locate Baltimore, Washington, D.C., and New Orleans by giving their approximate latitude and longitude.* (The exact answers are 39°17′N/76°37′W;38°54′N/77°01′W; pupils may estimate.)

e. *What waterway was used in the attack on Baltimore and Washington, D.C.?* (Chesapeake Bay)

f. *What is the distance from New Orleans to Washington, D.C.?* (793 mi, or 1,276 km; pupils may estimate the distance.)

4. Creative Writing. After pupils have read "Why another war with Britain?" on pp. 136–137, explain that the War of 1812 might not have occurred if there had been a "hot line" between the leaders of the United States and Great Britain. Ask the pupils to create a series of dialogues between President Madison and British Prime Minister Spencer Perceval that would have averted war. Encourage them to center their dialogues on the need for mutual understanding, respect, and cooperation.

LESSON 4 PAGES 140–143

JACKSONIAN DEMOCRACY

GOALS

1. To understand the meaning of Jacksonian democracy. **2.** To name groups of people not included in Jacksonian democracy. **3.** To appreciate the early efforts of women to gain human rights for all people.

TEACHING SUGGESTIONS

1. Questions and Answers. Have pupils answer the following questions based on their reading of "Victory for the common man" to "Trail of Tears" on pp. 140–141:

a. *In what war did Andrew Jackson serve when he was a young boy?* (Revolutionary War)

b. *What state did Jackson represent when he was a senator?* (Tennessee)

c. *Why was he popular in Tennessee?* (He was tough and Westerners had to be tough.)

d. *What nickname was Jackson given? Why?* ("Old Hickory" because he was thought to be tough like hickory wood)

e. *In what other wars did Jackson fight?* (War of 1812, against the Creeks of Alabama and Georgia, and the Seminoles in Florida)

f. *Whom did Jackson feel should run the government?* (Common people)

g. *What has Jackson's idea of government come to be called?* (Jacksonian democracy)

h. *When was Jackson elected President?* (1828)

2. Picture Reading. Have pupils study "Trail of Tears" on p. 141 and then describe the feelings and attitudes they think are represented in the artwork. Suggest that they examine the people's faces carefully, consider the conditions under which they appear to be traveling, and question the reason the military personnel are accompanying them.

3. Creative Writing. After pupils have read "Trail of Tears" on pp. 141–142, ask them to imagine that they made the journey to Oklahoma. Have them write diary entries in which they describe experiences as they traveled, their attitudes about leaving their homes, and their expectations for their future.

4. Role-Playing. Have pupils imagine that they are living at the close of Jackson's term as President and have come together to evaluate his presidency. Ask one pupil to volunteer to be President Jackson. Have the remaining pupils form several groups to discuss Jackson's treatment of Native Americans, blacks, and women. Ask them to formulate questions to ask "President Jackson" and then choose two or three spokespersons from their groups to present their questions. When the pupils have completed their questioning and have let "President Jackson" respond, have them evaluate his understanding of what democracy really means.

5. Understanding Primary Sources. Have pupils answer the following questions based on Sojourner Truth's speech to the Akron convention on p. 143.
a. *About what two groups of people was Sojourner Truth speaking?* (Blacks and women)
b. *What work did she do that men did?* (Plowed, planted, and gathered into barns)
c. *What could she do equal to a man?* (Work, eat, and suffer punishment)
d. *What special sadness did Sojourner Truth have to bear because she was a black woman?* (Her children were sold from her.)

e. *Why did she keep repeating the phrase, "And ain't I a woman?"* (Answers will vary. Pupils may say to dramatize her speech, to emphasize women's abilities, to plead for women's rights.)

6. Testing. Have pupils each make up a ten-question recall test using material in this lesson. Ask them to exchange tests and answer their partners' questions. Allow time for them to discuss their answers with their partners.

SUPPLEMENTARY INFORMATION

Three Great Native Americans. Many Native Americans stand out as great heroes during this period of our nation's growth. Osceola, a member of the Creek tribe, demonstrated courage and foresight when he fought against Andrew Jackson and his forces in the first Seminole War (1819). Osceola showed open contempt for the agreement signed in 1832 by a few members of the Seminole tribe of Florida with United States government officials. Under that treaty, the entire tribe was to surrender all its Florida lands and move to Indian territory (Oklahoma). Osceola organized Seminole resistance and carried on guerilla warfare against United States troops. In 1837 he was captured as he awaited General T.S. Jesup for a conference requested by the general to discuss peace. He was imprisoned and died there three months later.

Black Hawk, a Sauk of the Thunder clan, opposed the 1804 treaty which had taken away all Sauk homelands east of the Mississippi River. When he and his followers refused to leave their Illinois villages, they were evicted by soldiers and Illinois militia. Black Hawk was imprisoned, but was later released and sent on a trip to the East. There he was received as a hero. He visited President Jackson from whom he received a sword and a medal for his great leadership.

Sequoya, a Cherokee, had observed how important reading, writing, and printing was among whites. He succeeded in inventing an alphabet and in 1821 gave his tribe the first Indian writing system north of Mexico ever devised without help from whites. Within a short time many Cherokees learned to read and write. Sequoya gave much of his life to healing the differences between whites and Native Americans.

7/CHAPTER REVIEW   PAGE 144
Answers for Review Questions
1. Answers will vary. Pupils may say one great accomplishment of President Washington was that he served as a model for other Presidents or that he made the government that started with the Constitution work. Of President Jefferson they may say he doubled the size of the United States with the Louisiana Purchase. Of President Jackson they may say he extended democracy by believing that the common people could run the government.
2. Andrew Jackson was considered the hero of "the common man." George Washington was most trusted and admired; Thomas Jefferson, most talented.
3. Answers will vary. Pupils may say the United States and Great Britain agreed to work out all future problems peacefully. The War of 1812 gave the country two military leaders who later became Presidents—Andrew Jackson and William Henry Harrison. It gave the people of the United States a new way to look at themselves and at their country—they were proud of both. It gave Americans a greater sense of national unity.

CHAPTER 8   PAGES 146–163

A NATION CHANGES

THEME

By the mid-1800s America spread from the Atlantic Ocean to the Pacific Ocean. New land was acquired by war, treaty, purchase, and annexation. Making necessary a new means of transportation, the acquisitions in turn were developed by the improved means of transportation that they required. They created the need for many new inventions. They made possible an open invitation to thousands of people to immigrate to America.

PROJECTS

1. Have pupils show the growth of the United States from coast to coast by indicating on an outline map the original 13 states in 1776, the territory gained by the 1783 Treaty of Paris, the Louisiana Purchase (1803), the Spanish Cession of Florida (1821), the Texas Annexation (1845), Oregon Country Cession (1846), Mexican Cession (1848), and the Gadsden Purchase (1853). Have them give their map an appropriate title.
2. Have pupils make a scrapbook of great American inventions between 1800 and 1850. Direct them to include a picture or sketch of each invention included or its modern counterpart, the name of the inventor, and the date of the invention. Encourage them to find information about inventions not included in the text.
3. Have pupils research some early methods of "heading West" and write stories in which they imagine they were among the people who traveled West. Possible topics include Walking the Wilderness Road with Daniel Boone, Riding on a Turnpike, My First Steamboat Ride, and Wagons West!

LESSON 1 PAGES 146–151

A CHANGING WAY OF LIFE

GOALS

1. To understand why our nation needed improved forms of transportation and communication. **2.** To identify the major results of the improvements in transportation and communication. **3.** To know why many immigrants came to the United States between 1820 and 1860.

TEACHING SUGGESTIONS

1. Brainstorming. Before pupils begin to read p. 146, divide the class into five groups and assign to each group one of the following possibilities:
a. *What if there were no railroads in the United States?*
b. *What if there were no factories in the United States?*
c. *What if farmers had to use hand tools to farm?*
d. *What if there were no means of rapid communication such as the telephone and telegraph?*
e. *What if the writers of the Constitution had decided not to let people from foreign lands enter the United States?*

Have the pupils take about five minutes to consider possible consequences of their "what if's" before sharing them with the class.

2. Map Reading. Have pupils refer to the map on p. 148 to answer these questions:
a. *How might goods received in New York harbor be sent to Buffalo about 1845?* (Hudson River, Erie Canal)
b. *Could goods be sent from Buffalo to New Orleans by an all-water route?* (Yes)
c. *If you lived in Philadelphia in the 1860s and traveled by rail to New Orleans, through what cities might you ride?* (Baltimore, Washington, Chattanooga, Memphis)
d. *Through what cities might you ride going by rail from Milwaukee to Pittsburgh?* (Chicago, Cleveland) *About what distance would you travel?* (600 mi, or 961 km)
e. *Did most of the early railroads and canals run north to south or east to west?* (East to west)

3. Reading a Time Line. Have pupils refer to the time line on p. 148 to find which came first:
a. *The election of Jackson or the election of Jefferson?* (Jefferson)
b. *War with Mexico or the discovery of gold in California?* (War with Mexico)
c. *California or Texas becomes a state?* (Texas)
d. *Clermont steams up the Hudson or the Erie Canal is opened?* (Clermont)

Have pupils find how many years passed between statehood for Oregon and statehood for California (8); between Texas's declaration of independence and statehood for Texas (8); between Slater's arrival and first telegraph message sent (55); and between the appearance of the *Clermont* and the opening of the Erie Canal (32).

4. Dictionary Skills. Have pupils find the words *hath* and *wrought* in their dictionaries. Have them find what *archaic* means and then rephrase Samuel Morse's message as it might be sent today. Ask what Morse's message tells them about Morse's feelings about his invention.

● **5. Graph Reading.** Have pupils refer to the graphs on p. 151 to answer these questions:
a. *What was the population of the United States in 1820?* (9,600,000) *In 1840?* (17,000,000) *In 1860?* (31,500,000) Pupils will estimate.
b. *Was the population of the United States in 1860 twice that of 1820?* (No, 3½ times greater)
c. *About how many immigrants came to the United States between 1820 and 1830?* (129,000) *Between 1830 and 1840?* (540,000) *Between 1850 and 1860?* (2,815,000) Pupils will estimate.

d. *What was the total number of immigrants in 1860?* (4,984,000)

e. *Was the number of immigrants between 1840 and 1860 about the same as between 1820 and 1840?* (No, nearly double)

Make pupils aware that in 1860 immigrants made up about 1/6 or 15 percent of the total population of the United States. You might draw a pie graph on the chalkboard to show the relation between the number of immigrants and the total population of the United States.

You may wish to have pupils who have difficulty grasping the concepts look first at the upper graph and determine what the numerals 5.35 indicate. (Millions of people) Help them see that the bar for 1820 is more than 5 but slightly less than 10. Ask: *How close to 10 is the bar? Is it at 9 or over 9?* (Over 9) *About how many people, do you think, does the bar show?* (The exact answer is 9.6 million. The pupils will estimate.) Have the pupils study the second bar to see that it is more than 10 but not quite half the distance between 10 and 15. Have them estimate the population. (The exact answer is 12.9 million.) Continue to analyze each bar with them before studying the lower graph.

You may wish to have pupils who require a challenge report on some of the outstanding immigrants who came to the United States between 1820 and 1860.

6. Answering Checkup Questions. Divide the class into five groups. Assign each group the questions in the Checkup on p. 151. Allow time for class discussion of the answers presented by each group.

LESSON 2   PAGES 152–155

THE LONE STAR REPUBLIC

GOALS

1. To explain how defeat at the Alamo led to a victory for the Texans. **2.** To identify the land gained by the Treaty of Guadalupe-Hidalgo. **3.** To appreciate the contributions of Spanish Mexicans and Mexican Americans to American life and culture.

TEACHING SUGGESTIONS

1. Placing Events in Chronological Order. After pupils have read "Americans in the Southwest" to "War with Mexico" on pp. 152–153, have them place the following events in order of their occurrence:

a. General Santa Anna became president of Mexico. (2)

b. President Jackson tried to buy Texas from Mexico. (1)

c. Texas became independent. (4)

d. General Santa Anna attacked the Alamo. (3)

e. Texas became the twenty-eighth state. (5)

2. Reinforcing Information Gathered. Have pupils form small groups to read pp. 152–155 and find the names of at least ten persons associated with the Lone Star State and the contribution each made to its history. Ask a pupil in each group to write each name suggested on a separate card and the contribution of each person on a separate card. Then have the groups exchange their sets of cards and work out rules for card games that reemphasize what they have read.

3. Preparing Oral Reports. Have pupils choose people associated with the history of Texas whom they would like to know more about. Have them gather information from encyclopedias and other available materials. Suggest that they make appropriate drawings to enhance their presentations or select pictures from books that they might show the class using an opaque projector.

4. Summarizing. Have pupils write short paragraphs in which they summarize the War with Mexico and the Treaty of Guadalupe-Hidalgo using the following key terms:

a. Southern boundary of Texas
b. President Polk
c. 1846
d. General Zachary Taylor and General Winfield Scott
e. Rio Grande
f. Mexican Cession

5. Using Reference Works. Have pupils determine whether an encyclopedia or a dictionary would be a better source to answer these questions:
a. *About how many Mexican Americans now live in the United States?* (E)
b. *In which states do most Mexican Americans live?* (E)
c. *What is a mestizo?* (D)
d. *What does bilingual have to do with many Mexican Americans?* (D)
e. *What popular foods are of Mexican origin?* (E)
f. *Identify: Joseph Montoya, Junipero Serra, José Navarro, Romana Bañuelos, Cesar Chavez, Elfego Baca, Raul Castro, Juan Cortina, Rodalfo Gonzales, Ernesto Galarza, José Angel Gutierrey, George Isidore Sánchez, Hector Garcia, Vikki Carr, Lee Trevino.* (E)
g. *Do most Mexican Americans live in cities or on farms?* (E)
h. *When would you use a piñata?* (D)

Have pupils gain more information about Mexican Americans in our society by using an encyclopedia or dictionary to answer at least five of the questions. (Each person mentioned in **g** is considered a separate response.)

6. Making a Display. Have pupils find additional information on two important parts of the legend of the American West—the cowboy and the Indian. Then have them find appropriate pictures or make drawings depicting how cowboys and Indians of the Plains and of the Southwest lived and what they contributed to American culture. Have the pupils write appropriate captions for their display.

SUPPLEMENTARY INFORMATION
Romana A. Bañuelos (1925–). Romana Acosta Bañuelos was born in Miami, Arizona, and grew up in a Mexican mining village. She moved to Los Angeles and in 1947, with $400 capital, embarked on a business career with a taco stand. Her business grew and she became president of a $5-million-a-year company that packages Mexican food. In 1964, she founded the Pan American National Bank of East Los Angeles, the only United States bank owned and operated by Mexican Americans. In 1971 she became the thirty-fourth Treasurer of the United States. Bañuelos was the sixth consecutive female Treasurer and the first Mexican American woman to be named to such a high government post.

LESSON 3 PAGES 155–158

CALIFORNIA

GOALS
1. To describe the early settlement of California. **2.** To appreciate the rapid growth of California. **3.** To understand the meaning of inflation.

TEACHING SUGGESTIONS
1. Reading for Information. Have pupils read "Early Settlement" and "The Bear Flag Republic" on pp. 155–156 before answering the following questions:
a. *For what is Gaspar de Portolá remembered?* (Established presidios, or military forts, in California)
b. *What purpose did the presidios serve?* (Protected the settlers, held off England's claim to the west coast of North America)
c. *For what is Father Junipero Serra remembered?* (Built missions in California)
d. *What is meant by "California was settled by the sword and the cross"?* (The sword is the symbol of the military influence; the cross, the religious influence.)

e. *What peoples made up most of the population of California in 1840?* (Native Americans, Mexicans, and Spanish)

f. *Who owned California in 1840?* (Mexico)

g. *Did the people want to be under Mexican rule?* (No) *What did they want?* (To be part of the United States)

h. *What did the people do?* (Revolted and formed the Republic of California)

i. *What was the Republic of California also called?* (The Bear Flag Republic)

j. *What did Mexico do about the revolt?* (Nothing; it was too busy fighting the United States.)

2. Role-Playing. Ask pupils to imagine that they lived in 1848. Have two pupils volunteer to assume the roles of James Marshall and John Sutter and role-play the discovery of gold at Sutter's Mill. Refer them to "California gold fever" on pp. 156–158 to prepare the details of the discovery. Have other pupils volunteer to work out roles they identify in the reading. (Other workers at the sawmill, townspeople, newspaper reporters, merchants, travelers to Oregon, and people back east are some suggestions.)

3. Presenting Points of View. After pupils have read about inflation on p. 158, have them name groups of people who experienced the effects of inflation in California in 1848. (Merchants, nouveau-riche prospectors, unsuccessful prospectors, and people traveling to Oregon are some suggestions.) Have several pupils discuss the effects of inflation on one group of people and then choose a pupil to represent their group at a community meeting called by the people of Sacramento.

4. Gathering Information. Have pupils refer to pp. 155–158 to find the significance of the following dates:

a. 1769 (Gaspar de Portolá built presidio near present-day San Diego.)

b. 1846 (California revolted against Mexico.)

c. 1848 (California became a United States territory as part of the Treaty of Guadalupe-Hidalgo.)

d. 1848 (Gold was discovered near Sacramento.)

e. 1850 (California became the thirty-first state.)

5. Map Reading. Have pupils refer to the map on p. 157 to answer the following questions:

a. *In what year was the Mexican Cession added to the United States?* (1848)

b. *What present-day states were formed wholly or partly from the Mexican Cession?* (California, Nevada, Utah, Arizona, Colorado, New Mexico)

c. *What territory formed the northern boundary of the Mexican Cession?* (Oregon Country)

d. *What purchase gave the United States control of all its land from coast to coast?* (Gadsden Purchase)

e. *In what year was the Gadsden Purchase made?* (1853)

f. *In how many years did the United States grow from 13 states to a nation bounded by the Atlantic and Pacific Oceans?* (20)

g. *What territory did the United States add in 1867?* (Alaska)

h. *What was the last territory added to the United States?* (Hawaii)

i. *When was Hawaii added?* (1898)

j. *How are Alaska and Hawaii different from all other territories added?* (They are the only two territories not adjacent to any other part of the United States.)

SUPPLEMENTARY INFORMATION

Junípero Serra (1713–1784). Perhaps the best known of the Spanish missionaries in the Southwest was a Franciscan priest named Junípero Serra. Born on the island of Majorca, just off the east coast of Spain, he became a Franciscan at the age of 16. When he was 36, he sailed to the New World to work in the missions. From 1769 to 1784, Serra worked in what is now the state of California. He is remembered for starting the string of missions that were built in California—from Mission San Diego de Alcalá in the south to Mission San Francisco de Solano in the north.

Father Serra brought domestic animals and European methods of farming to California. For fifteen years he traveled from mission to mission. He felt especially close to the Penatian-speaking Indians. He often took up their cause against colonists who maltreated them.

LESSON 4   PAGES 158–161

THE OREGON TRAIL

GOALS
1. To know why people wanted to go to the Oregon Country. **2.** To recognize routes established by people who traveled to the West. **3.** To appreciate the contributions people made to the development of the West.

TEACHING SUGGESTIONS
1. Creative Writing. After pupils have read "Oregon fever" on p. 158, have them imagine that they are reporters on newspapers in Boston, New York, and Philadelphia who have been asked to write about Oregon fever, analyzing its causes, symptoms, and possible cures. (Causes: reports of the beautiful land and plentiful game in the Oregon Territory; symptoms: restlessness, fantasizing, new energy and hope; cure: "Oregon or bust.")

2. Map Reading. Have pupils refer to the map on p. 159 to answer the following:
a. *Where did the Oregon Trail begin?* (Independence, Missouri) *Where did it end?* (Portland, Oregon)
b. *Name the chief forts, rivers, and passes met in traveling the Oregon Trail.* (Fort Kearney, North Platte River, Fort Laramie, South Pass, Snake River, Fort Walla Walla)

c. *How long was the Oregon Trail?* [2,000 mi (3,200 km)]
d. *If travelers went to seek gold in Sacramento rather than continuing on the Oregon Trail, what trail might they have taken?* (California Trail)
e. *Where would they have crossed the Sierra Nevada Mountains?* (Donner Pass)
f. *Which cities did the Santa Fe Trail join?* (Independence, Missouri, and Santa Fe, New Mexico)
g. *What was the length of the Santa Fe Trail?* (780 mi, or 1,260 km)
h. *What trail was an extension of the Santa Fe Trail?* (Old Spanish Trail)
i. *What cities did it join?* (Santa Fe and Los Angeles)
j. *What river did the Old Spanish Trail cross?* (Colorado River)
k. *Through which states did the National Road pass?* (Maryland, Pennsylvania, West Virginia, Ohio, Indiana)
l. *What road joined Albany and Buffalo?* (Great Genesee Road)

3. Reading for Information. Have pupils read pp. 159–161 to find the three groups of people who went to Oregon and a representative from each group. (Mountain men—Kit Carson; pioneers—John Sager; missionaries—Narcissa Whitman or Marcus Whitman)

4. Interviewing. Have several pupils assume that they are about to interview people who have had experiences in the Oregon Country. Ask them to base their questions on the material on pp. 159–161. Have other pupils assume the identity of Kit Carson, Jim Beckwourth, Narcissa Whitman, Dr. Marcus Whitman, John Sager, John Sager's brother and sisters. Have them familiarize themselves with the material before they are interviewed.

5. Vocabulary Building. Have pupils choose ten words from the vocabulary in Chapter 8, review their meanings, and write a definition or description of each. Have pupils exchange papers and write the answers to the definitions or descriptions they are given. Allow time for discussion.

8/CHAPTER REVIEW   PAGE 162
Answers for Review Questions
1. Answers will vary.
2. The Industrial Revolution and changes in transportation helped each other in this way: the better transportation became, the more goods were shipped. The easier and cheaper it was to buy these goods, the more people wanted factory products. As more factories were built to produce goods, better transportation was needed to ship the goods.
3. Events that led up to Texas becoming independent in 1836 were: Mexico cut off immigration to Texas from the United States, which previously had been encouraged. General Antonio Lopez de Santa Anna took away much of the self-government that the people of Texas had enjoyed until that time. The Americans and some Texans set up a government, formed an army, and captured San Antonio. General Sam Houston defeated the Mexican army and held General Santa Anna.
4. As a result of the 1848 war with Mexico, the United States gained the Mexican Cession.
5. People went to California in the 1840s for gold. People went to Oregon inspired by reports of the beautiful land and plentiful game and filled with new hopes and dreams.

3/UNIT REVIEW   PAGE 164
Answers for Unit Review
1. "No taxation without representation" means no taxes were to be levied on British subjects without the consent of their representatives in the British Parliament.
2. The four major parts of the Declaration of Independence are the preamble, a statement of rights, a list of George III's wrongs, and a statement of independence.

3. Answers will vary. Pupils may include the following: leaders—Washington, Howe, Benedict Arnold, John Paul Jones, Francis Marion; foreign helpers—Lafayette, Kosciusko, Pulaski, de Kalb, von Streuben; ordinary men and women—Crispus Attucks, Molly McCauley, Deborah Sampson Gannett, Deborah Champion.
4. The three branches of the federal government are the legislative branch, or Congress, which makes the laws; the executive branch, or the President and his helpers, which carries out the laws Congress makes; and the judicial branch, or the courts, which decides on the meaning of the laws.
5. Answers will vary.
6. Pupils' scrapbooks will vary.
7. The states carved out of the Louisiana Purchase wholly or partially were Minnesota, Iowa, Missouri, Arkansas, Louisiana, North Dakota, South Dakota, Nebraska, Kansas, Oklahoma, Montana, Wyoming, and Colorado.
8. The War of 1812 is often described as the "second war for independence" because as a result of that war Europe respected our country as a strong nation, our country respected itself for its ability to fight a great power, and our country was free to go its own way.
9. Three groups of people that had few rights in the 1800s were women, blacks, and Native Americans.
10. The United States had changed greatly by the mid-1800s because the many roads, canals, steamboats, and railroads had improved means of transportation; the Industrial Revolution brought about changes in the production of goods, and inventions contributed to the growth of industry; new opportunities brought many immigrants to the United States.
11. New territories added to the United States were the Louisiana Territory added by purchase; Texas, by annexation; Oregon Country, by treaty; Mexican Cession by war; Gadsden territory, by purchase.

The United States Comes of Age

UNIT 4

THE UNITED STATES COMES OF AGE

Dear Parent,

Growing up can be a painful thing as well as a pleasant one. Perhaps you remember some times from your own childhood or adolescence that combined the pain and pleasure of growing up.

You might like to explain to your child that our nation had a "growing up" time just as people do. This is the focus of the new unit we will be beginning soon. A painful Civil War was necessary to establish this nation in a firm and united way. The promise of equality brought forth by that war was shattered by subsequent treatment of blacks, Native Americans, and some of the more recent immigrants to the United States. Yet the nation grew, learned from its mistakes, and matured into a powerful, distinctive industrial giant. All segments of the population have made vital contributions to this growth.

Perhaps your family has stories that go back to this time in the late nineteenth century. Were your ancestors among the immigrants at this time? Were they among those who helped build the railroads? Were they among the Native Americans who struggled proudly to maintain a traditional way of life? Were they among the black Americans who possessed inner strength and freedom even as they saw the outward signs of it snatched from their grasp? Did they join the hardy pioneers in the Great Plains? Were they farmers or city dwellers?

Personal accounts of this nature can do far more than enhance this study of history. They can help your children understand themselves better. And I am sure we both want that very much.

Sincerely,

THE UNITED STATES COMES OF AGE

BULLETIN-BOARD DISPLAY

Keep a "Good News . . . Bad News" bulletin board throughout this unit. Title the display The United States: 1850–1900. Divide the board in half—one side labeled Good News; the other Bad News. Make a "3 × 5" card for the major events or persons as each is discussed in this unit. Have pupils evaluate in which column the person or event should be placed. Do not hesitate to place cards in the middle if they do not fall clearly into either category. The evaluation can be a valuable review and the bulletin board itself a visual reminder of major events and people in the unit.

GETTING STARTED

Have pupils look at the unit opener on p. 165. Ask these questions:
a. *Do you recognize any of these people? Whom do you know?*
b. *What do you think these people represent?*
c. *Look at the unit title. What does "coming of age" mean?*
d. *What does this page tell you about the unit? What will you be studying?*

A NATION DIVIDES AND REUNITES

THEME

The Northern and Southern sections of the United States fought a bitter Civil War over the issues of slavery and states' rights. Gains were made in the area of civil rights as a result. However, these gains were largely erased by the latter part of the nineteenth century. By 1900, the disunity between the sections of the country had been ameliorated.

LESSON 1   PAGES 166–171

SLAVERY

GOALS

1. To find specific information on a time line. **2.** To describe the differences in farming in the three sections of the United States in the early 1800s. **3.** To name the section in which most slaves lived. **4.** To know how the Underground Railroad worked. **5.** To explain Lincoln's attitude toward slavery in the territories.

TEACHING SUGGESTIONS

1. Reading a Time Line. Have pupils study the time line on p. 168 and answer these questions:

a. *When did the Civil War begin?* (1861)
b. *How long did the war last?* (4 years)
c. *Did South Carolina leave the Union before Lincoln was elected?* (No)
d. *Was the Emancipation Proclamation issued before the Thirteenth Amendment was ratified?* (Yes)
e. *How many years did Reconstruction last?* (12 years)

PROJECTS

1. Many communities have ties to the Civil War. Are there monuments, memorials, records of troop involvement, pictures, or old newspapers from Civil War times available in your area? Have pupils find out in what way their community was involved in the Civil War. Visit a local museum or historical society. If nothing deals specifically with the war, find out what *was* going on in the community at that time.

2. Encourage pupils with an interest in the Civil War to research battles and make three-dimensional dioramas. Toy soldiers, if they are available, will add realism to the battle scenes.

2. Creative Writing. After pupils have read "Differences" on p. 166, divide the class into three groups. Assign each group a section of the country. Each pupil is to write a letter to a friend describing what life is like in his or her section. Pupils should tell where they live, what kind of work they and/or their parents do, and something about how they feel about the other sections of the country. You may wish to review the various parts of a correctly written personal letter before the class begins this exercise.

● **3. Making a Filmstrip.** Supply pupils with blank leader so that they can make a filmstrip on slavery. It may be necessary to divide the class into groups: some to draw pictures, others to write titles, and so on. Pages 166–170 and pp. 96–98 in Chapter 5 can supply enough background information for this activity. Sentences or phrases from the chapters can be used as titles for the frames within the filmstrip.

You may wish to select descriptive sentences from the text, and read them with pupils who have difficulty grasping concepts. Then have pupils look through picture history books and magazines for pictures that fit the sentences. These pictures can be used as models for the drawings in the filmstrip.

Those pupils who require a challenge may be asked to write and record a narration to accompany the filmstrip.

4. Building Vocabulary. Have pupils write these words on a sheet of paper: *studious, just, honest, humorous, eloquent, patriotic, intelligent.* Allow pupils to use dictionaries to find meanings for words they do not know. After they have read "Abraham Lincoln" on p. 170, have them find a statement in the text that shows how each of the words on the list applies to Lincoln. Have them write each statement next to the appropriate word.

5. Question and Answer. The following questions can be used to review the text:

a. *What is sectionalism?* (Feeling strongly about one part of the country and putting its interests first)

b. *How did it help lead to the Civil War?* (Answers will vary, but should include sectional rivalry and economic differences.)

c. *Why did the South still have slavery? Why did it no longer exist in the North?* (Southern economy was based on slave labor. Slavery was not profitable in the North.)

d. *Why was it so difficult for slaves to resist?* (Answers will vary.)

e. *What forms did resistance take?* (Open rebellion, work slow-down, damage to equipment, running away)

f. *What was Lincoln's attitude toward slavery?* (He did not like it and did not want it to spread to the territories.)

g. *Why did the South feel Lincoln's election was "an insult and a danger"?* (An insult to the Southern way of life and a danger to freedom of choice)

SUPPLEMENTARY INFORMATION

1. Harriet Tubman (1821–1913). Widely known as "the Moses of her people," Tub-man was one of the most active "conductors" on the Underground Railroad. She was born a slave in Maryland and escaped in 1849, traveling north via the loosely organized network of abolitionists who made up what was called the Underground Railroad. Over a period of about ten years after her own escape, Tubman risked her life repeatedly by returning to Maryland nineteen times to guide others to freedom. Her aged parents were among the more than 300 slaves so aided. At one time, rewards offered for her totaled $40,000, but she always evaded capture. Harriet Tubman became a friend of leading abolitionists, and John Brown conferred with her about his plan to seize Harpers Ferry. During the Civil War, she served as a nurse, scout, and spy for the Union army in South Carolina. After the war, she lived in Auburn, New York, where she worked to raise money for black schools and to establish a home for elderly and needy blacks. In 1908 such a home was opened and later became known as the Harriet Tubman Home. In 1914 the city of Auburn honored her memory by placing a bronze tablet at the entrance to the Cayuga County Courthouse.

2. Frederick Douglass (1817?–1895). Douglass was an abolitionist, an orator, and a journalist. Born a slave in Maryland, he was named Frederick Augustus Washington Bailey but assumed the name of Douglass after escaping from slavery and running away to Massachusetts in 1838. Although he was trained to work in a shipyard, Douglass had trouble finding work because other people refused to work with a black. Thus he was forced to take many menial jobs to stay alive. In 1841, Douglass successfully addressed a Massachusetts Anti-Slavery Society convention and was hired as a lecturer. In 1847 he published his autobiography, *Narrative of the Life of Frederick Douglass, an American Slave,* to answer those who doubted that a man of his abilities could ever have been a slave.

When publication of his autobiography exposed his past, friends helped raise money to buy his freedom. After a period in England, Douglass moved to Rochester, New York, and started an antislavery newspaper, the *North Star*. He wrote almost as much about the prejudice and discrimination against the free black person in the North as he did about the horrors of slavery in the South. Seeking justice for his race, he successfully fought an attempt to segregate the schools in Rochester. His house was a station on the Underground Railroad. During the Civil War, his sons served in the Union army. Douglass himself conferred several times with President Lincoln about the problems of slavery. After the war, he held several positions with the federal government, including recorder of deeds in Washington, D.C., and minister to Haiti.

LESSON 2 PAGES 171–177

A CIVIL WAR

GOALS

1. To compare and contrast the advantages and disadvantages of the North and South at the start of the war. 2. To identify important leaders on both sides. 3. To understand the importance of the Emancipation Proclamation. 4. To be able to locate important battle sites on a map.

TEACHING SUGGESTIONS

1. Making a Chart. Have pupils develop a chart listing Union Advantages and Confederate Advantages. Pupils should base the chart on the text section "Unequal Fight?" on pp. 172–173. The information on the chart can be used to answer the question: *Which side looked most unbeatable at the beginning of the Civil War?* (Answers will vary.)

2. Reading a Map. After pupils have studied the maps on pp. 172 and 175 and read text pp. 173–177, pose the following questions:

a. *Did every state in existence in 1860 line up on one side or the other?* (Yes)

b. *How many Union states were there?* (23) *How many Confederate?* (11)

c. *Were most battles fought in the North or the South?* (South)

d. *In which state were many battles fought?* (Virginia)

e. *Why, do you think, was this so?* (Answers may vary. Point out the location of the two capitals.)

f. *Which major battle was fought along the Mississippi River?* (Vicksburg) *Who won?* (North)

g. *Which major battle was fought in Maryland?* (Antietam) *Who won?* (North)

h. *Who won the first battle of Bull Run?* (South)

i. *How far north was a battle fought?* (Pennsylvania)

j. *Was a major battle fought in Washington, D.C.?* (No)

k. *Where did Lee surrender to Grant?* (Appomattox) *In what state is it?* (Virginia)

● **3. Reading Pictures.** There are two battle pictures in this chapter—a scene from the battle of Gettysburg on p. 167 and one from the battle of Petersburg on p. 174. There is another battle pictured on p. 40. Have pupils study these pictures and observe details such as uniform color, flags, types of weapons and other equipment, and use of animals.

For pupils who have difficulty concentrating on detail, you may wish to ask these questions:

a. *How are animals used in the picture on p. 167?* (Pulling artillery pieces, being ridden)

b. *Is it likely that the men on horseback are officers?* (Yes)

c. *What is one way to tell the two sides apart in the picture on p. 174?* (Flags) *What is another way?* (Color of uniforms)

d. *Which flag appears in all three pic-*

tures? (Union flag—the Stars and Stripes)

e. *What unusual piece of military equipment appears in the picture on p. 40?* (Balloon)

For those pupils who require more challenge, you may wish to pose the following questions:

a. *Why were battle scenes painted or drawn rather than photographed?* (Cameras of the time were too primitive to capture the rapid movements of battle on film.)

b. *Do you think these pictures present a particular point of view—favor one side over the other?* (Answers will vary.)

4. Interviewing. Pupils could arrange a news conference with Grant and Lee after the surrender at Appomattox Court House. Choose pupils who are particularly interested in this period to portray the generals. The rest of the class could be the reporters. Have each pupil prepare at least one question.

5. Discussion. After pupils have completed the study of text pages for this lesson, ask:

a. *In what ways, other than going to war, could the North and the South have solved their problems?*

b. *Why did Robert E. Lee, a man who disliked slavery, fight on the side of the South? Would you have done the same?*

c. *How did the Emancipation Proclamation influence the outcome of the war?*

d. *What are "turning points"? In what sense are the battles of Vicksburg and Gettysburg turning points of the Civil War?* (Answers to all these questions will vary.)

SUPPLEMENTARY INFORMATION

1. Battle of the Crater. At Petersburg, Virginia, General Grant had a chance to finish the war nine months sooner. His men had dug a tunnel 511 feet long (156 m) from a hidden place behind their line to a point under the Confederate line. Gunpowder was set off and a huge crater was blown in the Confederate line. A division of 10,000 black soldiers had trained for three weeks to rush around the top of the crater and attack the Confederate line. Only hours before the attack, Grant and General Meade ordered that a division of white soldiers go first. These soldiers lost time by going *into* the crater instead of *around* its top. The Battle of the Crater, on July 30, 1864, had failed. (The war settled into a long siege at Petersburg. See illustration on p. 174.) Grant later said that if the plan had not been changed and the blacks had gone first, "It would have been a success."

2. Digging for the *Monitor*. In 1973 undersea archaeologists discovered the final resting place of *U.S.S. Monitor*, off the coast of Cape Hatteras, S.C. In August 1979 a full investigation of the hull took place. The government in the meanwhile had designated the area a National Marine Sanctuary. It is unlikely that the ship will be raised since preservation would be extremely risky. Some artifacts were removed, however. The original plans for the ship were destroyed shortly after it was built, so these underwater investigations gave historians a chance to learn details about the ship's design. The *Monitor* sank on New Year's Eve in 1862.

LESSON 3   PAGES 177–183

RECONSTRUCTION

GOALS

1. To identify the purpose of the Thirteenth, Fourteenth, and Fifteenth Amendments. **2.** To name the President who was impeached. **3.** To tell who carpetbaggers and scalawags were. **4.** To discuss at least one accomplishment of Reconstruction governments.

TEACHING SUGGESTIONS

1. Making a Point. Give each pupil a piece of candy or something else that obviously will be enjoyed. Do not allow pupils to open their candy. Tell them that under a law you have passed, the candy is theirs. However, you will not allow them to eat it unless they meet certain conditions. These conditions can be anything that is nearly impossible—rubbing their stomachs and patting their heads, balancing pencils on the ends of their noses, reading a foreign language, and so forth.

After letting pupils try to meet the conditions, explain to pupils that their situation is similar to that of blacks after the Civil War. Three amendments gave them freedom and equality by law. For a time they were able to utilize their new status. Beginning in 1877, however, their freedoms were systematically denied by conditions often impossible to fulfill.

Discuss pupils' feelings about having something good but not being able to use it. Now have pupils read pp. 177–183— "Reconstruction."

● **2. Identifying Sources.** Write the following key statements from the Thirteenth, Fourteenth, and Fifteenth amendments on the chalkboard. Ask pupils to name the amendment from which each statement comes.

a. *"All persons born or naturalized in the United States . . . are citizens of the United States and of the State wherein they reside."* (14th)

b. *"The right to vote shall not be denied or abridged . . . on account of race, color, or previous condition."* (15th)

c. *"Nor shall any State deprive any person of life, liberty, or property, without due process of law."* (14th)

d. *"Neither slavery nor involuntary servitude . . . shall exist within the United States."* (13th)

e. *"Nor shall any State deny to any person . . . the equal protection of the laws."* (14th)

Refer those pupils who have difficulty understanding the amendments to the summary of the Constitution which is in Chapter 6. The amendments appear on p. 123.

You may wish to have pupils who require a challenge paraphrase each statement. Encourage pupils to use a dictionary to find the meanings of words they do not understand.

3. Building Vocabulary. Have pupils create a word-search puzzle using the vocabulary for this chapter. In a word-search puzzle words are hidden in the midst of meaningless letters. An added challenge can be introduced by writing the words diagonally and down as well as across. Pupils may exchange puzzles. Or you may wish to create a puzzle, duplicate it, and distribute copies to the class.

4. Discussion. Pose the following questions:

a. *Would Lincoln have been able to do a better job leading the country after the Civil War than Johnson? Why, or why not?*

b. *How did sharecropping differ from slavery?*

c. *Were Black Codes fair? Explain.*

d. *Why was Andrew Johnson impeached?*

e. *What, do you think, was the biggest problem during Reconstruction? What was the greatest accomplishment?*

(Answers to these questions will vary.)

5. Making Diary Entries. Ask pupils to imagine they are living in the South after the Civil War. Ask them to assume the identity of one of the following: An ex-Confederate soldier, a carpetbagger, a scalawag (try to get at least some pupils to take positive rather than negative views here), a black before 1877, and a black after 1877. Have pupils write a series of diary entries about this period in their lives.

SUPPLEMENTARY INFORMATION

1. After the War. We all know what happened to the Union leaders after the Civil War. Abraham Lincoln was assassinated. Ulysses S. Grant was elected President in 1868. But what happened to the two important figures of the Confederacy—Jefferson Davis and Robert E. Lee?

Jefferson Davis was not a universally popular President of the Confederacy. Many Southerners thought he had handled the war badly. Union forces arrested Davis after Lee's surrender at Appomattox. A grand jury indicted him for high treason. He sat in jail for two years waiting for his trial. In 1867 he was released on bail and went to his home near Biloxi, Mississippi. He was never brought to trial. He spent his time writing and attending reunions of Confederate soldiers. In 1881 he published a defense of his administration of Confederate affairs—*The Rise and Fall of the Confederate Government*. By the time he died in 1889, he was a widely respected figure in the South. Four Southern states observe his birthday as a legal holiday.

Robert E. Lee spent forty years as a soldier. The Civil War was both the high point and the end of his military career. Hoping to set an example for other Southerners, Lee applied for a full pardon under the Amnesty and Reconstruction Act of 1865. This pardon was not granted until after his death. He spent his last years (he died in 1870) as president of Washington College in Lexington, Virginia. "I shall devote my remaining energies to training young men to do their duty in life." Lee once said that *duty* was the sublimest word in the English language. Washington College was eventually renamed Washington and Lee to honor the person who brought it fame. Lee is buried in the chapel on the campus.

2. Andrew Johnson. The seventeenth President of the United States, Johnson was born in Raleigh, North Carolina. His father was a handyman and his mother a maid. Johnson had absolutely no formal schooling. He was apprenticed to a tailor when he was fourteen. It was at this point that he learned to read. When he was eighteen, he married. His wife taught him to write and to do simple arithmetic, and encouraged him to read and study.

Johnson took his politics from Andrew Jackson and, throughout his political career, sided with the "common man." He began his career in local politics as an alderman in Greenville, Tennessee. He went on from there to the state legislature, to the House of Representatives, to the governorship of Tennessee, to the United States Senate. On the national level, Johnson supported both the Union and slavery. In 1860 he was the only senator who refused to secede with his state. He was appointed military governor of Tennessee. The Republicans felt he was a natural choice for Vice President. One of his lawyers at the impeachment trial wrote, "He is a man of few ideas, but they are right and true, and could suffer death sooner than yield up or violate one of them." Johnson ended his political career as a United States senator; he was elected in 1874. He took his seat to a round of applause.

9/CHAPTER REVIEW   PAGE 184
Answers for Review Questions

1. The main differences between sections in the 1830s and 1840s were: Northeast—farms were smaller and factories and trade were important, merchants were leading citizens; Southeast—large-scale farming and the leading citizens were planters; West—large farms, developing industries.

2. The North had more of everything at the start of the war than the South did. The North also had to conquer the South in order to win while the South, in order to win, had only to hold out until the North grew tired of fighting.

3. The Thirteenth Amendment ended slavery; the Fourteenth Amendment extended the rights of citizens to blacks; and the Fifteenth gave the vote to black men.

4. Positive results of Reconstruction were the formation of public school systems; the building of roads, canals, and railroads; the creation of industry; and the broadening of the democratic base of Southern politics.

THE NATION EXPANDS

THEME

With the principle of "one nation, indivisible" firmly established by the Civil War, the United States was ready to expand. Aided by new inventions, miners, cattle ranchers, and farmers soon settled the western lands. Unfortunately, this settlement took place at the expense of Native Americans, who were pushed aside in order to "make room for progress."

PROJECTS

1. Have some pupils study the concept of cultural conflict by reviewing the history of contact between Europeans and Native Americans (Chapter 3). A report could cover what they learned from each other, how they helped each other, the results of the contact, and the conflict between "tradition" and "progress." Have other pupils research the treatment of Native Americans in the West. They could provide reports on Chief Joseph, Geronimo, Sitting Bull, Crazy Horse, General Custer, Sand Creek, Washita, Wounded Knee, the Plains tribes, and the buffalo.

2. Encourage class members to choose a character from the development of the West and keep a diary from that character's point of view. Suggestions are an early Great Plains farmer, a miner, a cowboy on the long drive, a sheep rancher, a homesteader, a railroad worker, an army leader, a Native American, Calamity Jane, Wild Bill Hickok, or a Bureau of Indian Affairs official. Pupils may undertake additional reading to make their diaries realistic and creative. Let pupils share their accounts and answer classmates' questions about the characters.

WESTWARD MOVEMENT

GOALS

1. To compare the prairies and Great Plains with farming areas in the East. 2. To understand how different tools and methods helped settlers in dry areas. 3. To explain why open-range grazing ended. 4. To define *recall*, *initiative*, and *referendum*.

TEACHING SUGGESTIONS

1. **Reading a Time Line.** After pupils have read the lesson and examined the time line on p. 188, ask the following questions:

a. *Were there farmers, miners, cattle ranchers, railroad workers, and Native Americans in the West in 1869?* (Yes)

b. *Was gold discovered in Colorado after the transcontinental railroad was completed?* (No)

c. *When was the first big cattle drive from Texas?* (1867)

d. *An important invention spelled the end to open-range grazing. What was it?* (Barbed wire in 1873)

e. *In 1898, what political reforms were allowed by South Dakota?* (Initiative and referendum)

f. *Who was President when the Homestead Act took effect?* (Lincoln, 1862)

g. *What year was James Garfield elected President?* (1880)

h. *Name the three Presidents after Garfield and the year each was elected.* (Chester Arthur in 1881, Grover Cleveland in 1884, and Benjamin Harrison in 1888)

i. *Was the Bureau of Indian Affairs established before the Homestead Act was passed?* (Yes)

j. *When did women gain voting rights in the Wyoming Territory?* (1869)

2. Reading a Map. After pupils have examined the map on p. 191, ask the following questions:

a. *Major cattle routes began in what state?* (Texas)

b. *In which direction did they head?* (North)

c. *In what city and state did the Western Trail end?* (Ogallala, Nebraska) *Chisholm Trail?* (Abilene, Kansas) *Sedalia Trail?* (Sedalia, Missouri)

d. *Dodge City and Wichita were called "cowtowns." Explain based on the map.* (Cattle were driven through these towns on their way to market.)

e. *How can you tell mining areas on the map?* (Symbol)

f. *True or false? Most mining areas are located in or near mountains.* (True)

g. *True or false? There was only one rail route from St. Louis to San Francisco.* (False)

h. *True or false? Railroads always went around mountains.* (False)

i. *True or false? In order to get from Salt Lake City to Los Angeles by rail at this time, you had to go through at least one other city.* (True)

3. Making Posters. Have pupils make posters advertising the benefits of the West at this time to people back East. Posters should appeal to all types of people: farmers, workers, adventure-seekers, women, and "get-rich-quick" types.

4. Making a Mural. Brown wrapping paper tacked along one side of the room provides a base for a wall mural. Use the Mississippi River and the Pacific Ocean as boundaries. Then water paint and crayons can be used to show scenes on the Great Plains including Native American villages, sod houses, buffalo herds, cowboys and cattle, boom towns and miners, homesteaders, and ranchers.

5. Debating. Let pupils collect information to substantiate or refute Major Stephen Long's evaluation of the Great Plains. Organize a debate on the topic—Resolved; The Great Plains are almost wholly unfit for farming.

6. Discussion. The conflict between the sheep ranchers and the cattle ranchers and between both of these groups and the homesteaders was often violent. Have pupils discuss the rights of each group and the effect of the invention of barbed wire.

7. Research. Western states were the first to try some new ideas such as recall, initiative, and referendum. Have pupils use an encyclopedia to find more information about how the measures work and their value. You may want to review the skills of note taking, proper citation of sources, and report writing at this time.

● **8. Writing Letters.** Let some volunteers imagine that they live on a homestead on the Great Plains in 1870. Have them write letters to a friend back in the East, describing their experiences and their life and emphasizing the differences from Eastern living.

For those who have difficulty getting started, you may wish to provide a topic, such as a recent storm, cattle trampling down a fence on the farm, the kind of crops raised, and so on.

You may suggest that those who require a challenge write several paragraphs describing the landscape, their home, and their schooling.

SUPPLEMENTARY INFORMATION

Farming Changes. In the Plains states, water is in short supply. Most places in the East have more than 20 inches (50 cm) of rainfall a year. Less than that makes farming a risky business. To irrigate their fields, the early farmers on the Plains dug ditches from the nearest stream. When there were no streams nearby, the farmers dug deep wells and built windmills to pump the water to the surface of the ground.

Early settlers in the West had crop failures because they brought the seeds and farming methods used in moist areas. When immigrants from Eastern Europe came, they brought varieties of hard wheat from the Black Sea region, which has a similar climate. They also used a method of farming more suited to the dry climate of the West.

In dry farming, farmers plow the land so that the soil helps hold the rain and snow when it falls. Furrows run across, instead of up and down, the hillsides. This forms a series of troughs in the land, one above the other, that hold the rain. Tilling the soil keeps out weeds that take moisture and nutrients from the soil. Factors that vary include the kind of soil, the rate of moisture evaporation, the intensity and season of the rainfall, and the amount of moisture a crop needs. After harvesting a crop, the farmer allows the land to lie fallow, or idle, until the next summer, thus enabling the land to store up moisture.

LESSON 2   PAGES 193–199

THE TRANSCONTINENTAL RAILROAD AND THE INDIAN WARS

GOALS

1. To explain what a transcontinental railroad is and why one was needed. 2. To tell how and why the federal government aided in the building of the transcontinental railroad. 3. To understand how the railroad affected the life-style of the Native Americans. 4. To discuss the plight of Chief Joseph and the Nez Percé.

TEACHING SUGGESTIONS

1. Questions and Answers. For a review of the content of the lesson, ask the following questions:

a. *When did the rail lines from the East reach Chicago?* (Before 1860) *In what year did the rail lines from Chicago reach the Mississippi?* (1854)

b. *Why was it necessary to build a railroad to California?* (California, which became a state in 1850, was separated by more than a thousand miles (1,600 km) of unsettled country from the nearest states: Texas, Arkansas, Missouri, Iowa.)

c. *What did the federal government do to help the railroad builders?* (The government gave the railroads sections of land 1 mile long (1.6 km) on alternating sides of the railroad track and gave loans ranging from $16,000 to $48,000 a mile, depending on the terrain.)

d. *What was a fundamental difference in the views of the land between the Native Americans and the settlers?* (Native Americans considered the land and all of nature as gifts to be cared for and shared. Crops were for the good of all. Settlers were looking for a better life, which included owning their own farms and ranches.)

e. *In what ways were the Native Americans treated unfairly?* (They were promised supplies and protection by the government but little was ever delivered. Sometimes they were not told what the treaty they signed really said; sometimes the boundaries and terms were changed after the treaty was signed.)

f. *What happened at the Little Bighorn in 1876?* (General George Custer and about 250 of his soldiers were killed in a battle with the Sioux.)

g. *Who said "I will fight no more forever," and why did he say it?* (Chief Joseph of Nez Percé when he finally had to surrender to the U.S. Army after a long, arduous flight.)

h. *Who was Major Edward Wynkoop? How did he treat the Native Americans?* (He was an army officer who became an agent for the Bureau of Indian Affairs. He treated the Native Americans decently, as did some other agents.)

i. *What was the content of the Dawes Act of 1887? What was its aftermath?* (The act divided tribal land among individual members of the tribe. They were to be educated and become farmers and United States citizens after 25 years. But few members wanted to farm; many sold their lands, and eventually they ran out of money. An act postponing citizenship was passed in 1906, and it was not until 1924 that Indians were made citizens. In 1934 another act returned land ownership to the tribes as a whole.)

● **2. Writing Character Sketches.** After reading about General Custer on p. 196 and Chief Joseph on p. 197, pupils could write character sketches describing their contrasting characters. Encyclopedias or other reference books can provide additional information. Have pupils try to find at least five adjectives to describe each man distinctively.

For those pupils who have difficulty getting started, you may wish to provide a few descriptive adjectives or phrases about each leader. Pupils can add to the word list and then combine their words into a brief paragraph.

You may wish to direct pupils who require a challenge to include stories or incidents to prove their opinions. Also, you may suggest other persons to be characterized, such as Major Edward Wynkoop, Sitting Bull, Crazy Horse, and Ely Parker.

3. Recordings. Have pupils look for recordings of cowboy songs that can be played in class. Lead a discussion of what life was like for cowboys: what they wore, what they ate, their pay, their attention to their horses, and some of the jobs they performed on the trail and on the ranch. Make a list of vocabulary words that pertain to their lives, such as *dogie, bronco, mustang,* *pinto, roundup, maverick, chuck wagon, yearling, tenderfoot, stampede, brand, wrangler, foreman, cowtown, corral, ride herd, rustler, chow.*

4. Ecology. Have pupils describe the Native American attitude toward the land and its use. Let them relate this to current concerns about air pollution and conservation of natural resources.

5. Book Report. Try to locate a copy of Helen Hunt Jackson's book, *A Century of Dishonor.* Let volunteers read sections of the book and report on the material to the class.

6. Role Playing. Assume that there has been a dispute between a Native American tribe and a homesteading family over water rights on a large tract of land. Have pupils take the roles of the family, tribal members and the Bureau of Indian Affairs agent. Let the class decide whether the dispute was decided fairly.

7. Current Events. Direct some pupils to look through the *Readers' Guide to Periodical Literature* for any recent references to Native Americans' pursuit of their rights and fair treatment.

8. Films. There are several outstanding films available on the treatment of Native Americans in this period of history. Three for this age group are *Tahtonka*, the story of the Indian's relationship to the buffalo; *I Will Fight No More Forever*, a dramatization of the classic retreat of Chief Joseph and the Nez Percé from lands promised them by treaty; and *End of the Trail: The American Plains Indian*, available in two parts, *Treaties Made, Treaties Broken* and *How the West Was Won*. One film or another can serve as a focus for final discussion.

SUPPLEMENTARY INFORMATION
Native Americans Today. About 800,000 Native Americans live in the United States. Although they can live wherever they

wish, about half make their home on a reservation. There are about 285 federal and state reservations, most of which lie west of the Mississippi River. Some residents prefer to live on a reservation so they can practice and preserve tribal customs and ways of life. Some reservations are owned by an entire tribe, and others are divided into individual plots. Some who live on the reservation farm the land or raise livestock. Some work in sawmills and businesses belonging to the tribe. Others have jobs in businesses owned by others, not Native Americans. The federal government has helped those who wish to move to cities by aiding them in finding housing, training, and jobs. Some have found good jobs in business and industry; others have entered professions such as education, law, and medicine.

In the late 1960s and 1970s, some Native American groups protested their treatment, citing injustices on the reservations and in cities and blaming chiefly the Bureau of Indian Affairs for such wrongs. Many Native Americans reject the militant tactics of some groups. The government, in turn, has begun to give Native Americans more opportunities for a stronger voice in controlling their own welfare and future.

10/CHAPTER REVIEW PAGE 200
Answers for Review Questions

1. The pioneers who settled on the Great Plains learned to use iron plows in the dried earth, wire fences instead of wooden fences, and corn cobs and grass stalks instead of firewood. They lived in dugouts cut into the ground or into the sides of small hills. Homes were built using sod strips; thick grass covered the roof. They used dry farming, allowing the land to lie idle every other year, and planted the kind of grain used on European steppes.

2. The discovery of a bonanza, a rich vein of silver ore, attracted people to Virginia City, Nevada, and it became a boom town until the mines gave out.

3. The peak of the cowboy era was from the 1860s to the 1880s. There were about 40,000 working cowboys at that time.

4. The Homestead Act of 1862 helped bring farmers westward by allowing free land to anyone who settled on the land for 5 years and improved it by planting crops and building a house.

5. A homesteader filed a claim by swearing that the land had been improved by putting a house on it.

6. The federal government helped build the transcontinental railroads by giving land on alternating sides of the railroad track and giving money for each mile of track, ranging from $16,000 for level land to $48,000 for mountainous terrain.

7. The Native American viewed the land and all of nature as gifts to be shared. Land belonged to the whole tribe, crops were for the good of all, and the land was to be treated with respect. Animals were hunted for food and skins. The settlers wanted to have sole ownership of the land they worked.

8. The federal government broke promises and treaties given to the Native Americans, deceived them about treaty terms, and changed the terms after treaties were signed. The government failed to provide the supplies and other help as promised.

CHAPTER 11 PAGES 202–219

A MODERN NATION EMERGES

THEME

Rapid changes occurred in the social structure of the United States between 1850 and 1910. A change from farming to industry as the primary way to make a living, the rise of big business, the labor union movement, increased federal control of business and labor, the influx of immigrants, and the population shift from rural to urban combined to make this a very different country in the course of this time period.

PROJECTS

1. Have pupils research what the community in which they live was like during the nineteenth century. Population growth by decades; listings of major businesses and industries; ethnic background of inhabitants are possible topics. The public library or local historical society are sources of information.

2. Divide the class into four groups and assign each a current events bulletin board. One group is to find articles and pictures on farming; another on business; a third on immigration; and the fourth on cities.

3. Have a group of pupils prepare a series of pantomime skits to be presented as this chapter is studied. Each skit is to have two scenes. The other pupils are to guess what is being shown. Possible topics are:

a. Nation of farms/Nation of industries

b. Farming by hand labor/Farming by machine

c. Life before the telephone/Life after the telephone

d. Life before the electric light/Life after the electric light

e. Rural population/Urban population

LESSON 1 PAGES 202–205

THE CONTINUING AGRICULTURAL REVOLUTION

GOALS

1. To explain the difference between subsistence and commercial farming. 2. To find specific information about a period of history from a time line. 3. To understand how organizations and political parties are formed to represent special interests.

TEACHING SUGGESTIONS

1. **Reading a Time Line.** Ask pupils the following questions based on the time line on p. 204.

a. *When was Standard Oil started?* (1867)

b. *Which was invented first—the telephone, the phonograph, or the typewriter?* (Typewriter)

c. *Which was formed first–the AFL or the CIO?* (AFL)

d. *In which year was Grover Cleveland elected to a second term?* (1892)

e. *When was Hull House started?* (1889)

● 2. **Building Vocabulary.** Before pupils read pp. 202–205, have them study the vocabulary words. Ask if anyone can define the words. Direct pupils to turn to the text to find the words that were not correctly defined and have volunteers read aloud the sentences where they appear and where they are defined.

For pupils who have difficulty, you may wish to write the vocabulary words on the board. You could then read the text material to these pupils and have them raise their hands as they hear the definition for each word.

You may wish to have those pupils who require a challenge use the vocabulary words in writing brief essays on Farming after the Civil War.

3. Drawing a Cartoon. Have pupils draw cartoons illustrating the following sentences from the text:

a. " 'Who is making all the money?' the farmers asked."

b. "They felt the government did not think their problems were very important."

c. "These changes seemed very revolutionary at the time."

Also see the Skills Development Activity on p. 219.

4. Discussion. After pupils have read pp. 202–205, have them consider the following questions:

a. *Why were so many people farmers in 1850?*

b. *What has made it possible for fewer farmers today to produce so much more?*

c. *How did the Grange help the farmers?*

d. *Are third parties like the Populists a good idea? Why, or why not?*

(Answers to all of these questions will vary.)

SUPPLEMENTARY INFORMATION

The Granger. The old Grange poster reproduced on p. 205 is now in the Library of Congress. It depicts the type of yeoman farmer that the Grange, and later the Populist party, was trying to help. The poster shows Grange activities and family life on a farm as well as the slogan "I pay for all," reflecting farmers' grievances.

Oliver Kelley, the founder of the organization, wisely provided that farm women as well as men were eligible to join the Grange. So, too, were young people of both sexes. In order to attract young members, Kelley said of the Grange: "In its proceed-

ings a love for rural life will be encouraged, the desire for excitement and amusement, so prevalent in youth, will be gratified." For old and young, the goals of the Grange were, in Kelley's words, "to advance education, to elevate and dignify the occupation of farmers, and to protect its members against the numerous combinations by which their interests are injuriously affected."

LESSON 2 PAGES 206–211

A REVOLUTION IN INDUSTRY

GOALS

1. To develop an outline on the growth of business and labor unions in the United States. **2.** To associate industrial giants with the industries they built. **3.** To explain how inventions have changed the way people live.

TEACHING SUGGESTIONS

1. Making an Outline. Have pupils read and outline the material on pp. 206–211. If reinforcement of outlining techniques is needed, pupils can review the Skills Development exercise on p. 29.

2. Reading a Table. After pupils have studied the table on p. 207, pose the following questions:

a. *Which inventions were important for farming?* (Cotton gin, cast iron and steel plow, barbed wire)

b. *Which were important inventions in communications?* (Morse code, linotype, vacuum tube, transistor, telephone)

c. *Transportation?* (Propeller, steamboat, air brakes, airplane, stoplight)

d. *Business?* (Typewriter, telephone, shorthand, adding machine, computer)

3. Creative Writing. Ask pupils to imagine what it would be like if the telephone or the electric bulb or the traffic light had not been invented. Have them write a description of a day in their lives without one of these inventions.

SUPPLEMENTARY INFORMATION

1. The Bessemer Process. The Bessemer process was invented in 1856 in England by Henry Bessemer. It involves blowing air through molten pig iron, thus burning out much of the carbon. Too much carbon makes iron too brittle for major industrial use. This cheap, efficient way to make steel was introduced in America by Alexander Holley, who combined Bessemer's ideas with those of William Kelley. The Bessemer process was also the basis for Andrew Carnegie's steel empire. The Bessemer process was most important during the 1880s. By 1900 it had been surpassed by the open-hearth method as the major steel-producing method.

2. Samuel Gompers (1850–1924). An English immigrant, Gompers was the first registered member of the Cigar-Maker's International Union when he joined at age fourteen. He made it into one of the most successful trade unions. As president of the AFL, he tried to make member unions rely on bargaining with management rather than appealing for government help or combining with political parties.

LESSON 3   PAGES 212–214

WELCOME TO OUR SHORES

GOALS

1. To understand why so many immigrants came to the United States. **2.** To know the countries of origin of large numbers of immigrants. **3.** To discuss the reasons for limiting immigration. **4.** To explain what a naturalized citizen is.

TEACHING SUGGESTIONS

1. Reading a Poem. Obtain a copy of "The New Colossus" by Emma Lazarus. Duplicate it and pass out copies to the class. Discuss it, line-by-line, with your pupils. Have pupils read "Why they came" on p. 212 and find lines in the poem that describe reasons given in the text.

2. Making a Bulletin Board. A world map and colored yarn are the materials needed. The pupils can run the yarn from the country from which they or their immigrant ancestors came to the section of the United States where they are living.

3. Research. Have pupils read "Changes in immigration" and "Closing the door" (pp. 213–214) and identify the major sources of immigrants from 1840 to 1920. Pupils can turn to encyclopedias and almanacs to find similar information for the period from 1920 to the present. Ask: *Why, do you think, has it been necessary to put limits on immigration?* Be sure pupils note the number of refugees who have found shelter in the United States. Ask: *What groups of people have found refuge in the United States in the last 50 years?* (German Jews, displaced persons after World War II, Hungarians, Vietnamese, boat people, Cubans, etc.)

4. Questions and Answers. Pose the following questions:
a. *What is the difference between an immigrant and an emigrant?* (Immigrant—person born in one country who comes to another to live; emigrant—one who leaves his or her native land)
b. *What are two ways one can become an American citizen?* (Native born—born in the United States or one of its territories; naturalized—taking an oath of allegiance to the United States after meeting certain requirements.)
c. *What is a ghetto?* (Ethnic neighborhood)
●**5. Writing a Letter.** Pupils can demonstrate writing skills by writing a letter to an

imaginary relative urging him or her to emigrate to the United States. They are to include reasons for leaving the old country as well as reasons for coming to the United States.

Pupils who have difficulties can tape their letters rather than write them. You may wish to extend the activity further by helping these pupils transcribe the taped material into formal letters.

Pupils who require more of a challenge can do some research into the lives of immigrants and write a series of letters based on their research.

SUPPLEMENTARY INFORMATION

1. Clearing Procedure on Ellis Island. An intelligence test was only one of the examinations that were administered to would-be immigrants before they were allowed entry into the United States.

Beginning in 1892, immigrants were assigned a number while they were still aboard the ship, before a barge or ferry carried them to Ellis Island. Inspectors called out numbers in German, Italian, Polish, Russian, Yiddish, and other languages. Once the immigrants were organized into small groups, the clearance procedure began. Doctors quickly evaluated the health of the immigrants. An "H" chalked on an immigrant's back referred to suspicion of heart disease; an "L" referred to a limp associated with rickets or other deficiency disease.

Two feared symbols were a circle with a cross in the middle, which referred to feeble-mindedness, and an "E," which referred to trachoma, a disease common among southern and eastern Europeans. Deportation was certain for any who wore these symbols.

The final ordeal was a series of questions from an immigration inspector. Those who survived the clearing process then changed their money into dollars at the currency booth. Those bound for places inland met a railroad agent or a ticket agent. Those planning to stay in New York might have met relatives, representatives from an immigrant aid society, or politicians looking for a vote.

2. Naturalization. The concept of naturalization of citizens developed during the 1800s. Until that time, people were considered to be citizens of the lands of their birth no matter where they lived. One of the causes of the War of 1812 was the British refusal to acknowledge the naturalization of British subjects in the United States. Not until 1870 did Great Britain recognize the right of a British person to become a citizen of another country.

Congress approved the first naturalization law in the United States in 1790; it set up certain courts to naturalize citizens. Only "free white persons" could be naturalized. Other groups eventually became eligible; for example, blacks in 1870 and Chinese in 1943. The Immigration and Nationality Act of 1952 did away with all racial bars to naturalization in the United States.

Today the naturalization procedure involves three steps. To file a petition for naturalization, a person must be 18, must have been a United States resident for five years, and must be of good moral character. The second step involves an investigation by and interview with officers of the Immigration and Naturalization Service. The prospective citizen must be able to read, write, and speak some English, have some knowledge of United States history and government, and provide two citizens who offer assurance of the qualifications of the person. The final hearing—the third step—is held in a public court. If approved for citizenship, the new citizen must denounce allegiance to foreign countries and pledge to defend and support the Constitution of the United States.

GROWTH OF THE CITIES

GOALS
1. To understand the shift within the United States from a rural population to an urban population. 2. To appreciate the problems caused by unplanned city growth. 3. To describe various methods of making city life more pleasant.

TEACHING SUGGESTIONS
1. **Reading Maps and Tables.** Pupils should study the maps on p. 215. Ask pupils to answer the question(s) found in the caption. Also ask: *How do the maps show some of the same information that is shown in the table?* (Growth of cities indicates a population shift.) Be sure pupils answer the questions in the text on p. 215, which deal with the table.

2. **Making Graphs.** Pupils can make a line graph based on the information given by the table. Distribute graph paper and give these directions:

a. *Write percentages by tens from 0 to 100 up the left margin.*
b. *Write the dates given across the bottom.*
c. *Plot the percentages from the information on the table. Use a solid line to connect the urban percentage points. A dotted line can be used for the rural information.*

Pupils who have difficulty in doing this work can work together and, with your help, create one large graph that can be used as a bulletin-board display.

Pupils who need a challenge can write a statement that summarizes what the graph says.

3. **Reading for Recall.** After pupils have read pp. 214–217, they should be able to answer these questions:

a. *What is a rural area?* (Countryside) *An urban area?* (City)

b. *What are the areas of small towns outside cities called?* (Suburbs)
c. *Where do most Americans live today?* (Urban areas)
d. *What is zoning?* (Dividing a city into parts)
e. *What problems resulted from rapid growth without planning?* (Crowding, poor housing, poor sanitation, pollution, few recreational areas, poor quality of life)
f. *What kinds of things were done to improve city life?* (Parks, laws improving housing, increased city services, settlement houses)

4. **Career Awareness.** Three occupations have been mentioned or implied in this lesson—landscape architect, social worker, and city planner. Have pupils gather information about these careers by considering these points:

a. Needed preparation
b. Kind of work involved
c. Average pay scale
d. Employment opportunities
e. Satisfaction derived

SUPPLEMENTARY INFORMATION
1. **Jane Addams.** Born into a comfortable Illinois family in 1860, Jane Addams was among the first generation of American women to attend college. After graduating from Rockford Seminary in 1881, she looked for a career where she could be of service to others. She found it on a trip to England in 1883, when she visited an English settlement house called Toynbee Hall. On her return to the United States, she and a college friend, Ellen Gates Starr, arranged for the purchase of the old Hull mansion, then in a poor neighborhood in Chicago. In 1889 Hull House opened its doors. Some 70 other settlement houses were to follow in American cities in the 1890s and early 1900s. Hull House remained, however, the most famous and the largest, growing to 13 buildings and a staff of 65 people.

Through her work in settlement houses, her writings, and her many reform activities, Jane Addams became known to millions. She shared the Nobel peace prize in 1931 for her work with women's peace organizations.

2. Skyscrapers. The first skyscrapers in the United States were built in Chicago and New York City. William Le Baron Jenney designed the first skyscraper in 1884. It was for the Home Insurance Company in Chicago. It was torn down in 1931. One of New York City's early skyscrapers was the Flatiron Building, which was twenty-one stories high and was erected in 1902. It is still standing. Iron girders provided the strong skeletons of the early buildings. Skyscrapers today have skeletons made of steel and concrete. Completed in 1931, the tallest skyscraper for many years was the Empire State Building in New York City (1,250 feet; 381 meters). During the 1970s, two taller buildings were completed—the Sears Tower in Chicago (1,454 feet; 443 meters) and the World Trade Center in New York City (1,350 feet; 411 meters).

11/CHAPTER REVIEW PAGE 218
Answers for Review Questions

1. Widespread use of farm machinery and the development of scientific farming were responsible for changes in agriculture after the Civil War.
2. Inventions improved industrial processes and created new industries.
3. Concerns about working conditions, workers' safety, child labor, etc. led workers to band together to seek improvements.
4. Before 1880 most immigrants came from northern and western Europe. After 1880 more came from southern and eastern Europe.
5. The 1920 census was the first to show a greater number of Americans living in urban rather than rural areas.

6. Zoning and city planning prevent a jumble of residential, commercial, and industrial development within a single area and provide patterns for orderly growth and use of city facilities.

4/UNIT REVIEW PAGE 220
Answers for Unit Review

1. Answers may vary. Most pupils, however, will probably answer that Lincoln was not interested in abolishing slavery in states where it already existed. He did not wish to see it extended to the territories.
2. Answers will vary.
3. Answers will vary.
4. Trappers, or mountain men, explored the West and made first contact with the Native Americans. Miners, ranchers, herders, and farmers developed the natural resources and created permanent settlements. Cattle and sheep have different grazing needs, but neither ranchers nor sheepherders wanted the open range restricted by the farmers' use of the land. Farmers fenced off their fields to protect their crops from roving livestock.
5. Answers will vary.
6. Commercial farming meant a financial investment in machinery and land. This often put farmers into debt from one harvest to the next. They were dependent on the railroads to ship their crops and were often charged high rates. The Grange, the Populist party, and legislation such as the Sherman Anti-Trust Act provided at least partial solutions.
7. Answers to this question about inventions will vary. The growth of big business led to a movement to form labor unions.
8. Answers will vary.
9. City planning and zoning laws made some difference in the pattern of city development after the 1890s.

UNIT 5

The United States in the Twentieth Century

UNIT 5

THE UNITED STATES IN THE TWENTIETH CENTURY

Dear Parent,

We are about to begin our final history unit in *The United States and Its Neighbors.* It is entitled, "The United States in the Twentieth Century," and covers the period in which the United States developed into a world power. Both foreign affairs, especially our involvement in two world wars, and domestic events are covered.

Perhaps members of your family helped make the history covered in this time period. By all means share stories of a personal nature from your family that relate to the information covered. Perhaps you remember where you were and what you were doing when you heard the tragic news of Kennedy's or King's assassination. Maybe you were involved in the Civil Rights movement. Might grandparents recall the attack on Pearl Harbor, the dropping of the atomic bomb, or even the Great Depression? Great grandparents might even have stories from World War I or the "Roaring Twenties." This personal contact with history is the best way imaginable to make this unit come alive for your child!

Thank you for being willing to share in the study of these important times. Perhaps your child will be able to share some aspects of your family's involvement with the class.

Sincerely,

THE UNITED STATES IN THE TWENTIETH CENTURY

BULLETIN-BOARD DISPLAY

Divide the class into eight groups. Assign each group a decade. One group would be responsible for 1900–1910; the next for 1911–20; and so on to 1980. Using picture history books such as those from Time-Life, magazines, vertical files, and other picture sources, pupils should collect the source material for drawings of events in United States history for their decade. The drawings—a composite from each group—should be displayed under the proper decade label.

GETTING STARTED

Ask pupils to study the figures pictured on p. 253. Ask these questions:
a. *Do you recognize any of these people?* (King, MacArthur)
b. *What do you know about them?*
c. *What does the person in the space suit represent?*
d. *What does the woman stand for?* (Pupils may be surprised to learn that women have been able to vote only during the last 60 years.)
e. *What do you think you will be studying in this unit?*

THE UNITED STATES BECOMES A WORLD LEADER

THEME

During the twentieth century the United States increased its involvement with the rest of the world. By gaining new territories and through participation in two world wars, the United States assumed a position of world leadership. This country has taken an active role in world affairs in a variety of ways.

PROJECTS

Debates are a useful way to present differing points of view. Many of the events discussed in this chapter were once debated by Americans. Assign two pupils to each of the topics listed below. Give them time to do the research to find arguments for and against the action. Have them present their findings to the class as each topic is discussed. The complexity of this task is greatly reduced by having pupils report on the pro and con side of the issue. Perhaps very advanced pupils could actually debate, but this would require extensive research.

a. Purchase of Alaska
b. Annexing Hawaii
c. Involvement in the Spanish-American War
d. Building the Panama Canal
e. Returning the Canal to Panamanian Control
f. Acquiring Overseas Territories
g. Involvement in World War I
h. Involvement in World War II
i. Joining the League of Nations
j. Use of the Atomic Bomb
k. Involvement in Vietnam
l. Boycott of 1980 Olympics in Moscow

EXPANDING BEYOND OUR SHORES

GOALS

1. To locate in time and place major overseas territorial acquisitions. 2. To explain reasons for United States' expansion into the Pacific. 3. To list the territory formed as a result of the Spanish-American War. 4. To explain the importance of building the Panama Canal. 5. To use a time line to see a cause and effect relationship between certain historical events.

TEACHING SUGGESTIONS

1. **Making a Map.** Distribute outline maps of the world after the class has read the text pages for this lesson. Have pupils locate the following places and label and key them according to directions.

a. RED—all new acquisitions between the Civil War and the Spanish-American War
b. BLUE—all acquisitions as a result of the Spanish-American War
c. GREEN—Panama Canal

2. **Discussion.** Point out that at this time in history the United States was part of a worldwide movement in which countries expanded beyond their borders. This policy was known as *imperialism*. Quite often the territory and people who were "expanded into" were not pleased and resisted. Ask pupils:

a. *How do you feel about this policy?*
b. *What if the imperialistic country honestly feels it will make life better for the people in the country it is going to control?*

c. *We think we in the United States have a wonderful system of government. Do we have a responsibility to share it with other countries?* This is a difficult concept to teach. It is possible to present imperialism in either a too positive or too negative fashion.

3. Reading for Recall. Pose the following questions after pupils have read the text:

a. *What were the causes of the Spanish-American War?* (Unrest in Cuba; U.S. feelings against Spanish rule in Cuba; destruction of the *Maine*)

b. *What territory did the United States gain as a result of the war?* (Puerto Rico, Philippines, Guam, Cuban protectorate)

c. *How did the Spanish-American War show the need for the Panama Canal?* (Necessity for navy to move quickly from ocean to ocean)

4. Reading a Time Line. Have pupils use the time line on p. 224 to answer the following questions:

a. *Could the Spanish-American War have been fought over the building of the Panama Canal?* (No)

b. *Did the Japanese attack on Pearl Harbor lead to United States entry into World War II?* (Yes)

c. *Could Hitler's becoming Germany's leader have been a cause of World War II?* (Yes)

d. *Was the Korean War a result of the cold war?* (Yes)

5. Recognizing Propaganda. Using the Spanish-American War as an example, point out the effect of propaganda on public opinion. The sinking of the *Maine* (see Supplementary Information) was used to inflame a public already outraged by atrocity stories that had been appearing in the Hearst and Pulitzer tabloids.

SUPPLEMENTARY INFORMATION

1. Great White Fleet. The picture on p. 223 is of the Great White Fleet entering Golden Gate in San Francisco Bay. The painting by Henry Reuterdahl is in the United States Naval Academy Museum collection.

The Great White Fleet was an idea of Theodore Roosevelt's. It was part of his "big stick" diplomacy. Thanks to his efforts, the United States was the second naval power in the world. Great Britain was the first. The Japanese were developing as the Asian power and were beginning to compete with the United States' influence in the Pacific. Roosevelt feared Japan's intentions toward the Philippines. He decided that a show of American power was not amiss. So in 1907 he sent sixteen new battleships, painted white, on an around-the-world cruise. The commander of the fleet stated that he was ready for "a feast, a frolic, or a fight." The fleet returned to the United States early in 1909—shortly before the end of Roosevelt's second term. Roosevelt felt that the rest of the world had been shown that the United States was now a great power.

2. "Remember the *Maine*." The sinking of the battleship *Maine* became a major cause of the Spanish-American War. Americans held the Spanish responsible for mining the Havana Harbor and went to war with Spain within two months after the tragic incident.

Initial reports by a Naval Court of Inquiry in 1898 supported the claim of Spanish responsibility. Spanish divers who also checked the wreckage in 1898 insisted, however, that an explosion inside the ship was the source of the tragedy.

In 1911 a third inquiry was held. This time the investigation took place in the open, as the water was removed from the *Maine* and it was salvaged. Copious notes, measurements, and photographs were taken. At the time, this investigation supported the original Naval Court of Inquiry report. However, the material from this inquiry has recently been studied again by the Taylor Naval Ship Research and Development Center and the Naval Surface Weapons Center. They still do not claim to know what caused the explosion that sank the *Maine*. Probably no one ever will. But as they examined the photographs showing the position of the hull sides and deck after the explosion, one thing was obvious—the explosion had come from the *inside!* The Spanish could not have been responsible for such an explosion.

Historians have long agreed that Spain could have gained very little by intentionally exploding a United States ship and have sought other solutions. Perhaps it was an accident. One popular theory blames Cuban rebels who were anxious to get the United States involved in their cause. The mystery only deepens now that the location of the explosion has been pinpointed.

3. Aguinaldo. The leader of the Filipinos in their bid for independence was Emilio Aguinaldo (1869–1964). He was involved in the Philippine independence movement while the islands still belonged to Spain. In 1898 he went into voluntary exile after accepting a financial settlement from the Spanish governor and getting his promise that liberal reforms would be made. He returned to the Philippines to aid the Americans in the war with Spain. Aguinaldo and other Filipinos fought with the understanding that the Philippines, like Cuba, would be granted independence at the war's end. The United States Senate refused, by a very narrow margin, to pass a resolution to this effect. The Filipinos were very embittered, and after the power of Spain had been broken, Aguinaldo broke with his American allies. The independence movement adopted a flag, organized an army, installed Aguinaldo as president, assembled a congress, and declared the existence of the Republic of the Philippines. Thus began the Philippine-American War. It was a particularly horrible, savage war with hideous barbarities practiced by both sides. The rebellion came to an end with the capture of Aguinaldo. He took an oath of allegiance to the United States, received a pension, and retired to private life. In 1935, he was defeated when he ran for president of the Commonwealth of the Philippines. The Japanese used Aguinaldo to make anti-American speeches after their successful invasion of the islands in 1941. After the Americans returned, he spent some time in prison for collaboration with the enemy. He was made a member of the council of state of the independent Philippines in 1950. The last years of his life were spent in fostering a growing spirit of nationalism and democracy in the Philippines and trying to find new ways of improving relations between his country and the United States. Aguinaldo published a book, *A Second Look at America*, in 1957.

LESSON 2   PAGES 228–234

THE WORLD WARS

GOALS

1. To appreciate the similarities and differences between World War I and World War II. **2.** To understand the difference in the attitude of the United States toward involvement in the League of Nations as opposed to the United Nations.

TEACHING SUGGESTIONS

● **1. Reading for Thinking.** Write the following questions on the chalkboard:

a. *Could World War I have been prevented? How?*

b. *In what sense did World War I cause World War II?*

c. *Why was the League of Nations unable to prevent World War II?*

d. *Why were Japanese Americans imprisoned during World War II? Should they have been?*

e. *Do you agree with President Truman's decision to drop the atomic bomb?*

Have pupils read pp. 228–234 to get the background necessary to answer these questions. These questions can be answered orally, or you may wish to have them answered as written work. In either case, answers will vary.

For pupils who have reading difficulties, you may wish to try the buddy system, pairing a poor reader with a good one.

Pupils who require a challenge could prepare outlines of the text material, which they can share with less-able readers to help them find the answers to the discussion questions.

2. Reading a Chart. Have pupils use the chart "Combat Casualties of World War I" and the text to answer these questions.

a. *Which country lost the most soldiers in World War I?* (Germany) *Why might that be?* (Answers will vary.)

b. *Which country lost the fewest soldiers?* (United States) *Why?* (Answers will vary.)

c. *To the nearest 100,000, how many total combat casualties did the Central Powers suffer?* (3,500,000) *The Allies?* (4,100,000)

d. *What is the total number of combat deaths in World War I?* (7,609,000)

e. *One historian has placed the total deaths related to World War I at 14 million. How could the difference between that figure and the total on the chart be explained?* (Chart only shows military casualties. Many civilians also died because of the war.)

3. Making Comparisons. Have pupils divide sheets of paper into two columns. One column should be labeled World War I; the other World War II. Tell them to fill in the following categories for each war: Year Started, Year U.S. Entered, President, Year Ended, Major Cause(s), Major Results, Role of Women. The textbook will provide the information needed.

4. Discussion. Ask: *Do you think the United States became a member of the United Nations after World War II because we did not join the League of Nations after World War I?*

You may wish to introduce this discussion by having a current events session dealing with UN activities.

5. Creative Writing. Ask pupils to study the picture on p. 229 noting what the conditions are, what they think might have just happened, and what the future might be for the people in the picture. Their thoughts about this picture should be the basis of a descriptive paragraph. Rules of grammar, spelling, punctuation, and proper paragraph formation should be observed.

SUPPLEMENTARY INFORMATION

WASPs. During World War II over 1,000 brave women served their nation in a very exciting way. These women were members of the Women's Airforce Service Pilots—WASPs for short. It was their job to fly warplanes to where they were needed. Women were not permitted to be combat pilots, but they could do this job and free men for combat duty. From 1942–1944 they did just that.

Twenty-five thousand women applied for the jobs. Nearly 2,000 were trained and over 1,000 actually became WASPs. The obstacles were overwhelming. They were resented by males who often refused to fly with them. In one case it is suspected that male sabotage of a plane caused the death of a WASP. Men simply could not get used to female pilots. The women were never allowed to join the armed forces. They received no military benefits, pensions, or funerals (38 WASPs died while on duty). Finally, Congress ordered them to cease functioning. The prejudice was too great!

Yet, the women performed skillfully and admirably. They flew over 60 million miles

(95 million km) in all types of planes. One of the first jet pilots was a WASP. WASPs tested new planes that one group of male pilots did not dare fly. Their bravery and performance under pressure left no doubts about their ability.

Long after their duty ceased, WASPs have finally received some of the recognition due to them. In 1977 President Carter signed a law giving them the same benefits as other veterans. The exploits of these unrecognized heroines are finally being told.

LESSON 3 PAGES 234–237

THE COLD WAR

GOALS
1. To explain the term "cold war." 2. To divide European countries into NATO and Warsaw Pact members and neutrals. 3. To describe how the cold war became "hot" in Asia. 4. To appreciate the peacemaking role of the United States.

TEACHING SUGGESTIONS
1. **Reading a Map.** Distribute duplicated copies of the following True-False questions. The questions are based on the map on p. 235 and the text on pp. 235–236.
a. *The countries to the east of the Iron Curtain are Warsaw Pact countries.* (T)
b. *Switzerland is a member of NATO.* (F)
c. *All the countries shown on this map are either NATO or Warsaw Pact members.* (F)
d. *Turkey is southeast of most Warsaw Pact countries.* (T)
e. *All NATO member countries are shown on this map.* (F)
f. *Yugoslavia could be described as being "behind the Iron Curtain."* (T)
g. *West Germany belongs to NATO and East Germany is one of the Warsaw Pact nations.* (T)
h. *The largest Warsaw Pact nation is Poland.* (F)

i. *Norway, Sweden, and Finland are all members of NATO.* (F)
j. *Most Warsaw Pact and NATO nations are part of the continent of Europe.* (T)
● **2. Writing an Editorial.** Have each pupil bring a newspaper editorial to class. Help pupils understand that an editorial can be an expression of opinion. It can also be an attempt to educate or provide background for an ongoing news story. Ask pupils to write editorials on the cold war.

For pupils who have difficulty grasping the concept, you can use the visual aid of a world map, color-coding Communist countries red; democracies red, white, and blue; neutral nations gray; and perhaps using a symbol to denote past, and present, and possible future trouble or "hot" spots.

Pupils who require a challenge could be asked to keep a scrapbook of newspaper articles that deal with the cold war. At the end of one week they are to write a summary of the articles.

3. Outlining. Pupils should make an outline of Lesson 3 by filling in information under the proper heading.
  I. The Cold War
 II. Hot War
III. U.S. Activities in the World.
See p. 29 for the correct form for outlining.
4. Discussion. Pose the following questions:
a. *Why have the United States and the Soviet Union fought a cold war since World War II?*
b. *How has the Peace Corps helped relationships between the United States and other countries of the world?*
c. *Should the United States send American soldiers to stop the spread of Communism in other countries?*
(Answers to all these questions will vary.)

SUPPLEMENTARY INFORMATION
President Nixon's China Trip. In 1972 President Nixon visited China for 7 days. The United States had recognized the exis-

tence of only one China since 1948 and that was the non-Communist government on the island of Formosa. For most of his political career, Nixon had been adamant in his stand against the recognition of the Communist Chinese government. This trip was historic because it marked a dramatic reversal for this former "cold warrior." In several speeches Nixon emphasized that there were reasons and opportunities for cooperation between the two countries even if we were ideologically opposed. As part of a ceremonial exchange of gifts, the Chinese gave the United States a pair of giant pandas. They are now in the National Zoo in Washington, D.C. This trip was the highlight of Nixon's administration. It stimulated a new interest in Chinese goods and culture. Chinese isolation behind the "bamboo curtain" had lasted for 25 years.

12/CHAPTER REVIEW   PAGE 238
Answers for Review Questions

1. Two reasons for United States expansion into the Pacific Ocean were naval bases and missionary zeal.

2. Cuba and the Philippines were Spanish colonies.

3. President Wilson thought a League of Nations would give nations a place to talk over their differences rather than fight.

4. The United Nations is a group of world nations that was formed with the idea of working together for peace and human rights. NATO is an alliance of the United States and several non-Communist European countries. The Peace Corps was formed to bring specialized knowledge to other nations.

5. The cold war became "hot" in Korea and Vietnam.

CHAPTER 13   PAGES 240–251

A TIME OF RAPID CHANGE

THEME

A country is as strong as its people. This chapter focuses on the people who have helped make the United States the nation it is in the twentieth century.

PROJECTS

1. Pupils can make scrapbooks of newspaper articles and pictures that describe life in the past, present, and future. The scrapbooks should be divided into three sections: Past, Present, and Future. Encourage pupils to add their own ideas and drawings as well.

2. Have pupils help you make a list of freedoms enjoyed by Americans. The list should include those freedoms guaranteed by the Bill of Rights such as freedom of speech, religion, assembly, and press; the right to petition; the right to trial by jury; the right to be faced by one's accusor; the right to vote; and so on. You may wish to have pupils review the constitutional amendments, which appear in summary on p. 123. Pupils could then prepare a mural or bulletin-board display showing these freedoms and rights.

LESSON 1 PAGES 240–247

THE UNITED STATES SINCE 1900

GOALS
1. To spell, pronounce, and define the vocabulary words and to be able to explain their use in the context of this lesson. **2.** To understand the importance of the domestic reforms in Theodore Roosevelt's administration. **3.** To name at least four new ideas and discoveries that changed the United States in this century. **4.** To explain the causes of the Depression and how Franklin Roosevelt used the power of the government to try to control it. **5.** To list a number of ways in which the 1980s will continue to be a time of change.

TEACHING SUGGESTIONS
1. Reading a Time Line. Pose the following questions based on the time line on p. 242.
a. *Could Theodore Roosevelt have ridden to his inauguration in a Model T?* (No)
b. *Could women have voted for Franklin Roosevelt?* (Yes)
c. *Who was President when a human being first walked on the moon?* (Nixon)
d. *In what year was Martin Luther King, Jr., assassinated?* (1968)
e. *In what year did a President of the United States resign?* (1974)
2. Making a Time Line. Assign each pupil a twentieth-century American. Be sure there is biographical information available in an encyclopedia. Include all the Presidents since 1900. People such as Martin Luther King, Jr., Eleanor Roosevelt, Wilbur Wright, Orville Wright, Henry Ford, Shirley Temple Black, Douglas MacArthur, Upton Sinclair, Connie Mack, Charles Lindbergh, Amelia Earhart, Walt Disney, W.E.B. Du Bois are also possible subjects. Pupils are to place the events in their subject's life on a time line: birth on the left side and death or most recent information on the right.

The time lines are to be neat, attractive, and if you intend to display them, large enough to be read at a small distance. You may also wish to have each pupil give a very brief oral report on his or her subject.
● **3. Vocabulary Quiz.** Use the vocabulary list on p. 240 for a quick quiz. Pupils can exchange papers to correct them.

For pupils who have difficulties, you may wish to make flash cards and work on word recognition and pronunciation.

Pupils who require a challenge can use each word in a sentence, as well as spelling it correctly.
4. Reading for Recall. After pupils have read "Theodore Roosevelt" and "Roosevelt and reform" on pp. 240 and 242, ask:
a. *What did Roosevelt do in the Spanish-American War?* (Colonel in Rough Riders)
b. *How did he become President?* (Upon death of President McKinley)
c. *Who were the muckrakers?* (People who wrote about wrongdoings)
d. *What is conservation?* (Saving important resources)
5. Creative Writing. Pupils are to pick one new invention, discovery, or product developed in this century and write an advertisement for it. You may wish to display a number of newspaper and magazine ads for inspiration.
6. Discussion. Ask: *Would you enjoy life as much without radio, TV, automobiles, or airplanes? What advantages would there by without these things? Disadvantages?* (Answers will vary. If pupils do not mention such things as air and noise pollution, depletion of resources, you may wish to make them aware of them.)
7. Reading for Information. Write these words and phrases on the chalkboard: *depression, bank closings, Dust Bowl, fireside chats, New Deal.* Pupils are to find sentences on pp. 244–246 that describe or define the items listed on the board.

(Depression—"In the 1930s it was because too many people were spending more money than they had.")

(Bank closings—"Soon many banks had to close because they had no money," or "Over 4,000 banks closed between 1929 and 1932.")

(Dust Bowl—"Poor farming methods and dry weather turned much of the farmland in the Great Plains to dust.")

(Fireside chats—"Often during his time in office, Roosevelt explained his programs and tried to make people feel better through a series of fireside chats!")

(New Deal—"He caused the government to create jobs and grant other types of aid to people.")

Ask these questions:

a. *What were some of the New Deal programs?* (Forestry projects; building dams, parks, sewers, schools, airports, roads, and public buildings; aid to farmers; grants to artists and writers. Make pupils aware of any WPA or CCC projects that were developed near your community.)

b. *What one thing made FDR different from all the Presidents who came before him and all who followed and will follow him?* (Four terms)

8. Reading for Thinking. After pupils have read "The post-war nation" and "A decade of change" on pp. 246–247, ask: *What in your opinion is the biggest problem facing the United States today? Why, do you think, is this problem greater than any other?* (Allow full and free expressions of opinion.) Now ask pupils to think about what can be done to solve the problems they have mentioned.

9. Reading a Map. After pupils have studied the map on p. 247 ask:

a. *What is the map about?* (Change in number of representatives each state has in the House)

b. *Upon what is the change based?* (Census; population shifts)

c. *How can you tell from this map that the* southern and western parts of the United States are growing in population? (More representatives)

SUPPLEMENTARY INFORMATION

Eleanor Roosevelt. Eleanor was much more than the President's wife. She changed the whole idea of what a "first lady" ought to be. Shy and retiring in her early life, she blossomed into an outstanding leader in her own right.

Eleanor, as most Americans called her, first emerged as Roosevelt's eyes, ears, and legs after his polio attack. Franklin found travel difficult, but Eleanor went everywhere. During the Depression and World War II, she traveled all over, assuring people that the government really cared about them. She even visited the troops in the Pacific. She became friends with Mary McLeod Bethune and other black leaders. These friendships resulted in jobs and other forms of help for black Americans who had been suffering from the effects of the Depression.

In addition to fighting for equal rights, Eleanor was a noted author. She wrote a newspaper column and four books.

FDR's death did not stop Eleanor. She served as an early delegate to the United Nations General Assembly. She helped write the "Universal Declaration of Human Rights." Her good works continued right up to her death in 1962.

LESSON 2   PAGES 247–249

THE STRUGGLE FOR HUMAN RIGHTS

GOALS

1. To define human rights. **2.** To name some of the important events in the struggle for human rights. **3.** To describe the work of Martin Luther King, Jr. **4.** To tell how the struggle for human rights applies to many people.

TEACHING SUGGESTIONS

1. Telling a Story. You may wish to tell your class about an experiment made by an elementary school teacher in the Midwest. She had a class with pupils who got along well with each other. One day she told them that from then on all blue-eyed children in the class were special. They would not be allowed to do what the other children could do. They would not be allowed to play at recess; they would have to walk at the end of the line when the class went to lunch, and so on. The other children could in time make up more rules that applied just to the blue-eyed children. This went on for several days and the children who had been good friends were becoming more and more unfriendly toward each other. Suddenly the teacher changed the rules and the brown-eyed children became the special ones. The same things happened. There were fights and tears and unhappiness. It took some time for the children in the class to return to their old friendly ways after the experiment was over. Ask: *What is this story about?* Instead of telling the story, you may wish to show the film *Eye to Eye*, which is about this experiment. The tone may be a little too mature for your pupils, but the actions and interactions of the children in the film will be easily understood.

2. Identifying People and Events. Ask pupils to write sentences identifying the following: 1954 Supreme Court decision, Martin Luther King, Jr.'s "dream," Rosa Parks, sit-ins, Robert C. Weaver, Thurgood Marshall.

3. Outlining. For homework, have pupils outline the section "Equality for all," which starts at the bottom of p. 248. Review the outlines in class and use the opportunity to discuss how certain groups of people must struggle for their rights.

4. Current Events. Ask pupils to bring to class newspaper or magazine articles about the struggle for human rights. They need

not limit themselves to the United States. This a worldwide struggle.

13/CHAPTER REVIEW PAGE 250
Answers for Review Questions

1. A national forest system was started to set aside or conserve western forestland.

2. The muckrakers were a group of people who wrote about wrongdoings in business and politics. They influenced President Theodore Roosevelt.

3. On an assembly line, each worker does one small part of the job as the product rolls past.

4. The Model T was popular because it was a simple and inexpensive car.

5. New Deal policies provided government-sponsored jobs and aid for those who had no work.

6. Dr. King organized the bus boycott, sit-ins, marches, and other challenges to what many felt were unjust laws.

5/UNIT REVIEW PAGE 252
Answers for Unit Review

1. Alaska—purchase; Midway, Samoa—treaty; Hawaii—annexation; Guam, Puerto Rico, Philippines—war. The Philippines are an independent republic today.

2. The answers to the first part of this question will vary. Pupils may have several answers to why the United States entered World War I—the most popular will probably be submarine warfare. The Japanese attack on Pearl Harbor was the reason the United States entered World War II.

3. Answers will vary.

4. Answers will vary. Possibilities are the United Nations, Marshall Plan, NATO, Korea, Vietnam, and Peace Corps.

5. Answer will vary.

6. Answers will vary. The basic idea is that Roosevelt felt this was a legitimate government function.

7. Answers will vary.

8. Answers will vary.

9. Answers will vary.

UNIT 6

The United States: A Land of Great Variety

THE UNITED STATES: A LAND OF GREAT VARIETY

Dear Parent,

Your child is about to start a unit of study on the geographic regions of the United States. The unit will begin with an overview of the nation as a whole, including landforms and resources and the reasons we have daylight and darkness and seasons. Following this overview, your child will study in more depth each of the seven regions: New England, the Middle Atlantic states, the Southeast, the South Central states, the North Central states, the Mountain West, and the Pacific states.

Your child will be learning about the landforms, climate, agriculture, resources, industry, population, and cities in each region. You could help your child by pointing out pictures and magazine and newspaper articles dealing with the various regions. If you have a road atlas or road maps, you might want to look on the map with your child for places of interest. Perhaps you could include your child in planning the route for any weekend or holiday trips you may take. If you have visited any national parks, your child might be permitted to bring to class souvenirs or photographs from your visit. A trip to the local library might produce some heavily illustrated books or magazines on the various regions.

If your family is new to our region, perhaps you could come to class and tell us about the region from which you have come. Anything you can do to help your child understand and enjoy our beautiful nation will be greatly appreciated.

Sincerely,

UNIT 6   PAGES 253–420

THE UNITED STATES: A LAND OF GREAT VARIETY

BULLETIN-BOARD DISPLAYS

1. Display on the bulletin board a large outline map of the United States showing state boundaries. Divide the class into seven groups and assign each group one of the seven regions in this unit. As each region is studied, have the group outline the region, label the states, and fill in the major cities, physical features, natural resources, and climate data for the region. Ask the class to develop standard symbols and a map key as they work on the display.

2. Ask pupils to collect pictures from magazines and travel agencies that illustrate the seven regions of the United States. Display the pictures with labels on the bulletin board.

GETTING STARTED

1. Have pupils imagine first that they live in a desert region and then in an Arctic region. Ask them to describe how their day-to-day lives would change in each region. Guide pupils to the conclusion that environment influences how people live. Discuss ways people have adapted to their environment and in some cases altered it.

Ask pupils how the area of the United States in which they live affects (a) the ways they dress, (b) their recreational activities, (c) the foods they eat, (d) their parents' jobs, and (e) the number of people living in their area.

2. Have pupils turn to the unit opening art on p. 253. Ask the following questions:

a. *If you were a dairy worker, how would geography affect the location of your job?*

b. *Why is an understanding of environment an important part of a park ranger's job?*

c. *How are factory workers' jobs affected by the geography?* (Example: Most cotton mills are located in the Southeast.)

d. *Why is a dockworker's place of residence dictated by his or her job?*

GEOGRAPHY OF THE UNITED STATES

THEME

The United States contains a rich variety of landforms, climate regions, and natural resources.

PROJECTS

1. Assign individual or group reports on the following topics about your state:
a. major landforms
b. major bodies of water
c. climate
d. forests
e. soils and farming
f. fuels, minerals, and metals
g. industries

2. The weather page in most newspapers will indicate the daily time for sunrise and sunset. Have pupils check this page for about a month. Have them draw a large graph (bulletin-board size) based on this information. A line graph would provide the best visual presentation of this material. Use the vertical axis to indicate time. Divide the horizontal axis into the number of days in the month for which you will be preparing the graph. Use two colors, one for each dot indicating sunrise and another for each dot indicating sunset. As the month passes, the class will see that the amount of daylight time between sunrise and sunset will steadily decrease if done prior to December 22 or increase if done after December 22.

LESSON 1   PAGES 254–260

TOOLS OF GEOGRAPHY

GOALS

1. To define the study of geography. 2. To know why and how the United States can be divided into regions. 3. To identify the major features of a political map. 4. To use a map key to identify the meaning of map symbols. 5. To read and compare geographical information on graphs, tables, and maps. 6. To understand the concept of population density. 7. To use the tools of geography to learn about people.

TEACHING SUGGESTIONS

1. **Reviewing.** You may wish to review Chapter 1, Reading Maps, with your class before teaching the concepts in this chapter. You may also wish to ask pupils to list and discuss some of the geographic features they learned about in earlier chapters. Some examples follow:
a. Chapter 2: Rivers as areas of settlement and as a source of water power.
b. Chapter 3: Vegetation, i.e., pine forests, as an economic base for the colony of North Carolina.
c. Chapter 5: Soil as a factor in determining farm size and crops.
d. Chapter 7: Rivers as transportation routes.
e. Chapters 7–8: Mountains as barriers.
f. Chapters 8 and 11: Mineral wealth as a factor in influencing settlement and industrial growth.

2. **Reading a Map.** Have pupils turn to the map on p. 255. Ask them to name the states in the New England, North Central, Mountain West, Pacific, South Central, Southeast, and Middle Atlantic regions.

Or distribute outline maps of the United States. Have pupils label and color each of the seven regions of the United States. Ask them to make a map key for the colors.

3. **Using Maps and Tables.** Using the table on p. 257, have pupils group states according to size. For example, they may divide the table according to states with areas of
a. 10,000 square miles (25,900 sq km) or less
b. 10,000–50,000 square miles (25,900–129,500 sq km)
c. 50,000–100,000 square miles (129,500–259,000 sq km)
d. 100,000–250,000 square miles (259,000–647,500 sq km)
e. 250,000 square miles or more (647,500 sq km or more)
Next, have them color code a key based on the above groups, and color states accordingly on an outline map of the United States.

●4. **Making a Graph.** Using an appropriate source book, have pupils research the population of the ten largest cities in your state. Distribute graph paper and ask pupils to present the information in bar graph form.

For pupils who have difficulty grasping the concept of reading graphs, you may wish to try the following activity. Have pupils turn to the graph on p. 258. Ask them to estimate the area of each state on the graph in thousands of square miles and/or thousands of square kilometers. Have them check their estimates against the figures on the table on p. 257. Then distribute graph paper and help pupils set up and label the grid in square miles or square kilometers. Ask them to make a bar graph showing the areas of Arizona, Idaho, Mississippi, Vermont, and Washington.

Pupils who require a challenge might do the following:
a. Add up the total population or area for each of the United States regions.

b. Calculate the percentage of the whole of the United States population or area represented by each region.
c. Show these regional percentages on a pie chart.
5. **Population Density.** Draw two squares, both the same size on the chalkboard. Place five dots in the center of the first square and 25 dots in the center of the second square. Ask pupils to tell which of the squares is more crowded by the dots. Next write Wyoming under the first square and Oregon under the second square. Have pupils turn to the table on p. 257 to see that the land areas of Wyoming and Oregon are about the same. Ask pupils if they can figure out why you placed five dots in the square that stands for Wyoming and 25 dots in the square that stands for Oregon. (Note on the chart that the population of Oregon is about five times the population of Wyoming.) Ask which state is more crowded. Then have pupils read "Using the tools of geography to learn about people" on pp. 259–260.

LESSON 2   PAGES 261–267

LANDFORMS OF THE UNITED STATES

GOALS
1. To identify the major features of a relief map. **2.** To define the following geographic terms: *plain, plateau, mountain, island, peninsula, source, delta, river mouth, channel.* **3.** To name and locate on a map the major land features and the twelve largest river systems of the United States and the Great Lakes. **4.** To read a cross-section map. **5.** To appreciate the importance of water.

TEACHING SUGGESTIONS
1. Reading for Information. Use the following questions after pupils have read pp. 261–264:

a. *What kind of map shows landforms?* (Relief or physical map)

b. *How would you describe a plain?* (A wide area of flat or gently rolling land)

c. *Where are the largest plains in the United States located?* (In the middle of the nation)

d. *What are the north-south boundaries of the Great Plains in the United States?* (Canadian border to Mexican border)

e. *What is a coastal plain?* (A plain bordered by a large body of water)

f. *Name the two large coastal plains in the United States.* (Atlantic and Gulf Coastal plains)

g. *How would you describe a plateau?* (A large, high area of level land)

h. *What large plateau is located in the Mountain West region?* (Colorado Plateau)

i. *What are mountains?* (High, steep lands that have a broad base and a narrow peak at the top)

j. *What do we call a group of mountains?* (A chain or range)

k. *Where are the highest mountains in the United States?* (Alaska)

l. *What is the highest point in those mountains?* (Mount McKinley)

m. *How high is Mount McKinley?* (20,320 feet, or 6,190 m)

n. *What do we call the longest mountain chain in the United States?* (The Rocky Mountains)

o. *Describe an island.* (A body of land completely surrounded by water)

p. *Describe a peninsula.* (A piece of land almost surrounded by water)

q. *Which state is made up of islands?* (Hawaii)

● **2. Using a Map.** Have pupils turn to the map on p. 263. Ask:

a. *What is the name of the largest eastern United States mountain chain?* (Appalachian Mountains)

b. *Name the states in the Great Plains region.* (Texas, Oklahoma, Kansas, Nebraska, South Dakota, North Dakota and Wyoming)

c. *The Atlantic Coastal Plain is bordered by what body of water?* (Atlantic Ocean)

d. *The Gulf Coastal Plain is bordered by what body of water?* (Gulf of Mexico)

e. *Which mountain range takes up the largest area of the United States?* (Rocky Mountains)

f. *Which states have elevations of 10,000 feet (3,048 m) and above?* (Alaska, Hawaii, New Mexico, Colorado, Wyoming, Montana, Idaho, Utah, Arizona, Nevada, California, Washington and Oregon)

g. *How many states do not have elevations below 1,000 feet (300 m)?* (Nine) *Name those states.* (Montana, North Dakota, South Dakota, Nebraska, Idaho, Wyoming, Colorado, New Mexico, and Kansas)

h. *Is Mount McKinley in northern or southern Alaska?* (Southern)

Pupils who have difficulty grasping the concept of elevation may want to label the major landform features of the United States on an outline map, using the map on p. 263 as a guide.

You may want to have pupils who require a challenge turn to the relief maps in the Atlas, pp. 466–476. Ask them to locate and name some of the world's major plains, plateaus, mountains, peninsulas, and islands.

3. Using a Cross Section. Have pupils lay a straight edge on the map on p. 263 so that it connects the northwest corner of North Dakota, where North Dakota, Montana, and Canada join, and the southeast tip of Texas, where Texas and Mexico border on the Gulf of Mexico. Tell them that they are going to take a trip across the United States following that line or route. To show them how a profile along this line would be different from the one shown on p. 263, ask them the following questions:

a. *Through which states does the line cross?* (North Dakota, South Dakota, Nebraska, Kansas, Oklahoma, Texas)

b. *Moving from north to south, what is the name of the first body of water you cross?*

(Missouri River) *In what state will you cross it?* (North Dakota)

c. *What is the second body of water you cross?* (Red River) *In what state will you cross it?* (Between Oklahoma and Texas)

d. *What landform do you cross between the Missouri and Red rivers?* (Great Plains)

e. *What other plain do you cross south of the Red River?* (Gulf Coastal Plain)

f. *What is the elevation of the land on the northern half of the route?* (2,000–5,000 feet, or 600–1,500 m)

g. *What is the elevation of the land as you cross the Red River?* (1,000–2,000 feet, or 300–600 m)

h. *What is the elevation of the land along the Gulf Coastal Plain?* (0–1,000 feet, or 0–300 m)

Distribute graph paper and ask pupils to make a cross section of the route from North Dakota to Texas, using the diagram on p. 263 as a guide.

4. Place Geography. Have pupils turn to the map on p. 265. Have them locate these twelve major rivers: Mississippi, Missouri, Yukon, St. Lawrence, Rio Grande, Arkansas, Colorado, Brazos, Columbia, Red, Snake, and Ohio. For each river ask the following questions:

a. *What is the source of the river?*

b. *Into what larger body of water does the river mouth drain?*

c. *Through what states does the river flow?*

5. Creative Writing. Have each pupil write several descriptive paragraphs on how he or she would spend a day on a river, lake, or ocean. At least one paragraph should describe the body of water selected.

LESSON 3   PAGES 268–274

THE EARTH AND THE SUN

GOALS

1. To define weather and climate. **2.** To read maps and graphs that show precipita-

tion and temperature in the United States. **3.** To understand the rotation of the earth and its effect on night and day. **4.** To understand the earth's revolution and its relationship to climate and seasons.

TEACHING SUGGESTIONS

● **1. Drawing a Climate Graph.** Obtain climatological data for your community or a community near you from a local weather station, newspaper, or nearby airport. Have pupils draw graphs showing monthly precipitation or monthly and average annual temperatures. Encourage them to use the graphs on pp. 268 and 271 as guides.

You may work in small groups with pupils who have difficulty grasping the concept of graphing precipitation. Guide them to set up the vertical and horizontal axes on graph paper, and teach them how to determine the precipitation and/or temperature intervals on the vertical axis. Then have them draw a line graph for temperature and a bar graph for precipitation.

You may wish to have pupils who require a challenge research and prepare oral reports on careers in climatology and meteorology. Pupils may choose to write to the National Weather Service, Washington National Airport, Arlington, Va. 22202, for information. If so, have them write a group letter, rather than several individual letters.

2. Calculating Averages. To help pupils understand how the figures for average annual precipitation and average monthly temperature are calculated, have them find the averages for the following examples:

a. Ask pupils to find out how many children there are in each class in grades five and six. Have them add the numbers of children in each class together, and divide the sum by the number of classes. Explain that the final answer shows the average class size for grades five and six.

b. Have pupils record the daily temperature for one school week. At the end of the week, ask them to add all the temperature figures together, and divide the sum by five (total number of days temperature recorded). Explain to the pupils that their answer shows the average daily temperature for the week.

c. The following monthly precipitation amounts were recorded in New Orleans, Louisiana. Write the amounts on the chalkboard. Ask the pupils to add the amounts together and divide by twelve to find the average monthly precipitation for New Orleans. (6.41 inches, or 16.3 cm)

January	13.63 inches	(34.6 cm)
February	2.53 inches	(6.4 cm)
March	2.67 inches	(6.8 cm)
April	3.44 inches	(8.7 cm)
May	9.72 inches	(24.7 cm)
June	7.82 inches	(19.9 cm)
July	10.34 inches	(26.3 cm)
August	14.68 inches	(37.3 cm)
September	2.98 inches	(7.6 cm)
October	0.00 inches	(0 cm)
November	4.67 inches	(11.9 cm)
December	4.42 inches	(11.2 cm)

Write to the National Climatic Center, Federal Building, Asheville, North Carolina 28801 for their list of climatological publications. The *Local Climatological Data* publication in particular provides information gathered from 300 National Weather Service stations located across the country. There are also climatological publications issued for each state.

3. Demonstration. Have pupils read pp. 273–274. Before discussing the text, perform an experiment with ice cubes. Set one bowl of cubes directly under a lamp—sunlamp, if possible. Place another bowl so that it receives indirect rays of the lamp. Discuss the reason why one set of ice cubes melts faster. **Do not permit pupils to look directly at the sunlamp or to touch it.**

Relate the experiment with the ice cubes to the seasons through a discussion of the following concepts:

a. Because the sun is more directly over-

head in summer, the earth receives more of the sun's heat.

b. In winter, the sun's rays are indirect, and the earth receives less of the sun's heat.

c. The variation in the directness of the sun's rays is caused by the change in the earth's position in relation to the sun.

d. As the earth's position changes, the weather changes, and we have seasons.

LESSON 4   PAGES 275–283

NATURAL RESOURCES

GOALS

1. To understand why the United States is considered rich with natural resources. **2.** To know the states that lead the nation in the production of lumber, coal, oil, iron ore, steel, wheat, corn, and/or cotton. **3.** To name at least five major industries found in the United States. **4.** To list and give two uses for at least five natural resources found in the United States. **5.** To use maps and graphs to survey the natural resources, and agricultural and industrial wealth of the United States.

TEACHING SUGGESTIONS

●**1. Skimming for Facts.** Ask pupils to make a list of all the natural resources mentioned in Lesson 4 as they skim pp. 275–282. Have pupils share their lists orally. Make a composite list from their lists on the chalkboard. The following resources should be on their lists: air, water, soil, forests, natural gas, petroleum, coal, and metals such as iron, gold, silver, copper, lead, aluminum, and uranium. Discuss what natural resources are and why they are important to us. Ask pupils to name products they use that are made from natural resources.

For pupils who have difficulty grasping concepts, you may want to use this lesson as an opportunity to review the skill of outlining. Outlining the lesson will also give these pupils extra practice with the vocabulary words.

You may wish to have pupils who require a challenge research and write about the mineral resources of their community, area, and/or state. Have them report their findings orally to the class. Lead a class discussion on the economic impact of those resources for their community and state.

2. Letter Writing/Gathering Information. Have pupils write a group letter to the National Wildlife Federation, 1412 16th St. NW, Washington, D.C. 20036, for information concerning forest- and water-conservation practices. Review with pupils the parts of a business letter—heading, inside address, greeting, body, closing, and signature. Also review the proper forms for the envelope—return address, use of 2-letter state abbreviations, and use of zip codes.

3. Reading a Bar Graph. Draw pupils' attention to the graph of lumber production on p. 275. Ask the following questions:
a. *Name the five leading states in lumber production.* (Oregon, California, Washington, Idaho, and Alabama)
b. *Which state produces the most lumber in the United States?* (Oregon) *How much lumber?* (690 cu ft, or 19 cu m)
c. *How does California rank in lumber production?* (Second)
d. *How much more lumber does Oregon produce than California?* (363 cu ft, or 10 cu m)

4. Reading a Line Graph. Draw pupils' attention to the line graph of United States Oil Production on p. 278. Ask the following questions:
a. *How many barrels (metric tons) of oil did the United States produce in 1955?* (2.5 billion barrels, or 480 million t)
b. *In what year did oil production dip back down to 1955 levels?* (1958)
c. *What year shows the highest levels of oil production?* (1970) *How much oil was*

produced that year? (3.5 billion barrels, or 680 million t)
d. *Oil production rose sharply from 2.8 billion barrels (480 million t) to 3.3 billion barrels (630 million t) between what years?* (1965–1967)
e. *Oil production gradually declined over a span of 10 years. What are those years?* (1970–1980)

SUPPLEMENTARY INFORMATION
Energy Alternatives. Each year great demands are placed on our fossil fuels. The main consumers are industry (30 percent), transportation (24 percent) and residential and commercial (25 percent). Fuel lost through conversion consumes 18 percent of our energy resources. Each of these energy consumers can take measures to conserve fossil fuels. But conservation of existing resources is not enough. Long-range energy alternatives need to be explored. Two natural power sources being developed are the following:

Solar Power—The collection and distribution of energy from the sun, through the use of solar batteries, is one of the most promising alternatives. Solar heat creates no noise or air pollution. The cost of operation, after initial installation, is very low.

Geothermal Power—The source of this energy is pressurized steam, which results when water comes in contact with hot rocks below the earth's surface. Today, Iceland derives some of its electricity from geothermal heat. The earthquake belt in California has excellent potential for the use of this power.

14/CHAPTER REVIEW   PAGE 284
Answers for Review Questions
1. A political map shows the names and boundaries of different countries or states. It might also show the location of cities. A physical or relief map shows the kinds of landforms of a continent, country, or state.

2. The largest state in the United States is Alaska. The smallest state is Rhode Island.
3. Five landforms found in the United States are plains, plateaus, mountains, islands, and peninsulas.
4. The highest mountains in the United States are found in Alaska.
5. The state that is made up entirely of islands is Hawaii.
6. Weather is the condition of the air at a certain time. Weather can change in just a few hours. Climate is the kind of weather a place has over a long period of time.
7. We have night and day because the earth rotates on its axis in a 24-hour period, and any given point on the earth faces the sun part of the time and faces away from the sun part of the time.
8. The tilt of the earth and its 365-day revolution around the sun cause the changing seasons.

14/SKILLS DEVELOPMENT   PAGE 285
Answers for Skills Development
1. Answers will vary.
2. The cities in the United States that have more than 1 million people are New York, Chicago, Los Angeles, Philadelphia, Houston, and Detroit.
3. Massachusetts has a higher population density than Nevada.
4. New Orleans is the city located at 30°N/90°W.
5. There are 18 cities located within 100 miles (160 km) of the large bodies of water shown. The other cities are on or near bodies of water that do not appear on the map.
6. The two states that each have three or more cities among the 25 largest cities in the United States are California and Texas.
7. The United States city that is one of the 25 largest cities in the world is New York City.
8. The continent that has the largest number of cities that are among the 25 largest cities in the world is Asia.
9. The southernmost city shown on the world population map is Santiago.
10. The northernmost city shown on the world population map is Leningrad.
11. There are 0–5 persons per square mile in most of Australia (0–2 persons per sq km).
12. The population density in most of central India is 100–500 persons per square mile (40–200 persons per sq km).

CHAPTER 15   PAGES 286–309

THE NEW ENGLAND STATES TODAY

THEME

The industry and agriculture of New England and the growth of its communities have always been influenced by its landscape, climate, and natural resources.

PROJECTS

1. Have pupils use tracing paper to make a New England map of their own. After making the tracing, they can mount the tracing paper cutout on a white background. Names of states, cities, rivers, lakes, and other places mentioned in the text can be filled in on the individual maps as the lessons are covered.
2. New England is rich in historical incidents and figures. Assign individual or group reports on the historical aspects of New England. Below are just a few suggested topics.
a. The founding of one of the first colonies
b. The role of Native Americans in the settlement of New England
c. The Salem witch trials

LESSON 1   PAGES 286–289

THE LAND AND CLIMATE

GOALS
1. To list the six New England states. **2.** To identify the two major geographical areas of the New England states. **3.** To state the relationship of the two geographical features to the New England climate. **4.** To read a table showing temperature averages and extremes of major New England cities.

TEACHING SUGGESTIONS
1. Making a Chart. The text mentions some "superlatives" associated with the New England states. They are
a. The highest mountain (Mt. Washington),
b. The largest lake (Lake Champlain),
c. The windiest spot (Mt. Washington),
d. The highest point on the Atlantic Coast (Cadillac Mountain), and
e. The longest river (Connecticut River).

Have pupils locate these references in the text and make a chart for display. The headings for the columns might read as follows: Feature, Name, Location, Statistics.
2. Using a Road Map. Because large parts of the New England states are sparsely populated, a New England road map offers pupils an excellent opportunity to practice using this important tool within a relatively simple context. Divide the class into groups of two or three pupils and provide each group with a road map of the New England region or with road maps of individual New England states. Give an assignment to each group. An assignment might consist of having the group provide directions for an automobile trip from one New England city or town to another. The same assignment might be given to more than one group to see if they select the same or similar routes. Ask a spokesperson for each group to explain the reason why each route was selected.

3. Questions and Answers. After pupils have read pp. 286–289, ask the following questions:
a. *What are the two main features of the New England landscape?* (Coastline and mountains)
b. *Which is the only New England state not bordering on the Atlantic Ocean?* (Vermont)
c. *How would you describe a promontory?* (High, rocky land that juts out into the sea)
d. *In what state does the Appalachian Mountain range begin in the north and in what state does it end in the south?* (Maine and Georgia)
e. *What is the longest river in the New England states?* (Connecticut River)
f. *What is meant by the term temperature extremes?* (Highest and lowest recorded temperatures)
g. *What are two examples of precipitation?* (Rain and snow)
h. *Snowfall in Maine can reach 100 inches (250 cm) in one year. How many feet is 100 inches (meters/250 cm)?* ($8\frac{1}{3}$ feet or 2.5 m)
i. *What are three factors that affect the climate of New England?* (Mountains, Atlantic Ocean, and northern location)

LESSON 2   PAGES 289–293

MINING, FISHING, AND OTHER INDUSTRIES

GOALS
1. To list nine industries of New England. **2.** To list four major mineral resources of New England. **3.** To recount the steps necessary to quarry stone in New England. **4.** To list at least four changes in the New England fishing industry. **5.** To identify the major reasons for the decline of the whaling, cotton, and shoe industries in New England. **6.** To identify the changes in New England's traditional shipbuilding industry.

TEACHING SUGGESTIONS

● **1. Using Maps.** Have pupils locate Vermont on a physical map and identify the mountain areas. These areas provide stone for Vermont's quarrying industry.

You may wish to have pupils who require a challenge divide into groups and follow these steps:

a. Procure a topographical map of the United States;

b. Select various states with a topographical structure similar to Vermont's;

c. Research appropriate texts to find out if each particular state does indeed have a stone-quarrying industry; and

d. Report to the class on findings made.

Pupils who might have difficulty with this type of hypothesis and research project could use a general reference source to research the stone-quarrying industry and make a list of all the major stonemining states. They could then locate these states on a physical map of the United States.

A comparison might then be made of the results of both types of research.

2. Researching an Industrial Process. Some pupils might research the methods employed to quarry granite and prepare it for various uses. At the conclusion of the research, a display of drawings demonstrating the process may be made. Explanations can be in the form of captions on large index cards.

3. Making a Chart. Practice presenting information in chart form can be provided by having pupils identify several uses for each of the minerals mentioned in the text and listing them under the following headings: Mineral, Mining Method, and Common Uses.

4. Making Comparisons. Using appropriate texts, pupils can locate pictures of New England fishing trawlers of the nineteenth century and those of the 1970s and 1980s. Pupils can then make their own drawings, including labels identifying the major elements of change.

5. Researching and Reporting. The clipper ship was a fast sailing vessel that was developed in the mid-1800s. Many of these ships were built in New England. Pupils will enjoy learning about the design, building, history, and races of these glorious sailing vessels.

The methods of fishing and seafood harvesting are both fascinating and unfamiliar to many children, who will enjoy finding out about this industry as it is practiced in New England.

● **6. Learning Consumer Skills.** The increased use of synthetic fabrics was one of the reasons for the decline of the New England cotton textile industry. Tell pupils that most of their clothes are labeled for fabric content. Ask them to check the labels on their own clothes to see how much of their clothing is made at least partly of some form of synthetic. They might bring examples of textile products into class and classify them according to whether they are made of natural or synthetic fabrics.

Pupils who require a challenge might research the cleaning and care necessary for a variety of synthetic fabrics as well as for natural fabrics, noting the differences in the suggested methods.

7. Taking Notes. While reading a lesson, pupils might obtain good practice in noting salient facts. A small notebook or even scrap paper can be headed Important Facts. Pupils could then be asked to jot down important facts concerning what they are studying. You might tell them that they are responsible for at least ten facts for this lesson. The notes may come directly from the text. At the end of the lesson, you might call on a volunteer to read his or her facts aloud. Ask the other pupils to raise their hands as each fact is read if it is included in their own notes. Pupils might be allowed to refer to their notes while answering "Checkup" questions or other testing material.

SUPPLEMENTARY INFORMATION

Continental Shelf. A narrow band of shallow water lies around the edges of the earth's landmasses. This area is called the continental shelf. The shelf off the coast of New England provides some of the richest fishing grounds in the world. In addition to fishing, the people of New England also harvest clams, oysters, lobsters, and scallops found along the coast. Although these are not true fish, they are considered part of the fishing industry. One seventh of the nation's fish comes from the New England states. Maine, Massachusetts, and New Hampshire are leaders in the lobster industry. Four fifths of the nation's frozen and packaged seafood come from the New England states.

LESSON 3 PAGES 294–299

AGRICULTURE AND FORESTS

GOALS

1. To name the agricultural crops of the New England states. **2.** To describe the relationship between climate and agriculture in the New England states. **3.** To describe the relationship between geographical features and agriculture in New England. **4.** To identify uses for the lumber from the New England forests. **5.** To explain the concept of renewable resources. **6.** To list the steps in the cutting and hauling of timber. **7.** To list the steps in making paper.

TEACHING SUGGESTIONS

1. Making a Report. Pupils eat meat and poultry without much thought about what is involved in raising the livestock. Have several groups of pupils select a type of livestock and use appropriate resources to report to the class what is involved in bringing an animal from birth to the table. Included should be definitions of terms commonly associated with the particular type of livestock, for example, *lamb*, *mutton*, *poultry*, *capon*, and *fryer*.

If any of your pupils are enrolled in a 4H club and are currently involved in raising livestock, they might wish to present to the class some of the facts and figures they have been required to keep. Most interesting would be the total amount of food fed to the animal and the total cost of care.

2. Researching. The history of the introduction of tobacco to Europeans is both interesting and funny. It is said that the first European seen smoking the rolled leaves was promptly doused by his manservant, who thought that he was on fire. Pupils might wish to learn more about the story of the tobacco plant. The story of tobacco can also be tied to the story of slavery in our country. Results of the research may be presented in oral or written form.

3. Doing an Experiment. The text relates the growing of the potato plant to conditions of climate and soil. Pupils can conduct their own experiment with these variables by following these steps:

a. Select several potatoes from the same bag and allow them to bud under exactly the same conditions.

b. After the potatoes have budded, raise each one under differing conditions of "climate" and soil. Plant the potatoes in containers with different types of soil, ranging from sand to fertile garden or potting soil.

c. If two containers of each soil type are prepared, then the "climate" can also be tested. Water one container every day and the other once a week.

d. Make sure potato plants receive sufficient light.

e. Keep a chart on the number of centimeters the buds grow over a period of a month.

f. Draw conclusions about the best conditions for potato farming.

Be sure to explain to the class that many modern farming methods are the result of such controlled experiments.

4. Researching a Problem Area. The text makes a short reference to the Indian families from Canada who help with Maine's blueberry crop. These workers are part of the migrant farmer population of the United States. Many pupils have no awareness of the problems of this minority group. Some pupils might be interested in researching this area and giving a presentation that would make the class better informed about this serious situation.

5. Cooking and Tasting. Maple syrup and candy are readily available in many stores. The class can make a pancake breakfast. One pupil might bring in the ingredients for the pancakes and another the syrup. (If real maple syrup is used, the cost should probably be shared more evenly.) Also, if each pupil can taste a piece of maple candy, an additional dimension to the study of maple sugaring will be obtained.

6. Making a Diorama. The old logging methods make excellent material for a diorama. Small sticks can be used to represent logs, and foil with transparent wrap can represent water. The oxen used for hauling may be made from modeling clay. Plaster of paris is a good substitute for the snow over which the oxen pulled the sleds loaded with logs.

7. Making Paper. Paper manufacturing is a huge mechanized industry; however, paper can be made by hand. Pupils might write to the American Paper Institute, Inc., 260 Madison Ave., New York, N.Y. 10016, for their pamphlet "How You Can Make Paper." This pamphlet provides very simple instructions on how to make paper at home, using a minimum of ordinary household equipment. The process could also be done fairly easily as a classroom project. Pupils who take part in the project can display their product on the bulletin board.

8. Questions and Answers. After pupils have read pp. 294–299, ask the following questions:

a. *Why is New England's soil unsuitable for growing wheat and oats?* (Most of the soil is too rocky and thin.)

b. *What kinds of farming have been successful on New England's thin, rocky soil and why?* (Hay can be successfully raised in thin soil when there is also a cool, moist climate, such as that of New England. Chickens and cattle can be raised successfully. They do not need rich, level land.)

c. *Where do New England farmers get the grain for their livestock?* (From the North Central states)

d. *Why is tobacco a good cash crop?* (It provides more income per acre than most other crops.)

e. *What makes the Aroostook River valley ideal for growing potatoes?* (Rich, silty soil and cool, moist summers)

f. *Where are Maine potatoes sold?* (Throughout the United States and Europe)

g. *Which of the New England states is the leading producer of low-bush blueberries?* (Maine)

h. *What is a bog?* (Wet, swampy land)

i. *Why are cranberries grown in bogs?* (Flooding the bogs helps control weeds and helps prevent the plants from freezing in early spring and late fall.)

j. *Is most of New England farmland, cities, or forest?* (Forest)

k. *What is a deciduous tree?* (A tree that loses its leaves in the fall)

l. *In what ways were the trees in New England's forests used in the early days of America?* (Forests sheltered the game people needed for food and clothing. The wood was used for firewood for cooking and heating. Logs and lumber were used as building material. Lumber was also used in building ships.)

m. *What are the steps in collecting maple sap for syrup?* (In early spring farmers bore holes in the maple trees. A tap is placed in each hole. The sap flows slowly into a container and the containers are collected every day. Some farmers have a system of tubes which bring the sap to the sugarhouse.)

n. *Why is it necessary for people to treat trees as "crops"?* Because such large numbers of trees are cut down, it is necessary to plant new trees as older ones are "harvested," or even before, to ensure that we have a supply of wood for the future.)

o. *How has transporting timber to the sawmills changed over the years?* (Logs are no longer hauled by oxen to the river and then floated downstream in the spring. Now trucks are used to transport the logs to the sawmill.)

p. *How did paper mills pollute streams and rivers?* (The water and chemicals used in the manufacturing process were discharged into the streams and rivers before the chemicals were removed and the water cooled.)

q. *What is recycled paper?* (Paper that has been used before is collected and goes through the paper-making process again.)

LESSON 4 PAGES 299–305

TOURISM, PEOPLE, AND COMMUNITIES

GOALS

1. To state at least four reasons why people travel to the New England states for vacation. **2.** To read a table showing urban centers in New England and answer pertinent questions. **3.** To define the term *metropolitan area.* **4.** To read a graph showing population changes in six New England cities since 1800 and answer pertinent questions. **5.** To state the name of the largest city in New England. **6.** To name and locate on a map six important New England cities and be able to give at least one important or interesting fact about each one.

TEACHING SUGGESTIONS

1. Keeping Records. Ask pupils who have traveled any distance to a vacation area to recall their experiences in writing. They may do this in the form of a log or diary. To get a practical idea of the meaning of the term *tourist industry,* pupils should be sure to include those items on which they or their family spent their vacation money. Such expenditures would be money paid for gas or some form of transportation, food, lodging, rental of a variety of equipment, tickets for admittance to special sites or events, souvenirs.

While pupils will probably not remember exact costs, simply enumerating the occasions for expenditures on vacations or while traveling will be a good indication of the size and importance of the tourist industry.

If any pupils are currently planning a trip or weekend vacation of some kind, they might keep a record of activities and expenditures and report to the class.

2. Making Comparisons. Many people who have not seen the *Mayflower II* have little idea of how small the original *Mayflower* was. Pupils can gain an appreciation of the conditions aboard such a ship and the bravery of the people who ventured across the Atlantic Ocean in such a tiny craft by researching the dimensions and construction of the original *Mayflower* and comparing it with modern ships.

3. Creative Writing. You may have some pupils who would enjoy re-creating life aboard the *Mayflower* in an imaginary account of the daily happenings on the voyage to America. Library references will give pupils an idea of some of the hardships, dangers, and fears faced by the Puritans. These references can become the springboard for a fictional diary.

● **4. Researching.** The text mentions that the government has taken a census every ten years since 1790. Many pupils are probably not familiar with this government func-

tion. Some pupils might research the history, scope, and functions of the census through primary and secondary sources. The following are suggestions for structuring such research:
a. Research the history of the census, using appropriate library materials; **b.** Research the methods of census taking; **c.** Research the kinds of censuses the government takes. (These are censuses of population, housing, agriculture, governments, business, manufactures, mineral industry, construction, and transportation.); and **d.** Find out the kinds of questions asked on the Census of Population and some of the reasons for those questions.

Much general information can be found in standard encyclopedias. Pertinent facts and statistics can be obtained from the *Statistical Abstract of the United States* and from the Bureau of the Census in Washington, D.C.

This is a challenging research project, probably requiring some adult assistance. However, pupils who might have difficulty with this type of research could easily conduct their own census, perhaps recording the number of members in each of their classmates' families, their sex, age, and so on. This will give pupils experience in composing pertinent questions and recording statistics. This activity might be extended to include the members of other classes, and statistics could be compiled and reported.

5. Questions and Answers. After pupils have read pp. 299–305, ask the following questions:
a. *Why did many New England communities grow up?* (They were at a crossroads for travelers or on a stream or river that provided transportation. A river also provided power to run a gristmill or small factory.)
b. *What is a metropolitan area?* (A city and the smaller cities and towns around it)
c. *What are some of the important indus-tries in the Boston area?* (Electronics, banking, insurance, publishing, and food processing)
d. *What lake does Burlington overlook?* (Lake Champlain)
e. *What is the major industry of Concord?* (Printing)
f. *What famous university is located in New Haven?* (Yale)
g. *To what city does Portland's pipeline carry oil?* (Montreal, Canada)
h. *By whom was Portland founded?* (Roger Williams)

6. Reading a Table. Have pupils use the table on p. 302 to answer the following:
a. *What is the largest city in the New England states?* (Boston)
b. *Name the states in which the largest city is also the capital.* (Massachusetts and Rhode Island)
c. *Which state has the smallest capital?* (Vermont)
d. *What is the population of Portland?* (62,000) *Montpelier?* (8,000) *Burlington?* (38,000)

SUPPLEMENTARY INFORMATION
Census. The Bureau of the Census is part of the Department of Commerce. Every 5 years it conducts censuses of agriculture, business, construction, governments, manufactures, mineral industries, and transportation. Every 10 years it conducts a Housing Census. The census that most people are aware of is that of population. In the past this was conducted once every 10 years. However, in 1976 the federal government passed legislation that requires a Population Census every 5 years.

In addition to finding out the actual numbers of people in the United States, the Population Census gathers such information as age, employment, education, income, marital status, race, and sex. Methods of securing census information include personal interviews and mailed questionnaires. The Census Bureau decides what information is necessary, what questions to include, and who is to gather the information. Mountains of data must be processed and tabulated. The Bureau then publishes the census statistics. Business; industry; federal, state, and local governments; social scientists; and many other organizations and people make extensive use of census statistics for a great variety of purposes. Many important decisions are made based on census information.

15/CHAPTER REVIEW   PAGE 308
Answers for Review Questions

1. The mountains and northern parts of New England are the coldest and have the greatest temperature extremes. The coastal areas are milder throughout the year. New England has some precipitation every month. Snowfall is heavy and cloudy skies are common. Some parts of New England have severe winters; but spring and fall are particularly colorful seasons, and the harsh coastal winds help keep some areas cool and pleasant in summer.

2. The Connecticut River is New England's longest, and the three other important rivers in the region are the Penobscot, Kennebec, and Merrimack.

3. New England's industries include the manufacture of many products such as textiles, silverware, firearms, machinery, leather goods, pulpwood and paper, and electronic equipment. Other industries include quarrying, fishing, lumbering, banking, publishing, shipbuilding, insurance, and tourism.

4. New England farm products include hay, livestock such as dairy cattle and chickens, potatoes, tobacco, blueberries, cranberries, and some vegetables. New England's trees may also be considered a "crop," as might maple-syrup products.

5. The two New England states in which the capital is also the largest city are Massachusetts (Boston) and Rhode Island (Providence). Montpelier, the capital of Vermont, is the smallest capital city in New England. Boston, the capital of Massachusetts, is the largest.

6. Answers will vary.

CHAPTER 16   PAGES 310–327

THE MIDDLE ATLANTIC STATES TODAY

THEME

The Middle Atlantic states are endowed with abundant natural resources, including good soil, energy sources, and waterways. As a result, much of this area is heavily urban and highly industrialized.

PROJECTS

1. Have pupils make a bulletin-board display of resources of the Middle Atlantic states. If they use a large hand-drawn map as a base, they can show water routes and city areas. Then as they progress through the chapter they can indicate farmlands, coalfields, and other areas; and they can bring in pictures of foods, fuels, and other products and paste them on these areas.

2. Have pupils do research on the ways open spaces—parks, recreation areas, historical areas, wildlife refuges—are being preserved in the heavily populated Middle Atlantic states. Pupils might wish to find out about the programs and open areas of one state and make a report to the class.

LESSON 1

PAGES 310–312

THE LAND

GOALS
1. To name the five Middle Atlantic states and locate them on a United States map. **2.** To understand the geographical terms *bay* and *harbor*. **3.** To name the two largest lakes of this area.

TEACHING SUGGESTIONS
1. Questions and Answers. After pupils have read the text and studied the map, ask:

a. *Why are these states called the Middle Atlantic states?* (They are located between the New England states and the Southeastern states, and all but one border the Atlantic Ocean.)

b. *What is a bay?* (Part of the ocean that cuts into the land)

c. *What is a harbor?* (Protected waters where ships can anchor safely)

d. *What are the foothills of the Appalachians like?* (Low tree-covered hills and rich green valleys)

e. *Why is the Great Valley important?* (It is good farmland.)

f. *Why are the lakes in the Middle Atlantic states important to this area?* (They draw thousands of visitors.)

2. Making a Topographic Map. Have pupils create a three-dimensional topographic map of the Middle Atlantic states. They will need a map of these states cut from a road map of the East Coast, some chicken wire, papier-mâché, and a board to accommodate the map. The chicken wire is shaped to form the skeleton of the Appalachians and stapled to the board in the approximate location of the range as shown on the map on p. 311. Pupils then apply three to four coats of papier-mâché to the chicken wire. After the papier-mâché dries, pupils may paint it and label major rivers, lakes, bays, towns, and the Atlantic Ocean.

3. Making a Model. Have pupils interested in geology make a model to demonstrate for the class how a bay is created. (See Supplementary Information, below). Using clay and a baking pan or pie tin, they can simulate the area surrounding Delaware Bay. The part of the model representing the present bay should be about ¼ inch (½ cm) below the rest of the land surface and ¼ inch (½ cm) higher than the ocean. The bay will be created as the pupils slowly add water to the ocean, raising its level until it moves into the lower land.

4. Synonyms and Antonyms. Often, language arts and social studies skills can be combined in one lesson. One way of doing that is to reproduce a paragraph from the text, underline certain words and have pupils find synonyms or antonyms for the underlined words. For example, you could have pupils find synonyms for the following words in paragraph 2 of column 1 on p. 314: *beautiful, region, supply, provide, enjoy, quiet, beauty.*

SUPPLEMENTARY INFORMATION
Bays. The three great bays of this region are really drowned river valleys. Much of Chesapeake Bay is the drowned valley of the Susquehanna River. Delaware Bay is the drowned valley of the Delaware River, and New York Bay, of the Hudson River. A drowned river valley is formed over thousands of years as the coastal plain sinks. As it sinks, the ocean water begins to cover the lowest land. Pupils can find drowned river valleys on a map by looking for rivers with a wide mouth. "Ordinary" rivers do not have this feature.

LESSON 2

PAGES 313–314

CLIMATE AND NATURAL RESOURCES

GOALS
1. To understand the weather and climate of the Middle Atlantic states. **2.** To read a

map of average temperatures. **3.** To locate Niagara Falls on a map. **4.** To name two sources of energy that the Middle Atlantic states have in abundance.

TEACHING SUGGESTIONS

1. Questions and Answers. For a review of the content of the lesson, ask pupils the following questions:

a. *What is the average winter temperature for this region?* (About 30° F, or −1° C)

b. *What is the average summer temperature?* (About 75° F, or 24° C)

c. *What is the average snowfall in southern New Jersey, Delaware, and Maryland?* (About 20 in., or 51 cm)

d. *Can these states provide for their lumber and paper needs from their woodlands?* (No)

e. *Why can't the people use all of the rivers and streams for drinking water?* (Some are too polluted.)

f. *How does Niagara Falls help meet the power needs of the people on the Canadian and United States sides of the Falls?* (The falling water is used to make electricity.)

g. *What is a more important fuel in this area than oil?* (Coal)

2. Making a Rain Gauge. Have pupils collect information about the precipitation in their hometown. A simple rain gauge can be made from a short, wide glass jar with straight sides. The jar must have a flat bottom. Pupils should use a grease pencil or permanent marking pen to calibrate the jar in ¼ inches or in centimeters. The gauge should be placed in an exposed area to catch the rainfall. Readings are made through the side of the jar.

3. Making a Model. A model of Edwin Drake's well can be built using pine 1″x1″ wood trim and ½″ flat pine molding. The model can be constructed on a plywood base and have explanations of the parts on index cards attached to the base.

4. Using the *Readers' Guide*. Because of the uncertainties in the future of our oil supplies, attention has returned to America's vast coal reserves. The Middle Atlantic states have a role to play in this "new" energy future. Using the *Readers' Guide to Periodical Literature*, pupils can learn about the problems and the promises of coal as an energy source. In doing such research they should also look carefully at the statistics that tell them of the changes in coal production in the Middle Atlantic states during the last decade or two.

SUPPLEMENTARY INFORMATION

1. Niagara Falls. Niagara Falls is located about 16 miles (26 km) northwest of Buffalo, N.Y. The Falls are part of the 36-mile-long (57.6 km) Niagara River, which drains four of the Great Lakes into the fifth. More than 3,500,000 people come to see this spectacular natural wonder each year.

There are two parts to the Falls, the Horseshoe or Canadian Falls and the American Falls. The boundary line between the United States and Canada passes through the Horseshoe Falls. The Horseshoe Falls are 160 feet (49 m) high and 2,500 feet (762 m) wide. The American Falls are slightly higher, 167 feet (50 m), but considerably narrower at only 1,000 feet (305 m). Every minute 500,000 tons (450,000 t) of water spill over the Falls. This quantity of water is capable of generating a considerable amount of power. That power was first tapped to run a sawmill in 1757. The first waterpowered electric generator was built in 1882. By the mid-1890s the first generators for the large-scale production of electricity were installed on both sides of the Falls. Today there are many plants converting the power of the falling water into electrical power for the people of the United States and Canada. The Niagara Falls hydroelectric capacity (over 4 million kilowatts) is one of the greatest in the world.

2. Hydroelectric Power. Hydroelectric power is power created by the movement of water. In the case of Niagara Falls, the movement is created by the effects of gravity on a large volume of water as it tumbles over a cliff. The falling water is converted into electricity by a turbine. The turbine is an updated waterwheel. The shaft of the turbine spins an electric generator, which rotates powerful magnets past coils of copper wire or copper bars. In some generators, the magnets are stationary and the coils of wire or bars move.

LESSON 3 PAGES 315–318

FARMING AND INDUSTRY

GOALS

1. To understand the importance of agriculture in the Middle Atlantic states and to name the different kinds of agriculture in this region. **2.** To include the fishing industry in a list of food production industries in these states. **3.** To define the term "Manufacturing Belt" in relation to these states and to list at least three important products manufactured here. **4.** To understand the contribution of water travel and the large coal reserves to the growth of the iron and steel industry in Pennsylvania.

TEACHING SUGGESTIONS

1. Questions and Answers. Use the following questions to check pupils' understanding as they progress through the lesson.
a. *What fraction of the land in Delaware is farmland?* (One half)
b. *Are the people of the Middle Atlantic region able to provide much of their food needs from their own farms?* (Yes)
c. *Are there more or fewer farms and farmers in this area than there once were?* (Fewer farms and farmers)
d. *If the number of farms and farmers has declined, how do these farms supply much of the food that is needed?* (The farms use modern methods and modern machinery.)
e. *What kinds of farms are common in New York and Pennsylvania?* (Dairy farms)
f. *What products can be found in southern Delaware?* (White corn, potatoes, and strawberries)
g. *What do poultry farms supply?* (Eggs and chickens)
h. *What is a truck farm?* (One that grows a large variety of vegetables)
i. *Why is the Middle Atlantic region called the Manufacturing Belt?* (Because it is one of the larger industrial areas in the United States.)
j. *What are some examples of synthetic fabrics?* (Nylon and Dacron)
k. *What is the definition of the term petrochemical industry?* (An industry that relies upon chemicals made primarily from petroleum)
l. *Which of the Middle Atlantic states is known for its iron and steel production?* (Pennsylvania)
m. *How do lakes and rivers play a part in the production of steel in Pittsburgh?* (Iron ore is shipped on barges to the mills in Pittsburgh. The coal needed for the furnaces is brought on ships and barges. Also, the products of the mills can be distributed on ships and barges.)
2. Constructing a Display (Farming). To help pupils understand and remember the differences between various kinds of farming in the Middle Atlantic states, a bulletin-board display can be constructed that will present the differences in a visual fashion. Such a display can include poultry, dairy, and truck farms. The variables to be compared might include such things as what is raised (chickens, vegetables, cattle, or cows) and the commercial food products (eggs, milk, vegetables).
3. Constructing a Display (Fishing). Modern fishing fleets are very different than most pupils imagine them to be. Pupils may be amazed to learn of the

sophistication of the new ships and methods for catching and processing the fish. A bulletin-board display illustrating the advances in this industry due to modern science would be a good complement to a display about modern farming.

4. Making a Model. Models of lobster traps are relatively easy to construct from ½″ flat pine molding strips and twine. A group of pupils can construct such a trap to scale and demonstrate how it works.

5. Research Report. The conflict between growing urbanization and the growing need for food—both farm products and fish and shellfish—creates many problems for this area. The dwindling amount of available farmland is an obvious problem. One less obvious problem, which pupils might be interested in researching, is the effect on the shellfish industries in Chesapeake and Delaware bays when river water is diverted to other uses. State agencies, such as the Division of Shellfisheries, in the New Jersey Department of Environmental Protection, should have information on this subject.

6. Reading Labels. The term *synthetic* might need further elaboration for pupils to fully understand the scope of products this term includes. This might be accomplished by having them draw up a list of synthetic fabrics. With the list in an easily visible location in the classroom, pupils can begin to read the labels on their shirts, coats, shoes, and sweaters. They might list beside each synthetic fabric-name the end products that are made from that fabric.

SUPPLEMENTARY INFORMATION

1. Modern Farming. The image many children have of the red barn and assorted animals running around the barnyard does not correspond to modern farm realities. For example, a modern poultry farm specializing in the production of eggs might have 60,000 chickens, each producing 250 eggs each year. The chickens lay their eggs in wire cages. The cages are constructed so that the eggs roll down the sloping wire bottom of the cage into a trough. There they are picked up and sorted.

The chickens live in a carefully controlled environment. Insulation, fans, and heaters maintain the temperature in a large building at a constant, comfortable level. The lack of windows allows the farmer to regulate the length of the "day." The content and quantity of feed is controlled. Close living increases the possibility of disease, so all the chickens must be inoculated and receive regulated dosages of vitamins and minerals.

To keep the operation profitable, each chicken must lay approximately 250 eggs during the year to year-and-a-half of its laying life. This necessitates accurate record keeping. The successful running of a poultry farm requires the farmer to be a bit of a scientist, businessman or woman, accountant, and veterinarian.

2. Urbanization and the Shellfisheries. Many people assume that the greatest threat of urbanization to the shellfishing industry is water pollution. However, pollution has been on the decline in recent years, as regulations have become more stringent. A less apparent problem is that of the multiple uses of the supply of fresh water. As more and more water is diverted from the rivers that flow into the Chesapeake and Delaware bays, the amount of fresh water in these bays decreases, and the ocean water moves in. As the salinity of the water increases, the shellfish are attacked by pests and diseases that could not survive in fresh water. The result is a drop in the shellfish harvest.

3. Manufacturing and Processing Industries. The greatest economic base of the Middle Atlantic area is to be found in the manufacturing and processing industries. This region earns about 18 times as much income from manufacturing and processing as it does from agriculture. The Middle Atlantic states rate among the top manufacturing states in the country. The success of these industries lies in the strategic location of this area. Natural resources such as coal and iron ore; availability of skilled workers, good harbors, and inland waterways; and proximity to extensive markets combined to produce the concentration of industry found in this area.

LESSON 4 PAGES 319–325

CITIES

GOALS

1. To read a population map. **2.** To name the five largest cities of this region and to explain the role of transportation in the growth of these cities. **3.** To cite New York City as the largest city in the country and the port of New York as the busiest port in the country. **4.** To locate New York City, Philadelphia, Baltimore, and Washington, D.C., on a map of the United States. **5.** To identify Washington, D.C., as the capital of our country, the center of the government of the United States, and the place where the President lives and works. **6.** To define the letters *D.C.* as "District of Columbia" and to understand that Washington, D.C., is not part of any state. **7.** To define the term *megalopolis*.

TEACHING SUGGESTIONS

1. Questions and Answers. Use the following questions for a review of the lesson.
a. *What state is the most densely populated in the country?* (New Jersey)
b. *How many people, on the average, live on each square mile or square kilometer of land in New Jersey?* (979 per sq mi, or 378 per sq km)
c. *Where are the factories and mills located?* (In and around the cities)

d. *Name the five largest cities in the Middle Atlantic region.* (New York, Baltimore, Washington, D.C., Philadelphia, and Pittsburgh)
e. *What do four of these five cities have in common?* (They are port cities.)
f. *Which city is not a port city?* (Washington, D.C.)
g. *How did access to water help these cities grow?* (In the earlier days of the country, most travel was by ship. Being close to water made transportation of people and products much easier.)
h. *Define the term* commerce. (The buying and selling of goods)
i. *Name two of the largest industries in New York City.* (Clothing manufacture and book publishing)
j. *What two rivers meet at Philadelphia?* (The Delaware and Schuylkill rivers)
k. *How can ships go from Baltimore to Philadelphia without going around Virginia's Cape Charles?* (By taking the Chesapeake and Delaware Canal)
l. *What industry has been in Baltimore since its earliest days?* (Shipbuilding)
m. *Why is Washington called the District of Columbia?* (It is not part of any state. It was built on land donated by the state of Maryland.)
n. *In what way is Washington, D.C., our most important city?* (The government of our country is located in this city.)
o. *How would you define* megalopolis? (One huge city made up of many cities that seem to touch each other.)
● **2. Constructing a Display.** The concept of population density might still be somewhat vague to fifth graders. This concept can be part of a bulletin-board display dealing with the population of the Middle Atlantic states. One part of the display can have a list of the states and their populations. Another might include the major cities and their populations.

For pupils who have difficulty grasping the concept of population density, you may wish to do the following. Have them make two areas, about one foot square (or 1 sq m if you are using the metric system), on the display. In one, three cutout paper dolls can be stapled or glued with the caption "Three people per square foot (meter)." In the other they can put twelve paper dolls with the caption "Twelve people per square foot (meter)."

For pupils who require a challenge, you may wish to encourage the use of graphing skills. The population information can be presented on charts, in a pictograph, and in bar and line graph form.

3. Making a Map. The New York metropolitan area is an interesting complex of waterways, which include many bays, rivers, inlets, and sounds. Using a detail map of New York City and the area, pupils can re-create and enlarge the map, placing emphasis on the intricate water system that has helped make this city the giant it is. While some pupils may wish to make an original map, others with less artistic ability can use tracing paper or an opaque projector. Another way to reproduce the original map and still emphasize the water system is to place a transparency over the original and outline the land areas while coloring the water areas. The finished transparency can then be projected on a screen or wall for class presentation.

Pupils studying the New York City ports should direct some of their attention to the location of the Statue of Liberty and Ellis Island and their significance to the millions of immigrants who entered the country through the New York port.

4. Making a Field Study. The text states that one of the major industries of New York City is the publishing industry. Some pupils may wish to check the accuracy of that statement through a simple field study. First they should learn a little about sampling techniques. They need to know that most studies they hear about (such as opinion polls and the Nielsen ratings for TV) are conducted by studying a small portion of the population. This sometimes leads to mistakes, but is impossible to ask every citizen his or her opinion on a given topic. Therefore the researchers ask a small, carefully selected portion of the population.

Once the pupils understand that a sampling procedure can allow supportable inferences, they can begin their own field study. If what the text states is true, it is reasonable to assume that many of the books in the school library were published in New York City, no matter where the school is located. Thus the pupils can formulate the hypothesis: More than 50 percent of the books in the school library were published in New York City.

Now teams of pupils can divide the task of conducting a field study to support or refute this hypothesis. It is important for them to know that it is not necessary to check every book in the library, but that they must check a representative sample. Everyone must think about and agree on the size of a reasonable sample. Ten percent is probably a workable size. The pupils then should learn the size of the "universe"—the total number of books in the library—so they can compute the size of their sample. Once they have done this simple mathematical procedure, the actual checking of books can begin. Books should be selected randomly from the entire library collection, rather than from just one area.

Pupils need only check the title page to discover the location of the publishing company. Sometimes the publishing company has several locations, but if New York City is listed, that book can be counted as being published there. Using simple math, pupils can compute the percentage of the books sampled that were published in New York, and, by inference, the percentage of the total library books published there. Then they must decide if they have met their original criterion (50 percent of the books published in New York City) to support the hypothesis.

Having completed this piece of research, pupils can now write up the entire study. They may profit from reading some scientific journals that publish original studies to find models for their written efforts. They should also realize that such research is often published in professional journals so that other professionals in the same field can read about the work and replicate the study (repeat it under the same conditions).

5. Writing a Business Letter. An interesting letter-writing project can be organized in which pupils write letters to government officials in Washington, D.C. They might write to the President, the Vice-President, Cabinet members, members of the Supreme Court, or to the representatives and senators from their state or area. One question they may wish to ask might concern the functions of each of those offices. The replies that they receive might make an interesting bulletin-board display.

6. Creating a Game. Pupils might enjoy working together to research and create a game that would further expand upon their knowledge of the major cities of the Middle Atlantic states. Two models for such a game are very familiar to most pupils; one is Monopoly. The rules may stay the same as for the short game in the Monopoly directions, but the names of the properties could be changed to incorporate the main attractions of the Middle Atlantic cities. Committees could assign values to the attractions—for example, the Statue of Liberty might equal Boardwalk. Independence Hall could equal some other property on the playing board. One way to assign these values would be for pupils to find out how many tourists actually visit these sites each year. The sites could then be ranked according to their drawing power in real life.

Another model for such a game is Chutes and Ladders, in which each player proceeds on an imaginary tour. Movement is determined by the number on the dice. The board should include a path or several paths leading from the starting point to the winner's square. Along the way would be some of the famous sites of each of the cities and dangers that carry a penalty, such as "flat tire, go back two spaces."

7. Research. The buildings, institutions, and monuments in Washington, D.C., offer interesting opportunities for research projects. The following are some particularly interesting topics: the Smithsonian Institution, the National Archives, the Capitol, the White House, the Library of Congress, the Bureau of Engraving and Printing, and Arlington National Cemetery.

16/CHAPTER REVIEW   PAGE 326
Answers for Review Questions

1. The Middle Atlantic states are New York, Pennsylvania, New Jersey, Delaware, and Maryland.

2. The chief physical features of this region are the Atlantic Coastal Plain and the Appalachian Mountains. There are many good bays and harbors and many rivers and lakes, including two of the Great Lakes. The climate is moderate, with colder temperatures in the northern parts and in the higher elevations. The precipitation varies, with the mountains getting more rain and snow than some of the other parts.

3. Answers will vary, but a list of natural resources might include good soil, water, forests, coal, and oil and natural gas.

4. Harbors and waterways were and still are important for transporting people, raw materials, and goods from one place to another.

5. The Liberty Bell is in Philadelphia, the White House is in Washington, D.C., and the Statue of Liberty is in New York City.

6. Answers will vary.

THE SOUTHEAST STATES TODAY

THEME

The Southeast is an important agricultural and mining region and is becoming increasingly important industrially as well. The warm climate and the variety of recreational opportunities make tourism vital to the Southeast's economy.

PROJECT

Have pupils find out about and collect or draw pictures and diagrams of the two kinds of coal mines, underground mines and strip mines. These visuals can serve as the focus of a large bulletin-board display. The various machines commonly used in the process of extracting coal from the ground can be shown and labeled. Information sources include the National Coal Association, Coal Building, Washington, D.C., 20036, as well as encyclopedia articles. When sending away for free materials, it is best to send one letter, from the class as a whole or from the teacher.

LESSON 1   PAGES 328–331

THE LAND

GOALS

1. To list the ten states of the Southeast. 2. To locate the Gulf Coastal Plain. 3. To differentiate tidewater from swamp. 4. To locate the Everglades and Lake Okeechobee on a map of Florida. 5. To describe the Florida Keys, the Outer Banks, and the Piedmont. 6. To list the major rivers of the Southeast states. 7. To list two accomplishments of the TVA.

TEACHING SUGGESTIONS

1. **Questions and Answers.** Have pupils read the text and answer the following.
a. *Name the states of the Southeast region.* (Virginia, West Virginia, North Carolina, South Carolina, Georgia, Florida, Alabama, Mississippi, Kentucky, Tennessee)
b. *What are the main geographical features of this area?* (Coastal plains, Piedmont, mountains, and lowlands)
c. *What is a temperate climate like?* (Neither extremely hot or cold nor extremely wet or dry)
d. *How are tidewater areas and swamps different?* (Tidewater areas are sometimes covered with water. Swamps are always covered with water.)
e. *What are some of the rules of a wildlife refuge?* (Hunting is not allowed. Building of houses and roads is not permitted.)
f. *What are the Florida Keys?* (A string of islands stretching 150 miles, 240 km, from southern Florida into the Gulf of Mexico)
g. *What are barrier islands?* (Islands that form a barrier that protects the mainland)
h. *In what way did the Outer Banks present a danger to ships?* (Ships wrecked on the shoals and reefs.)
i. *What is the Fall Line?* (A line marking the point at which one finds waterfalls on the rivers flowing towards the coast)
j. *What is the highest point of the Appalachian chain?* (Mount Mitchell in North Carolina)
k. *Where does the term Bluegrass country come from?* (The blue flowers in the grass that carpet the hills of Kentucky)
l. *Name the Southeast's four great rivers.* (Mississippi, Ohio, Cumberland, Tennessee)
m. *What do the initials TVA stand for?* (Tennessee Valley Authority)

n. *In what ways has the TVA helped people in the area?* (The TVA built dams to control flooding, provides water for irrigation, generates electricity, manufactures fertilizers, and introduced soil conservation methods to many people.)

2. Map Reading. Have pupils find the following on the map on p. 329.

a. *The rivers that form state borders* (Mississippi, Pearl, Chattahoochee, Savannah, Ohio, Potomac)

b. *The lakes and reservoirs shown* (L.M. Smith Reservoir, Lake Martin, Wheeler Lake, Guntersville Lake, Lake Sidney Lanier, Clark Hill Reservoir, Lake Cumberland, Dale Hollow Reservoir, Lake Marion, Hartwell Reservoir, Kerr Lake, Norris Lake, Kentucky Lake)

c. *The swamps shown* (Great Dismal Swamp, Okefenokee Swamp, Everglades)

3. Map Making. Pupils can feature the Southeast region on a classroom bulletin-board display. Such a display can include the state flags and a large map of the states showing their capitals and largest cities. Main products and interesting places to visit can be added to the map during Lesson 3. Much of this information is included on the table on pp. 344–345. The main products are listed in most almanacs, and encyclopedias include places of interest in their articles about states.

4. Research Report. The Everglades is one of the nation's great wildlife refuges. Not only is this park a beautiful place to visit, but the park is vital to the ecological balance of southern Florida. Pupils can use appropriate resources to learn about this function of a wildlife refuge. What kinds of animals and plantlife would be endangered by development of the Everglades? What have been some of the more recent threats to the park? Pupils can explore these issues using the *Readers' Guide* to find recent information.

5. Research Report/Geology. The text refers to reefs, shoals, and coral in discussing the Florida Keys and the Outer Banks. Pupils interested in science can explore the forces that shape these features and present their findings to the class.

SUPPLEMENTARY INFORMATION

Tennessee Valley Authority. The TVA was created in 1933 to develop the natural resources of the Tennessee River valley. The valley covers 40,910 square miles (105,960 sq km) in the states of Tennessee, Kentucky, Virginia, North Carolina, Georgia, Alabama, and Mississippi. It has rich deposits of coal, copper, gravel, iron, limestone, manganese, marble, sand, and zinc. Rivers in the valley have the potential to supply vast amounts of hydroelectric power.

Associated with the TVA is the atomic energy project in Oak Ridge. The TVA's steam plant can generate 2,558,200 kilowatts of electricity. About 650 miles (1,050 km) of the Tennessee River system can be navigated by small boats and barges. In the early 1970s, this system carried 25 million tons (23,000,000 t) of freight yearly. Chemical plants operated by the TVA act as national laboratories for research and for experimental production of fertilizers. The TVA also has provided over a billion seedlings and reforested 1½ million acres (600,000 ha) of land. Agents of the TVA actively promote better forest management in the valley.

LESSON 2 PAGES 332–333

CLIMATE

GOALS

1. To understand that the warmest parts of the region are in southern and low-lying areas. **2.** To explain the relationship between temperature and elevation and between temperature and latitude.

TEACHING SUGGESTIONS

● **1. Reading Tables.** After pupils have read pp. 332–333, discuss the tables with them. Pupils who have a firm grasp of latitude and longitude will easily be able to answer the text questions. Others may simply need to be reminded that the higher the number, the farther from the equator a given latitude is.

Use a map or draw a diagram for pupils who are having difficulty grasping the concept. Have one pupil call out the temperature as you point to each place in turn.

Later on, pupils will learn that distance inland and ocean currents affect temperature too. In fact, both factors may help account for temperature differences in the places on the bottom table. For simplicity's sake, these factors are not stressed here. However, you may wish to allow pupils who need a challenge to go ahead and research the effects of these two factors.

2. Questions and Answers. Use the following to review the content of the lesson.
a. *What does the term frost-free mean?* (The period of time when the temperature is always above freezing)
b. *How long does the frost-free season last in most coastal areas?* (6 months or more)
c. *What are two reasons for differences in temperatures in the area?* (Elevation differences and differences in latitude)
d. *If a place is humid, is it dry, or wet?* (Wet)
e. *What is a hurricane?* (A storm with high winds and heavy rainfall)
f. *Describe the "eye" of a hurricane.* (The calm, cloudless center of a hurricane, often several miles across)

3. Research Report. Have pupils do some research to find out why temperature is related to distance from the equator. Ask them to present the results of their research in the form of a bulletin-board display, a demonstration using a globe and a flashlight, or a short report.

4. Hurricanes. This topic is one that would interest many pupils in the fifth grade. Hurricanes pack a violent punch and often totally disrupt life in an area, as well as cause millions of dollars worth of damage. Sometimes lives are lost during a particularly bad hurricane. The topic can be developed in the form of book reports, movies, or essays. Pupils can seek to discover the causes of hurricanes, the course they take (from the ocean to inland areas), how they are predicted, and the impact of some of the more powerful hurricanes.

LESSON 3   PAGES 334–338

AGRICULTURE, INDUSTRY, AND RESOURCES

GOALS

1. To name some of the major agricultural products of the Southeast. **2.** To list some of the tourist attractions in the Southeast. **3.** To briefly describe the fishing industry and tree farming in the Southeast. **4.** To list some reasons textile mills have been successful in the Southeast. **5.** To list at least four important mineral resources of the Southeast. **6.** To name two methods of extracting coal from the ground, and to list three ways in which underground mining is dangerous to the miners. **7.** To explain why coal decreased in importance and why it is again an important fuel.

TEACHING SUGGESTIONS

1. Questions and Answers. As pupils read the text, have them find the answers to the following.
a. *Name four citrus fruits.* (Oranges, lemons, limes, grapefruit)
b. *What are two important nonfood crops from the Southeast?* (Tobacco, cotton)
c. *Why is cotton grown inland?* (Inland areas are drier than the coastal areas.)
d. *Name some of the tourist attractions of*

Florida. (Walt Disney World, the beaches of the Atlantic and the Gulf coasts, the Florida Keys, the Kennedy Space Center, and the Everglades)

e. *What are two historic villages that people may visit in the Southeast?* (Williamsburg and Jamestown)

f. *How is menhaden used?* (For bait, fertilizer, and oil)

g. *What is one thing that scientists on tree farms do?* (Try to develop fast-growing types of trees)

h. *Why are the textile mills of the Southeast successful?* (Good workers, well-run plants, and good transportation)

i. *What is one major use of the sand and gravel mined in the Southeast?* (The making of highways)

j. *Why did coal become less important?* (People were using more oil and gas.)

k. *What has made coal more important today?* (We are running out of oil and gas and both have become expensive.)

l. *What are some of the advantages of strip mining?* (It is safer and less costly.)

m. *What is one of the problems with strip mining?* (It destroys the land.)

n. *What would happen if mining companies did not restore the land after strip mining?* (The land would erode, little vegetation would grow, and the land would be ugly and of little value.)

o. *What are some of the dangers of underground mining?* (Cave-ins, poisonous or explosive gases, dust explosions, and black lung disease)

2. Research. While reading about the raising of citrus fruits, your pupils may profit from learning about the value of these fruits to human health. This can be fostered by a report concerning the importance of vitamin C to the diet. Also, pupils interested in history might find fascinating the reason English sailors were called "limeys." Using the library resources, pupils can discover that many years ago the English discovered that medical prob-lems caused by the lack of vitamin C on long sea voyages could be avoided by taking along a citrus fruit, the lime.

3. Life Skills. It may be hard for pupils to understand why they must learn about such topics as agriculture and industry. One way of relating these studies to pupils' lives is to have them think about future career choices. Ask each pupil to think of three jobs he or she might want. As a homework assignment, have each pupil find employment ads for at least one of those jobs or for a job in the same field. In class, discuss the ads, pointing out the meaning of abbreviations and showing pupils how they can determine whether the salaries are weekly, monthly, or yearly. Have pupils think of questions they might be asked by prospective employers and questions they might ask the employers.

SUPPLEMENTARY INFORMATION

1. Jamestown. The original Jamestown was established on a peninsula in the James River. The peninsula has since become an island. Visible at the site are the ruins of a church, foundation stones from some of the buildings, and many relics. The church ruins are under the care of the Association for the Preservation of Virginia Antiquities. The remaining area is under National Park Service jurisdiction.

2. Great Smoky Mountains National Park. This lovely park is noted for its virgin hardwood and red spruce forests and for its large variety of shrubs and flowering plants. The park is located on the boundary between Tennessee and North Carolina and contains within its 517,368 acres (206,947 ha) most of the section of the Appalachians designated by the name Great Smoky Mountains.

Of the many high peaks contained within the park (and the Smokies are among the highest in the Appalachians) is Clingmans Dome, which at 6,643 feet (2,025 m) is the highest in the Smokies.

POPULATION AND CITIES

GOALS

1. To name Florida as the state with the largest and fastest growing population in the Southeast. 2. To list four types of cities in the Southeast states, and give an example of each. 3. To describe some of the problems of Appalachia and to explain why conditions there are improving. 4. To use a grid, or coordinate system, to locate places on a map.

TEACHING SUGGESTIONS

1. **Questions and Answers.** Use the following for a review of the text reading.

a. *Where do most of the people in Florida live?* (In cities)

b. *Which Southeastern cities have more than 500,000 people?* (Memphis and Jacksonville)

c. *Name four types of cities and give an example of each.* (Manufacturing cities, trade centers, port cities, and resort cities. Examples will vary.)

d. *What is the National Center for Disease Control?* (A place where people look for ways to control outbreaks of diseases that spread from one person to another)

e. *Why do governments have consulates in Atlanta?* (Atlanta is the Southeast's center for foreign trade. People in the consulates help make agreements between business people from their countries and those from the Atlanta area.)

f. *Why has Birmingham tried to attract new industries?* (So the city would not be dependent upon just one industry)

g. *What important contribution to the lives of the blind comes from Louisville, Kentucky?* (Braille books)

h. *What three claims to fame does the port of Norfolk, Virginia, have?* (Exports more goods than any other Atlantic port, is the biggest coal port in the world, and has the largest naval base in the United States.)

i. *Why does much of the southern part of Florida have such a low population density?* (The Everglades are located there.)

j. *What factors contributed to the poverty in Appalachia?* (Difficult travel and hilly land made farming unprofitable; coal mines died when the demand for coal dropped.)

k. *What conditions have changed life in Appalachia in recent years?* (Renewed interest in coal, new methods and fertilizers to make farming profitable, the TVA electrification program, ski and resort facilities, and better roads)

2. **Reading a Table.** Have pupils look at the chart at the top of p. 339. Ask:

a. *Which state has the largest population?* (Florida) *The smallest?* (West Virginia)

b. *Which state has the highest percentage of people living in rural areas?* (West Virginia)

c. *Which state is mostly urban?* (Florida)

d. *Which states have more than four cities with populations of over 100,000 people?* (Virginia, North Carolina, Florida)

3. **Survey.** One information-gathering technique is the survey. Pupils can gain some experience with surveying while studying this lesson. Using the list of cities in the city index on p. 343, they can form the frame of a survey to learn which cities are most visited by members of the class or school.

A second survey can be built from the tourist areas of the Southeast. Using an encyclopedia, pupils can locate the major recreational sites for each state, and then make a questionnaire requesting each child and teacher in the school to check off the places they have visited. Your class would then compile the results and rank the recreational sites according to popularity. The final data can be "published" and distributed to each participating class.

4. Using Coordinates. Use the map on p. 343 to give pupils practice in using coordinates. Have them name the cities in a variety of boxes, such as A-3, B-2, and C-2. Then have them give the coordinates for a number of cities, such as Memphis, B-1.

SUPPLEMENTARY INFORMATION

Dismal Swamp. The Dismal Swamp is a marshland (750 square miles, or 1,940 sq km) on the Coastal Plain between Virginia and North Carolina. A portion of the swamp in Virginia was named a National Wildlife Refuge in 1974. Although there are clearings here and there throughout the swamp, the land is heavily wooded with juniper, water ash, pine, black tupelo, and bald cypress. Honeysuckle and woodbine vines abound. In addition to bears, deer, opossums, and raccoons, there are many species of snakes and birds, including the nearly extinct ivory-billed woodpecker.

In the middle of the eighteenth century, the swamp covered an area of 2,000 square miles (5,200 sq km). It was surveyed in 1763 by a team whose members included George Washington. Not long after that, about 62 square miles (161 sq km) were drained and the land reclaimed for agriculture. Over the years much of the marsh has been drained, until less than half of the original swampland remains. In the center of the swamp is Lake Drummond, which is connected to the Lake Drummond Canal by Feeder Ditch. The Lake Drummond Canal was built between 1790 and 1828. It is a part of the Intracoastal Waterway, linking Chesapeake Bay with Albemarle Sound in North Carolina. The canal is used in connection with lumbering activities in the swamp.

17/CHAPTER REVIEW   PAGE 346
Answers for Review Questions
1. The Atlantic Coastal Plain is located along the shore of the Atlantic Ocean. The Gulf Coastal Plain is along the shore of the Gulf of Mexico. Both plains stretch inland for several hundred miles in many places.
2. The Everglades are swampy lands covering most of Florida from Lake Okeechobee south. They have many kinds of plants and animals. The climate is warm and wet. Much of the area is composed of parks and wildlife refuges.
3. The Piedmont is the upland area located between the Atlantic Coastal Plain and the Appalachians.
4. TVA stands for Tennessee Valley Authority. The TVA built dams to control flooding, generate electricity, and provide irrigation water. It also makes fertilizer and has introduced soil conservation methods to many people in the area. The TVA has made the Tennessee River navigable from Knoxville to Paducah.
5. Temperature and latitude are related in that temperature generally decreases with distance from the equator (assuming that elevation and distance inland are about the same).

Temperature and elevation are related in that temperature generally decreases with rising elevation (assuming the latitude and distance inland are about the same). Note: Pupils will probably not include the material in parentheses in the above answers since these points were not stressed in the text.
6. Answers will vary.
7. Strip mining is a method of mining in which large shovels remove the earth covering the deposit of coal.
8. Answers will vary.
9. Life in Appalachia was hard at one time. The land was not very good for farming and the area was isolated. There were few ways of earning a living and poverty was widespread. Life is changing in Appalachia since coal mining is again providing more jobs; electricity and improved transportation are encouraging the growth of business and industry; and tourism is increasing.

THE SOUTH CENTRAL STATES TODAY

THEME

The South Central states are few in number but are of great importance in terms of mineral and agricultural resources.

PROJECTS

1. In the second lesson, pupils will read that irrigation is important in the agriculture of the South Central states. Many different types of irrigation are being used all over the world. Many other types have appeared in history. Pupils can find pictures of some of the various systems and reproduce these pictures on blank filmstrip. Permanent, fine-point markers must be used to make these drawings. The text to accompany the filmstrip can be recorded on a tape recorder. Pupils will enjoy putting in a chime or other signal to indicate the need to advance the filmstrip. Ambitious pupils may wish to select appropriate background music.

2. The value of plants in preventing erosion can be demonstrated in class by preparing two trays with backyard soil. One pan is left as is. In the other pan pupils can plant grass seeds. After the grass has grown and the roots have had sufficient time to become established, the two pans can be compared as to resistance to eroding conditions. To demonstrate the value of plants in resisting water erosion the two pans are tilted at the same angle, and water is sprinkled over the high portion of the pans. Make certain that the runoff water has a place to go. It is not advisable to let it drain in a sink since the drain may clog. An old bucket is best.

LESSON 1   PAGES 348–352

THE LAND AND CLIMATE

GOALS

1. To list the four states of the South Central region. 2. To describe the major topographical features and name the great rivers of the South Central region. 3. To describe the ways the Mississippi has been a boon and a problem to the people living by the river. 4. To describe the factors that give South Central farmers a long growing season. 5. To read temperature and precipitation charts.

TEACHING SUGGESTIONS

1. **Questions and Answers.** To make sure pupils have understood the reading on pp. 348–352, use the following questions:

a. *Name the four states of the South Central states.* (Arkansas, Texas, Louisiana, and Oklahoma)
b. *List four natural resources of all four states.* (Oil, natural gas, large forests, and rich, fertile soil)
c. *How would you describe a delta?* (Land built up by silt deposits at the mouth of a river)
d. *How did the* Llano Estacado *get its name?* (From early explorers who found the area so flat that they placed stakes in the ground to mark where they had been)
e. *In what way has the Mississippi River been of help to people?* (It has been a major water transportation route throughout the history of the United States.)
f. *Of what value is silt to the farmers near the river?* (It helps make the land fertile for farming.)

g. *What major problem does the river sometimes present? What is one of the ways people have worked to lessen that problem?* (Flooding. People have built levees to hold back the rising water.)

h. *What does the term Rio Grande mean in English?* ("Great River")

i. *Describe the natural warming system that keeps winters mild in the South Central states.* (Warm waters from the area around the equator flow into the Gulf of Mexico. This warm water warms the breezes that blow towards the land and, therefore, the air over the land surfaces.)

j. *What is a tornado?* (A violent storm marked by cone-shaped clouds with high-powered, twisting winds)

● **2. Map Reading.** As pupils read the text, have them locate on the map the various physical features mentioned.

For pupils who have difficulty with map reading, review the use of symbols by pointing out the symbols used on the map: circled stars for capital cities, dots for other cities, ticked line for canals, and triangles for mountain peaks.

For pupils who need a challenge, use Teaching Suggestion 3.

3. Three-Dimensional Relief Map. A rather simple relief map of the South Central states can be constructed using cardboard. Pupils should first cut from cardboard the outline of the region. This outline is used as a base. Then have pupils cut from cardboard pieces the shape of each land feature at a number of elevations. Finally, the shapes should be glued to the base map. The overall product has the appearance of a series of plateaus or terraces. However, this kind of map clearly shows changes of elevation.

4. Using the Overhead Projector. The overhead projector can be used very effectively to demonstrate certain points in a presentation. Pupils can use the projector to show the great number of states that border the Mississippi River. To do this

they would need to have a number of transparencies, a map showing the Mississippi River and the surrounding states, and permanent felt marker pens. The first transparency would show the general shape of the river. The second transparency might show Wisconsin and Minnesota. The third transparency would show Illinois and Iowa. Each succeeding transparency would show another set of states through which the river passes or whose borders the river touches. As each transparency is placed over the one on the projector, pupils see rather dramatically the size of the river and the scope of the land it affects. Major cities along the river can be marked on each of the states.

5. Believe-It-or-Not Report. The storm known as the tornado is most unusual in many ways. The power and speeds involved in such a storm can be the topic of a Believe-It-or-Not booklet created by a small group of pupils for distribution to the class. Such a booklet would have short sentences explaining the formation, effects, characteristics, and other interesting pieces of information about the tornado.

SUPPLEMENTARY INFORMATION

Landsat Satellites. A landsat satellite moves in a nearly circular orbit around the earth at an altitude of about 570 miles (917 km). It crosses the equator on the day side of the earth 14 times a day at about 9.30 A.M. local time. Each successive orbit is parallel to the previous orbit but crosses the equator at a point somewhat farther west, so that slightly different but overlapping views are obtained.

The Landsat's scanning system converts into electrical signals the different wavelengths of light given off by the various features on the earth. These signals are transmitted to a receiving station on the earth. (There are three stations in the United States, but only one is operational at present.) The data obtained by the scanning system can be stored on the Landsat until it passes within receiving distance of the station. The signals are used to produce black and white photographic images, which are then filtered to produce the characteristic colors of Landsat photographs. Growing vegetation shows up in shades of red. Rocks and soils range from bluish to yellows and browns. Water is in shades of blue to black depending on the depth and the amount of sediment. Cultural features such as towns and roads appear in distinctive patterns of bluish black.

Landsat data has applications in many fields, including agriculture, forestry, resource management, cartography, geology, oceanography, and environmental studies. Within these fields, Landsat data is used in a variety of ways, including measurement of land use, timber types and volume, crop types, pollution, flooding, and forest-fire damage.

LESSON 2 PAGES 352–354

AGRICULTURE

GOALS

1. To list seven crops grown in the South Central states. **2.** To read a chart showing rank in crop production by state. **3.** To list five ways machines are used in the harvesting and processing of sugarcane. **4.** To explain why rice fields are irrigated even in areas with abundant rainfall. **5.** To state the reasons Texas and Oklahoma are cattle-producing states. **6.** To list some of the tasks of the modern cowhand.

TEACHING SUGGESTIONS

1. Questions and Answers. Check pupils' comprehension of the text with the following questions:

a. *Name three factors that determine the type of crops raised in this area.* (Temperature, rainfall, and land features)

b. *What crops grow well in the warm, moist climate of the South Central states?* (Soybeans, rice, cotton, sugarcane, sweet potatoes, and citrus fruits)

c. *In what type of climate do sorghum grain and winter wheat grow?* (Drier and more temperate areas of the South Central states)

d. *Where are citrus fruits and vegetables grown?* (Along the Rio Grande and the Gulf Coast)

e. *Which is the leading state in the production of cotton?* (Texas)

f. *In what ways are machines used in the raising and processing of sugarcane?* (Preparing the fields, planting the cane, weeding, harvesting, and loading the cane onto trucks. Machines cut the cane, wash and crush the plants.)

g. *Name two products made from sugarcane.* (Syrup and sugar)

h. *Why are rice fields irrigated even though there is plenty of rainfall in Arkansas, Louisiana, and eastern Texas?* (Rice needs lots of water. The fields are irrigated to make sure that there is always enough water.)

i. *In what ways does winter wheat help save the soil?* (The roots of the wheat help prevent erosion during the dry winter.)

j. *Why are cattle sent to feedlots?* (To fatten them up before sending them to market)

k. *In what way has the work of cowhands changed from the days of the Old West?* (They now use jeeps and helicopters.)

l. *What does the word* rodeo *mean in Spanish?* ("Surround" or "round up")

●**2. International Comparison.** Have groups of pupils use the appropriate reference tools in the library to locate some of the other countries in the world that have the same agricultural products as the South Central states. Have pupils look for ways in which these countries are similar to the states now being studied. Direct attention to rainfall, land features, and temperature. Discuss whether any generalizations can be made from this comparison.

For pupils who have difficulty using research tools, provide guidance, either your own or that of a capable pupil.

Ask pupils who require a challenge to prepare tables and graphs to illustrate the similarities and differences.

3. Comparing Cattle Types. The text states that cattle ranching is the best known and most important agricultural activity in Oklahoma and Texas. What pupils may not know is that these two states are leading states in the raising of beef cattle not dairy cattle. Using appropriate reference books and encyclopedia articles, pupils may wish to compare these two categories of cattle. They will find many differences between beef and dairy cattle. Posters can effectively display the information pupils have learned.

4. Creative Writing. The excitement of the rodeo offers members of the class an opportunity for creative writing. Ask pupils what it would be like for a city boy or girl to enter a rodeo event after a little training. Ask how this brave soul would talk himself or herself into the ring. Pupils can reflect upon the fears and the sights and the sounds of the day of the rodeo. After researching the events, pupils in your class can probably describe the event itself and then write a logical ending to this drama.

LESSON 3   PAGES 355–359

RESOURCES AND INDUSTRY

GOALS

1. To list at least two mineral and two energy resources of the South Central states. **2.** To name Texas, Louisiana, and Oklahoma as leading oil-producing states. **3.** To give a brief explanation of how oil is obtained and to list five uses for refined oil. **4.** To state two reasons for oil spills and to list three dangers of oil spills. **5.** To name at least three other industries of the South Central states.

TEACHING SUGGESTIONS

1. Questions and Answers. Use the following for a check on pupils' understanding of the content of the lesson. You may wish to divide the questions into two or more groups, rather than using them all at once.
a. *What kind of mine is found in the state park near Murfreesboro, Arkansas?* (Diamond mine)
b. *If the United States can get bauxite from its own mines, why do we import bauxite from South America and Africa?* (The mines in the United States do not supply enough bauxite to meet the demands of our aluminum industry.)
c. *Name some of the ways sulfur is used.* (To keep rubber from becoming too sticky in the summer and too brittle in the winter; to make matches, gunpowder, and insect sprays)
d. *Aside from seasoning our food, what are some uses for salt?* (Making glass, preserving meat, and processing leather)
e. *Which three South Central states are leading oil producers in the United States?* (Texas, Louisiana, Oklahoma)
f. *What does the geologist study?* (The earth's surface and the layers of rocks below the surface)
g. *What are wells that don't yield oil or gas called?* (Dry wells or dry holes)
h. *What is a derrick?* (A tall, steel frame)
i. *How do workers get to the oil platforms in the Gulf of Mexico?* (Boat or helicopter)
j. *How long do workers stay on the platform at one time?* (Two to three weeks)
k. *Why are diamonds used on the drill bits?* (They are hard enough to cut through rock.)
l. *What happens to oil at the refinery?* (It is made into many products.)

m. *Name some uses of oil.* (Gasoline for cars, jet fuel, fuel for power for factories, fuel oil to heat homes, diesel fuel, fuel for camp stoves, solvents, asphalt, and lubricants)

n. *Name some products made from petrochemicals.* (Medicine, fertilizer for growing food, plastics, some clothes, and soaps)

o. *What are some of the problems presented by oil spills?* (Harm people, beaches, plants, and wildlife. Oil spills can ruin the life forms in the tidal pools, stick to the feathers of the birds, and pollute the water.)

p. *What other industries are located in this area?* (Tourism, electronics, lumbering, and the space industry)

2. Research Project. The text mentions that many minerals are to be found in the South Central states. Have the pupils select a mineral mentioned and learn how this mineral is mined and/or how it is used. Fifth graders are probably surprised to learn that salt has over 14,000 uses. Many probably cannot imagine how salt can be used for anything save flavoring hamburgers and French fries. A report of this nature, accompanied by class presentations, can open the eyes of many pupils.

3. Graphing. The general topic of petroleum offers pupils many opportunities to practice some of the graphing skills they have learned. The following topics lend themselves to graphing: Leading Countries in Oil Production; Changes in Cost of a Barrel of Oil over the Past Ten Years.

4. Making a Petroleum Dictionary. The oil industry has many terms that are becoming part of the general vocabulary. Pupils can collect many of these terms from appropriate library references and make a petroleum dictionary. Some terms include:

crude	Christmas tree	kelly
barrel	bit	roughneck
kerosene	casing	pipeline
refinery	rig	royalty
derrick	distillation	dry well

5. Career Exploration. Geology may be just the profession for some of the pupils in the class. A career research project might serve to enlighten an interested pupil in the possibilities in this profession. Such a career report might include such issues as educational requirements, places where geologists find employment, financial rewards, and future prospects for the need for geologists in our country.

LESSON 4   PAGES 360–361

POPULATION AND CITIES

GOALS

1. To name the three South Central cities that are among the 25 largest cities in the United States. **2.** To describe the Mardi Gras. **3.** To name two reasons for Houston's growth. **4.** To name Spanish as a second language and culture of San Antonio in particular and of the southwestern United States in general. **5.** To list at least two reasons for the importance of the Dallas/Fort Worth metropolitan area.

TEACHING SUGGESTIONS

1. Questions and Answers. Use the following to check pupils' comprehension of the lesson.

a. *What is the largest city in the state of Arkansas?* (Little Rock)

b. *What city was named after an important leader in the American settlement of Texas?* (Austin)

c. *Name some of the peoples who have lived in the New Orleans area over the years.* (Indians, French, Spanish, Africans, and Americans)

d. *What is the Mardi Gras?* (A festival celebrated in New Orleans during the two weeks before Lent)

e. *How do ships reach the port of Houston?* (Through a deepwater channel that connects the port with the Gulf of Mexico)

f. *What cultures have influenced life in the city of San Antonio?* (Spanish [Mexican] and American)

g. *Name some of the things that make Dallas/Fort Worth an important metropolitan area.* (The cities both have important aircraft industries, the area has very large oil reserves, and one of the busiest airports in the country.)

h. *How did Hot Springs get its name?* (From the hot mineral water that comes up from the ground)

2. Map Making. Using an opaque projector or a transparency on an overhead projector, have pupils enlarge and then trace a map of the South Central states. When they enlarge a map using visual projection equipment, they must alter the scale. Have pupils consider the best way to make the enlargement in order to create a new scale. They will probably decide to double the size of the map or enlarge it to the next unit of measure, e.g., inch to foot or millimeter to centimeter.

3. Research Reports. The following are descriptions of reports pupils might be asked to prepare.

a. The Changing of Hands. Pupils can undertake to learn about the various ways certain cities "changed hands" so many times in history. Some South Central cities, such as Baton Rouge and New Orleans, have flown several flags.

b. The Mardi Gras. This most unusual celebration gives New Orleans a unique charm. What the Mardi Gras is and how it is celebrated can be an enjoyable report.

c. Hot Springs. What are hot springs and from where do they come? For most pupils the idea of water bubbling up from the ground at 145°F (63°C) is hard to imagine. A report on this topic would lead the researcher into elements of geology.

● **4. Map Reading.** Have pupils locate on the map on p. 362 each city described on pp. 360–361. Have them give the grid coordinates and population category for each.

(Little Rock, A–4, 100,000–499,000; Austin, B–3, 100,000–499,000; Baton Rouge, B–5, 100,000–499,000; Oklahoma City, A–3, 100,000–499,000; New Orleans, B–5, 500,000–999,000; Houston, B–4, 1,000,000 or more; San Antonio, B–3, 500,000–999,000; Dallas, B–3, 500,000–999,000; Fort Worth, B–3, 100,000–499,000; Hot Springs, A–4, less than 100,000)

Help pupils who are having difficulty with the grid system by physically guiding their fingers across and down the map.

For pupils who need a challenge, provide several road maps and let them find on the map selected cities from the map index. These pupils could work in pairs, with one pupil choosing the city to be located and the other using the coordinates to find the city on the map.

18/CHAPTER REVIEW PAGE 364
Answers for Review Questions

1. The Llano Estacado got its name from the Spanish explorers, who to avoid getting lost in the flat prairie, put stakes into the ground to show where they had been.

2. Three important rivers of the South Central region are the Mississippi River, the Rio Grande, and the Red River.

3. The warm winds from the Gulf of Mexico make the winters mild and the summers warm and humid.

4. Answers will vary.

5. Answers will vary.

6. The cutting edges of an oil drill are made of diamonds because they are hard enough to cut through rock.

7. Answers will vary.

8. Any oil spill destroys the habitat of many types of animals, it destroys plants, pollutes the water, and coats the feathers of water birds.

9. The four South Central states are Texas, Louisiana, Oklahoma, and Arkansas. Their capitals are, respectively, Austin, Baton Rouge, Oklahoma City, and Little Rock.

CHAPTER 19 PAGES 366–385

THE NORTH CENTRAL STATES TODAY

THEME

The wealth of agricultural and industrial products from the North Central states makes this region the Heartland in more than location.

PROJECT

If possible, arrange to have a group of pupils interview a dairy farmer. Questions can be constructed from the text material and from additional reading. Make sure pupils realize that the interviewers must have enough information about the topic to ask intelligent questions. Some possible questions are (a) What kinds of cows are on your farm? (b) How much milk can a cow on your farm give in a good year? (c) What kind of bookkeeping must you do in order to make a profit? (d) Could a computer help a modern farmer and, if so, how? (e) What are some of the health/safety procedures you follow?

Urban children can have the opportunity to ask such questions by doing some aggressive searching for resources. Using a map of the North Central states, pupils can address a letter to the superintendent of schools of one of the rural towns listed on the map. The letter can explain that the class is located in an urban school and the pupils would appreciate having their questions forwarded by the superintendent's office to a local dairy farmer who might be willing to answer the questions. It may even be possible to find a dairy farmer with a child of the same age as the children in your class. In that case information about the respective environments could be shared, as well. The project could turn out to be an exciting one, extending far beyond the original scope of the assignment.

LESSON 1 PAGES 366–369

THE LAND

GOALS

1. To name the states and the most important physical feature of the North Central region. 2. To describe the area known as the Bad Lands. 3. To explain why the Great Lakes are called inland seas. 4. To name the major rivers of the North Central states. 5. To state one reason for the dams on the Missouri and its tributaries.

TEACHING SUGGESTIONS

1. **Questions and Answers.** Use the following to check pupils' understanding of the text reading.

a. *How wide is the North Central region from east to west? From north to south?* (1,000 miles, or 1,600 km; 800 miles, or 1,300 km)

b. *Name the states of the North Central region.* (Illinois, Indiana, Iowa, Kansas, Michigan, Minnesota, Missouri, Nebraska, North Dakota, Ohio, South Dakota, Wisconsin)

c. *What are two things that make this area a region?* (The plains and the farms)

d. *Of the 30 largest cities in the United States, how many are found in the North Central states?* (Eight)

e. *What is the highest point of the North Central region?* (Harney Peak)

f. *What are Bad Lands?* (Dry, rugged lands with little or no vegetation, deep gullies, and steep bluffs)

g. *How were the lakes of this area formed?* (Glaciers carved out hollows, which later filled with water from the melted ice.)

h. *Why are the Great Lakes called inland seas?* (They are so large that they are more like seas than lakes.)

i. *Name three major rivers of the area.* (Missouri, Ohio, Mississippi)

j. *What is one reason why dams were built on the Missouri River and its tributaries?* (To control the seasonal flooding)

● **2. Map Reading.** Give pupils practice in using a scale by having them find the distances between places on the map, p. 367.

For pupils who have difficulty with the concept of scale, bring in a chair from a dollhouse. Have pupils measure it and a classroom chair as well. Have them round off both measurements to make computation easier. Ask: *Why can't we sit in the dollhouse chair? If it were twice as big, how big would it be? Could you sit in it then? How much bigger would it have to be in order for us to use it, that is, how much would we have to enlarge it to bring it to the size of a classroom chair?* If necessary, take pupils through each multiple: three times as big, four times, and so on. Probably, someone will suggest using a larger multiple after a few trials with small multiples. If not, do so yourself to save time.

Relate this demonstration to map scale by pointing out that just as the dollhouse chair has to be smaller than a real chair to fit into the dollhouse, maps have to be drawn smaller than the real world in order to fit on a page. The scale line is like the dollhouse chair; the number at the end of the line is like the number used to multiply the size of the dollhouse chair. In the case of the map on p. 367, the line is about 1 inch long (25 mm if you are using metric measure). The number at the end is 200 miles (300 km). So every time you measure 1 inch (25 mm) you know that it stands for 200 miles (300 km).

Have pupils who require a challenge do Teaching Suggestion 3.

3. Three-Dimensional Relief Map. Pupils can make a relief map of the North Central region by using papier-mâché on a stiff cardboard base. The size of the cardboard can be related to the scale of the map used as a model. Metric measurement is much easier to use for the purpose of enlarging a map than is customary measurement.

4. Diorama. A model of the Bad Lands can be constructed in a shoe box to make a diorama. Sand can be sprinkled on a surface covered with white glue, and then painted to create the proper effect.

5. Research Report. The story of the ice ages is fascinating. Pupils can learn of the cycles of the glaciers' advance and retreat, the changes in topography, and the changes in animal life. After they learn some more about the conditions that are thought to have led to an ice age, pupils who require a challenge can reflect upon conditions in the world today as they relate to changes in climate.

6. Creative Writing. What would the ice age do to modern civilization? Could humans develop the technology to survive a marked drop in temperature and increase in the amount of ice cover? Pupils working in groups can attempt to either "design" the technology and the methods for human survival or write a story centering upon the struggle to live through the next ice age.

SUPPLEMENTARY INFORMATION

The Great Plains. The Great Plains extends for 2,500 miles (4,000 km) from Canada to Texas and about 400 miles (640 km) eastward from the Rocky Mountains. On the east the Great Plains is about 1,500 feet (460 m) above sea level. Sloping at a rate of 10 feet a mile (2 m per km) to the west, the Great Plains ends at 4,500 to 6,500 feet (1,400–2,000 m) above sea level at the base of the Rocky Mountains.

The Great Plains tends to be rather flat

and dry. In the early 1800s an Army explorer, Major Stephen H. Long, had this to say about the Great Plains, "In regard to this extensive section of the country, I do not hesitate in giving this opinion, that it is almost wholly unfit for cultivation, and of course, uninhabitable by a people depending upon agriculture for their subsistence." On his official map he labeled these thousands of square miles of land, "The Great Desert." So great was the disaffection with the Plains during the 1800s that it was felt by some to be a blessing in disguise since it would prevent too great an expansion of the population westward. An exception to this negative view was that of John Frémont, the most famous member of the Corps of Topographical Engineers of the United States Army. He wrote of the rich, arable soil, sparkling streams, and lush grasses. "Everywhere," he stated, "the rose is met with and reminds us of cultivated gardens and civilization." History has proved Frémont to be the visionary.

LESSON 2   PAGES 369–370

CLIMATE

GOALS

1. To describe the variations in temperature and precipitation from north to south and east to west in the North Central region. **2.** To explain the effects of the Great Lakes on temperature and precipitation in the areas near the lakes. **3.** To describe the water cycle.

TEACHING SUGGESTIONS

1. Questions and Answers. Use the following to check comprehension of the text.
a. *What are the extremes of temperatures in the northern states?* (−40°F to 100°F [−40°C to 38°C])
b. *What part of the region has the warmest winters?* (Southern areas)

c. *How do temperatures change as one travels west?* (It gets hotter in the summer and colder in the winter.)
d. *In what ways do the Great Lakes affect the temperature of the surrounding areas?* (The temperature is warmer in the winter and cooler in the summer.)
e. *Why do the Great Lakes have this effect?* (Large bodies of water get warmer and cooler more slowly than the surrounding landmasses.)
f. *Where does the most precipitation fall in the North Central states?* (In the southeastern part, along the Ohio River valley)
g. *According to the water cycle diagram, where does most of the water that evaporates to make rain-bearing clouds come from?* (From the ocean surface)
h. *How much of the water that evaporates comes from the land or is given off by the plants?* (18 percent)
i. *How would this difference account for the increase in precipitation in the area surrounding the Great Lakes?* (If 82 percent of the moisture that forms rain-bearing clouds comes from large bodies of water like the oceans or large lakes, then the land surfaces near such bodies will have far more moisture in the air to form the rain-bearing clouds than those land areas far from large bodies of water.)
2. Plotting a Temperature Graph. Using the weather statistics from the newspaper or other source, such as an almanac, let the pupils graph the average temperatures for several cities of the North Central states. Pupils can check their graphs to see if the generalities stated in the text (concerning the lowering of temperature in the northern part and the western part of the region) hold true.
3. Plotting a Precipitation Graph. Using the weather statistics as above, have the pupils plot the precipitation for selected cities for a given year. Again, compare the graphs with the generalities made in the text. (Pupils should be told that gener-

alities are statements that hold true in most but not all instances.)

SUPPLEMENTARY INFORMATION
Precipitation in the North Central Region. Precipitation in the eastern part of this region is affected not only by the Great Lakes but also by the Gulf of Mexico. Winds blowing inland from the Gulf of Mexico carry a great deal of moisture. As these breezes move northward they bring rain to the eastern part of the North Central states. This factor allows farmers a greater diversity in the selection of crops to plant.

LESSON 3   PAGES 371–374

FARMLANDS AND FORESTS

GOALS
1. To list at least four of the most important crops of the North Central region. **2.** To state one major use of wheat and at least five uses of corn. **3.** To define the term *gasohol*. **4.** To state the reason that cattle are sent to the Corn Belt before being shipped to market. **5.** To locate the Dairy Belt and explain why this area is sometimes called the Hay and Dairy Belt. **6.** To describe the work of the dairy farmer. **7.** To explain the dangers of cutting down forests.

TEACHING SUGGESTIONS
1. Questions and Answers. You may want to use the following as a review of the text reading, or you may have pupils read to find the answers.
a. *What conditions make the North Central states ideal for farming?* (Fertile and deep soil; frost-free season long enough for many crops; and enough rainfall)
b. *States in the North Central region rank among the top producers of which eight crops?* (Wheat, corn, soybeans, barley, oats, sorghum, rye, hay)

c. *Where is winter wheat grown in the North Central region?* (In the warmer southern areas from Ohio to Nebraska and Kansas)
d. *What are some of the ways wheat is used?* (Answers will vary.)
e. *How is it possible that part of the Wheat Belt can also be in the Corn Belt?* (The land area is so large that there is enough room for both crops.)
f. *How is it helpful to the farmer to have all of the crop at the same height?* (The harvesting machines are set at a given height. More of the crop is harvested if the plants are all almost the same height.)
g. *List some of the uses of corn.* (Answers will vary.)
h. *What are barley "pearls" used for?* (Making soup)
i. *Why is there a chart on p. 373 to show the products made from soybeans?* (Because there are so many products made from soybeans)
j. *What does the term market weight mean?* (The weight an animal must reach before it is sent to market)
k. *How does a modern farmer bring a hog to market weight?* (The quantity and quality of the food that is given to hogs is carefully controlled. The proper amount of each kind of food is mixed automatically, so the farmer can be sure that hogs are being fed well.)
l. *Name the leading dairy state.* (Wisconsin)
m. *In the Dairy Belt what happens to most of the crops that are raised?* (They are used as animal feeds.)
n. *In what ways do farmers try to prevent milk from going bad?* (Barns, milking machines, and milk storage areas must be up to cleanliness standards; cattle are inspected and the milk tested often.)
o. *Name some of the reasons a farmer must keep good records.* (To make sure that the value of the milk is greater than the cost of feeding and caring for the cows. The

farmer can also tell which cows are the good producers.)

p. *Why are there few forests in the western and central parts of the North Central states?* (There is not enough rainfall in the west, and the trees have been cleared in the central areas.)

● **2. Interpreting a Chart.** Have pupils look at the chart on p. 371. Ask them to name the top ten corn-producing states, the top six soybean-producing states, and the top seven oat-producing states.

Help pupils who are having difficulty in reading tables construct their own chart based on this one. Across the top of the chart would be the name of the crops as shown. Along the sides would be the words *First, Second, Third,* and so on. Then, for each crop, pupils should locate the state that is the number one producer. Have pupils write the name of each state in the appropriate column. Thus, in the column with the word *Wheat* at the top will be the name of the state that is the number one producer of wheat: Kansas. In the column with the word *Corn* at top will be the number one producer of corn: Iowa. Pupils should continue in this way, filling in the state that is second, third, and so on in each crop. This procedure will allow pupils to see the information in the chart in the text in a slightly different way.

Have pupils who require a challenge create a similar chart showing top-ranking states in livestock production. Information for such a chart can be found in the *Statistical Abstract of the United States,* a reference work similar to an almanac and available in most libraries.

3. Tasting Wheat Germ. On p. 371 of the text is a diagram of the wheat kernel. Point out to the class the location of the wheat germ. Using other sources, the pupils in the class may wish to find out more about this part of the wheat kernel. Many pupils may never have tasted wheat germ. Today wheat germ comes flavored with brown sugar and honey, and the taste is often well accepted by children of this age. One bottle of wheat germ can easily provide the class with at least a taste of this healthful part of the wheat kernel.

4. Baking with Cornmeal. A social studies lesson like this one offers pupils the opportunity to consider how production in one part of the country affects lives in other parts of the country. Corn produced in the Corn Belt finds its way to kitchen tables in Florida, Maine, California, and Alaska. This point can be made while pupils are in the process of creating muffins using cornmeal made, more than likely, from corn grown in this part of the country.

Have pupils closely examine the cornmeal, perhaps even under high magnification. Encourage them to compare cornmeal to the refined white flour made from wheat. Perhaps they can make a list of the ways these two flours are the same and the ways they are different, using the senses of taste, touch, and sight. Then, using a recipe, members of the class can bake muffins using cornmeal in one batch and white flour alone for a second batch. Again, comparisons can be made and a vote can be taken to find out what part of the class prefers the corn muffins and what part of the class prefers the wheat muffins.

5. Gasohol Research. Gasohol is a mixture of 90 percent gasoline and 10 percent alcohol. Industrial alcohol can be made from molasses, potatoes, or grains, chiefly corn. It can also be made by a synthetic chemical process. Because the Corn Belt is the chief area of United States corn production, the use of gasohol can both significantly aid the oil situation and help the farmers of the North Central states. Pupils may wish to learn more about the promise and the production of gasohol. To do so they should consult the *Readers' Guide to Periodical Literature* to find the most current information. In addition, pupils can write to major oil-producing companies for literature.

Finding the address of the corporate headquarters might require some old-fashioned footwork. The place to start would be a reference work called *The Thomas Register* at a local library. Failing that, pupils might try a local service station. Another place to look for information is at the auto section of a large department store or at an auto supply store. Gasohol can be purchased over the counter. The address of the producer should appear on the container.

6. Breakfast Cereals Research. Another chance for primary research can be created using common breakfast cereals. Pupils can construct a list of all of the cereals consumed by fifth graders in the school.

After making a list of the products, pupils can embark upon a campaign to accumulate the empty boxes of these cereals. Then a small group can study the ingredients to discover the types of grain used in each product. The outcome of such a study would be a list of the cereals eaten by their peers and the crops used in the manufacture of the cereal product. Arranging the list according to the popularity of the cereal would add to the interest in constructing and reading the list.

SUPPLEMENTARY INFORMATION

Wheat. The wheat plant is a grass that belongs to a group of grains called cereals. There are about 30,000 varieties of wheat grown in various parts of the world. Some are adapted to hot climates, some to cold climates, others to dry climates. Scientists are working hard to increase the output of this valuable crop by creating varieties that will resist cold and drought, various kinds of plant diseases, and insects. At present we grow about 200 kinds of wheat in the United States. The United States Department of Agriculture has collected for study about 15,000 varieties of wheat from around the world. The scientists with the

department are always seeking to find plants with some outstanding quality in order to produce a new variety that combines the outstanding qualities of several plants.

LESSON 4   PAGES 375–378

INDUSTRY AND RESOURCES

GOALS
1. To name three industries of the North Central region that are related to agriculture. **2.** To name some by-products of the meat-packing industry. **3.** To name three basic necessities for industrial growth. **4.** To name at least three mineral resources of the North Central region. **5.** To name some of the products used in the manufacture of motor vehicles.

TEACHING SUGGESTIONS
1. Questions and Answers. Use the following for a check on comprehension.
a. *Name at least three industries in the North Central region that are related to agriculture.* (Answers will vary.)
b. *What process is used to make milk safe to drink?* (Pasteurization)
c. *How is grain transported?* (Truck, train, barge)
d. *Name two animal products other than meat.* (Answers will vary.)
e. *What are three things necessary for the growth of an industry?* (Good market, raw materials, good transportation network)
f. *Name three mineral resources of the North Central region.* (Answers will vary.)
g. *What is taconite? An open-pit mine?* (A low-grade iron ore. A mine in the form of a large hole, rather than underground tunnels)
h. *Name some of the products used in the manufacture of motor vehicles.* (Answers will vary.)

2. **Making a Mural.** Different groups of pupils could make wall murals on large sheets of brown wrapping paper. One group could show the different steps and products of the dairy industry; another group, the grain industry; another, the meat-packing industry.

3. **Discussion.** Stress the ideas presented in "Farm machinery," p. 376. Make sure pupils realize that these three conditions are necessary for the growth of *any* industry, not just the farm-machine industry. Ask pupils whether they can think of one more basic necessity for industrial growth. (Labor supply) Ask pupils to consider what would happen if any one of these conditions was not met.

4. **Ecology.** There is an environmental problem associated with taconite mining: disposal of the waste products, or tailings. Have an interested pupil research this problem and present his or her findings to the class.

LESSON 5   PAGES 378–380

POPULATION AND CITIES

GOALS

1. To name the state in the North Central region that has the largest population and the state that has the smallest population. 2. To name the two largest cities of the North Central region. 3. To name three cities of the North Central region and tell at least one interesting fact about each one.

TEACHING SUGGESTIONS

1. **Questions and Answers.** Have pupils read the text to find the answers to the following questions.
a. *Which of the North Central states has the largest population?* (Illinois) *The smallest?* (North Dakota)
b. *Which cities have more than 1 million*

people? (Detroit and Chicago)
c. *What has helped Chicago grow to its present size?* (The port on Lake Michigan)
d. *Name two products carried on ships leaving the port in Chicago.* (Grains, ores, and other goods)
e. *What are some of the industries located in the Chicago area?* (Iron and steel, electrical equipment, machinery, publishing, foods, plastics, and construction)
f. *Why is the Sears Tower in Chicago famous?* (Tallest building in the world)
g. *What two resources have helped make Cleveland one of our major iron- and steel-manufacturing centers?* (Iron and coal)
h. *Where is the city of Detroit located?* (On the Detroit River between Lake Huron and Lake Erie)
i. *Where is one of the largest salt mines in the United States located?* (Under the city of Detroit)
j. *What does the Gateway Arch in St. Louis help us remember?* (That St. Louis was the starting point for many pioneers heading west)

2. **Classification.** This lesson makes reference to the 25 largest cities in the United States. Have pupils find these cities on the map on p. 285. Ask whether they can find any characteristics common to the 25 cities, such as proximity to water routes, region, or availability of natural resources such as oil or coal. (Refer pupils to the resource maps on pp. 277, 279, and 281.)

3. **Map Making and the Great Lakes.** Have pupils create a large map of the Great Lakes and locate the port cities along the lakeshores. Pupils who need a challenge can use the library to find information about the most used shipping lanes of the Great Lakes. These can be plotted on the map.

4. **Bulletin-Board Display.** At present, the world's largest building is the Sears Tower in Chicago. At one time the tallest buildings were the World Trade Towers in New

York City. Prior to that the Empire State building held the distinction as the world's tallest building. Children of the fifth grade are often fascinated by the superlatives of our world. Many seem to enjoy talk of the world's fastest, tallest, or greatest. These children would probably enjoy a display of the outlined drawings of the five tallest buildings in the world. Each drawing would be labeled with the name, location, date of completion, and height of the building. This information is available in the *Guinness Book of Records* and in many almanacs.

5. Research Report. Detroit is so famous worldwide for its automobile industry that the city is often referred to as Motor City. An interesting report would be a study of some aspect of this industry. Some suggestions are How the Assembly Line Works, Henry Ford and His Model T, and Early History of the Automobile.

6. Map Reading. The map on p. 381 shows very clearly the impact of the Great Lakes on population distribution. Make sure pupils notice the great concentration of cities on the shores of Lakes Erie and Michigan. Have pupils practice their skills at using the scale by measuring the distance between various cities.

19/CHAPTER REVIEW   PAGE 384
Answers for Review Questions
1. Glaciers changed the landscape of the North Central region by carving out hollows that later filled with water to form the lakes and rivers of the region. The glaciers also moved masses of earth and huge boulders.

2. The water cycle is the process by which water evaporates from the earth's surface, forms clouds, condenses, and returns to the earth in the form of precipitation.

3. Answers will vary.

4. Most cattle are raised on the grasslands of the Great Plains.

5. Our leading dairy state is Wisconsin.

6. The making of farm machinery is a leading industry of the North Central region because the region contains a good market, the raw materials, and a good transportation network.

7. Answers will vary but should reflect the idea that industries need one another.

8. The two cities in the North Central region with more than 1 million people are Chicago and Detroit.

19/SKILLS DEVELOPMENT   PAGE 385
Answers for Skills Development
1. In the first paragraph, one reads that Huck and Jim dangled their legs in the water. In the third paragraph one reads that frogs could be heard.

2. The author uses *sparks* instead of *light*.

3. The author uses the word *belch* to let you know that the sparks came in bursts.

4. The author uses *a whole world of* to let you know that there were lots of sparks. He uses *rain down* instead of *fall down*.

5. Answers will vary, but should reflect the fact that the origin of stars is the kind of topic discussed by people who are relaxed and at ease.

THE MOUNTAIN WEST STATES TODAY

THEME

The Mountain West states contain many well-known natural features. Most of these are part of our National Park System. This region is also known for its valuable mineral resources. Although these states are not heavily industrialized, they have a growing population.

PROJECTS

1. Have pupils develop on index cards state profiles to be kept for future reference. Cards might include such information as the capital, major cities, population growth, state symbols, geographical features, natural resources, agricultural and industrial products, and climate. (The chart on pp. 398–399 and an almanac may be sources for this kind of information.)
2. Have pupils make a bulletin-board display that locates and illustrates some of the national parks. Individual pupils might report on some of these and attach their reports to the bulletin board.

THE LAND AND CLIMATE

GOALS

1. To name the eight Mountain West states and locate them on a United States map. 2. To locate the Great Plains, the Rocky Mountains, the intermontane region, the Continental Divide, the Colorado and Snake rivers, the Great Salt Lake, and the Painted Desert on a map. 3. To note and compare the differences in climate in the region.

TEACHING SUGGESTIONS

1. **Questions and Answers.** Use the following questions for a review of the lesson.
a. *What is the most outstanding feature of this region?* (The Rocky Mountains)
b. *Where are the highest peaks of the Rockies located and how high are they?* (Colorado, over 14,000 feet, or 4,270 m)
c. *Where is the intermontane region located?* (Between the Rockies on the east and the Cascades and Sierra Nevadas on the west)
d. *What are the three major parts of the intermontane region?* (Columbia Plateau, Colorado Plateau, and the Great Basin)
e. *What are three important rivers of the region?* (Colorado, Snake, and Columbia)
f. *What is an arroyo?* (A dry streambed)
g. *Where is the Painted Desert located?* (Northern Arizona)
h. *Where is the Great Salt Lake located?* (Northwestern Utah)

2. **Outlining.** Have pupils outline the section on climate, pp. 389–390. Refer pupils to the Skills Development page on outlining at the end of Chapter 1, if they need to review methods of outlining.

3. **Longitude and Latitude.** Using the map on p. 397, have the pupils give the longitude and latitude for the following: the source of the Colorado and Snake rivers, the cities of Denver and Phoenix, the Great Salt Lake, and Yellowstone National Park. (Colorado River: 40°N/106°W; Snake River: 45°N/112°W; Denver: 40°N/105°W; Phoenix: 33°N/112°W; Great Salt Lake: Between 40°N and 41°N and between 112°W and 113°W; Yellowstone: Between 44°N and 45°N and between 110°W and 111°W)

4. Graphing. Have pupils make graphs using the climate information in the Supplementary Information below. When the graphs are completed, discuss them with the class. Point out that although Flagstaff and Phoenix are in the same state, Flagstaff is both colder and wetter because of its elevation. The same is true of Ely and Las Vegas in Nevada. Discuss the effects of northern location and distance inland.

SUPPLEMENTARY INFORMATION

1. Climate Data, Mountain West

Weather Station	Record Temperature Extremes		Average January Temperature		Average July Temperature		Average Yearly Temperature		Average Yearly Precip.		Average Yearly Snowfall	
	°F	°C	°F	°C	°F	°C	°F	°C	In.	Cm	In.	Cm
Flagstaff, Ariz.	97/−23	36/−31	28	−2	66	19	45	7	19	48	91	231
Phoenix, Ariz.	118/17	48/−8	51	11	70	21	70	21	8	20	Trace	
Alamosa, Colo.	93/−50	34/−46	23	−5	72	22	42	6	7	18	36	91
Pocatello, Idaho	104/−30	40/−34	17	−8	65	18	47	8	11	28	40	102
Helena, Mont.	105/−17	41/−41	18	−8	68	20	43	6	11	28	49	124
Ely, Nev.	99/−28	37/−33	24	−4	67	19	44	7	9	23	48	122
Las Vegas, Nev.	116/8	47/−13	44	7	90	32	66	19	4	10	1	3
Albuquerque, N. Mex.	105/−17	41/−27	35	2	79	26	57	14	8	20	11	28
Salt Lake City, Utah	107/−30	42/−34	28	−2	77	25	51	11	16	41	59	150
Casper, Wyo.	104/−40	40/−40	23	−5	71	22	45	7	11	28	75	191

2. Elevation, Latitude, and Longitude of Weather Stations on the Table.

Flagstaff: 7,006 feet (2,135 m); 35°08′N/111°40′W

Phoenix: 1,110 feet (338 m); 33°26′N/112°01′W

Alamosa: 7,536 feet (2,297 m); 37°27′N/105°05′W

Pocatello: 4,454 feet (1,358 m); 42°55′N/112°36′W

Helena: 3,828 feet (1,167 m); 46°36′N/112°00′W

Ely: 6,253 feet (1,906 m); 39°17′N/114°51′W

Las Vegas: 2,162 feet (659 m); 36°15′N/115°10′W

Albuquerque: 5,311 feet (1,619 m); 35°03′N/106°37′W

Salt Lake City: 4,221 feet (1,287 m); 40°46′N/111°58′W

Casper: 5,338 feet (1,627 m); 42°55′N/106°28′W

AGRICULTURE, RESOURCES, AND INDUSTRY

GOALS

1. To name five important mineral resources of the Mountain West. **2.** To know the major agricultural and industrial products of the region. **3.** To understand the importance of ranching to the economy of the Mountain West. **4.** To understand and appreciate the value of our national parks.

TEACHING SUGGESTIONS

1. Questions and Answers. Use the following for a review of lesson content.

a. *What are some of the agricultural products grown in the Mountain West?* (Potatoes, wheat, cotton, fruits, and vegetables)

b. *What allows crops to be raised in parts of Arizona and New Mexico?* (Irrigation)

c. *How much good grassland is needed to feed one cow?* (20 to 25 acres, or 8–10 ha)

d. *How large is the average ranch in the region?* (4,000 acres, or 1,600 ha)

e. *What are some of the fuel resources?* (Natural gas, oil, oil shale, coal, and uranium)

f. *What are some of the problems in removing oil from shale?* (Cost, waste disposal, and the need for large amounts of water)

g. *What is uranium used for?* (To produce nuclear energy)

h. *Where and when was the first transcontinental railroad completed?* (Near Ogden, Utah, in 1869)

i. *What are some of the nonagricultural products and industries of this region?* (Aircraft, electronics equipment, machinery, transportation equipment, wood products, chemicals, sports clothing and equipment, printing and publishing)

● **2. Making a Map.** Have the pupils make a map that shows what and where the main products of the region are produced. Include agricultural and industrial products.

You may decide to allow pupils having difficulty to work in small group situations. Each individual might be assigned a particular task.

3. Interviewing. Construction and use of nuclear power plants is quite controversial. Almost everyone has an opinion on the subject. Have pupils tape interviews with people on this subject. Some of the completed interviews may be played for the total group and used as the basis for a discussion.

4. Scale. Using the map on p. 387 have pupils calculate the distance between the following: Carlsbad Caverns National Park and Mesa Verde National Park (375 miles, 650 km); Rocky Mountain National Park and Grand Teton National Park (325 miles, 525 km); Zion National Park and Arches National Park (200 miles, 290 km); Petrified Forest National Park and Yellowstone National Park (650 miles, 1,010 km).

5. Community Resources. Have pupils check the local or county library to see whether they can locate any films or slides that illustrate some of the national parks in this region. They may also know someone who has traveled to some of the parks. This person might be willing to share his or her experiences with the class.

SUPPLEMENTARY INFORMATION

The National Park System. National parks are monuments to America's history and natural beauty. The National Park System began in 1872 when Congress established Yellowstone as our first national park. Today the park system includes nearly 300 areas, covering over 31 million acres (12,555,000 ha). Each year Americans make over 250 million visits to national, historical, and recreational parks in all regions of the United States, Puerto Rico, and the Virgin Islands.

The President has the power to proclaim national monuments on lands under federal jurisdiction. Congressional acts are necessary for designating all other areas as national parks. Further information may be obtained from the U.S. Department of the Interior, National Park Service, Washington, D.C. 20240.

LESSON 3 PAGES 394–399

POPULATION AND CITIES

GOALS
1. To know that the population of the Mountain West region is growing rapidly. **2.** To understand the conflict between Navajo values and coal mining. **3.** To name the major cities of the region.

TEACHING SUGGESTIONS
1. Questions and Answers. Use the following as a review of lesson content.
a. *Of the ten states whose population is growing most rapidly, how many are in the Mountain West region?* (Seven)
b. *Where do most of the Navajo live today?* (On a reservation in northeastern Arizona)
c. *From what sources do the Navajo gain income?* (The text lists the following sources: raising sheep, growing crops, owning and operating a lumber mill and an electronics company, and the sale of handcrafted jewelry and woven items. Pupils who have done research on the Navajo may be able to add other sources.)
d. *Three of the nation's fastest growing cities are in the Mountain West. Which cities are they?* (Aurora, Colorado Springs, and Albuquerque)
e. *What are some of the reasons why Phoenix has grown?* (Irrigation of the desert made it possible to grow crops; climate has brought people for health reasons; industry has attracted other people.)

f. *How did Denver get its start?* (As a mining town)
g. *Why is Denver often called the "Washington of the West"?* (Federal government has many offices there—mint, airforce base, arsenal, nuclear energy plant, and others)
h. *About how many of Utah's people live in or near Salt Lake City?* (Two thirds)

2. Using Scale. Using the map on p. 397, have pupils calculate the distance between the following: Tucson and Alamosa (480 miles, 775 km); Reno and Boulder (760 miles, 1,210 km); Casper and Boise (510 miles, 820 km); Salt Lake City and Phoenix (520 miles, 820 km); and Santa Fe and Albuquerque (60 miles, 100 km).

3. Making Charts. Have individuals use the charts on pp. 398–399 for reference in making charts for each state. Display the charts in the classroom. Pupils may wish to include maps of the states that show major cities and geographical features.

4. Using Latitude and Longitude. Have pupils trace the map on p. 397. Their maps should show only the Mountain West states and the lines of latitude and longitude. As pupils trace, they may notice that many of the state borders are straight lines. Point out that these lines follow lines of latitude and longitude. Ask:
a. *What is the latitude of the northern border of Arizona and of New Mexico?* (37°N) *Of Colorado?* (41°N) *Of Wyoming?* (45°N)
b. *What is the longitude of the border between Arizona and New Mexico?* (109°W) *Of Nevada's western border?* (120°W)
c. *Where do you see borders that follow or seem to follow natural features?* (Idaho/Oregon border: Snake River; Idaho/Montana: mountain range; Arizona/California: Colorado River; Arizona/Nevada: Colorado River)

5. Using the Gazetteer. Have pupils use the maps they traced in Teaching Suggestion 4 to do the following activity. List on the chalkboard a number of cities, such as Salt Lake City, Santa Fe, Carson City, Phoenix, Denver, and Ogden. Tell pupils to turn to the Gazetteer in the back of the text. Have them use the information on latitude and longitude to determine the placement of the cities on their maps. When the activity is complete, you may decide to have pupils read all the information listed in the Gazetteer entries used.

6. Oral Reports. Have individual pupils research different aspects of Navajo customs and culture. When the research is complete, have them present their findings to the total group.

20/CHAPTER REVIEW   PAGE 400
Answers for Review Questions

1. At the base of the mountains, vegetation consists of meadows and broadleaf trees. As one climbs higher, the broadleaf trees begin to give way to evergreens. The higher one goes, the more stunted and sparse the vegetation becomes, until one finally reaches the timberline. Trees do not grow beyond this point. The highest peaks are barren.

2. The three major parts of the intermontane region are the Columbia Plateau, Colorado Plateau, and the Great Basin.

3. The Colorado River system is important to the people of the Mountain West because it provides hydroelectric power and drinking water and irrigates many of the croplands.

4. A rain shadow is a region of little rainfall on the sheltered side of coastal mountains.

5. The state that produces the most potatoes is Idaho.

6. Mineral resources of the Mountain West include copper, lead, potassium, iron, molybdenum, gold, silver, uranium, natural gas, oil, oil shale, and coal.

7. The problems that must be solved before oil shale is used are as follows: (a) the expense of mining, transporting, and refining must be reduced, (b) a method of disposing the waste shale must be found, and (c) a large water supply must be obtained.

8. Some people object to the use of nuclear energy because they feel that laws controlling nuclear energy are not strong enough. Others think that nuclear energy is too dangerous to use.

9. The first national park was Yellowstone National Park.

10. Coal mining is a source of conflict for the Navajo because Navajo tradition and culture always believed in preserving the natural landscape. Coal mining changes it.

11. The two largest cities of the Mountain West are Phoenix, Arizona, and Denver, Colorado.

20/SKILLS DEVELOPMENT   PAGE 401
Answers for Skills Development

1. Phoenix: Named after a mythological bird

2. Boulder: From the many boulders visible after mining operations

3. Carson City: Named after Kit Carson, the frontiersman

4. Havre: Named after the French city

5. Moab: From the Paiute word *mohapa*, "mosquito-water"

6. Trinidad: Spanish for "trinity"

7. Yellowstone: The park was named after the river, which was named for a yellow rock near its mouth.

8. Rio Grande: Spanish for "big river"

9. Pocatello: Named after a Bannock chief of the 1800s

10. Utah: Named after the Ute tribe

11. Aurora: Latin for "dawn"

12. Mesa: Named after the landform

13. Alamosa: Adjective form of *alamo*, or "cottonwood"

14. Cody: After William F. (Buffalo Bill) Cody, cavalry scout and showman

15. Theodore Roosevelt Lake: Named after President Theodore Roosevelt

16. Arizona: From the Papago words *ali*, "small," and *shonak*, "place of the spring." (Originally, the "place of the small spring" was the site of rich finds of silver. The name was extended to cover all the surrounding territory. The spring is located in what is now Mexico.)

17. Tucson: Papago for "black base." The name refers to the base of a nearby mountain.

18. Helena: Named after the hometown of a man from Minnesota

19. Santa Fe: Originally named *La Villa Reál de la Santa Fe de San Francisco*, "The Royal City of the Holy Faith of Saint Francis," it was soon shortened.

20. Lewis Range: Named after Meriwether Lewis, the explorer

CHAPTER 21 PAGES 402–419

THE PACIFIC STATES TODAY

THEME

The Pacific region is one of great variety in landforms, agriculture, resources, industry, and peoples.

PROJECT

Help the class plan a program of songs and a filmstrip dealing with the entire unit. Some suggested songs are listed in Books and Other Media, pp. T22–T24. Pupils should prepare their own filmstrip, highlighting some of the interesting things they have learned about the seven regions they have studied. When the program is ready to be presented, have pupils write invitations to their parents.

LESSON 1 PAGES 402–406

THE LAND AND CLIMATE

GOALS

1. To name the Pacific states. **2.** To name the major landforms and rivers of the Pacific region. **3.** To name three factors that affect climate in the Pacific region. **4.** To describe earthquakes and volcanoes. **5.** To name the season of the year during which Arctic regions have the most daylight.

TEACHING SUGGESTIONS

1. Questions and Answers. For a switch that pupils will enjoy, have them make up their own questions on the text reading. Then have them exchange papers with one another and answer the questions. In case

it is not convenient to do the above, the following questions may be used for a comprehension check.

a. *What is the northernmost point in the United States?* (Point Barrow, Alaska) *The southernmost point?* (Ka Lae, Hawaii)

b. *What is special about Mount McKinley?* (Highest point in North America) *About Death Valley?* (Lowest in North America)

c. *What are the two major kinds of landforms in the Pacific region?* (Mountains and valleys)

d. *Name two major rivers in the Pacific region.* (The text names the Yukon, Columbia, San Joaquin, and Sacramento rivers)

e. *Why is the Salton Sea salty?* (It has no river flowing out of it. Water enters it and evaporates, leaving behind more and more salts.)

f. *What effect do mountains have on pre-cipitation in the Pacific states?* (Make the windward sides of the mountains wet, and the leeward sides dry)

g. *What effect does the warm ocean current have on the coastal lands from northern California to the Alaskan peninsula?* (Makes them wetter and warmer than the inland areas at the same latitude.)

h. *In addition to mountains and the ocean currents, what is another factor that affects climate in the Pacific region?* (Latitude; the farther north, the colder it is)

i. *Where would it be colder in winter and warmer in summer: in Seattle on Puget Sound, or in Spokane on the plains of eastern Washington?* (Spokane)

j. *What is permafrost?* (Ground that stays frozen all year round)

k. *What is the tundra and where is it found in the United States?* (A cold, dry, treeless plain in northern Alaska)

l. *When do the Arctic regions have the longest periods of daylight: in winter or summer?* (Summer)

m. *What happens during a volcanic eruption?* (Clouds of hot gases, water vapor, or ashes pour from the volcanic opening. Lava may also be emitted.)

n. *What is an earthquake?* (A movement of the ground, ranging from a gentle shaking or sharp jolt to a large tremor that causes cracks in the earth's surface and great damage to roads, bridges, and buildings)

2. Making a Model. A very popular project with children of this age is the construction of a model volcano. Pupils can build a papier-mâché mountain around an open jar. Baking soda is placed in the jar. To cause the "eruption," an equal amount of vinegar is poured on top of the baking soda. Newspapers should be placed around the mountain to catch any spills.

3. Making a Cross Section. Pupils can make a cross section diagram of one of the Hawaiian Islands, showing the base of the mountain beneath the sea. The school li-brary may contain reference materials that will help pupils with the scale; however, this is not vital. The main point is to show that the islands are really mountain tops.

4. Demonstration. With the aid of one or two pupils, you can show how the midnight-sun phenomenon works. Use a flashlight for the sun and a globe for the earth. Have the pupil holding the globe walk around the sun, making sure the earth is tilted at the appropriate angle. (The exact angle is 23½° to the perpendicular.) If the globe is anchored to a stand, day and night can also be shown, by having a second pupil twirl the globe on its axis.

LESSON 2 PAGES 407–411

AGRICULTURE, RESOURCES, AND INDUSTRY

GOALS

1. To name the nation's leading state in farm production and to identify the most important farming regions in that state. **2.** To name some major crops of the Pacific region. **3.** To name the leading lumber state. **4.** To identify the controversy over redwoods. **5.** To explain how oil is transported from the North Slope to the refineries.

TEACHING SUGGESTIONS

1. Questions and Answers. Use the following to review the text content.

a. *Which state leads the nation in farm production?* (California) *What are that state's two most important farming areas?* (Central and Imperial valleys)

b. *In which state are apricots, dates, and figs grown?* (California) *Apples and wheat?* (Washington) *Sugarcane, pineapples, and coffee?* (Hawaii)

c. *Which state is our leading lumber state?* (Oregon)

T165

d. *What is unusual about redwood trees?* (Great size and longevity) *How do people disagree about what should be done with the remaining redwoods?* (Some· want to preserve them, others want them to be used for lumber.)

e. *What is the purpose of a fish ladder?* (Provides a way for fish to travel past dams)

f. *Why is Alaska's North Slope important?* (Contains huge reserves of oil and natural gas) *How is oil transported from the North Slope?* (By pipeline to Valdez and then by tanker) *Why can't the oil be carried by tanker from Prudhoe Bay?* (The bay is blocked by ice for much of the year.)

g. *Name two national parks in the Pacific region.* (The text names Yosemite, Olympic, Crater Lake, Mount McKinley, and Hawaii Volcanoes. Others are North Cascade, Mount Rainier, Redwood, Sequoia, Kings Canyon, Lassen Volcanic, and Haleakala.)

2. Research Report. Have interested pupils find out about the current status of otters, seals, and whales. Help them use the *Readers' Guide to Periodical Literature* to locate magazine articles on the topic.

3. Writing a Business Letter. Pupils who do Teaching Suggestion 2 above can obtain further information by writing a group letter to the World Wildlife Fund, 1319 Eighteenth St., NW, Washington, D.C. 20036. Have the group ask for the Fund's list of rare and endangered species, as well as for information specific to otters, seals, and whales. At one time this list was printed on both sides of a narrow strip of paper about 5 feet (150 cm) in length. If it still comes in this form, pupils will be duly impressed by the length of the list of rare and endangered species.

4. Consumer Awareness/Ecology. Pupils can be made aware of two sides of the consumer coin by a discussion of some of the resources mentioned in this chapter. One such discussion might center on oil, a non-renewable resource. Remind pupils that oil is used for hundreds of products, including many that are essentially luxuries, such as the plastic bags and wrap used to package many consumer products. Point out that such packaging can be a gimmick to make us buy more of a product than we need or to get us to buy the product in the first place. Once people are aware of these gimmicks, they can refuse to buy in larger quantities than they need, resist the siren call of the pretty package, and reject over-packaged goods. By doing so they save themselves money (heads), and they help preserve valuable resources (tails). Similar points can be made with other resources.

LESSON 3 PAGES 412–416

POPULATION AND CITIES

GOALS

1. To name the state in the Pacific region with the largest population and the state with the smallest population. **2.** To name the five largest cities in the Pacific region. **3.** To name some problems minority groups have had to face. **4.** To name Los Angeles's two major problems. **5.** To read a map showing the chief canals and aqueducts that supply water to California.

TEACHING SUGGESTIONS

1. Questions and Answers. You may wish to use the following for a review of the text.

a. *Which state has the largest population?* (California) *The smallest?* (Alaska)

b. *What are the five largest cities in the Pacific region?* (Los Angeles, San Diego, San Francisco, San Jose, and Seattle)

c. *What problems have many Mexican Americans had to face?* (Discrimination, poor housing, jobs, education) *How have Mexican Americans tried to overcome these problems?* (Formed groups to draw attention to their plight and to encourage pride in themselves and their history)

d. *What other large group of people in the Pacific region has faced problems similar to those of the Mexican Americans?* (Asian Americans)

e. *Where are many of Alaska's cities located?* (Near waterways or along the coast)

f. *What is Hawaii's capital and largest city?* (Honolulu)

g. *What is Honolulu's leading industry?* (Tourism)

h. *What city served as the nation's link to the Alaskan gold fields and was again a chief link during the building of the Alaskan pipeline?* (Seattle)

i. *What has helped Los Angeles become the Pacific region's most important trade and manufacturing center?* (Rich farmlands and nearby oil deposits)

j. *What are Los Angeles's two major problems?* (Smog and providing enough water)

k. *Why are a large fishing fleet and a United States Navy base located in San Diego?* (Because of its natural harbor)

l. *What is the largest port of the Pacific Coast?* (San Francisco)

2. Map Reading. Have pupils refer to the map on p. 413 to answer the following questions:

a. *Which states of the Pacific region border on the Pacific Ocean?* (Alaska, Washington, Oregon, California, Hawaii)

b. *Which states of the Pacific region border on Canada?* (Alaska, Washington)

c. *What is the approximate distance from the Canadian border to the Mexican border?* (1,300 miles, or 2,090 km)

d. *Locate Barrow, Alaska, by latitude and longitude.* (71°N/156°W)

e. *Which of Alaska's important cities is an interior city?* (Fairbanks)

f. *What is the distance between Barrow and the capital of Alaska?* (About 1,070 miles, or 1,721 km)

g. *What is the capital of Washington?* (Olympia)

h. *In what part of the state is Oregon's capital located?* (Northeastern)

i. *On which island is the capital of Hawaii located?* (Oahu)

j. *In which direction do the islands in the state of Hawaii extend from the island of Hawaii?* (Northwest)

3. Reinforcing Learning. Give each pupil ten 3″ × 5″ index cards or ten pieces of paper of that size. Ask the pupils to choose five cities in the lesson and write the name of each on a separate card. Have them find an interesting fact about each city and write it on a separate card—for example, "Is the largest city in the Pacific region"; "Is located on Puget Sound." Then have the pupils form small groups and plan card games in which they share the information they have gathered.

4. Map Reading. Explain to the pupils that two plans that provide California with water are the Central Valley Project and the California Water Plan. Explain that the Central Valley Project begins at the Shasta Dam. Have pupils look at the map on p. 416. Ask:

a. *On what lake is the Shasta Dam located?* (Shasta Lake)

b. *In which part of California is Shasta Lake?* (Northern)

c. *Into what river does the Shasta Dam release water?* (Sacramento)

d. *What canal takes the water south?* (Delta-Mendota Canal)

Explain that in the California Water Plan water is released from Lake Oroville by the Oroville Dam. Ask:

e. *Into what river does the Oroville Dam release water?* (Feather)

f. *Where does the Feather River carry the water?* (Into the Sacramento River)

g. *By which two aqueducts is water carried from the Sacramento area to the coastal areas?* (North Bay Aqueduct and South Bay Aqueduct)

h. *Which is the longest aqueduct in California?* (California Aqueduct)

i. *Into what two branches does it separate?* (West Branch and East Branch)

j. *Which branch of the California Aqueduct supplies the Los Angeles area?* (West Branch)

k. *Where does the East Branch end?* (Perris Lake)

l. *How many pumping stations are shown on the California aqueduct and its two branches?* (Five)

Explain that work on the California Water Plan began in 1960. It is hoped that the work will be finished in 1990 and will meet southern California's future needs.

21/CHAPTER REVIEW PAGE 418

Answers for Review Questions

1. Mount McKinley in Alaska is the highest point in North America. Death Valley in California is the lowest point in North America.

2. The Salton Sea is salty because it has no rivers flowing out of it. (Water enters it and evaporates, leaving behind more and more salt.)

3. Mountains create a rain shadow on their protected sides, and they cause rain to fall on the ocean sides. Also, temperatures decrease with elevation. Ocean currents have a warming effect on the coastal areas. Temperatures tend to decrease the more northerly the latitude. (Both temperature and precipitation are also affected by distance inland.)

4. California's two most important farming areas are the Central Valley and the Imperial Valley.

5. Our leading lumber state is Oregon.

6. Redwood trees are unusual in that they have long life spans and can grow to enormous size. The disagreement concerning redwoods is that some people think the trees should be cut for lumber; other people feel they should be preserved for future generations to enjoy.

7. The mineral resource that we get from the North Slope is oil. The oil gets from Prudhoe Bay to the places where it is needed by pipeline to Valdez in southern Alaska and from there by tanker to refineries in Washington and California.

8. Life is often difficult for immigrant groups such as Mexican Americans and Asian Americans because many of them have been discriminated against and have had to settle for poor jobs, education, and housing.

9. Answers will vary.

6/UNIT REVIEW PAGE 419

Answers for Unit Review

1. The seven regions are New England, Middle Atlantic, Southeast, South Central, North Central, Mountain West, and Pacific.

2. Two major mountain ranges are the Appalachians and the Rockies. The high, dry inland plain is the Great Plains. The plains along the southern and eastern coasts of the United States are the Gulf Coastal Plain and the Atlantic Coastal Plain.

3. The three oceans that form parts of the United States border are the Atlantic, Arctic, and Pacific oceans. The five Great Lakes are Erie, Ontario, Huron, Michigan, and Superior. Pupils' choices of rivers will vary but should include the Missouri and the Mississippi. Answers will vary.

4. The higher the elevation, the lower the temperature. The Great Basin is dry because it lies in a rain shadow created by the Cascades and the Sierra Nevadas. The warmer and wetter place would be the one near the Atlantic coast.

5. Answers will vary.

6. Answers will vary.

7. The Manufacturing Belt is in the Middle Atlantic region. Answers will vary.

8. The areas of greatest population density are along the Atlantic coast from Washington, D.C., to southern Maine; along the shores of Lakes Erie and Michigan; along the Mississippi and Missouri rivers; and around a few of the major cities west of the Mississippi River—notably Los Angeles, Dallas, and San Francisco.

9. Answers will vary.

UNIT 7

Canada and Latin America

UNIT 7

CANADA AND LATIN AMERICA

Dear Parent,

In this unit your child will be studying Canada and Latin America. The chapter on Canada focuses on the five physical regions of the country. It discusses how Canada's climate and location have affected where people live and work. As your child studies this chapter, he or she will note that Canada and the United States have many similarities in their history, physical environment, and ways of living.

The chapter on Latin America reviews the history of Latin America with its Indian, European, and African cultures. The chapter also focuses on the climate and physical features of Latin America and how they have influenced where people live and where cities have grown. The physical environment, resources, economic activities, and major cities of the countries of Latin America are also discussed. The pupils will learn that, although parts of it are highly industrialized, Latin America is generally a developing area.

While your child is studying this unit, you might alert him or her to magazine or newspaper articles about Canada and Latin America. You might also take your child to a local library to find books on the countries discussed in this unit.

Sincerely,

CANADA AND LATIN AMERICA

BULLETIN-BOARD DISPLAYS

1. Have pupils display pictures or drawings of the flag of Canada and the flags of various Latin American countries. Have pupils write an explanation of the symbolism of the colors and design of each flag.

2. Display photographs of Canada and Latin America from newspapers, magazines, and travel brochures.

GETTING STARTED

1. Use the unit-opening art to stimulate class discussion on Canada and Latin America. Ask pupils whether they can guess where each person lives or what he or she does for a living. (Left to right, the figures are: a Royal Canadian Mounted Police officer, a lumberjack, a Peruvian Indian, and an oil worker.) If any of your pupils have lived or traveled in Canada or Latin America, you might ask them to share their experiences with the class.

2. Have pupils prepare a travel brochure on Canada or a Latin American country. The brochure should include drawings or other illustrations relating to the country. You might also have pupils refer to a travel guide on the country so that they can write brief descriptions of some interesting places to visit.

CANADA

THEME

Canada is a country with a variety of contrasting environments, both physical and cultural.

PROJECTS

1. Have pupils draw a large map of Canada and sketch in the boundaries of the five physical regions shown on the map on p. 427. If you have an overhead projector, you can project this map on to a large sheet of paper on the wall. Pupils can then trace the map. As pupils study each region, have them indicate on the wall map the physical features, resources, and cities of that region as indicated on the text map.

2. Have pupils bring in photographs and articles on Canada from newspapers and magazines. Have pupils prepare a display of material, organizing it by such topics as People, Government, Industry, Physical Features, Cities, Regions.

LESSON 1   PAGES 422–425

HISTORY AND GOVERNMENT

GOALS

1. To understand how Canada's history has contributed to its ethnic diversity. 2. To name and locate Canada's provinces and territories. 3. To compare the governments of Canada and the United States.

TEACHING SUGGESTIONS

1. **Discussion/Outlining.** After pupils have read from p. 422 to the end of the first column on p. 424, ask these questions:

a. *Who were the first people to come to Canada?* (Indians and Eskimos) *Where did they come from?* (Asia)

b. *Who were the first Europeans who came?* (Explorers)

c. *When did the first settlers come?* (Early 1600s) *Where did they settle?* (French settlers moved to the St. Lawrence Valley; British settlers came to what is now New Brunswick, Prince Edward Island, Nova Scotia, and Newfoundland.)

d. *Beginning in the late 1800s, what were the two great periods of immigration?* (From the late 1800s to the beginning of World War I; the 15-year period after World War II, 1946–1961)

e. *What similarities do you see between the history of Canada and the history of the United States?* (Both countries were first inhabited by Indians from Asia. Both countries were colonies of Great Britain. Both countries have had immigrants from many ethnic groups.)

Have pupils make an outline to show the sequence in which various ethnic groups began arriving in Canada.

2. **Research Report.** Have one or more pupils prepare an oral report on the search for a Northwest Passage between the Atlantic Ocean and the Pacific Ocean. The report should discuss the history of the search, the explorers who tried to find the passage, and what routes they took.

3. **Reading a Map.** After pupils have read the section on provinces and territories on p. 424, have them locate Canada's ten prov-

inces and two territories on the map on p. 423. Ask these questions:

a. *What is the national capital of Canada?* (Ottawa) *What province is it in?* (Ontario)

b. *Name the capital of each province and territory.* (Alberta—Edmonton; British Columbia—Victoria; Manitoba—Winnipeg; New Brunswick—Fredericton; Newfoundland—St. John's; Nova Scotia—Halifax; Ontario—Toronto; Prince Edward Island—Charlottetown; Quebec—Quebec City; Saskatchewan—Regina; Northwest Territories—Yellowknife; Yukon Territory—Whitehorse)

c. Have pupils make a list of states that border on a province or territory of Canada. Include those states in which the international boundary runs through a lake or river. Next to each state listed, have pupils indicate the province or territory it borders on. (Alaska—Yukon Territory, British Columbia; Washington—British Columbia; Idaho—British Columbia; Montana—British Columbia, Alberta, Saskatchewan; North Dakota—Saskatchewan, Manitoba; Minnesota—Manitoba, Ontario; Michigan—Ontario; Ohio—Ontario; Pennsylvania—Ontario; New York—Ontario, Quebec; Vermont—Quebec; New Hampshire—Quebec; Maine—Quebec, New Brunswick)

4. Comparison. After pupils have read the section on Canada's government, p. 425, write the headings Canada and the United States on the chalkboard. Then have the pupils compare the governments of the two countries, focusing on these items: (a) Form of government; (b) Head of government; (c) Lawmaking body; (d) Two houses of lawmaking body; (e) How members of two houses are selected; and (f) National capital.

SUPPLEMENTARY INFORMATION

Eskimos. Eskimos live in the Arctic regions of northeastern Asia and North America, including parts of Alaska and Canada. The word *Eskimo* means eaters of raw meat. Eskimos often do not cook their food because fuel is so scarce.

Unlike American Indians, Eskimos do not live in tribes. They have no regular form of government and no chiefs. The family is the main group in Eskimo life. Several families may live together in a settlement during the winter, but this is usually temporary.

There is no system of strict rules; rather, there are rules of good conduct. Public ridicule and banishment from the community are punishments for misconduct. The most important rule is that everyone must help in the search for food. Successful hunters are highly respected.

Eskimo children are rarely punished, but they learn that good behavior earns them respect. They are usually taught at home by their parents. Today many Eskimo children also attend government or mission schools.

Eskimos believe all objects have souls. The spirits of animals especially must be respected because animals provide food and clothing.

Eskimo life and customs today have become a mixture of old and new ways. Eskimos still hunt and fish, but many also work for mining and transportation companies in Alaska and northern Canada. Those who live in towns have discarded many of their old ways.

LESSON 2 PAGES 426–432

THE LAND AND CLIMATE

GOALS

1. To understand how physical geography, climate, and vegetation affect the choice of where people live. **2.** To name and locate the five physical regions of Canada. **3.** To identify the physical features, resources, and economic activities of those regions. **4.** To note similarities between regions of Canada and regions of the United States.

TEACHING SUGGESTIONS

● 1. **Reading for Comprehension/Reading a Map.** On the chalkboard list the five physical regions of Canada: (a) Appalachian region, (b) St. Lawrence Valley and Lakes Peninsula, (c) Canadian Shield, (d) plains region, and (e) western mountain region. Have pupils locate the five regions on the map on p. 427 and then read pp. 426–432. Ask these questions:

a. *Why are there large areas of Canada in which no people live?* (Large parts of Canada are too cold for most people. In many places the growing season is too short for crops. Often the land is too mountainous or rocky for farming.)

b. *In what area of Canada are most crops grown?* (In the south) *Why?* (The summers are warm enough and long enough for crops to grow.)

c. *What is the largest land region of Canada?* (Canadian Shield)

d. *What is the smallest land region of Canada?* (St. Lawrence Valley and Lakes Peninsula)

e. *In which region are most of Canada's cities located?* (St. Lawrence Valley and Lakes Peninsula) *Why do you think this is so?* (Climate, location along the St. Lawrence River and the Great Lakes, area of the earliest European settlements)

f. *Why is the Canadian Shield a very important region?* (It has vast resources— forests, minerals, and lakes and rivers that provide the energy to produce hydroelectric power.)

g. *What three regions are similar to regions in the United States?* (Appalachian region, plains region, and western mountain region) Point out that the Appalachian Mountains in Canada and in the United States are part of the same system. The plains of Canada and the Great Plains in the United States are part of the same

system. The western mountain region of Canada is part of the same system as the Rocky Mountains and the Coast Ranges in the United States.

For pupils who have difficulty in grasping the concept of *regions*, you may wish to try this activity. Have pupils trace the outline of Canada from the map on p. 427. Then have them color and label the regions.

For pupils who require a challenge, you may wish to use this activity. Have pupils make a chart for each of the five regions. Using the map on p. 427 for reference, have them list the cities and resources of each region.

2. Research Report. Have one or more pupils prepare an oral report on the St. Lawrence Seaway.

3. Essay. Have pupils write an essay comparing the plains region and the western mountain region. The essay should compare the following: (a) landforms, (b) climate, (c) resources, and (d) economic activities (industry and agriculture).

LESSON 3   PAGES 432–435

CITIES

GOALS

1. To identify and locate Canada's ten largest cities. **2.** To locate cities, using map coordinates. **3.** To rank the provinces and territories of Canada by area and population. **4.** To compare the population densities of Canada's provinces and territories.

TEACHING SUGGESTIONS

1. Reading for Comprehension/Analysis. Have pupils read the section on cities and study the chart entitled "Canada's Ten Largest Cities" on p. 432. Ask the following questions:

a. *How did most cities in Canada begin?* (As trading centers)

b. *What is an economic activity?* (One that has to do with the production or selling of goods or services)

c. *What are Canada's three most important economic activities?* (Manufacturing, mining, and agriculture)

d. *In which provinces are Canada's ten largest cities located?* (Quebec, Ontario, Manitoba, Alberta, British Columbia)

e. *What is Canada's largest city?* (Montreal) *How many people does it have?* (1,081,000)

f. *How many cities of 500,000 or more people does Canada have?* (Three) *What are they?* (Montreal, Toronto, and Winnipeg)

● **2. Reading a Map.** Have pupils use the map on p. 434 and the coordinates A–C and 1–9 to do this activity. Note: All Canadian cities of more than 100,000 are shown on this map and chart. The only cities of less than 100,000 people that are shown are territorial and provincial capitals. Ask for the coordinates for each of the cities listed below.

a. *Whitehorse, Yukon Territory* (A–1)

b. *St. John's, Newfoundland* (C–9)

c. *Victoria, British Columbia* (C–2)

d. *Saskatoon, Saskatchewan* (B–4)

e. *Calgary, Alberta* (B–3)

Then ask what cities are within the coordinates listed below. Have pupils name the province each city is in.

f. *C–6* (Kitchener, Ontario; London, Ontario; Thunder Bay, Ontario; Windsor, Ontario)

g. *B–6* (None)

h. *C–7* (Brampton, Ontario; Burlington, Ontario; Hamilton, Ontario; Laval, Quebec; Mississauga, Ontario; Montreal, Quebec; Oshawa, Ontario; Ottawa, Ontario; Quebec City, Quebec; St. Catharines, Ontario; Toronto, Ontario)

For pupils who have difficulty grasping the concept, you may wish to try this activity. On a separate sheet of paper, have pupils list these cities: Edmonton, Alberta; Halifax, Nova Scotia; Ottawa, Ontario; Windsor, Ontario; and Yellowknife, Northwest Territories. In another column have them list these coordinates: A–3; B–3; C–6; C–7; C–8. Have pupils use the map on p. 434 to match the cities with the correct coordinates. (Edmonton, B–3; Halifax, C–8; Ottawa, C–7; Windsor, C–6; Yellowknife, A–3)

For those pupils who require a challenge, you may wish to try this activity. Have the pupils use the list of cities on p. 434 to make a chart to categorize cities by province and population range. At the left of the chart, list Canada's ten provinces and two territories. Across the top of the chart, list the four population ranges from p. 434 (Cities with less than 100,000, and so on). Have pupils fill in the chart.

(Cities with less than 100,000: British Columbia—Victoria; New Brunswick—Fredericton; Newfoundland—St. John's; Northwest Territories—Yellowknife; Prince Edward Island—Charlottetown; Yukon Territory—Whitehorse

Cities with 100,00–499,000: Alberta—Calgary, Edmonton; British Columbia—Vancouver; Nova Scota—Halifax; Ontario—Brampton, Burlington, Hamilton, Kitchener, London, Mississauga, Oshawa, Ottawa, St. Catharines, Thunder Bay, Windsor; Quebec—Laval, Quebec City; Saskatchewan—Regina, Saskatoon

Cities with 500,000–999,000: Manitoba—Winnipeg; Ontario—Toronto

City with 1,000,000 or more: Quebec—Montreal)

3. Reading a Chart/Analyzing Data. Have pupils study the chart on p. 435. On the chalkboard list the numbers 1 to 12. Have the pupils rank the ten provinces and two territories of Canada by area from largest to smallest. (1. Northwest Territories 2. Quebec 3. Ontario 4. British Columbia 5. Alberta 6. Saskatchewan 7. Manitoba 8. Yukon Territory 9. Newfoundland 10. New Brunswick 11. Nova Scotia 12. Prince Edward Island) Then write the heading "Population" and list the numbers 1 to 12. Have pupils rank the provinces and territories by population from largest to smallest. (1. Ontario 2. Quebec 3. British Columbia 4. Alberta 5. Manitoba 6. Saskatchewan 7. Nova Scotia 8. New Brunswick 9. Newfoundland 10. Prince Edward Island 11. Northwest Territories 12. Yukon Territory) Ask these questions:

a. *Which province or territory has the largest area?* (Northwest Territories)

b. *Which province or territory has the smallest area?* (Prince Edward Island)

c. *Which province or territory has the largest population?* (Ontario) *What is its rank in area?* (3)

d. *What province or territory has the smallest population?* (Yukon Territory) *What is its rank in area?* (8)

e. *What are the three provinces or territories whose rank is the same in area as it is in population?* (Newfoundland, Quebec, and Saskatchewan)

Have pupils study the population density figures for each province and territory. Pose these questions:

f. *Which province or territory has the greatest population density?* (Prince Edward Island) *What is it?* (57 people per square mile, or 22 people per sq km) *What is the province's rank in area?* (12) *In population?* (10)

g. *Which province or territory has the smallest population density?* (Northwest Territories) *What is it?* (.03 people per square mile, or .01 per sq km) *How do the Northwest Territories rank in area?* (1) *In population?* (11)

h. *Which provinces or territories have a population density of 20 or more per square mile (8 or more per sq km)?* (New Brunswick, Nova Scotia, Ontario, and Prince Edward Island)

i. *Which provinces or territories have a population density of less than 20 per square mile (8 per sq km)?* (Alberta, British Columbia, Manitoba, Newfoundland, Quebec, Saskatchewan, Northwest Territories, Yukon Territory)

22/CHAPTER REVIEW PAGE 436
Answers for Review Questions

1. Most Canadians are descended from the English and French settlers.

2. Most French Canadians live in the province of Quebec.

3. Canada has a federal form of government. The federation is made up of ten provinces and two territories. Each province has its own government. The territories are run mainly by the federal government, although they do have some self-government.

The head of the government of Canada is the prime minister. There is also a governor-general who is appointed by the queen. The lawmaking body of Canada is called Parliament. It has two houses—the Senate and the House of Commons. The people of Canada vote for the members of the House of Commons. The members of the Senate are appointed by the governor-general.

4. The Commonwealth is an organization of nations that were once part of the British Empire.

5. The five physical regions of Canada are (a) the Appalachian region, (b) the St. Lawrence Valley and Lakes Peninsula, (c) the Canadian Shield, (d) the plains, and (e) the western mountain region.

LATIN AMERICA

THEME

Latin America is an area of great contrasts in physical environment, industrial development, and levels of wealth among its people.

PROJECTS

1. Have pupils select a Latin American country and make a booklet on that nation. The booklet could include some or all of these items:

a. An outline map of the country showing major physical features, rivers, the capital, and other cities.
b. A drawing or picture of the country's flag with a description of the symbolism of the colors and design of the flag.
c. A time line showing some important dates in the country's history.
d. Photographs or articles on the country from newspapers or magazines.
2. Have pupils make a list of the national holidays of various Latin American countries. Have them tell the name of the holiday, what it commemorates, and when it is celebrated.

LATIN AMERICA YESTERDAY AND TODAY

GOALS

1. To understand some similarities and differences between Latin America, Canada, and the United States. 2. To interpret information on a chart and to locate cities on a map by using coordinates.

TEACHING SUGGESTIONS

1. **Discussion.** Before starting this lesson be sure pupils understand the distinctions among Latin America, Middle America, and Central America that they learned in Chapter 3. Have pupils recall what they learned about the Mayas, Aztecs, and Incas and about the European explorers who came to Latin America.

Point out the following similarities and differences between Latin America and the United States and Canada:

a. In the English colonies in North America most of the early English settlers came to America to build permanent homes and to make a better life for themselves. Many of the early Spanish and Portuguese settlers came to the colonies in Latin America with the hope of getting rich quickly and then returning to Europe.
b. In both North America and Latin America the native Indian peoples were mistreated and taken advantage of by the Europeans.
c. Black people from Africa were brought to both North America and South America as slaves.
d. Two countries, the United States and Canada, were created out of the English colonies in North America. Over twenty countries were created from the Spanish and Portuguese colonies in Latin America.
e. In the United States and Canada the majority of people belong to the middle class. Most Latin American countries do not have a large middle class. There are a relatively few very wealthy people, while

the majority of the population is economically disadvantaged.

f. Like the United States and Canada, Latin America is rich in natural resources. While the United States and Canada are highly industrialized, developed countries, Latin America is a developing area. There are areas of Latin America, however, that are already highly industrialized.

● **2. Reading a Chart/Reading a Map.** On the chart on pp. 455–456 have pupils find the capitals of the countries listed below. Then have pupils find the coordinates for the capitals in the list of cities on p. 441. You might also ask what population range each city is in. After pupils have found the coordinates, have them locate the cities on the map on p. 440.

a. *Brazil* (Brasília; F–8; 100,000–499,000)

b. *Cuba* (Havana; B–4; 1,000,000 or more)

c. *Ecuador* (Quito; E–5; 500,000–999,000)

d. *Guyana* (Georgetown; D–7; 100,000–499,000)

e. *Mexico* (Mexico City; C–3; 1,000,000 or more)

f. *Paraguay* (Asunción; G–7; 100,000–499,000)

For pupils who have difficulty grasping the concept, you may wish to try this activity. Have pupils list ten countries from the charts on pp. 455–456. Ask them to name the capital of each country and give its population.

For pupils who require a challenge, you may wish to use this activity. Have pupils make a chart. Across the top write these headings: Argentina, Brazil, Cuba, Nicaragua, Paraguay. At the left of the chart, list these categories: Less than 100,000; 100,000–499,000; 500,000–999,000; 1,000,000 or more. Have pupils use the list of cities on p. 441 to fill in the cities for each country in the correct category. (Argentina: 500,000–999,000—Córdoba, Rosario; 1,000,000 or more—Buenos Aires. Brazil: 100,000–499,000—Brasília, Manaus, Santos; 500,000–

999,000—Belém, Curitiba, Fortaleza, Nova Iguaçu, Pôrto Alegre; 1,000,000 or more—Belo Horizonte, Recife, Rio de Janeiro, Salvador, São Paulo. Cuba: 100,000–499,000—Guantánamo, Santiago de Cuba; 1,000,000 or more—Havana. Nicaragua: 100,000–499,000—Managua. Paraguay: 100,000–499,000—Asunción.)

LESSON 2 PAGES 442–444

MEXICO

GOALS

1. To locate physical features and cities of Mexico on a map. **2.** To understand why only one eighth of Mexico's land is used for agriculture. **3.** To identify Mexico's resources on a map. **4.** To name the major crops of Mexico.

TEACHING SUGGESTIONS

1. Reading for Comprehension/Reading a Map. After pupils have read the section on Mexico, have them locate the Rio Grande, Sierra Madre Oriental, Sierra Madre Occidental, and the Yucatán Peninsula on the map on p. 444. Pose these questions:

a. *What is the largest country of Middle America?* (Mexico)

b. *What two nations border on Mexico?* (United States and Guatemala)

c. *Which two mountain ranges border the high plateau of Mexico?* (Sierra Madre Oriental and Sierra Madre Occidental)

d. *What is the climate in the mountains of Mexico?* (Cool most of the year) *What is the climate in the plateau?* (Dry, very hot in summer and warm in winter) *What is the climate in the lowlands in the south?* (Hot and wet)

e. *Why is only about one eighth of Mexico's land used for farming?* (The rest of the land is too mountainous or too dry. Also, large parts of Mexico have very little rainfall.)

f. *What is the major crop of Mexico?* (Corn) *Name some of the other crops grown.* (Beans, wheat, cotton, sugarcane, coffee, rice, henequen, fruits, and vegetables)

g. *Is most of Mexico's farming subsistence farming or commercial agriculture?* (Subsistence farming)

h. *Name six Mexican cities that are important manufacturing centers.* (Mexico City, Guadalajara, Puebla, Monterrey, Mazatlán, and Monclova) Have pupils locate these cities on the map on p. 444.

● **2. Reading a Map.** Have pupils identify the natural resources of Mexico shown on the map on p. 444.

For pupils who have difficulty grasping the concept, you may wish to try this activity. Select one natural resource from the map key on p. 444. Help pupils make a list of the countries of Middle America in which that resource is found.

For pupils who require a challenge, you may wish to use this activity. Have pupils make a chart with these headings: Industrial Areas, Plantation Areas, Petroleum, Natural Gas, Silver, Iron Ore, Bauxite. Have them use the map on p. 444 to identify all the countries of Middle America in which each item is found. Ask pupils to exchange papers to compare answers.

3. Research Report. Have pupils prepare a written report on land reform in Mexico. Remind pupils to use their skimming, notetaking, and outlining skills.

LESSON 3   PAGES 444–446

CENTRAL AMERICA AND THE CARIBBEAN

GOALS

1. To name the six countries and one colony in Central America. **2.** To describe the land and climate of Central America. **3.** To locate various countries and capital cities in Central America and the Caribbean.

TEACHING SUGGESTIONS

1. Research Report. Have pupils prepare an oral or written report on the history of the building of the Panama Canal.

● **2. Reading for Comprehension/Reading a Map.** After pupils have read the text, have them locate the six countries and one colony in Central America on the map on p. 444. Ask them to name the capital of each. (By the time this text is in the classroom, Belize may no longer be a colony. Early in 1981, Belize and the United Kingdom reached an agreement that called for Belize's independence in the middle of that year.) Pose these questions:

a. *What are the major landforms in Central America?* (Mountains cover most of Central America. Between the mountains and the sea are narrow coastal plains.)

b. *What kind of forests cover most of Central America?* (Tropical rain forests)

c. *What is the climate of Central America?* (Hot with heavy rainfall)

Have pupils locate Cuba, Jamaica, Haiti, the Dominican Republic, and Puerto Rico on the map on p. 444. Pose these questions:

d. *Of what country is Port-au-Prince the capital?* (Haiti) *Kingston?* (Jamaica) *Havana?* (Cuba) *Santo Domingo?* (Dominican Republic)

e. *What two countries share the island of Hispaniola?* (Haiti, Dominican Republic)

For pupils who have difficulty grasping the concept, you may wish to try this activity. On the chalkboard list these capital cities in a column: Managua, Mexico City, Nassau, San José, San Salvador. In a second column, list these countries: Bahamas, Costa Rica, El Salvador, Mexico, Nicaragua. Have pupils work in a group, using the map on p. 444 for reference. Ask them to match the capital cities with the countries. (Managua, Nicaragua; Mexico City, Mexico; Nassau, Bahamas; San José, Costa Rica; San Salvador, El Salvador)

For pupils who require a challenge, you may wish to use this activity. Refer pupils to the text material on pp. 445–446 and the charts on pp. 455–456. Have pupils make a chart or write an essay comparing Cuba, Jamaica, Haiti, the Dominican Republic, and Puerto Rico in terms of the following: (a) area, (b) population, (c) capital city and its population, (d) major crops and industries, and (e) the nation(s) that have influenced the history of the area.

LESSON 4 PAGES 447–448

SOUTH AMERICA

GOALS
1. To identify the major physical features of South America on a map. 2. To locate the major rivers of South America on a map.

TEACHING SUGGESTIONS
1. **Reading a Map.** After pupils have read pp. 447–448, point out that the Andes are part of the mountain system that runs through the western part of Canada, the United States, Mexico, and Central America. Turn to the map on p. 439. Have pupils locate the Andes, the coastal plain between the Pacific Ocean and the Andes, the two high plateaus (Brazilian Highlands and Guiana Highlands), and the plains (the Llanos, the Chaco, the Pampas, and Patagonia).

Locate the major rivers on the map: the Amazon, Orinoco, Paraná, and Paraguay. Point out that most of South America's cities are along the coast. Tell pupils that mountains and tropical rain forests make travel into the interior difficult.

For pupils who have difficulty grasping the concept, you may wish to try this activity. Write these terms on the chalkboard: *Llanos, Chaco, Pampas, Patagonia.* Have pupils look up these terms in the glossary and write the definition of each.

For pupils who require a challenge, you may wish to use this activity. Have them answer the following:
a. *What lakes in South America are shown on the map on p. 439?* (Lake Maracaibo, Lake Poopó, Lake Titicaca)
b. *What desert of South America is shown?* (Atacama Desert)
c. *What rivers of South America are shown?* (Amazon, Cauca, Caura, Colorado, Essequibo, Magdalena, Orinoco, Paraná, Paraguay, Río de la Plata, São Francisco, Salado, Uruguay)
d. *What mountain peaks in South America are shown?* (Aconcagua, Chimborazo, Cotopaxi, Huascarán, Tolima)
2. Research/Making a Map. Have pupils refer to an encyclopedia or atlas to make a map showing one of the following:
a. Rainfall in South America
b. Climate in South America
c. Land Use in South America
d. Transportation in South America

LESSON 5 PAGES 449–456

THE COUNTRIES OF SOUTH AMERICA

GOALS
1. To locate the 12 countries and 2 other political units of South America on a map. 2. To locate major areas under cultivation and to identify the major resources of South America on a map. 3. To understand that some areas of South America are highly industrialized while other areas have little industry.

TEACHING SUGGESTIONS
1. **Research Report.** Have pupils look in an encyclopedia or historical atlas to find the names of the colonies from which the countries of South America were created. Have them also find what European nation owned each colony. Ask pupils to present this information either in a chart or on a

map. You might also have them include the date each country of South America became independent.

- **2. Reading a Map.** Refer pupils to the resource map on p. 454. Work with the class to identify the countries that have plantation agriculture and/or intensive agriculture. Select several countries and have pupils identify the natural resources and crops shown for each country.

For pupils who have difficulty grasping the concept, you may wish to try this activity. Select one country on the map. Have pupils locate the various symbols shown on the map for that country. Have pupils work together to make a resource map of that country. Make sure they include a map key. Have them use the map key on p. 454 as a guide.

For pupils who require a challenge, you may wish to use this activity. Have pupils list the 12 countries and 1 colony of South America at the left of a chart. At the top of the chart, have them write these headings: Capital, Other Cities, Rank in Area, Rank in Population, Rank in Population Density. Have pupils use the map on p. 454 to find the capitals and other cities. Have them use the chart on pp. 455–456 to find the area, population, and population density. When pupils rank the countries and colony by area, population, and population density, have them rank from the largest (1) to the smallest (13).

(Note: In some countries the capital is the only large city. Capitals and other cities: Argentina—Buenos Aires [capital], Bahía Blanca, Córdoba, Rosario, San Justo; Bolivia—Sucre [capital], La Paz, Potosi; Brazil—Brasília [capital], Belém, Belo Horizonte, Curitiba, Fortaleza, Manaus, Nova Iguaçu, Pôrto Alegre, Recife, Rio de Janeiro, Salvador, Santos, São Paulo; Chile—Santiago [capital], Antofagasta, Valparaíso; Colombia—Bogotá [capital], Barranquilla, Buenaventura, Cali, Medellín; Ecuador—Quito [capital], Guayuquil; French Guiana—Cayenne [capital]; Guyana—Georgetown [capital]; Paraguay—Asunción [capital]; Peru—Lima [capital], Callao; Surinam—Paramaribo [capital]; Uruguay—Montevideo [capital]; Venezuela—Caracas [capital], Maracaibo.)

SUPPLEMENTARY INFORMATION

1. The Llama. A humpless member of the camel family, the llama stands about 4 feet (1.2 m) tall at the shoulder and can range in color from white to shades of brown or black.

The Indians of South America use the llama in a variety of ways. Young animals are used for meat, hair is made into clothing, and hides are used for sandals. Females are kept for breeding and furs, while males over 3½ years can be used as pack animals.

The llama is economical to maintain since it thrives on wild grasses, shrubs, and lichens. It can go for weeks without drinking water because it gets moisture from the plants it eats.

The llama has quite a personality. If its load is too heavy or if it feels overworked it will lie down, tuck in its front hoofs, and refuse to budge. If it is angry or frightened, it may spit a wad of foul-smelling saliva in its antagonist's face.

2. The Naming of Bogotá, Buenos Aires, and Rio de Janeiro. The original dwellers on the high plains of Colombia, where Bogotá is located, were the Chibcha Indians. They had an advanced civilization equal in some respects to the civilizations of such better-known Indian groups as the Aztecs, Incas, and Mayas. The Chibchas were conquered by the Spanish in 1538, but their heritage lives on in the name *Bogotá*, derived from the name of the Chibcha Indian chief, Bacatá.

Buenos Aires, a city of wide boulevards, imposing squares, and formal gardens with fountains and statues, is sometimes called the Paris of America. When Spanish explorers first sailed up the estuary of the Río de la Plata in the sixteenth century, their sailing ships were driven by favorable winds. For this reason, they named the region *Buenos Aires,* Spanish for "fair winds."

During an exploration voyage along the coast of South America, a Portuguese ship sailed into a beautiful bay on January 1, 1502. The navigator believed—incorrectly—that the bay was the mouth of a river. Because of that and because of the date, he named the spot Rio de Janeiro, meaning "river of January."

23/CHAPTER REVIEW   PAGE 457
Answers for Review Questions
1. Spain and Portugal were the two European countries that colonized most of Latin America.

2. Three ways in which developed and developing countries are different are as follows: (a) Developed countries are highly industrialized. Developing countries are becoming industrialized. (b) Developed countries are richer; developing countries are poorer. In developed countries, many people share in the wealth of the country. In developing countries most people do not share much in the nation's wealth. (c) Workers in developed countries produce much more than workers in developing countries. That is because workers in developing countries have fewer machines and much simpler tools than workers in developed countries.

3. Subsistence farming means that a farm family grows enough food to meet its own needs, but there is little, if any, left to sell. Commercial agriculture is the growing of crops or livestock to be sold.

4. Mexico is the largest country in Middle America. Its capital is Mexico City.

5. The 12 countries of South America are: Argentina, Bolivia, Brazil, Chile, Colombia, Ecuador, Guyana, Paraguay, Peru, Surinam, Uruguay, and Venezuela.

7/UNIT REVIEW   PAGE 459
Answers for Unit Review
1. There are a number of differences between the large forest areas of Canada and South America. The large forest areas of Canada are in the Canadian Shield. The climate there is cold and poor for farming. Lumbering has developed in areas that can be reached by land or water. Some animals in these forests are trapped for their furs.

The forests of South America are tropical rain forests. These forests have a hot, wet climate. Trees and vines grow thickly in such forests. Travel into and through the rain forests is difficult. There are few roads or railroads. Most travel is by boat.

2. The forest areas of Canada are very valuable to the United States, since this nation imports large amounts of paper and pulp from Canada.

3.a. Along the equator, the climate is usually hot and humid. If the land is high above sea level, as in Quito, Ecuador, the climate may be very pleasant. As you travel south from the equator toward Cape Horn, the climate changes. Generally it is still hot for most of the year, but the rainfall is less and comes mostly in the summer. Farther south, in central Chile, there is a small area with hot, dry summers and warm, rainy winters. As you travel from central Chile to southern Chile, the climate becomes colder and wetter. Southern Chile is cool in summer and cold in winter.

b. As you travel from the equator north toward Alaska, you would go through many climate changes. Central America has a hot climate with heavy rainfall. The lowlands in the south of Mexico are hot and wet. The plateau of Mexico is very hot in summer and warm in winter. It is also very dry. The mountains of Mexico are cool most of the year.

Most of California has a dry climate. Rainfall in summer is rare. Summers are hot, and winters are warm in most of southern and central California. The coastal areas from northern California, through western Canada, into the Alaskan peninsula and the Aleutian Islands have plenty of rainfall and milder temperatures than do the inland areas at the same latitude. Snowfall is heavy in the high mountains of Washington, Oregon, western Canada, and southern Alaska.

Generally, as you travel either north or south from the equator, temperatures become cooler. Also there is less precipitation as you travel away from the equator.

4. Answers will vary. Note: About 15 percent of the ships that use the Panama Canal are from the United States. Liberia, Great Britain, Japan, Panama, and Greece are also major users of the canal.

5. Some minerals that are obtained from Canada are coal, copper, gold, iron ore, lead, natural gas, nickel, petroleum, pitchblende, silver, tungsten, uranium, and zinc.

Some minerals that are obtained from South America are bauxite, coal, copper, gold, iron ore, lead, manganese, nitrates, petroleum, silver, tin, and zinc.

6. Canada has many industries and a great deal of commercial agriculture. In Latin America there are places that are highly industrialized, but generally Latin America is considered a developing area. Most workers in Latin America produce much less than workers in a developed country such as Canada. That is because many workers in Latin America have fewer machines and much simpler tools than workers in Canada. Also, although there is some commercial agriculture, much of the farming in Latin America is still subsistence farming.

7. The Canadian northlands have a very cold climate. The growing season is too short for most crops. Because of the cold climate, few people live in the northlands. The Amazon forest, on the other hand, has a very hot, humid climate. Few people live there because the climate is very uncomfortable.

8. The northernmost extension of the chain of mountains that extends from North America into South America is the Brooks Range in Alaska. The Rocky Mountains extend through western Canada southward into the United States. In Mexico the system is made up of the Sierra Madre Oriental and the Sierra Madre Occidental. The system narrows in Central America and then extends into South America, where the mountains are called the Andes.

9. Answers will vary.

10. The northern areas of Canada have very few people. The climate in the northern areas is very cold, the soil is poor, and the growing season is too short for most crops. In Latin America there are large areas of tropical rain forest, where few people live. The climate there is hot, humid, and very uncomfortable. Because of the thick vegetation, it is difficult to travel through the rain forests. There are also many mountain areas that are sparsely populated. Travel across the mountains is difficult. There are few roads and railroads. Often the soil is poor for farming.

11. The Canadian Shield has a cold climate and is rich in minerals and forests. As a result, mining and lumbering are important industries in the Shield. The Shield also has many lakes and rivers that are the source of energy for the production of hydroelectric power.

The Brazilian plateau is made up of savanna. The climate is warmer than that of the Shield. Brasília, Brazil, one of the few cities on the plateau, was built to encourage people to move to this region. Brazil is trying to develop more agriculture in the region. Coffee is an important crop. Cattle grazing is also becoming important.

TEACHER'S NOTES